THE COMPANY DIRECTOR
POWERS, DUTIES AND LIABILITIES

Eighth Edition

THE COMPANY DIRECTOR
POWERS, DUTIES AND LIABILITIES

Eighth Edition

Peter Loose MA(Oxon)
Solicitor
Partner, Edwin Coe, London

Michael Griffiths LLB, LLM, ACI Arb
Formerly Deputy Head of the School of Legal Studies at the University of
Wolverhampton

David Impey MA(Oxon)
Solicitor
Director, Jordans Professional Services Division

JORDANS
2000

First Edition 1953
Seventh Edition 1993
Eighth Edition 2000

Published by
Jordan Publishing Limited
21 St Thomas Street
Bristol BS1 6JS

British Library Cataloguing-in-Publication Data
A catalogue record for this book is available from the British Library.

ISBN 0 085308 409 2

Typeset by Mendip Communications Ltd, Frome, Somerset
Printed by MPG Books Ltd, Bodmin, Cornwall

ACKNOWLEDGEMENTS

The authors and publishers are grateful to Xenia Frostick who updated and substantially rewrote the chapter on directors' pensions and to Andrew Thornton of Erskine Chambers for providing the Specimen Executive Director's Service Agreement which is reproduced with his kind permission.

Appendix E, Draft Statement of Directors' Duties, Company Directors: Regulating Conflicts of Interests and Formulating a Statement of Duties (LAW COMMISSION No 261, SCOTTISH LAW COMMISSION No 173, Cm 4436) Crown Copyright reproduced by permission of the Controller of Her Majesty's Stationery Office.

The Combined Code has been reproduced by kind permission of Gee Publishing Limited, © The London Stock Exchange Limited.

PREFACE

In the preface to the last edition in 1993, we expressed our disappointment that the Companies Act 1989 had left the efforts to consolidate companies legislation in tatters.

Sadly, we have to report that, six years later, things are even worse. Nothing whatsoever has been done to catch up on consolidation and those amendments which are introduced tend to be the subject of unpredictable and unscrutinised secondary legislation. Changes of government seem to make little difference – the importance of company law as a framework for a dynamic business sector has never been recognised by our decision makers. Impending reforms of company law are sometimes announced and indeed three consultative papers have been put out since the last election by the Company Law Review Steering Group. These covered General Meetings and Shareholder Communications, Company Formation and Capital Maintenance and Overseas Companies. However, the validity of the consultation process must be open to doubt as a single example may illustrate.

The meetings document consults on whether public companies should, like private ones, be allowed to dispense with annual general meetings. Yet, no mention is made of the recent Combined Code on Corporate Governance which placed so much emphasis on the importance of quoted companies making the most constructive use of the annual general meeting. The Code is set out in Appendix D, but businessmen and professionals will be less willing to give their time to serve on committees such as those which led up to the production of this Code if their efforts are being disregarded in any subsequent consultation exercise.

The Queen's Speech heralded the Limited Partnerships Bill, an Insolvency Bill and the Electronic Communication Bill. Drafts have been published, but much of the detail is to be brought in by delegated legislation which is unlikely to be debated in Parliament. The Insolvency Bill covers three main areas. It will introduce a much needed procedure for a moratorium when a company is seeking a voluntary agreement. There will be a procedure for unfit directors to give an undertaking to the Secretary of State that they will not act as a director for a specified period as an alternative to the delay and expense of disqualification procedures in the courts. Finally, notice will have to be given before an administrative receiver is appointed. The draft provision on this last matter shows the absurdity of using delegated legislation when no apparent thought has been given to the substantive provisions. Notice will have to be given in the specified manner before an administrative receiver can be appointed. It must be served within the specified period leading up to the appointment. It must contain specified information and must also comply with other specified requirements. What are all these specified items? Wait and see – all will be revealed when the delegated legislation is finally unveiled by the Secretary of State. How can lawyers advise their clients on likely changes in the law when this is how it is being produced. At the best of times, it is difficult for Parliament to find time to scrutinise even substantive legislation. When everything is left to a statutory instrument, we are almost back in the world of Royal prerogative.

So, are there any other likely reforms that we can look forward to? A new Table A for small companies may be introduced of which the main new element would be some form of escape route from the company for dissatisfied shareholders as an alternative to bringing unfair prejudice proceedings under s 459 of the 1985 Act. In terms of judge-made law, the Court of Appeal has, at the time of writing this preface, just handed down its ruling in the case of *Secretary of State for Trade and Industry v Deverell*. For perhaps the first time, the definition of shadow director was considered as a central element in a case of disqualification. The judgment will, no doubt, be reported shortly, but the Court of Appeal appears to have widened the previous interpretation of the words 'a person in accordance with whose directions or instructions the directors of the company are accustomed to act'. The Court held that such directions and instructions do not have to extend over all or most of the corporate activities of the company; nor is it necessary to show a separate element of compulsion or a tendency to 'lurk in the shadows'.

A positive reform which we can welcome is the Law Commission's recommendation of a statutory statement of a director's main fiduciary duties and his duty of care and skill. The reader can see the draft statement in Appendix E. Amongst other things, it will, if enacted, give statutory force to the landmark judgment of Hoffmann LJ (as he then was) in *Re D'Jan of London Ltd*. He said there that the standard of skill and care of a director should be the same in negligence as in wrongful trading; he must reach the standard actually possessed by him *and* that which would be objectively expected of such a director. The old subjective test set out by Romer J in his judgment in *Re City Equitable Fire Insurance* will belatedly be given its last rites.

We may perhaps conclude on another positive, if surprising, note by congratulating the Companies Registry on converting itself into a practical, user-friendly and above all speedy arm of the DTI. Practitioners of 20 years ago would not recognise the new agency and it is a pleasure to acknowledge it.

Peter Loose
Michael Griffiths
David Impey

January 2000

CONTENTS

TABLE OF CASES

References are to paragraph numbers.

TABLE OF STATUTES

References are to paragraph numbers and Appendices.

TABLE OF STATUTORY INSTRUMENTS

References are to paragraph numbers and Appendices.

TABLE OF EUROPEAN MATERIAL

References are to paragraph numbers and Appendices.

TABLE OF ABBREVIATIONS

AGM	Annual General Meeting
AIM	Alternative Investment Market
APPS	Appropriate Personal Pension Scheme
AVC	Additional Voluntary Contribution
CGT	Capital Gains Tax
CJA 1993	Criminal Justice Act 1993
COMBS	Contracted-out Mixed Benefit Scheme
COMPS	Contracted-out Money Purchase Scheme
COSRS	Contracted-out Salary-Related Scheme
DTI	Department of Trade and Industry
EC	European Community
EGM	Extraordinary General Meeting
ESOS	Employee Share Ownership Scheme
EU	European Union
FA 1987	Finance Act 1987
FA 1992	Finance Act 1992
FIFO	First in First out
FSAVC	Free Standing Additional Voluntary Contribution
FURBS	Funded Unapproved Retirement Benefit Scheme
GMP	Guaranteed Minimum Pension
HMSO	Her Majesty's Stationery Office
ICP	Investment Protection Committee
ICTA 1988	Income and Corporation Taxes Act 1988
IHT	Inheritance Tax
IoD	Institute of Directors
LILO	Last in Last out
OPRA	Occupational Pensions Regulatory Authority
PAYE	Pay As You Earn
PRO-NED	Promotion of Non-Executive Directors
PSO	Pensions Schemes Office
RAC	Retirement Annuity Contract
RPRP	Registered Profit Related Pay
SARs	Rules Governing Substantial Acquisitions of Shares
SAYE	Save As You Earn
SERPS	State Earnings-Related Pension Scheme
SFO	Serious Fraud Office
SIPP	Self-Invested Personal Pension
SSAS	Small Self-Administered Scheme
SSAS Regulations	Retirement Benefit Schemes (Restriction on Discretion to Approve) (Small Self-Administered Scheme) Regulations 1991, SI 1991/1614 as amended by SI 1998/1315 and SI 1998/728
UURBS	Unfunded Unapproved Retirement Benefit Scheme

Chapter 1

THE COMPANY AND ITS LEGAL FRAMEWORK

1.1 BACKGROUND

This book deals with the powers and duties of directors of companies registered in Great Britain.[1] But before turning to the directors themselves, we should look briefly at the legal framework within which they work. What, then, do directors direct? The answer, for all practical purposes, is companies which are limited by shares and which are registered under the Companies Acts 1985 to 1989, or prior companies legislation, going back to 1844. The Joint Stock Companies Act 1844, introduced the principle of incorporation by registration which has been followed ever since. Limitation of liability was achieved by shareholders in 1855 and private companies were set apart from public companies in 1907. Company law was reformed by eight Acts between 1862 and 1981, and on each occasion the overall trend was towards greater disclosure by the company and greater powers of intervention by the State.

Before 1972, company law and its reform were purely domestic matters. Pressure for reform came largely from within the UK, and the strength of that pressure would determine the range and content of new Companies Acts. Some, like the 1948 Act, were thoroughgoing overhauls of company law, while others, like the 1967 Act, merely embodied proposals which appealed to the government of the day.[2] On its entry to the European Community (EC), however, the UK became obliged to give legislative form to EC Company Law Directives.[3] Thus, although the 1976 Act was essentially a 'domestic' Act, the 1980 and 1981 Acts were, to a considerable extent, designed to implement the EC Directives.

Directives by the EC Commission do not directly change UK law – it is the implementing UK Acts which have this effect. Nevertheless, it is a principle of community law, and this principle does bind English courts, that the implementing legislation should be construed in the light of the Directives and that the domestic courts should therefore refer to the text of the relevant Directive.[4]

Companies Act 1985
In 1985, the scattered provisions of the previous Companies Acts[5] were consolidated. 'Consolidation' does not involve any changes in the substance of earlier Acts,[6] but seeks to provide a coherent body of legislation setting out that substance in a single document and in a rational order.[7] The result was the Companies Act 1985, which contains nearly all the law previously contained in the 1948, 1967, 1976, 1980 and 1981 Acts. While the Companies Act 1985 has suffered many repeals, modifications and amendments, it remains the principal Act in relation to companies. Consequently, subsequent references to 'the Act' or 'the principal Act' are references to the

Companies Act 1985, and references to section numbers are to section numbers in the Companies Act 1985, unless otherwise indicated.

Associated Acts

At the same time, three 'satellite' Acts were passed. These were also consolidating measures drawn from the old legislation, and the reasons for their separation from the principal Act were a mixture of principle and expediency. The Business Names Act 1985, although derived from the 1980 and 1981 Companies Acts, regulated the trading names of partnerships and sole traders as well as companies, and it was clearly appropriate to remove this regulation from a 'pure' Companies Act. The Company Securities (Insider Dealing) Act 1985 (since repealed and replaced by the Criminal Justice Act 1993) dealt with trading in listed or advertised securities. Whilst it had considerable bearing on the conduct of company directors and management, it was not concerned with company structure as such and operated in an area where further legal and self-regulatory developments were already occurring. It was therefore convenient to sever these provisions from the principal Act. Finally, the Companies Consolidation (Consequential Provisions) Act 1985 contained a number of repeals and amendments of 'specialist' legislation[8] together with a number of necessary savings and transitional provisions.[9]

Table A

At the same time, the opportunity was taken to modify Table A, the statutory 'model form' for a company's Articles of Association. Section 8 removes Table A from the principal Act and provides that it shall be in the form prescribed by regulations.[10] This enables modifications to be made from time to time without disrupting the principal Act.[11]

Further developments prior to the Companies Act 1989

As is noted elsewhere, company law, as it affects directors, is, to a surprisingly large extent, the creation of the courts, not of Parliament. As far as statutory controls are concerned, however, the 1985 consolidation provided a welcome breathing space. It was no longer necessary to hunt through different Acts to root out an original provision and its amendment, and possible re-amendment or repeal. To a certain extent this remains true. In what follows, it is more often than not sufficient to refer simply to the 1985 Act. However, even in that same year of 1985, the Insolvency Act 1985[12] made many amendments and repeals to the principal Act, as well as introducing many new provisions. It was almost immediately overtaken by the Insolvency Act 1986, which sought to consolidate all insolvency legislation, in doing so repealing and replacing large parts of the principal Act itself. On a smaller scale, the Company Directors Disqualification Act 1986 sought to blend and consolidate the rules disqualifying directors and others from company management. The Financial Services Act 1986, among many other things, sought to regulate 'investment business' including public offers.

Companies Act 1989

As previously noted, the latest round of major legislative changes to company law were made by the Companies Act 1989. This Act introduced significant and far-reaching changes, such as the pruning of the ultra vires rule (see **1.5.2**), and a largely unsuccessful attempt at 'deregulation' of private companies (which has since had to be revisited in order to revoke anomolies). Particularly, the 1989 Act implements the EC Directives on regulation of auditors and in relation to group accounts. While those changes which are within the scope of this book are looked at in detail later, it is worth taking time at this stage to understand the way in which parts of the 1989 Act have been drafted.

A particular problem which warrants consideration is that large parts of the 1989 Act made changes to existing rules by lifting out parts, sections, or parts of sections, of the 1985 Act, and rewriting them, with the changes added or built in. The rewritten parts are then inserted back into the 1985 Act. References to certain parts, or sections, of the principal Act – the Companies Act 1985 – are therefore references to new versions of those parts or sections introduced by the 1989 Act.

The director faced with a reference to the Act must therefore ask whether the part or section of the Act referred to has been rewritten by the Companies Act 1989, or whether it is unaffected by the 1989 legislation. If it has been rewritten by the 1989 Act, he must then ask whether the rewritten part of the Act has been brought into force yet. The result is that the prudent director may well consider many of the 1989 changes better absorbed if received as advice from professional advisers, or from books like this one, than from the legislation itself. Sadly, this lack of accessibility is a hallmark of much modern legislation.

A related note of caution in respect of the 1989 Act is that some of the rules in the principal Act, affected by the 1989 Act have not actually changed, but they have been moved about in the 1985 Act as part of the general rewriting of that Act by the 1989 Act. For example, dormant companies continue to enjoy exemption from the requirement that their company accounts must be audited. However, the relevant rule, which appeared at s 252 of the Act in its pre-1989 incarnation, has been moved by the 1989 Act. It now appears at s 250 of the Act in its post-1989 incarnation.

At the time of publication, virtually all of the changes wrought by the 1989 Act are in force. The main exception is the new Part IV in relation to company changes intended to be introduced by the Companies Act 1989.

The Department of Trade and Industry (DTI) has indicated that the new Part IV will never be brought into force. Consequently, this text treats the 1989 Act reforms as if they were wholly in force, unless otherwise indicated and references to sections of the Act are to the Act as amended by the Companies Act 1989. For example, a reference to s 250 of the Act will be a reference to the section dealing with dormant companies. However, this will not apply to Part IV of the Act, in relation to which references are to the original version of the 1985 Act.

Statutory instruments

A further feature of the 1989 Act is that it is a classic example of a modern legislative trend of introducing Acts which delegate power to the Secretary of State to decide upon the substantive law to be introduced in relation to certain matters, rather than setting it out in the Act itself. The general area in which such a power may be exercised is specified in a particular section of the Act, and the Secretary of State can then legislate as he wishes within those parameters. He exercises this power by means of delegated or subordinate legislation, which takes the form of regulations set out in a document called a 'statutory instrument'. For example, the audit exempt company was introduced by the Secretary of State by means of the Companies Act 1985 (Audit Exemption) Regulations 1994[13] pursuant to a power given to the Secretary of State in that regard by s 257 of the Act.[14]

Traditionally, there were relatively few statutory instruments and they dealt only with peripheral housekeeping matters. For example, devolved powers were, in the past, exercisable in relation to relatively minor matters such as fees to be charged by Companies House or the format of statutory forms. However, as the example of the audit exempt company shows, the current trend is to devolve power in relation to a substantial number of quite significant matters. The director has only to consider the Table of Statutory Instruments at the beginning of this book for an inkling of their breadth and importance.

The advantage of statutory instruments is that they enable the Secretary of State to introduce changes swiftly and easily in response to immediate needs. Statutory instruments are not debated, and nor do they use up parliamentary time in the way that new, primary legislation (such as a new Companies Act) does, because they merely have to be 'laid' before Parliament.

However, one disadvantage is that there is a temptation to sacrifice attention to detail in the quest for speed. Unfortunately, this happens to an unacceptable extent. The upshot is that a depressingly large number of new statutory instruments are made to clear up ambiguities, inconsistencies or omissions in previous instruments. It is absolutely typical that, in the same year as the statutory instrument which introduced the audit exempt company, we were also treated to the Companies Act 1985 (Audit Exemption) (Amendment) Regulations 1994[15] and in 1995 to the Companies Act 1985 (Audit Exemption) (Amendment) Regulations 1995.[16] Two further amending statutory instruments were made in 1996, followed by three made in 1997.

The consequence of the existence of these amending instruments, is that the search for the latest version of a rule can involve labyrinthine investigation of a number of instruments to trace the original rule, and any subsequent amendments or repeals.

Of course, this problem would be eased if there were effective consultation prior to laying important new instruments. In the late 1980s and early 1990s, such consultation as took place was often perfunctory, resulting in the laying of many defective instruments. The defects were, of course, discovered by the hard-pressed practitioner who had to waste time, and his clients' money, struggling to comply. The tide seems to have turned in this respect and, these days, Companies House is able to cite a satisfyingly long list of topics upon which consultation is taking place prior to introduction of new instruments.

Another disadvantage is that, unlike an Act, there is a relative lack of publicity attached to the introduction of a new statutory instrument. Whilst most company lawyers will subscribe to the 'Daily List' of new statutory instruments issued by Her Majesty's Stationery Office (HMSO), few directors will and therefore rely on their advisers to alert them to relevant new instruments.

A third disadvantage is that, even if directors are aware of a new instrument, they may have difficulty accessing it. Whilst there are on-line and CD-ROM services which include the text of statutory instruments, few directors will subscribe to these so that the alternative is to order instruments from their nearest HMSO.

It would not be fair to suggest that the whole process could almost have been designed to introduce vast quantities of company law by the back door and keep it from the directors who need access to it, but directors could be forgiven for thinking that it looks that way.

A final characteristic of statutory instruments is that, in certain circumstances, the Secretary of State has power to amend primary legislation by means of a statutory instrument. For example, the European Communities Act 1972 permits him to make instruments which amend UK Acts of Parliament if the instrument is being introduced in order to implement an EC Directive. An example is the instrument which introduced the single member private company,[17] which amended both the Companies Act 1985 and the Insolvency Act 1986 in order to implement the EC Twelfth Directive. Similarly, the Deregulation And Contracting Out Act 1994 empowers the Secretary of State to amend primary legislation by statutory instrument, if for the purposes of deregulation of business.

These factors all make the task of finding the latest version of a particular rule, complete with all amendments and repeals, and whether in an Act or in a statutory instrument, even more problematic for the director and his advisers.

Since the Companies Act 1989
The tide of legislation arising as a result of the obligations of membership of the EU continues unabated.

For example, as mentioned above, single member companies were introduced in 1992. These companies are able to operate, if they are private companies, and subject to certain safeguards, with a sole shareholder, who may also be the sole director. In effect, sole traders are able to incorporate and parent companies no longer need to find a nominee to hold one share in their wholly owned subsidiaries if they are to retain limited liability.

More recently, the Public Offers of Securities Regulations 1995[18] have substantially amended the law relating to public offers of unlisted securities, as well as amending Part IV of the Financial Services Act 1986 in relation to offers of listed securities. These complex regulations were necessary as a result of the EC (Public Offers) Directive.[19]

The rules prohibiting insider dealing (see Chapter 7) in the Company Securities (Insider Dealing) Act 1985 have also been repealed and replaced by provisions in the Criminal Justice Act 1993 in the drive to create common laws as to insider dealing across the EU.[20]

The future
The advent of the Labour government has led to a major review of company law which is intended to result in root and branch reform in the new millennium to make the UK economy more competitive. This could result in wholesale changes to the

nature and operation of the business vehicles available in the UK and to the duties, burdens and responsibilities of those owning and managing them. The government has also indicated it intends to introduce an Electronic Communications Bill, rather earlier than the general company law reforms, which is likely to affect the administration of companies in areas such as company meetings and statutory filing and record-keeping, as well as in the general area of company contracts. However, at the time of writing the final legislative form these proposals will take is still unclear.

1.2   TYPES OF COMPANY

For all practical purposes, we are considering directors of companies limited by shares and registered under the Act, referred to here as 'registered companies'. These are not the only types of company which can exist, but they are by far the most numerous and significant and all references in this book are to such companies unless the contrary is stated. The full range of possibilities is as follows.

(1)   A registered company limited by shares, in which case the liability of a member is limited to the amount, if any, unpaid on his shares[21] and which in turn are subdivided into:

  (a)   a public company, ie a company limited by shares, whose Memorandum of Association states that it is a public company and which has been duly registered as such;[22] and

  (b)   a private company, ie all other companies limited by shares.

(2)   Registered unlimited companies, where a member's liability to contribute is unlimited.[23] Such companies are always private.

(3)   Registered companies limited by guarantee, where a member's liability is limited to the amount which he has guaranteed to contribute in the event of winding up.[24] Such companies are always private companies.

(4)   Companies incorporated by Royal Charter, for example, Hudson's Bay Co.

(5)   Companies incorporated by special Act of Parliament, for example, public corporations.

Types (4) and (5) do not concern us here and, of the registered companies, type (1) must have a share capital, type (3) must not and type (2) may or may not, as its promoters wish. Unlimited companies have the privilege of a general exemption from filing accounts[25] and may more easily repay or reduce their share capital than limited companies. Guarantee companies are often members' clubs, residents' associations and other non-commercial institutions.

We are, therefore, dealing here with directors of private and public companies limited by shares and the significant difference between such companies should be briefly looked at before we go on to consider the administrative machinery of limited companies generally.

1.3   PUBLIC AND PRIVATE COMPANIES

A public company is one registered with a Memorandum of Association which states that it is to be a public company. All other companies are private companies. Thus, the public company is the exception, and the private company (which accounts for over 99 per cent of registered companies) is the norm.[26] In general, both types of company are governed by the Act, but there are many provisions which are expressed to apply only to one type or the other.

The principal distinctions[27] between public and private companies are as follows.

(1) The name of a public company must end with the words 'public limited company' or, as an alternative the abbreviation 'plc'.[28]

(2) A public company must not commence business or borrow unless the Registrar has certified that he is satisfied that its allotted share capital is at least the statutory minimum of £50,000[29] and that at least one-quarter of the total allotted share capital, and any premium, is paid up.[30]

(3) A public company must have at least two members – it cannot be a single member company.[31]

(4) A private company need have only one director (although he cannot also be secretary). A public company must have two.[32]

(5) Restrictions on the tenure of directors aged 70 or over apply only to public companies and their subsidiaries.[33]

(6) A secretary of a public company must fulfil certain criteria.[34]

(7) Proxies may speak at general meetings of private, but not public, companies.[35]

(8) It is a criminal offence for a private company to offer its shares to the public.[36]

'Public' companies are not necessarily also 'listed' companies. Listed companies must, by definition, be public companies but the converse is not the case. A company may register as a public company and commence business with no intention of seeking a quotation.

1.4 THE MACHINERY OF THE COMPANY

All companies are now registered in the same way, although there are certain special requirements in the case of public companies.

The components to register a company limited by shares are as follows.

(1) The Memorandum of Association stating the name, domicile (England and Wales, or Scotland), objects, limitation of liability and authorised share capital[37] and subscribed, in the case of a private company, by at least one person, and in the case of a public company by at least two persons.[38] A public company's Memorandum must state that it is formed as such.[39] The authorised or nominal capital of a company stated in the Memorandum is not necessarily the same as its issued capital and, indeed, companies are often formed with an issued capital comprising a number of shares which is far greater than the share or shares which the subscribers to the Memorandum have agreed to take.

(2) The Articles of Association containing the internal regulations of the company which must be signed by the subscribers to the Memorandum.[40] Registration of Articles is not compulsory, as the specimen Articles known as Table A will apply automatically to any company, public or private, except as modified or extended. However, the Articles of a private company will very often contain restrictions

on membership not found in Table A and, in practice, Articles are virtually always registered.

(3) A 'statement of the first directors, secretary and registered office' (Form 10)[41] and a 'declaration of compliance with the requirements of the Act' (Form 12), together with the registration fee.

If all is in order, the Registrar of Companies issues a Certificate of Incorporation[42] whereupon the company becomes a legal entity separate from its members.[43]

Same day registration

It is possible to obtain a Certificate of Incorporation on the same day that the documents are filed. This can be extremely useful in the case of transactions such as reconstructions or acquisitions when secrecy might be essential until the parties are ready to complete the transaction.

The procedure is simple. The paperwork must be presented over the counter at any of the offices of the Companies Registry before 3 pm on the relevant day, together with a special fee. The sole caveat is that the proposed name of the company must not contain a sensitive word requiring approval of the Secretary of State or some other body or person (see **1.5.1**).

Public companies

Because of the need to ensure that public companies are adequately capitalised, extra rules apply to such companies. Foremost is the requirement that the authorised capital is at least £50,000,[44] since otherwise the company will not have sufficient shares to allot in order to obtain the certificate issued under s 117 (see below). The amount of authorised capital, together with the statement in (1) above as to public status, will be recorded in the Memorandum. The process leading to the issue of the certificate of incorporation is then similar to the incorporation of a private company. Thereafter, as already noted, the company must not trade or borrow until a further certificate has been issued under s 117. This certificate will be issued when the Registrar has received, verified and approved a declaration[45] by a director or the secretary specifying:

(a) the amount of the allotted share capital, which must be shares to a minimum nominal value of at least £50,000;[46]

(b) the amount paid up on each share, remembering the general rule that a public company must not allot a share unless it is paid up immediately as to at least 25 per cent of its nominal value and the whole of any premium;[47]

(c) the actual or estimated amount of preliminary expenses, and an indication of the person responsible for payment; and

(d) details of payments and other benefits received by promoters.

If a public company does trade or borrow before the issue of a certificate under s 117, both the company and any culpable officer (including a director) are liable to a fine. In addition, each and every director (whether culpable or not) is liable to indemnify the other party to that forbidden (but valid) transaction if the company for any reason fails to perform it.[48] These sanctions apply even though the uncertified company complies with all the statutory requirements, because the Act punishes the failure to obtain a certificate before transacting business and encourages directors to make sure that this does not occur.

Reregistration

A limited company's public or private status is not immutable. A private company's shareholders may decide by special resolution to reregister as public, and to alter the Memorandum and, if necessary, the Articles.[49] However, before a private company can be reregistered as a public company it must satisfy the capital requirements already mentioned, and its application to reregister must be accompanied by:

(a) a balance sheet not more than seven months old with an unqualified auditor's report;

(b) a declaration by the auditors that net assets are at least equal to the sum of the called-up share capital and undistributable reserves (see **4.4.2**);

(c) a declaration by a director or the secretary verifying the special resolution and the capital requirements and undertaking that net assets have not fallen below the required level since the balance sheet date;[50] and

(d) the altered Memorandum and Articles.

Conversely, a public company may reregister as a private company[51] by altering its Memorandum by special resolution, deleting the 'public company' clause and making any further amendments which may be necessary to the Memorandum and Articles. The amended documents and an application to reregister will then be sent to the Registrar. Registration is automatic, unless an objection is made to the courts by dissenting members holding five per cent of the shares (or any class of shares) or by 50 separate dissenting members. Such an objection must be made within 28 days of the resolution. If the court confirms the resolution, it may order the dissentients to be bought out and, in that case, the company will not only be reregistered, but have a reduced capital. But, this apart, there is no need for a public company which seeks reregistration actually to reduce its capital at all.

Same day reregistration

It is possible to obtain a Certificate of Incorporation on reregistration on the same day that the documents are filed. The procedure is the same as for registration of a new company on a same day basis. The paperwork must be presented over the counter at any of the offices of the Companies Registry before 3 pm on the relevant day, together with a special fee. The fee varies according to whether a substantive change is also being made to the company's name (that is, a change which does not constitute substituting 'public limited company' for 'limited' on a reregistration from private to public). Again, the proposed new name must not contain a sensitive word (unless it was already in the name prior to the reregistration), which requires approval of the Secretary of State or some other body or person (see **1.5.1**).

Members

The members own not the company but their shares in it, and perform their functions through the medium of the general meeting. However, even the general meeting is not a physical manifestation of the company itself, and its rights and powers depend upon the provisions of the Companies Acts and the Articles. The role of the general meeting vis-à-vis the directors is discussed in Chapter 3, and it will be seen that, far from being in control of the company's affairs, the general meeting may rather be regarded as playing second fiddle to the directors for most purposes.

Directors

The directors, since the company cannot act in person, are required officers of the company and are normally entrusted with the duty of managing its affairs. Regulation 70 of Table A states that 'the business of the company shall be managed by the directors', but the precise nature of their powers and duties depends upon the terms of the Memorandum and Articles in each case, subject to the overriding provisions of the Act and the general duties and responsibilities arising from cases decided in the courts. A private company must have at least one director and a public company (unless registered before 1 November 1929) must have at least two.[52] When the company receives its Certificate of Incorporation, the effect is to appoint those named in Form 10 (see (3) above) as the first directors and secretary[53] and, indeed, any attempt at this stage to treat someone not named in Form 10 as first director or secretary is void.[54]

Secretary

The secretary is also a compulsory requirement of the Act and must not be:

(a)   the sole director of the company; or
(b)   a corporation whose sole director is also sole director of the company; or
(c)   sole director of a corporation which is itself the sole director of the company.[55]

In the case of a public company, the secretary must meet certain criteria.[56]

Auditor

An auditor must, unless in the case of a private company the shareholders have passed an elective resolution to the contrary,[57] or the company is dormant[58] or an 'audit exempt' company[59] and therefore has no auditors, be reappointed annually by the shareholders, although the initial appointment and the filling of subsequent casual vacancies may be made by the directors.[60]

He cannot be:

(a)   an officer or servant of the company; or
(b)   the partner or employee of an officer or servant; or
(c)   if the auditor is an undertaking such as a body corporate, the auditor of a company which is one of its shareholders; or
(d)   a person precluded by (a) or (b) from acting as auditor of a parent, subsidiary or co-subsidiary of the company.[61]

He must be:

(a)   a member of a recognised supervisory body; and
(b)   eligible under the rules of that body to be an auditor.[62]

It is the directors' duty to check the qualifications of the auditors, as an unqualified appointment is a nullity and the Department of Trade and Industry (DTI) may then intervene and make the appointment.[63] The importance of the modern auditor cannot be overestimated, and the extent of his duties, and the identity of those to whom they are owed, are the subject of constant and fierce debate.[64]

Registered office

A registered office is required at all times after the company is formed.[65] The address must be in England and Wales, or in Scotland, whichever country is chosen as domicile in the Memorandum, and details must be filed with the Registrar. The purpose of the registered office is to provide an address to which communications and proceedings may be addressed since the company cannot be served in person. The posting of documents to the registered office is good service and a company which moves and fails to notify the Registrar has only itself to blame if judgment is obtained against it in default.[66] The office need not be its place of business and may freely be changed within the country of domicile upon registration of Form 287 by the Registrar. The company's name must be shown outside but there is no requirement that the Certificate of Incorporation should be displayed in the office.

1.5 MEMORANDUM OF ASSOCIATION

The Memorandum and Articles are of importance to every director. He should obtain copies and make himself familiar with their contents since he is deemed to know what is in them.[67]

The Memorandum of a private company contains five clauses, the name, domicile in which the registered office is to be situated, objects, liability and capital. The Memorandum of a public company will contain a sixth clause declaring its status as such.[68] These clauses common to all companies need more consideration.

1.5.1 Name

The name of a public company must always end in the words 'public limited company' or 'plc'[69] and that of a private company in 'limited' or 'Ltd'.[70] The use of those expressions anywhere else in the name is not permitted.[71] Private companies may not use a name ending in the words 'public limited company' or 'plc', nor may a public company use a name which implies that it is a private company.[72] On the other hand, certain private companies may dispense with the word 'limited' but only: (i) if they were licensed to do so on or before 25 February 1982 under s 19 of the 1948 Act; or (ii) if they are guarantee companies. In either case, the dispensation applies only to a company whose object is the promotion of commerce, art, science, education, religion, charity or a profession, and which prohibits dividends and distributions of assets to members.[73] There is, of course, no objection to the use, in the name, of expressions such as '& Sons', indicating a family business or a business to which there has been some succession.[74]

As to the substance of the name, there is, in principle, freedom of choice. There are, however, certain restrictions, and also various requirements as to the display and disclosure of names.

(1) The Registrar of Companies maintains an index of company names under s 714.[75] A company will not be registered with a name which duplicates an existing name,[76] nor will it be allowed to adopt a new name which does so.[77] The Registrar has no discretion to refuse to register a name on grounds it is similar to an existing name but, paradoxically, the DTI may direct a company to change its name within 12 months of registration in the index if it considers it to be the same as or 'too like' a name in the index.[78] Such directions are, in practice, made only following an objection, and investigations by the Registrar, by an aggrieved company.

(2) Registration will be refused if the name would, in the opinion of the DTI, be 'offensive', or if in the DTI's opinion its use would constitute a criminal offence.[79]

(3) The permission of the DTI is required for a name which implies a connection with central or local government, or which includes words or expressions specified in regulations under s 29.[80] Regulations made under earlier legislation, but still in force under the Act, have specified words such as 'Royal', 'Prince' and 'Windsor' (for obvious reasons) and also 'Group', 'Holding', 'Great Britain' and 'International' to prevent spurious claims to size or status.[81] Certain types of words may also require 'positive vetting', by a body designated in the regulations.[82] Such words are often referred to as 'sensitive' words.

(4) It is permissible for a company to trade (partly or wholly) under a name other than the name registered under the Act. If it does so, however, it is subject to the Business Names Act 1985[83] unless, in certain circumstances, the name merely indicates a business 'succession', for example, 'X and Sons'. The Business Names Act 1985 does not require registration of the trading name,[84] but does require the DTI's approval for any business to trade in Great Britain under a name:

   (a) suggesting a link with central or local government; or
   (b) including words or expressions specified in regulations made under the Act.[85]

(5) A company may be forced to change its registered name if the DTI considers it to give 'so misleading' an indication of the business as to be 'likely to cause harm to the public'.[86] The company may ask the courts to set the DTI's order aside, provided that it does so within three weeks, but, subject to that, the order must be complied with within six weeks, the new name taking effect as soon as the Registrar issues an amended Certificate of Incorporation. The change of name does not affect substantive rights and liabilities[87] or legal proceedings already commenced.

(6) A company may change its name voluntarily at any time by passing a special resolution and obtaining a new Certificate of incorporation from the Registrar.[88] The change becomes effective only upon issue of the Certificate, and not from the date of the special resolution. The new name is subject to the same screening process which applies when the company is first registered. As in the case of a compulsory change of name, there is no effect on existing rights or proceedings. It is possible to obtain a new Certificate on a same day basis. The procedure is that the special resolution must be lodged, over the counter, at any office of the Companies Registry in the relevant jurisdiction, prior to 3 pm on the day the

certificate is required together with the special premium fee. The proposed name must not include a sensitive word or expression within (2) or (3) above.

(7) When a company has gone into insolvent liquidation its name becomes a 'prohibited name' for the purposes of s 216 of the Insolvency Act 1986. The prohibition, which covers any name[89] by which it was known in the 12 months preceding liquidation, does *not* mean that no other company may adopt or continue to use the name. But anyone who was a director[90] of the insolvent company must not, for a period of five years from the liquidation, serve as a director of another company using the prohibited name or one similar to it,[91] or be concerned in the management of any unincorporated business using that name. Breach involves criminal liability (up to two years' imprisonment and an unlimited fine) and civil liability for the debts of the director's 'new' company – if it is an existing company he must resign.[92] He may, however, apply to the court for leave to act, either within a week of the winding up[93] or at any time during the prohibition. (If he does, he may continue to act for a period of six weeks after his application, or a period ending on the date the application is dealt with by the court, whichever occurs first.)[94] In addition, the Insolvency Rules 1986 allow him to act without leave of the court in the management of a company using a prohibited name if:

(a) that company took over the business from – in most cases – the liquidator and gives full details of the use of the name and the intention to appoint him to the creditors of the liquidating company; or

(b) that company was trading and known by the prohibited name for the whole of the 12 months preceding the winding up of the liquidating company.[95]

In addition, there are various requirements as to the display and disclosure of the corporate name.

(1) The company's registered name must be displayed legibly and conspicuously outside every place of business.[96] Where the Business Names Act 1985 applies (see (4) above) this requirement is reinforced by s 4 of that Act, which requires the registered name to be prominently displayed at each place of business to which the company's customers or suppliers have access, together with an address at which documents may be served on the company.

(2) The company's seal and its business letters, notices, bills, cheques and orders must display the registered name prominently and legibly.[97] In addition, its business letters, order forms, etc, must also show:

(a) the place of registration, for example, England and Wales, Wales or Scotland;

(b) its registered number; and

(c) the address of the registered office, or an indication that the address on the document, or if more than one, which one of them is the registered office.[98]

Where the company trades under a different name, s 4 of the Business Names Act 1985 requires all orders, business letters, invoices, receipts and written demands for payment to set out both the registered name and an address at which documents may be served on the company. Under this Act, an actual or potential customer may demand a written list of these particulars, which he must be given immediately.[99]

1.5.2   Registered office

By s 287, every company must have a registered office to which all communications and notices may be addressed. The memorandum contains a so-called registered office clause. This does not refer to the address of the office. This is contained in Form 10 (see **1.4**). It simply states that the company is incorporated in England and Wales (or Scotland if such be the case) and so establishes the law to which the company is subject. This clause cannot be altered.

1.5.3   Objects

Traditionally, if the director looked at the objects clause in his company's Memorandum he would see that it started with the words: 'The Company's objects are . . .'. There would then follow subclause (a), which contained a description of activities roughly corresponding to what the company actually did. Subclause (a) was usually referred to as the 'main objects clause'. This was followed by a long series of further subclauses apparently giving the company power to do almost anything under the sun. This form of omnibus objects clause has been supported by the courts,[100] and it was universally adopted in practice in an effort to avoid falling foul of the ultra vires rule under which the company could do nothing which was not expressly or impliedly authorised by its objects clause in the Memorandum.

The ultra vires rule still applies. However, the Companies Act 1989 sought to simplify objects clauses, by providing a statutory object and statutory powers for companies whose Memorandum of Association states that 'the object of the company is to carry on business as a general commercial company'.[101] It has done this by providing that such a company has, as its implied object, the carrying on of any trade or business whatsoever, and has implied power to do all such things as are incidental or conducive to the carrying on of any trade or business by it.[102] Existing companies may alter their Memorandum to take the new format on board.[103] Of course, the advantage of using or adopting the new wording is that the company will never need to alter its main objects again.

Regrettably, the 1989 Act leaves a number of large question marks about the construction of the new rule. Can a company state further objects in its Memorandum, in addition to the 'general commercial company' object and still enjoy the ability to carry on any trade or business? What of activities which many companies wish to carry on, such as payment of pensions to directors, employees etc, or subscription to charitable causes, which may not be incidental or conducive to trading activities?

The answer to the former question is probably no. It appears from the wording of s 3A(a) that such a company must have only one sole object if it is to enjoy the implied object and power under the Act. The answer to the latter is that companies which wish to carry out such activities should include in the statement of the objects of the company further provisions – not stated to be objects – which set out additions to the statutory object and power implied by use of the 'general commercial company' object. The problems and uncertainties created by the reforms introduced by the 1989 Act mean that, in practice, the 'general commercial company' object clause should be used only after appropriate professional advice or, in the case of, for example, a company registration agent, upon being satisfied that the agent has taken such advice.

Of course, new companies may continue to be incorporated with traditional style objects, rather than the 'general commercial company' object.

The ultra vires rule

This originally evolved in the courts as a means of protecting shareholders from having their share capital invested by the company in business ventures which they had not contemplated when they acquired their shares.[104] Hence, the courts held that any transaction which was not within the terms of the objects clause decided upon by the shareholders or was not reasonably incidental thereto was beyond the company's capacity (ultra vires) and could not be enforced, either against, or (probably) by, the company.[105] However, its original purpose was lost sight of and the rule became mainly a trap for unwary third parties, enabling the company or its liquidator to get out of paying debts freely contracted in good faith.[106] Moreover, if the members of the company themselves wished to change the objects it was not difficult for them to do so.[107]

As a result of successive reviews and reforms, culminating in ss 35, 35A and 35B of the Act, substantive changes have been made, both as to the effect of the ultra vires rule on the relationship between the shareholders and the directors, and the relationship between the company and third parties.

Dealing first with the relationship between the shareholders and the directors, s 35(2) allows a shareholder to step in and restrain the company from doing an act which is beyond the company's capacity. Since shareholders rarely find out about the activities of the directors until after the company is committed, this is not, in practice, much of an effective protection for a shareholder, since by then it is too late to prevent the transaction. However, the directors' duties to the company include a duty to observe any limitations on their powers which flow from the Memorandum of Association, so that if they commit the company to an act which is beyond its capacity, they will be liable for breach of duty. They escape only if the shareholders not only ratify the act, but also specifically agree to relieve the directors of their liability, in each case by special resolution. This is perhaps a more effective protection for the shareholders than their powers to restrain the directors, even though it does not result in the company escaping the transaction.

It is the second aspect of the changes which is of more significance – the relationship between the company and third parties. Since it is unrealistic for a third party to check the company's Memorandum of Association every time he becomes involved with a company, the new rules protect the third party against the consequences of the company exceeding its capacity. This protection is now so extensive that the application of the ultra vires rule to dealings between companies and third parties can be virtually ignored.

Now, neither the company nor the third party can try to escape their obligations by arguing that an act was beyond the company's capacity as defined in its Memorandum of Association. This is true whether the act is a commercial transaction, such as a contract, or a non-commercial matter, such as a donation to a charity, and whether or not the company or the third party knows that the act is beyond its capacity. Nor need the parties be acting in 'good faith', so that the act may even be, to the parties' knowledge, patently not in the company's interests. This means that the contents of the Memorandum of Association will be a matter of indifference to third parties.

However, an act might be called into question not only because it is beyond the capacity of the company, but also because the third party is dealing with the board of directors, or one or more of their number, or some other agent of the company authorised by the board and, as a result of some limitation under the company's constitution, the board or other agent does not have authority to bind the company. This problem is dealt with in s 35A(1). Such a limitation might appear in the Memorandum of Association, or the Articles of Association, or may be a limitation derived from a shareholders' resolution or agreement, or a class shareholders' resolution or agreement – it makes no difference to the application of s 35A(1).

The section applies only in favour of the third party, and not in favour of the company. It prevents the company from escaping its obligations by arguing that the board or other agent was not authorised to commit the company to those obligations. While the third party is protected whether the act is a commercial or non-commercial transaction, the third party must 'act in good faith'.

A third party will be treated as acting in good faith even if:

(1)   he does not bother to check the constitution or public record; or
(2)   he does check but does not understand the limitation; or
(3)   he checks and understands the limitation.

It seems that the third party must at least know that what the directors are doing is not in what they (the directors) honestly regard as being the best interests of the company. The net effect of these new provisions is that, in the absence of exceptional circumstances, the third party need not concern himself with the directors' authority to bind the company at all.

However, s 35A(1) only stops the *company* from trying to escape its obligations – what if the *third party* tries to escape by arguing, for example, that an act is beyond the powers of the board of directors? In that case the company may protect itself by ratifying the act, by special resolution of the shareholders, and enforce its rights.

The effect of these rules, coupled with the power to use the truncated 'general commercial company' object, is to provide a coherent and sensible regime, which is in tune with commercial realities. For example, as between shareholders and directors, a corporate parent controls its wholly owned subsidiary by far more practical and effective means than by relying on the legal niceties of the ultra vires rule. Similarly, as between companies and third parties, a company which tried to avoid obligations to a third party by relying on the ultra vires rule would soon find third parties – customers, suppliers, etc – giving it a wide berth, so that, in reality, trying to use the ultra vires rule to avoid its obligations was never a sensible commercial proposition.

However, the new rules might leave one loophole. Directors of the company might themselves take advantage of the rules to validate transactions which benefit them or their associates. To counter this, an exception is made of such transactions in s 322A. The exception provides that a transaction to which:

(1) a director of the company (or of its holding company); or
(2) a person connected with such a director; or
(3) a company with whom such a director is associated;

is a party, and in respect of which the board of directors have exceeded their authority under the constitution, is voidable at the instance of the company.

As a final 'tying up' of the ultra vires doctrine, it is made clear that, save in respect of registered charges, the doctrine of 'constructive notice', whereby a person is deemed to be aware of and understand all matters on the public record at Companies House, has been abolished.

One final word of warning is that charities are wholly excluded from these reforms, so that directors of, and third parties dealing with, corporate charities should beware! Likewise, the reforms have no application to statutory companies or companies formed by Royal Charter.

Change of objects

Whether a company has the 'general commercial company' object or not, s 4 permits a change of objects by special resolution and allows objectors with not less than 15 per cent of the whole or any class of the issued capital to apply to the courts within 21 days for cancellation. The courts have the power to order the company to buy out the objectors and to make a corresponding capital reduction. Objection on the ground that the alteration is outside the limits of s 4 can be made by any shareholder, however small his holding. But s 6(4) goes on to say that an alteration cannot be questioned on this ground unless proceedings are started within 21 days of the resolution.

If, therefore, the members are unanimous, they can change the objects to anything they like. No one can object and after 21 days the alteration becomes impregnable. A copy of the special resolution and of the Memorandum as altered has to be filed within 15 days,[108] and in addition:

(1) the Registrar must publish notice of receipt of the alteration in the *Gazette*;[109]
(2) the company cannot 'rely against other persons', on the alteration, unless it had been notified in the *Gazette*, or the third party had actual knowledge of it;[110]
(3) the third party may extend his period of protection to 15 days after notification in the *Gazette* if he was 'unavoidably prevented' from knowing of the alteration;[111] and
(4) a copy of the Memorandum of Association, as amended, must be filed with the Registrar within 15 days.[112]

The *Gazetting* requirements of s 711 apply not only to alterations of objects but also to, inter alia:

(1) Certificates of Incorporation;
(2) alterations of other parts of the Memorandum (for example, name or capital) or of the Articles;
(3) notice of change of directors;
(4) annual return;

(5)   notice of change of registered office.

1.5.4   Liability

The liability clause of a registered limited company states: 'The liability of the members is limited'.[113] In a sense, this is superfluous, since once the separate identity of the company is established there is no reason why the members should be liable for the company's debts. Their liability, if any, is to the company itself and is limited, as one would expect, by the terms of their contract with the company. They have taken shares and they must therefore pay for them – hence their liability is limited to the amount unpaid on those shares. This will include a share premium if the shares have been allotted to them on those terms, since the premium forms part of the company's capital.[114]

The main exception to the principle of limited liability derives from the rule that, save in the case of a single member company, if the minimum membership falls below two for more than six months, every member who knows of this is jointly and severally liable with the company for debts contracted during that time.[115]

Limited and unlimited private companies may reregister as unlimited and limited respectively under the procedure provided by ss 49 and 51, provided that they have not already reregistered the other way. These procedures were introduced in 1967 because of the abolition of the 'exempt private company' by the Companies Act 1967. The attitude of the legislature and of the Jenkins Committee, which recommended abolition, was that limited liability was a privilege to be paid for in the form of public disclosure of one's accounts. Hence, private companies were offered a simple choice – limited liability with disclosure or unlimited liability with privacy.

1.5.5   Share capital

The Memorandum must state the amount of share capital and its division 'into shares of a fixed amount'. This fixed amount is the 'nominal' or 'par' value of the share.[116] Thus, 'no par value' shares are not permitted, although they are often recommended.[117] The amount stated in the Memorandum is, of course, the authorised or nominal capital, and is simply the amount which the company is authorised to issue. It must be distinguished from the following.

(1)   Issued or allotted capital – that part of the authorised capital actually issued to members.
(2)   Paid-up capital – that part of the issued capital which has actually been paid for by the members.
(3)   Uncalled capital – that part of the issued capital not yet called up ie for which the company has not yet asked for payment.
(4)   Reserve capital – that part of the uncalled capital which the company has resolved not to call up except on winding up.[118]
(5)   Loan capital – which is not true capital at all but borrowings, often secured by debentures creating a fixed and/or floating charge. The debenture holders are not members but creditors of the company and the borrowings do not form part of the company's share capital. For this reason the restrictions on the allotment of securities, which are described below, do not generally apply to debentures, but

only to shares. However, those restrictions would be held to apply at least in some cases, on the issue of debentures which may be exchanged for shares of similar value often referred to as convertible loan stock.

(6) Stock – simply fully paid issued shares consolidated and expressed as units of currency.

Occasionally, the Memorandum also divides the shares into classes – preferential, ordinary, deferred, etc – and sets out their rights, but this is more usually done in the Articles. Shares may be denominated in any currency, indeed a multi-currency share capital is permitted.[119] However, in the case of a public company the requirement for a minimum issued capital of £50,000 means that the share capital of such a company must always include at least that amount in sterling, whatever the currency of the remaining share capital.

Substantial changes in the law governing share capital were introduced by the Companies Acts 1980 and 1981. In outline these are as follows. They are designed to ensure, particularly in the case of public companies, that the gap between the apparent and the real capital base of a company is not too great.

Payment for shares

(1) No company may allot shares at a discount, ie for a payment which is less than their nominal (or par) value.[120]

(2) Shares may be allotted for money or money's worth. This includes goodwill or know-how (for example, on transfer of a business to a company in return for shares).[121]

(3) A public company may allot shares only where they are paid up as to 25 per cent of nominal value and the whole of any premium.[122] An exception is made for shares issued under an employees' share scheme, defined by s 743 as a scheme to facilitate the holding of shares (or debentures) by, or for the benefit of, past or previous employees[123] of the company (or of its holding or subsidiary company or of another company in the same group).

(4) A public company must not allot shares as fully or partly paid up if the consideration for the allotment (or part of it) is an undertaking of some sort which may be performed more than five years after the allotment.[124] Nor may a public company ever accept an undertaking to do work or services in payment for its shares (or any premium on them).[125]

(5) Subject to the preceding rules, and provided its subscriber shares are paid for in cash (see (7) below) a public company may allot shares as fully or partly paid up for a non-cash consideration, provided that:

(a) it has obtained an independent valuation[126] of the consideration for the proposed allotment;

(b) it has received a report of that valuation in the six months before the allotment;[127]

(c) it has sent a copy of the report to the allottee.[128]

A copy of the report must be sent to the Registrar who will publish a note that he has received it.[129] This procedure need not, however, be followed by a company which is merely using its reserves or profits to pay up shares allotted to members by way of a bonus issue (often called either a scrip issue or a capitalisation of reserves),[130] nor does it apply on a merger or other arrangement with another company, provided that all the shareholders or relevant class members of the other company are allowed to take part in the arrangement.[131]

A common feature of all these provisions is that the allottee is liable to make up any deficiency in payment, with interest at five per cent, where a rule is infringed. The calculation of the deficiency will exclude any 'forbidden' consideration so that, for example, a public company allotment will infringe rule (3), above, if part of the consideration relied upon to make the shares 25 per cent paid up is in the form of work or services in contravention of rule (4), above. Further, a later holder of the shares will be liable to the same extent unless he can show that he is, or derived ownership of the shares from, a purchaser who acquired them for value and without notice of the infringement.[132] The Act preserves the enforceability against the allottee of 'forbidden' undertakings given as 'payment' for the shares.[133] Consequently, a person liable to make up a deficiency in payment is entitled to petition the court for relief,[134] for example, against having to pay for the shares and to perform the promised services. The court has a wide discretion when relief is sought, subject to two 'overriding principles':

(a) that the company shall have received money and/or money's-worth at least equal to the value of the shares and any premium, taking all the consideration for the allotment into account;

(b) that where the company has more than one remedy (for example, to call for the deficiency to be made up, and to enforce a 'forbidden' undertaking), it should be for the company to decide which remedy it wishes to pursue.

Contravention of the rules is also an offence by the company, and by any culpable officer of the company.[135]

(6) The rules described above apply equally to a private company which has passed a resolution to be registered under s 43 as a public company.

(7) Shares to be issued to a subscriber to the memorandum of a company which is being formed as a public company must be paid up in cash, with the whole of any premium.[136]

Redeemable shares

Any company may now issue shares of any class, on terms that they are redeemable at the company's or holder's option, provided that the Articles permit it and provided that there are, at the time of issue, at least some unredeemable shares.[137] In some circumstances, a private company may redeem such shares out of its capital.[138] For the rather complex provisions governing such repayments, see Chapter 7.

Alterations in capital

There are two main ways of altering the conditions in the capital clause:

(1) increase of capital, subdivision, conversion into stock or consolidation may be simply effected by ordinary resolution of the members.[139] Provided that it has not been issued, share capital may also be cancelled by ordinary resolution.[140] In each case, the resolution and a notice of increase of capital, subdivision etc is filed within 15 days;

(2) reduction of issued capital[141] is a more drastic step and is closely supervised since it conflicts with one of the fundamental principles of company law – the preservation of the company's capital for the benefit of the creditors. Reduction is only possible if it is:

    (a) authorised by the Articles, as under Table A, reg 34;

    (b) effected by special resolution (75 per cent majority); and

    (c) confirmed by the courts.[142]

A capital reduction may be sought because of a capital loss, or because the company is overcapitalised. In the latter case, at least, the proposed reduction may affect creditors, as when capital is being returned to the shareholders. They have the right to object and the courts will impose protective conditions before confirming the reduction.

Where the courts confirm a capital reduction by a public company to below the 'authorised minimum' of £50,000, the reduction will not normally take effect until the company has been reregistered as a private company.[143] Normally this would also require a special resolution, but the courts may permit reregistration without this and will then approve the alterations to the Memorandum and Articles required by the change of status.

The effect of a variety of other actions, such as the redemption of shares, or a purchase by a company of its own shares may also be to reduce or at least weaken a company's capital base. Further powers and controls are imposed by the Act and these are described in Chapter 7.

Reduction of capital is to be distinguished from reduction or loss of assets, although the consequences of the latter may be even more serious for the company, its members and its creditors. Consequently, the Act requires that when the directors of a public company discover that its net assets have fallen to 50 per cent or less of its called-up share capital, they must, within 28 days, convene an extraordinary general meeting to be held within 56 days of the discovery.[144] Although the Act does not make it clear whether constructive knowledge as well as actual knowledge will suffice to trigger the directors' obligations, it would be unwise to assume that a director who fails to see the obvious, or to make the sort of inquiry which the situation reasonably demands, will be treated as having no 'knowledge'. On the other hand, the criminal liability imposed by the section is attached to each director who 'knowingly and wilfully authorises or permits' the failure to call a meeting, so that there is scope for argument about the precise meaning of the requirements. The meeting itself will discuss the losses and is, presumably, intended to discuss possible remedial action. What positive steps the meeting may take and how much further the discussion may range (for example, as to directors' future conduct) is unclear, since the Act says, rather opaquely, that it does not 'authorise the consideration ... of any matter which could not have been considered at the meeting'.[145]

1.6   ARTICLES OF ASSOCIATION

1.6.1   In general

While the Memorandum regulates the company's dealings with the outside world and may be described as its charter, the Articles control its internal affairs and are more in the nature of by-laws or standing orders. For most purposes, they are of more daily concern to the director than the Memorandum and he should take particular note of their contents. Companies have almost complete freedom in their choice of Articles and from them the director can ascertain his powers and certain of the procedures which he must follow.

Since 1862, there have been various different versions of a 'model form' set of numbered regulations which the different Companies Acts have stated will apply as the Articles of each company limited by shares registered under the relevant Act unless a particular company lodges Articles of Association which exclude or modify its application. This model form is called Table A (to distinguish it from, for example, the model form of Memorandum and Articles of Association for a company limited by guarantee at Table C). The most recent version of Table A is set out in Appendix C to this book.

At one end of the scale, a director of a listed company will find that his company has lodged Articles which exclude Table A completely. Instead, they will comprise a set of regulations drafted to meet the company's specific requirements. At the other end of the scale, there are a very few companies which have not lodged Articles with the Registrar of Companies at all, so that Table A applies as the Articles of these companies in its entirety.

However, it is extremely rare to find companies which rely solely on Table A as their Articles. As Table A is so widely drafted, it is almost invariably inadequate to meet the needs of a particular company in some, or several, respects. Consequently, the great majority of companies lodge Articles of Association with the Registrar which state that Table A shall apply generally, but then set out various exclusions or modifications to specific regulations in Table A so that it is tailored to the company's particular requirements. This is so common that it can be said to be the usual practice. Since this means that the Articles cannot be easily understood except by cross-reference to Table A, a copy of it is often bound into the back of the Articles.

Since there have been many different versions of Table A, the question arises as to which Table A applies to a particular company. The rule of thumb is that the Table A which was in force at the date the company was incorporated will, unless the company's Articles exclude it completely, apply to the company subject to any modifications made to it by the company's Articles.

That Table A (as modified) will continue to apply notwithstanding that new versions of Table A may have been brought into force subsequent to the company's incorporation, unless and until the company's members pass a special resolution to adopt a whole new set of Articles. Upon passing such a special resolution, the version of Table A then in force (unless the company's new Articles exclude it completely) will apply to the company from then on,[146] subject to modifications to it effected by the Articles at the date of the special resolution. The different versions of Table A in force at various times were as follows.

Date of incorporation or adoption of new Articles	*Version of Table A*
1862 to 30 September 1906	1862 Act version
1 October 1906 to 31 March 1909	Statutory Rule 80.596/L15
1 April 1909 to 31 October 1929	1908 Act version
1 November 1929 to 30 June 1948	1929 Act version
1 July 1948 to 21 December 1980	1948 Act version
22 December 1980 to 2 December 1982	1948 Act version as modified by 1980 Act
3 December 1982 to 30 June 1985	1948 Act version as modified by the 1981 Act
1 July 1985 to 31 July 1985	Companies (Tables A to F) Regulations 1985 version
1 August 1985 to date	Companies (Tables A to F) Regulations 1985 version (as amended)[147]

In addition, various minor amendments were made to the 1948 version of Table A by the Companies Act 1967, the Companies Act 1976 and the Companies Act 1981. These are not mentioned in the above list. However, the 1980 Act changes are mentioned specifically because they were so significant. The resulting Table A, although nominally still based on the 1948 Table A can, in practice, be thought of as a new version. The Finance Act 1970 and the Stock Exchange (Completion of Bargains) Act 1976, also made changes to the Table A in force at the time of each.

Until the 1980 Act changes, Table A was divided into Parts I and II. Part I embodied regulations appropriate to public companies. Part II applied to private companies only. However, Part II worked by saying that Part I also applied to private companies, except for regs 24 and 53. It then set out alternative 'private company' versions of these regulations. It also included additional regulations specific to private companies such as the power for members to pass resolutions by written resolution in lieu of a general meeting – the familiar 'round-robin' procedure.

The 1980 Act swept away Parts I and II, so that Table A became a single set of regulations applicable to both private and public companies. This was a blessing in one respect, since a common mistake made by private company directors consulting the pre-1980 version of Table A was to consult Part I and then fail to realise that there was a Part II which modified the application of Part I to their company. They therefore followed the wrong regulations. For some reason, this was particularly common in relation to the quorum requirements, which were different in Parts I and II.

However, it was a curse in another respect, because it did make Table A even more general in its provisions, so that it became even more likely that companies would need to amend it to meet their particular needs – and there is no doubt that this happened.

It can be seen that most versions of Table A appeared in a schedule to whichever Companies Act introduced them. This had the disadvantage that amendments to

Table A required fresh legislation which, in turn, required parliamentary time. Now, however, s 8 of the Act provides for Table A to be introduced, and amended or replaced, by statutory instrument laid before Parliament. This is just as well because the current version, introduced on 1 July 1985 by the Companies (Tables A to F) Regulations 1985, had to be amended on 1 August 1985, a mere 30 days later, by the Companies (Tables A to F) (Amendment) Regulations 1985. At least this early hiccup proved that the new practice worked and enabled a swift response to the need for changes to the regulations.

As discussed at **1.1** above, the disadvantage of legislating by statutory instrument is that it makes it difficult for the director to monitor and keep abreast of changes. This is less of a problem in this context since changes to Table A do always involve substantial consultation and attendant publicity.

So far, we have discussed the effect of special resolutions to adopt a new set of Articles, which is to update the version of Table A which applies to the company. It should be noted that a special resolution which merely alters or amends the existing Articles, rather than adopting a whole new set, will not usually have this effect. Any Table A regulations which applied to the company prior to the passing of such a resolution will continue to apply to it afterwards.

A copy of a special resolution to adopt new Articles, or to alter existing Articles, should be inserted into all copies of the Articles, and all copies should be reprinted so that the text of the Articles reflects the terms of the resolution in each case. It is also good practice to insert a note at the beginning of the Articles, under the heading, referring to the date upon which the Articles were adopted, or if they have been amended, the date or dates upon which this occurred. Unfortunately, these practices are not always followed and a newly appointed director should make a company search and obtain copies of all resolutions which have been passed and any other information on the company's public record.

Directors of a company to which an old version of Table A applies will need to be aware that there will be limitations on the ability of their company to undertake certain transactions. For example, a company incorporated prior to the introduction of the Companies Act 1981 and to which a pre-1981 version of Table A applies, will be unable to buy back its own shares under the purchase of own shares procedure introduced by that Act. Consequently, any company incorporated prior to 1 July 1985, and which is contemplating a change to its Articles, should normally consider adopting an entire new set of Articles so that the current version of Table A applies, subject to such modifications as are appropriate to the company's needs.

1.6.2   In particular

The Articles govern almost every aspect of the director's activities and the relevant provisions of Table A and other common Articles are noted throughout the text which follows. Certain characteristic features of the Articles can usefully be summarised as follows.

(1) The Articles (and Memorandum) have the effect of a covenant or contract, signed and sealed by every member.[148]

(2) The director as such, is not a party to the contract but it can be enforced:

  (a) by the company against any member, for example, to refer a dispute to arbitration;[149]

  (b) by any member against the company, for exmaple, to compel the company to record his vote;[150]

  (c) by one member against another, for example, to compel another member to buy his shares.[151]

(3) The Articles do not themselves form a contract with the director *qua* director, but they may (unusually) form the basis of the director's service contract and provide evidence of its terms, for example, as to salary.[152] Even so, they are always liable to alteration by the members in the usual way, by special resolution (see (4)).

(4) The Articles are freely alterable by special resolution of the members (75 per cent majority),[153] subject to certain restrictions:

  (a) the alteration must not conflict with the Memorandum. This is not likely to occur, in any event, with a modern form of Memorandum which would not contain class rights or anything beyond the requirements of the Act;[154]

  (b) the alteration is subject to the terms of the Act, for example:

    (i) s 16 – it must not increase a member's liability to contribute capital to the company without his consent,

    (ii) s 127 – it must not vary class rights without following the procedure of the section which gives the right to object to 15 per cent of the class members,

    (iii) s 459 – it must not conflict with an alteration made by the courts under the procedure provided by this section for relief against 'unfairly prejudicial' behaviour.

  (c) Alteration must be bona fide for the benefit of the company as a whole,[155] ie not discriminatory against a particular group of shareholders.[156] However, the burden of proof of bad faith is heavy and in most of the reported cases the objector has failed to discharge it. The fact that the majority will, in practice, be the beneficiaries of the alteration, is not enough and the courts have been reluctant to overturn a majority vote even where the relative voting power of the objectors is being diminished.[157]

  (d) An alteration may be a breach of contract with a third party, for example, where it conflicts with a managing director's service agreement. He cannot prevent the alteration but he is entitled to damages.[158]

The Memorandum and Articles (and any alterations) are on file at Companies House and may be inspected and copied by anyone.[159]

1.7   THE ROLE OF THE DIRECTOR

Where, then, does the director stand on this corporate stage and what part does he perform? In fact, he plays several parts. The company is an artificial person but it cannot function without human agents. Those agents are the directors, and as company law evolved at a comparatively late stage in the history of English law, judges who were asked to define an office which fitted no established legal category exactly, utilised elements from various other branches of the law.

These elements are discussed in the text but include the following.

Agency

The director is acting not on his own behalf, but on behalf of the company. Therefore, he is, in some respects, an agent and has some of the rights and duties which characterise the principal and agent relationship, for example:

(1) on contracts within his authority, it is normally the company and not the director who is liable;[160]

(2) if he exceeds his authority, he may be liable to a third party for breach of warranty of authority;[161]

(3) like other agents, he must account to his principal for any personal profit made by him out of his position.[162]

And yet, he differs from other agents in that he himself, in conjunction with his co-directors, is in control of the affairs of his own principal and that principal is itself restricted in its freedom of action by the ultra vires rule.

Trusteeship

Directors are often described as trustees and this is certainly true in the sense that:

(1) any assets in their hands are held on a fiduciary basis for the company;[163]

(2) their powers must be exercised for the benefit of the company, for example, they must not issue shares for the purpose of maintaining their control[164] or refuse to register transfers when they have no power to do so[165] or transfer shares accrued by their company for no consideration to other companies;[166] and

(3) they are in a fiduciary position and their personal interests must not conflict with their duties to the company.[167]

It will be noted that the beneficiary is the company itself and not the members.[168] But the directors differ from trustees in the conventional sense in that:

(1) the 'trust' property is not vested in them; they are agents and not principals;

(2) their duties of management usually involve the running of what must, in some ways, be a speculative business – they must take risks which a trustee would not be permitted to take; and

(3) their duties of skill and care are probably lower than those of ordinary trustees, whose function is to hold and administer investments.

Master and servant

A non-executive director who confines his role to that of attending board meetings is not an employee,[169] but a full-time executive director is employed by the company[170] and for many purposes his position is similar to that of other employees. This was envisaged by the Companies Act 1948, which used the words 'any director holding a salaried employment or office in the company' in s 54(1)(b); and s 153(4)(c) of the 1985 Act refers to 'persons (other than directors) employed' by the company. In this situation the director is wearing two hats, one as a member of the board and one as an employee. It is the failure to keep these two capacities separate which has led to confusion in some of the cases.

Independent contractor

Insofar as the director is rendering services for reward, he must accept the burden of skill and care which falls on all such persons. The level of the duty was pitched very low in the leading authority on the duty of skill and care,[171] but it has probably risen in recent years, particularly where highly qualified or experienced directors are appointed to perform executive duties. Thus, there seems no reason why a chartered accountant appointed as finance director should not be expected to show the same objective standard of skill and care as if he were engaged to the work as a private practitioner.

1.8 WHO ARE THE DIRECTORS?

The appointment of directors is discussed in Chapter 2 but it must be borne in mind that the word is not confined to those who have been formally appointed. It may, in fact, have several meanings.

(1) A person duly appointed in accordance with the Articles and not subsequently disqualified by any provision in the Articles. He is a director for all purposes.

(2) A person appointed, but with some defect in his appointment; so far as third parties are concerned, his acts are validated by s 285.

(3) A person never appointed at all, either properly or improperly, but nevertheless, performing the functions of a director. This de facto director is converted into a director for some purposes of the Act and of the insolvency legislation, by cases such as *Re Lo-Line Electric Motors Limited*,[172] in which it was held that the meaning of 'director' would vary according to the context in which it was found, but could certainly include a 'de facto director' in many parts of companies legislation. The far-reaching consequences of this should not be underestimated. Its effect is that such a person may unknowingly incur many of the responsibilities and penalties imposed by the Act and other legislation affecting companies such as the Insolvency Act 1986, while at the same time having none of the authority of a proper appointment. Hence, he may find himself liable not only to statutory penalties or personally liable to third parties for the debts of the company under provisions such as the wrongful trading rules of s 214 of the Insolvency Act 1986, but also to the company itself for intermeddling in its affairs. The net has, since 1980, been thrown even wider to catch, officially, what are called 'shadow directors', for many parts of the legislation now regulate not only 'directors' but also 'shadow directors'. A shadow director is defined by s 741 as 'a person in accordance with whose directions or instructions the directors[173] are accustomed to act'. This will include all those who exercise a measure of regular control over the company (whether or not in some concealed or sinister manner) although it does exclude professional advisers acting as such. Another company may well be a shadow director whether or not it has placed its 'own men' on the board and it has been necessary to provide specifically that, in certain circumstances, holding companies are not invariably to be treated as shadow directors of their subsidiaries, although in all other circumstances this is a possibility.[174]

An interesting line of cases involving insolvent companies and their bank managers has created a frisson of concern, although that concern is probably overstated. Certainly, judicial comment swings first one way and then the other on this question. The cases generally involve a bank manager telling frightened company directors what to do to help their financially troubled companies – an urge which bank managers find hard to resist given that their loans to the companies are in jeopardy – or deciding which cheques the bank will bounce and which not. The liquidators in the subsequent liquidations are then keen to fix the bank with liability to contribute to the companies' debts as an alleged shadow director.

Company 'doctors' have also come under the microscope and need to act very carefully if they are not successful in nursing their corporate patient back to health to ensure that they are not fixed with some liabilities as shadow directors.[175]

Institutional investors, particularly those reserving the right to appoint a board member, perhaps in times of crisis, must also be alert to the possibility that their director's influence over the rest of the board might constitute them as a shadow director. Finally, shareholders in joint venture companies often have 'representative' directors on the board of the company and should take care to ensure that a shadow directorship is not inadvertantly created.

The question of whether a person has been notified to the Registrar of Companies by filing of Form 288a as a director has no bearing on the question of whether that person is a director or not.[176] Status as a director is not dependent upon such filing. Failure to comply is an offence by the company and any officer in default[177] but it does not confirm or invalidate the appointment. The presence or absence of the director's name on the company's file may, however, be relevant to the question of whether a person has been 'held out' as a director to third parties.[178] Note that s 288 (Register of Directors) treats a shadow director as a director and officer of the company.

1.9   WHO ARE THE OFFICERS?

The word 'officer' will often be found in the Acts when a person is being fixed with liability for company offences. Thus, s 288 of the Act, requiring registration of directors and secretaries, says that 'the company and every officer of the company who is in default is liable to a fine and, for continued contravention, to a daily default fine'. This is the characteristic language employed by the Act for the enforcement of its requirements. Several points may be noted.

(1)   Section 744 of the Act provides that 'officer' includes a director, manager or secretary. Thus, the definition is not exhaustive but will inevitably comprise all those engaged in management at a senior level, whatever they may be called. An auditor is an 'officer' for some purposes but not for others, but normally a person employed as an independent professional, such as a solicitor or accountant, does not fall within the definition.[179]

(2)   How then does an officer become liable to criminal proceedings and a default fine? He does so if he 'knowingly and wilfully authorises or permits the default, refusal or contravention mentioned in the enactment'.[180]

(3) What is the default fine itself? All fines (except those for serious offences tried before a jury) are subject to a 'statutory maximum' fine.[181] The current maximum is £5,000. Daily default fines vary from offence to offence under the Act but are either one-tenth or, more commonly, one-fiftieth of the statutory maximum.[182]

CHAPTER 1 FOOTNOTES

1 Section 745 of the Companies Act 1985.
2 Thus, the 1967 Act embodied a few of the very many proposals made by the *Report of the Company Law Committee Under the Chairmanship of Lord Jenkins* (The 'Jenkins Report'), Cmnd 1749 (June 1963).
3 The infamous s 9 of the European Communities Act 1972 (now repealed and replaced by ss 35, 35A, 35B, 36, 42 of the Companies Act 1985) itself was an attempt to comply with the first EC Directive on Company Law.
4 *Friedrich Haega GmbH, Re (No 32/74)* [1975] 1 CMLR 32, ECJ.
5 Together with certain other relevant provisions, such as s 9 of the Insolvency Act 1976 (disqualification of directors of insolvent companies).
6 Minor amendments were made before the consolidating legislation to remove anomalies.
7 But it does not form a comprehensive 'code' of company law. Many of the most important principles of company law are to be found only in decided cases, for example, as to directors' duties.
8 For example, repeal of the Insurance Companies Act 1982.
9 For example, in relation to companies which enjoyed 'public company' status until the reclassification of public and private companies introduced by the Companies Act 1980.
10 Companies (Tables A to F) Regulations 1985, SI 1985/805, with minor amendments in SI 1985/1052.
11 For discussion of Articles of Association, see **1.6**.
12 Which partly implemented and partly neutered the 'Cork Report', *Insolvency Law and Practice*, Cmnd 8558 (June 1982).
13 SI 1994/1935.
14 Altogether, 16 statutory instruments had been made pursuant to s 257 at the date of publication.
15 SI 1994/2879.
16 SI 1995/589.
17 Companies (Single Member Private Limited Companies) Regulations 1992, SI 1992/1699.
18 SI 1995/1537.
19 Directive 89/298/EEC, OJ 1989 L124/8.
20 Directive 89/592/EEC, OJ 1989 L334/30 (Directive co-ordinating regulations on inside dealing); and see **7.9** below.
21 Section 1(2).
22 Section 1(3). Registration or reregistration as a public company must have occurred on or since 22 December 1980, when this definition came into force.
23 Section 1(2)(c).
24 Section 1(2)(b).
25 Section 254. But see Partnerships and Unlimited Companies (Accounts) Regulations 1993, SI 1993/1820 for unlimited companies whose members are limited companies, or another unlimited company or Scottish firm each of whose members is a limited company.
26 Before the 1980 Act, the reverse was true and the 1948 Act treated private companies as the exception.
27 Further consequential distinctions will be found, in particular, in **1.5.4**, **4.4**, and Chapter 7 generally.
28 Or their Welsh equivalents, ss 25 and 27.
29 The company's share capital must therefore include shares to the nominal value of at least this amount in sterling, even if the remainder of the company's share capital is in a currency (or currencies) other than sterling. See *Re Scandinavian Bank Group plc* [1988] Ch 87.
30 Section 117(1), (2).
31 Section 24.
32 Sections 282 and 283.
33 Section 293.
34 Section 286.
35 Section 372.
36 Section 81.
37 Section 2.

38 Section 1, and the Companies (Single Member Private Limited Companies) Regulations 1992, SI 1992/1699.

39 Section 1. It will simply say, 'the Company is to be a public company'.

40 Sections 7 and 8.

41 The statement is required by s 10.

42 Section 13.

43 *Salomon v Salomon & Co Ltd* [1897] AC 22.

44 The 'authorised minimum', which is subject to alteration by Order under s 118. See also ss 11 and 117.

45 In Form 117.

46 See note 29 above.

47 Section 101. Subscribers' shares in a public company, together with any premium, must be paid up in cash (s 106). Companies House has indicated that an undertaking to pay the sum due is not sufficient, and will not issue trading certificates on the strengths of such undertakings, notwithstanding the wording of s 102, even if the undertaking is to be performed within five years. For further rules relating to allotment, see **1.5.5**.

48 Section 117(8).

49 Sections 43–46 (private to public) and ss 53–55 (public to private).

50 Any allotment for a non-cash consideration between the date of the balance sheet and the resolution must have been valued under s 108 and a report of the valuation must be sent with the application to reregister. Further, the consideration must have been independently valued for the benefit of the company within the six months preceding the allotment (s 44). Where a non-cash consideration is in the form of contractual undertakings by the allottee, further restrictions are imposed by s 45. Although these restrictions are relaxed in respect of employee share schemes (see **1.5.5**), shares held under these schemes are not to be counted towards the necessary minimum allotted share capital.

51 But not as an unlimited company.

52 Section 282.

53 Section 13(5).

54 Section 10(5).

55 Section 283.

56 Section 286.

57 Section 386.

58 Section 250.

59 See Companies Act 1985 (Audit Exemption) Regulations 1994, SI 1994/1935 as amended by SI 1994/2879, SI 1995/589, SI 1996/189, SI 1996/3080, SI 1997/220, SI 1997/570 and SI 1997/571 and ss 249A–249E.

60 Sections 385(3) and 388.

61 Sections 25–28 of the Companies Act 1989.

62 Sections 25–28 of the Companies Act 1989.

63 Section 387.

64 See further the reference to the *Caparo Industries* and related cases at **4.3**.

65 Section 287.

66 Section 725; *A/S Cathrineholm v Norequipment Trading Ltd* [1972] 2 All ER 538.

67 Copies as lodged at Companies House may be obtained through law agents or direct from the Registrar of Companies.

68 Section 2.

69 Sections 25(1) and 27. 'Cwmni cyfyngedig cyhoeddus' or 'ccc' may be used if the registered office is in Wales.

70 Sections 25(2) and 27. The Welsh equivalents are 'cyfyngedig' or 'cyf'. There are exceptions, but these do not relate to ordinary trading companies.

71 Section 26.

72 Section 33. Criminal liability is imposed on responsible officers.

73 Sections 30 and 31.

74 This is specifically permitted by s 1 of the Business Names Act 1985, as to which see note 83 below.

75 This includes not merely the names of companies registered under the Act but the names of certain other companies, including foreign companies with a place of business or branch in Great Britain.

76 Section 26(1)(c).

77 Section 28(6).

78 Section 28(2). The power extends to the case where the other name was not, but should have been, in the index when the 'objectionable' name was registered.

79 Section 26(1). A (relatively) well-known prostitute who sought incorporation of her business, or profession, encountered difficulties under the forerunner of this provision. The names 'Prostitutes Ltd' and 'Happy Hookers Ltd' were rejected.

80 Section 26(2).

81 Companies and Business Names Regulations 1981, SI 1981/1685, as amended by the Companies and Business Names (Amendment) Regulations 1982, SI 1982/1653; Companies and Business Names (Amendment) Regulations 1992, SI 1992/1196; and Companies and Business Names (Amendment) Regulations 1995, SI 1995/3022. Interestingly, words such as 'worldwide' and 'European' are not sensitive.

82 For example, if the name includes the word 'university', a written request must be made to the Privy Council to ascertain whether it has any objections.

83 Section 1. So are individuals and partners using trading names other than their own, a fact which in practice is often overlooked.

84 Before the Companies Act 1981, the name was required to be registered under the Registration of Business Names Act 1916. This, to some extent, made it easier to discover who was the 'real' owner of a business. The system was widely abused by non-registration; instead of strengthening the system, the government elected to save public expenditure by abolishing the register altogether. Efforts to produce private registers have not, to date, met with noticeable success.

85 Section 2. There are savings for names which were in use before the 1981 Act came into force on 26 February 1982 and there is also a 12-month period of grace for the transferees of a business under a transfer made after that date. As to regulations, see note 81 above.

86 Section 32.

87 But a company should bear s 32 in mind when it changes its objects or alters its business substantially.

88 Section 28.

89 Ie whether or not its registered name and including a name so similar as to suggest an association.

90 Including 'shadow director'.

91 Or be concerned in its promotion or formation.

92 Subject to the exceptions noted below. This liability is quite apart from the possibility of disqualification or personal liability for wrongful trading arising out of his involvement with the liquidating company, and also extends to anyone in management of the other company who, knowing of the prohibition, acts on his instructions.

93 Insolvency Rules 1986, SI 1986/1925, r 4.229, as amended.

94 In which case the Department of Trade and Industry may appear and oppose his application and the court may seek information from the liquidator. For instance, where the courts have considered s 216 applications, although they have not always been consistent in their approach. See *Re Bonus Breaks Ltd* [1991] BCC 546, and *Re Lightning Electrical Contractors Ltd* [1996] 2 BCLC 302.

95 Insolvency Rules 1986, SI 1986/1925, rr 4.228 and 4.230.

96 Section 348.

97 Sections 349 and 350. An explanation of the Welsh 'ccc' or 'cyf' is also required if these are in the name.

98 Section 351. If the company is an 'investment company' within the meaning of s 266 this must also be stated.

99 Non-compliance may lead not only to criminal liability in those responsible (which is the common sanction for default in all the requirements described above) but also to the unenforceability of contracts by the company. It is doubtful whether this policing of the Business Names Act 1985 by customers and trading standards officers is effective. As an enforcement 'system' it wears a distinctly anaemic air.

100 *Cotman v Brougham* [1918] AC 514.

101 Section 3A.

102 Section 3A(a) and (b).

103 Section 4.

104 *Sinclair v Brougham* [1914] AC 398.

105 *Bell Houses Ltd v City Wall Properties Ltd* [1965] 3 All ER 427.

106 *Re Jon Beaufort (London) Ltd* [1953] 1 All ER 634.

107 Section 4.

108 Sections 6(1) and 380.

109 Sections 711 and 744.

110 Section 42.

111 Section 42.

112 Section 18.

113 Section 2. Exceptions to the limitation will be found at several points in this book, but the principle remains paramount. The exceptions apply to directors or officers, who may happen also to be members, rather than to members as such.

114 Section 130.

115 Section 24.

116 Section 2(5).

117 *Report of the Company Law Committee Under the Chairmanship of Lord Jenkins* ('the Jenkins Report') Cmnd 1749 (June 1963), at para 34. Case-law appears to support the proposition that the nominal value of a share does not have to be legal tender. For example, a share with a notional value of 0.001p appears to be theoretically possible.

118 Section 120.

119 See *Re Scandinavian Bank Group plc* [1988] Ch 87.

120 Section 100.

121 Section 99(1).

122 Section 101(1).

123 Or their husbands or wives, widows or widowers, or children or stepchildren under 18 years of age.

124 Section 102(1).

125 Section 99(2). But, despite rules (2) and (4), bonus shares may still be allotted paid-up with sums which the company has set aside for the purpose.

126 Ie by a registered auditor or an expert approved by him.

127 In theory at least the members will see it, sooner or later.

128 Section 103(1).

129 Sections 111 and 711(1)(f).

130 Section 103(2).

131 Section 103(3), (4) and (5).

132 Section 112.

133 Section 115.

134 Section 113.

135 Section 114.

136 Section 106.

137 Section 159; Table A, reg 3, gives authority to issue such shares.

138 Section 171.

139 Section 121 and Table A, reg 32.

140 Sections 122 and 123.

141 Sections 135 and 136.

142 Section 136; *Re Lucania Temperance Billiards Hall (London) Ltd* [1966] Ch 98. Even when confirming a reduction reflecting a capital loss the court may impose conditions protecting present creditors: *Re Grosvenor Press plc* [1985] 1 WLR 980. In very exceptional cases an order may be made to protect future creditors as well: *Re Jupiter House Investments (Cambridge) Ltd* [1985] 1 WLR 975; but future creditors are normally adequately protected by disclosure of the reduction by advertisement and in the accounts.

143 Section 139.

144 Section 142.

145 One possible construction is that this restricts discussion to: (i) matters directly relevant to the losses; and (ii) such further relevant matters as may be specified in the notice convening the meeting, bearing in mind the powers of the directors to convene an extraordinary general meeting.

146 The further complication that, whilst most repeals and amendments are prospective, some affect existing companies, is ignored here for the sake of relative simplicity.

147 SI 1985/805, amended by SI 1985/1052. Interestingly, a 'dry run' preceding consolidation was made by Regulations issued in 1984 but which never came into force.

148 Section 14.
149 *Hickman v Kent or Romney Marsh Sheep-breeders' Assn* [1915] 1 Ch 881.
150 *Pender v Lushington* (1877) 6 Ch D 70.
151 *Rayfield v Hands* [1958] 2 All ER 194.
152 *Re New British Iron Co Ltd ex parte Beckwith* [1898] Ch 324.
153 Section 9.
154 For discussion of class rights generally, see **9.1.3**.
155 *Greenhalgh v Arderne Cinemas Ltd* [1950] 2 All ER 1120.
156 *Sidebottom v Kershaw Leese & Co* [1920] 1 Ch 154.
157 *Rights & Issues Investment Trust Ltd v Stylo Shoes Ltd* [1964] 3 All ER 628. The cardinal
     principle that courts are very reluctant to substitute their own commercial judgement for that of
     directors was reinforced in *Runciman v Walter Runciman* [1993] BCC 223.
158 *Southern Foundries Ltd v Shirlaw* [1940] 2 All ER 445.
159 Section 709. This applies to all documents kept by the Registrar.
160 *Elkington & Co v Hurter* [1892] 2 Ch 452. But see the case of *First Energy (UK) Ltd v Hungarian
     International Bank Ltd* [1993] BCC 533 in which a senior manager in the defendant bank, to the
     knowledge of the plaintiff, made an offer to the plaintiff which exceeded his actual authority,
     which the plaintiff accepted. The defendant claimed the manager lacked both actual and ostensible
     authority, so the bank was not bound. The court held that the manager did have ostensible
     authority to communicate the bank's offer and it was therefore bound.
161 *Firbank's Exors v Humphreys* (1886) 18 QBD 54.
162 *Industrial Development Consultants Ltd v Cooley* [1972] 2 All ER 162.
163 *Selangor United Rubber Estates Ltd v Cradock (No 3)* [1969] 2 All ER 1073.
164 *Piercy v S Mills & Co Ltd* [1920] 1 Ch 77.
165 *Morgan v Morgan Insurance Brokers Ltd* [1993] BCC 145, a case in which the directors
     concerned (who were also minority shareholders) were made personally liable for costs in a
     consequent application for rectification of the register of members under s 359 after reforming to
     register a transfer by the majority shareholder to his daughter.
166 *Bishopsgate Investment Management Ltd v Maxwell (No 2)* [1994] 1 All ER 261.
167 *Scottish CWS Ltd v Meyer* [1958] 3 All ER 66.
168 *Percival v Wright* [1902] 2 Ch 421.
169 *Re Lo-Line Electric Motors Ltd* [1988] 4 BCC 415.
170 *Boulting v ACTAT* [1963] 1 All ER 716.
171 *Re City Equitable Fire Insurance Co Ltd* [1925] Ch 407.
172 [1988] Ch 477. See also *Re Moorgate Metals Ltd* [1995] BCC 143.
173 Including de facto directors. From this, it is clear that shadow and de facto directors are quite
     different animals. See *Re Hydrodam (Corby) Ltd* [1994] BCC 161. See also *Re Unisoft Group Ltd
     (No 2)* [1994] BCC 766.
174 Section 741(3).
175 *Re Tasbian (No 1)* [1991] BCLC 54; *Re Tasbian (No 2)* [1990] BCLC 59; *Re Tasbian (No 3)*
     [1991] BCLC 792.
176 Section 288.
177 Section 730.
178 See **3.10**.
179 *Carter's Case* (1886) 31 Ch D 496.
180 Section 730(5).
181 Section 32 of the Magistrates' Courts Act 1980 (as amended by s 17(2)(c) of the Criminal Justice
     Act 1991). A different sum may be prescribed pursuant to s 143 of the Magistrates' Courts Act
     1980.
182 Section 730(4).

Chapter 2

APPOINTMENT OF DIRECTORS

2.1 ARTICLES DECIDE

A company, like any other artificial creature, can function only through its human agents, and those agents are 'directors', by whatever name they may be called.[1] How, therefore, are they appointed and by whom? The answer lies in the Articles of Association, as English law gives almost complete freedom to the promoters of a company in their choice of machinery for this purpose. The only exception is where two or more directors are to be proposed for election to a public company.[2] Thus, the Act does not say that directors must be appointed by the members in general meeting, although it does say that they may be removed in this way, no matter what the Articles may provide.[3] The inquirer must, therefore, look at the Articles and what he is likely to find there is summarised below.

2.2 APPOINTMENT OF FIRST DIRECTORS

This raises two distinct questions:

(1) how are appointments made?; and
(2) who has the power to make them?

Common sense suggests that these questions have been put in the wrong order but, as will be seen, the Act puts such force into the machinery for the appointment of the first directors that it, to a great extent, dictates the answer to the second question.

When it is sought to register a company, the Memorandum and, almost invariably, Articles must be filed with the Registrar. He may not, and will not, register the company, however, unless those documents are accompanied by a statement of the first directors.[4] That statement must be signed by the subscribers and each director named must sign a consent to his appointment. The statement will also give personal details of each director including his other directorships[5] and his date of birth. When the Registrar has issued the certificate of incorporation, the new company comes into existence with a ready-made board, and the appointment of the directors named in the statement thereupon takes effect.[6] Equally, however, any appointment made by the Articles but not mentioned in the statement is void[7] and appointments made by any other means would be equally ineffective unless followed by compliance with the procedure described above.

The effect of the Act is, therefore, to make the filed statement the only instrument by which the first directors may be appointed – it is not merely an official record of nomination and acceptance of office. However, the Articles may refer to the appointment of the first directors in one of three ways.

2.2.1   Articles may expressly confer the power of appointment upon the subscribers

Such a provision merely repeats what the Act says and does not usually appear in modern Articles. For example, while Table A, reg 75 in the 1948 Table A formerly had this effect,[8] a special provision would have to be inserted if the 1985 Table A applied. There have been instances in which an objection to a particular director's appointment has been anticipated. In such instances, Articles have been drafted which provide for appointment to be by a majority of the subscribers, rather than all of them. This is not usually effective, since the filed statement of first directors, etc must be signed by, or by an agent of, all the subscribers. Dissentients would therefore have a de facto veto in any event, prior to incorporating, unless the majority obtain a court order forcing them to sign.[9]

2.2.2   Articles may name the first directors

This occurs in Articles of old companies or, occasionally, in badly drafted recent Articles. Such a nomination is ineffective. Only the statement referred to above is effective to appoint the first directors. However, the subscribers, having agreed the terms of the Articles, are bound by the nominations made by them and should ensure that the Articles and the statement are consistent. Even a majority could be restrained, therefore, from attempting to name other directors in the filed statement, and the courts would probably be prepared to order reluctant subscribers to sign a statement listing those nominated by the Articles.

2.2.3   Articles specify appointor

It remains possible that the power is conferred upon some third party, for example, a parent company of the new company which might wish to have general power of appointment without the need to hold meetings. This is permissible once the company is incorporated, but is not effective in relation to the first directors.

Generally, whatever provisions are included in the Articles in relation to appointment of first directors, they must not provide for those directors to be appointed after incorporation of the new company (for example, by its first general meeting) because the company cannot be incorporated at all before the directors have been notified to the Registrar on the filed statement.

2.3   APPOINTMENT OF SUBSEQUENT DIRECTORS

When the first board has been constituted by virtue of the combined effect of the filed statement and incorporation of the company, and the company is a going concern the manner of subsequent appointments is governed by the Articles, with one exception. Section 292 provides that two or more directors of a public company cannot be proposed by a single resolution without unanimous consent.

The following are examples of provisions found in company Articles.

2.3.1   Appointment by ordinary resolution of members in general meeting

Regulation 78 of Table A provides that: '. . . the Company may by ordinary resolution appoint a person who is willing to act to be a director either to fill a vacancy or as an additional director'.

An ordinary resolution is also expressly prescribed by this regulation to determine the order in which additional directors are to retire.

Appointment by ordinary resolution is the procedure most commonly found in practice,[10] and the ordinary resolution requires a bare majority of those entitled to vote and who do vote at a general meeting of the company. This does not mean that specially loaded voting rights may not be exercised on such a resolution if provided for in the Articles. They are as permissible here as on other matters.[11]

Under s 381A (inserted by s 113 of the 1989 Act), it is possible for a private company to appoint a director by written resolution signed by all the members, in which case there is no need for a meeting. The procedure to be followed is described in Chapter 9. The section overrides procedural restrictions in the Articles and does not require the length of notice specified by reg 76 (see **2.3.2**) or any equivalent provision of the company's Articles.

2.3.2   Restrictions on the members' right to appoint

Regulation 78 is usually accompanied by reg 76 which is intended to prevent the members from giving too much of a shock to the board at general meetings. Regulation 76 provides that no one (except retiring directors or nominees of the board itself) shall be proposed for appointment unless notice of the proposal executed by a member and containing a consent by the prospective director, has been left with the company at least 14 clear days (and not more than 35 days) before the meeting.

For companies 'listed' on the London Stock Exchange, certain provisions must be included in the Articles. Among them is a requirement that the minimum period of notice for proposed appointments to the board should be seven days.[12]

Public companies are subject to the additional restriction of s 292, whereby two or more directors must not be proposed by a single resolution unless this is agreed unanimously by the meeting. Thus, the members cannot be presented with a situation where they have to choose all or none.

Although an appointment in contravention of s 292 is void, acts done in good faith by the director may be validated by s 285 (see **2.5.6**).

2.3.3   Nomination by specified parties

The Articles (although not Table A) sometimes provide that the majority may appoint (and remove) directors in writing. This may be useful where a company is a subsidiary or there are very few members or there may be inconvenience or difficulty in holding meetings. Similar provisions can be made for the right of holders of specific blocks of shares to nominate a proportion of the board. Cumulative voting rights of this type are common in the USA where they ensure that minorities have a voice on the board. They are rare under English company law where, in the absence of special Articles, 51 per cent of the members can appoint 100 per cent of the board.

There is no reason, however, why such rights should not be given by the Articles and there is much to be said for the greater use of them. For example, in the typical case of an 'incorporated partnership' with two or three equal shareholders, one party may be denied representation on the board if the others choose to absent themselves from meetings or succeed in voting down his nominee. The only remedy is an expensive, protracted and uncertain expedition to the Chancery Division.[13] This could be avoided if the Articles gave to each party the right to appoint, in writing, a specified number of directors.[14]

2.3.4   Nomination pursuant to agreement

It is quite common for a sale of strategic blocks of shares to provide for appointment to the board. For example, the seller may undertake that the purchaser or his nominee shall become a director, or the purchaser undertake that the seller acquires or retains a place on the board – which may, in many cases, be part of the 'price' of the shares. This private agreement cannot, of course, operate as a contract binding the other members in the same way as the Articles. The party giving such an undertaking can perform his agreement only to the extent that he commands the necessary votes.

The agreement may, in some cases, run into legal difficulties. In *Wilton Group plc v Abrams*,[15] the seller of some 14 per cent of the company's issued shares was promised a very lucrative service contract by the purchaser, whose agreement to buy was, in turn, conditional on his and his nominees' appointment to the board. The court refused to enforce the agreement, describing it as 'commercially disreputable' in the case of a listed company. The main reason for this was the service contract. This would have to be voted for by the new directors – the seller would be disqualified by his interest in the contract – and those directors would very probably be in breach of duty to the company. They would be voting in pursuance of the agreement and without proper regard to the company's best interests. This objection might, indeed, be made in the case of any company except a closely held private company; but the objection is particularly strong in the case of a listed company, many of whose members would have little chance of knowing what was happening.

Some commentators go further and argue that the *Wilton* decision extends to any agreement for board representation, even though untainted by any connection with private profit in the form of a service contract. This is probably going too far. Unlike the service contract, the board appointments will have to be voted at a general meeting. Here the members have a fairly good chance of observing which way the wind blows and voting accordingly; furthermore, the members voting pursuant to the agreement are in principle entitled to vote in their own interests as they see them. This is a principle which is dislodged only by evidence of serious misbehaviour prejudicing the interests of the company as a whole, which seems a somewhat exaggerated description of such an agreement.

2.3.5 Appointment by the directors

Regulation 79 of Table A, which is useful and is normally adopted, enables the directors (by a majority vote):

(1) to fill casual vacancies,
(2) to add to the board.

They must not exceed the maximum number specified in accordance with the Articles and their nominees retire at the next annual general meeting (AGM) when they may be re-elected. They are not counted in the number of directors who retire by rotation in the usual way under reg 73. Listed companies must provide for such retirement and submission for re-election by the members at the next AGM.[16]

The power to fill casual vacancies does not apply to vacancies occurring due to retirement by rotation or by effluxion of time as this cannot be 'casual', but there is nothing to prevent the board from making an appointment under their power to add to their number, if the general meeting does not elect (reg 79, Table A).

There is nothing to prevent the Articles from, apparently, giving the directors the sole power to make appointments, ie to the exclusion of the general meeting. A residuary power remains, however, with the members and such an Article will not take away their powers at all unless it so provides in the clearest terms.[17]

2.3.6 Appointment of successors or alternate directors

There are three possibilities to be considered here.

(1) The Articles or any agreement may (although not commonly) allow a director to assign his office. In that case the assignment is of no effect until approved by a special resolution (75 per cent majority) of the company (s 308 of the Act). This section overrides any agreement or Article to the contrary.
(2) Likewise, the Articles may allow a director to nominate his successor. If this may properly be construed as something other than an assignment, s 308 would not apply.
(3) The Articles may allow a director to appoint an alternative person (an 'alternate director') to act in his absence. Regulations 65 to 69 in Table A so provide. This is not caught by s 308 and is particularly useful in a small company where the directors are the proprietors. See, further, **3.3** at (7).

But note that neither of the first two powers are appropriate to the few listed companies which are not subject to the Companies Act 1985, where, in any event, the members must have the power to remove any director at any time by ordinary resolution.[18]

2.4 NUMBER OF DIRECTORS

(1) The Act requires a minimum of two for a public company and one for a private company (s 282).

(2)   Within these requirements the Articles are free to make any provisions which may be desired and whether as to maximum or minimum or both. Table A provides that the number of directors must be at least two but is not subject to any maximum unless the members fix a maximum by ordinary resolution (reg 64). In the case of a private company, the Articles very often vary Table A to provide for a sole director.

(3)   An alternative form of Article specifies both a maximum and minimum number of directors but there is little to be said in its favour unless the members wish to restrict the powers of the board. As in the case of qualification shares, the main effect of such an Article is to provide an unnecessary stumbling block if it is noticed, or an embarrassment if it is overlooked.

(4)   Effect of non-compliance with such Articles is as follows:

  (a)   if there are too many directors, the appointments of the supernumeraries are void but their acts done in good faith may be valid under s 285. On discovering the defect, they must cease to act until the permitted number is increased and they are reappointed;

  (b)   if there are too few, for example, because the number falls below the minimum, reg 90 of Table A (which is usually adopted) allows the survivors to act for the purpose of increasing their number or calling a general meeting but for no other purpose. Innocent third parties may not be prejudiced.[19]

But note that where a private company has only one director, he cannot also be secretary (s 283(2)), and there is no doubt that the idea of one-man management has, in the past, been viewed with some disfavour in certain circumstances. A private company seeking status as a bank (or licensed deposit-taking institution) need not have two directors, formally appointed; but (which may come to the same thing in practice) at least two individuals must 'effectively direct' its business.[20]

2.5   WHO CAN BE A DIRECTOR?

In 1998, the Institute of Directors introduced examinations on Company Direction enabling directors to fly their colours with a Royal Charter. Applicants, to take the examinations, must be over 28 and have certain qualifications and experience. As well as written examinations they will be interviewed by two experienced directors. After becoming a 'CDir' they have to agree to adhere to a Code of Professional Conduct. However, these examinations are wholly voluntary, and are likely to remain so for the foreseeable future. The position therefore remains that under the general law anyone can be a director unless he is disqualified for some particular reason. Thus, there is no qualification imposed by the law itself and therefore the following (among others) can be appointed directors unless the Articles forbid it:

(1)   a minor, ie a person less than 18;
(2)   another company;
(3)   a person of unsound mind;
(4)   an alien;
(5)   a director of another company;
(6)   a non-member;

(7)   the secretary (except where he would be the only director).

2.5.1   Disqualification by law

There is now a very wide range of statutory disqualifications. The most far-reaching disqualifications are those imposed under the Company Directors Disqualification Act 1986. This Act consolidates earlier company and insolvency legislation which had gradually increased the powers of the courts as public anxiety, as perceived from Westminster, had increased about the activities of fly-by-night or dishonest directors. The directors could trade through companies behind which they sheltered and from whose wreckage they would often reappear trading through yet another company. All references in paragraphs (1) and (2) below are to sections of this Act except where otherwise stated.

(1) Disqualification orders[21]

These are court orders banning a person from directorships[22] and from taking any part in the management of a company, whether directly or indirectly (for example, by giving instructions through a nominee director) except with leave of the court. An order may be made whether or not the person in question is made criminally liable for the conduct upon which the order is based. Contravention of an order is itself an offence (s 13).[23] In addition, the disqualified person may be made personally liable for debts and liabilities incurred by the company while he was acting in breach of the order (s 15). Furthermore, anyone else within the company, whether a director or not, can also be made liable[24] under s 15 for debts and liabilities of the company incurred at a time when it is shown that he was acting *or* 'willing to act' upon the instructions of the disqualified person and knew him to be disqualified. If it is shown that with such knowledge he has once acted upon such instructions, he is presumed to have been willing to continue to act on such instructions thereafter unless he proves the contrary.

Disqualification orders subsist for the period specified by the court: the maximum period which may be imposed is shown in brackets at the end of each description of order listed below.

(a)   *Conviction for indictable offence*[25] *(s 2).* An order may be made against any person convicted of an indictable offence in connection with the promotion, formation, management, liquidation of a company, on its striking off or on a receivership of its property. The order may be made by the court where the conviction takes place but may be imposed by the insolvency court or even, where the conviction is before magistrates, by another magistrates' court for the same area (five years in a magistrates' court; 15 years in any other court). In most cases disqualification is imposed to protect the public from someone who does not deserve the privilege of limited liability, and may therefore be based on neglect as well as on dishonesty. Under s 2, in contrast, there is a large penal function in disqualification. It follows that if the court imposes a light sentence for the offence, disqualification should rarely, if ever, be used as a 'topping-up' device. So, if the director is conditionally discharged because of exceptional circumstances, there should be no disqualification.[26] It is, perhaps, odd on any view that the trial judge in the Guinness prosecutions did not consider disqualification appropriate.

(b) *Persistent breaches of companies legislation (s 3)*. An order may be made against a person found to have been 'persistently in default' of Companies Act 1985 requirements as to company returns, accounts, notices or other documents required to be filed with the Registrar. The element of persistence[27] may be shown in any way but is conclusively proved by evidence that in the previous five years before the application for disqualification he has been 'adjudged guilty' of three or more such defaults. He is treated as 'adjudged guilty' if he was actually convicted in respect of his default or that of the company (ie as a responsible officer) or where a 'default order' was made in respect of a breach of duty under ss 242(4) or 245B of the Companies Act 1985 (delivery of company accounts or revised accounts) or s 713 of that Act (company's duty to make returns).[28] This type of order can be imposed by the High Court or by a county court with winding up jurisdiction (five years). In *Re Civica Investments Ltd*,[29] a one-year order was made where there had been nearly 300 accounting and annual return defaults. Most had been remedied, and some of the companies had done very little trading. This was enough to persuade the judge that the short term was sufficient. Where there has been no effective remedy, no attempt to comply with the Acts and no assurance to the Department that there will be compliance in the future, a four-year order has been made.[30] Even in a case like *Civica*, a longer term of disqualification would now be likely.

(c) *Fraud in a winding up (s 4)*. The winding-up court may make a disqualification order against a person whom it finds has been guilty of fraudulent trading or of any other fraud or breach of duty as an officer or manager of a company. Although the power is vested in the winding-up court, the fraud or breach of duty (for which he need not actually have been convicted)[31] need not have been in the course of a winding up. For example, the offence of fraudulent trading under s 458 of the Companies Act 1985 may be committed whether or not the company is in liquidation. It should also be noted that this section extends the net to catch shadow directors as well as other directors and officers (15 years).

(d) *On summary conviction for a filing or notice default (s 5)*. A magistrates' court convicting a person of any offence under the Companies Act relating to the filing of returns, accounts or notices may impose a disqualification order if, during the five years preceding the present conviction, the defendant has had three or more default orders (see (b) above) made against him or has had three such convictions (including the present one) or three default orders and convictions in aggregate. The purpose of this section is to give magistrates the power to disqualify in circumstances similar to those leading to disqualification for persistent default (see (b) above) (five years).

(e) *Unfit director of insolvent companies (s 6)*. This is a stronger provision since the court *must* make a disqualification order once satisfied that the section applies. The court must be satisfied that the person in question is or was a director of a company which has become insolvent; it need not have done so whilst he was still a director. 'Insolvency' for these purposes means that:

(i) it is wound up and unable to pay its debts and liabilities together with the expenses of winding up;

(ii) that an administrative receiver was appointed by a secured creditor; or

(iii) that an administration order was made in relation to the company.

The last of these is somewhat startling since the administrator may be appointed under s 8 of the Insolvency Act 1986 not with a view to insolvent winding up but to saving the company. Insolvency, however, is clearly a major possibility when an administrator is appointed and therefore the company is deemed for present purposes to become insolvent on his appointment. In addition, however, the court must also be satisfied that the director's conduct shows him to be unfit to be concerned in the management of a company. His conduct as director of the insolvent company is particularly relevant, but his conduct in relation to other companies may also be taken into account if it supports the contention that he is unfit. (Good behaviour in relation to other companies may not be brought before the court.) The court must look particularly carefully at his responsibility for matters connected with the insolvency of any of his companies but is certainly not restricted to insolvent situations when examining his conduct as a director generally. Once the court is satisfied that the director is 'unfit', he *must* be disqualified for at least two years; the maximum period is 15 years. As might be expected, this is by far the commonest ground on which disqualification is sought. In practice, the issues raised bear a very strong resemblance to those raised in cases concerning a director's personal liability for breach of duty. The manner in which the courts proceed under s 6 is described in Chapter 6.

(f) *Disqualification after investigation (s 8).* The DTI may also apply to the High Court for a disqualification order if, after receiving the report of company inspectors, or examining information or documents obtained in the course of a relevant investigation, it judges it to be in the public interest that a director or a shadow director, past or present, should be disqualified.[32] The court may then make an order if satisfied that that person's conduct makes him unfit to be concerned in the management of a company (15 years).

(g) *Disqualification for fraudulent or wrongful trading (s 10).* Under s 213 of the Insolvency Act 1986, the winding-up court may order anyone who has been knowingly concerned in the conduct of a company's business with intent to defraud creditors to make a contribution out of his own pocket to the insolvent company's assets. Under s 214, a similar contribution order may be made against a director or shadow director guilty of 'wrongful trading' (see **6.2**). Whether or not the court decides to make a contribution order, it may make a disqualification order against any person falling within those provisions (15 years).

These are, obviously enough, sweeping powers, although the court will exercise its discretion carefully. Certain factors are specifically declared by the Act to be of particular relevance *in all cases*:

(a) any misfeasance or breach of fiduciary or other duty owed to the company (for example, breach of a director's duty to exercise due care and skill);

(b) misapplication or retention of company money or property, or conduct giving rise to a duty to account to the company for money or property;

(c) the director's responsibility for the company's entry into any transaction intended to defraud creditors by removing company assets from their reach;

(d) the director's responsibility for the company's failure to comply with its statutory duties relating to accounting records, annual returns, registers of directors and members, and the registration of charges (security over the company's assets) given to creditors;

(e)   the director's responsibility for non-compliance with the board's obligations relating to the preparation of group accounts and the proper circulation, in any company, of annual accounts and the directors' report.

The emphasis on accounting duties, which has been underlined by the Companies Act 1989, is not accidental. It will be seen in Chapter 6 that both Parliament and the courts have begun to lose patience with directors whose inertia allows the company's true position to lie concealed behind delayed or non-existent accounts.

Where the company has become insolvent relevant factors declared by the Act will be:

(a)   the director's responsibility for the causes of the insolvency, and of any failure to supply goods or services for which payment has been received in whole or in part;

(b)   his responsibility for the company's entry into transactions liable to be set aside in a winding up;[33]

(c)   his responsibility for the board's failure to convene a creditors' meeting in a creditors' voluntary winding up;

(d)   his failure to comply with various obligations imposed upon him as a director when the company is subject to an administration order, administrative receivership or winding up.

Rather startlingly, the DTI has power to modify these criteria by statutory order. Constitutionally, this is perfectly proper since parliamentary veto is possible and, undoubtedly, a measure of additional flexibility is thus provided. Nevertheless, it is a strong measure that permits alterations to be made, almost certainly without effective parliamentary debate, to legislative rules which can effectively prevent a person from carrying on in business. As we have seen, a disqualification order prevents a person from taking any part in the management of a company. He cannot act as a financial adviser or negotiate as an agent of the company even if he describes himself as a 'management consultant' and holds no formal office or directorship in the company.[34] To be fair, as well as effective, these powers will have to be applied with an even hand by the courts. This is an easy enough aim where the insolvency courts, which are used to such applications, are concerned[35] but is difficult to ensure when magistrates' courts are involved. Most of these are staffed by amateur judges, and even stipendiary magistrates and qualified clerks who advise lay magistrates will have little or no experience of company management or, in all probability, of company law. To this extent, the criteria provided by the Act will act as a considerable safeguard to those who might otherwise be exposed to the hazards of the lower courts.

There is an underlying problem which may be insoluble. The 1986 Act allows considerably longer periods of disqualification to be imposed than was previously the case but, unless the courts are prepared to take advantage of these, disqualification will have more impact on the honest bumbler than on the criminally dishonest. The former will 'serve' his entire period of disqualification, short as that may be. The latter, however, may well be imprisoned as well as disqualified. This sounds severe, until it is remembered that the disqualification runs from the date of the order. This may produce the odd result that some or even all of the disqualification will be served while the offender sits peacefully in his cell, leaving him free to resume his activities when he emerges. Even if his widespread delinquency led to a series of disqualification orders, these run concurrently; there can be no 'consecutive sentences'. There is perhaps a further contradiction here. The courts tend to stress that disqualification is not principally a penal measure. Its object is mainly to protect the public generally, and potential creditors specifically, against the threat of continued activity by one who may have been thoroughly dishonest or, at the other extreme, thoroughly incompetent. If this is so, the courts should perhaps review their 'sentencing policy', since the effects of allowing a director to continue or resume in business are not necessarily less serious in the case of an incompetent than in the case of a fraudster. The only review to have been undertaken, however, has reinforced the approach which sees dishonesty as requiring a longer period of disqualification than incompetence.[36]

Even a disqualified director may act if he obtains the court's leave. This may be granted, for example, in the case of a family company, or where his absence will jeopardise the livelihood of employees,[37] but only if the court is able to impose some safeguard against a recurrence of the problems – for example, by requiring that there should be an independent director with financial control of the company, or that the auditors should attend board meetings.[38]

A register of disqualification orders is maintained by the DTI which is open to inspection (s 18). This can now be viewed on-line via various information providers including Companies House. This is a continuation of the register which was first created by s 29 of the Companies Act 1976.[39]

(2) Bankrupts

An undischarged bankrupt is disqualified from holding office as a director unless specifically authorised by the court (s 11) and something quite exceptional would be needed before the court authorised such an appointment.[40] He is also prohibited from taking part in company management, directly or indirectly, so, as in the case of a disqualification order, he may not shelter behind a nominee such as a member of his family. It is an offence for an undischarged bankrupt to do any of these things, so that further disqualification might be imposed under s 2 (see (1) (a) above). A similar disqualification applies where a county court is administering a person's estate; when revoking that order it may effectively disqualify him from office for up to two years. Any person acting in breach of ss 11 or 12 commits an offence (s 13). For what it is worth – probably very little – an undischarged bankrupt may also be made personally liable for company debts and liabilities incurred whilst he was wrongfully involved in its management. More to the point, those who knew of his disqualification are made similarly liable for debts incurred in carrying out his instructions (s 15).

(3) Other disqualifications

(a) The auditor of the company or of any company within its group, or associated with it, may not also be a director, secretary or employee of the company.[41] Nor may he be the partner or employee of such a person.[42]

(b) The secretary cannot be sole director of a private company;[43] and where something (such as the execution of a document) has to be done by the director and the secretary, the same person cannot act in both capacities.

(c)   A clergyman of the Church of England cannot be a director.[44]
(d)   A person of 70 years or over cannot be appointed director of a public company (or of its subsidiary) unless:
   (i)   the Articles provide otherwise; or
   (ii) the appointment is approved in general meeting by an ordinary resolution of which special notice, stating his age, has been given (s 293). For 'special notice', which is a technical term, see **9.4** and Chapter 11.

2.5.2   Disqualified by the Articles

The Articles can impose any qualification which may be desired such as that a director must be, for example, a shareholder or teetotal.[45] One must bear in mind that such qualifications cannot necessarily be overriden by the majority. Fifty-one per cent will serve to appoint a director but 75 per cent is required to alter the Articles.

2.5.3   Qualification shares

Articles occasionally require directors to hold a certain number of shares by way of a 'qualification'.

No such qualification is imposed by Table A or by the Act itself and there is little to be said in favour of such a requirement. Where it is found in the Articles, it is usually nominal, and then serves no purpose except as a nuisance. This is particularly so in private companies where a qualification share is allotted to an employee-director and is left outstanding after his employment has ceased. In the case of public companies, qualification shares are not a requirement of the Stock Exchange.

Table A makes no provision for shareholding qualification, but where such a qualification is fixed or specified in the Articles, the position is as follows.

(1) Two months' grace
The director must have his qualification shares within a period of not more than two months.[46] A shorter period may be specified by the Articles but, if not, the two months' period applies. The period runs from the date of appointment and, in the case of a poll, this is the date when the result of the poll is ascertained and not the date of the meeting.[47]

(2) Effect of failure to qualify
Where qualification shares are required and the director either fails to acquire them within the specified period (not exceeding two months) or ceases at any time to hold them, he forthwith vacates office (s 291(3)); Articles containing a share qualification may repeat this provision. Table A, reg 81 is to the same effect, although not referring to share qualifications as such.

(3) Effect of vacation of office under s 291(3)
Where a director vacates office because of s 291 the effect is as follows.

(a)   If he continues to act as director, he is liable to a fine and to a default fine for continuing to act (s 291(5)).

(b) If he acts inadvertently in this way, the courts can relieve him from liability under s 727.[48]

(c) His contract to serve as managing director at a salary is invalidated but he may have a claim on a *quantum meruit* for fair remuneration for work actually done in that capacity.[49]

(d) In the absence of a *quantum meruit* claim, he has no right to director's remuneration under the Articles and may have to repay what he has received.[50]

(e) Acts done before disqualification remain valid.[51]

(f) Acts done after disqualification by a person who continues to be held out as and to act as a de facto director are valid as regards both third parties and members (s 285),[52] unless they know of the defect.[53]

(f) The disqualified director cannot be reappointed until he has his qualification shares (s 291(4)).

(4) Meaning of share qualification

The meaning of share qualification depends upon the Articles, although s 291(2) provides that bearer shares will not suffice. Thus, the director must be on the register.

The following points have been decided and will apply in the absence of contrary provisions in the Articles.

(a) A joint holding will qualify.[54]

(b) A trustee holding, for example, under a settlement, will qualify even if the Articles require a holding 'in his own right', since the company does not recognise the trust and can safely treat him as the owner.[55]

(c) Conversely, a purely equitable right to the shares, for example, under an agreement to buy the shares, will not suffice if someone else's name is on the register.[56]

(d) A representative holding, for example, as executor or liquidator, will not qualify since here the company must recognise the representative capacity.[57]

(e) The source of the qualification shares does not matter,[58] but if they are a gift from a promoter or vendor there may be a liability for breach of trust.[59]

(f) The cost of the shares must not be lent, given or reimbursed to the director by the company whether in cash or in kind;[60] although there is no objection to the provision of qualification shares in a subsidiary since here they are held on trust for the parent, and the director therefore receives no financial benefit. In these circumstances a director normally signs a declaration of trust.

(g) Where the share qualification is increased, the director is not thereby disqualified but must obtain his increased holding within a reasonable time.[62]

(h) Where the Articles require the qualification before taking office, for example, 'no person shall be appointed unless, etc', the director cannot take advantage of the period of grace,[62] but the period will apply unless the Articles specifically exclude it.[63]

2.5.4 Vacation of office under the Articles

Table A, reg 81 requires a director to vacate office if any of the following events occur.

(1) If he loses his directorship by reason of a provision of the Act, for example, where a public company director 'passes' the AGM after reaching the age of 70 (s 293) or where a director parts with his qualification shares (s 291 and see **2.5.3**) or is prohibited by law from being a director (see **2.5.1**).

(2) If he becomes bankrupt or makes an arrangement with creditors. A person becomes bankrupt when a bankruptcy order is made against him. Bankruptcy lasts until discharge of the order (Insolvency Act 1986, s 278) and an undischarged bankrupt in any case commits an offence by acting as a director or, indeed, being concerned in the management of a company (Company Directors Disqualification Act 1986, s 11). The making of a voluntary arrangement with creditors need not lead to bankruptcy and, indeed, where the court has made an 'interim order' in respect of such an arrangement, no bankruptcy petition may be presented or pursued against the debtor (Insolvency Act 1986, s 252). In this respect, therefore, reg 81 of Table A goes beyond the statutory disqualification.

(3) If he becomes of unsound mind.

(4) If he resigns by notice in writing.

(5) If he is absent from board meetings without permission for more than six months.

Other provisions under which directors automatically vacate office may also be found in the Articles.

The effect of all these Articles is automatic removal from office and thus the purported appointment of a person caught by the 'automatic vacation of office' provisions would be a fruitless exercise. The board cannot waive the Article – the purported appointee would simply 'bounce' out of office again.[64]

2.5.5   Aliens

English company law imposes no restrictions on the appointment of an alien as director. However, his nationality must be stated on:

(1) the register of directors (s 289(1)(a)); and

(2) the particulars filed with the Registrar of Companies (s 288(2)).

In his capacity as an employee, he must, of course, comply with the regulations in force from time to time which govern the right of aliens to work in the UK.

2.5.6   Defects in appointment

A director must:

(1) have been properly appointed; and

(2) not have been subsequently disqualified by the operation of the Articles or the law; and

(3) not be caught by 'automatic vacation of office' provisions in the Articles.

If, for any reason, he does not satisfy these requirements, the question arises of his own position and whether third parties can rely on his acts.

Several factors may be relevant.

(1) Section 285 of the Act provides that 'the acts of a director or manager are valid notwithstanding any defect that may afterwards be discovered in his appointment or qualification'. Thus, a technical defect such as a director's temporary parting with his qualification shares will not invalidate a call made by a board of which he was an essential member.[65] However, in *Morris v Kanssen*[66] the House of Lords restricted the effect of the section by drawing a rather difficult

distinction between a defective appointment on the one hand (to which s 285 would apply) and a situation where there is 'no appointment at all' on the other. This seems to mean that s 285 will help a third party only where the defect is technical or procedural (such as insufficient notice of the meeting),[67] but one must bear in mind that the activities in *Morris v Kanssen* were of a fraudulent nature and the third party who sought to rely on s 285 knew that there was something wrong. This is very different from the situation where the third party is unaware of the defect and in those cases the courts would probably help him even though the director was, technically, out of office at the time he acted.[68] If the disqualification affects the collective capacity of the board to act – in particular, by making it impossible to assemble a quorum – the third party may be able to rely on s 35A if the court is prepared to regard the quorum rules as a 'limitation' on the board's power to bind the company.

(2) Regulation 92 of Table A contains a similar provision and it should be noted that both reg 92 and s 285 apply to defects 'afterwards' discovered. This means that the existence of the defect itself need not have been appreciated at the time of the appointment, although the parties may have known of the facts which caused the defect.[69]

(3) Minutes properly recording the appointment at general or board meetings are regarded as valid until the contrary is proved (s 382(4)) and the same will be true of appointments made under the new written resolution procedure available to private companies under s 382A.

(4) Quite apart from s 285, if the position of an innocent third party is that he is dealing with persons who are held out by the company as directors, he may hold the company responsible for their acts on the normal principles of agency.[70] Again, the third party may also be able to rely upon s 35A.

(5) Such a de facto director is likewise subject to all the duties and liabilities of a properly appointed director under the provisions of s 741: '. . . any person occupying the position of director, by whatever name called'.[71]

(6) An injunction may be obtained to prevent the de facto director from continuing to act.[72]

(7) The acts of the director or of the meetings which he attended may be ratified by a properly constituted board or meeting.[73]

Following logically from the principle that innocent third parties should normally be protected is the rule that those (whether directors or third parties) who know of the defect when entering into a transaction cannot subsequently complain of it or rely upon it.[74]

2.6 PUBLICITY

It is the object of the Act that members and third parties should always be able to ascertain who are the officers of a company. This object is achieved in several ways.

(1) The company must keep its own register at the registered office under s 238. This must contain the following details of directors (including de facto and shadow directors (s 288(6)):

   (a) full name and any former name;

    (b)   usual residential address;

    (c)   nationality;

    (d)   business occupation;

    (e)   other directorships either presently held or held within the previous five years (except for dormant companies (see **4.1.7**) and grouped companies, ie parents, subsidiaries or fellow subsidiaries where the subsidiaries are wholly-owned);

    (f)   date of birth.

Items (a) and (b) must also be included in the register in respect of the secretary. This register must be open to inspection to members (free) and the public during normal business hours, for at least two hours per day (s 288(3)).[75] The courts may compel an inspection (s 288(5)). Default in keeping the register or allowing inspection is an offence punishable by a fine of up to £5,000 on the company and any officer at fault, with a daily default fine of £500 (s 288(4) and Sch 24).

(2)   The same particulars of these officers and a signed consent to act as such, and of any changes, must be filed with the Registrar of Companies within 14 days (s 288(2)).

By s 711, the Registrar must publish these particulars in the *Gazette* or, in relation to companies incorporated in Scotland, the *Edinburgh Gazette*. Section 42 provides that the company cannot rely on a change of directors as against third parties until the day of such publication unless the third party knew of the change. Publication in the *Gazette* does not of itself, however, act as constructive notice, and a third party without actual notice is not bound by it.[76]

(3)   The annual return must set out the contents of the register at the date of the return save that other directorships are not required[77] (s 364).

(4)   A list of directors' names is not obligatory in business letters but they must set out each director's name (or initial) and surname if the name of any director appears (except if he is merely referred to in the text of the letter or is signing it) (s 305 (as amended)). Default carries a fine of up to £1,000.

CHAPTER 2 FOOTNOTES

1 Section 741.
2 Section 292 and see **2.3.2**.
3 Section 303.
4 Sections 10 and 12. The statement must be on Form 10.
5 Section 10 and Sch 1. All directorships held in the previous five years must be stated, unless the relevant company was dormant (see **4.1.7**) or grouped with the company supplying the statement. In the case of a proposed corporate director, its registered name and registered or principal office must be stated.
6 Section 13(5).
7 Section 10(5).
8 The provision disappeared with the 1985 form of Table A.
9 In practice, however, it would be simpler to abandon the company, perhaps with a view to substituting another with different subscribers.
10 Regulation 97 of the 1948 version of Table A corresponds broadly with reg 78 and expressly specifies an ordinary resolution to replace a dismissed director, and reg 94 specifies an ordinary resolution to increase or reduce the number of directors.
11 *Re NFU Development Trust Ltd* [1972] 1 WLR 1548.
12 *The Listing Rules*, App 1 to Ch 13 and 22.
13 *Re Lundie Bros Ltd* [1965] 2 All ER 692; *Re Westbourne Galleries Ltd* [1972] 2 All ER 492.
14 If a corporate member has the power to appoint a majority of directors it will become a holding company within the meaning of s 736 and a parent undertaking for accounting purposes under s 259.
15 [1990] BCC 310. The price of the shares had been reduced by 15 per cent in exchange for the more than reasonable salary specified by the agreement.
16 *The Listing Rules*, App 1 to Ch 13, para 21.
17 *Worcester Corsetry v Witting* [1936] Ch 640.
18 *The Listing Rules*, App 1 to Ch 13, para 23(d).
19 *British Asbestos Co v Boyd* [1903] 2 Ch 439.
20 Section 3 of and Sch 2 to the Banking Act 1987.
21 These orders also prevent a person from acting as an insolvency practitioner.
22 'Director' includes de facto directors (s 22) and in certain cases, mentioned in the text, shadow directors.
23 Punishable by up to two years' imprisonment and an unlimited fine.
24 Joint and several liability is imposed on each party – the creditor may therefore sue each until his claim is satisfied.
25 Ie serious enough to be triable by jury in the Crown Court even if, in fact, tried by magistrates.
26 *R v Young* [1990] BCC 549 (conviction of managing company while undischarged bankrupt might have warranted disqualification for two years, but delay in bringing the case to court and director's later success in business made the case exceptional).
27 'Persistence' does not require dishonesty or incompetence, merely repetition or continuation of default: *Re Arctic Engineering Ltd* [1986] 1 WLR 686. Absence of blameworthiness may mean, however, that no order is made, as in the *Arctic Engineering* case.
28 Other default orders are specified, but these relate to insolvency practitioners.
29 [1983] BCLC 456. The maximum period was, at the time, five years and the same conduct might now lead to a longer period of disqualification.
30 *Re Gilgate Properties* (1981) 1 Co Law 129.
31 It may be simply a breach of his civil law director's duty to the company.
32 Section 8 has been gradually widened in scope. Apart from Companies Act 1985 investigations and reports (as to which see Chapter 8), the application may now be based on: (i) inspector's reports into investment schemes and insider dealing (ss 94 and 177 of the Financial Services Act 1986); and (ii) documents discovered or information obtained in the course of investigations into an investment business (s 105 of the Financial Services Act) or serious fraud (s 2 of the Criminal Justice Act 1987 and s 28 of the Criminal Law (Consolidation) (Scotland) Act 1995) or (iii) information or documents required to assist overseas regulatory authorities (s 83 of the Companies Act 1989).

Rejecting the argument that the absence from s 8 of a minimum period of disqualification (a feature of s 6) meant that s 8 cases were to be treated relatively leniently, the court has instead pointed to the wide variety of circumstances which may trigger s 8 and the fact that there is the same maximum period of disqualification. Even an honest director who had lost money of his own and co-operated with the inspectors may be disqualified: *Re Samuel Sherman plc* [1991] BCC 699.

33 Ie property dispositions or share transfers after a winding up commences, and transactions at an undervalue or by way of preference (Insolvency Act 1986, ss 127, 238–240).

34 *R v Campbell* (1984) 78 Crim AR 95 and *Re Tasbian* (1990) BCC 318, CA – a 'company doctor' in each case.

35 Even here the Court of Appeal has noted that there has been an unfortunate discrepancy between the periods of disqualification imposed by the county courts and the High Court. The former are consistently more willing to impose long periods of disqualification. Perhaps they deal with smaller companies whose directors' misconduct is more obviously connected with the company's misfortunes – or, perhaps, because few of their judges have practised at the Chancery bar, they retain more of the outsider's distaste for director neglect and delinquency.

36 One of the problems is that as court lists have become 'case loads' the pressure has mounted to 'clear' them. Under the rules, a case with no substantial difficulties of law or fact may be disposed of summarily unless disqualification for more than five years is appropriate. There is thus a built-in tendency to divert marginal cases to a summary hearing which guarantees a lower period of disqualification.

37 *Re Lo-Line Electric Motors Ltd* [1988] Ch 477; *Re Majestic Recording Studios Ltd* [1989] BCLC 1.

38 And ensure that they are properly convened and conducted: *Re Chartmore Ltd* [1990] BCLC 673.

39 All orders must be reported by the court for registration with the Department of Trade and Industry. The register is open to inspection (both in hard copy format and on-line) free of charge (see the Companies (Disqualification Orders) Regulations 1986, 1986/2067 and Companies (Disqualification Order) (Amendment) Regulations 1995, SI 1995/1509), although the DTI has power to prescribe a charge.

40 *Re McQuillan* [1989] 5 BCC 105.

41 Section 27 of the Companies Act 1989. 'Association' is defined by s 52(3) as group membership; association through corporate directorships; or connection with group companies by employment or partnership.

42 Section 27 of the Companies Act 1989.

43 Section 283.

44 Section 29 of the Pluralities Act 1838.

45 *Govt Stock Co v Christopher* [1956] 1 All ER 490.

46 Section 291 of the Companies Act 1985.

47 *Holmes v Keyes* [1958] 2 All ER 129.

48 *Re Barry & Staines Linoleum* [1934] Ch 227; 'inadvertence' means blamelessness, not merely the absence of dishonesty (*Selangor United Rubber Estates Ltd v Cradock (No 3)* [1968] 1 WLR 1555, at p 1649).

49 *Craven-Ellis v Canons Ltd* [1936] 2 KB 403.

50 *Brown & Green Ltd v Hays* (1920) 36 TLR 330.

51 *Re International Cable Co* (1892) 66 LT 253.

52 *Dawson v African Consolidated Land & Trading Co* [1898] 1 Ch 6.

53 *Morris v Kanssen* [1946] AC 459.

54 *Grundy v Briggs* [1910] 1 Ch 444.

55 *Sutton v English & Colonial Produce Co* [1902] 2 Ch 502.

56 *Spencer v Kennedy* [1926] 1 Ch 125.

57 *Boschoek Proprietary Co v Fuke* [1906] 1 Ch 148.

58 *Re Hercynia Copper Co* [1894] 2 Ch 403.

59 *Re London & S W Canal Co* [1911] 1 Ch 346.

60 Section 151 of the Companies Act 1985.

61 *Molineaux v London Birmingham & Manchester Insurance Co* [1902] 2 KB 589.

62 *Channel Collieries Trust v Dover Railway Co* [1914] 2 Ch 506.

63 *Re International Cable Co* (1892) 66 LT 253.

64 *Re Bodega Co* [1904] 1 Ch 276.

65 *Dawson v African Consolidated Land & Trading Co* [1898] 1 Ch 6.

66 [1946] AC 459.

67 *Briton Medical Life Association v Jones* (1889) 61 LT 384; in contrast to the case where the appointers have no power to act at all.

68 *British Asbestos Co v Boyd* [1903] 2 Ch 439.

69 *Channel Collieries Trust v Dover Railway Co* [1914] 2 Ch 506.

70 *Hely-Hutchinson v Brayhead Ltd* [1968] 1 QB 549.

71 *Re New Par Consols (No 1)* [1898] 1 QB 573.

72 *Cheshire v Gordon Hotels* (1953) *The Times*, 13 February.

73 *Re Portuguese Consolidated Copper Mines* (1889) 42 ChD 160.

74 *Tyne Mutual Steamship Insurance Association v Brown* (1896) 74 LT 283.

75 By virtue of the Companies (Inspection and Copying of Registers, Indices and Documents) Regulations 1991, SI 1991/1998. For the public the inspection fee is £2.50 per hour. Copies may be taken (at £2.50 for the first 100 entries, £20.00 for the next 1,000 and £15.00 for every subsequent 1,000).

76 *Official Custodian for Charities v Parway Estates Developments Ltd* [1984] 3 WLR 525. Section 42 is not easy to interpret. It provides that for 15 days after publication the company may not rely on the charge against a person 'unavoidably prevented' from knowing of it. This seems to suggest that after 15 days, publication *should* constitute notice; but the Court of Appeal's contrary decision is consistent with the EC Directive which the section is supposed to implement.

77 The Companies (Forms) (Amendment) Regulations 1999, SI 1999/2356. While 'other directorship' details are not required on the annual return, they are still required on notices of appointment of a director (Form 288a) and changes in 'other directorships' therefore continue to be notifiable to Companies House (Form 288c).

Chapter 3

POWERS OF DIRECTORS

3.1 ARTICLES DEFINE POWERS

A company must have directors whether it appoints them or not, because those who actually manage its business will be 'occupying the position of directors' and so regarded as directors by the law.[1] Consequently, even in a company which had no directors and was managed by the members en bloc, each would probably fall within the definition of 'directors' in relation to their management activities – they would be likely to be treated as de facto directors[2]. Thus, there would be a board of directors and a body of members even though the composition of both was identical.[3]

Such an identity of ownership and management is common in small family companies, although the reverse is usually true of listed companies. There will be directors, therefore, in every company, whether de facto or de jure; what, then, is their power to direct? The answer to this question is not set out in the Act. The Act imposes many liabilities on directors, and many restrictions on their activities, but nowhere does it say what the directors may do.

This is, therefore, a matter which the legislature has left to the company to decide for itself and as it is an internal question, it will be dealt with in the Articles of Association, because it is essentially one of a division of powers within the organs of the company. The company itself has the powers given to it by law and by its Memorandum, within the ambit of the ultra vires rule. The Articles decide how those powers are to be allocated between such organs which the company has established for its management. The company must have a general meeting of members which has statutory powers and a general residuary authority, but it enjoys wide freedom as to what other functionaries there will be and as to the allocation of powers between them.

Thus, the Articles may, as does Table A, reg 70, delegate the general power of management to the directors; they may specify the powers which the members and directors are to have and subject to the provisions of the Act, which require that certain matters must be decided upon by the members, give residuary powers to one or the other; they may authorise the board to confer controlling powers of management on a single managing director or to executive directors carrying out specific functions or, indeed, to a management or service company which acts as director.[4]

Therefore, all, or nearly all, depends on the Articles and the newly appointed director should make it his first task to examine their contents. He must bear in mind, however, that the ultimate residuary authority does rest with the general meeting of members, in the sense that a company, like Parliament, cannot deprive itself of the right to reverse or repeal what it has done in the past. Articles can always be changed by special resolution (75 per cent majority, although the nature of the voting rights themselves are, in turn, a legitimate subject for the Articles, which can, in effect, decide what 75 per cent shall mean by giving weighted votes to specified shares or in specified circumstances).[5]

3.2   LIMITATIONS ON THE ARTICLES

We have noted that the members in general meeting have certain statutory and residuary powers and these are independent of and unaffected by anything which may be in the Articles. What are these limits on the company's freedom to regulate its internal affairs by its Articles?

They include the following.

(1)   An increase in the authorised capital or any consolidation subdivision conversion into stock or cancellation of unissued shares must be carried out by resolution of the members.[6]

(2)   A reduction in issued capital can be carried only by special resolution (75 per cent majority) of the members,[7] with the consent of the courts.

(3)   Alteration of the Memorandum of Association can only be carried out:

    (a)   as to the name by special resolution, subject to the DTI's statutory vetoes;[8]

    (b)   as to the object clause, by special resolution;[9]

    (c)   as to the liability clause, by special resolution to change from limited to unlimited[10] or from unlimited to limited (and subject always to the additional procedural requirements in each case);[11]

    (d)   as to the capital clause, by increasing or reducing in the way referred to in (1) and (2) above.

(4)   As a general rule, an alteration of the Articles of Association can only be carried out by special resolution.[12]

(5)   Voluntary liquidation of the company must be started by:

    (a)   ordinary resolution where its period of existence is limited by a provision in the Articles; or

    (b)   special resolution for any purpose; or

    (c)   extraordinary resolution where it is unable to continue because of insolvency.[13]

(6)   Directors (and auditors) can be removed from office by ordinary resolution of the members regardless of anything in the Articles.[14] This does not mean that other methods of removal of directors, which may be specified in the Articles, such as by special resolution or by co-directors by a majority shareholder or by a named member, are ineffective; merely that the ordinary resolution procedure can be used in any event. However, directors may resist removal if they are also shareholders, if their company's Articles contain provisions which, in effect, allow them to ensure that the ordinary resolution is not passed. Such Articles do not appear in Table A and must be specially drafted; they involve use of weighted voting rights in relation to such resolutions.[15]

(7) Every general meeting of the members at which accounts are laid must appoint an auditor,[16] unless the members have passed elective resolutions which alter this requirement.[17] Or the company is either dormant[18] or an audit exempt company.[19] The directors and the DTI have the right to make temporary or casual appointments but the members' right to appoint cannot be taken away. The effectiveness of this right is another matter, and is discussed in Chapter 9.

(8) The annual general meeting is a compulsory requirement[20] in each calendar year, unless the members have passed an elective resolution to dispense with this requirement.[21] The Act does not, however, specify anything that is to be done at the AGM. In practice, the accounts are often presented to it but this is not essential, as any general meeting will serve to receive them.[22]

(9) The directors may not allot shares without an authority to do so from the members. This may be conferred by ordinary resolution whether or not it amounts to an alteration of the Articles.[23]

(10) The giving of 'financial assistance', and the approval required on a purchase of own shares must be given by the company's members.[24]

(11) The right to demand a poll at general meetings cannot be excluded by the Articles, so long as the demand is made by at least:

(a) five voting members; or
(b) one-tenth of the voting rights; or
(c) one-tenth of the voting paid up capital.[25]

Moreover, proxies have the same rights as members for this purpose.[26]

(12) The right to appoint a proxy cannot be denied by the Articles to any member entitled to attend and vote.[27] This right must be stated in the notice calling the meeting and the proxy document cannot be required to be lodged more than two days in advance of the meeting.

(13) Reorganisations are provided for by special statutory machinery which is independent of anything in the Articles. This includes the following.

(a) Reconstruction under s 110 of the Insolvency Act 1986, whereby a company may go into a members' liquidation and pass a special resolution to exchange the company's assets directly for shares in another company.

(b) A scheme of arrangement under s 425 of the Act, whereby a compromise or arrangement can be made binding on all the parties affected where agreed to by 75 per cent in value and a majority in number at a meeting summoned by the courts, provided the scheme is then sanctioned by the courts. This procedure can be used where some variation of creditors' or shareholders' rights is the only solution to a difficulty and the courts have wide powers to take any steps necessary to implement the scheme.[28]

(c) Comulsory purchase of dissentients' shares under s 429.[29] This is a procedure designed to facilitate orthodox takeover bids, by enabling a bidder who has obtained 90 per cent acceptances[30] to acquire the remainder compulsorily on the same terms. There are stringent conditions which must be strictly complied with.

(14) The appointment of inspectors by the DTI is an important weapon in the armoury of shareholder protection and one which cannot be interfered with by the Articles.

    (a) Under s 431, the DTI may appoint inspectors 'to investigate the affairs of a company' on the company's application or on application by either 200 members or one-tenth of the issued shares.

    (b) Under s 432(1), the DTI must appoint such inspectors if the courts so order.[31]

    (c) Under s 432(2), the DTI may appoint on its own initiative if it suspects:

        (i) fraud, unfair prejudice to members, or misconduct in the company's formation or management; or

        (ii) that the members have not been given all the information about the company's affairs which they might reasonably expect.

    (d) Under s 442, the DTI may appoint inspectors on its own initiative to report on the control or ownership of shares, and must normally do so at the request of the members specified in (a) above.

    (e) Under s 446, the DTI may appoint inspectors if there is a suspicion that ss 323, 324 or 328 have been infringed. These sections relate to the prohibition on option dealing and to the notification of interests by directors and their families. The power to appoint may be exercised because of a complaint by members or any other circumstances giving rise to suspicion.

    (f) Under s 447, the DTI may require production of company documents. For these purposes, 'documents' includes information which is not in a legible form, such as computer records. This may, again, be done at the request of members and may be a preliminary to investigations. An order under s 447 should, if possible, specify which documents or classes of documents are sought by the DTI, particularly where it is likely that the documents will be removed from the company for a long period.'[32]

The DTI has wide powers of search and entry under these provisions, and there are severe penalties on directors or officers who withhold or suppress information.[33]

In the exercise of its statutory powers the DTI must act fairly, which is not merely a pious hope, but a legal requirement for it may be prevented from acting improperly; but it is a potential prosecutor, and it is not expected to show icy impartiality.[34]

(15) Directors' service contracts for more than five years must be approved by ordinary resolution[35] (although special notice provisions apply).[36]

(16) 'Substantial property transactions', regulated by s 320 et seq, whereby:

    (a) a director of the company (or its holding company) or a person connected with such a director acquires, or is to acquire, one or more non-cash assets of a requisite value; or

    (b) the company acquires or is to acquire one or more non-cash assets of a requisite value from such a director or person connected with a director, must be approved by ordinary resolution of the company (and, in certain circumstances, its holding company). The requisite value is currently

£100,000 or 10 per cent of the company's net assets, whichever is the lower, subject to an overall minimum of £2,000.

(17) Control over certain payments to directors is taken out of directors' hands, regardless of anything in the Articles.

(a) Remuneration cannot be paid to directors as a tax-free sum or a sum expressed to be net of the current rate of tax. If this is done, the net sum becomes a gross payment and is itself subject to tax.[37]

(b) The extension of loans or credits to directors or guarantees of such loans or credit are the subject of complex restrictions, with closely defined exceptions.[38]

(c) Compensation for loss of office must be approved by the members (ie by an ordinary resolution).[39]

(d) Payments to directors in connection with a sale of assets or shares must also be approved by the members.[40]

(18) Assignment of office by a director to a third party, even if in pursuance of a provision in the Articles, is of no effect unless approved by a special resolution.[41]

(19) Attempts in the Articles to relieve directors from liability for default or negligence are of limited effect, but the powers of a company to do this were greatly extended as a result of the Companies Act 1989.[42]

(20) The accounting duties of directors as to the form and presentation of accounts cannot be modified by the Articles.

3.3 POWERS IN THE ARTICLES: TABLE A

Having considered some of the limitations on the scope of the Articles, we can now see how powers are distributed, in practice, between the directors and the general meeting of members. Every director must look at his own company's Articles but he will usually find, at least in a private company, that they incorporate the whole or the greater part of the specimen Articles provided in Table A.[43] Table A is set out in Appendix C, but in this chapter we can take note of some of its salient features.[44] Most of them are then discussed separately in the relevant part of the text.

(1) Regulation 70 provides that 'the business of the company shall be managed by the directors'. This is, perhaps, the foundation stone of Table A, as upon it is built the management structure of the company. If reg 70 is adopted, as it usually is, then all powers of management except those specifically reserved by the Act, the Memorandum (which would be unusual) or by other Articles will be in the hands of the directors. The members 'cannot themselves usurp the powers which by the Articles are vested in the directors'.[45] In these circumstances, it is not true to say that the general meeting of members is in control of the company. It can alter the Articles by special resolution, or dismiss the directors by ordinary resolution, but what it cannot do is to tell the directors how to run the company's affairs.[46] The relationship between the board and the general meeting is discussed further in **3.8**. The directors' powers are, it should be noted, powers to manage the company, and this does not mean that they have a power to petition for the company to be wound up.[47]

(2) Regulation 2 provides that share rights and restrictions such as preferences as to dividend or capital (usually known as 'class rights') shall be fixed by the members by ordinary resolution in general meeting. Until the Companies Act 1980, the more important, or at least more immediate, decisions as to when, to whom, and at what price shares were issued, fell clearly within the directors' residual powers under what is now reg 70 (and until 1985 was reg 80). Now, however, the power to allot shares is 'overseen' by the members by virtue of s 80. The Articles may confer this power expressly upon the directors, in which case they must state the maximum number of shares which may be allotted by the directors (although this may be the whole of the unallotted share capital). If the Articles confer no such power, the directors must seek the company's authority to make allotments by asking for authority from a general meeting. In either event, the directors' authority will require renewal after the period specified in it, which may not exceed five years, unless the shareholders have passed an elective resolution dispensing with this requirement, in which case they may give an authority to the directors which either specifies a fixed period for the duration of the directors' authority, exceeding five years, or states that the directors' authority is for an indefinite duration,[48] and is revocable by the members at any time, even if it is contained in the Articles. The authority can be quite general, or conditional, or restricted to a particular allotment.[49]

All authorisations, variations or revocations under s 80 may be made by ordinary resolution even if the effect is to alter the Articles (which normally requires a special resolution). Equally, however, the resolution must be filed with the Registrar within 15 days, just like a special resolution, and a copy annexed to, or its substance embodied in, all copies of the Articles subsequently issued (s 380).

The rules govern not only allotments but also the grant of options, so that evasion is not easy. Infringement is a criminal offence, but s 80 itself does not invalidate the infringing allotment.

The directors may complete an allotment which was begun (for example, by offer or agreement) before their authority 'expired': s 80(7). The use of this word is a little unfortunate, since it leaves open the question what the directors may do if, between agreement to allot and the actual allotment, the authority does not 'expire' through lapse of the specified time but is actually revoked by the general meeting. If a revocation, or a variation of the authority, prevents the directors from completing the allotment, the company may be subject to an action for breach of contract; if, on the other hand, the directors ignore the new restriction in their powers then, even if the allottee's title to the shares on completion cannot be impeached, the directors will commit an offence by pressing on with the allotment.[50]

Section 80 does not, of course, apply to subscribers' shares recorded in the Memorandum. Nor does it apply to allotments made under employee share schemes as defined by s 743.[51]

(3) Regulation 32(a) allows increase of authorised share capital by ordinary resolution of the members.

(4) Regulation 34 allows reduction of share capital by special resolution subject to the consent of the courts.[52]

(5) Regulation 37 allows the directors to call extraordinary general meetings whenever they think fit, and also at the request of members specified in the Act.[53]

(6) Regulation 42 requires the chairman of the board to chair general meetings.

(7) Regulations 65 to 69 allow a director to appoint an alternate director to attend meetings and act in his place when he is unable to attend in person. He may appoint another director or a third party approved by a board resolution, and the alternate director has all his appointor's powers and voting rights. The alternate director's office is unremunerated, and his appointment may be revoked by the appointor in the same way as it is made, by notice to the company.[54]

(8) Regulation 82 leaves remuneration of the directors to be fixed by the members in general meeting (ie ordinary resolution).

(9) Regulation 71 allows directors to appoint attorneys or other agents for the company to act in the company's name.

(10) Regulations 85 and 86 require disclosure of a director's interests in contracts and, reg 94, provide rules for his dealing with the company (subject to the requirements of the Act and of the general law, discussed in Chapter 5).

(11) Regulation 87 allows directors to provide benefits, by way of gratuities, pensions, insurance or otherwise to retired salaried directors, including directors of subsidiaries.

(12) Regulation 81 provides for disqualification of directors in case of statutory or judicial disqualification, bankruptcy, insanity, resignation or six months' absence, without leave, from board meetings. Table A now makes no provision for removal of directors, since this is unnecessary in the light, of s 303 which gives the general meeting an entrenched power of dismissal by ordinary resolution.

(13) Regulation 73 provides for retirement of all directors at the first AGM and thereafter of one-third of the board at yearly intervals with eligibility for re-election.[55]

(14) Regulation 76 restricts nominations for the board (except by the directors themselves) to cases where notice is given to the company by a voting member not less than 14 or more than 35 days after a general meeting.[56]

(15) Regulation 78 allows the general meeting by ordinary resolution to appoint additional directors and to fix their remuneration.

(16) Regulation 79 allows the directors to fill casual vacancies on the board or to appoint additional directors – within the limits (if any) fixed by the subscribers or by the company, but reg 78 extends this power also to the general meeting of members.

(17) Regulation 88 allows the directors to regulate their meetings as they think fit; questions are to be decided by a majority of votes with a casting vote for the chairman. Any director may call a meeting at any time. A quorum is two unless the directors fix any other number (reg 89). They elect their own chairman (reg 91).

(18) Regulation 90 allows directors to continue to act despite vacancies but, where the number falls below the quorum, the survivor or survivors may act only to increase the number or call a general meeting.

(19) Regulation 72 allows delegation by the directors to such member or committee of the board as they think fit.

(20) Regulation 93 allows resolutions to be signed by all the directors, without the need for a meeting.[57]

(21) Regulation 72 allows the board to appoint a managing director upon such terms and with such of their powers as board members think fit. They may also delegate specified powers to any executive director.

(22) Regulation 99 requires the board to appoint the secretary (apart from the first secretary, whose appointment is governed by ss 10 and 13).

(23) Regulation 102 permits dividends to be:

  (a) declared by the general meeting (ie ordinary resolution); but
  (b) not to exceed the amount recommended by the directors.[58]

(24) Regulation 109 restricts members' rights to inspect the company's accounting records and other documents to cases where inspection is authorised by the directors, by the general meeting or, of course, by statute. These documents may be inspected by officers but members, as such, may only see the company's annual accounts themselves.

(25) Regulation 110 allows for capitalisation of profits, paying up issued shares, and issuing bonus shares. The general meeting must so resolve before these powers are exercisable.

(26) Regulation 118 indemnifies directors and other officers against liability incurred in defending proceedings (civil or criminal) provided:

  (a) they are successful; or
  (b) relief is granted to them by the courts under s 727.[59]

3.4   TABLE A: '1948 VERSION'

The current form of Table A came into effect on 1 July 1985. However, there will be many companies whose Articles are in the form set out in Sch 1 to the Companies Act 1948, either because:

(1) the company was formed before 1 July 1985, and did not exclude Table A; or
(2) the company adopted that form of Articles.

It is also possible that a company has adopted, or excluded, only parts of Table A (1948 version). It should be said that, unless the company is for some reason committed to the 1948 version, it would be simpler to adopt the current, 1985, version which may be done simply by moving and filing a special resolution to adopt new Articles and filing the resolution, and a reprinted copy of the new Articles at Companies House. It will make life easier, in most cases, to have the current version of Table A. Whether or not it has always made its intentions clear, Table A has moved steadily towards greater internal freedom of management and flexibility, and the '1948 version', in order that this process should be achieved, was considerably amended[60] over the years so that it might, by 1985, be fairly described as a scissors-and-paste job. Assuming, however, that a director is faced, at least for the time being, with the '1948 version', he will notice the following variations.

(1) The directors' power of management contained in reg 80 is similar to that set out in reg 70 (1985 version). This power is described as being subject to the restrictions imposed by the Act and by the Articles themselves, but unfortunately it adds that it is also subject to 'such regulations, being not inconsistent with' the Act or Articles, 'as may be prescribed by the company in general meeting'. No one is certain what these last words mean. On one view, they simply mean the Articles, as amended by the general meeting from time to time. If so, they are redundant. On another view, they refer to procedural matters and not the substantive management powers, in which case the words are either meaningless or misleading. A company which has an Article in this form should give consideration at once to ridding itself of these words and adopting reg 70 (1985 version).

(2) Regulation 4 provides that class rights may generally be varied with the consent of three-quarters of the members of the class. Companies registered before 22 December 1980 are subject to further provisions governing the procedure for variation, but these are redundant in the light of the procedure for variation introduced by the 1980 Act and described in Chapter 9. Indeed, the whole regulation is largely unnecessary.

(3) There is no power to appoint alternate directors.

(4) Regulation 77 requires no specific share qualification for directors, leaving this to be fixed, if at all, by the general meeting. This achieves so little that the 1985 version omits it, leaving it to companies who are rash enough to wish for a share qualification, to impose one by a special Article of their own devising.

(5) Regulation 79 delegates the company's borrowing power to the directors, including power to give mortgages on other security and (subject, however, to s 80 of the 1985 Act) to issue shares and debentures. These powers are inherent in the general management powers of the directors, and this express delegation served largely to introduce a limitation of the borrowing power to the amount of the issued capital, unless the general meeting consented. Regulation 80 then provides that this limitation will not bind a lender who had no actual knowledge that it was being exceeded. This may be thought to draw the sting from the limitation, but careful lenders, or prudent bankers, will exercise great care in any event to ensure that, to their knowledge, borrowing is within any limitations imposed upon the directors' powers.

(6) Regulation 85 allows the directors to determine how cheques and bills of exchange are to be signed.

(7) Regulation 93, governing nominations to the board, is similar to reg 76 (1985 version) but requires at least three and at most 21 days' notice to be given before the meeting (14 and 35 days respectively in the 1985 version).

(8) Regulation 96 allows the members to remove a director by ordinary resolution. In the light of s 303, this is redundant.

(9) Regulations 123 to 127 require proper accounts to be kept and presented by the directors. Again, the provisions of the Act make these obligations largely, if not entirely, superfluous.

(10) Regulation 135 requires the appointment of auditors, but again, in specifying that it shall be 'in accordance with' the Act adds nothing.

3.5   TABLE A: 'PRE-1948 VERSION'

A diminishing band of companies formed before 1948 may still be found with some or all of their Articles in one of the forms of Table A set out in the earlier Companies Acts. In certain respects, these Articles will differ from both the 1948 and 1985 versions of Table A, by the omission of powers and regulations which were introduced in 1948. Briefly, these are as follows.

(1) Regulations 66 (1948) and 58 (1985) provide that objections to a voter's qualifications can be made only at a meeting and not later, the chairman's decision being final. These Articles are completely effective to prevent disputes, at least in the absence of bad faith[61] but are not found in earlier versions of Table A.

(2) The newer forms of Table A (regs 71 and 61) set out a 'two-way' proxy form enabling a member to decide how his proxy is to be used at general meetings, and regs 73 and 63 preserve the validity of a proxy not withstanding its revocation.[62] Older Table A versions contain no such provision.

(3) Earlier versions did not expressly permit a director to be employed by, or have an interest in, the subsidiaries or associates of the company without having to account to the company for their fees or their benefits (now regs 78 (1948) and 85 (1985)).

(4) Regulations 81 (1948) and 71 (1985) empower the directors to delegate widely by power of attorney, with a further power for the attorney to subdelegate.[63] This is not found in earlier versions of Table A.

(5) Regulation 72 of Table A (1929) automatically disqualifies directors having an interest in a contract with the company, unless the general meeting consents. Directors of older companies must beware of this puritanical rule, which is very considerably relaxed by later versions (regs 84 (1948) and 85 (1985)).

(6) Regulation 87 (1948), was the first 'official' power for the board to pay pensions or gratuities to salaried colleagues on their retirement.

(7) Regulation 106 (1948) first introduced the useful rule allowing board resolutions simply to be signed by the whole board, instead of being passed at a formal board meeting. A court would apply the rule embodied in reg 106 in any event, but the presence of such an article discourages unnecessary disputes.

(8) Regulations 109 (1948) and 72 (1985) allow delegation to a managing director, and, in the later regulation, to any executive director. This did not appear in earlier versions of Table A, although it may have been implied from the power to appoint such a director (which the earlier versions did contain: reg 68 (1929)). No managing director should be willing to accept office in the absence of such a power as found in regs 109 (1948) and 72 (1985), since there seems to be no general power, apart from the Articles, to appoint and delegate to him.[64]

(9) Under Table A (1929) all dividends had to be paid in cash. By regs 120 (1948) and 105 (1985) the general meeting may authorise payment in kind on the board's recommendation.

(10) Regulations 128 to 129 (1948) and 110 (1985) allow the capitalisation of profits and the issue of paid up bonus shares by the general meeting, on the board's recommendation. Articles in the 1929 or earlier forms would require amendment to achieve this; in effect the board will need a 75 per cent majority to alter the

Articles instead of a bare majority (ordinary resolution) to apply the power contained in the later version of Table A.

Whilst some Tables A permit use of certain unrealised profits on revaluation of fixed assets, such as a revaluation reserve, to fund a bonus issue, pre-1980 Act versions may not.

3.6 PRIVATE COMPANY VARIATIONS OF TABLE A

Since the repeal of Table A, Part II, by the Companies Act 1980, no part of Table A has been geared exclusively to the use of private companies. The 1980 Act did, however, modify two rules in what was previously Part I to bring all companies into line with what had been the 'Part II practice' for private companies.

(1) Post-1980 versions of Table A, of which the latest incarnation is the 1985 Table A (to which all subsequent references to Articles will relate) set the quorum for the conduct of business at general meetings at two. The relevant Article in the 1985 Table A is reg 40. This regulation is a distinct improvement on its predecessor, reg 53 of the 1948 version, as modified in 1980, for it spells out clearly that each of the two persons present must be entitled to vote on the business to be transacted, or a proxy of such a person, or the authorised representative of a corporate member. It is often not understood[65] that corporate members are entitled to 'attend in person' by such a representative, and whilst it may be necessary to check his authority to attend and vote, he is not in any sense a proxy and is not therefore subject to the rules and restrictions governing proxies. A certified copy of a board resolution of the corporate shareholder, and proof of the identity of the authorised representative, is usually sufficient.

(2) By reg 53, a resolution in writing executed by or on behalf of all the members entitled to vote on it is as effective as a resolution passed at a formal meeting. This puts into the Articles a convenient manifestation of the 'principle of unanimity' by which an act which is clearly that of the whole membership dispenses with such a formality and is not treated as irregular (see **9.7**). To a considerable extent, reg 53 embodies common and reasonably sensible practice, backed by favourable decisions of the courts. Again, however, reg 53 represents an improvement upon its predecessors, including reg 73A of the 1948 version (inserted in 1980), for it makes it clear that there is no need for a single document; as long as each member has signed one of them there may be several 'instruments in like form'. Under ss 381A, 381B and 381C, a statutory procedure also exists as an alternative means of passing resolutions in writing of the members.[66]

The director of a private company will usually find that his company has adopted Table A, but with significant modifications of its own. These modifications tend to fall into a pattern, as most private companies use standard forms of Articles adopting and amending Table A, which are supplied by law stationers after settling by counsel. The object of the amendments will usually be to increase the board's freedom of action – subject to the Act – and the following are common amendments.[67]

(1)   Certain clauses of Table A are often excluded. These include regs 24 (refusal to register transfer of shares), 87 (payment of pensions) and 78 (power of general meeting to fill casual vacancies on the board) in the 1985 Table A.

(2)   The issuing of shares will usually be placed expressly in the hands of the directors, subject often to a proviso that new shares must be offered pro rata to existing shareholders, unless the general meeting decides otherwise. A common form is: 'The shares shall be under the control of the directors who may allot . . . as they think fit.' This must be read subject, however, to s 80, which prevents an open-ended delegation of allotment powers to the directors (see **3.3**); its relationship with the statutory pre-emption rights conferred by s 89 can be seen at **7.3**. Where the directors act under this form of Article, they do not (despite its wording) have a completely free hand, as they are always subject to an overriding fiduciary obligation to use their powers for the benefit of the company rather than for themselves or any group of individuals.[68]

(3)   The company's lien (or charge) for debts owing to the company is often extended to fully paid shares. Regulation 8 restricts the lien to sums due on partly paid shares, reflecting s 150, which restricts the lien of a public company to such debts.[69] There seems no reason why a private company's Articles should be so restricted and, indeed, a lien on fully-paid shares is clearly of more practical use in a private company whose members are likely to become indebted to the company. Regulations 9 to 11 in Table A regulate the sale of the shares if the member's debt is not discharged and could usually be adopted without substantial modification.

(4)   The Articles may restrict the transfer of shares. These restrictions are not necessary (as they were until 1980) for the company to maintain its status as a private company, but many companies will have adopted such restrictions both before[70] and after 1980. Most private companies simply give the board complete discretion over whether to register the transfer of shares. Such a discretion may invariably be exercised without the need for the board to give reasons. However, a significant minority of private companies prefer their shareholders to enjoy the right to freely transfer their shares within clearly defined limits. Provisions commonly found are:

(a)   a right to transfer freely to other members;

(b)   a right to transfer within a member's family;

(c)   a right of pre-emption for other members, ie a duty to offer shares to them before selling elsewhere; and

(d)   (occasionally) a right to transfer within a group of companies or between members of a particular trade or profession.

However, such companies will invariably also have an Article which gives the directors an absolute discretion, without giving reasons, to refuse registration of a transfer not within one of the special categories. Of course, wherever the directors are required to exercise any such discretion, and even if they do not have to give reasons, they must do so in the best interests of the company, in accordance with their general fiduciary duties.[71]

(5)   The maximum and minimum number of directors is often specified. One will suffice for a private company (s 282(3)) and even if a minimum of two or three is fixed there may be a reserve power for a sole survivor to function for all purposes

(and not merely to fill vacancies or call a general meeting, as under reg 90 of Table A).

(6) The 1985 version of Table A contains no restrictions on directors' borrowing powers, but reg 79 of the 1948 version limits their borrowing to the amount of the issued capital. The usual practice will be to exclude this and to delegate all (ie unlimited) borrowing powers to the directors. This is clearly necessary if the directors of companies with a small issued capital are to have any effective borrowing powers, but whether it is desirable is another matter. There is no immediate prospect of introducing a minimum paid-up capital for private companies and it is a harsh but undeniable truth that those who lend large sums to undercapitalised companies have only themselves to blame if the loans are lost, whether the lender is a bank or a director. The directors' borrowing powers are subject to s 80 (see **3.3** at point (2)).

(7) Regulation 94 prevents a director from voting at board or committee meetings on contracts or other matters in which he has, directly or indirectly, a material interest, but reg 94 itself says that this is subject to contrary provision in the company's Articles. Frequently, the rule is relaxed, enabling him to vote and to keep any resulting profit. This may be justifiable in the case of a director-controlled company, although it may not seem so to outside shareholders (ie those who are not members of the controlling group) and it is, in any event, subject to certain overriding prohibitions imposed by the Acts.

(8) 'Associate directors' may be provided for by the Articles. Here, the expression does not mean directors holding salaried office in the company, but officers or employees who are 'directors' in name, but not in fact – the opposite of de facto or shadow directors as defined by s 741. The Articles should expressly state, if that is the intention, that they are not directors for the purposes of the Act. Articles of this type will not necessarily use the expression 'Associate' – such employees or officers might be called 'local', 'special', 'executive' or 'divisional' directors, or some other term might be used. To determine the precise status of such employees or officers, the Articles should always be consulted.

(9) If the company opts not to have, or if it has one, opts not to use, a company seal,[72] and chooses to rely instead on the procedure for executing documents introduced by the Companies Act 1989,[73] or, in Scotland the Requirements of Writing (Scotland) Act 1995 (see **3.11**) the Articles will usually amend Table A, regs 6 and 101. These deal with sealing of share certificates, and signature of documents to which the seal is affixed. Such amendments will prevent a challenge to the validity or effectiveness of documents executed using the new procedure.

(10) Retirement at 70, which would otherwise be required for directorship of public companies and new subsidiaries under s 293 is often expressly excluded (even where it does not apply!) as are the rotation provisions of Table A, reg 73. In director-controlled companies, retirement by rotation is little more than a nuisance and may well be dispensed with. Indeed, if the shareholders pass an elective resolution to dispense with an AGM, this amendment will be essential. An alternative is to specify named directors as life or governing directors, but this is rarely found in post-1948 companies, and such directors can always be removed under s 303 (ordinary resolution) in any event if appointed after 18 July 1945.[74]

(11) Share transfer forms do not require the signature of the transferee if the shares are fully paid, and a special Article is often inserted to record this.

(12) The power to retain benefits, such as pensions, may be extended to authorise the grant of pensions to directors who have not held salaried office in the company, thus going beyond reg 87 of Table A. The Articles should also expressly authorise the directors to commit the company to pay for and maintain insurance for their benefit, within the limits set by s 310 of the Act.

(13) Even before the introduction of regs 65 to 69 of Table A (see **3.3**), many Articles provided for the appointment of alternate directors, enabling the alternate director to act in a way in which his appointor could act, for example, to attest the use of the seal, to make statutory declarations, and to vote and count towards the quorum. These Articles may also contain provisions not found in Table A, and which even those companies adopting regs 65 to 69 should consider:

(a)   that attendance at board meetings by the alternate director should prevent the appointor's directorship from being vacated by reason of his absence without permission from board meetings for more than six months (if this is not done, permission will have to be sought when the alternate director is appointed);

(b)   that the appointor may give written notice to the company that some or some specified part of his remuneration should be paid to the alternate director;

(c)   that the alternate director may represent more than one appointor, but shall count as one only for the purposes of establishing a quorum (reg 89 of the 1985 Table A probably has this effect, but only by implication) and, if it is decided to prevent an alternate director from dominating the board, shall have one vote for each appointor (as well as his own vote, if any) but shall not have any special or weighted voting rights of an appointor.

Although an alternate director's name need not appear on company letter headings (under s 305), it is probably necessary to notify the Registrar of an appointment (under s 288, Form 288a) and to otherwise enter the alternate director on the company's registers, such as the Register of Directors' Interests in Shares or Debentures.[75]

(14) UK company legislation and case-law take virtually no account of technological advances.[76] Directors seeking to take advantage of modern technology to ease the administration of their companies must therefore look to their Articles for their authority to do so. Modern Articles often contain provisions enabling electronic board meetings and electronic notice of such meetings. Certain safeguards should be included in any such provisions, such as provisions requiring that all directors should be able to hear each other and be heard at all times, and provisions governing where meetings are deemed to be held – for the directors 'present' at the meeting are, of course, not actually physically together in the same place.

Articles may also permit giving of notice of general meetings by electronic means such as e-mail. Again, including additional safeguards in the Articles may be prudent, such as a requirement that shareholders must have given their consent to receiving notices by e-mail, and the member concerned must be able to read the e-mail sent.

(15) Since 1992, it has been possible for a private company to be incorporated as, or to become, a single member company.[77] Private company Articles commonly contain a combination of provisions which:

    (a) prohibit transfers of shares (including elections by personal representatives to become registered as holders of a deceased's shares in their own right) except at the discretion of the director or directors of the company; and

    (b) suspend the voting rights which otherwise attach to the shares of a deceased member until the member's personal representatives either transfer them to some new shareholder or elect to become holders of those shares in their own right.

On the death of a single member who is also the sole director, this creates a problem. There is no director to approve a transfer or election by his personal representatives. Nor can the personal representatives vote to appoint new directors, for the deceased's shares carry no right to vote. There are, of course, no other shareholders or directors who could make such an appointment.

Modern Articles will provide for this and similar situations by allowing personal representatives in such circumstances to appoint a new director or directors. The new director(s) can then exercise their powers in the usual way, and either approve or refuse to register a subsequent transfer or election by the personal representatives. The deceased's shares are, in effect, enfranchised to the limited extent necessary to escape the lacuna which otherwise results.

(16) The rules regulating single person companies, such as the rule that the sole member may constitute a quorum, may apply to a company in any event, but well-drafted Articles will often include reminders of the rules.

3.7 LISTED COMPANY VARIATIONS OF TABLE A

3.7.1 Compulsory variations

At the end of March 1996, there were 11,500 public companies comprising 1.1 per cent of all effective companies in England, Wales and Scotland,[78] of which fewer than 25 per cent were 'listed' on the London Stock Exchange. Directors of listed companies will find that the Articles contain differences of two kinds from those in Table A:[79]

(1) those arising from the requirements of the London Stock Exchange;

(2) those adopted by the company to meet its particular requirements.

In this paragraph, we look at the requirements of the London Stock Exchange and thus at variations on Table A which will be found in the Articles of all listed companies.[80] The source of these requirements is as follows.

(1) The London Stock Exchange and the Midlands, Western, Northern and Scottish Exchanges were unified on 31 March 1973 and subsequently merged with the International Securities Regulatory Organisation in November 1986 to become

'The International Stock Exchange of the United Kingdom and the Republic of Ireland Limited' which trades as the London Stock Exchange by virtue of s 142 of the Financial Services Act 1986, the London International Stock Exchange is the 'competent authority' without whose consent no securities – including not only shares and stock but also debenture and other loan stock, warrants, etc, and public stock issued outside the European Community – may be admitted to the Official List. It is therefore responsible for dealing with admissions listing particulars, and the continuing obligations of companies whose securities are listed. Recent years have seen the London Stock Exchange alter from an essentially 'private' institution to a body which, although not governmental or quasi-governmental, can be regarded as a public body. First came three EC Directives – the Admission (ie to listing) Directive, the Interim Reports Directive and the Listing Particulars Directive.[81] These were followed by the drive to modernise investment institutions and increase competition among them, resulting in the Financial Services Act 1986. Most of that Act relates to the business and regulation of specialised investment companies and organisations which is a subject beyond the scope of this work.

Whilst the Directives impose a minimum level of requirements which the London Stock Exchange has no power to relax or waive, the London Stock Exchange is entitled to impose more stringent requirements than the Directives. It has done so in many cases. In the past, the extra requirements were a kind of 'voluntary code' but the listing rules have acquired a measure of statutory recognition as a result of the Financial Services Act 1986. As a result, the system is that peculiar mixture of law and semi-autonomy which is fashionably known as self-regulation. One effect – whether intended by the legislature or not – is that, in principle, decisions taken by the London Stock Exchange now appear to be subject to control by the courts in the form of 'judicial review'. This is the system under which a person aggrieved by the decision of a 'public law' body may seek a remedy in the High Court if that body has acted beyond its powers[82] or badly misused its discretion. It should be clearly understood that this is not the same thing as an appeal. The court is not interested in whether it would have made the same decision nor does it, in fact, make any decision on the matter before the body challenged. It looks only to see whether the decision taken was lawful, and if it concludes that it was not it quashes it or declares it void. Thus, for example, a disappointed applicant who successfully challenges a refusal to admit does not thereby obtain admission; that will be up to the London Stock Exchange, who will re-examine the application in the light of the court's decision.

(2) The various requirements are set out in a publication called *The Listing Rules*[83] (or, more commonly, the Yellow Book) issued by authority of the London Stock Exchange and now in loose-leaf form for ease of updating.[84] The Yellow Book contains, inter alia:

   (a) the procedure for application, and the requirements imposed on listed companies and their boards;[85]
   (b) the continuing obligations imposed upon listed companies;[86]

    (c)   requirements as to the company's 'constitutional' documents, including its
        Articles.

It is (c) above which concerns us here. In a listed company, the Articles must provide, inter alia, as follows.

(1)   That transfers, forms and other documents or instructions relating to or affecting the title to any shares will be registered without fee.
(2)   That fully paid shares must be free from liens and any restriction on the right of transfer.
(3)   That share certificates will be executed and issued free in the case of loss or transfer of part of a holding.
(4)   That unclaimed dividends will not be forfeited until 12 years after declaration or they become due for payment.
(5)   That a director will not vote on any contract in which he has a material interest other than an interest which is specifically permitted.
(6)   That casual or additional appointments to the board must submit themselves for re-election at the next AGM.
(7)   That a period of at least seven days be available during which nominations to the board can be made, and that the deadline for lodging nominations with the company be no earlier than seven days before the meeting.
(8)   That adequate voting rights will, in appropriate circumstances, be secured to preference shareholders.
(9)   That the share capital structure be stated in the Articles together with class rights, if any, and a one-third quorum for meetings to vary such rights.
(10) That any limit imposed on the number of members in a joint allotment must not prevent the registration of up to four persons.
(11) That non-voting shares be described as such, as must shares with restricted or limited voting rights.
(12) That proxies must be capable of being 'two-way' and that a corporation may execute a form of proxy under the hand of a duly authorised officer.
(13) If the company takes power to issue share warrants to bearer in its Articles, new warrants must not be issued to replace lost warrants unless the company is satisfied beyond reasonable doubt that the originals have been destroyed.
(14) If the company takes power to sanction members for non-compliance with a notice served under s 212, there are specific limits to the sanctions it can impose.
(15) There are restrictions on the powers which a company can take in its Articles to cease to send dividends to 'untraceable members' or to sell the shares of such a member.
(16) There are specific requirements as to the publication of notices by advertisement where power to do this is to be taken in the company's Articles. If the Articles provide that notices are to be given to members whose registered addresses are in the UK, members whose addresses are not in the UK must be entitled to nominate an address within the UK to be considered as his address for these purposes.
(17) Persons appointed by the board to fill a casual vacancy or as an addition to the board must retire from office at, or at the end of, the next AGM.

3.7.2   Optional variations

We have noted some of the provisions which directors of all listed companies will find in their company's Articles. We can now turn to some of the other modifications of Table A which they are likely to find in practice.

(1) Table A is usually excluded entirely and replaced by a complete set of Articles, drafted to meet the company's specific requirements, although reintroducing many of the clauses of Table A.

(2) There will, in the usual way, be a multiple-objects clause in the Memorandum containing many subclauses, each of which is described as independent. The directors should be given power in the Articles to pursue or discontinue any one of these branches of business as they think fit. Chapter 9, paragraph 1 of the Yellow Book also requires public announcements of major new developments in the company's activities which, because of their effect on assets or liabilities or the company's financial position or in the general course of its business, may lead to a substantial movement in share prices or significantly affect its ability to meet its commitments.

(3) Class rights should be specified, including rights on winding up.

(4) Variation of class rights should also be provided for, requiring a specified majority (usually 75 per cent of the members of the class[87]) with a quorum of at least one-third of the class.[88]

(5) Subject to s 80, issuing of shares is usually entrusted to the directors, subject also to the directions, of the general meeting, but, in any event, the Yellow Book (Chapter 9, paragraph 18) requires the directors to get the consent of the general meeting before any share issue for cash, otherwise than to existing equity shareholders.

(6) Power to pay underwritings and other commissions is usually taken, within the limits of the Act.[89]

(7) There may be discretionary powers to refuse to register transfer but only in respect of partly paid shares.[90]

(8) Forfeiture at the discretion of the directors may be allowed but only for non-payment of calls, and the procedure must be strictly complied with.[91]

(9) Power to increase or rearrange capital by ordinary resolution and to reduce by special resolution in the manner prescribed by the Act will usually be granted to the general meeting, often with wide discretion to the directors to resolve problems in regard to joint holders or fractional amounts.

(10) Procedure for calling and conducting general meetings may be left to Table A (regs 38 to 53) but it may be useful to provide that where a meeting is requisitioned[92] by members, no business shall be conducted beyond that stated in the requisition.

(11) Provisions for voting rights should specify the circumstances in which preference or other classes of shares have the right to vote.

(12) Qualification shares may be required for directors, in which case they must obtain them within two months or such less period as is stated in the Articles, otherwise they must vacate office.[93]

(13) Power to pay gratuities and pensions should also be widely drawn so as to apply to former directors and officers of all categories.

(14) Section 293 (retirement at 70) applies to public companies and their subsidiaries but may be excluded by the general meeting or the Articles (if the company was registered after 1946).

(15) Detailed provisions as to directors' interest in contracts will usually be found providing, inter alia, for:

(a) exemption from disqualification;

(b) exclusion from voting or quorum;

(c) retention of profit;

(d) permission to vote and be counted in a quorum for the purposes of fixing pension schemes and terms of employment (other than his own service contract);

(e) relaxation of this Article by ordinary resolution of the members.

(16) The board may be allowed to appoint local managers or 'directors' and local boards with such delegated duties as the board may decide.

(17) Special provisions will usually be included for the appointment and remuneration of the managing director, and other executive, departmental and branch directors as well as the chairman and vice-chairman.

3.8 EFFECT OF ARTICLES – DOMINANCE OF THE BOARD

Having looked at examples of Articles both in Table A and elsewhere, what can we conclude about the separation of powers which the Articles invariably prescribe? One feature which immediately strikes the eye is the supremacy of the constitution of the company (the Acts and case-law combined with the Memorandum and Articles) over the organs of the company which that constitution creates. The situation is analogous to that in a federal as opposed to a unitary State. It is neither the federal nor the provincial governments, nor the courts, which are supreme, but the constitution itself. So with a company, neither the general meeting nor the board of directors is the ultimate authority. That authority is the company's constitution which may be changed certainly, but until it is so changed it cannot be overridden by any one of the company's organs.

Thus, although the members may regard the company as 'their company' because they own it, they cannot override or usurp the powers which the directors have been given by them in the Articles. They can, of course, change the Articles by special resolution[94] or change the directors by ordinary resolution[95] but, until they do so, they must yield to the authority which the directors have been given,[96] and the general meeting cannot retrospectively reverse or annul the board's acts and decisions, even by special resolution.

To take an important example, the Articles normally include reg 102 of Table A which says that dividends may be:

(1) declared by the members in general meeting; but

(2) shall not exceed the amount, if any, recommended by the directors.

Thus, the directors decide whether there may be a dividend and if so, how much. The members may take it or leave it but they cannot initiate it. So a unanimous resolution by all of the members to declare a certain dividend will be of no effect whatsoever if it is not within the amount recommended by the directors.[97] This principle applies equally to all the exclusive powers which the directors may be given, including the general power in reg 70 of Table A to manage the business of the company. So, a resolution of the members that the company should not acquire some leasehold premises could be disregarded by the directors who had already decided to the contrary.[98] Regulation 70 is so wide that the members' powers are effectively limited to those specifically given to them, such as the power to remove directors or to increase capital. The directors are thus the repositories of all residuary powers and, as such, have become the dominating element in the corporate machinery, as has occurred in most constitutions of the federal or power-sharing type.

3.8.1   Exceptions

Two exceptions are worth noting to the general principle that the members must keep to the place which the Articles have allotted to them.

(1)   If the directors will not act, either from choice, or because of a dispute or lack of quorum, the general meeting may do so, for example, to appoint an additional director[99] or to sue.[100]

(2)   Regulation 70 makes the directors' powers subject to the Articles and to 'any directions given by special resolution'. This may prove to be a troublesome provision. Its 1948 predecessor, reg 80, subjected the directors to 'such regulations . . . as may be prescribed by the company in general meeting'. The difficulty of interpreting this provision has already been referred to (see **3.4** at point (1)). It seems unlikely that reg 80 enabled the members to interfere with the directors' substantive powers,[101] and (if it had any effect at all) it was probably limited to procedural matters. Regulation 70, like reg 80, refers to the restrictions placed upon the directors by the Articles themselves, and substitutes 'directions . . . by special resolution' for the earlier 'regulations . . . prescribed'. We are, therefore, dealing with a special resolution which, apparently, may not formally have altered the Articles; but it is not easy to see what effect such a special resolution can have unless it is to inhibit the exercise of powers contained in the Articles. The question is, therefore, whether reg 70 permits the imposition of substantive, or merely procedural, inhibitions upon the board. There is nothing to limit 'directions' to procedural matters and it is probably the case that reg 70 now allows a majority large enough to pass a special resolution to give the board specific directions as to its conduct. Regulation 70, in any case, makes it clear that no such 'direction' is to have retrospective effect.

3.9   BORROWING POWERS

It is necessary to look separately at one of the more important powers which are given specifically to directors – quite apart from the general sweeping-up power under reg 70. The usual position with regard to borrowing powers is as follows.

(1) The Memorandum will contain a power for the company to borrow and to give security of all kinds.[102] The power will be implied in a trading company.[103]

(2) The Articles, if adopting 1948 Table A, reg 79 (see **3.4** at point (5)), will allow directors to exercise the company's borrowing powers.

(3) Private company Articles often delete the proviso in reg 79, but subject to the proviso that the aggregate amount borrowed should not exceed the issued capital of the company without the consent of the general meeting.[104]

(4) There is no regulation in the 1985 Table A which provides especially that the directors may exercise the company's borrowing powers, but most forms of Articles supplied by law stationers contain a specific borrowing power for directors, without any limit, thus corresponding to the proviso in reg 79.

The importance and frequency of company borrowings is such that every director will want to ensure that both loan and security are within the powers both of the company and the board. If not, he may find himself liable both to the lender for breach of warranty of authority and to the company for breach of duty. He will also bear in mind the strict obligation to file particulars of certain charges, for registration by the Registrar of Companies within 21 days of their creation[105] (charges include mortgages, floating charges, debentures, etc). In practice, registration of particulars is usually effected by the lender, because it is the lender who may lose his security if registration does not take place. Legally, however, the obligation to file particulars of the charge lies with the company. Indeed, if particulars are not registered the company may become liable to a fine and the loan becomes immediately repayable. For these reasons, if the lender does insist on registering the particulars, the company's officers should always check that it has done so within the time-limits and will, in any event, require the original certificate of registration of the charge issued by Companies House (which is conclusive evidence that the particulars have been properly registered) to be forwarded to them by the Registrar.

Thus, a fixed loan for 20 years which is not registered within the time-limit could be converted overnight into one repayable on demand, merely through inadvertence or a delay in the post. If the 21-day limit is not met,[106] the only remedy is to apply to the court for an order allowing the charge to be registered out of time. The court's powers to make such an order are discretionary, and the order may make the charge subject to rights acquired by creditors between the date the charge should have been registered and the date it actually was.[107] The importance of complying with these registration requirements cannot be too strongly emphasised. The nature of the debt secured and the assets charged must be accurately described in the form of particulars, since otherwise the form will be rejected by the Registrar and this may result in failure to re-submit the corrected particulars within the 21-day time-limit, with the consequences described above.

There are various other ways in which a company may obtain finance. It may acquire supplies on hire purchase or instalment sales terms, under a reservation of title clause or under an equipment lease. It may sell its customers' accounts to a factoring or discount company. These transactions are not, strictly speaking, borrowing and, in general, the board will be free to enter into them in the ordinary course of business. A secured lender (such as the company's bank) may insist upon an Article excluding or restricting such transactions. Irrespective of whether such an Article binds third parties who are unaware of it, the board should observe the restrictions since the lender may reserve powers in its security to appoint an administrative receiver if, for example, the company sells its accounts. The law relating to security and de facto security such as hire purchase and retention of title is regarded by many as highly unsatisfactory and reform may well be undertaken. However, the announcement by the DTI that proposed new provisions in the Companies Act 1989, designed to replace entirely the current law relating to registration of charges under the principal Act, would never be brought into force because of dissatisfaction with its terms is likely to have deflated any major initiatives in this direction for the foreseeable future.

3.10 POWERS EXERCISED COLLECTIVELY

The directors do not enjoy individual rights to act on behalf of the company, as do partners, and the general rule is that they must act collectively as a board.[108] Regulation 88 of Table A provides as follows.

(1) They may regulate their proceedings as they think fit.
(2) Any director may call a meeting or require the secretary to do so.[109]
(3) Each director has one vote (an alternate director having two, in the absence of his appointor, if himself a director) and all questions are decided by a simple majority, with a casting vote for the chairman, if necessary.

Thus, an individual director is not, as such, entitled to bind the company although, in practice, there may be exceptions to the general rule, which we can now consider.

(1) The Articles (as reg 72) may entitle the board to delegate, its powers, or some of them, to such one or more directors as they think fit. If they do this, the director(s) will have actual authority.
(2) The Articles may expressly confer individual management powers on a managing director. (Regulation 72 does not do this, but leaves it to the board to decide what powers the managing director shall have which may include powers to act on his own as if he were the full board.)
(3) So far as third parties are concerned, managing directors are normally 'held-out' as having authority to bind the company, regardless of the actual extent of their delegated powers, and even if they have never been formally appointed.[110] This is called the 'ostensible' authority of the managing director. Similarly, a finance director may have ostensible authority in relation to, for example, instructing the company's brokers or financial advisers, so that the company is bound even if the finance director does not in fact have authority to bind the company.
(4) An individual may be so effectively in control of a company that he will be regarded as having actual or ostensible authority to act on its behalf.[111]
(5) Regulation 93 allows the directors to dispense with a board meeting altogether where a resolution is signed by all of them.

In general, it may be said that business practice is at variance with the law on the question of the directors' duty to act collectively as a board. In practice, business people do deal with a single director whether or not he is the managing director and whether or not he has any delegated powers. They treat him as they would a partner in a professional firm. It may be that they run some risk in doing so, although the courts may be able to help them by the 'holding out' principle. This has now been extended even to the secretary, who is regarded as having ostensible authority to bind the company on 'administrative' matters, such as the ordering of office equipment and hire cars.[112] The law had tended in the past to regard the secretary as a person of insignificance with no authority whatsoever, long after the time when he had developed into a most important officer, often playing a larger role than some of the individual directors. As a last resort, a third party, whose contract is repudiated by the board, may have a claim against the offending officer for breach of warranty of authority.[113]

It may be noted that a director (and, indeed, any officer) has an individual right to inspect the company's accounting records at all times by virtue of s 222. Even books which are not accounting records seem to be open to inspection by a director, and the courts will force disclosure unless there is clear evidence that he is about to be removed, or is likely to misuse confidential information.[114]

3.10.1 Delegation of powers

As we have seen, directors may not delegate their powers unless specifically permitted to so do and such permission is granted by reg 72. Regulation 72, or an expanded version, is always likely to be adopted and the usual position is as follows.

(1) The directors may delegate to a committee comprising one or more of themselves as they think fit. There is no legal objection in this context to a committee of one.[115]

(2) The board cannot deprive itself of the right to revoke a delegation of powers (although such revocation may amount to a breach of contract with a managing or executive director, as we shall see below).

(3) The board may appoint a managing director and may confer such of their powers upon him as they think desirable, and indeed they can do so in the case of any director holding executive office.

Thus, in any specific case, a director must consider first the extent of delegation permitted by the Articles and secondly, the extent to which it has actually taken place. If the first is adequate, the second may well be presumed in practice as there may be a de facto managing director even if no formal appointment has been made.[116] However, it is clearly in the interests of all parties to have the delegation expressly made, since the board must always be aware of their ultimate collective responsibility, and any director who is to be given specific responsibilities, whether as managing director or otherwise, should ask his board for the appropriate resolution or provision in his service agreement, job description or whatever, to be approved and minuted.

The special questions arising from the removal of the managing director are discussed in Chapter 11, but it must always be borne in mind that the extent of his powers, as of any other director or committee, are entirely at the discretion of the board who may make exclusions or impose limits as they think fit, subject to the terms of his service agreement.

Thus, if the service agreement or resolution specifies, as it commonly does, that the managing director shall perform such functions as the board may assign to him, he may not be able to complain if they decide to confine him exclusively to one of the subsidiaries.[117]

3.10.2   Directors exceeding powers

(1) Ultra vires the company

Having ascertained the extent of his powers, the director can now consider the consequences if he exceeds them. There are two levels at which this may occur, the first limited by the powers of the company itself, and the second by those of the board. In this paragraph we are concerned with acts which are ultra vires the company itself, that is beyond the capacity of the company as limited by the Memorandum; although it should be noted that in either case there is a breach of the director's duty to the company which may lead to a liability on his part to compensate the company if it suffers loss. What, then, is the position where a director enters into a contract which is ultra vires the company, for example, where he borrows money for a business which the company is not authorised to carry on?[118]

(a)   The contract is prima facie void[119] and cannot be ratified even by the unanimous vote of all the members.[120]

(b)   An important exception appears in s 35, whereby the validity of an act done by a company shall not be called into question on the ground of lack of capacity by reason of anything in the company's Memorandum.

This means that neither the company nor any third party can escape their obligations arising from such a contract on grounds that it is beyond the company's capacity as set out in the Memorandum of Association. This effectively eliminates the need to consider whether an act is ultra vires the company or not – in terms of the parties' rights against each other, it does not matter.

This ability to disregard the Memorandum applies whether the act in question is a commercial transaction, such as a contract to borrow money, or a non-commercial transaction, such as a donation to charity.

It will also apply irrespective of whether the limitation on the company's capacity derives from its statement of objects or from any other provision in the Memorandum. For example, it appears that an allotment of shares which causes the company's issued share capital to exceed the authorised share capital stated in its Memorandum will not be void under the section.

The rule operates to prevent not only the company, but also the third party, from arguing that an act is void. Previous versions of the rule operated only in favour of the third party, and not in favour of the company.

There is no requirement of good faith so the third party is under no obligation to inquire as to the powers of the company or the directors, nor to consider whether the act is in what the directors honestly believe to be the best interests of the company. Indeed, the third party and the company may be fully aware that the act is neither within the company's capacity nor in its best interests, and the section will still save the transaction. Generally, a third party is not deemed to have knowledge of the contents of the Memorandum simply because it appears on the public record at Companies House, for the doctrine of 'constructive notice' of such matters of record has been abolished.[121] As a result of s 35, the content of the Memorandum has become irrelevant in considering the validity of acts as between the company and third parties. As a corollary to this emasculation of the Memorandum and, in particular, the reduction in the significance of the statement of objects in a company's Memorandum of Association, fundamental reforms, introduced by the Companies Act 1989,[122] now enable companies to operate using a truncated form of objects.

Indeed, even where a company adopts a more traditional statement of objects, evasion or even total exclusion of the operation of the ultra vires rule by the draftsman of the Memorandum is often allowed by the court. This was generally the aim when drafting the Memorandum, and such drafting was upheld by the courts in such cases as *Bell House Ltd v City Wall Properties Ltd*,[123] where the ultra vires rule was cut down by the simple expedient of empowering the company to carry on 'any other trade or business whatever which can in the opinion of the directors be advantageously carried on'; and, in *Newstead v Frost*,[124] an Article permitted the company to do everything which a 'capitalist may lawfully do' and to 'undertake and carry on and execute all kinds of financial commercial trading or other operations'. But the cases have tended to go in cycles. The *Cotman v Brougham*[125] clause (providing that each subclause of the 'objects' was to be treated as separate, and not as a dependent or ancillary power) was itself cut down in the *Introductions Ltd* case on the basis that some powers are inherently incapable of constituting 'objects' in their own right, for example, the borrowing of money and the giving of guarantees.[126] The exercise of such an ancillary power for an ultra vires purpose – a purpose beyond the scope of the 'real' or main objects – may be ultra vires, therefore, even though the act is actually authorised in itself by the Memorandum. Until recently, however, the position in such a case was that the act would be ultra vires only if the third party knew that the purpose was outside the main objects, as to which he need not inquire.[127] But more recently, it has been decided that if the express ancillary power is used in a transaction which could be intra vires, it does not, in any circumstances, become ultra vires merely because the directors are acting for some purpose beyond those set out in the memorandum.[128] Consequently, if a transaction, on the true construction of the objects of the company, comes within these objects, the underlying purpose of the transaction will not cause the transaction to be ultra vires.[129] This restores the position as it was before the *Introductions Ltd* case and, logically, gives the 'ancillary' power at least the status of an independent object.

If the courts had been left to go round in circles in this fashion, life would obviously have been difficult for directors, if profitable for their advisers. However, ss 3A and 35 have made life far easier, and have provided a coherent set of interrelated rules which are in tune with commercial reality.

(2) Ultra vires the board

The second type of ultra vires situation in which a director may find himself occurs where his act (or that of the board, or some other agent of the company) is beyond the powers of the board or, indeed, beyond his own authority as a single member of that board. The position here is as follows.

(a) Whether or not the transaction is within the powers of the company, it can be ratified[130] by special resolution of the members in general meeting.

(b) If the transaction is within the powers of the company, it can be ratified by ordinary resolution of the members in general meeting.

(c) If it is merely beyond the authority of a single director, it may be ratified by the board in the same way.

(d) The *Turquand* rule may apply.[131] This provides that if a transaction is not inconsistent with the external public documents (Memorandum and Articles, special resolutions, etc) of a company, an outsider is not concerned with internal irregularities. Thus, if the directors are entitled to borrow with the authority of an ordinary resolution of the members, the outsider may assume that they have obtained it. He cannot do so, however, if he knows of the irregularity or if he is an insider, for example, a director.[132]

(e) Sections 35A and 35B may apply. Section 35A provides that, in favour of a person dealing with a company in good faith, the power of the board of directors to bind the company, or authorise others to do so, shall be deemed to be free of any limitation under the company's constitution.

This means that the company cannot escape its obligations arising from an act of the board, or a person acting under the authority of the board, on grounds that the board (or such person) was exceeding its actual authority. It is irrelevant whether the act is a commercial transaction, or a non-commercial transaction, such as a donation to charity – the third party may still enforce his rights.

There is no requirement that the third party be dealing with the board of directors as a whole – he has protection irrespective of the agent of the company with whom he is dealing. However, the third party must be acting in good faith.

The sections make it clear that the requirement of good faith does not refer to his knowledge of whether the board (or other agent) is exceeding its authority. He may:

(i)   have no knowledge of the lack of authority, or

(ii) know of, but not understand, the lack of authority, or

(iii) know of, and understand, the lack of authority,

yet still be dealing with the company in good faith. It seems that it refers to his knowledge of the act itself – he must, at the very least, not only be aware that the act exceeds the board's authority, but that it is not in what the board honestly believes to be the best interests of the company. The onus of proving lack of good faith is on the company – otherwise good faith is presumed.

Finally, it is made clear in the Act that the nature of the limitation is irrelevant. It may appear in the Memorandum, the Articles, a resolution of the shareholders, or some class of shareholders, as an agreement entered into by the shareholders, or some part of them.

These rules, together with ss 3A and 35, merit some praise – at last, a sensible and clear set of guidelines, which bear some relation to commercial realities.

(f) The company may be bound by the contract if it has 'held out' the director as having authority to make a contract of that type.[133] This is important for third parties, because the legal restrictions on the authority of individual directors are widely disregarded in practice; innocent outsiders inevitably find themselves dealing with people who have been put in a position to make contracts, whether or not they have been authorised or indeed appointed as directors at all. Fortunately, the courts are taking note of the realities of these situations, as in *Ford Motor Credit Co v Harmack*[134] where the affairs of three companies were so intermingled that the dominant shareholder was to be regarded as having authority to act for any of them. Thus, where the board allowed one of its members to represent himself as being in the position of a managing director they and the company were bound by indemnities and guarantees which he signed.[135]

(g) The directors who have exceeded their authority will have a potential liability to the company for breach of duty,[136] and to the third party for breach of warranty of authority.

3.11 VALIDITY OF DIRECTORS' ACTS

Technical defects in the qualifications or appointment of a director are corrected for the benefit of third parties by s 285 and reg 92 of Table A (which is usually adopted). Both provide that his acts are not invalidated by any defects which might be afterwards discovered in his appointment or qualification, and reg 92 extends the protection to acts of the board, or of committees, to directors who have vacated their office and to votes by a director not entitled to vote. Some features may be noted.

(1) Acts done in relation to members as well as outsiders are validated as where calls were made by an unqualified director.[137]
(2) They do not cover cases where there has been no appointment at all, as where a person, who had never been appointed, purported to attend a board meeting and to appoint another director.[138]
(3) They do not validate acts which could not have been done even by a properly appointed director, such as the appointment of an unqualified director as managing director.[139]

Other procedural matters may be noted here.

(1) In High Court proceedings, the former rule that a company must appear by counsel and not in person through an officer does not appear in the Civil Procedure Rules 1998. However, it has been held by the Court of Appeal[140] that the new Rules[141] implicitly provide that a body corporate may act without a legal representative and contained no provision against carrying on proceedings in person and allowed an employee authorised by the company to appear at trial on its behalf by its managing director.[142]
(2) Directors may, however, appear as the company in person in magistrates' courts but will not be entitled to legal costs.
(3) Proceedings started without authority by a director may be ratified by the liquidator on winding up.[143]
(4) By s 41, documents or proceedings may be authenticated by a director, secretary or authorised officer and do not require the common seal.

(5) By s 36, contracts or other documents otherwise required by law to be executed in writing under seal under the law of England and Wales (for example, share certificates, leases or conveyances of land) may be made on behalf of the company under its common seal.[144]

Alternatively, the contract or document may be executed in accordance with s 36A. All such documents may now be executed without using the common seal. Instead, they need simply to be signed by two directors, or a director and the secretary, provided they contain appropriate wording. The wording will depend upon whether the document is intended to be a deed or not. If the document is not intended to be a deed, such as a share certificate, the document must be expressed (in whatever form of words) to be executed by the company. In the case of a document intended to be a deed, such as a conveyance of land, the document must make it clear on its face that it is intended by the persons making it to be a deed. In the case of this latter type of document, the document is presumed delivered as a deed on the date it is executed, unless a contrary intention is proved.

It is important to note that the new procedure does not permit execution by any authorised signatory who is not a director or secretary, whereas such an authorised signatory may countersign the common seal in certain circumstances.

It follows that a company may now dispense with use of the common seal altogether, although, in fact, companies are reluctant to switch from a familiar and tested procedure for executing documents, and the vast majority have retained their common seal.

In relation to documents subject to Scots law, Parliament has, in recent years, created legal and practical mayhem for company officers and their advisers. The original intention had been to enact a private member's Bill, tabled in 1988, to amend Scots law as to execution of documents. This was based on recommendations made by the Scottish Law Commission. Regrettably, the Bill fell by the wayside because of the usual timetabling problems.

The consequence was that certain parts of the aborted Bill had to be incorporated into the Companies Act 1989, which therefore purported to reform both English and Scots law as to execution of documents and to make the company seal optional in both jurisdictions. The new law was brought into force in July 1990.

Unfortunately, the 1989 Act effectively created a nonsense in relation to Scottish documents. For example, at one point in the 1989 Act the new Scots law was made subject to previous statutes and at another those previous statutes were repealed. The consequence was that Parliament had to make some hasty additions to a Bill already on its way to the statute book, the Law Reform (Miscellaneous Provisions) (Scotland) Bill, to deal with these difficulties. This became an Act and was brought into force in December 1990. It repealed the 1989 Act rules and, of necessity, retrospectively validated those defective documents executed between July and December.

However, on 1 August 1995, the Requirements of Writing (Scotland) Act 1995 came into force, which substantively and radically reformed Scots law. The 1995 Act represents to a large extent the fruits of the Scottish Law Commission's deliberations, referred to above, so it could be said that our legislators had at last caught up with, and managed to introduce, the reforms proposed in the aborted private member's Bill of 1988. The result is a less complex – even comprehensible – set of rules relating to execution of documents under Scots law.

The 1995 Act specifies circumstances in which a written document is required in relation to a transaction, signed by the granter. These are in addition to the circumstances in which a written document is required under any other enactment. Where the granter is a company, the document is signed by the company if it is signed by a director, the secretary or by an authorised signatory at the end of the last page. 'Annexations' do not generally need to be signed, provided that the document refers to them and they are identified on their face as being the annexations referred to in the document. However, annexations do need to be signed if they are annexations to a document relating to land. If the annexation is a plan, drawing, photograph or other representation it must be signed on each page. If it is an inventory, appendix, schedule or other writing it must be signed on the last page.

There is no need for the company to have or to use the company seal because the 1995 Act provides that the requirement in any enactment for the use of the common seal is satisfied if the document is signed or subscribed in accordance with the 1995 Act. The word 'enactment' is expressly stated to include a statutory instrument so that this also applies to any requirement to use a company seal specified in Table A, such as the requirement in reg 6. However, directors of a company would be well-advised, when next considering asking members to make changes to the company's Articles, to also make consequential amendments to the Articles to reflect the optional company seal.

'Authentication' of documents is required if the document is to be acceptable for registration or recording in the Register of Sasines or the Books of Council and Session or in Sheriff Court Books, and documents are often authenticated in any event. The effect of authentication is that it creates a presumption that the document was subscribed by the granter and, if the date and place where it was signed or subscribed are specified, that the document was executed at such date and place.

In order for a document executed by a company to be 'authenticated', it should either:

(a) bear to have been subscribed by a director, the secretary or an authorised signatory and bear to have been signed by a witness to that subscription and include the witness's name and address; or
(b) bear to have been subscribed by two directors, a director and the secretary or by two duly authorised signatories, without witnesses.

In each case, it should state the date and place of the granter's subscription.

However, there is no presumption that a purported director or secretary subscribing the document is in fact an officer of the company, or that a director, secretary or authorised signatory has actual authority to subscribe on the company's behalf so that precautions will be required to be taken by any person requiring an authenticated document from the company.

Whilst the law in relation to documents executed under Scots law now seems clear and sensible, it cannot be stressed enough that it is still highly dangerous to carry out any transaction with a Scots law element without the advice of Scottish-qualified professionals.

(6) By s 36(1)(b), contracts between individuals which are made in writing or by word of mouth may likewise be made for the company by 'any person acting under its authority express or implied', under the law of England and Wales.

(7) Regulation 101 provides that the board may decide who is to be authorised to countersign the company's seal. If they make no special determination, every document to which it is affixed must be signed by a director,[145] and counter-signed by the secretary or by a second director. Alternatively, any person may be authorised to countersign, whether a director or secretary, or not, if the board so resolves. In any event, the board, or a committee of the board, must specifically authorise every use of the seal. An alternate director cannot, it is thought, sign twice. The Article, in any case, requires the document to be signed; it does not require the signatories actually to witness the sealing.

(8) Section 74 of the Law of Property Act 1925, provides that sealing is valid in favour of a purchaser if attested by a director and the secretary or his deputy. This implies that in such cases, the purchaser is not concerned with any limitation in the Articles. However, there is a relationship between the companies legislation governing execution by companies generally and s 74 governing execution of documents in relation to land transactions in England and Wales. The two sets of provisions are difficult to reconcile. Particularly, the circumstances in which a document is presumed duly executed under each statute sit uncomfortably with each other. The Law Commission has proposed a series of reforms,[146] including a new Instruments (Formalities) Bill but, at the time of writing, nothing has been enacted. Directors and company secretaries need to be aware that there are inconsistencies and ensure they take expert advice in every transaction involving land.

(9) By s 37, cheques, bills or promissory notes bind the company, if signed 'in the name of, or by or on behalf or on account of, the company by any person acting under its authority'.

By s 349(4), any officer who signs a cheque, bill of exchange or other specified instruments without stating the company's full name[147] becomes personally liable to the third party for the relevant amount, although the courts have indicated that they are prepared to tolerate mere typographical errors in certain circumstances.[148]

The use of the abbreviations 'Ltd' for 'limited' and 'plc' for 'public limited company' is permissible,[149] as is 'Co' for 'Company'[150] and almost certainly the ampersand '&', but the temptation to use such abbreviations should be resisted. Where the third party is himself responsible for the incorrect statement of the name, he cannot rely upon it to enforce personal liability under s 349 against the signatory.[151] Where liability does arise under the section, it only becomes enforceable if the company does not pay. But the signatory is not in the position of a guarantor, and (unlike a guarantor) his liability once it has arisen is not extinguished by any indulgence shown by the holder of the instrument.[152] The hazards of signing a negotiable instrument must always be borne in mind, quite apart from s 349, for even where the company's name is correctly recorded it is wise to ensure that the signature appears with or near to the words 'For and on behalf of' the company. This prevents any argument that the signature was a personal endorsement.[153] Further, unless the director really intends to act as an endorsee, he should never put more than one signature on the instrument. If he does – for example, on the back – the courts will probably deduce, if not assume, that he intends to act as endorsee and, even if the second signature is adjacent to the words 'For and on behalf of the company . . . Director', evidence may be led that the intention was to endorse the instrument.[154] An endorsee incurs personal liability, in effect guaranteeing payment, quite apart from the Companies Act.

3.12   COMMENT AND REFORM

Shareholder power

We have seen that the board of directors is, in practice, the dominating element in the corporate structure, even though the members retain the ultimate sanction in the form of their right to remove and replace directors at any time by ordinary resolution, under s 303, and to prescribe their actions by virtue of provisions in the Memorandum or Articles. It has been suggested that these rights may be more apparent than real in listed companies, in the sense that the marshalling of 51 per cent of the votes in a widely dispersed public company is a herculean (and expensive) task. The directors, on the other hand, are in control of the proxy machinery and, in effect, of their own remuneration. Thus, it is said that the board will tend to evolve into a self-perpetuating and self-remunerating oligarchy.

Against this, it may be objected that there are many checks and balances to prevent the assumption of excessive power by the directors.

(1)   The right of the members to decide the composition of the board by ordinary resolution is paramount, whether or not they choose to exercise it. There is no limit to what a determined shareholder may achieve, even if he remains in a minority.[155]

(2)   New appointments in a public company, made by the board itself, invariably have to seek re-election at the next AGM.

(3)   Details of remuneration must be disclosed in the accounts and the directors' report.

(4)   The DTI has wide powers under Part XIV of the Act to investigate the affairs of a company and it may exercise these powers at the request of a single shareholder.

(5)   The restrictions upon the board's powers to issue shares (s 80) give the membership a method of controlling one of the greatest potential sources of abuse.

(6)   The Act contains disclosure requirements which to some extent at least enable directors' personal and corporate excess of power to be 'flushed out' – sooner or later.

It is very difficult, however, to hit upon additional methods of shareholder control which do not risk (in the words of Jenkins in 1962) hampering 'the activities of honest men in order to defeat an occasional wrongdoer'. Whilst there may be criticism based on a perception that boards of directors tend to be dominated more and more by full-time executives who are more concerned with their own position and remuneration than the interests of the shareholders, the answer perhaps should rather be to persuade shareholders – particularly institutional shareholders – to exercise their rights more effectively than to confer additional rights upon them. Indeed, Jenkins pointed out, even back in 1962, that the Act 'provides shareholders with powerful weapons provided that they choose to use them and even if practical considerations make them difficult for the small investor to wield, the same cannot be said of the institutional investor'.[156] Since then, of course, new weapons have been devised, and occasionally an institutional investor does act as a soi-disant Robin Hood for all the members.[157]

But traditionally, the institutions have generally remained inert provided that a substantial, often short-term, yield is produced for their funds. However, the institutional worms may be turning. In this respect, the activities of bodies such as the British Insurer's Investment Committee and the Investment Protection Committees (IPC's) may gain in importance. IPCs have been described as the trade representatives of the major UK institutional investors[158] and issue guidance to their members as to how they should use their votes in relation to certain matters. This has two important consequences. The first is that it creates peer pressure among institutions to be seen to take an interest in the companies in which they invest and provides them with a defence to the traditional cries of 'disinterested short-termism' which issue against them from the boards of listed companies. Secondly, and more importantly, it provides a powerful constraint on the behaviour of directors on such boards, for whom the certain prospect of a united vote by the institutions on its share register in favour of, or against, certain prescribed matters is, albeit de facto, as effective a control as their de jure obligations as set out in the Yellow Book.

Worker participation

A second criticism is that the interests of workers are not represented on the board. In this respect, the long-standing wrangle over the question of worker participation in the draft Fifth Directive comes sharply into focus.

The Fifth Directive began life as a proposal that it should be mandatory for listed companies throughout the EC to have a 'two-tier' board structure, following the practice which exists in many European countries such as Germany (where it originated). Under this system, a large company must have two boards of directors. First, a supervisory board appointed by the shareholders and employees in defined proportions and, secondly, a management board appointed by the supervisory board and responsible to it. On certain matters, the management board cannot act without the consent of the supervisory board and no one can be a member of both boards.

The argument about two-tier boards is essentially one of flexibility against uniformity. The Bullock Report,[159] as long ago as 1977, favoured single-tier boards with worker representatives, but with no special voting rights for those representatives and no majority for them on special issues such as redundancy or lay-offs. Furthermore, the Report treated 'worker' and 'trades union representative' as synonymous. Notwithstanding the Bullock Report, three alternative forms of company management developed in practice.

First, the traditional, non-executive board which directs but does not manage. All the directors are non-executive and management is in the hands of senior managers under the supervision of the board, a two-tier board in all but name but with the freedom to change if circumstances require. Such boards are now extremely rare.

Secondly, the mixed board, which unites outside, non-executive directors with one or more senior executive directors, usually including a managing director. This has been found to work in practice and is common among listed companies but it does have the disadvantage (if such it be) of combining two roles in the same individuals. The executive directors share responsibility for the supervision of management, of which they themselves form part.

Thirdly, the close company board where management, supervision and indeed ownership coincide in the same persons. This is characteristic of the smaller private companies in the UK and is one of the factors which make them so different an animal from the typical listed company.

These forms of management clearly disregard worker participation, and the rejection of worker participation on any basis other than at the company's option remained a constant plank of Conservative party policy throughout the 1980s and into the 1990s.[160] (Perhaps the nearest the current legislation gets is that s 309 now obliges the boards of all companies to have regard to the interests of employees generally.) As a result of this policy, the Fifth Directive generated a great deal of political heat in the UK. It also encountered fierce and powerful opposition from other Member States,[161] primarily because of its provisions in relation to worker participation.

Such was the fury generated by the Fifth Directive that, until recently, it could be said to have sunk – not, perhaps, completely without trace, since work continued on it in the Brussels backrooms – but certainly with very little trace. Its transformation from a mere proposal to adoption as a Directive could safely be predicted as being many years away.

However, the Fifth Directive is, in its turn, linked to the proposal for a European Company Statute. The latter provides for a pan-European company which would be established under a Community company law regime drafted specifically for the purpose of creating and regulating such companies and they would be governed partly by such law and partly by the law of the Member State in which they registered. The link with the proposed Fifth Directive is that the proposed European Company Statute also contains provisions for worker participation in European Companies. Consequently, the European Company Statute has also been opposed by the UK.

A third link in the chain is the Works Council Directive, which has been adopted by the EC but has not been implemented by the UK. The Directive provides for information to, and consultation with, Works Councils of employees by certain undertakings with 'complex structures' (including many whose headquarters are not within the Community). The UK, true to form, opposed the Directive on grounds its provisions as to employee involvement were mandatory rather than voluntary. Strictly, the Directive is part of the Social Chapter, with its emphasis on employment and social protection. The UK therefore opted out of it at Maastricht.[162] However, in practice, many UK companies are likely to be affected by the Works Council Directive in any event because it will affect their operations outside the UK. On one view, therefore, the effect of opting out of the Social Chapter was to disenfranchise the UK from influencing rules to which many employees of many UK companies or their subsidiaries will in fact be subject.

That said, it is hard to see why the UK opposes the Directive so virulently, as its main fault seems to be that, far from being the first stirrings of a tidal wave of worker's rights, it is too anodyne to offer workers any real benefits. This blandness is to be expected since the Vredeling Directive from which it evolved was subject to such blasting criticism, even from non-members doing business in Europe,[163] that the provisions of the new Directive were always bound to smack of conciliation and compromise to the employers affected by them.

However, the important point to make about this Directive, in this context, is that it has provided a fresh impetus to the European Company Statute because it provides an alternative, and more palatable (at least to non-UK members of the EU), means of involving workers in management decision-making than those proposed in the Fifth Directive. Encouraged by the successful adoption of the Works Council Directive, the EU is therefore in the process of revisiting the European Company Statute with a view to substituting the problematic Fifth Directive provisions with the more acceptable Works Council Directive provisions.

But the Fifth Directive has not been consigned to the scrap heap. Paradoxically, the adoption of the Works Council Directive has also opened the door to reconsideration of the Fifth Directive itself and it may be that it resurfaces at some stage with watered down provisions akin to those in the Works Council Directive. Of course, if the Fifth Directive is adopted by the Council of Ministers, all EU members will be bound by its provisions. This could mean that, in the future, UK companies not caught by the Works Council Directive (because of the opt-out and because they do not operate outside the UK) may find themselves subject to worker information and consultation provisions in any event, as a result of adoption of a revised Fifth Directive. How this will be resolved will depend on the political complexion of the UK government of the day.

If the worker participation provisions of the Fifth Directive should, at some stage in the future, be adopted and implemented in the UK, UK companies subject to it, and their directors, may get a number of additional, unexpected shocks. The spotlight to date has focused almost exclusively on its worker participation provisions in the Fifth Directive, yet it also contains proposals in relation to joint and several liability for directors for breach of their duties by one or more of them, a right for 10 per cent of the members to bring proceedings against directors on behalf of their company,[164] new proxy rights for shareholders at general meetings and strengthening of the duties and liabilities of auditors, including to third parties.[165] All of these are contentious in their own right and companies and their directors would be well-advised to take an early view on whether they welcome or reject these provisions as events unfold and make their view known as loudly as they can.[166]

Finally, there is another draft Directive[167] which could require disclosure of information to employees or unions and for consultation on proposals which would significantly affect the work force. This would apply to all undertakings employing more than 1,000 (counting employees of subsidiaries) and would – if, again, ever enacted – probably be more far reaching than any reform of board structure. However, it has to be said that the prospect of either this or the Fifth Directive materialising into law is distant.

Co-operatives

Two further developments may be noted. First, the 1980s saw a growing number of 'employee buy-outs' by which a company facing dismemberment or liquidation was taken over (by purchase rather than sit-in!) by its workforce, or part of it. Apart from a few, and generally ill-fated, attempts to apply co-operative structures to such undertakings,[168] they had little new to show in the way of management structure. Some were merely buy-outs by senior management. Others involved the offer of shares to each employee. It is only the second category which is remotely likely to have a two-tier board structure. Secondly, government policy after 1979 was to encourage wider shareholding by the public and by employees, particularly through share issues on the 'privatisation' of major statutory undertakers. As yet, these have hardly been a long-term political success, as distinct from a source of capital for the Treasury, but the Conservative government of the 1990s continued, sometimes with a touch of desperation, to introduce, and enlarge on, incentives to widen share ownership. Tax concessions for Employee Share Ownership Schemes (the ESOS), the set of Table G Articles for employee share ownership companies (which may be prescribed as a result of the Companies Act 1989, but in respect of which there are no current signs of activity) and relaxations of the prohibitions whereby a company may not give financial assistance to a person to enable him to acquire shares, where such person is participating in an employee share scheme, are all evidence of legislative tinkering to this end. If shareholdings become more diffused and less institutionalised in the years to come, the question of distribution of power between the board and the membership and of employee participation will not go away. The form in which the question is raised will, however, depend upon the political complexion of the majority of the day in Parliament.

3.13   THE CADBURY REPORT

If a final push was needed to consign the issue of two-tier boards to oblivion, at least in the case of listed companies, it came in the form of the Cadbury Report in December 1992. The Report was the result of an 18-month review of standards of corporate governance, dealing with the control and reporting functions of directors, and the role of auditors. It concentrated specifically on financial aspects such as the way in which boards set financial policy and oversee its implementation and the process whereby they report to shareholders on the activities and progress of the company. It was given special impetus in that it overlapped or followed closely on the heels of a number of business scandals such as the BCCI and Maxwell affairs and was carried out in an atmosphere of public discontent over issues such as significant directors' pay rises in the face of worldwide recession.

The Report attracted much comment, both constructive and destructive, during its compilation. But there is little doubt that, the Committee having taken such comments seriously, enhanced the quality of the final Report. Bodies such as the Institute of Directors, which had been unenthusiastic about aspects of the Report at the draft stage, eventually took the view that the final Report would go a long way towards removing public concern over such matters. The authors of the Report believe that, had it been in operation at the time, a number of unexpected company failures and cases of fraud would have received attention earlier.

Certainly, the Report put the supporters of unitary boards firmly into the driving seat and dealt a severe knock to the distinction between 'doers' and 'checkers' implicit in the two-tier board structure. The recommendations in the Report, and the associated Code, (now mostly incorporated into the Combined Code – see below) sought to strengthen the unitary board and make it more effective. Indeed, the Report expressly endorsed the unitary board structure.

Central to the Report was a Code of Best Practice, which dealt with issues such as the composition and operation of the board; division of responsibilities on the board; non-executive directors; directors' access to advice; disclosure of emoluments; and delegation, reporting and controls. It did not have statutory force since the intention was not to regulate, but to raise, business standards. However, it was recommended in the Report that the boards of all listed companies registered in the UK should comply with the Code. The Report also urged non-listed companies to strive to comply. This resulted in inclusion of a new rule 12.43(j) in the Yellow Book which required listed companies to include a statement in their report and accounts saying whether or not they had complied with the Code throughout the period covered by the accounts and giving reasons for any non-compliance. The auditors were required to review parts of the statement before publication.

Many of the recommendations in the Report were familiar, since much of the approach of the Cadbury Committee was to bring together the existing good practices of many large companies into a coherent Code. This is not to say that the Report was not radical in its effect. The exercise of bringing all of these practices together gave them new force and shareholders had, at last, a yardstick against which to assess the governance of their companies.

In return, the Report laid stress on not only the rights, but also the responsibilities of shareholders. One clear intention behind its recommendations was to ensure that shareholders had sufficient guidance about what constituted best practice, and were then given sufficient information by their companies to judge whether they were measuring up to those requirements. Ideally, these two factors were to promote greater interest in their companies from shareholders who, even at the level of institutional investors, often gave the impression of being moribund and uninterested.

Another key feature of the Cadbury Report was the importance it placed upon the non-executive director. These were clearly considered a key safeguard by the

Committee, ideally placed to review the performance of the executive board on a continuing basis.

3.14 THE GREENBURY RECOMMENDATIONS

Hard on the heels of the Cadbury Report came the Greenbury Study Group on Directors' Remuneration. This was established at the instigation of the Confederation of British Industry and its objectives were to identify good practice in determining directors' remuneration. The consequent Report, published in July 1995, made recommendations in relation to establishment and composition of remuneration committees; disclosure and approval of annual remuneration committee reports; remuneration policy; and directors' service contracts and compensation. Perhaps inevitably, given continued and vocal public dissatisfaction with the remuneration enjoyed by big industry 'fat cats' at the time,[169] the Group's findings included the recommendation that existing statutory rules about disclosure of directors' remuneration were insufficient. Like the Cadbury Committee, the Group produced a Code of Best Practice and recommended that this be incorporated into the Yellow Book. Again, like the Cadbury Committee, the Greenbury Group indicated its hope that the Code would also be followed, as far as possible, by non-listed companies.

The Yellow Book was duly amended to reflect certain of the requirements of the Greenbury Code. Rule 12.43(w) required a statement in the report and accounts saying whether or not the company had complied with the Code and explaining and justifying any areas of non-compliance. Rule 12.43(x) also required a report from the remuneration committee to the shareholders to be included in the report and accounts containing specific disclosures in relation to directors' remuneration. The auditors were required to cover certain of the disclosures made under rule 12.43(x) in their report and state if, in their opinion, the company had not complied with them.

3.15 THE HAMPEL COMMITTEE

Both the Cadbury and Greenbury Committees recommended that a further Committee should be established to review the implementation of their recommendations. To this end, the Hampel Committee on Corporate Governance was set up in November 1995. Its remit included specific review of the implementation of both the Cadbury and Greenbury Reports, but it also addressed ways to promote high standards of corporate governance in the interests of investor protection; to enhance the standing of listed companies; the role of shareholders; the role of executive and non-executive directors; and the role of auditors in corporate governance. The Committee published its Report in January 1998.

The Report endorsed the vast majority of both the Cadbury and Greenbury Reports. However, the Hampel Committee's approach was to place emphasis on the basic principles underpinning good corporate governance, and justifying the specific rules required to achieve good governance by reference to those principles.

Under this approach, the Hampel Committee treated governance as the art of managing relationships with the many different groups having a stake in each company. This included not only the shareholders, both present and future, but also groups such as employees, suppliers and those in the communities affected by the company's activities and governance. Like Cadbury before it, the Hampel Report saw shareholders as having responsibilities as well as rights and looked to them to hold boards accountable for decisions and activities.

The Hampel Committee worked throughout early 1998 to produce a fresh Code, which combined aspects of the Cadbury and Greenbury Codes and incorporated its own conclusions about best practice, and the London Stock Exchange consulted widely in relation to its provisions. The result was the issue, in June 1998, of a new Principles of Good Governance and Code of Best Practice (the 'Combined Code') by the London Stock Exchange, which was introduced as an appendix to the *Listing Rules* on 1 January 1999.

At the same time, rule 12.43(j) was replaced by new rule 12.43A in the Listing Rules. Under this rule, companies are required to disclose the extent of their compliance with both the new principles and the specific requirements of the Combined Code in relation to accounting periods ending on or after 31 December 1998.

The Combined Code is in two parts. Part 1 deals with directors, directors' remuneration, relations with shareholders, and accountability and audit and Part 2 deals with institutional shareholders. There are also schedules which provide for the design of performance-related remuneration and for the contents of remuneration reports. The Code is reproduced at Appendix D.

3.16   THE FUTURE

While the provisions of the various Reports and the consequent Combined Code have great merit in the abstract, it remains to be seen whether they will achieve the aims of protecting investors and enhancing the standing of listed companies – or being perceived as doing so – in the long term. There is a danger that the costs and practical difficulties attached to compliance will, unless the benefits are evident and measurable in terms of effectiveness of boards and greater shareholder satisfaction and involvement, breed either disaffection or indifference to the Code. It may come to be seen as merely bureaucratic and superfluous.

Particularly, like its predecessors, the Combined Code places great emphasis on the effective involvement of non-executive directors – but where is the necessary pool of experienced men and women to be found from which companies may make non-executive appointments? This problem is at its most intense among those involved with smaller and medium-sized listed companies.

It is hard to see a solution to the difficulty of finding non-executive directors of sufficient numbers and calibre. Certainly, organisations such as the Institute of Directors (IoD) and Promotion of Non-Executive Directors (PRO-NED) provide ample and irrefutable reasons why independent, competent non-executives should play a critical role in listed companies. Jettisoning the idea of non-executives completely is clearly not an option. An alternative is to educate non-executives and potential non-executives more effectively. The IoD provides training and the

Institutional Shareholders' Committee, one of the sponsors of PRO-NED, has produced a Statement of Best Practice for non-executive directors, linked to the recommendations in the Greenbury Report. These and other initiatives are to be applauded but the overall conclusion must be that, for the foreseeable future, a continued scarcity of suitable non-executives must probably be accepted as a fact of life.

One certainty is that the issues the Combined Code addresses show no signs of going away. Certainly, the strong message is that, if directors fail to keep abreast of developments in corporate governance, they are storing up trouble for themselves. As the Cadbury Report made plain, failure of directors to comply with the standards of corporate governance of the day is likely to result in Parliament replacing the principles of self-regulation, espoused by that and subsequent Reports, with external regulation – probably statutory – with all the ramifications which ensue when regulation based on principles is replaced by regulation based on the letter of the law.

CHAPTER 3 FOOTNOTES

1 Section 741.

2 See **1.8**.

3 The temptation to characterise the members, in such a case, as 'shadow directors' is to be resisted, since there must, in the first place, be 'directors' accustomed to act upon the shadows' directions or instructions.

4 Which might itself become a director or shadow, and is certainly likely to be concerned in the management of the company for the purposes, for example, of disqualification (see **2.5.1**) or fraudulent trading (see **6.2.11**).

5 *Bushell v Faith* [1970] AC 1099.

6 Section 121(2)(a). Note that this does not concern the power to issue or allot the shares, which is often in the hands of the directors but is subject to s 80 (see **3.3**).

7 Section 135(1). Note that a reduction of unissued authorised capital serves little purpose and would be carried out only in unusual circumstances.

8 Section 28.

9 Section 4.

10 Section 49 (private companies only).

11 Section 51 (no reregistration as a public company).

12 Section 9.

13 Section 84 of the Insolvency Act 1986. An extraordinary resolution requires the same majority (75 per cent) as a special resolution and the only practical difference is that it can be called on 14 days' instead of 21 days' notice.

14 Section 303.

15 As discussed and sanctioned by the House of Lords in *Bushell v Faith* [1970] AC 1099.

16 Sections 384–385A. As to 'dormant' companies, see **4.1.7**.

17 Sections 252 and 386.

18 Section 250, see **4.17**.

19 Sections 249C–249E, and 388A. See **4.17**.

20 Section 366.

21 Section 366A.

22 Section 241 merely requires the directors to 'lay before the company in general meeting' copies of the accounts in respect of each financial year.

23 Section 80, see **3.3**.

24 Section 157, and ss 164–167, and 173.

25 Section 368.

26 Section 373.

27 Section 372. Except in the case of a company limited by guarantee.

28 Part I of the Insolvency Act 1986, together with the Insolvency Rules 1986, SI 1986/1925, as amended, provide also for a 'voluntary arrangement' under which the board of a company in difficulty may propose a scheme to pay off debts in an orderly manner (the initiative need not, however, come from the board in all cases). Such an arrangement may lead to the appointment of an administrator to manage the company's affairs (if one has not already been appointed); so may a scheme under s 425 of the 1985 Act. Although this may sound like a terminal illness, the intention of these provisions is to save the company, if this is possible.

29 As substituted by Sch 12 to the Financial Services Act 1986.

30 Or 90 per cent of any class or classes of shares to which the offer related. Section 430 sets out in detail the consequences of a notice served under s 429. Conversely ss 430A–430B confer a right to be bought out by an offeror on a minority shareholder.

31 The former duty under s 165(1)(a) of the 1948 Act to investigate if the company passed a special resolution to this effect was abolished in 1981. An ordinary resolution would now attract the DTI's discretion. The investigation procedure remains a relatively effective and useful alternative to hazardous litigation by aggrieved members. The powers under ss 431 and 432 may also be exercised where, in the course of a voluntary winding up, the liquidator believes that an offence has been committed by a past or present director or any member. He must then notify the Director of Public Prosecutions (or, in a Scottish winding up, the Lord Advocate). The court may order him

to make such a report if he fails to do so. If the DPP requires further information, he may refer the matter to the Department of Trade and Industry for investigation under the Act; ss 218 and 219 of the Insolvency Act 1986.

32 *R v Secretary of State for Trade ex parte Perestrello* [1981] QB 19.

33 Sections 447–451A.

34 *Norwest Holst Ltd v Secretary of State for Trade* [1978] Ch 201.

35 Section 319.

36 Section 320.

37 Section 311; *Owens v Multiflux Ltd* [1977] IRLR 113.

38 Sections 330–338.

39 Section 312.

40 Sections 313–316. These sections are discussed in Chapter 10.

41 Section 308. It will be seen that the required majority (75 per cent) is greater than that required for the appointment of a director in the ordinary way. Thus, in practice, s 308 can always be circumvented if the director can get a bare majority of support for his proposed assignee.

42 Section 310. This section applies to any officer or auditor and includes provisions in contracts as well as in the Articles.

43 Table A, as set out in the Companies (Tables A to F) Regulations 1985, SI 1985/805, as amended by SI 1985/1052, has been modernised to accord as closely as possible with company practice. The Specimen Memoranda in Tables B–F, on the other hand, are distinctly thin and, despite the reference in Table F to 'electronic equipment' manufacture, somewhat antiquated. This may simply reflect the coherence of the law relating to company management (the Articles) as against company objects (the Memorandum).

44 The director of a company when looking at his own Articles should bear in mind that the 'relevant' Table A will depend on when his company was incorporated, see **1.6.1**.

45 *John Shaw & Sons (Salford) Ltd v Shaw* [1935] 3 All ER 456, per Greer LJ.

46 *Scott v Scott* [1943] 1 All ER 582.

47 *Re Emmadart Ltd* [1979] Ch 540.

48 Section 80A.

49 Which must state when the authority expires, or that it is of indefinite duration. In practice, many, if not most, Articles will (subject to s 80) give the directors power to issue shares.

50 Provided that the directors act within their authority under s 80 and bona fide in the company's interests, the allotment of shares by them will be unimpeachable: *Mutual Life Insurance Co of New York v The Rank Organisation Ltd* [1985] BCLC 11.

51 Running a share scheme for bona fide employees or ex-employees of the company or group, or their immediate families, does not constitute an 'investment business' on the company's part within the meaning (and controls) of the Financial Services Act 1986. Ibid, Sch 1, para 20.

52 Section 135.

53 One-tenth of paid-up voting capital: s 368.

54 This is a useful power, and there is nothing to prevent a single person from being appointed as alternate for more than one director. See further **3.10**.

55 In the case of close private companies, there is much to be said for deleting this Article as it serves little purpose except as a nuisance.

56 Regulation 77 then provides for the necessary notice to members. Notice under regs 76 and 77 must be accompanied by disclosure of existing directorships and a statement of willingness to act.

57 The Act also permits a one man board for private companies and formal meetings might be considered unnecessary in such cases (s 282). However, see *Neptune (Vehicle Washing Equipment) Ltd v Fitzgerald* [1995] 1 BCLC 352; s 317 and **5.6.3**.

58 This is the classic example of separation of powers by the Articles and means that the members, even by a unanimous vote, cannot exceed the directors' recommendation. The question is discussed in **3.8**.

59 This regulation does not conflict with s 310 which we have already noted, as the section expressly allows an indemnity in these terms.

60 One of the last amendments was to delete references to old Acts and to substitute references to the 1985 Act: s 27 of the Companies Consolidation (Consequential Provisions) Act 1985.

61 *Wall v London & Northern Assets Corpn* [1899] 1 Ch 550; *Wall v Exchange Investment Corpn* [1926] Ch 143.

62 But reg 63 (1985) applies only to the 'determination' of a proxy's authority, leaving the general law (or special Articles) to determine whether events specified by reg 71 (1948) – such as death and insanity – will in fact terminate a proxy's authority.

63 As distinct from the power to delegate to committees of the board in reg 102 (1948) and 72 (1985) which is also in Table A, reg 85 (1929) and reg 91 (1908).

64 *Boschoek Proprietary Co Ltd v Fuke* [1906] 1 Ch 148.

65 Although reg 74 (1948) tried to make this clear.

66 This procedure, introduced in 1990, has been amended by virtue of the Deregulation (Resolutions of Private Companies) Order 1996, SI 1996/1471.

67 In the case of the 1948 version, it would also be common to exclude regs 79 (the proviso relating to borrowing powers), 88 (requiring all directors to sign the minute book), 96 (removal from office) and 126 (appointment of auditors). These do not appear in the 1985 version, which indicates that they are of doubtful or no real utility and in the last two cases add nothing to statutory requirements.

68 *Bamford v Bamford* [1969] 1 All ER 969. This important subject is discussed in Chapter 5.

69 Except in the case of credit-granting companies. The restriction is pursuant to the EEC Second Directive. Listed companies have never been able to have a lien on fully-paid shares as this would restrict freedom of transfer.

70 Even when restrictions were imposed by the now repealed Table A, Part II, many companies wished to expand the list.

71 *Popely v Planarrive Ltd* (1996) *The Times*, 24 April.

72 Sections 36 and 36A.

73 Ibid.

74 The few appointed before then are irremovable: s 14 of the Companies Consolidation (Consequential Provisions) Act 1985.

75 Section 324 et seq.

76 There is some recognition of the fact that company registers and records may be held electronically – for example, in ss 722 and 723 of the Companies Act 1985 and in the Companies (Registers and other Records) Regulations 1985, SI 1985/724.

77 The Companies (Single Member Private Limited Companies) Regulations 1992, SI 1992/1699.

78 DTI Report, *Companies in 1995–96*.

79 Adoption of Table A is sufficient to constitute a public company but, in practice, a full set of special Articles is always adopted.

80 The expression 'listed' to describe the admission of securities to the official list replaced 'quoted' in June 1972.

81 Originally implemented by the Stock Exchange (Listing) Regulations 1984, SI 1984/716 repealed and replaced by the Financial Services Act 1986 and now amended by the Public Offers of Securities Regulations 1995, SI 1995/1537.

82 Ultra vires, but a distant and more refined cousin of the company law doctrine.

83 These replaced the previous *Admission of Securities to Listing* (also called the Yellow Book) on 1 December 1993. However, the *Listing Rules* are based very substantially on the previous *Admission of Securities to Listing*.

84 Obtainable from the Head of Listing, The London Stock Exchange, London EC2N 1HP, tel 020 7797 1000.

85 Previously it was necessary for the company to subscribe to the 'listing agreement' by board resolution. This has now been dropped, but the effect of Chapter 5 of the Yellow Book is very much the same as that of the agreement. The need to comply with the listing particular requirements has added force in the light of the Financial Services Act 1986. Copies of the particulars must be filed with the Registrar of Companies by the date of publication (s 149) and the directors are responsible for their contents (s 152) with possible liability to pay compensation for error and omission (s 150).

86 There is a general duty on applying for admission to disclose enough material concerning assets, liabilities, financial position, profits, losses, prospects and the rights attaching to the shares for an 'informed assessment' to be made (Financial Services Act 1986, s 146) including any significant

changes occurring before dealings begin (s 147). Those responsible for this, and in particular the directors, may be held liable for loss sustained by an investor as a result of misstatements or non-disclosure.

87 As provided by Table A, reg 4 (1948).

88 Where one member holds all the class shares, he can constitute a meeting on his own. *East v Bennett Bros Ltd* [1911] 1 Ch 163.

89 The limit is 10 per cent of the issue price: s 97.

90 The Articles must provide that fully paid shares are free of restrictions and not subject to any lien.

91 See Table A, regs 18–20.

92 Section 368.

93 Section 291.

94 Section 9. It is probably the case that no contract made by the company can deprive the members of their right to alter the Articles: *Punt v Symons & Co Ltd* [1903] 2 Ch 506. No term will be implied into a contract which binds the company to such an undertaking unless the intention is very clear: *Allen v Gold Reefs of West Africa Ltd* [1900] 1 Ch 656, at p 673. If a company makes a contract not to alter its Articles, the members may ignore it: *Cumbrian Newspapers Group Ltd v Cumberland & Westmoreland Herald Newspaper & Printing Co Ltd* [1986] 3 WLR 26, at p 44. The company may itself then act on the altered Articles (indeed, it may have to) but is then liable for breach of contract: *Southern Foundries (1926) Ltd v Shirlaw* [1940] AC 701, at p 740.

95 Section 303.

96 'A company cannot by ordinary resolution dictate to or overrule the directors in respect of matters entrusted to them by the Articles': *Bamford v Bamford* [1970] Ch 212, at p 220 per Plowman J.

97 *Scott v Scott* [1943] 1 All ER 582.

98 *Salmon v Quin & Axtens Ltd* [1909] AC 442.

99 *Barron v Potter* [1914] 1 Ch 895.

100 *Marshall's Valve Gear Co Ltd v Manning Wardle & Co Ltd* [1909] 1 Ch 267.

101 *Thomas Logan v Davis* [1911] LT 914 (except by amending the Articles).

102 Although it will often lack the power to guarantee the debts of associated companies, and a change in the objects clause may be called for by banks and other lenders, particularly where several companies' trading and accounts are not being kept distinct. The effect of 'cross-guarantees', where company A guarantees company B's debts, and vice versa, can be quite devastating when backed by charges on each company's property, which then becomes available as security in the other's insolvency. Even assuming that each company, and each board, has power to execute such securities, a director of both companies runs immediately into potential conflicts of interest if asked to sign or approve such guarantees.

103 *General Auction Estate Co v Smith* [1891] 3 Ch 432.

104 Regulation 79 in the 1948 Table A.

105 Section 395 (or, in Scotland s 410). Strictly speaking, 'creation' means the date when the charge is executed, even though the advance and the dating of the document occur later, unless the charge relates exclusively to property not yet acquired by the company. This only adds to the dangers of this notorious section: *Esberger & Son Ltd v Capital & Counties Bank* [1913] 2 Ch 36.

106 *Watson v Duff Morgan & Vermont (Holdings) Ltd* [1974] 1 All ER 794. The Registrar himself may not waive the 21-day time-limit: *R v Registrar of Companies ex parte Esal* [1986] QB 1114.

107 Section 404. See *Re Telematic Ltd* [1993] BCC 404 for a case in which the court refused to exercise discretion.

108 *Re Haycraft Gold Reduction Co* [1900] 2 Ch 230.

109 Meetings are considered in detail in Chapter 9.

110 *Hely-Hutchinson v Brayhead Ltd* [1968] 1 QB 549. But see *Mitchell & Hobbs (UK) Ltd v Mill* [1996] 2 BCLC 102 where a managing director was held not to have ostensible authority to instruct solicitors on behalf of the company.

111 *Ford Motor Credit Co v Harmack* (1972) *The Times*, 7 July, CA.

112 *Panorama Developments (Guildford) Ltd v Fidelis Furnishing Fabrics Ltd* [1971] 3 All ER 16. In the case of other officers, a holding out of authority may be the result of the way in which the officer is allowed to carry out his tasks (*Ebeed v Soplex Wholesale Supplies Ltd* [1985] BCLC 404) or the authority implicit in his job-description, for example, where he is called a 'branch manager' and there is evidence that 'branch managers' in a particular area of business, such as in finance, usually have the authority upon which the third party relied: *British Bank of the Middle East v Sun Life Assurance Co of Canada (UK) Ltd* [1983] 2 Lloyd's Rep 9. An employer

(including a company) may be liable even for the fraud of an employee who has been held out to have authority to act, but unless there is a holding out (or, of course, actual authority) he is not liable because of the misplaced assumption by a third party that an officer (for example, a 'vice-president') has certain authority: *Armagas Ltd v Mundogas SA* [1986] AC 717.

113 *Firbank's Executors v Humphreys* (1886) 18 QBD 54.
114 *Conway v Petronius Clothing Co Ltd* [1978] 1 WLR 72.
115 *Re Fireproof Doors Ltd* [1916] 2 Ch 142.
116 *Freeman & Lockyer v Buckhurst Park Properties (Mangal) Ltd* [1964] 1 All ER 630.
117 *Harold Holdsworth & Co (Wakefield) Ltd v Caddies* [1955] 1 All ER 725, HL.
118 *Re Jon Beauforte (London) Ltd* [1953] 1 All ER 634, where the lenders were excluded from proving in the company's liquidation.
119 *Rolled Steel Products (Holdings) Ltd v British Steel Corpn* [1986] Ch 246.
120 *Ashbury Railway Carriage and Iron Co v Riche* (1875) LR 7 HL 653.
121 Section 711A.
122 Section 3A.
123 [1966] 2 QB 656.
124 [1980] 1 All ER 363.
125 [1918] AC 514.
126 *Introductions v National Provincial Bank* [1970] Ch 199. In the absence of an 'independent objects' clause, such acts would almost automatically be given the status of powers, not objects.
127 *Re David Payne Ltd* [1904] 2 Ch 608 (borrowing powers).
128 *Rolled Steel Products (Holdings) Ltd v British Steel Corpn* [1986] Ch 246.
129 Ibid.
130 *Bamford v Bamford* [1969] 1 All ER 969. Presumably this is the position where the *Rolled Steel* principle applies, but if so the minority's position is very weak.
131 *Royal British Bank v Turquand* [1856] 6 E & B 327.
132 *Morris v Kanssen* [1946] AC 459.
133 *Freeman & Lockyer v Buckhurst Park Properties (Mangal) Ltd* [1964] 1 All ER 630.
134 (1972) *The Times*, 7 July, CA. Note also Lord Denning's remark in *Wallersteiner v Moir (No 1)* [1974] 3 All ER 217: '. . . they were just the puppets of Dr Wallersteiner . . . I am of the opinion that the Court should pull aside the corporate veil and treat these concerns as being his creatures – for whose doings he should be and is responsible.'
135 *Hely-Hutchinson v Brayhead Ltd* [1968] 1 QB 549.
136 Unless the members resolve not to sue them or unless the courts give relief under s 727 because they have acted honestly and reasonably and ought fairly to be excused.
137 *Dawson v African Consolidated Land & Trading Co* [1898] 1 Ch 6.
138 *Morris v Kanssen* [1946] AC 459.
139 *Craven-Ellis v Canons Ltd* [1936] 2 KB 403.
140 *R H Tomlinssons (Trowbridge) Ltd v Secretary of State* (1999) *The Times*, 31 August.
141 Civil Procedure Rules 1998, r 48.6(6).
142 *Frinton & Walton UDC v Walton & District Sand & Mineral Co Ltd* [1938] 1 All ER 649.
143 *Danish Mercantile Co Ltd v Beaumont* [1951] 1 All ER 925.
144 'Contracts' in the usual sense of the word do not have to be under seal and thus can be made in writing or by word of mouth under s 36.
145 But where a transaction is authorised by the directors, it may be valid even though signed not by a director but on his behalf by his attorney.
146 The Execution of Deeds and Documents by or on behalf of Bodies Corporate (LC No 253, Cm 4026).
147 Ie its registered name, and not a business name under which it trades: *Haxford SpA v Mariani and Goodville Ltd* [1981] 2 Lloyd's Rep 54.
148 *Jenice v Dan* [1994] BCC 43.
149 Section 27.
150 *Banque de l'Indochine et de Suez SA v European Group Finance Ltd* [1981] 3 All ER 198.
151 *Durham Fancy Goods Ltd v Michael Jackson (Fancy Goods) Ltd* [1968] 2 All ER 987.
152 *British Airways Board v Parish* [1979] 2 Lloyd's Rep 361.

153 But, in principle, a director's signature adopts not only the figures drawn on the cheque but also the company's name and account number so that there should be no argument that he is *personally* liable unless he has done something more than sign: *Bondina Ltd v Rollaway Shower Blinds Ltd* [1986] 1 All ER 564.

154 *Rolfe Lubell & Co v Keith* [1979] 1 All ER 860.

155 In *Wallersteiner v Moir (No 2)* [1975] 1 All ER 849. Mr Moir, a small shareholder, pursued the controlling director to the Court of Appeal, recovered £234,773 for his company and secured an indemnity for his own costs.

156 *Report of the Company Law Committee*, Cmnd 1749, para 106.

157 As in the *Prudential Assurance* litigation: see **7.15.1**, and Chapter 7, note 129.

158 See Birds and Leighton *Secretarial Administration* (Jordans, loose-leaf).

159 *Report of the Committee on Industrial Democracy*, Cmnd 5706 (1977).

160 Following the lead set by Mrs Thatcher in this respect.

161 Even from the Germans, upon whose domestic law the worker participation provisions in the Fifth Directive are based.

162 Which resulted in the Treaty of European Union.

163 Which included the Japanese.

164 Thereby riding a coach and horses through the rule in *Foss v Harbottle*. See **7.15.1**.

165 See discussion of the *Caparo Industries* and related cases at **4.3** below.

166 Although at the date of publication, the DTI has already consulted in relation to shareholder rights and remedies and The Law Commission is reviewing the rule in *Foss v Harbottle*.

167 The so-called Vredeling Directive.

168 This means, if the so-called 'Rochdale principles' are applied, that each member receives one share in the enterprise and cannot acquire more. A whole-hearted application of these principles removes the enterprise from the capitalist camp, but not from the capitalist battlefield.

169 Including that shown by shareholders of British Gas against what they perceived to be the excessive remuneration of Cedric Brown, the chief executive. Their very public protests were enlivened by the presence of a magnificent pig filmed (by a delighted press) with his snout deep in his trough. Perhaps not entirely coincidentally, the pig was also called Cedric.

Chapter 4

ACCOUNTS

4.1 BACKGROUND

The Companies Act 1989 introduced significant new accounting provisions primarily in relation to group accounting. As ever, the EC provided one impetus for reform.'[1] Having said that, the EC did not provide the sole motive for change. The report of the Dearing Committee on the making of accounting standards[2] also provided a major justification. Part of the Committee's brief involved consideration of the relationship of accounting standards with company law, and the related issue of how best to monitor and enforce the application of accounting standards. The nub of the problem is the decision whether accounting standards should be given force of law. On the one hand, force of law would give certainty and specific remedy in the event of default. On the other hand, the standards would, if entrenched in statute, be subject to formalistic legal interpretation. This may restrict the application of the standards, as the courts give effect to their letter, and not to their spirit. Additionally, in the event of a need to change the standards, their entrenchment in statute will make this all the more slow and cumbersome. The report recommended that accounting standards and company law become more closely entwined, but did not recommend that the standards be given statutory effect. The recommendations in the report have, to a large – although insufficient – extent, been included in the regime introduced by the 1989 Act, for example, the requirements that companies reveal in their accounts the reasons for any material departure from applicable accounting standards[3] and that civil action be available to require companies to produce proper accounts (ie accounts which comply with the Act and, in consequence, with applicable accounting standards).

Of course, preparation and submission of accounts is pre-eminent amongst the directors' responsibilities to their shareholders. A compact and authoritative summary both of the statutory requirements and of the best practice will be found in the booklet *Financial and Accounting Responsibilities of Directors*, and we shall confine ourselves here to a brief summary of the general duties imposed by the Act. These are as follows.

4.1.1 Accounting records

These are dealt with by ss 221 and 222. In general terms, accounting records must be kept which enable the company's transactions to be explained and which also disclose the company's financial position at any given time with 'reasonable accuracy'. They must enable the directors to ensure that the balance sheets and profit and loss accounts prepared under the Act comply with the requirements of s 221(1). In particular, they must record amounts and details of receipts and expenditure, assets and liabilities and, where applicable, details of stock held at the end of each financial year, details of the stock-takings from which these figures emerged and (except in the retail trade) sufficient details to identify buyers and sellers of goods (s 221(3)). These accounting records (or books of accounts) must (save in the event of an insolvency):

(1)   be kept either at the registered office or such other place as the directors specify;[4]
(2)   be open to inspection by the company's officers at all times; and
(3)   be preserved for three years in the case of a private company, and six years in the case of a public company (s 222).

Failure to comply constitutes an offence by every officer in default, as does the failure by any officer to take all reasonable steps to ensure the preservation of the accounting records (s 222(4)). Where there is a failure to comply, an officer in default is liable unless he can show that he 'acted honestly and that in the circumstances in which the company's business was carried on the default was excusable'. The penalty is a maximum of two years' imprisonment and/or an unlimited fine, or on summary conviction six months' imprisonment and/or a fine of up to £5,000. Neither the imposition of criminal liability nor the availability of a defence directly affects the directors' general duty of care under *Re City Equitable Fire Insurance Co* (**5.8**), which requires the directors to display the usual degree of skill and diligence in the manner in which tasks are delegated and supervised.[5] In fact, the powers of the Inland Revenue to raise assessments up to 20 years after the relevant period means retention for at least 20 years is prudent.

4.1.2   Annual accounts

The directors must prepare a profit and loss account for every financial year, together with a balance sheet as at the last day of that year (s 226). They must then lay the accounts before the general meeting (usually the AGM) or, in the case of a private company, if the members have passed an elective resolution to dispense with this requirement, the accounts must be sent to the members (s 252); more specifically, their duty is to lay before the meeting or send to the members copies of every document required to be in the accounts (s 241), which comprise:

(1)   the profit and loss account and balance sheet;
(2)   the directors' report (see **4.2**);
(3)   the auditor's report (see **4.3**); and
(4)   (where applicable) the group accounts (s 227).

The balance sheet must give a 'true and fair view of the state of affairs of the company as at the end of the financial year', an obligation which, in the event of any conflict, takes precedence over the more detailed requirements of Sch 4 to the Act (below) and any specific provisions of the Act relating to material to be included in the accounts or in notes to the accounts (s 226(4), (5)). This may require additional information of a qualifying nature to be included in the accounts or notes, and even if that is insufficient to provide a 'true and fair view' it may justify a departure (within the reasons stated) from the Act's requirements, although, obviously enough, this is not a matter in which a prudent board will act without seeking professional advice. One recommendation of the Dearing Committee[6] was that only accounts which complied with applicable accounting standards would be presumed to give a true and fair view. A material departure would therefore have to be justified by those arguing that, notwithstanding the departure, the accounts still presented a true and fair view. This recommendation was not enacted since the courts would be likely to treat compliance with accounting standards as prima facie evidence that the accounts presented a true and fair view in any event. However, Part III of Sch 4 to the Act does require a note to the accounts to state whether the accounts have been prepared in accordance with applicable accounting standards and particulars of, and reasons for, any material departure from those standards.

Copies of these documents must be sent to every member,[7] every debenture holder and every other person who is entitled to notice of general meetings,[8] at least 21 days[9] before the meeting (s 238) or, if an elective resolution has been passed to dispense with the meeting, sent to the members and others not less than 28 days before the end of the 7 or 10-month period referred to below. In such circumstances, the accounts must be accompanied by a notice to each member, telling him of the right to require a general meeting to be held to consider the accounts (s 253). This right must be exercised within that 28-day period, and in writing. In the case of a public listed company, it is possible, in certain circumstances, to send 'summary financial statements' rather than full accounts (s 251[10]). A copy of the accounts and other documents must be filed with the Registrar of Companies (s 242). The time-limit for laying and filing the accounts is 10 months (private companies) or 7 months (public companies) from the end of the financial year (s 244). A company with overseas interests may extend the period by 3 months by written notice to the Registrar, and the DTI has power to authorise any company to extend the period. The accounts and documents delivered to the Registrar are placed on the company's file and are available for public inspection. Consequently, care should be taken to exclude the kind of detailed trading or management accounts which are not required to form part of the statutory accounts and which are intended to remain confidential. In addition to the obligations already outlined, the company must supply any member or debenture holder with a free copy of the accounts on demand (s 239).

4.1.3 Signature

Copies of the balance sheet must always state the name of the director who signed the balance sheet on behalf of the board following its approval by the board. Copies of the directors' report must always state the name of the director or secretary who signed it on behalf of the board following its approval by them, and every copy of the auditor's report must state the name of the auditor. The originals delivered to the Registrar must bear 'live' signatures in each case (ss 233, 234A, 236).

4.1.4 Penalties

Schedule 24 to the Act sets out a statement of offences under the Act and of the prescribed penalties. In relation to the signature, delivery, etc, of accounts, various offences attend non-compliance with these requirements, including the following:

Nature of offence	*Person(s) liable*	*Penalty*
(a) Laying, filing or circulating unsigned accounts	Company and every officer in default	£500
(b) Failure to send accounts to persons entitled to receive them	Company and every officer in default	Unlimited fine, or £5,000 on summary conviction
(c) Failure to lay or file accounts in time	Directors	£5,000 or £1,000 on summary conviction

It is a defence in case (c) that the director took all reasonable steps to secure compliance with the Act; but it is no defence merely to show that the documents had not been prepared in time. In addition, failure to file accounts gives rise to a civil penalty recoverable from the company by the DTI increasing with the period of default as follows (s 242A). In each case, the 'length of period' means the period between the expiry of the period allowed for delivering the accounts, and the day upon which they are actually delivered. The penalties differ according to whether the company is private or public.

Length of period	*Public*	*Private*
Not more than 3 months	£500	£100
More than 3 but not more than 6 months	£1,000	£250
More than 6 but not more than 12 months	£2,000	£500
More than 12 months	£5,000	£1,000

It is no defence to prove that the documents were not in fact prepared as required by the Act.

4.1.5   Accounting requirements

The Companies Act 1981 radically reshaped the statutory requirements governing the form and content of company accounts. In doing so, it implemented the Fourth Directive on company accounts, while taking advantage of the increased flexibility which the Directive permitted. These rules have been further amended by the 1989 Act. The principal features are as follows.

(1)   The accounts prepared under s 226(1) must, as we have seen, give a 'true and fair' view of the company's affairs (see **4.1.2**). Subject to this requirement, they must comply with Sch 4 with respect to the form and content of the balance sheets and the profit and loss accounts, together with extra information required to be given by way of notes to the accounts. Thus, additional material may be required and, as we have seen, departures from the Schedule (with reasons) are permissible.

(2)   Schedule 4, Part I, specifies the 'format' of the accounts, there being two choices for the balance sheet and four for the profit and loss accounts. Once a format has been adopted, it must be continued unless the directors believe (and state in a note to the accounts) that there are 'special reasons for a change' (Sch 4, Part I, para 2).

(3)   Items.

   (a)   Goodwill may be included only to the extent that it has been acquired for valuable consideration (Sch 4, Part I, balance sheet, note 3).

(b) Gross profit must be disclosed by showing the major items between turnover[11] and pre-tax profit.

(c) Stock must be subdivided between raw materials, work-in-progress, finished goods, and payments on account.

(d) Debtors must be subdivided between trade, group undertakings and undertakings in which the company has a participating interest,[12] other items and prepayments.

(e) Creditors must be subdivided between 'due within one year' and 'due after one year', debentures, banks, payments on account, trade, bills of exchange, group and related companies, tax and social security, accruals and deferred income.

Requirements which may particularly affect directors are the inclusion in the accounts of:

(a) loans (see **10.4**);

(b) directors' emoluments (including 'golden hellos') (see **10.6**);

(c) waived emoluments (see **10.6**);

(4) Accounting principles by which the figures in the accounts are to be, broadly, determined, are set out in Sch 4, Part IIA. They are:

(a) a presumption that the business is a going concern;

(b) a consistent application of accounting policies from year to year;

(c) a prudent determination of profits (which must have been realised) and losses and liabilities (which must be allowed for, even if they become apparent only between the time when the balance sheet is prepared and the time when it is approved and signed);

(d) the accrual of income and charges by reference to the period to which they relate, regardless of the actual date of receipt or payment.

(5) Accounting rules are set out in Sch 4, Parts IIB and C. Part IIB sets out the 'Historical Costs Accounting Rules' which are to apply unless the company adopts Part IIC. The historical costs rules require, among other things, that:

(a) fixed assets are shown at purchase price or production cost and depreciated over their estimated life, with additional depreciation where there is a permanent diminution in value. Conversely, any recovery in value should be written back;

(b) development costs (but not research costs) may be capitalised, but the period of amortisation must be stated;

(c) goodwill (where treated as an asset) must be written off systematically over a period not exceeding its useful economic life;

(d) current assets should be shown at purchase price or production cost, or at net realisable value if lower;

(e) the price or cost of stocks may be fixed by the FIFO (first in, first out) or LILO (last in, last out) method, by a weighted-average price or any other similar method, whichever is most appropriate in the circumstances and provides the fairest practicable approximation to actual cost.

Any departure from the rules must generally be disclosed and explained.

The company may choose to adopt the alternative accounting rules set out in Part IIC which provide for current cost accounting and the revaluation of assets. Where they are adopted there must be a note as to the valuation basis of each item. The effect of this is that:

(a) intangible fixed assets (other than goodwill) may be stated at current cost;

(b) tangible fixed assets may be stated at their market value on the last valuation date or current cost;

(c) fixed asset investments may be shown as at last valuation or as deemed appropriate, with reasons, by the directors;

(d) current asset investments may be stated at current cost;

(e) stocks may be stated at current cost;

(f) any difference between an 'alternative' basis valuation and an historical cost figure must be debited or credited to a revaluation reserve, shown on the balance sheet and available only for transfer to profit and loss account where it had previously been charged to that account or represents a realised profit or on capitalisation, ie the payment up in full or in part of unissued shares to be allotted to members of the company by way of bonus issue;

(g) provision for deferred taxation must be stated separately from provision for other taxation.

(6) Schedule 4, Part III, lists those items which may be shown by way of a note, if not shown in the accounts themselves.

These include:

(a) disclosure of the company's accounting policies and whether the accounts have been prepared in accordance with applicable accounting standards;

(b) any material departure from applicable accounting standards and the reasons for it;

(c) in relation to the balance sheet, particulars of capital, redeemable shares, allotments (with explanations), fixed assets and changes therein, revaluations, interests in land and buildings, investments, reserves, creditors (distinguishing those debts payable more than five years hence), charges to secure the liabilities of other parties, contingent liabilities, and loans for acquisition of shares in the company; and

(d) against the profit and loss account, particulars of interest on loans, taxation, turnover (analysed in terms of business class and market), average number of employees, wages, social security costs and pensions.

Section 231 and Sch 5, require additional information to be disclosed in notes to the accounts or in some cases attached to the annual return, in order to prevent the accounts themselves from becoming too unwieldy.

These relate to:

(a) particulars of any subsidiary undertakings and other shareholdings;

(b) certain financial information relating to subsidiary undertakings;

(c) where the company is itself a subsidiary undertaking, the identity of its ultimate parent company;

(d)   section 390A also requires disclosure of fees for audit work in the profit and loss account and s 390B allows the DTI to make regulations requiring disclosure of fees for non-audit work.[13]

It should also be remembered that s 232 requires that particulars of emoluments of directors, loans, 'quasi-loans' and certain other transactions in favour of directors are to be disclosed in notes to the accounts and imposes a similar requirement in respect of transactions with officers other than directors. Details of the disclosure required are contained in Sch 6 to the Act.

Schedule 6, Part I requires disclosure of details of emoluments paid to or receivable by directors (including those waived), directors' pensions and compensation for loss of office. Since 1997, [14] the disclosure requirements have covered 'excess retirement benefits', long-term incentive schemes and gains made by directors on the exercise of share options (if the company is listed).

When the aggregate of the benefits provided equals or exceeds £200,000, details must be given of the highest paid director's emoluments etc.

(7)   Where accounts laid or filed are defective (ie in not complying with the rules described in outline above) the directors may voluntarily prepare revised accounts.[15] There is a special procedure to be observed in relation to these revised accounts, depending upon whether they have been laid before the company in general meeting, or delivered to the Registrar. It is therefore possible to find two (or more!) sets of accounts on the public record in respect of the same period!

The Secretary of State may also raise his own queries in respect of the accounts, and whether they comply with the Act. He may require an explanation from the directors. The explanation is requested by notice indicating the matters in respect of which he has a query, and the directors are given one month to provide an explanation, or prepare revised accounts. If he is still not satisfied, a court application may ensue.[16]

There is no criminal penalty if accounts are approved which do not comply with the Act unless the directors know of the non-compliance, or were reckless as to whether the accounts complied or not.[17] A director who is party to approval of such defective accounts is presumed to be aware of, or reckless as to, their non-compliance unless he shows that he took all reasonable steps to prevent their approval.

4.1.6   Small and medium-sized companies

The Act permits relaxation of certain of the rules relating to company accounts if the company is either small or medium sized.

A medium-sized company must (subject to one concession relieving the company from the requirements of para 36A of Sch 4) always prepare a full set of accounts for presentation to its shareholders. However, if it wishes to reduce the information made available in its accounts filed with the Registrar of Companies, it may prepare a second set of accounts in an abbreviated format, for filing purposes. These abbreviated accounts will be acceptable to the Registrar (s 246).

A small company is in an even better position. First, it is entitled to prepare a set of accounts for presentation to its shareholders which include simplified versions of the balance sheet formats prescribed by the Act and with a directors' report which is also in a simpler format than that usually required.[18] If it wishes to take advantage of these entitlements (and it may choose whether it does and, if so, to what extent), additional statements as to its entitlement to these special exemptions must be included in the balance sheet and/or directors' report as appropriate. Secondly, whilst the small company may file its accounts with the Registrar of Companies (whether those accounts are in a simplified format or not), it may also, like the medium-sized company, prepare a second set of accounts in an abbreviated format, for filing purposes. These abbreviated accounts contain even less specific information than the simplified version of the company's accounts (s 246).

To qualify as a small or medium-sized company, a company must satisfy two of the following criteria for both the current and the previous year.

	Turnover	Balance sheet total	Average employees per week
Small must not exceed	£2.8m	£1.4m	50
Medium must not exceed	£11.2m	£5.6m	250

A qualifying company has one year's grace if it fails to meet the conditions in any one year. The relaxations are not available to public, banking or insurance companies, or companies authorised under the Financial Services Act 1986, or to companies in a group containing any such companies.

Small companies

A small company's accounts can be made up to comply with Sch 4 (in which case they will be the same as the full accounts prepared by larger companies), with Sch 8 (the provisions of which allow small companies to simplify their accounts to the full extent) or with any combination of the provisions of Schs 4 and 8.

The directors' report may also omit certain information, such as amounts to be paid as dividend, substantial differences between market and book values of interests in land and certain matters relating to employee involvement.

If the small company also wishes to prepare a second set of abbreviated accounts for filing purposes, the small company files:

(1) a modified balance sheet showing main headings in accordance with one of the formats specified in Part I of Sch 8A;
(2) modified notes to the accounts, showing only the items specified in Part II of Sch 8A;
(3) no directors' report;
(4) no profit and loss account;
(5) no details of directors' emoluments etc; and
(6) a statement by the directors and auditors of their entitlement to these exemptions.

Thus, the small company's filed accounts will give no indication of the profits for the year apart from the differences in the balance sheet item for profit and loss accounts.

Medium-sized companies

A medium-sized company is not entitled to prepare simplified full accounts, but if it wishes to prepare a second set of abbreviated accounts for filing purposes, the medium-sized company files:

(1) a full balance sheet and notes;
(2) a modified profit and loss account, starting with gross profit and thus omitting turnover and intervening items;
(3) a directors' report; and
(4) statements by the directors and auditors as to their entitlement to these exemptions.

4.1.7 'Dormant' and 'audit exempt' companies

Dormant companies

Sections 250 and 253 permit a company, whether public or private, to exempt itself from the provisions of the Act relating to the audit of accounts and (it follows) to lay and file unaudited accounts. The essential precondition is that the company is at the time 'dormant', that is to say that over the relevant period there have been no 'significant accounting transactions', which are transactions which would normally be entered into the accounts (and, of course, audited).

The company, not the board, claims the exemptions, by passing a special resolution.

(1) A company dormant since incorporation (perhaps an 'off the peg company' awaiting a buyer) may pass a resolution at any time.
(2) Where the company has completed its first financial year before becoming dormant (so that some audited accounts will have been laid), the special resolution may be passed at any time after copies of the annual accounts for that year have been sent out in accordance with s 238(1),[19] provided that:

    (a) the company has been dormant since the end of the financial year to which the accounts relate and remains dormant;
    (b) it is not required to present group accounts; and
    (c) it qualified as a small company for the year in question, or would have done if not in an ineligible group.

(3) The dormant company may then file 'small company' modified accounts omitting:

    (a) any reference to an audited account; and
    (b) any directors' statement of small company qualifications but showing, immediately above the directors' signatures on the balance sheet, a statement of dormancy.

Audit exempt companies[20]

A company which meets the total exemption conditions in respect of a financial year is exempt from the provisions of the Act relating to the audit of accounts in respect of that year (s 249A to s 249).

The company is also exempt from the obligation to appoint auditors. If the entitlement to exemption ceases the directors have power to appoint auditors. In default, the power may be exercised by the members in general meeting (s 388A).

The total exemption conditions are met by a company in respect of a financial year if:

(a)   it qualifies as a small company in relation to that year;
(b)   its turnover in that year is not more than £350,000;
(c)   its balance sheet total for that year is not more than £1.4m (s 249A(3)).

A company is not entitled to the exemption from audit under either s 249A(1) in respect of a financial year if, at any time within that year, it was a public, banking or insurance company, an authorised person or appointed representative under the Financial Services Act 1986 or an insurance broker. It is also not entitled to the exemption if it was a parent company or a subsidiary undertaking unless, in the latter case, it is a dormant subsidiary undertaking throughout a financial period (s 249B) or, in either case, it is a member of a small group meeting the conditions set out in s 249(B)(1C).

Any member or members holding not less in aggregate than 10 per cent in nominal value of the company's issued share capital or any class of it may, by notice in writing deposited at the registered office of the company during a financial year (but not later than one month before the end of that year), require the company to obtain an audit of its accounts for that year. The effect of the deposit of such a notice is that the company is not entitled to the exemption in respect of the financial year to which the notice relates (s 249B).

A company is not entitled to the exemption under s 249A(1) unless its balance sheet contains a statement by the directors to the effect that:

(a)   for the year in question the company was entitled to exemption;
(b)   no notice has been deposited in relation to its accounts for the financial year; and
(c)   the directors acknowledge their responsibilities for ensuring that the company keeps accounting records which comply with the Act and for preparing accounts which give a true and fair view of the state of affairs of the company as at the end of the financial year and of its profit or loss for the financial year, and otherwise comply with the requirements of the Act relating to accounts which are applicable to the company.

Such a statement must appear in the balance sheet above the signature of the director signing on behalf of the board (s 249B(2)). It should be noted that charities which operate as limited companies are subject to a separate regime in these respects (s 249A(2)).

4.1.8   Groups of companies

These attract special requirements which are intended to ensure that the shareholders of the parent company will receive more or less the same information which would be available to them if the group's business was carried on by a single company operating through a number of different departments or branches.

The Companies Act 1989 introduced a new and wide definition of parent and subsidiary undertakings for the purposes of determining matters to be included in group accounts. The EC Seventh Directive required introduction of the new definition. The main effect of the new definition is to determine the parent/subsidiary relationship by reference to factual control of the subsidiary by the parent, rather than simply a legalistic test based on holding a majority of voting equity. The result is that group accounts may now have to include financial affairs of bodies which were not included prior to the new rules. This prevents an abuse known as 'off-balance sheet financing' under which a company was previously able to, for example, borrow money through an undertaking over which it had factual, but not legal, control, without the transaction appearing in its balance sheet.

(1) Section 227 requires a company with subsidiary undertakings (and which is not itself a subsidiary undertaking of a company incorporated within the EU) to prepare both the company's own accounts and consolidated group accounts. However, there are new exemptions for groups of companies,[21] whereby in certain circumstances, group accounts need no longer be prepared. The exemption is based on the concept of the 'small group' and 'the medium-sized group'. These are familiar concepts, save that the old exemption allowed delivery of modified group accounts. The new exemption removes the requirement to prepare group accounts at all.

To be a qualifying group, the group must satisfy two of the following criteria for both the current and the previous year. Alternative net and gross figures are included, either of which will confer qualification (s 249).

	Turnover	Balance sheet	Average employees per week
Small must not exceed	£2.8m net	£1.4m net	
	£3.36m gross	£1.68m gross	50
Medium must not exceed	£11.2m net	£5.6m net	
	£13.44m gross	£6.72m gross	250

The relaxations are not available if any member of the group is a public, banking or insurance company, or a company authorised under the Financial Services Act 1986.[22] Group accounts, together with any notes to them, must give a true and fair picture of the state of affairs and profit and loss of the parent company and the subsidiary undertakings dealt with by the accounts as a whole, so far as concerns the members of the parent company (s 227(3)). As in the case of individual accounts, this is an overriding requirement which may justify deviations from the more specific statutory requirements relating to form and content of accounts.

(2) Group accounts need not deal with a particular subsidiary undertaking if in the opinion of the parent's directors:

(a) its inclusion is not material for the purposes of giving a true and fair view. In determining whether inclusion is material, all subsidiary undertakings proposed to be excluded must be aggregated;

(b) severe long-term restrictions hinder the exercise of the parent's rights over the subsidiary undertaking;

(c) it would involve disproportionate expense or delay;

(d) the interest in the subsidiary undertaking is held solely for resale and the undertaking has not previously been included in group accounts; or

(e) the two businesses are so radically different that it would be incompatible with providing a 'true and fair view' to combine their accounts.

Finally, to avoid doubt, the Act states that, if all subsidiary undertakings fall within these exemptions, group accounts are not required.

(3) Group accounts must be consolidated, ie combining the accounts of the parent and subsidiary undertaking into a single set of accounts. The directors therefore have no discretion as to the way in which the group information is presented, particularly:

(a) by using more than one set of consolidated accounts; or
(b) treating each individual subsidiary separately, supplemented by explanatory statements.

(4) Other matters dealt with by the Act may be briefly noted. First, directors of a parent company must ensure that the financial years within the group coincide unless there are good reasons against this (s 223(5)). Secondly, whether a company is required to prepare group accounts, or is within one of the exemptions, special provisions apply as to the formats of the group of individual accounts, and notes to them.[23]

4.1.9   Publication of company accounts

This is the situation in which a company publishes, issues, or circulates its accounts publicly, or at least to a section of the public – 'its accounts' meaning the accounts as required to be laid or filed under the Act.

In the case of full company accounts,[24] the company must also publish the auditor's report (s 240(1)). If it is required to publish group accounts then, if it publishes its individual accounts, it must publish the group accounts with them; and a company which publishes the group accounts without the individual accounts must publish the auditor's report which will (among other things) state whether the group accounts represent a true and fair picture of the financial position of the company and its subsidiaries. A company may also publish 'abridged accounts'; that is summarised accounts or the preliminary announcements made by listed companies.[25] In that case, no auditor's report on the full accounts may be published with the abridged accounts, but the company must state:

(1) that these are not the full accounts;
(2) whether full accounts have been filed;[26] and
(3) whether there is an unqualified auditor's report. This is designed to ensure that abbreviated abstracts, press releases and advertisements do not carry the authority of the auditor's report.

4.2   DIRECTORS' REPORT[27]

This is a document which by definition is of particular concern to the board. It is the sole responsibility of the directors and although once a short, formal addition to the accounts, it has become of much more central significance.[28] The most general requirement, under s 234(1), is to prepare, for every financial year, a report:

(1) containing a fair review of the development of the company's business and that of any subsidiaries during the financial year and of the position at the end of it;

(2) stating any proposed dividend; and

(3) stating any amount proposed to be carried to reserves.

The last two items were a traditional part of the 'old-style' and very bare directors' report; the first requirement follows the wording of the Fourth Directive and, whilst it undoubtedly represents an addition to the directors' obligations, it leaves considerable discretion as to the degree of detail which is provided. However, s 234 goes on to make quite a large number of more specific requirements.

The report must contain the following information.

(1) The names of all those who have been directors at any time during the financial year.

(2) The principal activities of the company and any subsidiary undertakings and any significant changes in them, during the financial year.

(3) Details of the following:

    (a) substantial differences between market and book value of interests in land at the end of the financial year;

    (b) any director's interests in shares or debentures of the company or group at the beginning and end of the financial year, including share options granted;[29]

    (c) donations for political or charitable purposes;

    (d) events affecting the company or group since the end of the financial year;

    (e) future likely developments in the business;

    (f) research and development activities;

    (g) the direct or indirect acquisition by the company of its own shares, and charges taken over them;

    (h) where the average weekly payroll exceeds 250, the employment and training opportunities for the disabled;

    (i) the involvement of employees in the affairs, policy and performance of the company;

    (j) if the company is public or in a group whose parent company is public (and, in the latter case, the company is neither a small nor a medium-sized company) during a financial year, the report for the next following financial year must state its policy and practice as the payment of creditors.[30]

The directors' report, approved by the board and delivered to the Registrar of Companies must be signed either by a director or the secretary. The name of the signatory must appear on every copy.

However, as noted at **4.1.6** above, a small company may include in its individual accounts a version of the directors' report which omits all or any of:

(1) the fair review of the development of the company's business, the amount to be paid as dividend and the amount to be carried to reserves;

(2) substantial differences between market and book values of interests in land;

(3) events affecting the company since the end of the financial year;

(4) details of the involvement of employees in the affairs, policy and performance of the company provided that the directors' report includes an appropriate additional statement as to the company's entitlement to these exemptions.

An innovation of the 1981 Act (now s 235(3)) was the imposition of a duty on the auditors to extend their scrutiny of the company's affairs and to consider whether the information given in the directors' report is consistent with the accounts, and to note the fact if they form the opinion that it is not. The not uncommon practice under the old law of obtaining the auditor's assistance in preparing the report is not directly affected by this development; but the auditor's advice is given very great weight, and the onus on them to act independently of the board is accordingly increased. One effect of s 235(3) is to place considerable weight, in cases of doubt, upon the auditor's interpretation of some of the vaguer statutory requirements. For example, it is not always easy to see how (2) (above) (land interests) is to be applied. No company is obliged to have its real property revalued each year, but they must, nevertheless, consider its value (although whether on a break-up basis or not is not specified) and assess all other relevant factors such as taxation, planning permission, relocation costs, and even possibly the effects of liquidation. If a 'substantial' difference in the total value of the land emerges, they must disclose it, but they are entitled to draw the members' attention to these other factors. 'Substantial' must exclude merely trivial changes, but there is certainly no need for a major or decisive shift in value before disclosure is necessary. The point of s 235(3) is that it is no longer enough for the directors to have acted honestly and reasonably; in the end the interpretation both of the Act and of the facts is a matter for the auditors to determine.

4.3 AUDITOR'S REPORT

Every company must have an auditor, unless it has taken advantage of s 250 (dormant companies: see **4.1.7**) and still retains that status or is exempt from the provisions of the Act relating to audit of accounts by virtue of s 249A (primarily, that its turnover is less than £350,000). The auditor's qualifications are noted in paragraph (6) below. His position in relation to the directors (which was much strengthened by the Companies Act 1976) and the company is as follows.

(1) He reports to the members on the accounts and every balance sheet, profit and loss account and group account presented during the term of his appointment (s 235). The auditor's report must be annexed to the accounts, and open to inspection by any member (s 241).

(2) The report must state:[31]

    (a) whether the accounts have been properly prepared in accordance with the Act;

    (b) whether they give a true and fair picture of the company's state of affairs and profit or loss for the financial year; and

    (c) whether the directors' report is consistent with the accounts.

The auditor's report to the company, delivered to the Registrar of Companies, must state the name of the auditor and be signed by him. Every copy of the report must state the name of the auditor.

It is the auditor's duty in preparing the report to ensure that proper accounting records have been kept, and to state in his report if this is not so, or if he has been unable to obtain the required information, or if the accounts do not tally with the company's accounting records (s 237). For these purposes, he has a right of access at all times to the company's books and papers, and to such information and explanations from the directors and officers as he considers necessary and, if any of these are not forthcoming, he should qualify his report.

(3) These are statutory obligations. The precise scope of the auditor's duties to members and others at common law remains uncertain, but is more likely to go beyond what follows than to fall short of it in any future developments in the courts. An auditor will owe a contractual[32] duty of care to the company and must perform his obligations not only honestly but with the care and skill currently expected from a person with his professional qualifications.[33] Although he has no contract with the members, he will be liable for false information knowingly given to them[34] and very probably for false information or unsound opinions negligently given.[35] He may also owe a duty of care to potential investors. But the case which decided this, *J E B Fasteners Ltd v Marks Bloom & Co*[36] has since been dealt a blow by the case of *Caparo Industries plc v Dickman*.[37] In the *Caparo* case, the House of Lords took the view that the accounts and auditor's report were intended to provide members with adequate and reliable information to enable them to vet the company's affairs, make judgements on its management and thereby exercise an effective control over the company when collectively making decisions in general meeting. In order to establish whether a duty of care was owed by the auditor to a member who was buying, selling or retaining shares, when preparing the accounts and report, the court asked whether the auditor prepared his report for this purpose, ie to enable members to decide whether to buy, sell or retain shares – as they did not, there was no duty of care owed to members or potential members if the accounts and report were used for that purpose. Nor was the auditor specifically made aware that the report would be relied upon in this way.

It is now unlikely that members, or potential members, will be able to argue that the audited accounts and auditor's reports were a proper basis for making an investment decision. In practice, the issue in *J E B Fasteners* should not commonly arise, since a prudent purchaser in the plaintiffs' situation will obtain a warranty by the directors that the audited accounts were accurate, and that there has been no material change since the end of the financial year. The auditor's statutory duties are performed by forwarding his report to the secretary. He is not personally responsible for presenting it to the members.[38] However, he has a statutory right to notice of any general meeting and to attend and speak at it, and his common law duties, referred to in the previous paragraph, may require him to exercise that right. Furthermore, his position vis-à-vis the board is strengthened in a number of ways:

(a) 'special notice' procedure (see **9.4**) is required for most appointments: ss 388 and 391A;

(b) the same procedure applies if it is proposed to remove an auditor prematurely. When the company receives the special notice of the resolution, it must send a copy to the auditor.[39] He is then entitled to make written representations, which must be circulated to the members (s 391A (4)) and he has a further right to address the meeting;

(c) in the event of any cessation of office by an auditor, the auditor must give a written statement, which must either state that all is well or explain the circumstances connected with the cessation of office, which he feels should be brought to the attention of the members or creditors (s 394). In the case of a resignation, he may also demand that an extraordinary general meeting should be called to consider these matters (s 392A).

Failure by the company to comply with these requirements is visited by criminal liability.

(4)   The auditor's responsibilities extend to certain other cases.

    (a)   If a company's accounts do not make the requisite disclosures of loans and other transactions with directors and of the remuneration of directors and higher-paid employees, the auditor must include a statement in his report on the balance sheet giving as many particulars as he reasonably can (s 237).

    (b)   He must supply supporting reports in the case of:

        (i)   financial assistance for the acquisition of shares in the company (s 156(4));

        (ii)   entitlement to deliver modified accounts (small and medium-sized companies) and compliance with the modified accounts rules (s 247B);

        (iii)   proposals to finance a share purchase or redemption out of capital (s 173(5)).

(5)   While auditors' reports must be published with the full annual accounts, they must not be published with 'abridged' reports (see **4.1.9**), although there must be an accompanying statement of whether the full accounts have been audited and, if so, whether the auditor's report was qualified or not. The Act refers to these as accounts 'relating to a financial year'. Whether interim or half yearly accounts fall within this definition is open to debate in view of these words; but certainly the kind of summarised financial statements, often not merely published, but circulated to employees, as well as members, will fall within the rule.

(6)   The Companies Act 1989 made significant changes to the rules regulating capacity to act as, and conduct of, auditors.[40] This part of the 1989 Act reflects the requirements of the Eighth Directive, the intention of which is to standardise minimum criteria for education and training of auditors, and for their ethical regulation. This has resulted in a regime under which auditors must be members of, or subject to the rules of, recognised supervisory bodies. To gain qualification, from a recognised supervisory body, the auditor must be independent of the companies audited by him, and must hold 'appropriate qualifications'.

The recognised supervisory bodies are:
-   the Institute of Chartered Accountants in England and Wales;
-   the Institute of Chartered Accountants of Scotland;
-   the Association of Chartered Certified Accountants;
-   the Institute of Chartered Accountants in Ireland;
-   the Association of Authorised Public Accountants;
-   the Association of Accounting Technicians;
-   the Association of International Accountants; and
-   the Chartered Institute of Management Accountants.

However, one reform which the director may notice is that auditors are entitled to practise through limited companies and other bodies corporate.

(7) An auditor is often called upon to value shares, under the terms of the Articles, and must then act with reasonable care in the interests of third parties if he knows that his professional skill is being relied on. Generally speaking, it does not matter whether his assistance is invoked as an arbitrator or as an expert, for he has no immunity from the ordinary law of negligence unless he can show that an existing dispute between two parties has been referred to him to resolve in a 'judicial' capacity.[41] When giving advice, he may attempt to disclaim responsibility. A disclaimer is effective at common law[42] unless a statement is made fraudulently,[43] but would probably fall within ss 2 and 3 of the Unfair Contract Terms Act 1977 and require justification as a 'reasonable' clause.

One thing which should be borne in mind is that liability in negligence is one thing; the liability of the parties to the contract for the valued shares is another. Thus, the courts may readily construe a contract in such a way that the parties remain bound even if the valuer makes a mistake (even a negligent mistake) particularly where the valuer is not required to give reasons.[44]

4.4 DIVIDENDS

The power-sharing aspects of this important subject were considered in **3.8**. As we saw, the usual regulation (reg 102 of Table A) provides that 'the company may by ordinary resolution declare dividends in accordance with the respective rights of the members, but no dividend shall exceed the amount recommended by the directors'. Thus, the dividend is the joint responsibility of board and members, but the control and initiative remain firmly with the directors, as it must where there are so many inhibiting factors to be considered.

4.4.1 Profits available for distribution

Section 263(1) states the basic rule: no company may make a distribution[45] except out of profits available for the purpose. These are defined as:

Accumulated, realised[46] profits
minus
Accumulated, realised losses[47]

In computing realised profits, allowance must be made for profits shown on revaluation[48] of fixed assets (ie any assets other than current assets) provided that account is taken of sums written off or retained for depreciation of the assets. Certain distributions are, in effect, exempted by s 263(2) – in particular distributions for paying up bonus shares – but unrealised profits may not be used to pay up debentures or issued shares.[49] These rules have now been in force for over 10 years, and have considerably narrowed the sometimes rather generous view which some companies (in particular small companies) used to take of the concept of 'profits'. In addition, very permissive decisions which, for example, allow payments to be made even when revenue losses from previous years had not been made good[50] are swept away.

4.4.2 Restrictions on public companies[51]

Further restrictions are imposed by s 264, which permits a public company to pay a dividend only when the distribution does not reduce its net assets below the combined value of called-up share capital and undistributable reserves, the latter meaning:

(1) the share premium account;
(2) the capital redemption reserve;
(3) the excess of accumulated, unrealised profits over accumulated, unrealised losses; and
(4) any other reserve which the Memorandum, Articles or other statutory provision precludes from distribution.

4.4.3 Relevant accounts: s 270

A dividend must be based upon the following items:

(1) profits, losses, assets and liabilities;
(2) provisions (for depreciation, diminution in asset value, retentions to meet liabilities, etc); and
(3) share capital and reserves, including undistributable reserves.

These items are determined by the relevant accounts, which are not necessarily the latest audited annual accounts. As a general rule, these are the 'relevant' accounts, but if the distribution infringes s 263 or s 264, and if based on those accounts, the determination is to be made by such interim accounts as are necessary to form a reasonable judgement of the amounts of the items in (1) to (3) above. Where the distribution is proposed during the first financial year (or 'accounting period') of a company, 'initial accounts' must be used.

There are strict requirements concerning the preparation of the relevant accounts which must be satisfied before a distribution may be based upon them – s 271 (the annual accounts), s 272 (interim accounts of a public company) and s 273 (initial accounts of a public company). Where the annual accounts only are used, they must be strictly in accordance with the Acts and the subject of an unqualified auditor's report, unless the auditor has stated whether a qualification is material to the proposed payment and that it complies with s 263 or s 264, and the statement has been filed with the Registrar of Companies.

4.4.4 Successive distributions: s 274

Where successive distributions[52] are proposed by reference to the same accounts, they are treated as cumulative, ie the amount of the proposed distribution is treated as increased by the amounts already diminished. Section 270 then applies in the ordinary way to determine whether the company has distributable profits for the purposes of s 263 and s 264.

4.4.5 General

Among other things, these requirements end speculation by directors on 'long-term' and anticipated profits. Generally, this will be a good thing, although in some cases it is bound to damage a company which has a reasonable and legitimate expectation of profits. Breach of the requirements does not involve any criminal sanction. However, directors must, at all times, remember fiduciary obligations and, quite apart from that, s 277 requires a member who received an improper distribution to restore it if he knew, or had reasonable grounds to believe, that it contravened the Act.

Directors themselves should remember that, even before these statutory rules applied, they were held jointly and severally liable to the company for dividends paid out of capital,[53] although they might seek an indemnity from members who knew of this:[54] and the recipient of a dividend which is unlawfully paid in breach of the Act will often have to account to the company for the payment.[55] Further, distributions should be in cash, unless the Articles provide otherwise; reg 105 of Table A permits this subject to certain conditions, but the issue of shares in lieu of dividends is taxable as income.

4.5 TAKEOVERS AND MERGERS

Directors involved in such situations are bound to take specialist advice, but it may be useful to draw attention to some of the main features of the takeover scene.

(1) The general duty of directors is the usual one of acting bona fide in the interests of the company as a whole; this is liable to be complicated by their obligation under s 309 to consider the interests of employees as part of their general duty, for the interests of the 'company as a whole' and of the workforce will by no means invariably coincide. Since it is 'the company' which enforces the duty under s 309, there is an obvious danger that the interests of the workforce will be subordinated to those of the incoming shareholders, who will certainly put their own interests first; but directors must give honest and reasonable consideration to their duty under the section. Apart from that, where an offer for shares is being made, it is not 'the company' but the shareholders whose interests are primarily at stake; and the directors must not seek to put assets out of the shareholders' reach,[56] nor to block the bid by an unnecessary share issue.[57] Since the directors' duties are normally owed to the company and not to the members, these rules are explained on the basis that the directors must use their powers only for the purposes for which they were conferred, but what is really being protected is the members' right to sell their shares in a manner which realises the full value of the company's assets.[58]

(2) Parliament has tended to hold back from imposing direct control over the conduct of takeovers, friendly or hostile. The *City Code on Takeovers and Mergers* (the 'Code') has effectively become part of the 'membership' rules, binding those carrying on investment and other financial business and governed by the Financial Services Act 1986; in this way, the 'private' rules of the Code have been given indirect legal force. In the meantime, the legislature has preferred to rely, in general, on disclosure rules, progressively tightened, and to deal with specific problems such as insider trading on an ad hoc basis rather than as an aspect of any wider regulation. Competition law is concerned more with the effect of, than with the conduct of, takeovers. The Companies Acts have, for many years, however, governed the position of small minorities left after a successful takeover, and these rules – which may have some impact on the way

in which an offer is formulated and conducted – have been redrawn and tightened by the Financial Services Act 1986, from which the following sections of the 1985 Act are taken in their modified form.

The rules apply when certain conditions are satisfied. First, the offer must have been made to all members on identical terms or, if it covers more than one class of share, on identical terms in relation to all the shares of each class (s 428(1)).[59] Secondly, aggregating his pre-offer holding and acceptances,[60] the offeror must have obtained 90 per cent in value of the equity of the target-company (or of any class of share to which the offer related). Provided this 90 per cent holding is acquired within four months of the offer,[61] the offeror may then serve a 'compulsory purchase' notice[62] on the remaining minority of members or class members; he must, however, do this within two months of the last acquisition or purchase contract needed to take his holding to the required 90 per cent (s 429(1) to (3)). On service of the notice, the offeror becomes entitled, and also bound, to acquire the minority shares on the terms of the offer itself (s 320(2)), although if the offer gave offerees the choice of a non-cash consideration which it is no longer possible to provide, the offeror must instead pay the cash equivalent, calculated as at the date of the notice (s 430(4)). The minority has six weeks in which to make its choice[63] where alternative consideration was offered, and at the end of six weeks from the notice the offeror must, in any case, send a copy of the notice to the company and pay over to it the price of the minority shares[64] together with an instrument of transfer; the offeror must then be registered as holder of the shares. The target-company then holds the consideration on trust for the minority (s 430(5) to (10)). Even where the offeror prefers not to make a compulsory purchase, the minority shareholders, who by now are well and truly 'locked in', have a right to demand that the offeror buys them out. This arises in the same circumstances, ie a 90 per cent holding, except that it makes no difference that some of that holding was built up by purchases outside the terms of the offer (s 430A(1)). The offeror must serve notice on the minority, setting out their rights, within one month of the date of expiry of the offer, giving the minority at least three months from the closing date of the offer in which to decide whether or not to sell (s 430B). Each minority shareholder can thus require the offeror to buy him out (s 430B(2)) and may choose which form of payment specified in the offer he will take,[65] unless a particular method is now impossible, in which case he must be paid the cash equivalent computed at the date when he required the offeror to buy him out.

Matters may be more complex where the offeror does not make all acquisitions himself. Section 430E deals with 'associates', that is to say nominees, concert party members, group companies, companies controlled through compliant boards or a one-third voting power at general meetings and, in the case of an individual, immediate family members. An offer is still treated as an offer for the 'whole' of the relevant equity, even though it excludes not only the offeror's holding but also holdings of associates, present or future. However, associate holdings and acquisitions do not count as acceptances entitling the offeror to make a compulsory purchase unless they are acquired at a price no higher than the offer or revised offer price. In contrast, they always count towards the acceptances which, at the 90 per cent level, enable the minority member to demand that the offeror buys him out. These rules will link with the rules requiring disclosure of acquisitions to 'lift the veil' from team effort takeovers – if the disclosure rules themselves operate effectively.

(3) However, the director's duty of good faith must inevitably come under sharp scrutiny when a bid is made or imminent, since his status as a director may be at stake and the result is bound to affect his personal position. He must act scrupulously, and must bear the following standards in mind.

   (a) The right of members to all available information, on an equal basis, before deciding whether to sell.
   (b) The complete suppression of personal interests.
   (c) The avoidance of the need for 'death-bed repentances' which indicate only that directors have not done their job in the past.
   (d) The desirability of following the procedure of the Code.
   (e) The importance of taking advice even in the earliest and most tentative stage of discussions in order to avoid breaches of the Code and other mistakes before the board realises they are happening.
   (f) The need for care and advice, especially but not only where the directors control the company, before becoming committed to a particular offer. Directors must avoid situations in which shareholders may be deprived of a better offer from another source, although they must equally be prepared themselves to assess the likelihood, and quality, of other offers.
   (g) An absolute prohibition on anything resembling insider dealings.
   (h) Where the company operates in the public eye, the greatest care in statements made publicly or which may find their way into the press.

(4) The Code[66] applies primarily to listed companies, but also to:

   (a) unlisted public companies;
   (b) companies whose equity has been listed in the previous 10 years;
   (c) companies, in whose equity dealings have been regularly advertised in newspapers for a continuous period of at least six months in the previous 10 years;
   (d) companies on the Alternative Investment Markets (AIM);
   (e) companies who have filed a prospectus for an equity issue at the companies' registry within the previous 10 years.

Directors of listed companies must follow the Code but some of the companies affected may be private companies and to that extent the Panel on Takeovers and Mergers (the 'Panel') will apply the Code 'with flexibility in suitable cases'. It has no legal force in itself but violations may be subject, after hearing, to private reprimand and public censure or, in an extreme case, exclusion from the securities market. It is administered by the Panel, which also acts as the consultative and disciplinary body and whose purpose is the enforcement of good business standards, not of the law.[67]

The principles of the Code are of wide application and should be heeded even by directors of companies not subject to it. These are, in essence, as follows.

(a) The spirit as well as the letter of the Code must be observed.

(b) Acceptance that the Code inevitably limits the freedom of action of the parties involved.

(c) Shareholders must be treated even-handedly, none being given information withheld from others, and must have sufficient information and time to make their decision. No relevant information should be withheld.

(d) Once a bona fide offer is made or believed to be imminent, the target-company's board must do nothing which might frustrate the offer or deprive the members of an opportunity to decide on the merits, without their consent in general meeting.[68] Such consent should always be obtained when a question arises which may involve a Panel ruling so that the members may share the responsibilities.

(e) The object of all parties must be to avoid the creation of a false market in the shares of either company.

(f) The board, once approached, must normally seek competent and independent (ie disinterested) outside advice.

(f) Rights of control must be exercised in good faith and there must be no oppression of a minority.

(h) Documents and advertisements addressed to shareholders must be prepared with the highest standards of care and accuracy.[69]

(5) Although the director's duty is owed primarily to the company and not to the members, there are areas where a direct duty to the shareholders will arise. Directors addressing advice in recommendations to the members must take responsibility for what they say (r 19.2 of the Code) and in a case where directors sent out a recommendation omitting to mention an adverse report from the stockbrokers, it was held that they had a legally enforceable duty to their own shareholders 'to be honest and a duty not to mislead'.[70] Moreover, any dissenting shareholder could properly complain if he were wrongfully subjected to compulsory purchase under s 429 (above) as a result of such a breach of duty. A personal duty will also arise if the directors hold themselves out to the shareholders as their agents for the purpose of negotiating a takeover or amalgamation.[71]

(6) The listing rules of the London Stock Exchange will apply to any listed company engaged in a takeover, but these incorporate the Code. Listed companies and AIM companies resident in the British Isles are also subject to the *Rules Governing Substantial Acquisitions of Shares* (SARs).[72] These relate to the offeror, and restrict the speed with which a purchaser may increase his holdings and voting rights to an aggregate between 15 per cent and 30 per cent. The SARs also require accelerated disclosure of share acquisitions relating to such holdings.

(7) The Fair Trading Act 1973 applies to monopoly and merger 'situations'. A monopoly exists where one-quarter or more of the market in the supply of a particular type of goods or services[73] is in the hands of one company (or connected group of companies).[74] A relevant merger arises when a takeover or merger will either lead to, or strengthen, a monopoly, or where the gross value of the assets taken over will exceed £15m. (There are also special rules for newspaper mergers.) Neither is presumed, itself, to be contrary to the public

interest, nor does either require advance notification (although the Code may require offer documents to disclose the possibility of a merger reference).

The Director General of Fair Trading may make monopoly references to the Monopolies and Mergers Commission, but only the DTI may commence a merger reference, and this power may be exercised in anticipation of a 'merger situation' arising. Having made a reference, the DTI has wide powers, including the power to stop the merger from proceeding until the Commission's report is issued. If the Commission reports that a merger is contrary to the public interest, the DTI may (at its discretion) prohibit or even undo the merger if it has already taken place. These powers are so sweeping that a clearance is often sought in advance where the bid will fall within the Act.[75]

(8) Finally, directors involved on either side of a takeover or merger must not overlook the effect of ss 151 to 154 (see **7.5**) prohibiting financial assistance by a company for the purchase of its own shares. These provisions may be a particular problem where the offeror company, or its financiers, expect to recoup their outlay from assets of the offeree companies but, even if this is not the situation, it will be necessary to examine the overall financial position of the offeror, before and after the anticipated purchase, with great care. Quite apart from the criminal sanctions for breach, there will be civil liability which can be enforced by any shareholder by derivative action.[76] Having said this, it may also be remembered that the prohibitions do not apply where the principal purpose of the transaction is not to give assistance and the transaction is made in good faith in the interests of the company (s 153).

CHAPTER 4 FOOTNOTES

1 EC Seventh Directive on Company Law (83/349/EC); EC Eighth Directive on Company Law (84/253/EC).

2 *Report of the Review Committee on the Making of Accounting Standards*, published 9 November 1988.

3 Schedule 4, para 36A.

4 Where the records are kept outside Great Britain, the accounts and returns must be made to the company at least every six months and must be sufficient to facilitate the preparation of proper annual accounts under the Act.

5 A director or other officer may, however, apply for relief by the courts under s 727.

6 See note 2, above.

7 Whether or not he is entitled to receive notice of the general meeting.

8 Section 238(1).

9 Meaning 'clear days', and excluding therefore the date of sending and the date of receipt.

10 As amended by the Companies Act 1985 (Amendment of Sections 250 and 251) Regulations 1992, SI 1992/3003.

11 Ie income from the company's ordinary activities, deducting trade discounts and VAT.

12 Companies in which the accounting company has acquired an equity stake with a view to a contribution to its own activities (presumed once a 20 per cent stake is achieved).

13 Section 390A and Companies Act 1985 (Disclosure of Remuneration for Non-audit Work) Regulations 1991, SI 1991/2128 as amended by the Companies Act 1985 (Disclosure of Remuneration for Non-Audit Work) (Amendment) Regulations 1995, SI 1995/1520. There are limited exceptions from this requirement for small and medium-sized companies.

14 Company Accounts (Disclosure of Directors' Emoluments) Regulations 1997, SI 1997/570.

15 Section 245 and Companies (Revision of Defective Accounts and Reports) Regulations 1990, SI 1990/2570.

16 Section 245A—245C.

17 Section 233.

18 Section 246. Companies Act 1985 (Accounts of Small and Medium-Sized Enterprises and Publication of Accounts in ECUs) Regulations 1992, SI 1992/2452: Companies Act 1985 (Miscellaneous Accounting Amendment) Regulations 1996, SI 1996/189 and Companies Act 1985 (Accounts of Small and Medium-Sized Companies and Minor Accounting Amendments) Regulations 1997, SI 1997/220.

19 Companies Act 1985 (Amendment of Sections 250 and 251) Regulations 1992, SI 1992/3003.

20 Companies Act 1985 (Audit Exemption) Regulations 1994, SI 1994/1935 and Companies Act 1985 (Audit Exemption) Regulations 1997, SI 1997/936. Also see Companies Act 1985 (Audit Exemption) (Amendment) Regulations 1995, SI 1995/589 and Companies Act 1985 (Audit Exemption) (Amendment) Regulations 1996, SI 1996/3080.

21 Section 248.

22 Section 255.

23 Sections 230–231.

24 Including the modified accounts of small or medium-sized companies.

25 Section 240.

26 Or that the company was an exempt dormant company.

27 Not to be confused with the chairman's report which is not a statutory document and is used for a general review.

28 A process beginning with the 1967 Act and considerably accelerated by the 1981 Act, implementing the Fourth Directive.

29 Schedule 7 permits this to be given by way of notes to the accounts instead.

30 Companies Act 1985 (Miscellaneous Accounting Amendments) Regulations 1996, SI 1996/189 and Companies Act 1985 (Directors' Report) (Statement of Payment Practice) Regulations 1997, SI 1997/571.

31 Section 235.

32 Even an auditor without a contract and appointed only by resolution would be liable in the case of negligence for any lack of skill and care and, probably, for misfeasance proceedings.

33 *Re Thomas Gerrard & Sons Ltd* [1967] 2 All ER 525, indicating that the standards required might be proved by the relevant Statement on Auditing issued by the Institute of Chartered Accountants in England & Wales.

34 *Derry v Peek* (1889) 14 App Cas 337.

35 *Hedley Byrne & Co v Heller & Partners Ltd* [1964] AC 465. Liability was said to arise because the defendant assumed a duty to speak, and therefore to speak carefully. The *JEB* case described below imposed liability on the wider principle that loss to a party such as the plaintiff was reasonably foreseeable.

36 [1983] 1 All ER 587.

37 [1990] 1 All ER 568. *Caparo* has been followed at first instance in *Morgan Crucible Co plc v Hill Samuel Bank Ltd and Others* [1990] 3 All ER 330.

38 *Re Allen Craig & Co (London) Ltd* [1934] Ch 483.

39 This applies also to a retiring auditor who is being replaced and a resigning auditor whose resignation produces a casual vacancy which is now being filled.

40 Part II of the Companies Act 1989. This is one part of the 1989 Act which does not operate by reuniting, adding to or deleting the 1985 Act, so that statutory reference to rules introduced by Part II will in fact be references to the 1989 Act.

41 *Arenson v Casson, Beckman, Rutley & Co* [1978] AC 405.

42 *Hedley Byrne & Co Ltd v Heller & Partners Ltd* [1964] AC 465. See also note 35 above. On the *Hedley Byrne* principle, a disclaimer is not an 'exclusion' since it prevents a duty arising; on the *JEB* principle, a disclaimer is an exclusion.

43 *Commercial Banking Co of Sydney v R H Brown & Co* [1972] 126 CLR 337.

44 *Baber v Kenwood Manufacturing Ltd* [1978] 1 Lloyd's Rep 175.

45 A distribution means every kind of distribution of assets to members, in cash or kind, but not an issue of fully or partly paid bonus shares, a redemption out of capital or unrealised profits, certain types of capital reductions, and distributions on winding up. For tax purposes, s 209 of the Income and Corporation Taxes Act 1988 (ICTA 1988) defines distribution.

46 Guidelines for determining the amount of realised profits and losses are given by s 275, based on accepted accounting principles. Account is taken of revaluations (below). Section 276 deals with distribution in kind. Where the asset contains an element of unrealised profit, it is to be treated as although realised for the present purposes. This is primarily intended to facilitate 'demergers' though it could apply equally to a distribution to a single member, especially where s 264 does not apply because the company is a private company.

47 Unless previously written off in a capital reduction or reorganisation.

48 Meaning 'any consideration by the directors' of a fixed asset value at any particular time, whether or not there is an actual revaluation.

49 Special provision is made by s 278 for companies which, before 22 December 1980 were authorised by their Articles to issue bonus shares paid up in part or in full.

50 *Ammonia Soda Co v Chamberlain* [1918] 1 Ch 266.

51 Special provision is made by s 265 for 'investment companies'.

52 Including the use of distributable profits to give financial assistance for the acquisition of its shares or in connection with a purchase or redemption of its own shares.

53 *Flitcroft's case* (1882) 21 ChD 519.

54 *Moxham v Grant* [1900] 1 QB 88.

55 *Precision Dippings Ltd v Precision Dippings Marketing Ltd* [1985] 3 WLR 812.

56 *Savoy Hotel Investigation* (s 432 (s 165(6), of the 1948 Act)) (HMSO, 1954).

57 *Hogg v Cramphorn Ltd* [1967] Ch 254.

58 *Re A Company (No 008699 of 1985)* [1986] BCLC 382.

59 Terms are 'identical' if variations are made only to take account of restrictions which a foreign legal system imposes on the form of consideration which an overseas member may accept for his shares: s 428(3). 'Class' probably means 'class created by the Articles or terms of issue', not by special contract with a particular member.

60 Ie acceptances of the offer terms. Purchases made on special terms are liable to run into problems with the *Takeover Code* and, where a director is selling, may call his good faith into question – especially if he has recommended the offer. Nevertheless, the real damage is done only if the

special deal invoked a better price than the offer. Accordingly, s 429(8) allows special deals to be treated as 'acceptances' if the price did not exceed the offer or increased offer price.

61 A new offer starts time running afresh. But a revision pursuant to the terms of the original offer and counting earlier acceptances of the revised offer is not a 'new' offer and time runs from the date of the original offer: s 428(7).

62 Serving a copy on the target-company together with a statutory declaration that all the requisite conditions are met: s 429(4). Where the offeror is 'nearly there' in terms of a 90 per cent holding, he may be authorised by the court to serve notice under s 429 if there is an untraceable member whose shares would, if purchased, tip the balance and the court considers the price 'fair and reasonable': s 430C(5). But the court is unlikely to make an order if the minority comprises a large number of members who did not accept the offer.

63 Or to object to the court (s 430C) which can exempt his shares or alter the terms of acquisition. Costs will not normally be awarded against the objector unless he delayed or is thought to be making trouble unnecessarily. An objection 'freezes' the compulsory acquisition: s 430C(2).

64 Or allot to the target-company if the offer is share for share: s 430(8).

65 He or the offeror may ask the court to lay down the terms of acquisition: s 430C(3). An offeror who applies to the court will normally pay the costs of the application.

66 *The City Code on Takeovers and Mergers* issued on the authority of the Panel on Takeovers and Mergers, and amended periodically. Copies can be obtained from the Secretary of the Panel, PO Box 226, The Stock Exchange Building, London EC2P 2SX.

67 But it is judicially reviewable. Although decisions of the Panel can be challenged on the basis of serious error (and not merely error) the fact that the court can review the panel's decisions (*R v Panel on Takeovers and Mergers ex parte Datafin* [1987] 2 WLR 699) does not lead automatically to the conclusion that the Code is enforceable between the parties of a takeover. It may in the near future effectively become a term of membership of investment exchange, however, and this may enable compensation to be recovered under the Financial Services Act 1986 in some cases.

68 See note 58 above.

69 In which case the 'spirit' of the Code may be extremely difficult to ascertain. It does seem to be accepted that the Code is not broken by a profit forecast which turns out to be wrong, provided that it was prepared with due care.

70 *Gething v Kilner* [1972] 1 All ER 1164.

71 *Allen v Hyatt* (1914) 30 TLR 444, where they had to account for their personal profit on the sale of the shares. The shareholders (and not merely the company) were able to take action because of the directors' implied agency on their behalf.

72 Together with certain companies traded under Stock Exchange Rules.

73 Or export of goods.

74 Or where there is a cartel.

75 Under the Code, an offer may have to contain terms dealing with the effect of a reference to the commission.

76 And, notwithstanding, that the company entered into an 'unlawful' transaction, it too may be able to sue: *Selangor Rubber Estates Ltd v Craddock (No 3)* [1968] 1 WLR 1555.

Chapter 5

DUTIES OF DIRECTORS

5.1 SOURCES OF DUTIES

The duties of directors derive from their position in relation to the company, as this has evolved through decisions of the courts. Although successive Companies Acts have increasingly regulated particular types of transaction involving directors, they do not impose any general duty of good faith or competence. It is necessary before going any further, therefore, briefly to analyse the position of directors in terms of the general law. It is an amalgamation of several elements.

(1) *Agent*, in that the director acts not on his own behalf but that of the company.
(2) *Trustee*, in that although he does not own company assets he controls the assets and exercises powers for the company's benefit and not his own. As such, he owes fiduciary duties to the company.
(3) *Employee*, in that a paid, executive director has similar rights and duties to those of any other employee.
(4) *Professional adviser*, in that he renders services for reward (even as a non-executive fee-earner) and must accept the burden of skill and care which falls upon independent contractors of that type.[1]

The director does not fall exactly within any of these categories since his function is unique, but his duties derive from principles applicable to them, and break down into two broad types – duties of 'good faith' and duties of skill and care. Virtually every duty or liability can be seen to fall under one of these headings, and the obligations imposed by the Act may be categorised in a similar way.

There is, as we shall see, not a great deal of debate about the content of the duties gathered under the heading 'good faith'. Those gathered under the heading 'care' raise more problems. There are various reasons for this. First, current case-law may well understate the extent of a director's ordinary obligation to exercise a reasonable level of diligence and skill in the performance of his functions. Secondly, increasing statutory duties almost certainly carry over into increased demands upon the director to show proper competence and attention to his functions. Thirdly, the lengthening arm of insolvency law imposes direct liability and possible disqualification for certain types of misbehaviour, which may include inattention or incompetence. Not only does this have immediate implications for directors; insofar as insolvency law imposes greater burdens on directors than those previously imposed by the courts, it may well be the cue for the courts themselves to do the same. Fourthly, where a company is insolvent, there are significant signs that insolvency officers such as liquidators, taking their lead from the reformed insolvency laws, are subjecting the conduct of directors to much more rigorous scrutiny, as a matter of routine, than was the case even a few years ago. This is particularly so since late 1994 when the DTI adopted a far more rigorous approach to the pursuit of unfit directors.

(A useful and authoritative guide to the practical and ethical aspects of this subject is published by the Institute of Directors (*Guidelines for Directors*).)

5.2   DUTIES TO WHOM

The general rule is that directors' duties are owed to the company and not to individual shareholders,[2] nor to the company's creditors.[3] This was recently confirmed by the Court of Appeal in *Stein v Blake*.[4] The plaintiff and the defendant were each 50 per cent shareholders in the relevant companies. The defendant was the sole director of these companies and he transferred their assets to other companies which were under his control. The plaintiff claimed that the defendant had been in breach of fiduciary duty in misappropriating the assets and sought to recover the loss sustained by him in the diminution in the value of his shares as a result of the misappropriation. It was held that the plaintiff had no separate cause of action. The loss was one that was recoverable only by the company and not by the shareholder. Indeed, the Court of Appeal felt that the case was so hopeless that leave to appeal should never have been granted in the first place and set aside the leave which an earlier Court of Appeal had granted. Possible exceptions to this general rule will be discussed as they arise. First, however, the general rule leads inevitably to the question – how is the company to enforce those duties when the directors are in control of its affairs, including the commencement of proceedings? The courts have never found a satisfactory answer to this question, although the so-called 'derivative action' by a minority shareholder is an established possibility.[5] Since the duty is owed to the company, and the company in general meeting can usually ratify, or indeed pardon, a director's defaults, majority control will often prevent action being taken by the company itself. Questions will always arise where the director in question votes his own shares in support of such a resolution,[6] but this is the sort of interference with the director's proprietorial right to vote his own shares which the courts will countenance only in exceptional cases.[7] In 1980, Parliament provided shareholders with the right to complain to the court of conduct which was 'unfairly prejudicial' to their interests; but it has only been in recent years that the courts' interpretation of this remedy, confirmed by amendment to the legislation, has begun to give it real teeth, and then usually only in the case of smaller and private companies.

5.2.1   'The company'

When the director is told that his duties are owed to the company, he may well ask what this means. The company is an abstraction: is he to have regard to the interests of the present members, or those of future members, or some combination of the two? The question is most acute where the two interests conflict, for example, where there is a choice between paying profits by way of dividend and retaining them against future needs. Here the director is entitled and indeed bound to exercise his business judgement in striking a balance between two legitimate but competing demands.[8] Similarly, where directors receive a takeover offer unwelcome to them, they must tread carefully so as not to prevent the present membership from having a fair and informed opportunity to consider and accept the offer. There may be genuine grounds for belief, however, that the offer is not in the long-term interests of the company (including perhaps those of the workforce: see **5.2.3**) and the directors may, on that basis, refuse actively to promote an offer which merely provides the present membership with the best currently available price for their shares.[9] To say that directors must always promote such an offer would, of course, come dangerously close to a breach of the general rule that duties are not owed to shareholders as such.

5.2.2   Creditors

The established rule is that directors owe their duties to the company, and not to its present or future creditors as such (see **5.2**). There have, in recent years, been judicial comments which might be construed in the opposite sense. In *Winkworth v Edward Baron Development Co Ltd*,[10] Lord Templeman said:

> 'a company owes a duty to its creditors, present and future . . . to keep its property inviolate and available for repayment of its debts. The conscience of the company, as well as its management, is confided to its directors. *A duty is owed by the directors to the company and to the creditors* of the company to ensure that the affairs of the company are properly administered and that its property is not dissipated or exploited for the benefit of the directors themselves to the prejudice of the creditors'. (Emphasis added.)

Despite this, the law does not appear to have changed so as to afford a direct personal remedy to a creditor who claims that directors have mismanaged the company's affairs or even misappropriated its assets. Indeed, in *Kuwait Asia Bank EC v National Mutual Life Nominees Ltd*,[11] Lord Templeman said 'A director does not by reason only of his position as director owe any duty to creditors or to trustees for creditors of the company.' Thus, there seems no possibility that a creditor could personally bring an action against a director for breach of duty. The real development appears to have been the recognition that, once the company is insolvent,[12] a major change in interest takes place. The members' residual interest in the company's assets is replaced by the interest of the creditors, who will be repaid, if at all, from those assets. This is reflected by a change in the substance of the directors' duties; in exercising their functions, they must now have regard to the interests of the creditors.[13] *It does not follow that the duty is owed to the creditor, or to any particular creditor*, and there are indeed very sound reasons why not. The interests of creditors will often vary as widely as their ability to safeguard themselves. The whole point of insolvency law is to impose a regime of equality on these divergent interests – an impartial insolvency officer[14] is appointed to ensure that, as far as may be, the assets are efficiently gathered in, realised and applied in discharging the company's debts on a pro rata basis. This may be an equality of misery for the creditors, but it is based on the premise that to allow creditors to continue to take their own actions against the company would benefit only those strong enough to pressure the company into payment or swift enough to obtain judgments which it is still able to pay. The insolvency officer therefore represents the interests of all the creditors; he has a wide variety of redress against delinquent management, and it would be both pointless and damaging to have his functions bypassed by a particular creditor making a claim on his own account. The true position is reflected in *West Mercia Safetywear Ltd v Dodds*.[15] Here a director used company funds to pay off a debt owed by its holding company, which he had personally guaranteed. He knew at the time that both companies were insolvent. The liquidator of the subsidiary recovered the payment from the director on the basis that he was in breach of duty to the company, 'when, for his own purposes, he caused the £4,000 to be transferred in disregard of the interests of the general creditors'. In this case, the Court of Appeal adopted the approach of the Australian court in *Walker v Wimbourne*[16] and the New Zealand court in *Kinsela v Russell Kinsela Pty Ltd*.[17] In particular, Dillon LJ approved the following dictum of Street CJ in the Kinsela case:

> 'In a solvent company the proprietary interests of the shareholders entitle them as a general body to be regarded as the company when questions of the duty of directors arise. If, as a general body, they authorise to ratify a particular action of the directors, there can be no challenge to the validity of what the directors have done. But where a company is insolvent the interests of the creditors intrude. They are respectively entitled, through the mechanism of liquidation, to displace the power of the shareholders and directors to deal with the company's assets. It is in a practical sense their assets and not the shareholders' assets that, through the medium of the company, are under the management of the directors pending either liquidation, return to solvency or the imposition of some alternative administration.'

The interests of creditors, then, supply the content of a duty which continues, nevertheless, to be owed to the company itself. Frequently, the duty will actually be enforced not by the company but by an insolvency officer who, on appointment, not only takes over the company's claims but also has a battery of remedies of his own.

There are, however, further considerations. The onset of financial difficulties which marks the shift in content of directors' duties outlined above will also be the trigger for an obligation, imposed by s 214 of the Insolvency Act 1986, to begin to act in protection of the interests of creditors.[18] Very often, the only way to protect those interests will be to have an insolvency officer appointed, in which case management of the company will be removed from the board. Secondly, the 'interests' of creditors are frequently conflicting rather than uniform; some may benefit from an immediate realisation of assets, others from keeping the healthier parts of the business intact. Specifically, secured creditors are in a much stronger position than unsecured creditors, since assets are already earmarked for the discharge of the debts owing to them and they are able, therefore, to look after themselves. Although it would be wrong for the directors altogether to ignore the interests of secured creditors,[19] they may legitimately consider that those of the unsecured creditors require more immediate protection.

Finally, there is a problem which has yet to be considered by the courts, which tends to divide the world into members on the one hand, and creditors on the other. Many modern forms of lending give the lender rights of control or participation in the company which begin to blur this distinction. Although the issue is unlikely to arise except in relation to larger, and probably listed, companies, there remains a question of how such interests are properly characterised in terms of the 'director's duty to the company', discussed above.

5.2.3 Employees

Directors are now obliged by law to have regard to the interests of the company's employees in general when performing their functions (s 309). The Act makes this obligation a part of the director's fiduciary duties and, as such, it is owed to the company and not to the employees, still less to any one employee in particular.[20] Consequently, it is 'enforceable in the same way as any other fiduciary duty', that is to say primarily by the company, and not by any employee or trade union. In the last resort, a minority – which may, of course, include employee-members – may be able to enforce s 309, but this possibility will be hedged around with the restrictions applying to any minority action (see **7.1**). Nor does the section give the board carte blanch to put the interests of the work-force higher than those of members. This is the sort of commercial judgment with which both Parliament and the courts have been reluctant to interfere. The significance of the section lies in a statutory recognition which what may loosely be described as 'social' criteria – the interests and welfare of the workforce[21] – may imperceptibly merge with, and become, legitimate commercial considerations for the board. In a sense, it is misleading to describe this as a duty. Rather it is a defence when directors are criticised by shareholders for acting with social responsibility towards employees. Suppose, for example, that a board of directors were to make ex gratia redundancy payments to employees who were being laid off and the members complained that the payments were excessively high. This statutory provision would provide a defence for the directors who could argue that they were under an obligation to have regard to the interests of the employees as well as to the interests of its members. Accordingly, the members as a body would in these circumstances have no ground for complaint.

5.2.4 Nominees

Where a director is a nominee of a parent company, or of a shareholder or creditor, or of a union or of the workforce, he must bear in mind that there is no such thing as a delegate director in English law. Every director has exactly the same responsibility to the company as a whole and, if he neglects that responsibility in the interests or on the orders of his principal, he will be guilty of a breach of duty. Thus, he must not starve a subsidiary out of business merely because it suits the parent company to do so,[22] nor must he be guided solely by the interests of the group as a whole, at least where the subsidiary has separate creditors.[23]

This principle is widely disregarded in practice, and nominee directors often see themselves simply as watchdogs for those who put them on the board. They are wrong in adopting this approach to their duties and, before accepting office, they should remember that the law expects them to devote their loyalty to the company as a whole. On the other hand, the obligation imposed by s 309 (see **5.2.3**) spares the employee director much embarrassment, for it means that he must have regard to the interests of the workforce. Even now, however, he must be careful. He must not represent only those appointing him. He must look to the interests of 'the company's employees in general' (s 309(1)) and he, like any other director, must also balance these, where necessary, with those of the membership comprising the company.

5.3 DUTY OF GOOD FAITH

Essentially, the director's duty is to act bona fide in the interests of the company and to use his powers for the purposes for which they were conferred. It will be seen that these are not necessarily the same things. A director will be acting bona fide if he genuinely considers that he is acting in the company's interest and the test is thus subjective.[24] But while still acting in this belief, he may, none the less, use his powers for a purpose for which they were not intended. In this case, there is no bad faith, but there is a breach of duty and this time the test is objective. A characteristic example of the second type of situation is where directors issue shares, not to raise capital needed by the company but, for example, to forestall a takeover bid which threatens their control of the company.[25] In *Re Smith and Fawcett Ltd*,[26] Lord Greene MR said that directors must act: 'Bona fide in what they consider – not what a court may consider – is in the interests of the company, and not for any collateral purpose'. In *Hogg v Cramphorn Ltd*,[27] Buckley J said that this meant that directors would be in breach of their duty to the company if they acted either:

(1)   not bona fide in the interests of the company (in other words, a subjective test); or
(2)   for some improper purpose (in other words an objective test) even if they themselves believed reasonably that they were acting bona fide in the interests of the company.

The director's duty is commonly described as one of absolute loyalty and utmost good faith to his company. Like many attempts to summarise a complex relationship, this is accurate, as far as it goes. But as we have already seen, more than good faith is required. A director may act honestly but be in breach of duty; he may not have enriched himself at the company's expense, but may still be liable to account for a personal profit.[28] It is for these reasons that the use of the word 'trustees' in the next three sections is not merely fanciful.

We can now look at some examples.

5.4   TRUSTEES

5.4.1   Of powers

The director's duty is to use his powers for the purposes for which they were intended, that is for the benefit of the company as a whole and not for any 'collateral purpose'.[29] The courts will not interfere in the exercise of the director's discretion or business judgement,[30] and must therefore be satisfied that the purpose is unauthorised. Thus, the power to issue shares (itself controlled by s 80) must be used for the purpose of raising capital for the company and not to defeat a controlling member[31] or to defeat a takeover bid.[32]

In *Bamford v Bamford*,[33] directors issued shares to another party for just such a purpose. The allotment was held voidable, but since the company as a whole was the injured party it could, after full disclosure, approve the allotment by ordinary resolution at a general meeting. The case illustrates that:

(1)   honesty or good faith alone are insufficient to prevent a breach of the director's duty of good faith;
(2)   misuse of power for an improper purpose is a breach of duty, albeit not of the duty to act in good faith;

(3) where, however, there is good faith the company may usually ratify or adopt the improper act.[34]

The directors' duties in this most important area of the issuing of shares have come into question on a number of occasions. The law has come close to saying that there may be no issue except for the purpose of raising capital to meet the company's needs, and in the following examples the directors can be seen to have overlooked this limitation on their powers.

(1) Where directors fearing a bid issued shares to trustees for the employees, confident that the trustees would support the board in the coming struggle. They honestly believed that they were acting in the company's best interests, but were held to have misused their powers. The share issue, although prima facie invalid, might be 'ratified' by the general meeting, but the new shares could not be voted.[35]
(2) Where directors sought to place valued company assets beyond 'the speculator's grasp' by issuing shares to trustees of a staff benevolent fund.[36]

Even rights issues may fall foul of this rule, as where directors made rights issues which they knew the minority could not take up, in order to gain total control and create tax advantages for the majority[37] or reduce the minority's share of the profit on a proposed (but undisclosed) sale.[38]

Conversely, in *Howard Smith Ltd v Ampol Petroleum Ltd*,[39] the board supported a takeover bid and, faced with a 55 per cent majority proposing to reject it, issued sufficient shares to the bidder to reduce the objectors to below 50 per cent and thus to enable the bid to proceed. The Privy Council held that even though the company in fact needed new capital, the primary purpose of the issue was to facilitate the bid; even though there was no self-interest, this was enough to have the issue set aside.

The question arises whether shares may *ever* be issued except for the purpose of raising capital. In the *Howard Smith* case, the Privy Council acknowledged that, in theory, a company's Articles may allow shares to be issued for other purposes. An obvious example would be the issue to a director of any necessary qualification shares. Beyond such 'routine' issues, however, it is the results of the cases which are striking rather than any theory based on the construction of the Articles, and these results do strongly suggest that for practical purposes shares may never be issued to alter the balance of power within the company. It more or less follows that they may not be issued simply to facilitate or obstruct an offer. This seems to be confirmed by decisions which have considered the position of directors when bids are made or expected. It is accepted that directors are under no duty to recommend any bid, even the better of two offers (as long as they do not mislead the members),[40] but they must not do anything which prevents the members from considering and accepting an offer.[41] If this is so, it is hard to see how a share issue designed to tilt the balance against a superior offer, or in favour of an inferior one, could ever be upheld, let alone an issue designed to manipulate acceptance or rejection of the only available offer. Indeed, directors must take care that an imminent offer does not paralyse their power to issue shares altogether. Suppose that an issue is proposed in order to finance the purchase of a new business or new assets. This is perfectly legitimate. Either the issue, or the purchase itself, may serve to defeat or discourage the offer. Does this make the proposal illegitimate?

To answer the question posed above, it is necessary to go back to basics. Directors must exercise the powers for the purposes for which they are granted, which means for the benefit of the company as a whole. Assuming that they have given the matter proper consideration and are acting in good faith, the proposed purchase will satisfy that basic criterion. As long as the directors proceed carefully – in particular, as long as the records of their deliberations truthfully record the commercial basis on which they are acting – their *primary* purpose is legitimate and any challenge to the exercise of their powers will fail, even if there is evidence that they were also very happy to think that their actions would deter or defeat a bidder.[42] If, on the other hand, the transaction is window-dressing for an effort to retain control, the primary purpose is not to benefit the company. If directors knowingly use their powers for a wrongful purpose, they break their duty of good faith, and if they do so unknowingly, they, in effect, break their duty of skill and care.

This approach is confirmed in the judgment of Lord Wilberforce in the *Howard Smith* case:

> '. . . it is . . . too narrow an approach to say that the only valid purpose for which shares may be issued is to raise capital for the company. The discretion is not in terms limited in this way: the law should not impose such a limitation on directors' powers. To define in advance an exact limit beyond which directors must not pass is . . . impossible. This clearly cannot not be done by enumeration, since the variety of situations facing directors of different types of company in different situations cannot be anticipated. . . . It is necessary to start with a consideration of a power whose exercise is in question, in this case a power to issue shares. Having ascertained, on a fair view, the nature of this power, and having defined as can best be done in the light of modern conditions the, or some, limits within which it may be exercised, it is then necessary for the court, if a particular exercise of it is challenged, to examine the substantial purpose for which it was exercised and to reach a conclusion whether that purpose was proper or not. In doing so it will necessarily give credit to the bona fide opinion of the directors if such is found to exist, and will respect their judgement as to matters of management; having done this, the ultimate conclusion has to be as to the side of a fairly broad line on which the case falls. . . . There may be reasons other than to raise capital for which shares may be issued.'

The learned judge then went on to cite with approval the decision in *Harlowe's Nominees Pty Ltd v Woodside (Lakes) Entrance Oil Co*[43] where an issue of shares was made to a large oil company in order to secure the financial stability of the company. This was held by the court to be within the powers of the directors notwithstanding that it had the effect of defeating an attempt by a bidder to secure control of the company by buying up the company's shares.

Perhaps an alternative way of looking at the role of the directors in issuing shares, other than to raise capital, is to consider the division of power within the company as between the members in general meeting and the board of directors. It could be argued that, in the absence of a contrary provision in the Articles, the issue of shares is primarily a matter for the members rather than for the directors. This is reflected in the requirement of s 80 that the authority of the members is needed if the directors are to make an issue of equity shares. Any such issue made by the board without members' approval must be looked upon as being beyond the powers of the directors.

This balance of power is reversed in the case of a wholly owned subsidiary. Here the power is very clearly in the hands of the shareholder (the parent company) with the board of directors usually being treated as little more than managers.

5.4.2 Of assets

Just as directors are trustees of the powers entrusted to them, so it is with the company's property. The ownership of the assets is not vested in the directors so that in this respect they differ from the trustees of, for example, a will or a settlement. However, the assets are in their hands and under their control and they have all the duties of trustees in their dealings with them. Thus, if they dispose of the assets without consideration and merely because they have been ordered to do so by the majority shareholder who nominated them, they will have a liability for misapplication which can be enforced by the minority shareholders.[44] This principle applies to any disposal or use of the company's property which is unauthorised or not bona fide in the interests of the company. So, if only the full board of directors has power to pay remuneration for services rendered to the company, no single director or committee of the board can make a valid contract binding the company to pay and the company will be entitled to recover any payments actually made.[45]

In these circumstances, the directors must repay what they have misappropriated, whether or not they acted honestly, for example, as follows:

(1) where they apply assets for an ultra vires purpose;[46]
(2) where they pay compensation for loss of office without disclosure to and approval of the members under s 312;[47]
(3) where they pay dividends otherwise than from available profits;[48]
(4) where they provide financial assistance for the purchase of the company's own shares in breach of s 151.[49]

We may note that 'property' or 'assets' bears an extended meaning for the purpose of the directors' duties as trustees. The trust extends to:

(1) assets which are received by the directors in circumstances which oblige them to hold for the company's benefit, as where they are paid commission by third parties on company contracts;[50]
(2) inventions, discoveries, technical or confidential information acquired by directors in the course of business;[51]
(3) business advantages, such as opportunities to enter into contracts, which directors obtain by virtue of their position whether or not the company could have taken full advantage of them.[52]

It will be seen that cases of this type also illustrate the principle that a director must not make an unauthorised personal profit out of his position. This question is discussed below but it is really the other side of the same coin. The director as trustee is liable if he misapplies the company's assets; and, if he directs them into his own pocket, he is equally liable on the alternative ground that he must not use his position to enrich himself.[53]

5.5 ASSETS: FIDUCIARY DUTIES UNDER THE ACT

In 1980, Parliament intervened in an effort to stop suspect asset dealings at source as far as possible. This was done by requiring 'substantial property transactions' between the company and a director to be given prior approval by the company. Section 320, which now embodies the main rule, requires an ordinary resolution of the general meeting to approve any 'arrangement'[54] by which:

(1) a director acquires[55] a non-cash asset from the company; or
(2) a director transfers a non-cash asset to the company.

A 'non-cash asset' means just that – anything except money.[56] Section 320 is not intended to catch small transactions, which may be quite legitimate and will not usually be dangerous enough to justify the statutory intervention. It applies therefore only if the asset in question is worth £100,000, or 10 per cent of the company's asset value[57] and, in any event, must be worth more than £2,000.[58]

The results of a breach of the approval requirement are set out in s 322 and resemble the remedies developed by the courts.

(1) The company may rescind the arrangement, and restore the status quo. But, like rescission in general, this may require timely action by the company, for the arrangement is not absolutely void and the power to rescind is lost if:

   (a) restitution of the asset or the price has become impossible;
   (b) the company has been indemnified in full against any loss caused by the transaction;
   (c) rescission would prejudice third party rights acquired in good faith and in ignorance of the breach of s 320; or
   (d) the transaction has been affirmed by the general meeting within a reasonable time.

   These are similar to bars on the right of rescission in equity. The last bar is, apparently, designed to encourage prompt disclosure of transactions for which approval should have been sought when they were first entered into. If such disclosure is not made, the power to rescind will endure for a considerable period (subject to (a) to (c) above) since the transfer may well not be revealed to the members until the next accounts. By then a 'reasonable time' may well have lapsed (unless, perhaps, that time is measured by the next accounts) and affirmation within (d) above will be out of time. 'Affirmation' does not; in any case, seem to require a resolution to be passed[61] and acquiescence by a general meeting to which disclosure has been made seems to be sufficient. But even though statutory affirmation will exclude the right of rescission under s 322 only if it occurs within a reasonable time, there is nothing in s 322 to prevent the company from giving positive approval to the transaction by ordinary resolution. This it may do whether or not the statutory period for affirmation has elapsed, and the effect will be to waive the irregularity for all purposes.

(2) Whether or not the arrangement is rescinded, the director in breach (with any other directors authorising the arrangement) will be liable:

    (a) to account to the company for any profit made; or

    (b) to indemnify the company for any loss suffered. See *Duckwari plc v Offerventure Ltd*[59] and *Re Duckwari plc*[60] discussed below.

Authorising directors have a defence of ignorance of the circumstances constituting the contravention, but this will require a considerable degree of innocence, if not actual negligence, and will not be an easy defence to sustain.

These statutory liabilities are, it must be remembered, imposed over and above the fiduciary duties already imposed upon directors by the courts. Quite a number of breaches of s 320 are likely to occur in all innocence but, even where this is so, many will be breaches of fiduciary duty. In that event, outsiders acquiring company assets with actual or constructive knowledge of the director's breach of duty will become constructive trustees of those assets and liable to make restitution to the company. Where the misapplication of assets falls within s 320, the Act makes special provision for certain third parties:

(1) shadow directors, who are treated in the same way as directors (s 320(3));

(2) outsiders 'connected' with a director, who are subject to the same liabilities as the director unless they can show ignorance of the circumstances constituting the contravention.

'Connected persons' are defined elaborately and at length by s 346. Briefly, they comprise:

(1) the director's spouse, children, and step-children up to 18 years old;

(2) companies with which he is 'associated' by control:

    (a) of one-fifth of the equity by nominal value, or

    (b) of one-fifth of the voting rights;

(3) trustees[62] for the director, or any of the foregoing;

(4) partners[63] of the director, including partners in Scottish 'firms'.

The net cast by s 320 also catches transactions involving subsidiaries and the directors of holding companies. These will require prior approval by both companies. The section has to stop somewhere, however, when the point is reached that transactions, if not actually harmless, can harm only the participants. Consequently, s 320 does not apply at all to intra-group transactions where the subsidiaries are wholly owned. Nor is prior approval required for a party to receive a non-cash asset 'in his character as a member' (s 321(3)). This seems to cover an entitlement, under the Articles, to receive payment in kind,[64] but it may not be very wise to rely upon this exemption; a court may take a different view of the dual capacity of the director/member from that taken by those who authorised the transfer.

In *Re a Company (No 0032314 of 1992), Duckwari Plc v Offerventure Ltd*,[65] the defendant company had entered into a contract to buy land for £495,000. In making the contract, it had paid a 10 per cent deposit to stakeholders. The defendant company was in fact connected with a director of the plaintiff company. This director had arranged for the benefit of the purchase contract to be assigned to the plaintiff company without the necessary approval of a general meeting of the members of that company. It was held that there had been a transfer to the plaintiff company of the benefit of the defendant company's interest under the purchase contract. The value of the asset acquired was at least £49,500, the amount of the deposit. As this was greater than had been 10 per cent of the asset value of the company as shown by its last accounts, the arrangement was one which required approval of the members.

An enquiry was ordered by the Court of Appeal as to what damage, if any, had resulted to the company for the purpose of assessing any indemnity which should be payable to the company under s 322(3)(b). This enquiry was subsequently reported as *Re Duckwari plc*.[66] Here, Judge Paul Baker QC found that there was no recoverable loss. The only mischief which s 320 sought to avoid was the acquisition by a company at an inflated value or the disposal by a company at an undervalue. If the company either could not or chose not to avoid the transaction, the recoverable loss would include the difference between the market value at the date of the transaction and the price paid. However, since in this case the asset would be returned, no claim for a loss of value could arise.

In *British Racing Drivers Club v Hextall Erskine*,[67] solicitors who failed to note the need for a s 320 resolution in a joint venture were held to be liable in negligence. In *Demite v Protec Health*,[68] s 320 was held to apply to sales by receivers.

5.5.1   Liability for ultra vires transactions

It will be recalled that ss 35 and 35A (as inserted by the 1989 Act) provide that the company may be bound by transactions which are ultra vires the Memorandum or beyond the limits of the directors' power to act on its behalf. Standing alone, these sections might well have validated a transaction even though the other party was a director or some other person closely connected with the company. This would have been an odd result, given that ultra vires and unauthorised dealings by the board have always been very clear breaches of duty[69] and that ss 35 and 35A are at pains not to cast doubt on that basic proposition (see **1.5.2** and **3.10.2**). To make this clear, s 322A specifically enables the company to avoid any transaction with a director[70] in connection with which the board exceeded its powers under the company's constitution.

Whether or not the transaction is avoided, the director and those who authorised the transaction are liable to account for any direct or indirect gain which results to them, and to indemnify the company against any resulting loss.[71] This is quite apart from any non-statutory liability for breach of duty or any liability which might arise for breach of some other statutory provision such as breach of s 320. The transaction itself will cease to be voidable by the company in a number of situations:

(a)   where restitution of the subject-matter is no longer possible;
(b)   where the company has been indemnified;
(c)   where an innocent third party[72] has acquired rights for value and in good faith and would be adversely affected if the transaction were avoided; and
(d)   if the company ratifies the transaction in general meeting.[73]

It should be noted that a resolution which ratifies such an action does not of itself affect any liability incurred by the director or directors concerned or by any other person. Section 35(3) expressly provides that relief from any such liability must be agreed to separately by a further special resolution.

Although, as noted above, these provisions are meant to preserve and clarify what was already to a great extent the law, they may focus third parties' attention on the need to ensure absolute compliance with the Memorandum and Articles[74] or obtain prior shareholder approval for all deals which involve or may involve directors and connected parties. If so, it may well be felt that Parliament has somewhat overstepped the mark – the philosophy of ss 35 and 35A is to free third parties from the need to check on the company's capacity and the directors' authority, but this is precisely what a cautious third party may wish to do in the light of s 322A.

5.6 TRUSTEES OF THEIR POSITIONS

5.6.1 Personal profit

Flowing naturally from the director's position both as agent and as trustee is the rule that he must not make a personal profit from his position beyond what he receives in the form of authorised remuneration. The leading case of *Regal (Hastings) Ltd v Gulliver*[75] is worth noting as it indicates the width and strictness of the rule. In that case a company owned a cinema and wished to purchase two others with a view to selling all three as a going concern. It formed a subsidiary to buy the two additional cinemas but could only afford to contribute £2,000 of the required share capital of £5,000. Accordingly, the remaining 3,000 shares were taken up by the directors. The shares in both companies were sold off and the profit on the subsidiary's shares (2,000 being sold by the company and 3,000 by the directors) amounted to £2.80 per share. The new owners of the parent company then caused it to sue the directors for the profit which they had made and it was held by the House of Lords that they must repay.

The case teaches many hard lessons in the sphere of directors' duties, including the following.

(1) The fact that they acted in good faith and that the company itself could not have subscribed for the shares was no defence. The directors' opportunity came to them because of their position and this was sufficient to require them to 'disgorge' their profits.

(2) There was no merit in the claim because it benefited only the buyers who were presumably content with the price which they had agreed to pay for the shares. So the recovery of the directors' profit came as an unmerited windfall. If anyone was to benefit, it should have been the original outside shareholders who sold their shares at a price which did not reflect that part of the profit which the directors were eventually required to pay over. This is a problem which can always arise where a company changes hands after some breach of duty has occurred but before any proceedings are taken.

(3) Directors should therefore bear in mind that what they do today, confident in the knowledge that the general meeting will support them, may fall tomorrow under the hostile scrutiny of strangers or indeed of a liquidator or inspector. All their actions should be decided by the criterion of whether they will stand such scrutiny.

(4) Where directors do have majority support at the general meeting, there is nothing to prevent them submitting proposals of the *Regal* type for ratification by the members by ordinary resolution. This will protect them in the future provided there is no fraud on the minority.[76] Thus, in a later case, the directors escaped liability where they had been confirmed in office by the company after it was aware of the facts.[77]

(5) The very harshness of *Regal* strengthens its value as a guideline for directors. If they retain or account for profits or benefits on the principles of that case, they are unlikely to be open to attack; and if in doubt they should seek approval of an ordinary resolution at the next general meeting.

As Lord Russell of Killowen said:

> 'The rule of equity which insists on those, who by use of fiduciary position make a profit, being liable to account for that profit, in no way depends on fraud, or absence of bona fides; or upon such questions or considerations as whether the profit would or should otherwise have gone to the plaintiff, or whether the profiteer was under a duty to obtain the source of the profit for the plaintiff, or whether he took a risk or acted as he did for the benefit of the plaintiff, or whether the plaintiff has in fact been damaged or benefited by his action. The liability arises from the mere fact of a profit having, in the stated circumstances, been made. The profiteer, however honest or well-intentioned, cannot escape the risk of being called upon to account.'

5.6.2   Examples of personal profits

Other illustrations of this principle may be noted.

Conflict of interest

Boardman v Phipps[78] indicated the continuing authority of *Regal*. In that case a trust held shares in a company and an opportunity arose to acquire further shares. The shares were not an authorised investment and so one of the trustees and the trust solicitor acquired the shares for themselves. It was held, as in *Regal*, that they must account to the trust for their profit, but the additional factor of conflict of interest was present, as is always likely when an opportunity is presented to the company and the directors must decide whether the company will take it. In *Phipps*, the conflict derived from the fact that the defendants could not advise impartially as to whether the trust should seek, from the courts, the power to acquire the shares itself.

There were indications in *Phipps* that information acquired by a director, while acting as such, might not always give rise to an obligation of this type, but there would have to be evidence of full disclosure and rejection of the opportunity by the company. Moreover, if the director had been involved in the board decision to reject, his burden of proof would be correspondingly greater.

Ratification insufficient

To the general principle that a director may keep his personal profit where it is ratified by the members in general meeting, there must clearly be an exception where the directors are themselves in the majority and use their votes to pass the resolution.

Otherwise the minority could be expropriated at will. Thus, in *Cook v Deeks*,[79] the directors used their position to obtain in their own names a contract which should have benefited the company. They passed an ordinary resolution which was carried by their own votes to the effect that the company should have no interest in the contract, but the Privy Council held that none the less the contract 'belonged in equity to the company and ought to have been dealt with as an asset of the company'. Obviously, *unanimous* approval by the members would be a different matter[80] and it appears that even where the breach of duty is not ratifiable in the sense described above, an independent majority of the remaining members may determine that the company will not take proceedings against the delinquent directors.[81]

Having said this, it was clearly stated in *Regal (Hastings) Ltd v Gulliver*[82] that ratification could have taken place. Lord Russell of Killowen insisted that the directors 'could, had they wished, have protected themselves by a resolution (either antecedent or subsequent) of the Regal shareholders in general meeting. In default of such approval, the liability to account must remain'. How then is it possible to reconcile this with the decision in *Cook v Deeks*[83] where the purported ratification was said to be ineffective. Perhaps the answer lies in the fact that in *Cook* the contract which was misappropriated was looked upon as an asset of the company. On the other hand, the directors in *Regal* had not misappropriated property of the company. Rather, they had used information which had come to them in their capacity as directors of the company and, in so doing, had taken advantage of a business opportunity which could have been used by the company.

Fees from subsidiaries

Where a director is put on the board of a subsidiary or in some other position where he receives fees or benefits as a result of the action of his company, he is prima facie liable to account for them on the principles discussed above. However, reg 85 of Table A allows such a director to retain his fees (provided he has disclosed to his board the nature and extent of his interest, which is hardly an onerous obligation).

Post-retirement profits

In *Industrial Development Consultants Ltd v Cooley*,[84] the director failed to get a contract for the company but was then asked by the customer if he would take it up in his private capacity. He then got himself released from his service contract on the grounds of ill health, took up the contract and, not surprisingly, found himself ordered to pay over his profit to the company. There was a clear case of conflict of interest and the opportunity to get the contract arose out of his position as director. If he had vacated his office before receiving the approaches which led to the contract, the position might have been different as fiduciary duties cease on termination of the trustee relationship.[85] It may also be relevant that when the director leaves office the company has little more than a general hope of obtaining the business which the director later acquires. In *Island Export Finance Ltd v Umunna*,[86] the company had a contract with a third party but was at no relevant time in pursuit of further business from that source. The company's action against a director who had resigned and later obtained orders from the third party failed. There was no real opportunity which had been diverted from the company; moreover, the director's main reason for resigning was his dissatisfaction with the company. Too much should not, however, be read into this decision. Had the director resigned mainly in order to conduct business with the third party, or at a time when there was a real or imminent business opportunity for the company, the result would almost certainly have been different: in those circumstances, the director's fiduciary duties *would* have survived his resignation.

Bribes

It naturally follows from these rules that benefits paid to the director by third parties in connection with the company's affairs, must be accounted for. This applies, particularly at the time of incorporation, to payments from promoters or sellers of property to the company,[87] to takeover bids and to payments from contractors.[88]

A good example of a secret profit arose in *Boston Deep Sea Fishing and Ice Co v Ansell*.[89] The defendant was a director of the plaintiff company. On behalf of the company, he placed orders for the building of some fishing smacks and also for some dry ice. Unknown to the company, he was being paid a commission by the shipbuilders and he was also a shareholder in the company supplying the dry ice, and this latter company paid bonuses to shareholders who ordered ice from it. It was held by the Court of Appeal that the defendant had to account to his company for both the commission and the bonus. This was so, even though the bonus could never have been received by his company because it was not itself a shareholder in the company supplying the dry ice.

To encapsulate the philosophy of these cases, one might take the proposition of Lord Hodson in *Boardman v Phipps*:[90]

> 'No person standing in a fiduciary position, when a demand is made upon him . . . to account for profits acquired by him by reason of his fiduciary position and by reason of the opportunity and knowledge, or either, resulting from it, is entitled to defeat the claim upon any ground save that he made the profits with the knowledge and assent of the other person.'

5.6.3   Interest in contracts: principles

Where a director has a personal interest in a contract or other transaction with his company, he is clearly placed in a situation where questions of conflict of interest, personal profit and breach of fiduciary duty are bound to arise. The law has, therefore, been active in this field since the development of commercial companies in the mid-nineteenth century. The main features are as follows.

(1) The general rule is that a director must not have such an interest[91] unless:

    (a)   he discloses it under s 317 (see below); and
    (b)   the Articles permit it; or
    (c)   it is ratified by ordinary resolution of the members.

(2) The effect of a breach of this rule is that:

    (a)   the director must account for the profit made; and
    (b)   the contract is voidable if the company chooses to avoid it.[92]

(3) The rule applies to interests of any kind (however small) including:

(a) a partnership in a firm;
(b) a shareholding in a company[93]

and to any other situation where a conflict of interest may arise.

(4) Disclosure of interests in contracts and other transactions,[94] actual or proposed, is required by s 317. Certain transactions involving loans or 'quasi-loans' to directors or connected persons are treated as giving rise to interests automatically (s 317(6)).[95] In other cases,[96] a transaction must be such as to give rise to an interest (but see (3) above). Section 317 provides as follows.

(a) The director[97] must disclose the nature of his interest at a board meeting.
(b) This must be the first meeting at which the transaction is considered or the first meeting after he acquires his interest, whichever is later.
(c) A general notice of interest will suffice, either in the form of a notice that he is interested in a specified firm or company, or that he is interested in any transaction between the company and a person connected with the director.[98] He must take reasonable steps to ensure that the notice is read at the next meeting of the board after it is given.

Default in giving statutory notice is punishable by a £5,000 fine (or an unlimited fine in the case of a Crown Court conviction). Section 317 provides a mechanism for disclosure which is necessary to comply with the Act. It used to be thought that failure to comply with s 317 did not itself make the dealing void or voidable. For example, in *Guinness v Saunders*,[99] Lord Goff said that he could not see that 'A breach of s 317 . . . had itself any affect upon the contract'. In so doing, he cited Lord Pearson in *Hely-Hutchinson v Brayhead*:[100] 'it is not contended that s 199 (the forerunner of s 317) in itself affects the contract. The section merely creates a statutory duty of disclosure and imposes a fine for non-compliance'. Similarly in *Runciman v Walter Runciman plc*,[101] Brown J said that s 317 applied to service contracts and to variations of service contracts. Even though a director's interest in his service agreement might be regarded as self-evident, it was nevertheless necessary for him to declare his interest at the board meeting at which it was being considered. Having said this, the learned judge regarded a non-declaration of interest in such circumstances 'as purely technical as it could ever be'. Accordingly, the non-disclosure had no affect on the service contract under consideration.

If this is the law, then it is unsatisfactory. It is absurd that a director should be permitted to make a profit at the expense of his company at a time when he is in breach of a specific statutory provision. Having said this, it might be that the *Guinness* and *Hely-Hutchinson* cases stand on their own in that the Articles of both the relevant companies required compliance with the statutory provision and so the courts did not have specifically to address their minds to the breaches of the statutory provisions. Likewise, in *Runciman* the obligation to make disclosure was regarded as purely technical. Brown J said:

> 'I remain profoundly reluctant to conclude that a director must solemnly declare an interest in his own service agreement – a contract which by its very nature involves his interest – before any variation is made concerning his salary or other terms of employment.'

Coming as close as it does to saying that a director apparently need not follow an obligation imposed upon him by statute, the reasoning behind this observation may be regarded as being flawed.

A different approach was adopted in *Neptune (Vehicle Washing Equipment) Ltd v Fitzgerald*.[102] In this case, a sole director had ceased his employment with his company and upon so doing had purported to authorise a payment to himself of some £100,000. At the board meeting at which he had made this payment, he had not apparently made his s 317 declaration of interest. Lightman J regarded the s 317 declaration as being mandatory, even in the case of a director's meeting in a company with a sole directorship. A full trial was then heard on these facts as *Neptune (Vehicle Washing Equipment) Ltd v Fitzgerald (No 2)*.[103] Here again, AG Steinfeld QC sitting as a deputy judge of the Chancery Division regarded the declaration of interest as mandatory.

> 'To allow validity to the transaction here where no such declaration is found to be made on the ground that such was "a mere technical non-declaration" as all the relevant facts were known to the director would be, in effect, to negate altogether the requirement for such a declaration to be made at all. For, wherever there is a sole director he must know all the facts to which the declaration was to relate.'

Accordingly, in this case, the declaration not having been made, the £100,000 payment was recoverable by the company.

(5) In practice, the Articles normally contain an enabling provision and Table A, reg 85 permits a director:

    (a)   to be a party to or interested in any transaction or arrangement with the company or in which the company is interested;

    (b)   to be a director, officer or employee of any other company promoted by his company or in which the company has an interest, or to be a party to any transaction or arrangement between the two companies.

This is subject:

    (a)   to the Act, which may prohibit or regulate the transaction,[104]

    (b)   to making disclosure to the board of the nature and extent of any material interest.

Regulation 86 specifies what is to be sufficient disclosure for the purposes of reg 85, and allows a director to give general notice that he is to be regarded as having an interest of the nature and extent specified in any transaction in which a specified person or class of persons is interested.[105] Such a notice will cover all the company's dealings with the other party. Where such general notice has not been given pursuant to reg 86, however, it appears that some judges will require notice of interest to be given specifically, formally and in *exactly* the manner required by s 317 itself,[106] disclosure during informal discussions preceding the relevant meeting will not be sufficient, still less disclosure at a time or in a manner which does not relate directly to the transaction raising the conflict of interest. The effect is to permit the director to contract with the company and keep his profit (reg 85(c)) provided that he has complied with reg 86.[107] Furthermore, he may not vote or be counted in a quorum when an interest of his (direct or through a connected person) is involved except where:

(a) he is being given an indemnity or security against company loans or obligations which he has taken on himself; or

(b) the company is giving security to the third party in respect of such obligations; or

(c) his interest arises because he is taking or underwriting shares or debentures in the company or any of its subsidiaries; or

(d) the business relates to a retirement benefit scheme approved or requiring approval by the Inland Revenue.

He may, however, be counted in the quorum, and may vote, on any appointments other than his own (reg 97).[108] Moreover, reg 96 allows the general meeting by ordinary resolution to suspend or relax restrictions in the Articles prohibiting a director from voting at board meetings. This makes it clear enough that there is no objection, in principle, to the relaxation of directors' liabilities in this way and specially adapted Articles may go beyond reg 85, as where a director is permitted to vote and be counted in a quorum on his own contract.[109] But such an Article must be strictly complied with and the burden of proof will lie on the director himself.[110] Regulation 86(6) also provides that an interest of which the director is, reasonably, unaware is not to be treated as an interest of his; but this dispensation, useful as it is, is restricted to the Table A disclosure requirements under reg 85. Thus, a director who fails to disclose an interest of which he is unaware may not necessarily be in breach of reg 85. But as soon as he does become aware of the interest, it must, of course, be disclosed.

5.6.4 Interest in contracts: features

We have looked at the principles governing directors' interests and seen that, in practice, the severity of the rule is mitigated by reg 85 or variations on it. Some other features should be noted.

Ratification

In the unlikely event that the rule is not relaxed by the Articles, the director, in addition to disclosing under s 317, must get the contract approved by the members in general meeting. For this purpose, the directors may vote their own shares,[111] so long as this does not amount to a 'fraud on the minority' or on creditors once the company has run into financial difficulties.[112]

Listed companies

In listed companies, the Articles must exclude the director's right to vote where he has a 'material interest'.[113] Exceptions may be specified in the Articles but they require the consent of the Council of the Stock Exchange.

Failure to comply

Where a director fails to disclose, or fails to comply with the specific terms of the saving Article, the contract does not become void but two main consequences follow.

(1) If it is not too late to do so, the contract may be rescinded by the company.

(2) The director must account for his profits.[114]

The question remains whether the director is entitled to invoke the general rule that an agent or trustee who 'has exercised exceptional skill to the significant advantage' of the principal or beneficiary should receive some allowance for this. Although to deny the director any reward may be to enrich the company at his expense, this appears to be the result of the decision in *Guinness plc v Saunders*.[115] Here it was alleged that a director had received a large sum for services connected with a takeover being pursued by the company. The sum had been paid under a contract between the director and a sub-committee of the board. There had been no disclosure of the director's interest to the full board. Although the company had not, in fact, chosen to rescind the contract, it was still able to recover the payment because, under the Articles, the sub-committee had no authority to make the contract, which was therefore void. The director had to repay the company and, it was decided, had no claim to *any* payment for his services;[116] the importance of the rules controlling conflicts of interest and duty outweighed the general rule referred to above.

It should not be forgotten that the duties of a director may affect not only the relationship between the director and his company, but also that between the director and a third party. In *Wilton Group plc v Abrams*,[117] a director had agreed to sell shares. It was also agreed that he was to have a well-remunerated service agreement with the company which would be approved, of course, by the board votes of the purchaser and 'his' new directors. The court refused to order the sale to be completed. The court found that this sort of arrangement may be unexceptionable in a private company where all the members agree to the proposal, but is commercially disreputable in the case of a public company whose members would have no idea that the service contract was approved for any reason but the best interests of the company, or that it was in fact part of the arrangements for the private sale of shares. It seems likely that the most which the vendor can achieve by such a term is an entitlement to a service contract if, other things being equal, an independent board could consider this to be in the company's best interests.[118]

Additional disclosure

We have seen that disclosure under s 317 is to the board only, but further requirements are also imposed by the Act.

(1) Section 232 added by the Companies Act 1989, requires that certain types of transaction in which directors or shadow directors are interested should be disclosed by way of notes to the accounts of any financial year in which such transactions were entered into or subsisted (ie were still in force). Schedule 6 to the Act lays down very elaborate rules governing the matters to be disclosed and the particulars to be given. Briefly, the following must be disclosed:

(a) loans, quasi-loans and certain other forms of credit provided to directors, or the provision of security for a director who has already been given credit by a third party;

(b) agreements to enter into such transactions;

(c) any other transaction[119] in which a director has a direct or indirect material interest.

All transactions in (1)(a) or (b) above must be disclosed if they involve a director of the company or its holding company, or a person connected with him (under s 346 (see **5.5**)).[120] Materiality of interest is in effect presumed in these cases. As long as the directorship or connection existed at some time during the financial year, it need not have lasted for the whole of that year; similarly the connection or the subsidiary-holding company relationship need not exist at the time the transaction is entered into provided that it existed at some time during the year. Disclosure remains necessary even if it reveals a loan or other transaction prohibited by s 330 (see **10.4**), which may well be the case. On the other hand, there is the *de minimis* principle excluding the requirement of disclosure if the total debt did not exceed £5,000 at any time during the year (in aggregate if there is more than one transaction).

As to (1)(c) above, there must be a 'material interest'. No interest at all arises merely because a person is a director both of a parent company and its subsidiary. Further, the word 'material' leaves some discretion with the directors; if they[121] have considered the matter, their judgement of materiality appears to be conclusive (in sharp contrast to s 317 which requires disclosure to the board of any interest, however trivial). Conversely, s 232 and Sch 6 impose much more precise requirements as to the details to be disclosed (see below). Again, there is a *de minimis* exemption for transactions:

(a) of a value of £1,000 or less; and
(b) in other cases, not exceeding £5,000 or one per cent of the net assets (whichever is less and aggregating the figures if there is more than one transaction).

(2) Broadly, similar requirements apply to transactions involving company officers.
(3) Contracts of service do not have to be noted under s 232.[122] They must, however, be open to inspection by members (s 318) except where terminable without compensation within 12 months. This requirement extends to service agreements with shadow directors.
(4) Every director and shadow director must notify the company of his shareholdings and other interests in the company's securities at the time he takes office, and also of his dealings in such shares or securities (s 324). The information will be filed by the company in its register of directors' interests (kept under s 325) and will be open to inspection by members of the company and by the public (see **7.11** et seq).

Extent of disclosure

As already mentioned, where s 232 requires disclosure in the notes to the accounts of contracts in which a director has a material interest, Sch 6 requires very detailed particulars to be stated. Briefly, these are as follows:

(1) the fact that the transaction was made, or subsisted, during the financial year;
(2) the name of the director or shadow director and (where relevant) the person connected with him;
(3) where the transaction is not a loan, quasi-loan or similar contract, the nature of the director's interest in the transaction;

(4)   in the case of a loan or similar arrangement, the amount due at the beginning and end of the year, the maximum liability during the year, any arrears of interest, and any provision made for default;

(5)   in the case of a guarantee or other security, the amount of potential liability, and of accrued liability or actual payment made by the company;

(6)   in any other case, what the value of the transaction is.

Section 232 is restricted to loans and credit transactions (which are deemed to give rise to a material interest) and those other transactions in which there is a material interest. In contrast, s 317 is not restricted to 'material' interests in contracts and it requires the 'nature' of the interest to be declared. What does this mean? Surely that the director must do more than say 'I declare an interest in this contract.' He must go further and say what form his interest takes, whether he is an owner, shareholder, or director of the contracting party and (if relevant) what is the extent of his personal stake.[123] Unfortunately, the section confuses the issue by providing (s 317(3)) that a general notice of membership in a specified company or firm or connection with a specified person shall be sufficient notice of interest in all future contracts with that company. This is all very well for the situation where the director has given a general notice that he has shares in a large listed company. No doubt, this will serve adequately for any contracts which his company may make in the future. But what of the case where he is in control of the third party and stands to make a very large personal profit from the transaction under discussion? Can he rely on a general notice of an (unspecified) interest which he gave years earlier and allow the contract to go through without saying a word? The answer must be 'no' and the reason must lie in his wider duty of good faith. He may have complied with s 317 but the general fiduciary duty requires him to go further and to inform the board of the specific facts which he knows to be relevant to its decision.[124]

Procedure
An example of the procedure followed in one public company may be useful.

(1)   Directors give general notice of all their directorships and shareholdings in other companies under ss 317 and 289.

(2)   At each board meeting the chairman draws attention to s 317 and requests disclosures under that section of any interest in contracts on the agenda.

(3)   Directors disclose specifically any material interest in contracts either on the agenda or otherwise pending.

This procedure faces the problem discussed above, that general disclosure under s 317 is not enough and that specific disclosure of any material interest is also required. Moreover, a director should not in any circumstances enter into a contract where abnormal personal gain accrues to him. In other words, full disclosure and compliance with the Articles is not a passport to contractual freedom. It is only the first test which a contract must pass, the second being the overriding duty of good faith. The director will meet this requirement only if the contract is one which he could justify to the members at a general meeting after all the facts were disclosed.

5.7 CONTRACTS WITH THE COMPANY: OTHER RESTRICTIONS

Apart from the general question of interest in contracts, there are other statutory restrictions on the company's dealings with its directors.

(1) Loans to directors are generally prohibited.[125]
(2) Substantial property transactions between a company and its directors are subject to approval by the general meeting.[126]
(3) Tax-free payments to directors are prohibited and any agreement to make such a payment is treated as an agreement to pay the sum stated, but subject to deductions of tax, ie as though the net sum were a gross sum.[127]
(4) Compensation for loss of office requires disclosure and approval by the members, ie by ordinary resolution.[128]
(5) Disclosure of remuneration and compensation for loss of office is required in the accounts.[129]
(6) Service agreements, or details if not in writing, must be available for inspection by any member, unless terminable without compensation within 12 months.[130] The Stock Exchange also requires copies of such agreements to be available during the AGM period of listed companies. In addition, contracts for five years or more must be approved by ordinary resolution.[131]
(7) The directors' report must disclose each director's interests in company or group company shares at the beginning and end of the financial year.[132]
(8) Dealing in options is prohibited in the case of listed companies.[133]
(9) Interests of the directors in securities of the company or its associates must be notified to the company and recorded in its register[134] in addition to the general duty to disclose individual and group acquisitions of voting shares.[135]

5.7.1 Competition

One would expect that a director would be prevented by his fiduciary obligations from competing with the company, as he would be if he were a partner.[136] However, this is not necessarily the case and the position appears to be as follows.

(1) He may accept a directorship in a competing company[137] and may be able to compete directly on his own account.[138] But an executive or managing director may certainly not compete on his own account if he does so whilst ostensibly on the company's business.[139] Even where he is not engaged on the company's business, an executive director must not generally compete with the company, since his duties will impliedly, if not expressly, preclude such competition.[140]
(2) Even where competition is permissible, there is a serious risk of a conflict of interest and thus of a breach of fiduciary duty, and the courts might restrain him by injunction from continuing to act in both capacities.[141]
(3) Apart from the general duty of good faith, the competing director is also vulnerable to attack on the grounds that his conduct is prejudicial to the members[142] 'if he subordinates the interests of the one company to those of the other'.[143] In practice, it is difficult to see how a man can sit on the boards of two competing companies and still do justice to each of them.

(4) Covenants against competition after vacation of office, which may appear in the director's service agreement, are subject to the general rules concerning restraint of trade and are discussed in Chapter 10. A director who is wrongfully dismissed is usually freed from such covenants in any event.[144]

5.7.2   Confidentiality

One of the inevitable difficulties which a competing director faces is that of conflict with his wider duty of confidentiality. How does he avoid giving the rival business the benefit of confidential information which he has acquired as a director?

The duty of confidentiality itself forms part of the duty of good faith and restricts the director from using, either during or after his term of office, anything which belongs to the company for his own purposes. Property in the normal sense is clearly included, but also intangible property in the form of trade secrets,[145] lists of customers, company documents and other confidential information.[146] The sort of information which must not be disclosed includes commercial as well as technical secrets, for example, prices being paid for supplies, the state of current negotiations, fast-moving product lines, and new or proposed product ranges.[147]

In *Baker v Gibbons*,[148] it was held that the duty in respect of confidential information applied 'with particular force' (as one would expect) to a director as compared with other employees and agents. But the duty was not broken by the director in this case who, after dismissal, recruited some of the company's selling agents to join his own competing business. He had simply memorised their names and addresses and had not stolen any documents or confidential information. Moreover, the courts are always reluctant to interfere, at the request of an employer, with the efforts of a former employee to earn his living.

5.8   DUTY OF SKILL AND CARE

5.8.1   Principles

We have been looking at duties which fall within the general category of good faith; a largely negative obligation to do nothing which conflicts with the director's duty to the company. But what of the positive side? What is a director expected to do to promote the company's welfare?

Until recently a fairly cynical answer could be given to this question: very little. The courts did not require any particular level of competence in a director, nor did they require a very high level of diligence. The judicial refusal to impose liability upon directors for anything falling short of 'gross' negligence reached its high point in *Re City Equitable Fire Insurance Co*[149] where Romer J formulated three propositions with which all considerations of the present position must still begin.

(1) A subjective test of skill

A director need not exhibit in the performance of his duties a greater degree of skill than may reasonably be expected from a person of his (subjective) knowledge and experience. So, for example, there was no liability on directors of a rubber company who, knowing nothing of the trade, had presided over massive losses arising from speculation in rubber.[150] Neville J said a director 'is, I think, not bound to bring any special qualifications to his office. He may undertake the management of a rubber company in complete ignorance of anything connected with rubber, without incurring responsibility for the mistakes which may result from such ignorance'. Having said this, he then went on to explain that if a director were to have special knowledge relevant to the business of his company, then he must give the company the benefit of that knowledge when carrying on the business of the company.

(2) Periodic attendance
He is not bound to give continuous attention to the company's affairs. His duties are of an intermittent nature, to be performed at periodic board meetings. He is not bound to attend all such meetings, although he ought to whenever he reasonably can. A most extreme example of this approach is *Re Cardiff Savings Bank, The Marquis of Bute's case*.[151] Here, the Marquis of Bute, who had been appointed president of the bank when he was only six months old, escaped liability when losses occurred because of irregularities in the operation of the bank in spite of his having attended only one board meeting in 38 years. Sterling J said 'Neglect or omission to attend meetings is not, in my opinion, the same thing as neglect or omission of a duty which ought to be performed at those meeting'. (This should, however, be contrasted with reg 81 of Table A, which provides that if a director misses more than six months board meetings without consent, his fellow directors may vote that he should no longer be a director.)

(3) Delegation to executives
He is entitled to trust an official to perform such duties as can properly be entrusted to him in accordance with the Articles.

What had happened in *Re City Equitable* was a catastrophic fraud by the managing director, who had been given a free hand by his colleagues. He had concealed the fraud by showing items in the balance sheet as 'loans at call' and 'cash in hand' but the other directors never enquired about these items – in fact the loans were mainly to himself and the cash included a very large sum in the firm of stockbrokers of which he was a partner. Even by the relaxed standards set out by Romer J, the co-directors were negligent.[152]

Although, these standards have been applied until comparatively recently,[153] there are good reasons for believing that they no longer represent the law.

(a) They are manifestly addressed to the non-executive director of the old school, who lent his name, sometimes his presence, and perhaps his connections, to the board, but who was rarely expected to exhibit business or financial skills.[154] Even Romer J's tests would require a professional or a business person to live up to his own, presumably higher, standards, and thus where he is appointed as an executive director an objective standard will apply; he must exercise reasonable skill in the performance of his contractual duties.[155]

(b) There was a view that if the members appointed directors who proved incompetent or idle, it was for the members to remove them. Although in other areas of the law this model of shareholder control may still survive, it is so obviously unrealistic in many professionally managed companies that it can hardly be used to justify insulating management and the board from liability for loss caused to the company.

(c)   There has always been a reluctance to 'second-guess' management acts and decisions by saying, with hindsight, that they were negligent. If directors were, in one sense, 'trustees' of the assets of the company, they were very different from ordinary trustees – they were entitled to take business risks and to make investments which no private trust could countenance. This understandable reluctance to evaluate the quality of management was one thing, however; a refusal to intervene when there was no effective or competent management was quite another. It completely overlooks the fact that the positive duty to look after the assets must involve a correlative duty not, by physical or mental inertia, to allow them to be lost or squandered.

Consequently, the law has probably reached the position that, whatever level of *skill* may be required of a director, he must show the *care* that an ordinary person would be expected to take in his own affairs.[156] This goes beyond saying that if he acts, he must act with care; it clearly implies that in certain situations, the duty to take care requires the director to act. This applies to executive and non-executive directors equally[157] and is reinforced by legislative developments. For now, that directors are required to approve the company's annual accounts, the very least that each director must do is to satisfy himself, as far as he is able, that the accounts comply with the statutory requirements.[158]

Furthermore, those directors particularly responsible for preparing the accounts, and those who profess accounting or business knowledge and experience, will have special responsibility in performing this function. They may also be required to be alert for signs of financial problems facing the company and which would be reasonably apparent to a competent professional or business person reading the accounts and making the necessary inquiries. This is partly because, as we have seen, a director must have particular regard to the interests of creditors when he knows the company is insolvent. It would not be difficult for a judge to backdate that duty to the time when the director knew or should have realised that the company faced financial difficulties which threatened the interests of creditors (and also, therefore, the credit and welfare of the company, even if it avoided insolvency).

Indeed, to some extent these extended duties already exist, for both the Insolvency Act 1986, s 214 (imposing liability for wrongful trading) and the Company Directors Disqualification Act 1986, s 6, focus considerable attention on the question: should the director – professionally qualified or not – have realised that the company was in difficulties? It is inevitable that these statutory requirements will come to supply some of the content of the duties of skill and care imposed on directors by the general law. It follows that the directors must have regard not only to the present discussion but also to the accounts of the statutory rules which follow it.

That the law has moved on to the requirement of an objective standard from directors seems to be confirmed by two judgements of Lord Hoffmann. In *Norman v Theodore Goddard*,[159] Hoffmann J (as he then was) accepted, without hearing any argument, that the standard of care expected of a director was accurately stated in s 214(4) of the Insolvency Act 1986. In other words, he had to show the general knowledge, skill and experience that might reasonably be expected of a person carrying on the same functions as were carried out by that director in relation to the company. The same learned judge repeated this in *Re D'Jan of London Ltd.*[160] Here Hoffmann LJ (as he then was) said 'In my view, the duty of care owed by a director at common law is accurately stated in s 214(4) of the Insolvency Act 1986'. Having said this, the latter case can be easily explained on the basis that the director concerned had not even met his own subjective standard of skill. At the time of writing, it is believed that a new s 309A may shortly be enacted by statutory instrument to put *Re D'Jan of London Ltd* on a statutory footing. This has, inter alia, been recommended by the Law Commission in its September 1999 Report.

Let us now turn to some particular aspects of the duties of skill and care, remembering that the 'subjective' nature of the duty to exercise proper skill, expounded by Romer J, is probably being turned on its head: *all* directors must show some skills, but professionally qualified or experienced directors must show more.

5.8.2 Examples

Cheque signing
In *Re City Equitable*,[161] the following tests were suggested.

(1) In the absence of suspicious circumstances, a director who is asked to sign a cheque may trust the officers as to whether it is properly required and whether it is duly applied for the stated purpose.
(2) He should satisfy himself as to an authorising resolution, either in advance or by way of confirmation.
(3) Such resolution should preferably specify payees and amounts.

Obviously, these suggestions are impracticable for large companies, but even there the proper procedure for delegating powers under the Articles must be followed. Once there has been delegation to an apparently competent and honest officer (or co-director), the law does not require each board member constantly to supervise his activities, or to query and investigate every transaction performed within the scope of the delegated power. On the other hand, if there is anything which seems to be a bit odd – for example, an unusual payee, a payee with whom the company does not, to the director's knowledge, do business, a payee known to be associated with a director or officer, an unusually large amount, a cheque drawn at an unusual time – the very least that any director should do is to inquire. A director must accept that on occasions his duties to the company (and self-protection) require him to ask irritating and embarrassing questions. This is all the more so where the delegation of power within the company is both total and casual. An extreme example of a complete failure to have regard to these requirements may be found in *Dorchester Finance Co Ltd v Stebbings*.[162] In this case, one director had been left in complete control of the company's affairs; no board meetings were ever held, the other directors being content that this was, as one director suggested in evidence, the practice 'in the vast majority of wholly owned subsidiaries'. The result was that the company made unsecured loans and irregular payments to other group companies and businesses in which the active director was interested. The other two directors – one a chartered accountant and the other with accountancy experience – had facilitated this not only by their inactivity but also by signing blank cheques. One of these directors said in evidence:

> 'As I was very rarely at head office, a secretary would sometimes ask me to sign cheques in blank so that payments could be made whilst I was away and this I willingly did, assuming that they were used to pay expenses.'

This was to be excused, he suggested, on the basis that he was a non-executive director. The court rejected this extraordinary argument and held the two directors liable for specific negligence in signing blank cheques,[163] and more generally for failing to exercise any of their duties, let alone to exercise due care and skill. Two of the three directors in the case were chartered accountants and all three were experienced businessmen. The signing of blank cheques by such persons must be regarded as acts of almost unbelievable stupidity.

Directors may, of course, rely upon professional advisers properly appointed by the company to carry out their functions honestly and efficiently. Thus, for example, directors are justified in handing a cheque to a solicitor and relying upon him to see that it is put to proper use.[164]

Investments

Romer J also suggested that:

(1) each director is responsible for ensuring that funds are properly invested, except insofar as delegation may be permitted by the Articles; and
(2) safe custody of the securities may properly be entrusted to an appropriate full-time officer such as manager, accountant or secretary.

Now whether investments are 'proper' in the sense of not being poorly chosen and ruinous to the company, is one question (see *Negligence*, below). Whether they are 'proper' in the sense of authorised and duly made is quite another and, as in the case of cheques, it is probable that Romer J's views would now be seen as too generous to the director. Even if the proper officer is making the investments, the basic duty of each director will be to ensure that the company's assets are being managed as required by the Articles, and by any stated board policy; a failure to check upon this, from time to time, would expose directors to the same criticisms as the abstention from supervision which occurred in the *Dorchester Finance* case (see above).

Professional advice

Directors are entitled to rely on qualified professional advice where appropriate. They may, indeed, be obliged to do so, for example, to get an independent valuation of a property offered to them as mortgage security.[165] Having obtained that advice, they may, and as a general rule must, exercise their own judgement; for example, as to whether, on the basis of a mortgage valuation it is in the company's best interests to proceed with a contemplated transaction.

Although the matter is one of degree, there will be some situations where their duties require them to obtain advice and to act upon it with very little room for their own judgement and discretion. Perhaps the best example of this is the board of a financially troubled company. As we shall see, there is an increasingly sophisticated body of corporate insolvency and quasi-insolvency law and practitioners. Not only that law, but the directors' duties towards their company (including, as we have seen, consideration of the interests of its creditors) may require the board and individual directors to put the direction of their company's affairs to a qualified insolvency practitioner. The sort of advice they receive will often be of critical importance to the survival of the enterprise, or parts of it, or to its orderly dissolution. This will almost inevitably be the sort of advice which leaves the director with very little scope for the exercise of his own judgement.

In those cases where the general rule is that a director may seek advice but must then exercise his own judgement, the corollary is that the directors, in doing so, make decisions informed by expert opinion, but they are not expected to be experts themselves. 'A director of a life insurance company does not guarantee that he has the skill of an actuary or physician'.[166] A good example of the degree to which delegation may take place arose in *Norman v Theodore Goddard*.[167] Quirk, a chartered surveyor, was a director of a property company. The shares in this company were the main assets of an off-shore trust administered in the Jersey office of Theodore Goddard, a major firm of London solicitors. Bingham, who had been a partner in the firm until his expulsion, had specialised in trust work. Bingham suggested to Quirk that tax would be saved if considerable sums of surplus cash belonging to the company were deposited with another company which Bingham said was controlled by his firm. Quirk accepted this advice and the surplus cash was deposited with the latter company which was in fact controlled, not by Theodore Goddard, but by Bingham personally and was a device for stealing money from various trust funds administered by Theodore Goddard. It was held that Quirk had not been negligent in relying upon Bingham's advice. While a director who undertook the management of a company's properties was expected to have reasonable skill in property management, he was not expected to have a similar level of skill in off-shore tax avoidance. Business cannot be carried on upon principles of distrust. Men in responsible positions should be trusted until there is a reason to distrust them. In all the circumstances of the case, Quirk had not been negligent. Bingham had given him information which, if true, would have been a proper basis on which Quirk could have acted. He had acted reasonably in accepting the information which he had been given.

These principles are subject to the expected qualifications: an executive director's standards of skill may be implied from the terms of his employment; and a non-executive director appointed by reason of a particular expertise must show more skill, in that field, than one appointed for other reasons.

Diligence

Romer J's statement that a director's duty is to attend board meetings when, in the circumstances, he is reasonably able to do so, is clearly too lenient to meet modern requirements. Under the old standard, Romer J was able to excuse a director who lived in Aberdeen and found it difficult to attend board meetings in London, and another director whose illness had meant his absence from meetings for five years. A judge today is likely to say that in those circumstances the appointment should never have been accepted, or that the office should have been relinquished when the difficulty emerged. Even in companies where board meetings are a formality – and how can this be predicted with absolute confidence even in a closely held private company? – there is the routine business of the company to supervise. Where this has been delegated to a competent and reliable officer, the burden of *statutory* duties laid upon the company and directors requires a degree of attention to the company's affairs, if only sufficient to check that the company is not in default of its duties. This is not to mention the embarrassing possibility that the delegate proves to be less competent or reliable than appeared;[168] how can a director ensure that functions are properly delegated and carried out without some degree of attention to the company's affairs? Even in the nineteenth century, when there were some spectacular examples of unsanctioned free-riding by directors, it was said that, 'It should be understood that a director consenting to be a director, has assumed a position involving duties which cannot be shirked by leaving everything to others'.[169] Furthermore, the law will make little distinction between an executive and a non-executive director, once satisfied that the director in question has not even sought to check that the company was managed in accordance with the Companies Act.[170]

On the other hand, there will frequently be differences between the standards expected of different directors when it comes to the actual conduct of the company's affairs. If a director assumes a specific responsibility for a particular task or for continuous involvement in management, whether by way of service contract or otherwise, his responsibility (express or implied) will be determined by the terms of his engagement. This may include a positive duty to take the initiative in pursuing business opportunities, even to the extent of changing to some other business which the company may lawfully undertake.[171]

Negligence

In a sense, this heading covers everything which has gone before. In the narrower sense which we shall now examine, it means a judgment that a director has failed to measure up to the appropriate standards of skill and care in the exercise of his functions. For example, in *Dovey v Corey*,[172] bad debts were included in the balance sheet on an assurance by a manager that they were good. As a result, dividends were unlawfully paid out of capital. The House of Lords refused to hold a director liable in negligence, on the basis of proper delegation: 'The business of life could not go on if people could not trust those who are put in a position of trust for the express purpose of attending to details of management'. Would the position have been any different if the defendant had been a director with management functions, or with responsibility for credit management?

Traditionally, the answer may well have been 'only slightly, if at all'.[173] There may have been liability for an obviously careless mechanical slip in recording the debts, but not for the assessment of the debts. The reason would be, in other jurisdictions as well as in England and Wales, the 'business judgment' rule. This simply reflects judicial reluctance to evaluate the performance of management and to second-guess its decisions. It assumes that, rather like a physician making a difficult clinical judgement, a manager has exhibited the basic professional skills and is not to be blamed if the resulting decision does not turn out for the best. Criticism of the manager is the task of the members, not the court. Having said this, delegation would not exonerate directors from liability if such delegation is to obviously incompetent or unsuitable employees.

The content of this rule can easily change without any alteration to the rule itself. All that is required is an increase in the demands made for the 'basic' skills, or in the areas which are not treated as falling within pure, unreviewable, management decision-making powers – or, of course, both. As to the first, we have seen that the day of the incompetent amateur is surely past. As to the second, we now have statutory regimes:

(1) requiring disqualification of directors of insolvent companies whose conduct shows them to be unfit to manage a company (Company Directors Disqualification Act 1986, s 6); and

(2) imposing personal liability on directors who, when they should have realised that the company faced insolvency, failed to take all available steps to minimise the loss to creditors (Insolvency Act 1986, s 214).

These rules inevitably involve the courts in evaluating the quality of management decisions. This is likely to reduce the courts' reluctance to do so in other areas[174] and, if this is the case, it is equally inevitable that decisions on these Acts will colour the general law of director's duties.

Finally, it must not be forgotten that if there is a service agreement there may well be implied a duty to satisfy an objective standard of reasonable skill and care higher than the law might otherwise have demanded. The same may be true, although not necessarily to the same extent, where a director simply undertakes a particular function within the company. This is probably confirmed by decisions such as *Henderson v Merrett Syndicates Ltd*,[175] where it was held by the House of Lords that where a person assumes responsibility to perform professional or quasi-professional services for another who relies upon those services, the relationship between the parties is itself sufficient to give rise to a duty on the provider of the services to exercise reasonable skill and care in so doing.

5.8.3 Reliance on others

Romer J suggested that directors were entitled to rely on the relevant officers in the absence of circumstances calling for inquiry, and directors have escaped liability on this principle in *Dovey v Corey* and other cases. The same holds true for reliance on a properly delegated sub-committee of the board.[176] As we have seen, however, this entitlement is heavily qualified by duties to supervise and inquire into the conduct of the company's affairs.

Likewise, the default of one director does not necessarily impose liability on the others.[177] However, failure to supervise or inquire where there are suspicious circumstances or other reasons for doing so, may involve the innocent director in the breach of duty; for example, where the chairman signed a minute and reported to the general meeting on an ultra vires investment effected by his colleagues.[178] And where he is, in fact, supervising a delegated task he cannot claim that he did not know what was going on.[179]

CHAPTER 5 FOOTNOTES

1 These aspects of the directors' position are also considered in **1.7**.

2 *Percival v Wright* [1902] 2 Ch 421.

3 *Multinational Gas and Petrochemical Co v Multinational Gas and Petrochemical Services Ltd* [1983] Ch 258.

4 [1998] 1 All ER 724.

5 *Wallersteiner v Moir (No 2)* [1975] QB 373, p 508n. But it is rarely a simple matter to bring such an action: see **7.15.1** and **8.3.5**. Another possibility which should not be ignored is an action by new controllers of the company, or by an insolvency officer.

6 In *Hogg v Cramphorn* [1967] Ch 254 the court excluded wrongfully issued shares from the resolution ratifying the directors' conduct in issuing them.

7 *Northern Counties Securities v Jackson Steeple & Co* [1974] 1 WLR 1133.

8 See Megarry J's remarks in *Gaiman v National Association for Mental Health* [1970] 2 All ER 362: 'The interests of some particular section or sections of the [company] cannot be equated with those of the [company] and I would accept the interests of both present and future members of the [company] as a whole as being a helpful expression of a human equivalent.'

9 *Re a Company (No 008699 of 1985)* [1986] BCLC 382.

10 [1987] 1 All ER 114, at p 118, HL.

11 [1991] 1 AC 187.

12 Or, perhaps, once insolvency is a real possibility.

13 It follows that no member can complain if his interests are thus subordinated to those of the creditors.

14 Ie a liquidator or, less commonly, an administrator.

15 [1988] BCLC 250, CA.

16 (1976) 137 CLR 1.

17 (1986) NSWLR 722.

18 For a discussion of s 214, see **6.2.4**.

19 And extremely dangerous, since they may be able summarily to dismember the company.

20 See *Parke v Daily News* [1963] 2 All ER 929.

21 Employment policy is now to be reported by the directors: see Sch 7 to the 1985 Act and **4.2**.

22 *Scottish Co-operative Wholesale Society v Meyer* [1959] AC 324. Here the 'company as a whole' included the minority interests in the subsidiary.

23 *Charterbridge Corporation v Lloyds Bank Ltd* [1970] Ch 62.

24 *Re Smith & Fawcett Ltd* [1942] 1 All ER 542.

25 As in *Hogg v Cramphorn Ltd* [1967] Ch 254.

26 [1942] Ch 304.

27 [1967] Ch 254.

28 *Regal (Hastings) Ltd v Gulliver* [1942] 1 All ER 378.

29 *Re Smith & Fawcett* [1942] 1 All ER 542.

30 *Pergamon Press v Maxwell* [1970] 2 All ER 809.

31 *Howard Smith Ltd v Ampol Petroleum* [1974] AC 821 (issue also designed to favour one of two competing takeover bids). Similarly, a board which knows that it is about to be voted out by the members must not make contracts which seriously inhibit the management powers of the incoming directors: *Lee Panavision Ltd v Lee Lighting Ltd* [1991] BCC 620, CA. In many such cases (but not this), such actions might be vulnerable for lack of good faith.

32 *Hogg v Cramphorn Ltd* [1967] Ch 254. (General duties on a bid are considered in **4.5**, where the provisions of the City Code are also noted.)

33 [1970] Ch 212.

34 Even, it seems, when a member of the board has profited from the action, as where the directors acknowledged an otherwise statute-barred debt owed to one of them: *Re Gee & Co (Woolwich) Ltd* [1974] 2 WLR 515.

35 *Hogg v Cramphorn Ltd* [1967] Ch 254.

36 *Savoy Hotel Investigation*, HMSO second report (1954).

37 *Pennell v Venida Investments Ltd* (1974) unreported, but discussed by Burridge in (1981) *Modern Law Review* 40.

38 *Report on First Re-investment Trust Ltd and other Companies*, HMSO (1974).

39 [1974] AC 821.

40 *Re a Company (No 008699 of 1985)* [1986] BCLC 382. But the Articles may sometimes require the directors actively to facilitate the highest available offer, as in *Heron International Ltd v Lord Grade* [1983] BCLC 244.

41 *Re a Company (No 008699 of 1985)* [1986] BCLC 382, at p 389. The duty of the board to ensure that the best terms are available to the members means that an agreement or undertaking to support an offer is subject to the directors' overriding duty to promote the best interests of the company and the shareholders, and the bidder cannot complain if the directors later lend support to a better offer: *John Crowther Group plc v Carpets International plc* [1990] BCLC 460; *Dawson International plc v Coats Paton plc* [1990] BCLC 560.

42 As to the 'primary purpose' test, see the *Howard Smith* case, above.

43 (1968) 121 CLR 483.

44 *Selangor United Rubber Estates Ltd v Cradock (No 3)* [1968] 2 All ER 1073.

45 *Guinness plc v Saunders* [1990] 2 AC 663. If the payee is himself a director, further considerations arise: see **5.6**.

46 *Re Claridge's Patent Asphalt Co Ltd* [1921] 1 Ch 543; *Aveling Barford Ltd v Perion Ltd* [1989] BCLC 626.

47 *Re Duomatic Ltd* [1969] 1 All ER 161.

48 *Re Sharpe* [1892] 1 Ch 154.

49 'Every director who is a party to a breach of [s 151] is guilty of a misfeasance and breach of trust, and is liable to recoup to the company any loss occasioned to it by the default': *Wallersteiner v Moir (No 1)* [1974] 3 All ER 217, per Lord Denning MR, at p 239.

50 Even if the company itself could never have received the commission: *Boston Deep Sea Fishing and Ice Co v Ansell* (1889) 39 ChD 339.

51 *Cranleigh Precision Engineering Ltd v Bryant* [1965] 1 WLR 1293.

52 Even where the third party would not have placed the contract with the company because of his personal objection to it: *Industrial Development Consultants Ltd v Cooley* [1972] 2 All ER 162.

53 *Regal (Hastings) Ltd v Gulliver* [1942] 1 All ER 378.

54 Usually a contract, but not necessarily so.

55 Where a director has already agreed to transfer an asset to the company (with, it is hoped, the necessary approval), the company's agreement to release him from that obligation is itself an arrangement for an acquisition by him, even though the asset already belongs to him.

56 Ie tangible property (land or goods) or intangible property (for example, shares or other securities; debts; patents, trademarks and similar rights; and, probably, the goodwill of a business). See also s 739.

57 Based on the accounts for the last financial year, or the paid up capital if those accounts have not been laid by the time of the arrangement.

58 Those who challenge the transaction must prove the value of the asset: *Joint Receivers of Niltan Carson Ltd v Hawthorne* [1988] BCLC 298.

59 [1995] BCC 89.

60 [1997] BCC 45.

61 Except where a holding company must approve an arrangement involving a subsidiary: s 322(2)(c).

62 When acting as such.

63 See note 62.

64 It does not cover transfers *to* the company.

65 [1995] BCC 89.

66 [1997] BCC 45.

67 [1996] BCC 727.

68 [1998] BCC 638.

69 And remembering that a transaction which falls within the terms of the Memorandum and Articles may still be a breach of duty under a 'lesser' head such as acting for the wrong purpose: see *Rolled Steel Products (Holdings) Ltd v British Steel Corp* [1986] Ch 246.

70 Or a director of a holding company, or any other person or company connected or associated with such directors.

71 Those other than directors have a defence if they can show that they did not know that the directors were exceeding their powers.

72 Ie a complete stranger to the improper transaction.

73 Which may be done in some cases by ordinary resolution, but in a case falling within s 35 would require a special resolution.
74 Including resolutions and agreements which limit the board's powers.
75 [1942] 1 All ER 378.
76 One of the many galling features of *Regal* for the directors is that they were apparently in a majority and so could have had their share purchase ratified if they had troubled to do so, there being no dishonesty involved; see **5.6.2**.
77 *Lindgren v L & P Estates Co* [1968] 1 All ER 917.
78 [1966] 3 All ER 721.
79 [1916] 1 AC 554.
80 *Re Gee & Co (Woolwich) Ltd* [1974] 2 WLR 515.
81 *Smith v Croft (No 2)* [1988] Ch 114.
82 [1942] 1 All ER 378.
83 [1916] 1 AC 554.
84 [1972] 2 All ER 162.
85 *Nordisk Insulin Laboratorium v CL Bencard* [1953] 1 All ER 986.
86 [1986] BCLC 460.
87 *Re London & South Western Canal Co* [1911] 1 Ch 346.
88 *Boston Deep Sea Fishing and Ice Co v Ansell* (1889) 39 ChD 339; there may be criminal liability for corruption, but not in many cases for 'stealing' payments from the company (*A-G's Reference (No 1 of 1985)* [1986] 2 WLR 733).
89 (1889) 39 ChD 339.
90 [1966] 3 All ER 721.
91 *Costa Rica Rly Co Ltd v Forwood* [1900] 1 Ch 746.
92 *Aberdeen Rly Co v Blaikie Bros* [1854] 2 Eq Rep 128, HL; *Guinness plc v Saunders* [1990] 2 AC 663.
93 *Transvaal Lands Co v New Belgium Land Co* [1914] 2 Ch 488.
94 Any arrangement or transaction counts for this purpose even if it is not a binding contract.
95 For 'quasi-loans' see **10.4.1**.
96 Whether or not they are themselves breaches of the Act.
97 Or shadow director, as defined by s 741.
98 For 'connected persons' see s 346, discussed at **5.5**.
99 [1990] 2 AC 663.
100 [1968] 1 QB 549.
101 [1993] BCC 223.
102 [1995] BCC 474.
103 [1995] BCC 1000.
104 In particular if it involves a property dealing (see **5.5**) or a loan or quasi-loan (see **10.4**).
105 A director or a partner or employee of his may act in his professional capacity for the company and be paid accordingly; but none of them may be an auditor: s 27 of the Companies Act 1989.
106 *Lee Panavision Ltd v Lee Lighting Ltd* [1991] BCLC 575. The Court of Appeal ([1991] BCC 620), held that there was insufficient evidence that the directors knew of the interest so that the niceties of disclosure did not arise.
107 *Costa Rica Rly Co Ltd v Forwood* [1901] 1 Ch 746.
108 Provided that resolutions appointing others are put separately from any resolution to appoint or reappoint him.
109 Such an Article is clearly desirable in single-family companies where all the members of the board would otherwise be disqualified.
110 *Gray v New Augarita Porcupine Mines Ltd* [1952] 3 DLR 1, PC.
111 *Northern Counties Securities v Jackson Steeple & Co* [1974] 2 All ER 625.
112 As in *Cook v Deeks* [1916] 1 AC 554, PC; 'Fraud' on a minority means 'oppression' rather than dishonesty: against creditors it connotes a deliberate, although not necessarily dishonest, depletion of assets which the creditors were entitled to have kept intact for their benefit: *Re DKG Contractors Ltd* [1990] BCC 903.
113 The word 'material' limits the effect of this requirement; the general law applies to interests of any kind.
114 *Hely-Hutchinson v Brayhead Ltd* [1968] 1 QB 549.
115 [1990] 2 AC 663.

116 Not only did the judges deny remuneration, at the same time they refused any right to payment under an Article entitling a director to remuneration for professional services on the basis that, although he was a lawyer, his skills in the present case were not being exercised in a professional capacity.

117 [1990] BCC 310.

118 Although the purchaser may have a claim for damages if the shares are not transferred to him, it by no means follows that the vendor has a claim for lost earnings if he is not awarded the service contract. If the purchase price of the shares was reduced to take account of the service agreement, it may be possible to award the vendor the difference; but the court would be rewriting the agreement if it did this.

119 Effectively any dealing between a company and a director or a person connected with him.

120 There are broadly parallel provisions for group accounts.

121 Ie the directors preparing the accounts, who may decide by a majority (excluding the interested director).

122 Schedule 6.

123 *Gray v New Augarita Porcupine Mines Ltd* [1952] 3 DLR 1, at p 14, PC, where Lord Radcliffe said '. . . if it is material to their judgment that they should know not merely that he has an interest but what it is and how far it goes then he must see to it that they are informed'.

124 This was certainly the view of the inspectors in the investigation in connection with the National Group of Unit Trusts (*First Re-investment Trust Ltd and other Companies*) (HMSO, 1974). In a situation of this type, they pointed out that a general declaration was 'almost valueless'. Only a full and specific declaration could have enabled the other directors to appreciate the significance of the decisions they were being called upon to make.

125 Section 330, discussed in Chapter 10.

126 Section 320, discussed at **5.5**.

127 Section 311: *Owens v Multiflux* [1977] IRLR 113.

128 Section 312, see **11.6.2**. Compensation is distinct from a bona fide payment by way of damages for breach of contract: s 316(3).

129 Section 231, Sch 5, discussed in Chapter 4.

130 Section 318.

131 Section 319, discussed in Chapter 10.

132 Section 235.

133 Section 323.

134 Section 324.

135 Section 198, discussed in Chapter 7.

136 Partnership Act 1890, s 30.

137 *London & Mashonaland Exploration Co Ltd v New Mashonaland Exploration Co Ltd* [1891] WN 165. It may be that this case rests on the fact that the director concerned was a mere figurehead. Christie (1992) 55 MLR 506 suggests the case is wrongly decided, although the decision was approved by Lord Blanesborough in *Bell v Lever Bros* [1932] AC 161, at p 195.

138 *Bell v Lever Bros* [1932] AC 161 per Lord Blanesborough, at p 195. On the other hand an executive director may have to disclose the misconduct of other employees; *Sybron Corp v Rochem Ltd* [1984] 1 Ch 112.

139 *Thomas Marshall (Exporters) Ltd v Guinle* [1979] Ch 227.

140 *Hivac Ltd v Park Royal Scientific Instruments Ltd* [1946] 2 All ER 350.

141 The *Mashonaland* case (see above) appears to suggest the contrary, but the modern authorities suggest a more vigorous approach.

142 Section 459. See Chapter 7.

143 *Scottish Co-operative Wholesale Society v Meyer* [1959] AC 324 per Lord Denning, at p 368.

144 *General Billposting Co v Atkinson* [1909] AC 118.

145 *Cranleigh Precision Engineering Ltd v Bryant* [1965] 1 WLR 1293. Outside confederates may also be made subject to an injunction on this ground.

146 *Printers & Finishers Ltd v Holloway* [1964] 1 All ER 54.

147 *Thomas Marshall (Exporters) Ltd v Guinle* [1979] Ch 227. What is to be regarded as a 'trade secret' attracting *automatic* protection is something which, in the end, can be determined only by the particular circumstances and not by the company's view of its 'confidentiality': *Faccenda Chicken Ltd v Fowler* [1986] 3 WLR 288.

148 [1972] 2 All ER 759.

149 [1925] Ch 407.

150 *Re Brazilian Rubber Plantations and Estates Ltd* [1911] 1 Ch 425.

151 [1892] 2 Ch 100.

152 They were in fact relieved of liability by an Article which made them liable only for wilful neglect or default. Such an Article would now be void under s 310.

153 *Huckerby v Elliott* [1970] 1 All ER 189. They were also recited more recently in the Privy Council in *Kuwait Asia Bank EC v National Mutual Life Nominees Ltd* [1990] 3 All ER 404, at p 420, but there the question to be decided was whether a shareholder with indirect representation on the board by two of the five directors owed a duty of care to the company's creditors. Not surprisingly the answer was 'No'. This should be read in the light of the discussion of 'shadow directors' at **6.2.9**.

154 One director in the *Brazilian Rubber* case had no knowledge of business and was induced to join the board by the assurance that it would give him a pleasant part-time activity with no responsibility. And this was not the 75-year-old, deaf director!

155 *Lister v Romford Ice and Cold Storage Ltd* [1957] AC 555.

156 *Dorchester Finance Co Ltd v Stebbings* [1989] BCLC 498.

157 Ibid, at p 505.

158 This is quite apart from the criminal sanctions imposed by s 233(5), as inserted by s 7 of the 1989 Act.

159 [1992] BCC 14.

160 [1993] BCC 646.

161 [1925] Ch 407.

162 [1989] BCLC 498. The litigation actually took place in 1977.

163 Since this allowed the active director to do as he pleased, it became more a matter of a very careless delegation of power than reasonable reliance on an officer to whom power has been properly delegated. In 1974, inspectors reporting to the DTI took the view that co-directors were responsible for the default of a colleague who dominated the board and submitted his investment decisions to it merely for rubber-stamping: *Report on First Re-investment Trust Ltd and other Companies* (HMSO, 1974).

164 *Re The New Mashonaland Syndicate* [1892] 3 Ch 577.

165 *Fry v Tapson* (1884) 28 Ch D 268.

166 *Re City Equitable Fire Insurance Co* [1925] Ch 407.

167 [1992] BCC 14.

168 For an example involving no element of dishonesty: a company is often exposed to swingeing criminal liability for breaches of social or environmental legislation. Even the most reliable compliance officer must be subject to some sorts of periodic checks by the board (quite apart from the unpleasant Parliamentary habit of tacking director fines onto corporate liability).

169 *Drincqbier v Wood* [1899] 1 Ch 406, per Byrne J.

170 *Dorchester Finance Co Ltd v Stebbings* [1989] BCLC 498, per Foster J.

171 *Fine Industrial Commodities Ltd v Powling* [1955] 2 All ER 707.

172 [1901] AC 1477.

173 See **5.8.1** at point (1), above.

174 When, however, it comes to *minority*, as distinct from company, action against directors it can equally confidently be predicted that the court will refuse to investigate a bona fide decision or dealing approved by the majority: see **6.4.1** and **7.15.1**.

175 [1994] 3 All ER 506.

176 *Land Credit Co of Ireland v Lord Fermoy* (1870) 5 Ch App 763. One consequence of EC membership may be, however, to change the law so that each director becomes liable for damage caused to the company by *any* director's wrong-doing, unless he proves that it occurred without fault on his part. This proposal is not supported by the UK: see DTI Consultative Document, *Amended Proposal for a Fifth Directive on the Harmonisation of Company Law in the EC*, January 1990.

177 *Huckerby v Elliot* [1970] 1 All ER 189, where the director failed to inquire whether a gaming licence had been obtained but had no reason to be suspicious; *Norman v Theodore Goddard* [1991] BCLC 1028, above.

178 *Re Lands Allotment Co* [1894] 1 Ch 617. He will have a right of contribution from those
responsible: *Ramskill v Edwards* (1885) 31 Ch D 100: Civil Liability (Contribution) Act 1978.
179 *Department of Health and Social Security v Wayte* [1972] 1 All ER 255, where a director who had
gone out of office on liquidation was made liable for National Insurance contributions which
should have been paid while he was a director.

Chapter 6

LIABILITIES OF DIRECTORS

6.1 CONSEQUENCES OF BREACH OF DUTY

What steps are open to the company or others where there has been a breach of one or
more of the duties discussed in Chapter 5?

6.1.1 Company to sue

Because a director's duties are owed to the company, and any loss resulting from
breaches will be presumed to be losses to the company, it is the company which is the
party primarily entitled to bring an action against the delinquent director. Where the
company cannot or will not sue (in particular where the wrongdoer controls it), it is
possible for one or more shareholders to bring a 'derivative' action in their own name,
but on behalf of the company. This form of action is so hedged about with limitations,
however, that it cannot be regarded as a primary remedy for breach of duty and is
considered separately in the context of shareholder remedies generally (see **7.15**).

6.1.2 Insolvency

After the company has gone into winding up, the liquidator may bring proceedings
under s 212 of the Insolvency Act 1986 for any breach of duty relating to the company.
This section is designed to allow the liquidator to recover from delinquent
management in the course of the winding up, and without commencing separate
proceedings. It does not actually widen directors' liabilities, but allows speedy
recovery where there is liability under the general law. It should be noted that the
jurisdiction extends not only to officers, but also to any person who 'is or has been
concerned, or taken part, in the promotion, formation or management' of the company
and even to any person who has acted as liquidator, administrator or administrative
receiver of the company. Although, therefore, it will not catch those who exercised
clerical or other non-management functions,[1] it will catch those who exercised
management functions, whether or not they are members of the board or, indeed, of
the company.

There is no similar summary remedy for an administrator appointed by the court or an
administrative receiver appointed by a creditor. Since each of these effectively takes
over the function of the board, each is able to bring an ordinary action, in the
company's name, for breach of duty. The remedy under s 212 can, however, be sought
by a creditor or contributory and may be available not only against a director who has
been guilty of breach of fiduciary duty but also against one who has merely been
negligent. For example, in *Re D'Jan of London Ltd*[2] Hoffmann LJ, sitting as an
additional judge of the Chancery Division, held that the director concerned had

clearly been negligent in signing a fire insurance proposal form (containing an untrue statement) and, as such, was susceptible to proceedings being brought against him by the liquidator.

6.1.3   Measure of recovery

Where the basis of the claim is loss caused to the company, this is the basis on which the sum recovered will be measured. It may often be difficult to quantify the liability of a director who is responsible, but nevertheless was not directly involved in the dealings which caused the loss. Loss to the company is irrelevant, however, if the company's claim is based on a right to an account of money or assets improperly taken or dealt with by the respondent. For example, if a director has been contracting on behalf of the company with another firm in which he is interested, his evidence that the firm charged the company only a commercial rate is more or less irrelevant once it is established that there was an unauthorised conflict of interest; he will be ordered to repay the whole profit made by the firm.[3] In liquidation, the court may restrict the claim to the amount required to pay the company's debts.[4] The director cannot set off any debt owing by the company to him.[5] It may, of course, be the case that a director receives payments from his company in breach of a number of different statutory provisions. For example, he might at the same time be liable under s 212 for misfeasance, s 214 for wrongful trading and s 239 for a preference. In *Re DKG Contractors Ltd*,[6] John Weeks QC held that liability under the various provisions was not cumulative. A payment ordered to be made under s 239 or s 212 should be taken as satisfying an order under s 214. On the other hand, in *Re Purpoint Ltd*,[7] Vinelott J found that there was no injustice in ordering the payments under both ss 212 and 214 so long as the director against whom the orders were made was not required to pay more than was needed to meet the liabilities of the company.

6.1.4   Defendant

Proceedings may be brought not only against a director properly appointed but also against:

(1)   a de facto or shadow director;[8]
(2)   a retired director;[9]
(3)   the estate of a deceased director;[10]
(4)   a bankrupt director.

6.1.5   Limitation of actions

Most actions are barred after periods of three or six years by the Limitation Act 1980. These limits do not apply, however, to actions for fraud, fraudulent breach of trust or for the recovery of trust property which has passed through the defendant's hands.[11]

6.2   DISQUALIFICATION AND WRONGFUL TRADING

Attention has already been drawn to the likelihood that the law relating to disqualification of those unfit to act as directors will have a considerable influence on the content of directors' duties under the general law. This is particularly important in relation to those duties summarised as obligations of skill and care.

Similarly, personal liability of directors who have failed to act to minimise losses to the creditors is based on considerations which bear directly on the general duties of directors.

Although these statutory rules do not involve directors' duties to the company in the traditional sense that the company may take action for a wrong done to it, their practical relevance is obvious and far-reaching.

6.2.1   Disqualification

The various statutory headings under which the court may or must disqualify a director from being concerned in company management are summarised at **2.5.1**. One heading in particular calls for comment.

Unfit directors of insolvent companies

The court must disqualify a person who is or has been a director of a company which has become insolvent at any time[12] if it is satisfied that his conduct (including his conduct as a director of any other company[13]) makes him unfit to be concerned in the management of a company: s 6 of the Company Directors Disqualification Act 1986. In *Re Bath Glass Ltd*,[14] Gibson J said that the provision:

> 'widens the meaning of the references to a person's conduct as a director of any company or companies so as to include, where that company or any of those companies has become insolvent, that person's conduct in relation to any matter connected with or arising out of the insolvency of that company. . . . The requirement as to conduct may be satisfied by looking at the conduct of the respondent as a director of the insolvent company alone or by looking not only at that conduct but at the respondent's conduct as a director of one or more other companies.'

Put another way, the conduct of the director in relation to other companies may be looked at by the court as an indication that the director should be disqualified. It may not be looked at in mitigation of his conduct in respect of the insolvent company.

The Act sets out a number of criteria to which the court must have regard. These are set out in full at **2.5.1**, but are not repeated here because what has happened in practice is that the courts, no doubt with an eye on the criteria, have formulated their own guidelines.

Safeguarding the public

The primary objective is not to punish delinquent directors but to disqualify where that is necessary to protect the public against *future* misconduct; the past conduct provides the judge with a measure of the threat posed by the respondent. Neither is disqualification directly related to breach of duty. Since, however, the court is using past conduct as the basis of the respondent's fitness for office, it is effectively laying down minimal standards which will inevitably colour the director's duties to the company itself.

Misfortune, misjudgment and mismanagement

There was a tendency in the earlier cases to say that disqualification should be reserved for directors who had committed a breach of 'commercial morality' or a lack of 'commercial probity', although this might include extreme cases of gross negligence or total incompetence.[15] The decision of the Court of Appeal in *Re Sevenoaks Stationers Ltd*[16] made a break with this line of reasoning, treating unfitness as a question to be decided on a case-by-case basis and certainly not dependent upon a finding of 'total' incompetence. It remains true, however, that disqualification is unlikely to be ordered where bad luck and unforeseeable misfortune has played a large part in a company's downfall. Examples of this would include the unexpected departure of key directors or employees[17] and the sudden termination of a profitable distribution agreement.[18] Similarly, an ordinary commercial misjudgment as to the profitability of a line of business or investment would not make a director unfit to hold office.[19]

The important task, therefore, is to find the middle ground between bad luck and the sort of wilful disregard of the interests of creditors and the company which undoubtedly merits disqualification and falls little short of dishonesty.[20] Most of the reported cases concern quite small companies and many, perhaps most, seem to have been undercapitalised. Merely to create and do business with a company which is short of capital is not, generally, conduct which in itself calls for disqualification. It often leads directly to such conduct however. First, it makes it more than ever inexcusable if proper accounting records are not kept and proper accounts made. Secondly, there is a real prospect that such a company will trade at the expense of its creditors. These are, perhaps, the commonest features of disqualification cases. For example, in the Sevenoaks case (above), the respondent, a chartered accountant, had been a director of five companies which had become insolvent. The following formed the basis of the disqualification order.

(1)   Two of the companies had been trading when insolvent and known to the respondent to be in difficulties. This was at the expense of those creditors who did not press for immediate payment. These included, as is usually the case, the Crown in respect of PAYE deductions and VAT collections. But there is nothing special about the Crown's status as a creditor. It is simply one of the creditors which tends to be slow to press for payment, and it is the practice of paying only those who are pressing, and keeping the business going with funds which should be used to pay the other creditors of the business, which is objectionable.

(2)   There were never audited, let alone filed, accounts (and, in one case, no accounting records at all).

(3)   Company funds were used to make what were obviously irrecoverable inter-company loans or improper payments by one company on another's behalf, and one company was made to guarantee another at a time when the latter was known to be in severe difficulties.

(4)   Trading went on when the respondent knew the companies to be in difficulties, which each company was after a short period of business.

A distinct question which sometimes arises is whether directors show themselves 'unfit' if their remuneration is excessive. No simple answer can be given to this. Even though profits may be falling and the business doing poorly, directors with a high payment package, including, perhaps, expensive cars, are probably on safe ground until it can be said that the company is facing such difficulties that they are enjoying their remuneration at the expense of the creditors.[21] Conversely, the fact that the director has lost his own money in the company and is suffering like other creditors is likely to count in his favour if the case is borderline, and may also reduce the period of disqualification if it is not. An example of personal loss by a director being taken into account as a mitigating factor in respect of the length of his disqualification arose in *Re Cargo Agency Ltd*.[22] Here the director against whom disqualification proceedings were taken had lost a considerable amount of his own money. Having said that, the public had suffered as a result of his continuing trading and no reasonable person could have properly so continued. Accordingly, a disqualification order had to be made. In the circumstances, Harman J felt that a two-year disqualification period was appropriate.

In *Re Living Images Ltd*,[23] Laddie J found that the repayment of a loan to a creditor in circumstances amounting to a preference was sufficient to justify disqualification. In *Secretary of State for Trade and Industry v Richardson*[24] Ferris J said that misconduct in this regard by a director was not confined to what he described as 'statutory preferences'.

Reliance on others

We have already seen that, under the general law, a director is allowed to rely upon others to whom functions have been properly delegated. This is true in the present context as well, but subject to similar qualifications. First, the sole executive director of a small company will be assumed to be directly concerned in all aspects of its business.[25] Secondly, no director may ignore his responsibility to see that the company keeps proper accounts and, as far as he has the skills to do so, that it is subject to proper financial controls.[26] This does not mean that disqualification follows automatically from every failure of overall board supervision. In one case, a company failed to produce audited accounts or annual returns because the responsible director had, on a mistaken view of his task, allowed auditing difficulties to bring the process to a halt. He could not, as a chartered accountant, be excused, but it was held that his co-director might be excused because he had relied on somebody he had 'good and sufficient cause to believe was a proper person to rely on' and with whom he shared the overall responsibility.[27] Some of this generosity extended to the responsible director, who was disqualified for the minimum period of two years because the company, having ceased trading, had no creditors which were injured by the lack of accounts. It would be different for both directors if third parties had suffered, or if there had been a failure to keep any accounting records at all.

6.2.2 Periods of disqualification

Once a finding of unfitness is made, the director *must* be disqualified. The minimum period, under s 6, is two years, the maximum is 15. The court in the *Sevenoaks* case (see above) laid down the following tariff.

(1) Only serious cases should fall within the 11 to 15 year bracket. These would include directors who had been disqualified in the past.

(2) The minimum bracket of two to five years should be applied where, although disqualification is mandatory, the case is relatively not very serious. It is only at this point on the scale, of course, that the court is likely to exercise its power to give the respondent leave to act as a director notwithstanding the disqualification. For example, a young director of a company formed to take over his father's business was disqualified for two years for a combination of trading at the expense of creditors (because of chronic undercapitalisation and a failure to see that proper accounts were kept). He was nevertheless given leave to act as a director of his new company provided that proper monthly board meetings were held and attended by representatives of the auditors. Leave was given for one year only, on the basis that when he applied for an extension the court could determine if he had continued to conduct the new company prudently.[28] The fact that the respondent has *already* shown some signs of mitigating prudence may also be relevant. For example, a director who has run more than one company into insolvency and who has filed no accounts or returns is likely to be heading towards the middle period of disqualification (below), and, as we have seen, cannot totally escape responsibility for matters which are within the supervisory function of all directors. If, however, he at some point took on a qualified person such as an accountant or chartered secretary to look after the 'paperwork', this may lead the court to view the matter more generously.[29]

(3) The middle period of 6 to 10 years should be reserved for serious cases not meriting the top bracket. This includes those directors who have been milking the company for their own gain[30] unless the degree or repetition of their misconduct takes them into the top bracket.

6.2.3 Procedure

Applications for disqualification under s 6 are made by the DTI or by the Official Receiver, who may be instructed to apply by the DTI where the company is being compulsorily wound up (s 7). This action will usually be triggered by a statutory report by an 'office-holder', ie the liquidator, administrator or administrative receiver appointed to a company, or the official receiver himself when acting as liquidator. See the Insolvent Companies (Reports on Conduct of Directors) Rules 1996, SI 1996/1909. Applications are normally barred 'after the end of the period of two years beginning with the day on which the company of which [the respondent] is or has been a director *becomes insolvent*' (s 7(2)) (emphasis added). This has been interpreted to mean that the period runs from the *first* event qualifying as 'insolvency'.[31] So, for example, if the company goes into administrative receivership or administration on 1 January, and then directly into liquidation on 1 July, the period runs from 1 January and does not start afresh when the liquidation commences.[32] Section 7(2) commences 'except with the leave of the court, an application for the making under that section of a disqualification order . . .' may not be made more than two years after the commencement of the insolvency. Accordingly, it is clearly envisaged that the court may grant an extension of the two-year limitation period. However, the legislation is deficient in two vital areas. First, it gives no guidance as to the procedure to be followed in applying for an extension. Secondly, it gives no guidance as to the ground on which an extension may be sought. In *Re Probe Data Systems Ltd (2)*,[33] Millett J said that an applicant should apply ex parte to the registrar for leave. Where leave is needed, it is for the applicant to apply in the first instance ex parte to the registrar for leave, putting before the registrar the whole of his evidence both for leave and on its merits. If the registrar considers that there is a prima facie case for granting leave, he should then give directions to the applicant to serve the respondent with the summons or other application for leave and the evidence in support. The respondent would then be entitled, if he so wished, to argue that leave should not be granted. On the other hand, in *Re Crestjoy Products Ltd*,[34] Harman J felt that this was an unsuitable procedure as it introduced an extra and unnecessary stage in the proceedings. He felt that the:

> 'Secretary of State should issue an originating summons for leave, serving it and making it good before the judge (possibly before the registrar) with the respondents to the summons for leave present, following which, if leave was granted, the disqualification summons would then be issued. If leave is refused the originating summons will be dismissed. Either way the originating summons for leave to issue proceedings for disqualification will have been disposed of.'

As has been said, the statute gives no indication as to the grounds on which an extension of the limitation period may be granted. In *Re Copecrest Ltd*,[35] Hoffmann LJ quoted with approval the judgment of Scott J in *Re Probe Data Systems Ltd (3)*[36] where he said:

> 'In considering an application s 7(2) for leave to commence proceedings out of time the court should, in my opinion, take into account the following matters:
> (1) the length of the delay;
> (2) the reasons for the delay;
> (3) the strength of the case against the director; and
> (4) the degree of prejudice caused to the director by the delay.'

In the latter case, Hoffmann LJ said that the two-year period must be treated as having a built-in contingency allowance for unexpected delays for which the Secretary of State is not responsible. In *Secretary of State for Trade and Industry v Murrall*,[37] an extension was not allowed where there had been a delay of some eight months in circumstances where no satisfactory explanation had been put forward by the Secretary of State. In *Secretary of State for Trade and Industry v Davis*,[38] the Court of Appeal, having cited with approval the criteria of Scott LJ in *Re Probe Data Systems Ltd (3)* (above) said that the Secretary of State had to show good reason for being granted the extension of time which he sought, but that this was not the same as having to show a good reason for the delay. Obviously the better the explanation for the delay, the easier it will be for an extension to be obtained. However, even where the explanation of the delay is not a good one, the court may still extend the two-year limitation. In this particular case, the allegations, against the director concerned were in respect of false accounting and trading while the company was insolvent. Having regard to the seriousness of the allegations and the public interest in their being determined, an extension should be granted. In *Secretary of State for Trade and Industry v Martin*,[39] Judge Weeks QC struck out an application for disqualification proceedings for unfitness following two periods of delay, one of six months and another of nine months after the expiry of the two-year period. These were said to be inordinate and inexcusable. Such a delay meant that the memories of those involved were less fresh than they should have been. The purpose of disqualification is to protect the public not to punish delinquent directors. Still less is disqualification designed to give revenge to creditors.

A further procedural oddity concerns the need to give notice of the ordinary application[40] for a disqualification order. Where the application is made to the winding-up court – and in no other case – the Act specifically requires 10 days' clear notice to the respondent (s 16(1)). The rules of natural justice require the DTI, quite apart from s 16, to give the respondent adequate warning of the case against him so that a proper defence may be mounted *at the hearing*. Since the 10 days' notice *before application* is unlikely to afford him enough time to persuade the DTI to stay its hand at that point, the courts have decided that a failure to comply with this requirement does not necessarily invalidate the application.[41] The respondent will have to show that a short period of notice actually prejudiced him.

Procedure for disqualification

The decision to start proceedings is that of the Secretary of State and the applicant is either him or the Official Receiver. The procedure for disqualification is governed by the Insolvent Companies (Disqualification of Unfit Directors) Proceedings Rules 1987, SI 1987/2023. An application is made to the High Court by originating summons or to county court by originating application. Accordingly, the Rules of the Supreme Court 1965 or the County Court Rules 1981 (now replaced by the Civil Procdure Rules 1998) apply as relevant, but the designations and procedures introduced by the Civil Procedure Rules will take effect as soon as those Rules are fully extended to Insolvency Proceedings. When the summons (ie the originating summons or application) is issued, there must be filed in court evidence in support of the application, copies of which must be served together with the summons on the respondent. The evidence must be by way of affidavit except where the applicant is the Official Receiver in which case it may take the form of a written report. In *Re Circle Holiday International plc*,[42] Micklem J allowed an administrator's affidavit which included hearsay. That this was correct was confirmed in *Re Rex Williams Leisure*.[43] Affidavits by an applicant for disqualification were said to fall into a special category of fact finding affidavit and so were said to be exempt from the hearsay rule under Ord 20, r 10 of the County Court Rules 1981. In *Secretary of State for Trade and Industry v Ascroft*,[44] Millett LJ gave three reasons why hearsay was acceptable in these circumstances. First, it was obtained by a professional. Secondly, it had been considered by the Secretary of State as worthy of credence. Thirdly, the respondent would have an opportunity to challenge it. On the other hand, in *Re Oakfame Construction Ltd*,[45] Reid QC, sitting as a Deputy High Court Judge, struck out affidavits sworn by two accountants on behalf of the respondents to director disqualification proceedings on the grounds that they consisted mainly of hearsay, advocacy and submissions rather than expert evidence.

The summons must be endorsed to the effect that the application has been made in accordance with the Rules and must specify the possible length of the disqualification order which may be made against the respondent. The endorsement must also state that a disqualification order for up to five years may be made immediately at the hearing and that if, at the hearing, the court is minded to impose a disqualification of more than five years, it will adjourn the application for the hearing of further evidence at a later date. Finally, the endorsement must also state that any evidence which the respondent wishes to be taken into consideration must be filed in court in accordance with time-limits imposed under the Rules. It is then for the respondent, within 28 days, to file in court any affidavit evidence in opposition to the application which he wishes the court to take into consideration. At the same time, he must serve a copy of such evidence on the applicant. The applicant must, within 14 days of receiving the copy of the respondent's evidence, file in court any further evidence which he wishes the court to take into account.

Summary procedure

When disqualification proceedings are taken for unfitness, it is possible for the court to follow an agreed summary procedure if there is little or no dispute on factual matters. In *Re Carecraft Construction Co Ltd*,[46] Ferris J allowed the case to proceed on the summary procedure on the basis that there was some disputed evidence which established unfitness within the lowest disqualification bracket of two to five years. The disputed evidence did not have such a significant potential impact upon the seriousness of the conduct as to require there to be a full hearing at which it could be evaluated. This procedure was confirmed, again by Ferris J in *Re Aldermanbury Trusts plc*.[47] Here there were more than 20 pages of agreed facts running to some 131 separate paragraphs. Again, it was said that the disputed facts were not sufficient to move the disqualification order into a higher bracket. Accordingly, the summary procedure could be used. The *Carecraft* procedure is now regulated by *Practice Direction No 2 of 1995*,[48] under which the parties must inform the court, submit a statement of the undisputed facts, and specify the period of disqualification which the court will be invited to order. Alternatively, they can specify the relevant brackets (two to five years; 6 to 10 years; 11 to 15 years) under the principles in *Re Sevenoaks Stationers* (above). However, a severe word of warning was sounded on the *Carecraft* procedure in *Secretary of State for Trade and Industry v Rogers*.[49] This case was an appeal from a decision of Harman J under which the learned judge had imposed an eight-year disqualification at a summary hearing. The director concerned was a member of a professional chartered association (we are not told in the report which profession but it is believed he was a chartered accountant). He was prepared to admit the majority of the allegations made against him but he vigorously denied a number of allegations of dishonesty. In spite of the denial of the allegations of dishonesty and in spite of the fact that no evidence had been produced to support them or tested in court, Harman J astonishingly added to the transcript the words 'that was dishonest' to his finding that the director had 'clearly acted for his own benefit and to the harm of the companies of which he was a director' and that he was dishonest. The director appealed, not against the disqualification (which he obviously had accepted by asking for the summary procedure to be followed), but against the finding of dishonesty. Accordingly, the Court of Appeal, very properly, set aside the finding of dishonesty. Having done so, the Court of Appeal confirmed that a disqualification was appropriate on the admissions of the director and imposed afresh a disqualification period of eight years. Scott V-C sounded a warning on the limits of the *Carecraft* procedure:

> 'The . . . procedure can effectively, and without the judge's consent, limit the facts on which the judge can base his judgment as to the order that should be made; but the *Carecraft* procedure cannot oblige the judge to make a disqualification order and cannot bind as to the period of disqualification to be imposed. It is important, in my opinion, in

cases where the *Carecraft* procedure is to be used, for the judge to have an opportunity to read the papers in advance. If the judge on reading the papers has any doubts as to whether a disqualification order should be made or as to whether the period should fall within the agreed bracket, the doubts should be voiced at the earliest possible moment so that parties may consider whether they, or either of them, would prefer a full trial. It would, I anticipate, be a very rare case in which any such doubts were entertained.'

Voluntary undertakings not to act as a director

In *Secretary of State for Trade and Industry v Rogers* (above), Scott V-C said:

'I have on previous occasions expressed the personal belief that it would be very sensible, in a case where the Secretary of State and director agree that the director's conduct warrants and the public interest would be satisfied by a disqualification for a specified period, if the disqualification could be imposed by a formal undertaking entered into by the director without the necessity of a court order. A statutory amendment would, however, be necessary in order to give such an undertaking the same effect as a court order.'

In so saying, Scott V-C was reiterating what he had stated in an introductory note to the Practice Note referred to above:

'under the 1986 Act, there is no alternative but for all applications for disqualification orders, no matter what state of agreement there may be between the parties, to be processed through the court machinery and made by a judge or registrar after a court hearing. I regard this as unnecessary and avoidable. I would recommend, accordingly, that the Secretary of State give consideration to the possibility of introducing amending legislation, under which an agreement between the director and the Secretary of State, or the Official Receiver, as to the disqualification period to be applied to the director, be given the same effect as a court order imposing the disqualification period.'

Even without such legislation, there have been a few cases recently where such undertakings have been considered. In *Re Homes Assured Corporation plc*,[50] Robert Walker J accepted an undertaking by a director, Sir Edward Du Cann, that he would not act as a director and granted a stay to disqualification proceedings being brought against him. In so doing, he said:

'The outcome of a stay of proceedings is no doubt not wholly satisfactory from the point of view of either party before me but it is right to say as Counsel has said and I echo, that approach and my approval of it is dictated by consideration of the state of health of Sir Edward who is now nearly 72 years of age. I have read a good deal of medical evidence about Sir Edward's condition. I do not propose to go into it in any detail except to mention that it covers both Sir Edward's heart condition and problems with his short-term memory and powers of concentration. The medical evidence satisfies me that it would be hazardous and difficult to embark on a trial which would be of several weeks duration.'

A similar decision was reached by Lloyd J in *Secretary of State for Trade and Industry v Cleland*.[51] Here the director concerned was 60 years of age. He was suffering from medical conditions attributable partly to stress and overwork and had been advised not to work. He had retired three years before the hearing and said that he had no intention of seeking an appointment as a director in the future. In these circumstances, Lloyd J was prepared to allow the application for disqualification to be stayed. On the other hand, in *Secretary of State for Trade and Industry v Davies (No 2)*,[52] Rattee J refused to accept such an undertaking. He regarded the earlier cases as standing on their own particular facts and that, in the absence of some compelling reason to the contrary, there should be a hearing at which a disqualification order is made. He said:

> 'I accept the Secretary of State's submission that the legislature has in the 1986 Act laid down machinery for protecting the public by disqualification orders made by the court. There is no suggestion that the Secretary of State did not act perfectly properly in bringing the present proceedings, although of course those proceedings are hotly disputed. It seems to me wrong in principle for the court to intervene to stop such perfectly proper proceedings against the Secretary of State on the sole ground that the respondent to them has offered undertakings, whose effect may well, in many respects, be likely to be as practically efficacious as an order under the Act but which do not have the same effect as Parliament has thought fit to give an order made under the statutory machinery.'

This decision was in fact confirmed sub nom *Re Blackspur Group plc (No 2)*.[53] In giving the judgment of the Court of Appeal, Lord Woolf MR said:

> 'The purpose of the 1986 Act is the protection of the public, by means of prohibitary remedial action, by anticipated deterrent effect on further misconduct and by encouragement of higher standards of honesty and diligence in corporate management, from those who are unfit to be concerned in the management of a company. . . . Once proceedings have been brought to trial, it is for the court, not for the Secretary of State or for any other party, to decide whether a disqualification order should or should not be made . . . The unique form of the order and the special procedure for obtaining it is as prescribed by the 1986 Act. Significantly the 1986 Act does not expressly equip the court with a discretion to deploy the armoury of common law and equitable remedies to restrain future misconduct (injunction or undertaking in lieu of injunction), to punish for disregard of restraints imposed by court order (contempt orders of imprisonment or fine), to compensate for past loss unlawfully inflicted (damages) or to restore benefits unjustly acquired (restitution).'

At the time of writing, it is believed that delegated legislation will soon be introduced to permit unfit directors simply to give an undertstanding not to act as an alternative to going through disqualification proceedings.

The effect of disqualification by s 1 of the Company Directors Disqualification Act 1986

When a disqualification order has been made against a person, he may not, without the leave of the court:

(1) be a director of the company;
(2) be a liquidator or administrator of the company;
(3) be a receiver or manager of the company's property;
(4) be concerned in any way, whether directly or indirectly, in the promotion, formation or management of a company;

for the period of time specified beginning with the date of the order.

Contravention of a disqualification order carries both criminal and civil liabilities. By s 13, if a person acts in contravention of a disqualification order he commits a criminal offence carrying, on indictment, imprisonment of up to two years and an unlimited fine. By s 15, a person who acts in contravention of a disqualification order and is involved in the management of the company also becomes personally responsible for all the relevant debts of that company. This is a joint and several liability for those debts together with the company and other persons who may be held liable for them. The relevant debts of the company are such debts and liabilities of the company as are incurred at the time when that person was involved in the management of the company. A similar liability falls upon any person who is involved in management in circumstances where he is acting upon the instructions of a person whom he knows at the time to be subject to a disqualification order or to be an undischarged bankrupt. It is important to note that disqualification does not prevent a person from earning a living. He can engage in business as a sole trader or (probably) as a partner. What he most certainly is precluded from is hiding behind the privilege of limited liability. It is suggested that the decision of the Court of Appeal in *R v Holmes*[54] is wrong. Here the appellant had pleaded guilty to a charge of fraudulent trading and had been sentenced to 9 months' imprisonment, suspended for 2 years, and disqualified from acting as a director for 12 months. He was also ordered to pay £25,000 to a creditor whom he had defrauded under s 35 of the Powers of Criminal Courts Act 1973. He appealed against the compensation order. The Court of Appeal quashed the compensation order. Tucker J, giving the judgment of the Court said:

> 'We have difficulty in reconciling the two orders which the judge made, one for payment of the compensation which depended on the viability of an existing company and the other disqualifying the appellant from acting as a director which effectively prevented him from operating the company from which profit could be generated. It deprived him of a businessman's best asset, that is the recognition in the eyes of the public that he is fit to act as a director of a limited company.'

Such an assertion is contrary to one of the underlying principles of the disqualification legislation. For example, under s 10 of the Company Directors Disqualification Act 1986, where a court makes a finding of fraudulent or wrongful trading against a director it can, of its own volition, disqualify that person as a director for a period of up to 15 years. Such a finding presupposes that the director concerned will be ordered to make a contribution to the assets of the company. Therefore, the ability to pay compensation is not regarded by Parliament as being negated by a prohibition against acting as a director. Moreover, the learned judge seems to ignore the fact that a person can earn a living without the benefit of limited liability, as indeed he had himself when he practised at the Bar.

It is probable that the offence is one of strict liability. In *R v Brockley*,[55] the Court of Appeal held that it was an offence of strict liability for an undischarged bankrupt to act as a company director.

Partial disqualification

It is clearly envisaged by s 1 that a person generally disqualified as a director may be permitted by the court to act as a director or otherwise take part in the management of a specified company or companies. In *Re Lo-Line Electric Motors Ltd*,[56] a person was disqualified for a period of three years. He was, however, permitted to remain as a director of two family companies so long as his brother-in-law, whom the court found to be capable and responsible, was connected with both of the companies, one as a director and the other as controlling shareholder, and was responsible for the financial management of the companies. A similar decision was reached in *Re Majestic Recording Studios Ltd*.[57] Here the person concerned was disqualified for a period of five years. He was, however, permitted to continue as a director of a named company

'If and so long as he has with him during that period as a co-director an independent chartered accountant approved by the court who is willing to act with him'. In reaching this decision, Mervyn-Davies J referred to the director concerned as 'a chastened man'. A slightly different approach was adopted in *Re Chartmore Ltd*,[58] where permission was granted for a disqualified person to remain as a director of a named company so long as board meetings were held monthly and were attended by the company's auditor or his representative.

A disqualification order cannot debar a director from acting simply in respect of a particular class of company. In *R v Goodman*[59] the Court of Appeal was asked to consider whether a disqualification order would debar the person concerned simply from being the director of a public company whose shares were traded on the Stock Exchange. It was held that there was nothing in the Act which permitted the court to make such an order. Any application to act as a director while disqualified may be made at any time, either at the hearing when the disqualification order is imposed or subsequently. Ideally the application should be made at the initial hearing. In *Re Dicetrade Limited*[60] Dillon LJ said:

> 'It is in everyone's interests that if it is envisaged before the disqualification application comes on for hearing, and if the director has advised it will have been envisaged, then it should be heard at the same time because, from the point of view of the director, it is desirable that if he or she is going to be allowed to continue as director of that company there should be no time passing before the leave is granted.'

In *Re Gibson Davies and Co Ltd*[61] Mervyn-Davies J allowed the applicant to remain as a director subject to certain conditions. The conditions were that no cheque should be signed by the director concerned alone, he should draw no more than £380 per week by way of emoluments, there were to be implemented agreed accounting controls and monthly management accounts produced by the company's auditors. It is to be questioned whether such conditions are a dangerous precedent and whether an undertaking on the part of the director would be more advisable. Since they were expressed by the judge to be conditions the question arises as to what would be the effect of the director disregarding one of the conditions. Would he then be acting as a director while disqualified? The position would be much clearer if the director were required to give undertakings, breach of one of which would then be enforceable as a contempt of court.

6.2.4   Wrongful trading: introduction

Section 214 of the Insolvency Act 1986 enables the court, on application by the liquidator, to declare a director liable to contribute to the assets of an insolvent company. While this power has long existed in the case of *fraudulent* trading (see **6.2.11**), the sweep of s 214 is much wider, since it is based on a form of negligence. Further, the statutory description is misleading, since liability need not be based on the company's 'trading', let alone upon particular transactions. Rather, the whole of the director's conduct in relation to the company is held up for scrutiny; what he knew and what he did is compared with what he should have known and done.

The section applies to a director or shadow director if:

(1) the company has gone into insolvent liquidation. This occurs when, at the time of the winding-up resolution (voluntary winding up) or petition (compulsory winding up) the company's assets are insufficient to meet its debts and other liabilities and the expenses of winding up;

(2) at some earlier time,[62] the respondent knew that there was no 'reasonable prospect' of avoiding insolvent liquidation *or* 'ought to have concluded' that this was so; and

(3) at that time, he was a director or shadow director.

The respondent may then be held liable unless the court is satisfied that he subsequently took every step with a view to minimising the potential loss to the creditors that he ought to have taken.

It will be seen that there is a double yardstick to measure the respondent's performance: what should he have realised, and what should he then have done? If, on the first test, the respondent should have realised that the company was in severe difficulties but failed to do so, it is unlikely that he will escape under the second test. Consequently, what will often be decisive is *timing*. When should the respondent have woken up and reacted? In *Re Produce Marketing Consortium (No 2) Ltd*,[63] draft accounts for 1984–85 and 1985–86 were eventually submitted to the company in January 1987. They revealed a disaster, the auditor stating that the company was insolvent and could continue trading only with the continued support of its bank which was already calling for reduction of its overdraft. For the purposes of s 214, the court imputed knowledge of the 1984–85 accounts to the respondent directors *as at the end of July 1986*, when the accounts should have been available if the company had complied with its accounting duties under the Companies Act 1985. Specifically, they ought to have known not only that there was a deficiency of assets against liabilities but also its size. The reasoning affects all directors. The judge accepted that the reference in s 214 to the director's 'functions' meant that the court must examine the particular company and its business.

> 'It follows that the general knowledge, skill and experience postulated will be much less extensive in a small company in a modest way of business, with simple accounting procedures, than it will be in a large company with sophisticated procedures'.

This is an echo of a theme which runs through the ordinary law of directors' duties, through the disqualification cases, and also through earlier Acts imposing specific liability on directors for their company's defaults.[64] But this theme is increasingly qualified, and the judge continued:

> 'Nevertheless, certain minimum standards are to be assumed to be attained. Notably there is an obligation laid on companies to cause accounting records to be kept which are such as to disclose with reasonable accuracy at any time the financial position of the company at that time'.

Furthermore, the directors actually knew that turnover was dropping, which meant a substantial loss was being incurred (which would increase the asset deficiency).[65] The inevitable conclusion was that, at the end of July 1986, the directors ought to have realised that there was no reasonable prospect of avoiding insolvent liquidation. Given this, liability had to follow, since they had simply gone on trading for a further year, so increasing rather than minimising the loss to the company's creditors.

It should be noted that in the *Produce Marketing* case, one of the respondents was very much the driving force of the company, full of energy and optimism; the other was a bookkeeper with accounting experience promoted to the board but not in a good position to influence the other unless he steeled himself to take a very firm line. Both were held liable.[66]

Section 214(4) clearly imposes a duty to make the necessary inquiries about the company's affairs. Once there are warning signs these may be enough *in themselves* to trigger the section, as in *Re Purpoint Ltd*,[67] where even the company's 'exiguous' accounting records should have revealed its hopeless position. In other cases, the warning signs will trigger the director's responsibility to make checks and investigate. In *Re DKG Contractors Ltd*,[68] the directors became aware that creditors were pressing for payment and that one supplier was withholding deliveries. The court held that they should have instituted some form of financial control at this point. That, in turn, would have revealed the company's position, and that was the stage at which s 214 came into operation.

6.2.5   Wrongful trading: the 'functions' of directors

In the cases discussed above, all the companies were small and had small boards. In these circumstances, some allowance is made for the lack of sophistication of the directors, but not for ignorance of their role or of the requirements imposed by law upon companies. Furthermore, since they are so few, and the business is so closely controlled, it is easy enough to apply the principle that every director has a residual supervisory function which includes monitoring the company's financial position.

The recognition of differing degrees of skill among directors becomes more significant as the company and the board grow larger, for here there will, and often must be, de facto, if not always formal, division of functions. Each director is in principle judged by the same statutory test: what should he have known, and what should he have *ascertained* (the word is used in the Act)? The standard to be applied is that of the 'reasonably diligent person' having not merely the general knowledge, skill and experience of the director in question, but that 'reasonably' to be expected of a person in his position and carrying out his functions.

It may therefore be relevant to inquire whether the director is an executive or non-executive director; how closely he is expected to be involved in day-to-day management; whether he is responsible for planning or finance, and so on. Although there is no reference to the reason for his appointment, this may become material. He may have been appointed purely because of some technical expertise. He may, therefore, be expected to have enough grasp in his professed area of competence to foresee that a project is failing or that an area of business is likely to damage the company financially but not, perhaps, to grasp as readily as a director appointed for his business acumen that the company is entering a financially dangerous period. This assumes that even where no formal or defined 'function' is allocated to a director, his expected role as adviser, consultant or resident expert may still be a 'function', which seems to be what the section intends. Of course, where a specific function is allocated to a particular director, the objective criterion of 'reasonably expected' knowledge, skill and expertise means that his failings will not be excused merely because he lacks the required levels of knowledge, etc. On the other hand, the actual level of expertise which he possesses may mean that more than normal could be 'reasonably expected' of him. There is, therefore, an element of 'heads I win, tails you lose' about s 214; liability may be imposed on the inadequate by reason of their inadequacy, and upon the more-than-adequate for performing below their own higher standards.

Re Produce Marketing Consortium Ltd,[69] concerned two directors, one of whom was perceived by the court to be more responsible for the insolvency of the company than the other. Knox J declared that the directors were jointly liable to make a contribution of £75,000 to the assets of the company in the liquidation. This was expressed as a joint and several liability. However, as between the two of them the more culpable director should indemnify the less culpable as to £50,000 and then above that figure there should be a joint liability. Accordingly, the more culpable director would have to pay £62,500 and the less culpable £12,500.

6.2.6   Wrongful trading: avoiding trouble

It is clear that s 214 requires some level of financial understanding and diligence of every director. Although the reported cases concern active directors, it would be folly to rely upon the principles of *Re City Equitable* (**5.8.1**) in the present context.

The question then arises: What can the 'average' director do to meet those obligations? Timing is all-important, since s 214 applies once the time comes when the director knows or, more stringently, ought to have concluded that insolvent liquidation was effectively the only reasonable prospect for the company. This means that the director must be constantly vigilant, not only to anticipate the moment at which he ought to conclude that insolvency is unavoidable, but also in order to 'take steps' so as to avoid his own liability (below). In general terms, therefore, he must at all times keep a careful eye on the company's performance and prospects. He must not be content with reading the last set of accounts and balance sheets – although his competence in doing this is now more important than ever before. He must look at all materials supplied to the board and to the members, and remember that he is judged not only by what he knows but by what he should ascertain. He must therefore be prepared to inquire, and to persist in inquiries, if there is any apparent cause for unease; the more awkward his inquiries, and the more embarrassing, the more he must be ready to persist. More specifically, he may take the following precautions.

(1) He should ensure that an accurate record is kept of his own activities in and out of board meetings, whether in the form of minutes or otherwise, and must be ready to make such a record and present it to his fellow directors if he feels that his actions or views are not properly reflected in the company's own records.

(2) He must satisfy himself that those records, and the financial and other information supplied to the board and to the membership, are sufficient. He should, if he feels it necessary to do so, go behind the formal accounting information supplied and investigate the basis on which that information has been supplied.

(3) If he has the slightest doubt about the company's present position or its prospects – whether or not this stems from a perceived inadequacy in the information supplied – he must be prepared to seek independent advice from an accountant or similar expert. This may be a considerable step to take, particularly on the basis of mere suspicions and is unlikely to make him popular. Traditional views would

hold this to be disloyalty at best, particularly if he passes confidential information to the adviser; but such an adviser is bound to respect the confidence and is the only practical source of informed assessment for a director who is not himself a financial expert. The advice he will be seeking may be comparative – how similar companies are performing – or based on other factors such as marketing problems, general business growth (or its absence), or particular peculiarities of the company itself, such as a weak capital base. It may be possible to apply a financial model to the company, often through a computer program which, although rather rough and ready, will help to determine whether the company's performance is within tolerable distance of the 'norm'. Such advice cannot always be right, but seeking it shows that a director was alive to his duty and the advice given ought to be very material in determining what he 'ought to have concluded' if the worst does happen.

(4) Once he believes that there may be problems, the director must be ready to put these to the board. If necessary, he must insist upon a board meeting for this purpose. At best, this may mean that the whole board will share his concern; failing that, he may at least recruit some allies; at worst, he will have placed a considerable onus upon those who resist him if and when insolvency arises for he will have put them on notice of the perils which at least one director foresaw. The stronger are his fears, the stronger must be the case which he puts. He may even suggest that trading must cease, and if he does so the rest of the board must in turn consider the impact upon themselves of s 214. 'Trading out of difficulties' is now an approach to be adopted only after careful thought and advice, particularly since it might attract an accusation of fraudulent trading in addition to an attack under s 214. Nevertheless, an honest and reasonable decision to trade on may be justifiable objectively, in relation both to the question of the board's 'conclusions' concerning insolvency and to the necessary steps to minimise losses (see **6.2.7** below).

(5) Inevitably, he will consider resignation. This would be something of a risk, however, in view of the fact that:

   (a) once he ought to have concluded that insolvent liquidation was inevitable, he is prima facie liable whether or not he remains on the board; and

   (b) resignation is unlikely to afford him any defence.

6.2.7   Wrongful trading: the 'defence'

Having identified the moment at which the director ought to have concluded that insolvent liquidation was for practical purposes unavoidable, the court will move on to consider imposing liability unless it is satisfied that he 'took every step with a view to minimising the loss to the company's creditors as . . . he ought to have taken' (s 214(3)).

This defence[70] calls for comment. First, it is not, as it might sound, a question of what this particular director should have done, for s 214(4) again imputes to him the general knowledge, skill and experience that are reasonably to be expected of a person carrying out his functions. Secondly, it is becoming clearer that the director must look to the interests of existing and potential creditors,[71] and this reinforces the conclusion that resignation from the board will rarely be sufficient, or advisable. Indeed, in *Re*

DKG Contractors Ltd,[72] a director against whom wrongful trading proceedings was taken had earlier purported to resign as a director. This purported resignation was held by John Weeks QC as insufficient to relieve him of his duties as a director and, accordingly, he was treated as remaining a director of the company until it went into liquidation. What, then, does the defence entail? First, he must act as quickly as possible. Secondly, the precautions already outlined remain very relevant. Thirdly, he should ensure that the board or, failing agreement, such directors as he can persuade, seek immediate advice from an insolvency practitioner as to the appropriate steps to be taken in the expected insolvency, and he must then do his utmost to see that the advice is followed. For the reasons already mentioned, trading on (except as a short-term measure and preferably on advice) is risky, and resignation possibly more so. Whatever advice is received should be followed. For example, it may be possible to reach a voluntary arrangement with certain creditors. On the other hand, such an arrangement may injure other creditors and may even be challengeable, quite apart from s 214. It is to deal with such problems that the director must seek independent advice. Sometimes the advice will be to invite the company's bank to appoint an administrative receiver or to petition the court to appoint an administrator. Often, circumstances will dictate the former course, but where the latter is open it must be given serious consideration. This is because, unlike the receiver, the administrator's basic function is to look after the interests of *all* the creditors. A short account of administration is given in **6.2.10**.

Finally, it must be said that the defence, if indeed it is a defence, is almost impossible to prove. The director concerned must show not simply that he took all reasonable steps to minimise the loss to creditors, but that he took every step. During the debate on the Insolvency Bill, Lord Denning had tried to persuade the House of Lords to substitute 'every reasonable step' for the expression 'every step' Parliament could not, however, be persuaded to do this. Accordingly, the defence is that the director took 'every step' to minimise the loss to creditors. In *Re Produce Marketing Consortium Ltd, Halls v David*,[73] an attempt was made by directors against whom disqualification proceedings were being brought to rely upon the defence afforded by s 727 of Companies Act 1985. This provides:

> 'If in any proceedings for negligence, default, breach of duty or breach of trust against an officer of the company or a person employed by a company as auditor (whether he is or is not an officer of the company), it appears to the court hearing the case that that officer or person is or may be liable in respect of the negligence, default, breach of duty or breach of trust, but that he has acted *honestly and reasonably*, and that having regard to all the circumstances of case (including those connected with his appointment) he *ought fairly to be excused* for the negligence, default, breach of duty or breach of trust, that court may relieve him, either wholly or partly, from his liability on such terms as it thinks fit.' (Emphasis added.)

It was held by Knox J that this general defence was inapplicable to proceedings for wrongful trading. Parliament did not intend s 727, which required the court to look at all the circumstances of the case to see whether the director in question had acted honestly and reasonably and ought fairly to be excused, and s 214, which contained objective tests, to be operated at the same time.

6.2.8 Wrongful trading: the court's order

Even when the liquidator has made out his case, he is not absolutely entitled to a contribution order. Normally, of course, the court will exercise its discretion to make an order. The amount it orders to be paid is entirely at its discretion. Essentially, there are two ways to assess liability. First, it can be based on the net increase in the deficiency of assets against liabilities which occurred since the moment when the duty to act arose, and which was caused by the director's conduct[74] or secondly – more ominously, and perhaps in cases where the conduct verged on recklessness – on the depletion in the assets 'attributable to the period' after the directors should have realised insolvent winding up was inevitable. Much depends on the degree of culpability: those who have disregarded not only warning signs, but also advice may be required to dig deeper into their pockets. This may mean picking a completely different measure, such as the amount of trade debts incurred during the period of liability,[75] a measure which might be resorted to in cases where the absence of proper records means that it is easier to measure the new debts than assets and liabilities. Whatever measure is adopted, it is agreed that s 214 is compensatory, not penal, and the contribution is made for the benefit of all the creditors with claims in the winding up, and not for the benefit of any particular group.[76] The court can also order that interest at commercial rates should be paid on the contribution, with effect from the date of the order.

A final warning. Where a contribution order is made under s 214, the court may impose a disqualification order for up to 15 years upon the director in question, under the Company Directors Disqualification Act 1986, s 10. In determining whether or not to do so, the court must look, in particular, at the following factors, of which account must be taken by directors who view their company's prospects with misgivings.

(1) The extent of the director's responsibility for the cause of the insolvency.
(2) The extent of his responsibility for the company's failure to supply goods or services which have been paid for, even partly.
(3) His responsibility for any transaction entered into by the company which is liable to be set aside as an undervalue transaction or a preference.
(4) His responsibility, once insolvency has led to winding up commencing, for various breaches of the Insolvency Act 1986, including wrongful dispositions of company assets.

6.2.9 Shadow directors

It has become almost second nature for Acts imposing restrictions, liabilities or disqualifications upon directors to extend also to shadow directors, and s 214 is no exception. The Insolvency Act 1986 defines a shadow director in the standard way, ie:

> 'a person in accordance with whose directions or instructions the directors of the company are accustomed to act (but so that a person is not deemed a shadow director by reason only that the directors act on advice given by him in a professional capacity).' (s 251)

Who then fits the bill? The first, and certainly the main, category, is the stringpuller who is really an insider because of his control over shares or the board, but who has insulated himself from membership of the company, or of the board, and is not performing the functions of an informal de facto director. This was certainly the person caught by the formula (minus the words in brackets) set out above when it first appeared during the First World War.

The formula may have acquired a wider meaning in recent years. It became so popular in company-related Acts that for brevity the simple but dramatic label 'shadow director' was, adopted in 1980 (explicitly to cover the same people as before). For some reason the professions became so greatly agitated that the words in brackets were added to calm them, and the pregnant negative in these words bore the implication that non-professional outsiders *might* be caught. There are not many situations where this really matters, but unfortunately disqualification is one and s 214 is another.[77] Under s 214, it was argued in *Re MC Bacon Ltd*,[78] that a bank which had prepared a report on the company's affairs in consequence of which various steps were taken by the directors to right its affairs had become a shadow director. It was held that this argument was not weak enough to be thrown out before the trial, but it was subsequently abandoned with the full approval of the trial judge. If it is correct that outsiders such as banks may become shadow directors, a considerable degree of interference is probably necessary, nevertheless, before this happens. Merely requiring the execution of security or the implementation of financial controls is unlikely to be sufficient. Dictating corporate strategy or requiring the cessation or commencement of a line of business might be enough. Having said this, there is no recorded case where a bank has actually been found liable as a shadow director. In *Re Tasbian Ltd (No 3)*,[79] a finance company appointed a chartered accountant to act as company doctor to one of its corporate borrowers. It was assumed that a mere watchdog or adviser was not, as such, a shadow director. On the other hand, this adviser had been instrumental in the transfer of the company's labour force to a shell company as part of an unsuccessful scheme to restore the company to – rather nominal! – going concern solvency. The vital question, according to the court, was whether this was conceived and carried through by the 'adviser' (in which case he would be a shadow director) or was it really a decision of the board, albeit on his advice (in which case he would not). In *Re Hydrodan (Corby) Ltd*[80] a parent company, although not its directors, was held to be a shadow director of a subsidiary company.

There is a now a risk in dealings with any troubled company, therefore, since it cannot be pretended that the judges have thrown much light on the outer limits of 'shadow status'. It cannot be the case that *any* contract with a company amounts to a direction or instruction on which its directors are accustomed to act. So, for example, a distribution agreement requiring a company to order minimum quantities of the manufacturer's products does not make the manufacturer a shadow director of the distribution company. There may, however, be dangers in a contract which facilitates continuing control over a company, not directly by its terms, but by substituting the discretion of the other party for that of the board in the conduct of the company's affairs or some major part of them. There will be even more danger if that situation arises without a contract, for then it will be much clearer that the directors are 'accustomed' to acting on the other party's instructions and are not merely doing what a contract requires the company to do. So, for example, outsider control over hiring and firing of important employees will, if shadow directorship does indeed extend to outsiders, be the sort of interference to be approached with great caution.

How far a shadow director will risk liability under s 214 will depend upon: (i) the degree to which he is in a position to know or inquire about its affairs, including its financial position; and (ii) the 'functions' which he fulfils, and against which what he ought to know and do will be measured. It can probably be assumed that to pass muster as a 'shadow director' at all requires a degree of influence at least as great as that of a powerful non-executive director, and this is probably to be regarded as the baseline standard. The more the shadow director is thrust, or thrusts himself, into the company's affairs, the greater the level of knowledge, skill and experience which is likely to be required.

6.2.10   Administration

This is a type of insolvency proceeding of which every director should be aware, since it is one of the procedures which should be considered by any company in financial difficulties (see **6.2.7**). The following is an outline of the subject.[81]

Administration was introduced in 1986 to fill a gap between winding up and receivership. A liquidator, whose task is to look after the interests of all the company's creditors, is able to carry on the company's business only for the purposes of maximising the asset value in the short term before the assets are cashed in and distributed to the creditors. A receiver – under the Insolvency Act 1986, almost invariably an 'administrative receiver' – has wide powers of management and is able, in theory, to restore a business to some kind of health or at least arrange its affairs so that the assets achieve a higher price; but his primary object is to see that the particular creditor who appointed him is repaid, and any benefit to the company, its business or its other creditors is a secondary consideration. Part II of the 1986 Act enables the court to appoint an administrator, whose powers are similar to those of an administrative receiver,[82] and whose function will be to achieve one or a combination of the following:

(1) the survival of all or part of the company as a going concern;
(2) the approval and implementation of an arrangement between the company and its creditors;[83]
(3) a more advantageous realisation of the assets than on a winding up.[84]

Often, (1) and (3) will be combined in the same order on a 'wait and see' basis. Even if the administrator cannot save the enterprise, he will get a better price for those parts which are actually or potentially profitable if he can sell them as a going concern and not on a break-up basis. He will certainly be able to impose some sort of order within the insolvent company – and as the cases in the preceding paragraphs have shown, disorder is almost a defining characteristic of many insolvent enterprises.

Administration has two real 'edges'. The first is that from the moment the petition for an order is presented, creditors' hands are stayed. No winding-up orders may be made,[85] and no security enforced, no goods held on hire-purchase, conditional sale, retention of title or lease terms repossessed, and no action or enforcement commenced or continued against the company unless with leave of the court or the administrator once he is appointed. A de facto freeze usually follows the appointment of an administrative receiver, too, but it lacks the absolute and unarguable quality of that imposed by administration proceedings. Secondly, the administrator must act for the benefit of all the creditors. Specifically, this means that he cannot prefer one class to another as the receiver, by definition, will.

From the point of view of the worried director, therefore, administration may well be a strong possibility – a way to 'minimise the loss to creditors' as required by s 214. There is a practical problem, which is that in many companies the appointment of an administrator may be vetoed by the bank or other major creditor which has security over all the company's assets[86] and this veto is an exception to the general freeze on creditors' remedies. Such a creditor may prefer 'his' man, the administrative receiver, to the administrator. Sometimes, however, even a creditor with the statutory veto may prefer an administrator, for example, because his debt is small, the problems of the company are so intractable that an administrator may save him a great deal of effort, or to avoid the public perception that he has acted selfishly in appointing a receiver. Another instance where an administration may be preferable is with a company trading through many branches where it would be: (i) impracticable for receivers actually to seize the assets at each branch; and (ii) where probably the leases of many of the branch premises provide that a receivership will mean the end of the lease. The moratorium brought about by the administration petition overcomes these problems.

Nor should directors present a petition[87] until they have sought advice from an experienced insolvency practitioner and supplied him with all available information about the company's affairs and prospects. This is because the court must be convinced that there is a chance of administration achieving one of the specified objects – it need not be a 50:50 chance, but it must be a real one. Only an affidavit by a qualified outsider will usually persuade the court of this. For the same reason, major creditors will have to be consulted. They will be asked to accept the administrator's proposals and can wreck the process by voting them down. Furthermore, they – or someone – will often have to provide funds to operate the business during the administration and the process can also be wrecked if funding is unobtainable. The court will know this – apart from anything else, the creditors are entitled to appear in opposition to the petition and will make the position all too clear.

The directors will also have to bear in mind that, quite apart from their statutory obligations to co-operate with the administrator, he has, in the last resort, control over the composition of the board, and may remove and appoint directors. In conclusion, administration should not be approached lightly or without advice, but must be considered by the board of any troubled company.

6.2.11   Fraudulent trading

Civil liability is governed by s 213 of the Insolvency Act 1986, which, unlike s 214, applies in any winding up, whether the company is insolvent or not. Again, unlike s 214, it is a long-established head of liability previously found in the Companies Acts and firmly based on dishonesty, not negligence. Contribution to the company's assets may be ordered against any person, including a director, who is knowingly a party to the company's business being carried on[88] with intent to defraud creditors of the company or of any other person, or for any other fraudulent purpose.

Although the words of the Acts have changed little, the courts have, over the years, widened their scope. First, it is not necessary that the fraud occurs in the context of trading activities. Cheating the Crown out of revenue collected on its behalf can constitute fraudulent 'trading',[89] as may the collection of assets acquired in the course of business and the distribution of the proceeds in payment of debts, if accompanied by the necessary dishonest intention.[90] On the other hand, there need not be a continuous course of fraudulent conduct, for fraud on a single creditor in the course of a single transaction is sufficient, for example, taking the price of goods knowing they cannot be supplied[91] or taking goods knowing that they cannot be paid for.[92]

For many years, the precise dishonest intention required was in doubt. That there should be real moral culpability, or a breach of common notions of fair trading, was not in doubt. But it was uncertain whether the director had to believe that the other party would *never* receive the goods, services or payment due to him.[93] It now seems that a dishonest intention to cause any prejudice may be enough and, in particular, awareness that payment will not be made when or shortly after it falls due is sufficient: an intention never to perform is not necessary.[94]

The director's cronies and other third parties may also be caught, such as a creditor who receives money or property from the company knowing that it has been obtained dishonestly.[95]

As in the case of wrongful trading, the sum which the director is ordered to pay will become part of the general assets of the company in the hands of the liquidator.[96] Insofar as s 213 is designed to be compensatory, the sum payable is probably limited to the amount owing to those creditors proved to have been defrauded; but this can be measured in a rough and ready way as the amount of the trading loss incurred during the period of fraudulent trading, deducting any items which were not on any view attributable to the fraud (such as incidental losses on the sale of premises or equipment). However, unlike s 214, s 213 entitles the judge to include a punitive element in the order. So, in *Re a Company (No 001418 of 1988)*,[97] the court, having awarded £131,420 in compensation, added a further £25,000 to the order because:

(1) the director knew that the company was trading with an excess of current liabilities over current assets and with severe cash flow problems;

(2) the director had gone on trading for nearly two years with no reason to think that the company could pay its debts, meanwhile drawing remuneration which was high in the context of a very troubled company and having a caravan at the company's expense; and

(3) the director had swapped the company's name with that of a subsidiary, and then back again, a transaction which, if not fraudulent, had at least been a source of confusion to creditors and, indeed, the company's bank.[98]

As to criminal liability, see **6.5**.

6.3   OTHER PERSONAL LIABILITIES OF DIRECTORS

It may be convenient to summarise here some of the other liabilities which may affect directors.

6.3.1   Contract

Where a director enters into a contract on behalf of his company with proper authority to do so, he incurs no liability to the other party since he is merely acting as the company's agent. There are, however, a number of circumstances in which he will risk personal liability, and these are now considered.

6.3.2   Personal liability

Where the director contracts without disclosing the company's interest, the other party may hold him liable. Moreover, if he signs or authorises any:

(1) bill of exchange;
(2) cheque; or
(3) order for money or goods

in which the company's name is not mentioned in full he is, under s 349, personally liable to the third party if the company does not pay and also subject to a fine of £1,000.[99] The full and correct registered name must be stated (as to permissible abbreviations see **3.11**(9)). Thus, for example, the description 'M Jackson (Fancy Goods) Ltd' would not do for 'Michael Jackson (Fancy Goods) Ltd,' although in the case where this arose, the plaintiffs could not rely on the error, as they were themselves responsible for it because they had actually written out the words on which they now tried to hold the director personally liable.[100] This result is not beyond question[101] and there is no prospect of a director avoiding liability in any other case by pleading unfairness.[102] In *Hendon v Adelman*,[103] a cheque was drawn on behalf of a company 'L & R Agencies Limited'. The cheque omitted the '&' and it was held that the directors who had signed the cheque were personally liable when it was dishonoured. Likewise personal liability was imposed on a director in *Barber and Nicholls Ltd v R & G Associates (London) Ltd*,[104] where the word in parenthesis 'London' was omitted from a cheque. On the other hand, the harshness of the rule was to some extent limited by R Titheridge QC, sitting as a deputy High Court Judge, in *Jenice v Dan*.[105] Here the company was called Primekeen Ltd. Its cheques bore the name 'Primkeen Ltd'. It was held that the signatory on the cheque was not personally liable when the cheque was dishonoured on the basis that this was a simple spelling or typographical error. However, this decision must be regarded as extremely doubtful since the requirement of s 349 is that the company's name shall appear on, inter alia, all cheques. If the name is misspelt, then the company's name does not so appear. The learned judge expressly said 'I am not over attracted in principle by matters of semantics'. This is a rather strange assertion by someone charged with interpreting the wording of a statutory provision. Similarly, a director who authorises the placing of an order on a form of contract which omits or misstates the company's name is potentially liable; if he is aware that orders have regularly been placed on such forms, he may perhaps be taken to have adopted that practice and will accordingly incur liability under s 349 just as if he had expressly authorised the use of the defective form.[106]

6.3.3 Breach of warranty of authority

We have said that the directors do not normally incur personal liability for company contracts. But where he purports to make a contract which fails to bind the company and which the company repudiates, he may be liable to the third party on the ground of breach of warranty of authority. As the name indicates, this liability is based on the assumption that the director has impliedly warranted to the third party that he has the authority to enter into the contract. If it then turns out that it is beyond the powers either of himself, or of the board, or of the company itself, he has broken that warranty and is liable accordingly. Examples may be noted.

(1) Where the director negotiates a loan which puts the total borrowing beyond the company's limits (*Chaples v Brunswick Permanent Building Society*).[107]
(2) Where directors induce the bank to pass cheques in the absence of a mandate (*Cherry and McDouglas v Colonial Bank of Australia*).[108]

It may be noted that these are both cases where the third party had no reason to think that the position was different from that represented by the director. But where the lack of authority is apparent from the Memorandum or Articles, it might be objected that the third party is presumed to know this and cannot complain. Fortunately for those who have to do business, this objection had little force at common law[109] and is now unsustainable in the light of s 35B of the Companies Act 1985 which provides that an outsider dealing with the company is not bound to check on the powers of the board (or indeed of the company). The tradition which previously imposed constructive notice of their contents upon those dealing with the company was, after all, designed for the protection of the company and not of those individuals who have ignored the limitations upon their powers to act on its behalf.

Moreover, the likelihood in practice of having to rely on this remedy against the individual directors is itself lessened by two developments which tend to save contracts from being repudiated on the ground of lack of authority. These are:

(1) the 'holding out' principle, whereby the company will itself be liable in most cases where the director is allowed to deal with third parties in a way which would normally imply authority to enter into such contracts;[110] and
(2) ss 35A and 35B, which free the board's powers from any limitations 'under the company's constitution' in favour of a person dealing with the company in good faith, and remove the duty to inquire as to any such limitations.

These sections replace the old s 35, and appear successfully to implement the First Directive on Company Law, issued by the EEC in 1968 – albeit some 17 years after the first effort by Parliament to do so. Constructive notice of limitations in the 'constitutional documents' is no longer imputed to the person dealing with the company. This means he is not bound by any limitations on the board's powers set out in the Memorandum, the Articles, or in any shareholder resolution or agreement. Consequently, he may hold the company bound despite any such restrictions. He must be dealing with the company in 'good faith' to rely on s 35A. It is, however, for the company to lead evidence of bad faith if the issue is raised.

Furthermore, a person who has actually read the documents containing the limitations but has failed to understand them can still be treated as dealing in good faith; and another company would not be treated as acting in bad faith merely because one of its officers, not involved in the present dealing, had learned of the limitations in the course of previous dealings. Beyond this, if the Act is to follow the Directive, bad faith ought to mean something akin to deliberately closing one's eyes to the obvious.

The new sections do not entirely supersede the holding out rules, however, for they apply only to limitations upon the powers of the *board of directors* to bind the company, or to authorise others to do so. So, if the board has exceeded its powers directly when dealing with a third party, s 35A will apply. Similarly, it applies if the board gives authority to a committee, or a single director, or an officer, and, in doing so, exceeds its own power to delegate. If the third party dealt not with the board but with such a committee, director or officer, s 35A assists him if the board decided to delegate its power, even though in doing so it went beyond what the 'constitution' permitted. But there s 35A stops, and for a good reason. An individual may legitimately repudiate liability on a contract or other dealing on the basis that he never authorised the 'agent', who negotiated the deal, to act on his behalf. It was never the intention of the Directive to put a company in a worse position than such an individual – merely to remove some of the legal technicalities[111] which often put a company in an unmeritoriously superior position. It remains open to the company to argue, therefore, that there *never in fact was a decision to delegate power* to the committee or individual with whom the third party has dealt. If that is indeed the case, there is nothing for s 35A to bite on, and the third party has dealt with an 'agent' who had no actual authority. Here, only agency law in the form of the holding-out rules (or 'ostensible authority') can help. The same seems to be true if there is an actual delegation, but in dealing with the third party the delegate assumes for himself a wider authority than was given to him by the board.

6.3.4   Torts

The basic principle of separate corporate entity[112] means that it is generally the company alone which can sue or be sued for torts (civil wrongs such as negligence, trespass, libel or deceit) which are alleged to have been done to or by it. Thus, the directors will not have personal liability merely because the wrongful act could be done only on their authority.[113] But if it can be proved that they were actively involved in directing or procuring the wrongful act, they may be jointly liable with the company,[114] although liability is most likely to be imposed where the director knew that the act was wrongful or at least took a risk that this was so.[115] The extent to which the company itself is liable for the torts of the director depends on the ordinary principles of an employer's vicarious liability for the action of servants committed in the scope of their employment. If a tort falls within this category and is committed by a director in a position of authority (whether express for implied), the company will be liable.[116] It might be thought that an ultra vires act could never be within the scope of employment, but if the board commits a tort in the course of pursuing an ultra vires object, it could hardly be right to deny the injured party his right of compensation from corporate funds merely on this ground.[117]

In *Adams v Cape Industries plc*,[118] a US subsidiary was sued for damages for personal injuries allegedly caused by the exposure of victims to asbestos fibres from an asbestos factory in the USA. The Court of Appeal had to consider whether a judgment given in the US courts was enforceable against the English registered parent company. The English company did not itself have a place of business in the USA and accordingly could not be present there. The plaintiffs tried to avoid the effect of this by three different means. First, they sought to argue that the parent and the subsidiary were part of a single economic unit. Secondly, they sought to lift the veil of incorporation. Thirdly, they tried to argue that the US subsidiary was the agent of the English parent company. The Court of Appeal held that all three arguments should fail. The single economic unit argument failed because the Court of Appeal regarded itself as concerned with law rather than economics and therefore refused to regard the subsidiary as an extension of the parent. The lifting of the veil of incorporation failed because it was felt that the separate corporate entities of the defendant company and its subsidiary could not be disregarded. The agency argument failed because, while there is nothing to prevent a company from being present in a foreign country by means of an agency, such an agency is not presumed in the relationship between a parent company and its subsidiary. A similar decision was reached in *Williams v Natural Life Health Foods*.[119] Here the plaintiffs had approached the defendant company (the franchisor) to franchise a retail health food shop in Rugby. The defendant company had been formed the previous year by a Mr Mistlin. The brochure selling the franchise held out the defendant company as having expertise to operate as franchisors and to give reliable advice to franchisees because of Mr Mistlin's involvement over a period of time in the health food business. The venture failed and the plaintiffs brought proceedings against the defendants and, when the defendants were wound up, joined Mr Mistlin as a co-defendant. Both the court of first instance and the Court of Appeal found Mr Mistlin personally liable on the *Hedley Byrne* principle. However, the House of Lords said that Mr Mistlin was not personally liable. For personal liability, he would have had to have assumed personal responsibility and liability for the advice which he had given. In the event, there had been no personal dealing between Mr Mistlin and the plaintiffs. All the pre-contractual negotiations had been done using company notepaper. Accordingly, there could be said to be no personal liability. A similar decision was reached in *Ord v Belhaven Pubs Ltd*.[120] Here the plaintiffs had bought the lease of a public house from the original defendants, Belhaven Pubs Ltd, and had invested money in it. Subsequently, they discovered that figures on which they had made the purchase were incorrect. Accordingly, they issued a writ claiming rescission and damages. By the time the case came to court, Belhaven Pubs Ltd no longer held any substantial assets and so an application was made to substitute either another company in the same ownership as Belhaven Pubs Ltd or its parent company. At first instance, an order was made that the parent company should be substituted. This decision was based on *Creasey v Breachwood Motors Ltd*.[121] The Court of Appeal overruled this. What the plaintiffs were really trying to do was to impose personal liability on the shareholder of the selling company when they had actually dealt with the company itself. In reality, this was a new course of action. It could be seen as a continuation of the previous action if it could be established that suing the original defendant had been wrong. However, this was clearly not the case. The judge had been wrong to order the lifting of the corporate veil. Nothing improper had been done. The company was not a mere façade. Transactions within the group had not been at an undervalue. For the lifting of the veil of incorporation, there must have been wrongdoing. The proper procedure in such a case is to proceed against the original defendants. If it is found there has been a wrongful disposal of assets, the proper way to proceed is to bring proceedings under s 423 of the Insolvency Act 1986. The House of Lords has confirmed the Court's unwillingness to go behind the corporate veil in *Williams v Natural Life Health Foods*.

6.3.5   Company crimes

The company can be prosecuted for the crimes of directors, if the relevant statute is construed as extending liability to employers,[122] despite the fact that it is clearly impossible for the company to have a guilty intention or *mens rea*. However, for such criminal liability to be imposed, it seems that there must be evidence of active involvement in the crime by those actually managing the company's affairs, whether properly appointed directors or not.[123]

Thus, an intention to deceive by the secretary and branch manager were held to be sufficient to make the company liable where they were the responsible officers in the area of activity in which the offence occurred.[124] What the courts are doing therefore is to attribute the mental state of the directing officers to the company itself.

Needless to say, any director who is responsible for the commission by the company of a crime (or a tort) may well be liable to his own company for breach of duty, unless he can get relief from the courts.[125]

It has also been held that a company may be guilty of a common law offence. This was established in *Re P&O European Ferries (Dover) Ltd*.[126] This was the case which arose out of the Zeebrugge disaster when the ferry *Herald of Free Enterprise* capsized with the loss of nearly 200 lives. The company was charged with manslaughter and it was held at first instance that the indictment was valid. In the event, the prosecution was unable to establish specific liability either upon the company or any of the managers who had been charged with the offence. (For details, see Law Commission Consultation Paper No 135 'Criminal Law: Involuntary Manslaughter 1994'.) The first ever conviction of a company for manslaughter was in the case of OLL Ltd on 8 December 1994 at Winchester Crown Court. This arose out of the Lyme Bay canoeing disaster when four young people had been drowned as a result of inadequate supervision. Both the company and its managing director were found guilty of manslaughter. The managing director was sentenced to three years' imprisonment which was reduced on appeal to two years. The company was fined £60,000 which was said by the court to represent its entire assets.

Moreover, where a company gives an undertaking in the course of proceedings and then breaks it, a director may also find himself personally liable for contempt.[127] Once the director is aware that an undertaking has been given by the company, he must take reasonable steps to ensure that it is observed. He may rely on a reasonable belief that another director is doing this, but otherwise he must act himself. The same is true when any order is made against the company by the court, for example, to refrain from a specified course of conduct. Indeed, if a copy of the order is served on the director, a failure to supervise or investigate may lead to the director's committal or the sequestration of his assets.[128] Given the readiness of the courts in recent years to issue orders freezing or restricting corporate assets or activities, directors should take this liability very seriously.

Occasionally the company may figure as the victim of offences by its directors. As to this, see **6.5**.

6.4 RELIEF FROM LIABILITY

A director who has committed a breach of duty may, nevertheless, escape liability in certain circumstances. Three possibilities are open to him:

(1) ratification by the members in general meeting;
(2) indemnity in the Articles or by agreement; or
(3) relief by the court.

6.4.1 Ratification by general meeting

By majority vote
A breach of duty which does not involve unlawful or ultra vires acts may be pardoned or ratified by an ordinary resolution of the members[129] or by their unanimous approval (whether at a meeting or not).[130]

The qualifications to this principle are that:

(1) the director may vote his own shares,[131] unless to do so would be a fraud on the minority, as in some cases where he directly or indirectly controls the meeting;[132]
(2) he must, in any event, have acted honestly, so that the duty broken must have been one of care and skill, or one where liability in no way depends upon fault.[133]

Examples of breaches which may be ratified in this way include:

(1) allotting shares for the wrong purpose;
(2) failing to disclose an interest in a contract;
(3) obtaining a secret profit, but without damage to the company; or
(4) negligence or lack of diligence,[134] except where this results in a substantial benefit to the directors.[135]

Examples of non-ratifiable breaches include:

(1) infringements of members' personal rights;[136]
(2) those involving fraud or dishonesty;[137]
(3) 'fraud on the minority', as where directors seize a business opportunity which should have been made available to the company, as in *Cook v Deeks*.[138] Here the defendants may not use their shares to obtain ratification precisely because this is a wrongful appropriation of the assets. Contrast *Regal (Hastings) Ltd v Gulliver*[139] (**5.6.1**) where the company could not have taken the opportunity and so the directors could have had their share purchase ratified had they only thought to do so.

The term 'ratification' is subjected to considerable strain in these examples. In some cases, it simply means that the members takeover the decision-making process: if, for example, the court finds that a share issue has been made for the wrongful purpose of defeating a takeover and requires the issue to be put to the existing membership, this is not so much ratification as a transfer of function. Quite apart from this, the term has two distinct meanings, that the general meeting is asked: (i) to adopt or legitimise a transaction; or (ii) simply to waive the breach of duty and its consequences. Examples (2) and (3) above of non-ratifiable breaches show an extreme impropriety which cannot be countenanced even with majority approval (the availability of an effective minority remedy is another matter, considered in Chapter 7). In practice, the dividing line is not so easy to draw. For example, a director who, in breach of duty, votes on a board resolution making him managing director has not committed a fraud on the minority and the breach is ratifiable; but, if the remuneration were clearly 'excessive', it might constitute a fraud on the minority as an expropriation of assets.[140] Ratification is impossible if it occurs in circumstances where the breach of duty by the directors caused prejudice to the interests of creditors in circumstances where the company is insolvent. This was the finding of the Australian courts in *Kinsela v Russell Kinsela Pty Ltd*,[141] which was approved by Dillon LJ in *West Mercia Safetywear Ltd v Dodd*.[142]

By special majority

To the categories of acts, set out above, which may not be ratified by ordinary resolution, may be added two more:

(1) acts which are ultra vires or illegal, such as the payment of dividend out of capital;[143]
(2) acts requiring a special procedure, such as the passing of a special resolution or, when a dividend is declared, the provision of audited accounts without a material qualification.[144]

As to acts requiring special resolutions, the same principle applies, and they may be ratified by the agreement of all the members. As to acts which are ultra vires, the company and the directors remain bound to observe the company's constitution, even though the doctrine of ultra vires has largely been abolished as far as it affects third parties. An ultra vires act may be 'ratified', in the sense of being legitimised, by a special resolution: s 35(3) (and 'only' by special resolution). The section leaves the directors liable for breach of duty in respect of the act in question, unless the members pass a *separate* special resolution relieving them from liability. The old rule was that ultra vires acts simply could not be 'ratified' in any sense. A number of questions arise in relation to the new rule.

(1) What is the position if there is no special resolution but all the members agree? The answer is that this is probably effective in favour of the directors, *but* at the very least the court would have to be convinced that the members understood the difference between legitimising the ultra vires act and relieving the directors from liability.
(2) What if there were some other taint, such as fraud? Nothing in the new rules suggests that this can be ratified. Indeed, there is a possibility that in cases which are on the margin of 'fraud on the minority' the use of the directors' votes in favour of a s 35 special resolution might itself constitute part of the fraud.

If the defect is merely that the directors have exceeded their own powers, without involving the company in an ultra vires act, the breach of duty can certainly be waived by a special resolution or unanimous consent, but subject to the same two stages – first, validating the act, secondly, relieving the directors of liability.

6.4.2 Ratification by the Articles: s 310

Exemption from liability was frequently conferred upon the directors by the Articles and, indeed, the *City Equitable* directors although negligent, escaped by means of such an Article. However, the law was subsequently changed and s 310 now declares that any Article (or contract) is void insofar as it exempts or indemnifies any officer or auditor for liability, in relation to the company, for:

(1) negligence;
(2) default;
(3) breach of duty; or
(4) breach of trust.

It appears from *Movitex Ltd v Bulfield*[145] that any Article which seeks to modify or reduce the duty itself, rather than merely exempting the director from the consequences of breach of duty is also void.

Examples of such a reduction are to be found in reg 85 of Table A, which: (i) allows a director to keep benefits accruing to him from associate companies; and (ii) allows him to keep his profit from contracts with the company, provided he declares his interest (reg 94) and does not vote (reg 95); although reg 96 allows even the restrictions on quorum and voting to be suspended or relaxed by ordinary resolution.[146] Since it would be absurd for part of Table A to be held void, the court in *Movitex* (above) reasoned that the conflict of interest rules are not really 'duties' within the meaning of s 310. They are disabilities – if a director puts himself into a position where there is such a conflict, he cannot keep the benefits unless specifically permitted to do this, which, of course, is exactly what reg 85 provides. This is a neat piece of judicial footwork, but it would be very unwise to assume that 'mere disabilities' extend beyond conflict of interest cases.

On the other hand, s 310 does permit an Article or contract under which the company will indemnify the director against costs incurred in either:

(1) successfully defending himself; or
(2) obtaining relief from the courts.

Furthermore, since its modification by the 1989 Act, the section expressly permits the company to buy liability insurance for its directors and officers – previously it had been open to question whether old s 310 allowed this. Liability insurance tailored to the UK market is becoming more readily available.

6.4.3 Relief granted by the courts

Even if a director is found in breach of duty or trust or otherwise in default, he may yet escape personal liability, by virtue of s 727, if the courts decide that he has acted honestly and reasonably and ought fairly to be excused.

Note that all three requirements must be present, the first two being matters to be proved and the third being a matter for the courts' discretion. Failure on any one count will thus be sufficient to deprive the director of relief.[147] It follows that s 727 can never operate in relation to a director liable because of negligence, since by definition he will not have acted 'reasonably'.[148] Examples of the workings of s 727 are as follows.

(1) The apprehensive director need not wait for proceedings to be brought against him, as he can take the initiative in applying to the courts for relief (s 727(2)).
(2) Relief has been given for:

   (a) ultra vires acts when carried through in good faith and on legal advice;[149]
   (b) failure to get approval for remuneration as required by the Articles;[150]
   (c) failure to take qualification shares;[151]
   (d) breach of duty, and of s 151, in using company assets to purchase shares, the director's object being to save rather than injure the company.

(3) Opposition to the granting of relief by the members is not conclusive.[153]
(4) Relief has been refused:

   (a) where directors allowed an unqualified person to make up a quorum for fixing their remuneration;[154]
   (b) where directors neglected their obligation to get approval for compensation for loss of office for a dismissed director;[155]
   (c) where directors misapplied company funds by slavishly following the orders of the controlling shareholder.[156]

(5) Relief is not available where the primary breach of duty is by the company itself and the director is made liable to third parties for that breach. This will be the case where a statute imposes a liability on the company and makes a director liable in default.[157]

Finally, we may note that directors also have the usual right to the protection of the Limitation Act 1980 after six years, except where:

(1) there is a fraud, in which case the time does not run until it is or should have been discovered;
(2) where the director has the company's property, in which case time does not start to run at all.

6.5   CRIMINAL LIABILITIES

Despite the principle of a separate corporate identity established by *Salomon v Salomon & Co*, there are many statutory provisions which impose personal liability on directors as well as on their companies.

The opportunities for individuals to commit a breach of the Companies Acts are truly abundant (Sch 24 lists some 200 offences) and the consequences can be horrifying. The practice of the DTI has been to abstain from prosecution except in flagrant or protracted cases or offences which have been fraudulent or damaging to others. But the risk is always present, and should be borne in mind by those who are asked to serve as directors of companies with which they may have little influence or regular contact.

The characteristic mechanism of the Act consists of the imposition of a duty, such as that to file the annual return,[158] accompanied by the sanction that: 'the company and every officer of it who is in default is liable to a fine and, for continued contravention, to a daily default fine'.

The effect of such a provision is that: (i) a director, as an officer, is liable if he knowingly and wilfully authorises and permits the default;[159] and (ii) he is further liable to a fine of one-tenth or one-fifth of the 'statutory maximum'[160] for every day of the default. Moreover, many sections also include a liability to imprisonment. Where conviction is in a magistrate's court the maximum sentence is six months' imprisonment. Where conviction is by jury, the maximum sentences vary from two years (for example, for a false declaration in relation to an assisted purchase of a private company's shares under s 155) to seven years. Most of these offences involve an element of fraud or serious impropriety.

(1)   Any officer who destroys, mutilates or falsifies company documents, or makes a false entry, or is privy to such an act, is liable to up to seven years' imprisonment and/or a fine.[161]

(2)   Payment of dividends otherwise than from profits available under the Act is not only a breach of duty but may amount to a criminal conspiracy, as may any agreement to use the company's assets dishonestly, ie for a purpose which is not honestly believed to be in the company's interests.[162]

(3)   Any officer who, with intent to deceive, publishes a misleading or false statement, commits an offence punishable with up to seven years' imprisonment.[163] The statement must be false 'in a material particular', which it may be if false when taken as a whole even though there is no specifically untrue statement in it. Thus, in the leading case of *R v Lord Kylsant*,[164] a prospectus quite truthfully said that dividends had been paid each year between 1921 and 1927. It omitted to say that trading losses had been made in each of those years and dividends had been maintained only out of non-recurring exceptional items following the end of the war. The implication, that the company had been trading profitably, was a statement which was false in a material particular.

(4)   There are various other offences specifically dealing with those who make false statements or declarations. Examples include the board's justification for disapplying the statutory pre-emption rights (s 95) or allotments for non-cash consideration (s 110), statements to the auditors (s 389A) and, in relation to a private company, assistance for the purchase of its shares or payments out of capital (ss 156 and 173). In the last two cases, liability is imposed if the statement is made without reasonable grounds for believing it to be true, which may catch the negligent as well as the dishonest. False statements in notifications of share interests are also offences (s 328).

(5)   The old regime governing misleading prospectuses and inducements to investors has now been replaced by the Financial Services Act 1986. We have seen that directors may incur civil liability for false or misleading listing particulars – including material omissions – and a similar liability is imposed by s 166 of the 1986 Act in relation to misleading statements in a prospectus for unlisted securities. The Act imposes criminal liability for contravention of many of the highly complex controls over the advertisement and issue of such shares and in relation to the ban on private company advertisements offering shares for sale

(unless exempted by the DTI). The old and inadequate Prevention of Frauds (Investments) Act 1959 is replaced by much more sweeping controls over the conduct of investments business generally. For present purposes, it is enough to note that making false markets in securities or dishonestly and recklessly making misleading, false or deceptive statements, promises or forecasts or the dishonest concealment of material information is a criminal offence, if done with a view to inducing investments, and is punishable with up to seven years' imprisonment and/or a fine.[165]

(6)   Liquidation is the occasion for other criminal liabilities (in particular offences involving dishonesty, under ss 206 to 211 of the Insolvency Act 1986) and the courts (in a compulsory liquidation) may direct the liquidator to institute a prosecution or refer to the Director of Public Prosecutions.[166]

> Unfortunately, the costs come out of the assets and such a prosecution should be ordered only against the wishes of those entitled to the assets, if they have a duty to prosecute as good citizens.[167]

Following the decisions of the Court of Appeal in *Attorney-General's Reference (No 2 of 1982)*[168] and *Re Philippou*,[169] a director can apparently steal from his own company. In the former case, directors of a property company were convicted of stealing from the company when they appropriated its funds for their own private use by drawing cheques on the company's bank account. Kerr LJ said:

> 'It does not by any means follow that the members and directors of a company which is wholly owned by them cannot properly be charged with theft of the company's property . . . Their appropriate defence in such cases is provided by s 2(1)(a) (of the Theft Act 1968), the belief of a defendant, which must of course be an honest belief, that he has in law the right to deprive the other (the company) of it (the property).'

In the latter case, the defendants were the sole shareholders and directors of a group of three travel companies which had gone into insolvent liquidation. Prior to the liquidation, they had bought a block of flats in Spain with sums drawn from the bank account of one of the companies. Again, this was found to be theft. O'Connor LJ explained that the key factor was the drawing of money from the company and using it to purchase the block of flats. From this, the jury could infer, not only that the transaction was dishonest, but that it was intended to deprive the company permanently of its money. For this reason, there had been an appropriation for the purposes of theft.

The director's burden of proof in these cases will depend partly upon the words of the governing section; whether, for example, they include 'knowingly', 'fraudulently' or 'wilfully' and whether they impose a presumption of guilt which the director has to disprove. There are several alternatives.

(1)   The typical offender is 'every officer . . . who is in default'. This is defined by s 730(5) as 'any officer . . . who knowingly and wilfully authorises or permits the default . . .'. This is an important safeguard for the non-executive director and means that he cannot be made liable unless he had some direct involvement in and knowledge of the offence or deliberately shut his eyes to what was going on.

Thus, a director was excused in a case where he did not learn of a failure to file an allotment contract until after the default had occurred and then attempted to correct it.[170]

Since it is clearly impracticable, especially in a large company, for all the directors to supervise compliance with the statutory requirement, this section confirms the general principle, that having appointed officials (particularly the secretary) whom they reasonably believe to be competent, they should not be personally liable for their defaults, in the absence of grounds for suspicion.[171]

(2) Some sections expressly incorporate this principle, for example s 234, which makes any person holding the office of director immediately before the end of the accounting year liable for any failure in complying with the statutory duties in respect of the directors' report. He has a defence if he can show 'that he took all reasonable steps to secure compliance' with the Act. This is a rather tougher requirement than that referred to in (1) above.

(3) Some statutes go further and presume guilt on the part of the director for the company's offence unless he can prove the contrary, or that he took all the steps which he should have done to prevent it.[172]

(4) Some statutes impose criminal liability on the director if an offence is proved to have been committed by the company with his consent or connivance, or is attributable to his neglect.[173]

(5) The winding-up provisions (ss 206 to 211 of the Insolvency Act 1986) impose a particularly formidable set of criminal penalties for directors, mainly in connection with concealment or alteration of documents or information, or failure to co-operate with the liquidator. An attempt by a director to procure the cancellation of a debt owing from him to the company was held not to be a criminal transfer under these sections,[174] although such a transaction might now fall foul of the modified rule against preferences (s 239 of the Insolvency Act 1986), leading to an order for repayment.

Whether or not the company is being wound up, a director may be prosecuted for fraudulent trading pursuant to s 458 of the Companies Act 1985. The essential elements of the offence are the same as those upon which civil liability is based (see **6.2.11**), but – since winding up need not be occurring – the question of defrauding creditors, as such, need not arise. In *R v Kemp*[173] for example, the defendants had simply committed a common or garden variety of fraud on the company's customers by claiming that they had placed orders for stationery and were held properly convicted.

CHAPTER 6 FOOTNOTES

1 *Re Clasper Group Services Ltd* [1989] BCLC 143. In this case the respondent was the controlling shareholder and sole director's 17-year-old son. He was at one stage a signatory of company cheques, but this appeared to be only for the purpose of getting the 'family name' on to the cheques and did not alter his 'lowly status' within the company.

2 [1993] BCC 646.

3 *Re Purpoint Ltd* [1991] BCC 121.

4 *Re Home & Colonial Insurance Co* [1930] 1 Ch 102.

5 *Re Anglo-French Co-operative Society* (1882) 21 ChD 492. *Manson v Smith* [1997] 2 BCLC 161.

6 [1990] BCC 903.

7 [1991] BCC 121.

8 For a discussion of the difference between a de facto and shadow director see *Re Hydrodan (Corby) Ltd* [1994] BCC 161, per Millett J.

9 *Curtis's Furnishing Stores Ltd v Freedman* [1966] 2 All ER 955.

10 Except, it may be, under s 212 of the Insolvency Act 1986, which seems to require an order to be made against the respondent personally. Given that the section is designed as a procedural aid to the liquidator, however, where there is existing liability, it is not inconceivable that a different view may prevail.

11 Sections 2, 5 and 21 of the Limitation Act 1980.

12 Ie whether he was then a director or not. Insolvency here means winding up or the approval of a voluntary arrangement with creditors; going into administration; and going into administrative receivership. As to the last two, see **6.2.10**.

13 Insolvent or not.

14 (1988) 4 BCC 130.

15 *Re Lo-Line Electric Motors Ltd* [1988] Ch 477.

16 [1990] 3 WLR 1165.

17 *Re Bath Glass Ltd* (1988) 4 BCC 130.

18 *Re Cladrose Ltd* [1990] BCLC 204.

19 *Re McNulty's Interchange Ltd* [1989] BCLC 709.

20 Examples include improper payments or undervalue transfers of assets, often to directors and associates.

21 *Re Keypack (Homecare) Ltd* [1990] BCLC 440. In other cases, judges have spoken in terms of 'living high off the hog' or 'feathering their own nests', but descriptions like these add very little to the admittedly very vague test stated in the text.

22 [1992] BCC 388.

23 [1996] BCC 112.

24 [1998] 1 BCLC 110.

25 *Re Probe Data Systems Ltd (No 3)* [1991] BCC 428.

26 *Re Lo-Line Electric Motors Ltd* [1988] Ch 477.

27 *Re Cladrose Ltd* [1990] BCLC 204.

28 *Re Chartmore Ltd* [1990] BCLC 673.

29 *Re Rolus Proterties Ltd* (1988) 4 BCC 446 (disqualification for two years only despite overall seriousness of the case).

30 *Re T&D (Timber Contractors) Ltd* [1990] BCC 592.

31 *Re Tasbian Ltd* [1989] BCLC 720.

32 *Re Tasbian Ltd No 3* [1992] BCC 358:

33 [1990] BCC 21.

34 [1990] BCC 23.

35 [1993] BCC 844.

36 [1992] BCC 110.

37 [1996] BCC 229.

38 [1997] BCC 235.

39 [1998] BCC 184.

40 Ie where there is no need to apply for leave to proceed out of time.

41 *Re Cedac Ltd, Secretary of State for Trade and Industry v Langridge* [1991] BCC 148. Complete failure to serve the notice would be another matter.

42 [1994] BCC 226.

43 [1994] BCLC 555.

44 [1997] BCC 634.

45 [1996] BCC 67.

46 [1993] BCC 336.

47 [1993] BCC 598.

48 [1996] 1 All ER 445.

49 [1997] BCC 155.

50 [1996] BCC 297.

51 [1997] BCC 473.

52 [1997] BCC 488.

53 [1998] BCC 11.

54 [1991] BCC 394.

55 [1994] BCC 131.

56 [1998] Ch 477.

57 (1988) 4 BCC 519.

58 [1990] BCC 673.

59 [1992] BCLC 623.

60 [1994] BCC 371.

61 [1995] BCC 11.

62 Note before 28 April 1986 when the section took full effect.

63 [1989] BCLC 520.

64 As in *DHSS v Evans* [1985] 2 All ER 472, on the now defunct liability of directors for unpaid National Insurance contributions.

65 This need not always be so, of course, but in this case the company's profitability was directly linked to turnover.

66 Although the judge gave the second director a partial indemnity against the other, this was less because of the latter's seniority than because he had seen to it over the last seven months of the company's life that the company reduced its bank debt which he had personally guaranteed.

67 [1991] BCC 121.

68 [1990] BCC 903: Warning signs which are adequately explained by an adviser on whom the director is entitled to rely would not trigger liability: *Norman v Theodore Goddard* [1991] BCLC 1028.

69 (1989) 5 BCC 399.

70 The government intended that it should be up to the liquidator to prove that the director did *not* take the necessary steps. Whether the section leaves the final burden on the liquidator, or upon the director, remains to be resolved, and may never be since, if the evidence is so finely balanced as to make the outcome depend on who has the burden of persuading the court, it would be very unlikely to make an order against the director. The text, therefore, treats s 214(3) as a defence, which is how in practice it is treated.

71 *Re Purpoint Ltd* [1991] BCC 121, at p 125. This is also relevant to any order made (see **6.2.8**).

72 [1990] BCC 903.

73 (1989) 5 BCC 399.

74 *Re Produce Marketing Consortium (No 2) Ltd* [1989] BCLC 520, at p 553.

75 *Re DKG Contractors Ltd* [1990] BCC 903.

76 Almost in the same breath as saying this, the judge in the *Produce Marketing* case, above, said that the contribution would be caught by a floating charge given to the company's bank and was therefore payable to the bank. This is generally regarded as a slip; if correct, it would often deprive the liquidator of any incentive to pursue delinquent directors.

77 For others, see the account of statutory controls of directors' dealings with their company set out earlier in Chapter 5.

78 (1988) 4 BCC 425 (reported as *Re a Company, 005009 of 1987*).

79 [1992] BCC 358. In his active role of negotiating with the company's creditors and bankers, and the Crown, the respondent may well have come very close to de facto director status.

80 [1994] BCC 161.

81 For a full account see *Gore-Browne on Companies* (Jordans, 44th edn, loose-leaf publication) **31.1** to **31.23**.

82 In fact, they are slightly greater in one respect since, subject to safeguards, he may deal with assets free of security and similar interests taken by particular creditors.

83 Which is possible without administration but does not involve the statutory freeze on creditors referred to in the text.

84 With the emphasis on 'realisation': only the liquidator makes a distribution as such.

85 Or, directors should remember, winding-up resolutions passed. Once directors present a petition they are committed, and may withdraw only with the court's leave.

86 Which must include a floating charge, and almost invariably will. Such a creditor must be served with notice of an administration petition, and may exercise the veto up to the moment when an administrator is appointed.

87 The position seems to be that: (i) the board as a whole must present the petition; but (ii) once a resolution is passed to do so, each director may (and must) see that a petition is presented and if this is not happening do it himself: *Re Equiticorp International plc* (1989) 5 BCC 599. It does not seem to be open to a single director to petition where the board has thrown out proposals for administration.

88 Generally this means being an insider. An outsider can be liable only if he is privy to the conduct of someone within the company's management who acts fraudulently: *Re Augustus Barnett Ltd* [1986] BCLC 170. See also note 95 below.

89 *Re L Todd (Swanscombe) Ltd* [1990] BCLC 454.

90 *Re Sarflex Ltd* [1979] Ch 592.

91 *Re Gerald Cooper Chemicals Ltd* [1978] Ch 262.

92 *R v Grantham* [1984] 1 QB 675 (CA).

93 *Re William C Leitch Bros* [1932] 2 Ch 71 and *Re Patrick & Lyon Ltd* [1933] 2 Ch 786, decisions of the same judge, Maugham J.

94 *R v Grantham*, above.

95 *Re Gerald Cooper Chemicals Ltd*, above. Of course, this will usually render the recipient liable to the company for receiving assets diverted by the director in breach of his duty. If they have been dissipated, the liquidator (who is all too often the only person representing the forces of good) may still mount attacks under the Insolvency Act, and will not be confined to claims under ss 213 and 214. He may, for example, bring proceedings under s 423 – transactions to defraud creditors.

96 *Re Cyona Distributions Ltd* [1967] Ch 889, at p 904 (Lord Denning MR).

97 [1990] BCC 526. A reader who wishes to pierce the veil of anonymity thrown over the participants by this coy and unmemorable form of citation has merely to read the report of the case to identify the parties.

98 Strictly, the judge should have found this to be dishonest before including it as a factor in a penal award.

99 *F Stacey & Co Ltd v Wallis* (1912) 106 LT 544.

100 *Durham Fancy Goods Ltd v Michael Jackson (Fancy Goods) Ltd* [1969] 2 QB 839.

101 Because s 349 is so clear that it might be held to prevail over the 'equity' invoked in the case: *Blum v OCP Repartition SA* [1988] BCLC 170, CA. In *Lindholst & Co v Fowler* [1988] BCLC 166, the director was liable because of the omission of 'Ltd'.

102 *Rafsanjani Pistachio Producers Co-operative v Reiss* [1990] BCLC 353.

103 (1973) 117 SJ 631.

104 (1981) 132 NLJ 1076.

105 [1994] BCC 43.

106 *John Wilkes (Footwear) Ltd v Lee International Footwear* [1985] BCLC 444.

107 (1881) 6 QBD 696. The fact that the company may be bound by the agreement by virtue of s 35 makes no difference. The director in fact has no authority, and s 35A preserves his liability even if the company is bound.

108 (1869) LR3PC 24.

109 *West London Commercial Bank v Kitson* (1883) 12 QBD 157, where the directors were personally liable for accepting a bill of exchange even though the memorandum showed that they had no power to do so.

110 *Hely-Hutchinson v Brayhead Ltd* [1968] 1 QB 549. The extent of the holding out is critical. Where an officer represents himself as having authority which the company has not: (i) given him; (ii) held him out as having; or (iii) authorised him, or appeared to authorise him, to represent himself as having, then the company may repudiate his dealings without liability: *Armagas Ltd v Mundogas SA* [1986] AC 717.

111 Particularly the constructive notice rule. Quite apart from s 35B, s 711A, when it is brought into force, will *almost* abolish the rule across the board.

112 *Salomon v Salomon & Co Ltd* [1897] AC 22.

113 *British Thomson-Houston Co v Sterling Accessories Ltd* [1924] 2 Ch 33.

114 *T Oertili A-G v E J Bowman (London) Ltd and Others* [1956] RPC 282.

115 *C Evans & Sons Ltd v Spritebrand Ltd* [1985] 1 WLR 317.

116 *Rudd v Elder Dempster & Co Ltd* [1933] 1 KB 566.

117 *Campbell v Paddington Corporation* [1911] 1 KB 869.

118 [1990] BCC 786.

119 [1998] 2 All ER 577.

120 [1998] BCC 607, CA.

121 [1992] BCC 638.

122 *Pearks, Gunston & Tee Ltd v Ward* [1902] 2 KB 1.

123 *Tesco Supermarkets Ltd v Nattrass* [1971] 2 All ER 127.

124 *Moore v Bresler Ltd* [1944] 2 All ER 515. *Meridian Global Funds Management v Securities Commission* [1995] 3 All ER 918.

125 *Selangor United Rubber Estates Ltd v Cradock (No 3)* [1968] 2 All ER 1073.

126 (1990) 93 Cr App R 72.

127 *Biba Ltd v Stratford Investments* [1972] 3 All ER 1041, where the unfortunate director was a solicitor who had no responsibility for day-to-day management.

128 *AG for Tuvalu v Philatelic Distribution Corpn Ltd* [1990] BCLC 245, CA.

129 *Hogg v Cramphorn Ltd* [1967] Ch 254.

130 *Re Gee & Co (Woolwich) Ltd* [1974] 2 WLR 515.

131 *Northern Counties Securities v Jackson Steeple & Co* [1974] 2 All ER 625.

132 *Cook v Deeks* [1916] 1 AC 554.

133 As in the exercise of power for a wrongful purpose, which may be perfectly honest.

134 As in *Pavlides v Jensen* [1956] 2 All ER 518, where a minority complained that a mine was sold at an undervalue but the sale was properly ratified by the general meeting, even though the directors were in the majority.

135 *Daniels v Daniels* [1978] 2 All ER 89, see **6.1**. 'Gross' negligence does not form a special unratifiable category: *Multinational Gas & Petrochemical Co v Multinational Gas & Petrochemical Services* [1983] Ch 258, at p 269.

136 For example, a refusal to register a share transfer: *Re Smith and Fawcett Ltd* [1942] 1 All ER 542.

137 *Atwool v Merryweather* (1867) LR 5 Eq 464n.

138 [1916] 1 AC 554.

139 [1942] 1 All ER 378.

140 *Foster v Foster* [1916] 1 Ch 532.

141 (1986) 4 NSWLR 722.

142 (1988) 4 BCC 30.

143 *Flitcroft's Case* (1882) 21 ChD 519.

144 *Precision Dippings Ltd v Precision Dippings Marketing Ltd* [1986] Ch 447.

145 [1988] BCLC 104.

146 See, for example, *Joint Receivers and Managers of Niltan Carson v Hawthorne* [1988] BCLC 298.

147 As in *Re J Franklin & Son Ltd* [1937] 4 All ER 43, where the directors had wrongly paid a director's widow out of the company's money and relief was refused.

148 *Re Produce Marketing* [1989] BCLC 513 (liability for wrongful trading).

149 *Re Claridge's Patent Asphalte Co Ltd* [1921] 1 Ch 543.

150 *Re Duomatic Ltd* [1969] 1 All ER 161.

151 *Re Barry and Staines Linoleum Ltd* [1934] Ch 227.

152 *Marine & Industrial Generators Ltd v Mercer* (1982) New LJ 65.

153 *Re Gilt Edge Safety Glass Ltd* [1940] Ch 495.

154 *Re J Franklin & Son Ltd* [1937] 4 All ER 43.

155 Section 312: *Re Duomatic Ltd* [1969] 1 All ER 161.

156 *Selangor United Rubber Estates Ltd v Cradock (No 3)* [1968] 2 All ER 1073.
157 *Customs and Excise Commissioners v Hedon Alpha Ltd* [1981] QB 818.
158 Section 365.
159 *Beck v Board of Trade Solicitor* (1932) 76 SJ 414; where the Act refers to an 'officer who is in default' it means the same: s 730(5).
160 Currently the statutory maximum fine is £5,000.
161 Section 450. Similar penalties apply in a winding up; s 209 of the Insolvency Act 1986.
162 *R v Sinclair* [1968] 3 All ER 241.
163 Section 19(1) of the Theft Act 1968. This is quite apart from the specific fraud offences created by that Act and the Theft Act 1978 (for example, obtaining property by deception).
164 *R v Lord Kylsant* [1932] 1 KB 422.
165 Financial Services Act 1986, s 47. Although appearing under the general heading 'Conduct of Investment Business' and not in the part of the Act dealing with publicity for issues, s 47 catches directors of a company whose shares are being offered. It does, however, go far wider than *merely* making false statements in a prospectus, which was the relevant offence under the Act.
166 Section 218 of the Insolvency Act 1986.
167 *Re London & Globe Finance Corporation* [1903] 1 Ch 728.
168 [1984] 2 All ER 216.
169 (1989) 5 BCC 665.
170 *Beck v Board of Trade Solicitor* (1932) 76 SJ 414.
171 *Huckerby v Elliott* [1970] 1 All ER 189.
172 For example, Borrowing (Control and Guarantees) Act 1946, Sch 3(4).
173 For example, Deposit of Poisonous Wastes Act 1972, s 6. This type of provision is now very common indeed; see, Trade Descriptions Act 1968, s 20; Fair Trading Act 1973, s 132; Consumer Credit Act 1974, s 169; Consumer Safety Act 1978, s 7; Banking Act 1987, s 96; a full list of relevant offences will be found in *Directors' Personal Liabilities*, published by the Institute of Directors (1992).
174 *R v Davies* [1954] 3 All ER 335.
175 [1988] BCLC 217.

Chapter 7

RELATIONS WITH SHAREHOLDERS

7.1 TRANSFER OF SHARES

One of the duties of the board is to register share transfers (when duly stamped) and, in the case of listed companies, they will have no discretion, as fully paid shares must be transferable without restriction. However, as we have seen, private companies may and often do restrict the right to transfer their shares. What, then, are the duties of the directors of a private company when a share transfer is presented to them for registration? All depends upon the Articles which will contain the restrictions but directors should remember that, in the absence of some impediment, they must register a duly stamped transfer accompanied by the share certificate and the prescribed fee (if any). The stamp duty is at present 0.5 per cent on the consideration,[1] but under the Stock Transfer Act 1963 the transfer can be in the form specified in that Act and does not need the signature of the transferee.[2] Thus, the prima facie right to have his shares transferred rests with the shareholder[3] and it is for the directors to show why it should be denied in any particular case.

When they refer to the Articles, the directors will usually find restrictions of two kinds.

(1) A power for directors, 'in their absolute discretion and without assigning any reason therefor' to decline to register any transfer.
(2) A power for the members to transfer freely within the membership or the family, but with a right of pre-emption for insiders before there is a transfer to an outsider.

Articles frequently combine the two forms of restriction in such a way that the directors' powers under (1) will only come into play if the possibilities in (2) have been exhausted and a transfer to an outsider is in prospect.[4] For example, if the Articles provide that a member may not transfer his shares to an outsider if any member or his relative is willing to purchase them, the directors have no power to register a transfer if they know that the shares have not first been offered to the members and their families.[5] It is, nevertheless, sensible to make it clear that the pre-emption rights are a condition precedent to the directors' power to register transfers[6] and also to spell out the procedure for compliance with the pre-emption rights.[7]

The directors must, of course, satisfy themselves that a transfer submitted under (2) above complies with the relevant Article but, subject to what is said above, the exercise of their discretion arises only under (1) above and it is here they may be in need of guidance.

The following factors may be relevant.

(1) Their primary duty is to exercise their discretion (like all other powers) in the interests of the company.[8]

(2) The burden of proving bad faith or improper purpose lies on the person alleging it. It was held that this burden was not discharged in a case where a surviving director and 50 per cent shareholder refused to register a transfer unless half of the shareholding was sold to him. It was held that there was nothing to show that he was not acting in the company's interests.[9]

(3) Where the Articles give the directors an absolute discretion to decline registration without giving reasons, the directors would be well advised to give no reason for their refusal. If they give none, there is nothing to be attacked.[10]

(4) Their duty is to act in good faith in the interests of the company, with due regard to the member's right to transfer his shares, and fairly to consider the matter at a board meeting. Thus, if they take no action at all, the transfer must be registered.[11]

(5) They must give notice of refusal within two months (s 183(5)), otherwise they are liable to a default fine, and the transferee will usually be entitled to demand registration.[12] This is obtained by his applying to the court under s 359 for rectification of the register (see (6) below). The directors must exercise their power of refusal without undue delay, and the statutory limit dictates the absolute limit of delay which is permissible. If, during that period, there are no directors, or no directors capable of acting, the transferee's prima facie right to registration does not crystallise, for it is possible that directors may be appointed who might refuse registration. Therefore, he cannot claim membership of the company until it is too late for the directors' powers of refusal to be exercised.[13]

(6) The remedy for a disgruntled transferee is to apply to the courts for rectification of the register under s 359, not for a winding up.[14]

(7) Transmission on death, bankruptcy or liquidation of a member gives rise to two consequences:

   (a) the company must accept the probate etc, as evidence of the right of the representative to deal with the shares (ss 183 and 187); and

   (b) the company is not automatically bound to accept the representative as a member. Most Articles will provide that the rules relating to the transfer of shares apply to the notice or instrument by which the representative asserts the transfer to him of the share, so that, for example, they may, even under Table A, decline to register the representative if the share is not fully paid and they do not approve the representative (Table A, reg 24). Similarly, if the Articles do give a discretion to refuse registration in any circumstances, that Article will apply to the representative (Table A, reg 30). Perhaps curiously, a personal representative who has taken shares by transmission has locus standi to bring proceedings for unfair prejudice under s 459.

On the death of a joint holder, the survivor becomes the sole member.

7.1.1   Pre-emption rights: valuing the shares

Unless the price is fixed by the Articles or can be agreed by negotiation, some mechanism must be found to value the shares. This is vitally important; overvaluation may nullify the pre-emption rights, while undervaluation may leave the transferor with a grievance. It is surprising how casual many Articles are in this respect.

Often the question is simply left to the judgement of an independent accountant. If so, the underlying principle is that he will act as a valuer, and *not* as a judge or arbitrator. Consequently, neither the transferor nor other members have an absolute right to make representations to him. Further, he cannot be forced to give reasons for his valuation. If he gives none, his 'non-speaking' valuation is very difficult to challenge unless there is good evidence from his report or from other documents or the surrounding circumstances that he acted in bad faith[15] or has stepped outside the terms of his instructions, but not on the grounds that it is wrong (even significantly wrong).[16] A valuation which gives reasons is more readily challengeable in the practical sense – it will be easier to detect such a vitiating factor – but the legal grounds on which the challenge may be mounted are no wider. In either case, a valuation may be challenged if it is shown, for example, to relate to the wrong number of shares, or the wrong company, or that the valuer has personally valued assets which he was instructed to have independently valued by an expert, but not on the basis that he has excluded from his valuation of the shares assets which one of the parties considers should have been taken into account.[17] The following are examples of factors which may be relevant to unfair prejudice proceedings under s 459 or to challenging the decision of an arbitrator but which would not in themselves nullify a valuation. They might well become relevant to a valuation if the aggrieved party claims not to upset the valuation itself, but to sue the valuer for professional negligence. A decision fixing the value of a 40 per cent shareholding as 40 per cent of the company's net asset value was wrong; the proper measure was the value of the shares in the market, which might well apply a discount to the value of a minority holding.[18] A genuine offer for the shares by an outsider should be taken into account as evidence of their value and may preclude any minority discount if made in respect of all the company's shares.[19] Since potential buyers often value shares by profit and dividend streams, these should be taken into account, together with any special rights or restrictions applying to the shares.[20]

Some Articles provide that share valuations are to be made as if a transfer notice had been served in respect of *each* of the shares. This choice of words is not neutral – several courts have held that they exclude consideration of the size of the holding and therefore exclude any minority discount;[21] and, it seems, a valuation which took the size of the holding into account could be challenged on the basis described above.

When Articles are drafted, it is impossible to foresee all the circumstances in which a share valuation may have to be undertaken. If the mechanism or formula worked out is not obviously capricious or unfair, insistence by the other members that a would-be transferor submit to the pre-emption rights and valuation procedures set out in the Articles, will not usually be a ground on which the transferor can complain of unfair treatment. Where, on the other hand, a minority tries to sell out against the background of an *existing* shareholder dispute, the court may well stop the board – or the majority – from invoking pre-emption rights precisely because the embattled minority will have no opportunity to challenge a non-speaking valuation.[22]

7.1.2 Paper-based and paperless share dealings

The traditional system of share transfer is set out in ss 183 to 186 of the 1985 Act. There must be a proper instrument of transfer, which need not be sealed but in practice often is; if the Articles require a particular form of transfer, it must be followed.[23] When the form is produced, the company must normally issue a share certificate to the transferee within two months – this certificate is not a guarantee of the holder's title, although it is prima facie evidence and also an assurance that proper transfer documentation was presented to the company.

For some time, less formal transfer documents have been permitted under s 1 of the Stock Transfer Act 1963. The certification procedure is, however, somewhat cumbersome when applied to listed companies, for shares may pass through several hands before reaching the eventual transferee. The Stock Exchange rules therefore permitted the transferor's broker to give the certificate to the Secretary of the Share and Loan Department, who would certify the transfer and forward the certificate to the company, which would make out a new certificate in the name of the final transferee. Registrars dealing in transfers of shares in companies having a Stock Exchange listing were until recently using the Talisman system. This was superseded in July 1996 by the fully computerised CREST system. The necessary legal changes were brought about by Part IX of the Companies Act 1989 and the Uncertificated Securities Regulations 1995, SI 1995/3272. This is the new settlement system for shares and other securities developed by the Bank of England and operated by CREST Co Limited, Trinity Tower, 9 Thomas Moore Street, London, E1 9YN. This company is owned by a broad spectrum of participants in the UK Securities Market. Under the system, shares and stock will be held in paperless electronic form on a computer record rather than in the physical form of a share certificate. There is no obligation on individual shareholders to commute their share certificates for a CREST electronic record and, indeed, unless they trade frequently in the shares, it would seem sensible for them to continue to keep their certificates.

In order to enter the CREST system, a company must go through the following stages.

(1) A resolution must be passed to disapply those clauses of its Articles of Association which relate to share certificates. This may be done either by resolution of the Board of Directors or alternatively by altering the Articles of Association by special resolution in a general meeting of the company in the usual way.

(2) Notice of the proposal to pass such a resolution must be given to all shareholders in the company, not merely to the holders of those shares of classes to which the resolution applies. The notice must be given prior to, or within 60 days of, the passing of the resolution. Where the resolution has been passed by the directors, it may be over ruled by an ordinary resolution of the members of the company.

(3) Following the resolution, the company must apply to CREST Co for permission for the shares or stock concerned to be transferred to the CREST System. The granting and timing of such permission is at the discretion of CREST Co.

Shareholders may move their holdings to the CREST System either by:

(a) using a bank or a nominee company of a stockbroker which has become a member of CREST; or

(b) by becoming a sponsored member of CREST. This is achieved by a sponsored membership agreement which could be provided only by an authorised CREST sponsor such as a bank or a stockbroker. A sponsored member may be either a private company or an individual shareholder. A charge is made by CREST Co to its CREST sponsors for each sponsored member.

Where shares are held through a nominee company, the individual share holdings will be recorded in the record of the nominee and only the total holding of the nominee will be recorded on the company's register of shareholders. Dividends will be paid to the nominee and the nominee will account subsequently to the beneficial owners. Many nominees will use designated accounts and each designation will be a separate share holding in the register of the company.

Where shares are held by a sponsored member of CREST, the name of the sponsored member will appear on the register of the company and dividends will be paid directly to that member.

Shares represented by certificates may be transferred to CREST by the use of a prescribed form (see the Stock Transfer (Additions and Substitutions of Forms) Order 1996, SI 1996/1571). Conversely, shares can be transferred out of CREST into a certificated format.

Shares held by a sponsored member of CREST may have their registered particulars altered through the CREST sponsor. Interests in shares held by nominee companies will be transferred, or details altered, by the use of internal documentation of the nominees.

Shares are transferred within the CREST System on the instructions given electronically by system members such as the stockbrokers or banks concerned. The authorised CREST sponsor will be the system member for the holdings of a sponsored member.

7.2 COMPULSORY ACQUISITION OF SHARES

We have noted the directors' responsibilities in connection with the restriction of share transfers. What powers may they enjoy in the opposite direction – that of compelling share transfers? There are several possibilities.

7.2.1 Lien

The Articles may give them a lien (or charge) on shares for any debts[24] due from the members of the company. In that case, the Articles usually also give a power of sale, at the directors' discretion, with further power to execute a transfer.[25] Table A, regs 8 to 11, contain such provisions but are restricted to sums owed in respect of partly paid shares.[26]

However, the special Articles of private companies often extend this to fully paid shares, which is clearly of more practical use to the company, in view of the rarity of partly paid shares.

7.2.2   Compulsory transfer

The Articles may also provide that a member shall transfer his shares on specified terms in the event of:

(1)   his bankruptcy; or
(2)   breach of some regulation of the company.

Transfer under (1) cannot be resisted by the trustee in bankruptcy unless he can show unfairness in the price. It is not therefore inherently objectionable.[27] A resolution by the directors (or members) for compulsory transfer under (2) will be enforceable if bona fide in the interest of the company as a whole, as where it is used to get rid of a competing shareholder.[28]

It will not be bona fide, however, if the objective is simply to expropriate the minority[29] or to force a sale without reference to the needs of the company.[30]

7.2.3   Deprivation of pre-emptive rights

A shareholder may be deprived of his pre-emptive rights (ie his rights to have first refusal in respect of the shares of the other members) by an alteration of the Articles, since every shareholder takes the risk that such alterations may be made – provided the change is made bona fide and is not a fraud on the minority.[31]

7.3   STATUTORY PRE-EMPTION RIGHTS

One sort of pre-emption right – the right of members to purchase the shares which other members wish to dispose of – has been discussed above. A second sort of pre-emption right arises when the company itself is proposing to make a capital issue, and is obliged to offer the new shares to the existing membership first. The reason for such a right is obvious enough; the new issue may well raise the desired capital, but it will equally dilute existing holdings in terms of voting power and quite possibly in terms of value. This is at least one of the reasons for placing the ultimate control over share issues in the hands of the general meeting rather than the board (see s 80, **3.3** above). Sections 89 to 95 provide complementary safeguards.

(1)   The general rule is that a company proposing to allot equity securities must first offer them to the existing equity shareholders, each member being offered a number of shares in proportion to his existing holding. This 'pre-emptive' offer must be on terms at least as favourable as the terms proposed for allotment to outsiders (s 89(1)). An equity share is defined in s 94. It is a share which carries a right to participate in surplus profits by way of a distribution or a return of capital. (See particularly (3) below.)

(2)   If the Memorandum or Articles themselves impose a similar obligation to make pre-emption offers in relation to shares of a particular class, the general statutory obligation does not apply in relation to members who accept offers made under such an obligation: s 89(2), (3).[32]

(3) 'Equity securities' excludes subscribers' and bonus shares together with preference shares, with limited rights of participation in dividend and capital; but the expression does include any form of right to subscribe for other types of shares or to convert a security of any sort into an equity security (s 94).[33]

(4) The general rule does not apply where the new shares are to be paid up, wholly or partly, for a non-cash consideration, nor to shares to be held under an employees' share scheme (s 89(4), (5)).

(5) The mechanism for making pre-emption offers under (1) and (2) above is prescribed by s 90. Offers must be posted to members, and take effect at the time when the offer letter would normally be delivered in the ordinary course of post. The offer must be for a period of at least 21 days and may not be withdrawn during that period. Thus, no offers may be made to third parties until the period has expired or replies have been received (in respect of every pre-emption offer (s 89(1)(b))). These rules override any contrary provision in the Memorandum or Articles: s 90(7).

(6) Contravention of these requirements renders the company and any officer who knowingly authorised or permitted the contravention jointly and severally liable to compensate shareholders suffering loss as a result, provided that an action to recover the loss is commenced within two years of the delivery of the allotment return to the registrar (shares) or the date of the grant (other securities) (s 92).

(7) An interesting case concerning the application of these pre-emption rights was *Re Thundercrest Ltd*.[34] The company had three shareholders, one of whom was the plaintiff. Each of the three shareholders held 50 shares. There was a proposal to issue a further 30,000 new shares, 10,000 to each shareholder. A letter of provisional allotment and form of acceptance was sent by Recorded Delivery post to the plaintiff shareholders. However, this was returned undelivered by the Post Office. The other two shareholders took up the shares which might otherwise have been taken by the plaintiff. At this time, these other two shareholders were aware that the letter of provisional allotment had not been delivered to the plaintiff. They also knew that the plaintiff was eager to take up the shares. The plaintiff brought proceedings under s 359 for rectification of the register. It was held by Judge Paul Baker QC that rectification should be ordered. The defendant shareholders could not rely on the provisions of the Articles deeming the provision letter of allotment to have been delivered by being sent to his registered address. The deeming provisions could not be relied upon where it was manifest that the letter had not been delivered.

There are, however, certain exclusions and savings from the general rules.

(1) The whole rule, or part of it (for example, in relation to the method of making the pre-emption offer) may be excluded by the Memorandum or Articles of a private company (although obviously this is not the effect of provisions referred to in paragraph (2) above) (s 91).

(2) The requirement to make pre-emption offers does not enable the company to override any statutory rule which forbids a company to offer or allot its shares: s 93. For example, s 84 forbids an allotment of shares in a public company unless the issue is fully subscribed or the terms on which the offer is made specifically allow allotment despite only partial subscription; and by s 454 share issues may

be forbidden by the courts or the Secretary of State. Those sections have precedence over s 89.

(3) Where the directors have been given power by the general meeting to make allotments generally (see s 80 at **3.3**), they may also be given power by the Articles or by special resolution (75 per cent majority) to ignore the statutory pre-emptive rights (s 95). They may also seek a special resolution authorising them to disregard those rights in a particular case, whether they have a general authority to make allotments or merely authority to make the particular allotment in question.[35] In this case, they must recommend the resolution to the members and circulate with the notice of the meeting a statement of their reasons, of the amount to be paid to the company under the allotment, and their justification of that amount.[36] For no obvious reason, no similar procedure applies in the case where the directors are seeking general authority to ignore the statutory pre-emption rights.

Pre-emption rights have been the subject of a long battle in the case of listed companies. As far as the last government was concerned, they represented an obstacle to wider share-ownership, given that institutional shareholders have an entrenched holding of well over two-thirds of listed shares. As far as the institutions are concerned, disapplication of pre-emption rights under s 89 is a threat to their position. For the Stock Exchange, allowing directors to override pre-emption rights is not undesirable in itself, but it hands the directors a major power which must be subject to regular shareholder scrutiny. The attitude of the present government is at the moment unknown. Rumours that the 1989 Act would abolish pre-emption rights proved unfounded. While hostilities may resume at any time, the position at the time of writing is that:

(1) listed companies *may* disapply pre-emption rights, but only for a limited period. The disapplication resolution must expire within 15 months or by the next annual general meeting, whichever is sooner;[37]

(2) the institutions will not oppose special resolutions allowing an issue equivalent to five per cent of the ordinary shares, with an upper limit of 7.5 per cent over any three-year period.

Effectively, therefore, annual approval must be sought for the board of a listed company to make issues, except on the rateable statutory basis.

7.4   SHARE CAPITAL RULES

Extensive changes in the law governing dealings affecting share capital were made by the Companies Act 1981. In particular, new powers were introduced enabling:

(1) private companies to give financial assistance for the acquisition of their own shares;

(2) all companies to issue redeemable shares;

(3) all companies to purchase their own shares;

(4) private companies to redeem or purchase their shares out of capital.

In the following sections the main features of these rules are described. They make for a considerably greater degree of flexibility than previously existed in relation to capital structure and represent a considerable inroad upon the 'hands off' policy of the older Acts. There is a corresponding danger to the capital base of the company, of course, and in an effort to avert this danger the rules are hedged about with qualifications. Directors should be aware of the opportunities offered but should beware of the statutory pitfalls. They will usually need expert advice before taking advantage of the opportunities.

7.5 FINANCIAL ASSISTANCE FOR ACQUISITION OF SHARES

7.5.1 The general rules

Section 54 of the 1948 Act, contained a general prohibition on such assistance although with some exceptions. This was repealed in 1981 and is now replaced by ss 151 to 155, which restate the prohibition in more carefully thought out terms and contain various entirely new exceptions. The effects are as follows.

(1) A company must not give assistance directly or indirectly for the purpose of an acquisition of shares in itself or its holding company (s 151(1)). Purchase of shares in a subsidiary is not within the prohibition.

(2) Where the shares have already been acquired and the acquirer has incurred a liability for the purpose of making the acquisition, such as a loan, neither the company nor any subsidiary may give direct or indirect assistance for the purpose of reducing or discharging that liability (s 151(2)) or to help to restore his financial position (s 152(3)(b)).

(3) Financial assistance means a gift, loan, indemnity, guarantee, assignment or other transaction by which the acquirer is directly or indirectly put in funds (s 152(1)). Any other transaction may amount to assistance if it materially reduces the company's net assets, for example, the payment by a target company of the legal fees of a bidder company on a takeover.

At this point some of the improvements made by the new formulation may be noted. The old s 54 was justly criticised for its ineffectiveness, but when, in later years, the courts began to give it teeth, the opposite danger appeared, namely that it would catch legitimate commercial transactions. Section 151 lays emphasis upon the purpose of the assistance, unlike s 54 which applied whenever assistance was given *in connection with* a share acquisition. Thus, when a company made a purchase of assets for proper commercial reasons, but also with a subsidiary view to assisting the vendor to purchase shares (or perhaps merely knowing that it was his intention to use the price for that purpose), there was a serious danger that the purchase amounted to prohibited financial assistance.[38] In an effort to avoid this, the courts then introduced requirements, in particular asking whether the impugned transaction was in the 'ordinary course of business'.[39] First, the removal of the italicised words (above) leaves the courts – and the board and its advisers – free to look solely at the question whether assistance is given for the purpose of the share acquisition. No doubt even under s 151 some marginal cases will arise where there are mixed motives and the courts must consider whether the dominant motive is to furnish assistance, but this has at least the merit of concentrating attention upon the appropriate issue and excluding those cases where assistance is unintentional or merely incidental (but see **7.5.2**).

Secondly, s 151 applies to assistance for the acquisition of shares rather than (as under s 54) purchase or subscription. Thus, s 151 clearly covers acquisitions which are not for cash.

Thirdly, as will be seen below, the new scheme makes the timing of assistance crucial.

Fourthly, the detailed definition of what constitutes 'financial assistance' (s 152(1)) should be a considerable improvement on the contortions necessary to determine this question under s 54. Apart from those transactions which are actually specified (see paragraph (3) above), the definition concentrates attention on the material reduction of the assisting company's 'net assets', ie its aggregate assets less its aggregate liabilities.[40] Even under s 54, however, a mere alteration in the character of the assets to make the company more inviting to the purchaser was not 'financial assistance'. Thus, where a holding company restructured the debts owed to it by a subsidiary in order to facilitate a 'buy out' by its finance and sales director, that was not financial assistance, nor had the subsidiary given 'indirect' assistance when it surrendered tax losses to the parent company in return. For at least, where the subsidiary is not making a profit, its tax losses are of little use to it unless someone will buy them. Even if the surrender involved a net transfer of assets from the subsidiary, this was no more than a change in the character of the assets; if anything, the parent had given assistance to the subsidiary, not to the purchaser.[41] The moral is simple. Even if the purpose is to provide assistance, the transaction escapes the statutory prohibition if it does not actually constitute financial assistance within the meaning of the Act.

7.5.2   Exceptions

The Act then makes a series of general exceptions to the prohibitions imposed by s 151.

(1)   Where the assistance is given in good faith in the interests of the company and the share acquisition (or subsequent reduction or discharge of the acquirer's liability) is not the principal purpose or is incidental to some larger purpose:[42] s 153(1) and (2). A previous edition of this book warned that although this is intended to place a further bar on the types of speculation indulged in under s 54[43] and to confirm that bona fide commercial dealing is not caught by s 151, the criteria stated are vague and might well fail in this objective. Unfortunately, this warning has been justified by the decision of the House of Lords in *Brady v Brady*.[44] Two brothers fell out and decided to split up the family business. A bought all the shares in the family company held by B. The price paid by A was reduced to take account of the transfer of a large part of the assets to B, leaving A to carry on what was left of the company's business, while an entirely distinct business was started up by B with the transferred assets. The object of the exercise was clearly a legitimate division of a business into separate parts, and it certainly had the support of the shareholders. But what was clearly legitimate in

family, shareholder and business terms unquestionably involved the old company assisting A to buy its shares by giving B part of his price in company assets. One might expect this to be treated as incidental to the principal or larger purpose of the reorganisation. After all, no one was hurt, everyone knew what was going on and there was no precariously balanced lending backed by company assets. The House of Lords held, however, that the arrangement was *not* to be excused under s 153. It was necessary:

> 'to distinguish between a purpose and the reason why a purpose is formed. The ultimate reason for forming the purpose *may, and in most cases probably will, be more important to those making the decision than the immediate transaction itself. But "larger" is not the same thing as "more important" nor is "reason" the same as "purpose".'* (Emphasis added.)

The arrangement remained prohibited, therefore, even though it was admittedly in good faith and in the interests of the company, which it saved from dissolution while injuring no creditors.[45] The House of Lords stressed that s 153 must not be interpreted so widely as to strip s 151 of its intended effect, which is presumably beneficial, but it is hard to be confident that the *Brady* decision leaves any room in practice for the application of s 153. The only safe course is to utilise the private company exemptions discussed in **7.5.3**, where these are available.[46]

(2) Where the assistance takes the form of a lawfully paid[47] dividend or distribution made in the course of winding up (s 153(3)(a)) or the allotment of bonus shares (s 153(3)(b)).

(3) Where it effects a reduction of capital confirmed by the court under s 137 (s 153(3)(c)) or by virtue of a redemption or purchase of shares under ss 159 to 181 (s 153(3)(d)).

(4) Where it implements a court order under s 425 (scheme of arrangement), a sale by a liquidator (s 110 of the Insolvency Act 1986) or an arrangement with creditors with a view to winding up (Part I of the Insolvency Act 1986) (s 153(3)(e) to (g)).

(5) Where it is a loan in the ordinary course of business by a money-lending company (s 153(4)(a)).

(6) Where assistance is provided by the company or a subsidiary to facilitate acquisitions under or for the purposes of an employees' share scheme for the benefit of bona fide employees (including directors) or their dependants (s 153(4)(b) and s 153(4)(bb), as amended by the Financial Services Act 1986 and the Companies Act 1989). The assistance may be direct (a loan) or indirect (a guarantee of borrowings by scheme trustees). The only limitation is that the assistance must be given in good faith; in particular, directors may not set up a scheme in order to make the company less attractive to potential bidders for the shares (action which would probably be a breach of directors' fiduciary duties under the general law).

(7) Where a loan is made to a bona fide employee (other than a director) for the acquisition of fully paid shares (s 153(4)(c)).

However, paras (5) to (7) above apply to a public company only if s 154 is satisfied, ie it has net assets which are not reduced, or if the reduction comes out of distributable profits. A loan will not normally reduce net assets as the cash payment will be balanced by a book debt owed to the company.

7.5.3   Private company exemptions

The Act proceeds to offer special exemption to private companies, which may give financial assistance in the following circumstances.

(1) Where the company has net assets[48] which are not reduced by the assistance, or the assistance is provided out of distributable profits (s 155(2)).

(2) A declaration of solvency must be made by the directors[49] giving details of the proposed assistance and stating that:

    (a) immediately thereafter the company will be able to pay its debts as they fall due; and

    (b) that it will be able to pay its debts within 12 months (if winding up is intended) or (if not) as they fall due during the following 12 months (s 156(2)).

(3) This must be supported by an auditor's report stating that after inquiry they can see nothing unreasonable in the directors' opinion (s 156(4)).

(4) The members must approve by a special resolution (75 per cent majority of those voting) (s 155(4))[50] at a general meeting at which the statutory declaration and auditors' report have been available and which must be held within one week of the date of the declaration (s 157(1), (4)).

(5) The declaration, report and resolution must be filed with the registrar within 15 days of the resolution (s 156(5)). Then timing becomes even more crucial. The assistance must be given between four weeks after the resolution and eight weeks after the statutory declaration (s 158) unless an application for cancellation has been made.

(6) Holders of 10 per cent or more of the nominal value of the share capital (or any class of it) may, within the initial four-week period, apply to the courts to cancel that resolution and the courts may then cancel, confirm or adjourn on such terms as it sees fit (s 157).

(7) Contravention of any of these provisions (including making a statutory declaration without reasonable grounds) is an offence. Punishments vary from a fine of £5,000 (failure to file a statutory declaration) to two years' imprisonment and an unlimited fine (prohibited assistance, statutory declaration without reasonable grounds). The Act says nothing about the civil consequences of breaches; presumably because to do so would be superfluous. Prohibited assistance involves an unlawful (indeed criminal) misapplication of company funds which in turn involves a clear breach of the directors' duties as quasi-trustees of the assets. Even where the directors control the company, this is an unratifiable breach of duty and a minority shareholder will be able to enforce the duty by means of a derivative action. Furthermore, those to whom the assets are paid over will be liable to a claim to 'trace' the misapplied assets[51] and if they receive or handle those assets with notice of the breach of duty they will remain liable to account to the company even after parting with the assets.[52]

In *Brady* (above) the House of Lords had decided that the financial assistance could not be justified under s 153. However, it then stated that 'where an agreement can be performed in alternative ways, one lawful and one unlawful, it is to be presumed that the parties intend to carry it out in the lawful and not the unlawful manner'. Accordingly, it was still possible for the financial assistance to be given so long as the s 155 procedure, described above, will follow it. This was the case because the company had sufficient distributable profits from which the assistance could be given. However, for this to apply the company must be solvent. In *Plaut v Steiner*,[53] it was held in a case where the situation was very similar to that in *Brady* that s 155 would not be applied because the company did not make the appropriate declaration of solvency.

7.6   ISSUE OF REDEEMABLE SHARES

Redeemable preference shares have been permissible since the Companies Act 1948 (s 58). It was only in 1981, however, that a power to issue redeemable shares of any type was introduced. Redemption will involve a reduction of issued capital, and the power is subject to statutory conditions which must be observed. The scheme is as follows.

(1)   Shares may be issued which are redeemable at the option of the shareholder or the company, or automatically to be redeemed by the company at a fixed date (s 159(1)). At the time of the issue, however, there must be one or more issued shares which are not redeemable[54] (s 159(2)).

(2)   Redemption may take place only if the shares are fully paid[55] and the terms of redemption must provide for payment on redemption (s 159(3)).

(3)   The Articles must authorise the issue (s 159(1)). The Articles must also specify the circumstances in which the shares are redeemable and most other terms and conditions of redemption. They may, however, leave it up to the directors to determine the date(s) for redemption but, if so, this determination must be made *before* the shares are issued. Again, the price payable on redemption need not be specified but, if not, the Articles must adopt a formula by which to calculate the price and the formula must be self-sufficient, not leaving any part of the calculation to the discretion of the directors or any third party (s 159A, inserted by s 133 of the Companies Act 1989).

(4)   The shares must be redeemed out of distributable profits[56] or from the proceeds of a fresh issue made for the purpose (s 160(1)). Any premium on the shares payable on redemption must come from distributable profits (s 160(2)).

(5)   The redeemed shares are cancelled (s 160(4)) reducing the issued capital but not the authorised share capital.

(6)   A new issue of shares may be made to replace the redeemed shares. An issue may be made before redemption, if the new issue does not exceed the nominal value of the redeemed shares (s 160(5)).

(7)   The company must file a return with the Registrar relating to the shares which it has purchased within 28 days of the first acquisition.

The sections represent a fairly major change in emphasis, since the *Jenkins Report*[57] did not favour a general power to issue redeemable capital. The new power, together with those powers discussed in the next section, is a response to a perceived demand for such capital, particularly to attract outside investment, at a minority level, in private companies.

On redemption the amount by which the capital is reduced is to be transferred to the capital redemption fund under s 170 (see **7.7**).

7.7   PURCHASE OF A COMPANY'S OWN SHARES

The principle that capital should be preserved for the benefit of creditors requires a rule which outlaws the purchase by a company of its own shares. Such a rule was established by the courts[58] and is set out in s 143 of the Act. The practical effect of the section is very greatly reduced by the exceptions to the rule referred to in it. These include cases where shares are acquired:

(1)   otherwise than for valuable consideration;[59]
(2)   pursuant to an approved capital reduction;
(3)   pursuant to court orders for the alteration of objects, dealing with objections to reregistration with private company status or granting relief to members under ss 459 to 461; and by forfeiture for non-payment.

The greatest erosion of the principle lies in the powers now given to issue redeemable shares (**7.6**) and, under the conditions discussed in this section, simply to purchase the company's own shares. This power may be exercised in relation to non-redeemable shares, or in relation to redeemable shares where for some reason s 159 (**7.6**) does not apply, for example, because the redemption date is still in the future. But it is only a power, not a right; there is nothing in these sections (as there may be in the terms of issue of redeemable shares) which enables the company to compel a member to sell his shares to the company.

There are three overriding requirements:

(1)   the company must be authorised by the Articles to make such a purchase[60] (s 162(1));
(2)   the purchase must leave at least one member holding non-redeemable shares (s 162(3)) and at least two members in all (s 1);
(3)   as in the case of redemption, the price must be paid out of distributable profits or from the proceeds of a fresh issue (see **7.6**) (s 162(2)). Premiums must be paid out of distributable profits. Purchased shares are cancelled and the nominal share capital reduced accordingly.

The Act then distinguishes different types of purchase.

7.7.1   Off-market purchases

A purchase is off-market if the shares are:

(1)   not purchased on a recognised investment exchange; or
(2)   although purchased on such an exchange are not subject to a marketing arrangement on that exchange.

A 'marketing arrangement' means that the shares are listed or traded on the unlisted securities market or can be dealt in without any prior approval being required by the Stock Exchange or other investment exchange on which they are traded[61] (s 163).

Such purchases must comply with s 164:

(1) there must be an approved contract; the proposed purchase must be approved by special resolution of the members. In the case of a public company, the resolution must state the date on which the authority to purchase expires, which must not be more than 18 months later. All such resolutions (public or private company) may be varied, revoked or renewed;

(2) in the case of an off-market purchase, the votes of the shares to be purchased must be disregarded;

(3) a copy or memorandum of the contract must be available for inspection at the registered office for at least the 15 days before the meeting, and at the meeting itself. This must disclose the names of the proposed vendors, and it should therefore be clear who is unable to vote at the meeting;

(4) the proposed contract may itself be varied, but variation is subject to the same procedure as the original contract;

(5) approval may be given pursuant to the private company written resolution procedure introduced by s 381A. This requires 'unanimity', so instead of disregarding 'interested' votes ((2) above) Sch 15A treats the members in question as not entitled to vote on this issue – so there can and must be unanimity among the holders of all the other shares. Those members must be supplied with the documentation referred to in (3) above, no later than they receive a copy of the resolution for their signature.

7.7.2 Market purchases

It would be difficult to obtain authorisation for market purchases by the procedure described above since there may be no specific purchases or shares in mind. Consequently, a much relaxed procedure applies to the purchase of shares traded on an investment exchange recognised for the purposes of the Financial Services Act 1986. This relaxation does carry a risk of malpractice by the creation of rigged or artificial prices; to some extent, at least, this danger may be reduced by the Company Securities (Insider Dealing) Act 1985 (see **7.9**). The requirements of s 166 for market purchases are as follows:

(1) there must be prior approval by the general meeting, but only an ordinary resolution is required, and whilst this may be conditional, or limited to certain classes or descriptions of shares, it may equally well be a general authority to purchase;[62]

(2) the authority must specify the maximum number of shares which may be acquired, the maximum and minimum prices payable,[63] and an expiry date no more than 18 months later. The authority may be revoked, and may be varied or renewed (subject to the same limitations);

(3) purchases must be completed within the period specified in the resolution ((2) above) unless the resolution permits a purchase contracted during that period to be completed after it has expired;[64]

(4) the resolution must be filed with the Registrar of Companies within 15 days. In addition, the company must file a return within 28 days of the first acquisition (s 169).

7.8   CAPITAL RULES AND TAXATION

In the ordinary way, purchases and redemptions by a company of its own shares (**7.6** to **7.7**) would count as 'distributions' for tax purposes and would thus attract liability as if the payments were to come. The powers to issue redeemable shares and to purchase own shares would be stripped of much of their effect by such a tax disincentive. Section 53 of, and Sch 9 to, the Finance Act 1982, accordingly, attempt to help, rather than hinder, the creation of a ready market in unquoted shares by providing reliefs; and since the object is to create a new market, and not to bolster an existing one, these reliefs do not apply except for the benefit of unquoted trading companies or their 75 per cent owned subsidiaries. A number of conditions must be satisfied, and in particular the purpose of the transaction must be to benefit the company's trade and not, in effect, to pay out a tax-free dividend. Although it is not particularly easy to see why, the 'benefit' test is generally accepted to be satisfied where the member parts with the whole of his shareholding. To take advantage of the reliefs, the conditions set out in Sch 9 must also be satisfied, namely:

(1) the vendor must be resident in the UK in the year of sale;
(2) he must have owned the holding for at least five years;
(3) all his holding must be sold, or there must be a substantial reduction in it, ie at least a 25 per cent reduction in nominal value.

If there is any doubt about these conditions, advance clearance may be obtained from the Inland Revenue, and no attempt should be made, in any case, to operate these reliefs without professional advice. It is advisable to obtain Inland Revenue clearance in all cases.

There is a further relief where the purchase of shares is made to discharge an inheritance tax (formerly capital transfer tax) liability; this is available only where that liability could not be discharged from other sources without 'undue hardship' and, again, there is an advance clearance procedure to ensure that the relief really is available as far as the Inland Revenue is concerned.

It is also necessary for those taking part in share transfers to consider stamp duty. Since the last edition of this book, this has been a highly mobile target. The following is a brief summary of the main developments (if that word is strong enough).

(1) In 1986, the rate of duty applying to the *transfer* of securities was reduced to 0.5 per cent. At the same time the scope of the charge was widened to include depositary receipts. More importantly, a new tax was introduced, Stamp Duty Reserve Tax, the main aim of which was to impose a similar rate of charge on dealings during a single Stock Exchange accounting period, which often escaped stamp duty. Unfortunately, this tax hit many unintended targets, and might, for example, be relevant in connection with share transfers on a divorce.

(2) In 1988, the capital duty of one per cent chargeable on the *issue* of shares was abolished.

(3) In 1989, the Treasury took powers to make regulations adapting stamp duty and the stamp duty reserve tax to take account of the new non-paper dealing system TAURUS was subsequently abandoned and replaced by CREST (see **7.1.2**). The two taxes were to lead the way into the high-tech era. The Inland Revenue had already announced measures to do this when, 12 months later, the Finance Act 1990 *removed* stamp duty from all transfers of 'defined securities' (including shares, stock, interests in or dividends arising out of shares and stock, and options and similar rights) and *abolished* the stamp duty reserve tax. These provisions were to take effect from a date to be fixed.

Between 1986 and 1990, therefore, stamp duty went from frontline status to obsolescence. Until the return of a Labour government in 1997, it had been intended that stamp duty on share transfers would be abolished; whether this is still the intention remains to be seen. Until then, all transfers remain subject to the existing stamp duty or reserve tax rules. Companies should be particularly mindful that stamp duty will usually be attracted to the returns made to the Registrar when they make purchases of their own shares under the 1985 Act.

7.9 INSIDER DEALING: COMMON LAW AND STATUTORY CONTROL

In this and the following section, we look at the director's position when he or someone close to him buys or sells shares in the company. The underlying rule of the common law derives from a decision of a single judge in *Percival v Wright*,[65] and is generous to a fault. In that case, a group of shareholders approached the directors, asking them to buy their shares. The directors did this without disclosing that a sale of the company's business was pending, which made the value of the shares far higher than the price paid for them by the directors. Nevertheless, the directors were held not liable to the vendors:

(1) because their duties are owed to the company and not to the individual members; and

(2) because there had been no misrepresentation or unfair dealing, and it was the members who approached the directors.[66]

Therefore the transaction could not be set aside. This case set an absurdly low standard of behaviour and the facts might well be viewed differently today under the rough justice embodied in the principle of *Regal (Hastings) Ltd v Gulliver*[67] that directors must not derive personal profit from information acquired by them as directors. As we have seen, absence of damage to the company is irrelevant in such a case and the inside information may be regarded as company property (see **5.6**). However, it would then be the company and not the vendors which would reap the benefit – perhaps the reason why no such action has ever been reported – but this would at least be better than nothing, and it is arguably right that the company, and only the company, should benefit from the use of insider information. Furthermore, the public spirited member who pursues such an action to a successful conclusion, benefiting all the members, could expect an indemnity for his costs on the basis of *Wallersteiner v Moir (No 2)*.[68]

It is possible that the same analysis will apply if the situation in *Percival v Wright* is reversed, ie directors have sold their shares to members or to outsiders without disclosing that the company is in difficulties. Again, the company suffers no immediate or direct loss, but the vendors are still taking advantage of their position and misapplying information held by them as fiduciaries. Accordingly, they may be under a duty to account to the company at least for the artificially inflated part of the price received. Even if the company or the members as a whole are unwilling to enforce the directors' duties, the same reluctance will not be shown by a receiver[69] or a liquidator.

There are obvious dangers in pressing this analysis too far. A director is bound to have some price-relevant inside information about his company, and while *Regal* is hard to stop once on the move, it cannot be sensible to press directors' positions as fiduciaries to the point where they can hardly trade the company's shares at all. What is objectionable is conduct which takes conscious and unfair advantage of inside knowledge. What, therefore, is necessary is a careful consideration by the director, in each case, of whether he has inside information which is material to the price of the shares which, if disclosed, would have more than a minimal impact on their selling price. Would the information affect the decision of the prudent buyer or seller in agreeing to the sale and to the terms? If the answer is affirmative, the director should beware. If he presses on with the transaction, he is taking a legal risk.

Part V of the Companies Act 1981 was the first major effort by Parliament to check the worst abuses which can stem from the abuse of a privileged position and the confidential information going with it. The same provision was re-enacted in the Company Securities (Insider Dealing) Act 1985. This Act was repealed by Part V of the Criminal Justice Act 1993 (henceforth CJA 1993) which came into force on 1 March 1994 and which implements the EC Directive on Insider Dealing. Those activities which are covered by CJA 1993 are in essence the same as those covered by the Company Securities (Insider Dealings) Act 1985. These are under the prohibitions on insider dealing which include dealing with shares, whether as a principal or agent with a view to:

(1)   procuring another to deal, again whether as a principal or agent;
(2)   encouraging another to deal who might reasonably be expected to do so;
(3)   disclosing information other than in the proper performance of one's duties (CJA 1993, ss 52 and 55).

The principal change brought about by CJA 1993 is that for procuring and disclosing it is no longer necessary for the prosecution to show that the insider knew or should have realised that someone would deal.

CJA 1993 covers transactions on a regulated market for transactions entered into either in reliance on or by a person acting as a professional intermediary (ss 52, 59 and 60). Accordingly, dealings on all European securities and derivatives exchanges are covered and also all other dealings by or arranged through British and overseas market makers and security brokers such as Eurobond dealers. Furthermore, the definition is sufficient to include many corporate finance transactions of merchant banks and stock brokers brought about either as principal or agent, including underwritings, firm placings, rescue packages and the obtaining of irrevocable undertakings to accept takeover bids (s 59).

The Company Securities (Insider Dealings) Act 1985 covered nearly all regularly traded corporate securities and their derivatives, including Footsie contracts and Stock Exchange bids, although there were some anomalies. CJA 1993 goes even further, adding public sector debt instruments and associated derivatives and LISSE contracts in short-term interest rates, even though there may be no underlying security (CJA 1993, Sch 2). However, the Insider Dealing (Regulated Markets and Securities) Order 1994, SI 1994/187 has restricted the investments covered to those dealt in, on or under the rules of, or which have their price quoted on, a regulated market or any off market derivatives thereof.

CJA 1993 applies primarily to persons who may be classified either as insiders or tippees, although the Act itself does not specifically use the word tippee. An insider is any person who has inside information through being a director, employee or shareholder of the company or other body which issues securities, or anyone else who has access to this information by virtue of his position. This would include persons such as auditors, bankers and solicitors who, in the course of acting for a client company, could acquire such information. A tippee is anyone else who has inside information from an insider or whose direct or indirect source was such an insider (s 57). There does not have to be any clear connection between the insider and the securities about which he has information. An insider is anyone who in fact obtains information through his job, whether inside or outside a company or with some other issuer of securities. A tippee is anyone who obtains such information from someone whom he knows to be an insider or whose source is such an insider. It is unclear whether the tippee has to know the exact identity of the insider.

Inside information is information which:

(1) relates to particular securities or to a particular issuer of securities or to particular issuers of securities (including information affecting the company or company's business prospects) and not to securities generally or to issuers of securities generally;
(2) is specific or precise;
(3) has not been made public; and
(4) if it were made public would be likely to have a significant effect on the price or value of any securities (ss 56 and 60).

The information may be either specific or precise. The Company Securities (Insider Dealing) Act 1985 used the word specific. The Directive on which CJA 1993 was based used the word precise. Specific was retained in CJA 1993 because it is thought that defendants might be able to argue, for example, that although they were aware that a takeover bid was going to be made, they did not know the precise timing and price of the bid.

Guidance is given in the Act as to when information can be treated as having been made public. It is made public if it is:

(1)   officially published as required by a regulated market, for example, through the company's announcement office or its overseas equivalent;

(2)   contained in statutory required records (for example, at Companies House);

(3)   readily available to those likely to deal in the relevant securities; or

(4)   derived from information which has been made public (for example, the analysis of company accounts) (s 58).

It is possible that information may be treated as having been made public even though:

(1)   it can be acquired only by persons exercising diligence or expertise;

(2)   it is communicated to a section of the public and not to the public at large;

(3)   it can be acquired only by observation;

(4)   it is communicated only on payment of a fee; or

(5)   it is published only outside the UK (s 58).

With the wider definition of insider dealing brought about by CJA 1993, the defences which are available become even more important. There are, as was the case with the Company Securities (Insider Dealing) Act 1985, defences available to market makers. An individual is not guilty of insider dealing by virtue of dealing in securities or encouraging another person to deal if he shows that he acted in good faith in the course of his business as a market maker or in his employment for the business of a market maker. In this context, the market maker is a person who holds himself out at all normal times in compliance with the rules of the regulated market or an approved organisation as willing to acquire or dispose of securities and is recognised as doing so under those rules. An approved organisation for this purpose is a self-regulating organisation approved under para 25(B) of Sch 1 to the Financial Services Act 1986.

An individual has a defence to a charge of insider dealing by virtue of dealing in securities or encouraging another person to deal, if he can show that the information which he had as an insider was market information and that it was reasonable for an individual in his position to have acted as he did despite having had that information as an insider at the time. In considering reasonableness in this regard, particular account must be taken of the content of the information, the circumstances in which the individual received the information and in what capacity, and in the capacity in which he was acting when he was committing the alleged offence. An individual is not guilty of insider dealing by virtue of dealing in securities or encouraging another person to deal if he can show that he acted in connection with an acquisition or disposal, which was under consideration or the subject of negotiation, and with a view to facilitating the accomplishment of the acquisition or disposal and that the information which he had as an insider was market information arising directly out of his involvement in the acquisition or disposal.

Market information is information consisting of one or more of the following facts:

(1)   that securities of a particular kind have been or are to be acquired or disposed of or that their acquisition or disposal is under consideration or the subject of negotiation;

(2)   that securities of a particular kind have not been or are not to be acquired or disposed of;

(3) the number of securities acquired or disposed of or to be acquired or disposed of or whose acquisition or disposal is under consideration or the subject of negotiation;

(4) the price at which securities have been or are to be acquired or disposed of or the price at which securities whose acquisition or disposal is under consideration or the subject of negotiation may be acquired or disposed of;

(5) the identity of the persons involved or likely to be involved in any capacity in an acquisition or disposal (CJA 1993, Sch 1).

As well as the specific defence for market maker, there are also a number of general defences set out in s 53.

An individual is not guilty of insider dealing if he shows that at the time of dealing:

(1) he did not expect the dealing to result in a profit attributable to the fact that the information in question was price sensitive in relation to the securities; or

(2) he believed on reasonable grounds that the information had been disclosed widely enough to ensure that none of those taking part in the dealing would be prejudiced by not having the information; or

(3) he would have done what he did even if he had not had the information.

An individual is not guilty of insider dealing by encouraging another person to deal in securities if he can show that:

(1) he did not at the time expect the dealing to result in a profit attributable to the fact that the information in question was price sensitive in relation to the securities; or

(2) at the time, he believed on reasonable grounds that the information had been or would be disclosed widely enough to ensure that none of those taking part in the dealing would be prejudiced by not having the information; or

(3) he would have done what he did even if he had not had the information.

A person is not guilty of insider dealing by virtue of disclosure of information if he can show that:

(1) he did not at the time expect any person, because of the disclosure, to deal in securities in the circumstances mentioned above; or

(2) although he had such an expectation at the time, he did not expect the dealing to result in a profit attributable to the fact that the information was price sensitive information in relation to the securities.

In the case of a merger or takeover of a public company, the City Code on Takeovers and Mergers (the Code) prescribes a code of practice administered by the Panel on Takeovers and Mergers. The Code is a long-established example of 'self-regulation'. There is no question of its being directly enforceable in the courts, whether between exchange members or the companies whose shares are traded under the Code. On the other hand, it may be indirectly enforceable to the extent that it is binding on those authorised to carry on an investment business under the Financial Services Act 1986 and the Conduct of Business Rules issued by the Securities and Investment Board.[70]

Further, the courts will, in appropriate circumstances, refer to the Code in order to help formulate the desired standards of conduct by those to whom the Code applies.[71]

It is also close enough to legislation for its meaning to be a matter for the judge rather than the jury in any criminal proceedings arising out of a takeover,[72] and for the functions of the Takeover Panel itself to be subject to review by the courts.[73] Those prepared to risk prosecution under the Company Securities (Insider Dealing) Act 1985 may or may not be deterred by the Code, and the Panel is from time to time criticised for being too closely identified with the buccaneering spirits it is supposed to supervise. The blame for this, if true, may lie less with the Panel than with financial and legal advisers who have sometimes seemed to regard their role as pushing back the boundaries of acceptable conduct rather than determining for their clients where those boundaries presently lie.

The Code warns that the spirit as well the letter of its rules must be observed, and that the result will inevitably impinge upon the freedom of action of boards. The Code first sets out certain interlocking 'general principles' which are particularly relevant.

(1)   When an offer is in contemplation or under way, neither the offeror nor the offeree company or their advisers may furnish information to some shareholders which is not available to all (general principle 2).
(2)   Shareholders must be given enough information and advice (and time) to enable them to reach a 'properly informed decision' (general principle 4).
(3)   All the parties must use every endeavour to 'prevent the creation of a false market' in the shares of either company (general principle 6).
(4)   Directors[74] of each company must act only as directors when advising shareholders and disregard all personal and family interests (general principle 7).

These general principles (which are quasi-rules in themselves) are elaborated in a series of specific rules which may well be interpreted in the light of the principles. The following rules relate to insider dealing.

7.9.1   Information

Rule 20.1
Information about the companies should be made equally available to all shareholders as far as possible at the same time and in the same manner. Directors must see that nothing is left out which makes what is published misleading (Rule 19.2).

Rule 23.2
This applies general principle (4) and requires a timely and sufficient supply of information. It specifies, however, that the offeror's duty in this respect extends to the offeree's shareholders as well as its own.

Rule 25.1
Disclosure of information now includes a requirement that if the offeree's board is divided the views of the minority as well as the majority should be published.

Rule 27.1
When either party sends out documents to shareholders of the offeree, later documents must contain details of material changes in information previously published, including shareholdings and dealings.

7.9.2 Secrecy and confidentiality

Under Rule 2, there must be absolute secrecy before an offer is announced. Those privy to confidential information, especially if it is price sensitive, concerning an actual or contemplated offer must treat that information as secret and may only pass it on where it is necessary and where the recipient is made aware of the need for secrecy.[75] A watch must be kept for rumours and speculation, particularly if discussions are going to bring in 'more than a very restricted number of people' or there are signs of 'untoward movement' in the offeree's shares.

7.9.3 Restrictions on dealings

Even where the desired equality of information and secrecy are achieved, insiders may still have an unfair advantage. Therefore, there are restrictions on dealings.

Rule 4
This imposes rules very similar to those contained in CJA 1993. There must be no dealings in shares of the offeree (including option dealings) by anyone apart from the offeror who has confidential price-sensitive information between the time when an approach or offer is contemplated and its announcement, nor may he give tips or encouragement to others; and there must be no such dealings in the offeror's shares except where the offer is not price sensitive in relation to those shares. During the offer period the offeror and those acting 'in concert'[76] with the offeror must obtain Panel clearance and give 24 hours' public warning before selling any shares in the offeree company.

Directors must not deal in the shares in any way which is inconsistent with the advice they have given to the members. When it is decided not to proceed with an offer, no dealings in the offeree's (or sometimes the offeror's) shares may be transacted by the offeror or an insider until there has been an announcement of the decision.[77]

7.9.4 Disclosure requirements

There are also disclosure requirements in the Code over and above those imposed by ss 198 to 206 of the Companies Act 1985 (see **7.12**), which include disclosure of directors' interests.

A general duty of disclosure has been discussed by the Department's inspectors in an investigation under what is now s 432 of the 1985 Act.[78] They pointed out that although a director's duties are owed to the company, there must be an implication in the 'information' sections of the Act (which of course are stronger now than then) that directors should supply to shareholders all the information concerning the company's affairs which they might reasonably expect to receive, particularly when they are being invited to vote on a resolution in general meeting. The inspectors pointed out that this interpretation is supported by s 432 itself, which empowers the Department to appoint inspectors if it considers 'that the company's members have not been given all the information with respect to its affairs which they might reasonably expect'. This may imply a general duty to provide information going beyond the specific statutory obligations in respect of accounts, reports, shareholding, etc.

It has certainly been held that, in the case of a takeover, directors in supplying information and making a recommendation, have a duty to their own shareholders to be honest and not to mislead.[79] Although this is well short of a duty of disclosure, it might come to be regarded as inherent in the board's duty to see that the members are informed of what is, in the board's opinion, the best available set of terms.

7.9.5   Special deals

Rule 16
Neither the offeror nor anyone acting in concert with the offeror may deal in the offeree's shares on specially favourable terms not being extended to all shareholders, without the Panel's consent. This is not primarily aimed at insider dealing; it is concerned rather with matters like 'top-ups'[80] and payments to shareholders for promoting the takeover. Given that an insider may wish to deal and may be prepared to give special terms, Rule 16 indirectly affects his ability to do so – provided, of course, that he is allowed to deal at all, which will often not be the case.

7.10   OPTION DEALINGS

The first move toward statutory regulation of insider trading was made by the Companies Act 1967, with the prohibition of option dealing by directors of listed companies (see also **10.3**). Under what is now s 323 of the 1985 Act:

(1)   a director commits a criminal offence if he buys an option to:

    (a)   call for delivery (a 'call' option),
    (b)   make delivery (a 'put' option), or
    (c)   call or put at his election (a 'double' option),

    listed shares or debentures in his company or any other group company;
(2)   the maximum punishment on indictment is two years and/or an unlimited fine; trial by magistrates, six months and/or a £5,000 fine. There is no civil sanction;
(3)   spouses and children under 18 are also prohibited from option dealing; s 327. For what it is worth, it is a defence to prove that they had no reason to believe that their spouse or parent was a director of the company in question;
(4)   the prohibition extends to option purchases for non-money consideration, but does not apply to options to subscribe for shares (ie from the company itself) nor to the purchase of convertible debentures. Thus, shares options remain possible as a form of remuneration, although they will have to be registered and disclosed;
(5)   if it appears that there has been a contravention of s 323, the Department may order an investigation (s 446).

In the ordinary way, option dealing is a straightforward piece of gambling but it is difficult to refute the argument that there is no difference in principle between using inside information to deal in options and using it to deal in the shares themselves. For example, Rule 4.1 of the Code, banning insider dealings before the announcement of an offer prohibits all dealings, including option business.

7.11 DISCLOSURE

7.11.1 Directors' share interests

The preceding sections have described how attempts are made to impose standards of conduct and fair dealing in company affairs by regulation.

Until recently, the underlying philosophy of UK company law was that regulation was unnecessary, or too inflexible; rather it was thought that directors would not deal improperly in their company's shares if their dealings were reported and thus became subject to comment and criticism by the members.

Since the Companies Act 1967, and more especially the Companies Acts of 1980 and 1981, the 'disclosure' philosophy has begun to yield supremacy to the 'regulatory' approach, but this has involved placing a greater emphasis on the latter rather than reducing the importance of disclosure.

Many obligations are imposed on directors in this respect, and we look first at the position with regard to their own shareholdings, and its relevance to the monitoring of insider dealings.

The duty to disclose directors' shareholdings is enforced by the following requirements of the Companies Act 1985.

(1) Every director (and shadow director) must notify his company of his interests in its shares or debentures (s 324(1) and (2)).

(2) Written notice must be given within five days of his becoming a director if he already owns the shares; otherwise, within five days of his acquiring the interest (or of his learning of it, if later) (Sch 13, Part II). The same period of notice must be given of any change in his interests (sale, purchase, contract, rights issue from an associate company, etc).

(3) The notice must state the number, amount and class of the shares or debentures (s 324) and the price (Sch 13).

(4) Failure to disclose,[81] or making a deliberately or recklessly false statement, is an offence punishable by up to two years' imprisonment and/or an unlimited fine.

(5) A listed company notified by a director of any acquisition, etc, of its listed securities must notify the Stock Exchange, or other investment exchange on which the securities are listed, by the end of the next following day (other than weekends and bank holidays) (s 329). Failure to do this carries a fine[82] of up to £1,000 with a daily default fine of £100.

These primary obligations are reinforced by a formidable array of definitions which, in general, extend the duties imposed by ss 324 and 329:

Interests to be notified (Sch 13)

(1) 'Interest' includes any kind of interest, direct or indirect, immediate or remote, sole or joint, disregarding any restraints or restrictions attached to its enjoyment or use.

(2) Where trust property includes shares or debentures the beneficiary is taken to have an interest in them.

(3) 'Interest' will arise when a person contracts to acquire shares or debentures (for cash or any other consideration), or becomes entitled[83] to exercise or control rights attached to them (except as a mere proxy or representative of a corporate shareholder), or by control of a company[84] or of its board, or by one-third control of another company which in turn controls the voting power in the company.

(4) 'Interest' also includes a right to call for delivery or a right or obligation to acquire an interest (apart from a right to subscribe).

(5) Joint interests are included, as are interests in unidentifiable shares (for example, where the shares form an individual part of a trust holding).

Interests which need not be notified[85]

Interests which need not be notified are as follows.

(1) Interests in reversion or remainder under a trust (ie where someone else is entitled to the income until his or a third party's death).

(2) Interests of a bare trustee (ie where the beneficiary can call for delivery at any time, as in the case where the director is a mere nominee).

(3) A unit trust holding.

(4) Interest as a proxy.

(5) A right of pre-emption under the Articles.

(6) Interest as a trustee or beneficiary of certain superannuation or retirement schemes.[86]

(7) Interests of a director of a wholly owned subsidiary, where he is also a director of the parent company which maintains its own register (see below).

(8) Interests of a director of a wholly owned subsidiary in shares of a foreign holding or associate company.

Spouses and children

Section 328 extends the disclosure duty to the interests of directors' spouses and children of under 18 years of age (unless they are themselves directors and therefore directly obliged to make disclosure). Moreover, the director must notify the company of the grant or exercise of any right given to them by the company to subscribe for shares or debentures in the company.

The notice

Notice under s 324 or s 328 must be written and must state that it is given in fulfilment of the duty of disclosure under the Act.[87] Provided that it comes to his attention when he is still a director, the director must give notice of any of the following events:

(1) that he has become or ceased[88] to be interested;

(2) his contracting to sell shares or debentures in the company;

(3) his assignment of a right to subscribe; and

(4) the grant to him of a right to subscribe in a subsidiary, holding or associate company, and the exercise or assignment by him of such a right.

The time-limit for giving notice is five days[89] from:

(1) the day following his appointment, in respect of existing interests;

(2) the day following the relevant 'event' by which an interest arose or ceased; or

(3) the day after he became aware of it, when he was unaware of the relevant interest or event in case (1) or (2).

The register (s 325)

Every company must keep a register of notices received under s 324 (including notices relating to the interests of spouses and children).

(1) The information must be recorded within three days[90] after receipt.[91]

(2) It must be indexed, unless it is itself in the form of an index. The forms in common use for the notices can themselves serve as a loose-leaf index.

(3) Entries for each name must be in chronological order.

(4) Where the company grants a right to subscribe, or such a right is exercised, the company must itself record the information. This does not apply to spouses and children because in their case the directors must give the usual notice.

(5) The register must be open to inspection by members (free of charge) and the public (£2.50 per hour). It must be at the registered office or where the register of members is kept and, in the latter case, notice of the address must be given to the registrar. It must also be open for inspection throughout the AGM. Anyone may request copies (£2.50 for the first 100 entries, £20.00 for the next 1,000 and £15.00 for each subsequent 1,000) to be supplied within 10 days of the day on which the request is received.

(6) Failure to comply is punishable by a fine of up to £1,000, with a daily default fine of £100 (except in respect of availability at the AGM). The criminal liability extends to every officer in default. The courts may order inspection and the supply of copies.

(7) Inspectors may be appointed by the DTI to investigate suspected contravention of ss 324 and 328 (s 446). The power to appoint inspectors under s 442 in order to investigate ownership and control may also be used to look into share dealings.

(8) The directors' report, or notes to the annual accounts, must include particulars of the directors' interests in the company or other group companies as recorded under s 325 (s 234, as substituted by s 8 of the 1989 Act, and Sch 7, para 2).

(9) For the purposes of the registrar, a shadow director is treated as a director.

A number of points may be noted by way of summary.

(1) There may be overlaps between the various requirements, so that the total extent of the interests notified may exceed the number of issued shares. For example, if a director and his wife hold a hundred shares jointly on trust for two of their children, four separate notices are required and the register will show a total of 400 shares.

(2) The duty to notify under ss 324 and 328 is not in any way restricted to public or listed companies, and applies in its full severity to all companies however small or closely held. The director of a 'one-man company' must give notice to himself. In contrast, s 323 (option dealings) and s 198 (notification of acquisitions[92]) apply to listed and public companies respectively.

(3) The disclosure requirements are very complex and far-reaching, and non-compliance may easily be the result of inadvertence. The only safe advice which can be given to a director is that any doubt should be resolved by giving notice at once.

(4) Peculiarly, there is no obligation upon a company to enter information on the register until it has received it. Logically, the company might be thought to have knowledge of the fact that it has issued shares to a director, but the Act does not require it to act upon such knowledge. It must receive it first from the director.

7.11.2   Inspection of documents

An important aspect of the principle of disclosure and of relations between board and members is the right of the latter to inspect many important documents and registers. Clearly this is not as effective as a right to receive information, but the existence of the right to inspect must have some influence on those whose papers may be inspected.

To summarise, the Act gives shareholders a right to inspect:

(1) copies of contracts to purchase the company's own shares (s 169);
(2) the register of debenture holders (s 191);
(3) the register of share interests (s 211: see **7.13**);
(4) the auditor's report on the accounts (s 241);
(5) the register of directors and secretaries (s 288);
(6) directors' service contracts or memoranda thereof (s 318);[93]
(7) the register of directors' interests (s 325: see **7.11.1**);
(8) the register of members (s 356);
(9) the minutes of general meetings (s 383);
(10) the register of charges (s 408).

Moreover it has been held that:

(1) members taking actions against the company are entitled to see reports obtained on behalf of the company unless protected by privilege;[94]
(2) where directors hold shares as trustees they are not obliged, for that reason, to disclose information acquired as directors.[95]

So far as other books and documents of the company are concerned (including ledgers and accounts), the members have no rights of inspection except where the Articles permit. Thus, for example, there is no inherent right to see minutes of board meetings.[96] Regulation 109 of Table A expressly provides that no member shall have a right to inspect any accounting records,[97] and a member may, accordingly, claim a right of inspection only if conferred by:

(1) statute;
(2) the decision of the directors; or
(3) the general meeting, by ordinary resolution.

If a member specifically asks for information which does not fall within any of the specified categories, the directors should not, of course, divulge anything which they would not communicate to the members as a whole.

7.11.3   Inspection of registers

Some of the rights of inspection noted above deserve special mention, apart from the register of directors' interests which was considered in **7.11.1**. Below we look at the registers which must be kept.

7.12 REGISTER OF MEMBERS

The register of members must be kept, under s 352.

(1) This must show:

    (a) names and addresses of each member;

    (b) date of registration as a member;

    (c) date of termination of membership;[98]

    (d) the shareholding (numbered where the shares are numbered) and identifying the class of shares held;

    (e) the amount paid or payable on each share.

(2) The register may be bound or loose-leaf provided that it is secure (s 722) and must be indexed if there are more than fifty members, unless it constitutes an index in itself. It is prima facie evidence of its own accuracy (s 361).

(3) It must be kept at the registered office, or at the office of the company's own registrar if it has appointed one for the task (s 353).

(4) Inspection must be allowed during business hours to any member (without charge) and to any member of the public (£2.50 per hour) and copies of any part must be furnished to any person who asks for them within 10 days (£2.50 for the first 100 entries, £20.00 for the next 1,000 and £15.00 for each subsequent 1,000) (s 356).

(5) It may be closed for up to 30 days per annum by newspaper advertisement to that effect (s 358).

(6) The register may be rectified by the courts if it is shown that a name is wrongly entered, omitted, or not removed (s 359).

(7) No notice of any trust can be entered on the register (s 360).

Thus, the company is always free to deal only with the registered proprietor.[99] So, for example, a vendor of shares who remains unpaid despite delivery of the transfer and share certificate to the buyer cannot require the company to take note of his claim.[100] The only way in which an unregistered party can protect himself is by service of a 'stop notice' by filing an affidavit and notice in the High Court and serving copies on the company. This does not entitle him to any priority as such, but is a procedural device; he must be given 14 days' notice of any transfer, during which he must apply to the courts for an injunction.[101]

7.13 REGISTER OF SUBSTANTIAL SHAREHOLDINGS

This register is the legislative reaction to concern at the accumulation of large shareholdings by stealth or by sudden attacks. The Companies Act 1967 attempted to deal with the former by introducing a '10 per cent disclosure' rule, which has gradually been whittled down to a three per cent threshold. The latter, the so-called 'dawn raid', was the subject of a major part of the 1981 Act, together with 'concert parties' in which apparently independent purchases are in fact made in a coordinated plan to acquire a major shareholding, and at as low a price as possible. These rules are now set out in Part VI of the Act, the main features of which are as follows.

(1)   The rules apply to voting shares in any public company, whether or not it is listed[102] (s 198).

(2)   Section 198 requires any person who acquires a notifiable interest or who disposes of such an interest to notify the company, and (as applied by ss 199(5)(b) and 200) also to notify the company of material changes in such an interest. The section places major emphasis on the party's knowledge of events at the relevant time and, in summary, the duty to disclose arises where a party:

    (a)   knowingly acquires a three per cent interest by nominal value in the share capital or any class of it; or

    (b)   knowingly sees his interest fall below that percentage; or

    (c)   knows that the percentage level of his holding, while remaining above three per cent has changed; or

    (d)   later becomes aware that any of these situations has arisen.

(3)   Once the duty to notify has arisen, the party in question must serve written notice on the company, identifying each registered holder, the number of shares held, any option or conditional purchase arrangements, and the fact that he no longer has a notifiable interest (s 202). It must be served within two days, although in practice this means three, since service must be within the two days following the day on which the duty arises (disregarding weekends and bank holidays). Where the party concerned is a director, his notice must state that it is served in pursuance of ss 198 to 202, so as to distinguish it from his quite separate obligations under s 324 (see **7.11.1**) (s 210).

(4)   'Interest' is defined by ss 207 to 209 in a way which corresponds with the definition of 'interests' discussed in **7.11.1** in relation to the directors' interests. The present definition is somewhat more complex, however, because of the complicated rules applying to 'concert parties' (see (5) below), and the need to keep the emphasis upon the party's knowledge. Moreover, assuming that an 'interest' exists, s 203 requires notification of certain other parties' interests:

    (a)   those of his spouse, or under-age child, or step-child;

    (b)   interests held via another company, or string of companies, where there is control through a one-third voting power.[104]

(5)   'Concert parties' are the subject of special disclosure requirements set out in ss 204 to 206. The expression is a commonly used shorthand to describe parties acting in coordination but each on his own, individual account, with the result that no party individually may acquire a notifiable interest. The sections treat the parties as if each obtained an interest in the others' shareholdings, and is therefore under a separate obligation to disclose them to the company.

There must be:

    (a)   an agreement to acquire shares involving obligations or restrictions[105] as to their use, retention and disposal; and

    (b)   actual acquisition of shares in pursuance of the agreement.

If those conditions have once been fulfilled, the sections continue to treat each party as being interested in all acquisitions, whether or not further acquisitions are made, and regardless of changes in the 'personnel' of the concert party and any variation (or rescission) of the agreement. But it is not just the shares acquired pursuant to the agreement which go into the aggregate to determine if a 'notifiable interest', ie three per cent or more, has arisen; shares already held, or acquired in some other way, go into the pot as well for this purpose (s 205(1)).[106] Since each party to the agreement comes under a separate duty of disclosure, arising because of other parties' acquisitions as well as his own, each party must know what the other parties are doing. There is therefore a separate and additional obligation under s 206 on each party to keep the others notified of existing interests, acquisitions and disposals.[107] The duty arises on his first acquisition made in pursuance of the agreement and then applies again on subsequent acquisitions or disposals. The obligation is to give written notice to the other parties within two days:

(a) stating that he is a party to the agreement;
(b) detailing the other parties; and
(c) specifying those shares which are included in the notice as acquired pursuant to the agreement.

As in the case of notification of direct or imputed interests (see (4) above), the concert party member's duty arises by virtue of his knowledge; for this purpose, receipt of notice from a fellow member of the party is taken to be knowledge (s 207(5)). The obligation to notify the company, as we have seen, falls upon each and every party, but the obligation may be satisfied by one party giving notification to the company on behalf of all.

(6) Default in compliance with any of the notification requirements or the deliberate or reckless making of false statements is an offence (s 210) carrying up to two years' imprisonment and/or an unlimited fine on indictment, and six months' imprisonment and/or a fine of up to £5,000 on conviction in a magistrates' court. Prosecutions may be brought only by or with the consent of the Department or the Director of Public Prosecutions (s 732). On conviction the Department may impose a 'freeze' on the relevant shares.

(7) A public company may itself conduct investigations into the ownership of its shares. Its powers are as follows.

(a) It may require any person,[108] a member or not, whom it knows or reasonably believes to have had an interest[109] in its shares within the preceding three years to confirm or deny this (s 212).
(b) Where there has been such an interest the party can be required to give details and identify, if possible, other interests in the company's shares during the three-year period. Other members of 'concert parties' must also be identified, so that the company may check holdings for connections which may not be apparent at first sight.
(c) Members holding one-tenth of the paid-up voting capital can require the company to exercise its powers, specifying how and stating reasonable grounds for the requisition (s 214). The company must prepare a report, or at least an interim report, within three months and thereafter at three monthly intervals until the investigation is completed (s 215). The company must notify the requisitionists within three days that the report is available at its registered office.

(d) Any other information obtained by the company of its own motion must be made available at the registered office for inspection and copying in the same way as the register of interests (s 219). Separate parts of the register will record interests notified to the company (which must be entered within three days of receipt) and information obtained by the company itself.

(e) If, on such an investigation, a company feels it has not received proper information, it can apply to the court under s 216(1) for a freezing order in respect of the shares. This effectively removes all shareholder rights in respect of the shares. (See *Re F H Lloyd Holdings plc*[110] and *Re Geers Gros plc*.)[111]

7.14   REGISTER OF DIRECTORS AND SECRETARIES

Section 288 requires every company to maintain a register of directors and secretaries. The requirements of that and other related provisions are as follows.

(1) The register must be kept at the registered office (s 288(1)) and must be open for inspection during business hours for at least two hours per day. Members may inspect free of charge, and any other person may inspect for a charge of (£2.50 per hour) (s 288(3)).

(2) Where a director is an individual, the register must state (s 289(1)(a)):

   (a) his christian name or forename and his surname and any former names;
   (b) his usual residential address;
   (c) his nationality;
   (d) his business occupation, if any;
   (e) particulars of other directorships, including past directorships, except:
      (i) directorships which ceased more than five years earlier,
      (ii) directorships of other companies within the same group,[112]
      (iii) where the other company is (and where relevant has for the past five years been) 'dormant';[113]
   (f) his date of birth.

Where the director is itself a company, the register must state its corporate name and its registered or principal office (s 289(1)(b)). The disclosure requirements extend, in the case of individuals, to shadow directors whose other directorships, including shadow 'directorships', must be registered. This piece of statutory wishful thinking (minus the description 'shadow') dates back to the First World War.

(3) These particulars must be notified to the Registrar of Companies within 14 days of the appointment of the first directors (s 10; Sch 1). Any change in the registered particulars or in the directorships must also be notified within 14 days (s 288(2)). The Registrar must then publicise this in the *Gazette* (s 711) and it is possible to identify the directors not only from the company's own register but from the Registrar's files. Until notification (including *Gazetting*) has occurred, the company may not rely on a change in directors as against a third party who is

unaware of it; consequently, if he has dealt with directors whose names appear in the latest returns and whose retirement is unknown to him, he may treat the company as bound by their actions.[114]

(4) Similar particulars of secretaries must be given under s 290, except that their age, occupation and other directorships need not be stated.

(5) In the event of non-compliance, or a refusal to allow inspection, an offence is committed. The maximum fine is £5,000, with a daily default fine of £500. Liability is imposed both on the company and any officer in default.

(6) The current state of the register must be recorded in the annual return submitted under ss 363 or 364 (where details must be added of other directorships held by any *corporate* director of the company).

7.15 OPPRESSION AND UNFAIR BEHAVIOUR

Directors will be understandably reluctant to regard this subject as having any relevance to their own position. They should beware of what follows, however, for two reasons; the 'bad cases' in what follows give an indication of what the courts require as positive standards to be observed; and the cases show that sometimes conduct may be oppressive or unfair in the eyes of the courts when the directors, in all honesty, might not agree.

The question usually arises when the directors constitute, or represent, a majority of the company's members and the minority complains that it is being treated unfairly.

Typical grounds for complaint might be that the majority are paying themselves the whole of the profits in the form of directors' remuneration (which, depending on the circumstances, the board might honestly feel to be justified) or that they are using their position to further private interests instead of those of the company.

7.15.1 The rule in *Foss v Harbottle*[115]

The common law gives no general remedy to a minority of members wishing to complain about the conduct of the majority, even if that majority is in control both of the board and the general meeting. This follows from two principles. First, if the real complaint is that the wrongdoers are damaging the company, it is the company which is the proper plaintiff. Secondly, it is for the majority in most cases to determine whether the company should proceed with an action. These are not just technicalities. The courts have always feared that, if a minority is able to bring all its grievances to court, the company and its management may become bogged down in the distractions and costs of litigation at the expense of its business and, ultimately, of all the members. Consequently, the courts are wary of actions brought by minority shareholders, especially those which are in reality inter-shareholder disputes which can be ventilated under statutory remedies designed for the purpose (see **7.15.2** and **7.15.3**).

Together, the principles referred to above produce the 'rule in *Foss v Harbottle*' precluding minority actions in respect of wrongs done to the company or complaining of technical irregularities. There have to be exceptions to the rule, however, if it is not to become a charter for illegal or oppressive conduct by the majority. The exceptions have become increasingly technical in nature as the courts have sought to funnel shareholder disputes away from the common law and towards the special statutory remedies. The following are the accepted cases to which the rule does not apply and where some form of redress is available at common law:

(1)   where the act complained of is ultra vires the company or otherwise illegal;
(2)   where the individual rights of the member have been infringed;
(3)   where a special procedure has not been followed;[116] and
(4)   'fraud' on the minority by those controlling the company.

Now it *might* be expected that a member has a right to have the company's affairs lawfully managed, so that exception (2) (above) would commonly eat up the rule and the other exceptions and allow a member to bring an action in his own name, complaining that his rights as a member are being infringed by improper conduct of the majority. There are occasionally decisions which seem to move in this direction[117] (as well as decisions which arguably go too far in the opposite direction[118]), but in practice this exception is confined to a range of rights which are clearly conferred on a member by his status as such, such as the right to have his vote duly recorded at company meetings, and the right to have special procedures followed where applicable under the Articles – which, of course, generates the exception to *Foss v Harbottle* in (3) (above).

It might also be expected that the courts would be particularly keen to uphold the exception mentioned in (1) (above) and allow a personal action by a member alleging ultra vires or illegal acts by the majority. As far as ultra vires acts go, the position is slightly different. As far as the *future* is concerned, the law has always allowed a member to stop the company from acting ultra vires its constitution, and this is confirmed by the Act subject to the limitation imposed by s 35.[119] But at least one court has held that the position is different in respect of an ultra vires act already committed and that since, in most cases, the complaint relates to the resulting loss to the company, the company is the proper plaintiff, not the minority.[120] Thus, the minority can only bring an action in the company's name, and this may be stopped if there are passed special resolutions: (i) ratifying the action; and (ii) relieving those responsible from liability to the company.[121]

As regards the member's right to bring an action on his own behalf and in his own name, therefore, this right exists where there is an outright illegality, to restrain the company from anticipated ultra vires acts, and in those cases where the member's rights as such have been infringed. In other cases, the minority must borrow the company's cause of action and bring what is known as a 'derivative' action. This is a true exception to *Foss v Harbottle*, since it cuts across both the principles underlying the rule. When may a derivative action be brought? There are two cases. The first is in respect of ultra vires acts already committed, the second where there is fraud on the minority (see (4) above). 'Fraud' here is not defined to its popular connotations of dishonest trickery. It is more accurate to think of it as a serious wrong done to the company which would go unsanctioned if the majority were allowed to stop proceedings against the wrongdoers.[122] The clearest example is the misappropriation of company assets or business opportunities,[123] and here majority control cannot stop a derivative action by the minority because such acts are so improper that they cannot be 'ratified' in any sense of that overused word. Indeed, whatever the position 'on the ground' – where the majority may be using its votes to exercise control – the legal position is that the wrongdoers who try to use their votes to insulate themselves from an action by the company are not entitled to vote at all,[124] and may actually be perpetrating a further fraud on the minority by purporting to do so. But some deliberate wrongdoing is required – negligence is not enough to allow a derivative action,[125] unless it is not only serious negligence but also results in the wrongdoers themselves pocketing a benefit at the expense of the company.[126] How far abuse of power or position without profit can be fraud on a minority is uncertain. Acts done in bad faith are usually regarded as unratifiable, and it follows as a matter of logic such acts are outside majority control and therefore outside the constraints of *Foss v Harbottle*; the same would not be true of a good faith exercise of power for an improper purpose.[127]

Before the fraud-based claim can proceed it is also necessary: (i) that the action should be substantially for the benefit of the company;[128] and (ii) that the wrongdoers are shown to be in control of the company. This can be done only by showing that efforts to get the company to sue have been thwarted by the use of the wrongdoers' majority of votes, or that a majority including the wrongdoers has approved the fraud. It is not enough to allege the sort of de facto control that can often be exercised over a public company by a party without a numerical majority of votes.[129] Wrongdoer control does *not* have to be shown in order to bring a derivative claim for a past ultra vires act. It does seem, however, that even where the minority therefore has standing to bring an action in the company's name, they will be defeated if a majority of the shareholders other than the wrongdoers wishes for proper reasons not to pursue the action. In *Smith v Croft (No 2)*, for example, the court took into account the fact that the majority of the 'independent' shareholders opposed the action, fearing that if it proceeded the defendants would leave the company, causing more harm to the members' investment than the conduct alleged against them.[130]

There are further obstacles to a minority action. In the 'fraud' case, the plaintiff must have a strong prima facie case before the court will allow him to proceed. He is not allowed merely to *allege* fraud and wrongdoer control, nor to fight out these issues at the preliminary stage when his standing is challenged, since the company would then be involved at once in the very sort of dispute and expense which *Foss v Harbottle* is intended to spare it. Secondly, he must bear in mind that while he may be given an indemnity against his costs in the action, he is not entitled to legal aid even if he has ruined himself by bringing the case.[131]

7.15.2 Winding up

The ultimate remedy for an oppressed shareholder is to petition for a winding up by the courts under what is now s 122(1)(g) of the Insolvency Act 1986 on the ground that it is 'just and equitable' to do so. Orders have been made where:

(1) the company's basic object has failed;
(2) the business is illegal or fraudulent;

(3) the company is in substance a partnership and there is deadlock or a complete breakdown of confidence;[132]
(4) there is an underlying obligation to allow the petitioner to participate in management, which has been broken;[133]
(5) there has been a repudiation of basic obligations contained in the Articles or a shareholders' agreement.

While the normal case for a winding up under this head is the small firm or 'quasi-partnership' in which there has been a breakdown of confidence between the 'partner' members,[134] it is possible (although rare) to obtain an order in relation to a different type of company.[135] But winding up is a remedy of last resort, and certainly a very final way of sorting out shareholder disputes. It was with this in mind that what is now s 459 was devised to provide a way by which dissentients could be extracted from deadlocked or unfairly run companies, or could less commonly be allowed to buy out their opponents. There is every reason to think that s 459 is achieving most of what was hoped of it (see **7.15.3**). The significance of this is that the court need not make a winding-up order under s 122 if s 125(2) applies, ie there is some other remedy available to the petitioner and he is acting unreasonably in not pursuing that remedy. There is no objection to a member petitioning under both s 122 and s 459, although he should not do so unless winding up is the preferred remedy or may be the only relief available.[136] In *Re Abbey Leisure Ltd*,[137] the court gave surprisingly little weight to these considerations. A joint venture company had run its course and there was little doubt that the petitioner (who had no management role) could in principle have the company wound up under s 122 and cash in his 40 per cent holding. The question was whether having him bought out was an alternative remedy which he was unreasonable in not accepting, and the court held that it was not. First, a buy out following the Articles *may* be a suitable alternative remedy, but not where, as here, the other members were not obliged to pay if they considered the price too high.[138] Secondly, an offer to buy at a valuation was a suitable alternative to winding up, but the petitioner was not acting unreasonably in refusing it, because the valuation might apply a 'minority holding discount' (see **7.1.1** and **7.15.4**). How damaging this decision is to the hope that s 495 would supplant s 122 as the obvious way of settling shareholder disputes, remains to be seen. The court considered that the s 459 cases show a 'general inclination' towards an undiscounted valuation – and, on this basis, s 459 will be the norm since it will offer a reasonable alternative to winding up. But it is far from settled that a s 459 buy out will always or even usually be on an undiscounted basis, with the result that a disgruntled member will often be able to wave *Re Abbey Leisure Ltd* over the heads of the other members.

The recent consultation document on *Shareholder Remedies* (Law Com Consultation Paper No 142) considered the relationship between a buy out Article and s 459 remedy. A major problem with the s 459 remedy is its expense. Frequently, the litigation will be in two stages. First, there will be proceedings for an interlocutory injunction to prevent the dissipation of assets from the company pending the outcome of the substantive unfair prejudice proceedings. Secondly, there will be the substantive action. If there is an escape route available, as there is an Article under which the aggrieved member can require the other members to buy him out, the court is likely to strike out a s 459 action as an abuse of process (see for example, *Re A Company (003096 of 1987)*).[139] This was not done in *Re Abbey Leisure Ltd* where the company was extremely liquid and where the discounting on a valuation which would be likely to occur were the auditor to value the complainant's shares would have been very much to the complainant's disadvantage. However, it is always extremely dangerous for a petitioner to commence s 459 proceedings where there is a viable escape route available. The Law Commission recommended that there should be a regulation included in Table A for small companies which provided that a disgruntled shareholder could ask that his shares be bought back either by the other members or by the company itself.

7.15.3   Relief under s 459

Any member[140] of a company may apply to the courts for relief on the ground that:

'. . . the company's affairs are being or have been conducted[141] in a manner which is unfairly prejudicial to the interests of its members generally or some part of its members or that any actual or proposed act or omission of the company . . . is or would be so prejudicial.'

This represents a more liberal approach than its predecessor (s 210 of the 1948 Act) which required the petitioner to establish oppressive rather than unfairly prejudicial behaviour. It used to be necessary also to establish that a 'just and equitable' winding up (**7.15.2**) would be justified by the petitioner's complaints, but this is no longer so.[142] This is important, since it does mean that some degree of blameworthiness on the petitioner's part will not be an absolute bar to relief. The petitioner cannot be defeated, therefore, merely by showing that he was lazy, or incompetent, or even that he was partly responsible for the breakdown of trust between the parties if he was not the main cause of it.[143] Such blameworthiness may still be relevant in at least two ways, however. It may mean that the 'other side's' conduct, although prejudicial, is not unfairly prejudicial, since the courts have begun to look at the effect of the conduct and not its motivation.[144] Secondly, it may affect the courts' discretion under s 461 when considering the form and substance of the appropriate relief if the petition is successful.

There are two important points to keep in mind when considering the impact of s 459. First, it is an enabling rather than a rulemaking provision. It leaves it to the court to conclude what constitutes unfair prejudice in a particular case. The courts may narrow its impact, by holding that specific types of conduct are incapable of being unfairly prejudicial or do not affect the members' interests, but cannot and are not intended to provide a checklist of what *is*, automatically caught. Further, even when a court makes a finding of unfair prejudice, it has a wide range of remedial powers and a discretion under s 461(1) to give no remedy at all. These characteristics are unlikely to endear s 459 to those who like absolute predictability in their affairs but are probably the necessary price of a provision which, unlike the common law rules on directors' duties with which it overlaps, is designed to provide a general relief from unfair management practice rather than automatic liability for particular types of misconduct. Secondly, s 459 was modified by the 1989 Act to make it clear that there can be unfair prejudice even though the conduct complained of affects *all* the members including quite possibly the alleged wrongdoers. An example would be persistent non-declaration of dividends when there are available profits. It is therefore no absolute answer to a s 459 complaint that there was no intended or unintended discrimination against the complainant (although proof of discrimination will undoubtedly help the complainant's case). In more general terms, s 459 looks for conduct which, viewed in the light of its effect on the complainant is 'unfair' and prejudices him – it is *not* necessary to show bad faith or some other impropriety.

The scope of s 459 is confined only by the scope of the word 'interests'. It is clear enough that breaches of directors' duties and infringements of member's *rights* can fall within the section. It will not matter whether or not these are actionable by the complainant at common law since the object of s 459 proceedings is to examine their effect, not whether there is a remedy elsewhere. It should be noted, however, that the court has power under s 461 to authorise action by the *company*, and s 459 does, to that extent, enable *Foss v Harbottle* **(7.15.1)** to be outflanked. Beyond strict legal rights and duties, the courts take an approach similar to that taken under s 122(1)(g) of the Insolvency Act 1986 **(7.15.2)** and look at the company as a whole to determine the legitimate rights, duties and expectations of the parties. The smaller the company, the more probable that the complainant had a legitimate interest in participating in management or receiving regular and full information about the conduct of the company's affairs. Equally, it will be easier to find that a relationship of trust and co-operation was necessary to run the business and that this has gone. The larger the company, particularly if it is a public company, the less likely it is that such small company characteristics will be present. For example, it is quite possible that in a small company there is a tacit agreement between the members that certain Articles will not be altered, but this is highly improbable in the case of a public company.[146] It is also possible that a member's interests will change with time. Where, for example, a small company prospers and expands, a director who is excluded from management may have a s 459 complaint *at that time*, but if he accepts the position and acts as a more or less passive minority, his expectations will subsequently be judged on that basis and not on the basis of his earlier interest in taking part in management.[147] It by no means follows that public companies fall outside s 459, merely that the unfairness of management's conduct will have to be judged independently of any 'quasi-partnership' interests. This seems to be rather too readily overlooked by public company boards.

What, then, can constitute 'unfair prejudice'?

(1)   an infringement of the petitioner's rights under the Articles, for example, breach of his pre-emption rights;

(2)   breaches of the Companies Act 1985 (for example, failure to hold general meetings and lay accounts before the members or issuing shares at invalid meetings[148]);

(3)   breaches of the general law, ranging from a crude misappropriation of assets[149] to the exercise of directors' powers for a wrongful purpose or the wrongful exercise of majority voting power (for example, where there is fraud on a minority (see **7.15.1**) or where the majority alters the Articles without regard to the interests of the company as a whole (see **1.6.2**[150] at point (4));

(4)   'pure' unfair prejudice, ie conduct which involves neither the infringement of legal rights nor the commission of specific breaches of the company's Articles or the general law;

(5) failure to provide proper information to the petitioner about how the company is being run (see *Re R A Noble*[151]);

(6) increase of issued share capital in circumstances which amount to a breach of duty by the directors *Re a Company (002612 of 1984)*[152] and *Re DR Chemicals Ltd*;[153]

(7) mismanagement (see *Re Elgin Data Ltd*[154] and *Re Le Macro (Ipswich) Ltd*[155]).

We have already seen that one of the main areas of dispute is exclusion from management or removal from the board, which can fall within (4) above where the complainant is able to establish that he became a member with the understanding or legitimate expectation that he would have a role in management. While this often constitutes unfair prejudice, where there is no separate complaint – for example, of diversion of assets to the wrongdoers – a petition will often fail if the complainant has been made a fair buy out offer.[156] Secondly, s 459 covers cases where the petitioner's shareholding has been seriously diluted. For example, a rights issue strictly in accordance with the Articles may still be held unfairly prejudicial if its timing shows that it was made deliberately in the knowledge that the petitioner would be unable to take up the offer.[157] Thirdly, there may be financial questions. Section 459 can accommodate challenges to directors' remuneration[158] or persistent non-payment of dividends, or payment of very low dividends.[159] It must be remembered, however, that these are just convenient descriptions of areas of conflict – s 459 is not intended to draw the hard and fast lines of which lawyers are fond and almost any conduct is capable of constituting unfair prejudice in appropriate circumstances. This does not mean that the courts regard s 459 as an invitation wholly to abandon their reluctance to 'second-guess' directors' decisions, although unquestionably it is a factor in the gradual weakening of their refusal to do so. Where, for example, a court finds that it may be a breach of duty and unfair prejudice, where there are rival takeover offers, to deprive the petitioner of the chance to sell to the highest bidder,[160] it is not telling the directors what they *must* do; it is indicating that failure to give accurate advice to the members and a rather too-slick adjournment of an extraordinary general meeting (EGM), which allowed the unfavoured higher offer to lapse, is not fair procedure and prejudices the petitioner by costing him an opportunity to realise his investment more advantageously. It also illustrates another important point. Section 459 allows a petition to be based on a single act or omission. There is no need to allege a continuous course of conduct, still less one which persisted up to the date of the petition.

7.15.4   Remedies for unfair prejudice

If the court is satisfied that a petition under s 459 is well founded, it may make such an order as it sees fit. In particular, it has power under s 461 to:

(1) regulate the future conduct of the company's affairs;[161]

(2) require action to be stopped or taken;[162]

(3) authorise civil proceedings to be taken in the name and on behalf of the company by such persons as it directs (outflanking the rule in *Foss v Harbottle*, see **7.15.1**);

(4) order the purchase of the petitioner's shares or those of the wrongdoers. This is an exceptional case in which capital can be returned to the members and the court may order a corresponding capital reduction;

(5) alter the Memorandum or Articles,[163] or freeze the company's power to do so without the court's leave.

It is (4) above which has become the norm since, in the nature of most of the petitions filed with the court, it is clear that there must be a parting of the ways. It is unusual to order that the wrongdoers be bought out, but if their conduct shows that they are unfit to run the company it can be done.[164] Since even the wrongdoer has an investment to protect, it may be necessary to attach conditions to such an order. For example, in *Re Nuneaton Borough AFC Ltd (No 2)*,[165] the company's affairs had been allowed to slide into such confusion that shares were issued by the 'purported board' beyond the authorised capital limits, and the petitioner had been induced to buy non-existent shares.[166] The controller himself had made substantial loans to the company. These might well prove irrecoverable as a matter of strict law if he sought recovery by legal action. Nevertheless, the court, while ordering him to sell his majority holding to the petitioner, made it a condition that these loans be repaid, since they had been intended to benefit, and had in fact benefited the company. Although this form of order is unusual, it is noteworthy because it seems to recognise that the investment which a court may wish to protect in unfair prejudice proceedings need not always be an investment in share capital. It is by implication possible that the more normal order, requiring the *petitioner* to be bought out, could also require repayment of loans or other indirect investment in the company.

The most contentious issue is usually the valuation of the petitioner's shares and the question whether they should be valued pro rata or subject to a 'minority holding' discount (see **7.1.1**). There can be no absolute rule, since the Act empowers the court to do what is necessary to give relief in particular cases. The leading decision indicates a preference for a pro rata valuation in the case of a minority holding in a small company which is in reality an incorporated partnership where the members enter the company expecting to take part in management.[167] In other cases, a discounted valuation may be appropriate, since the shareholding is more in the nature of a straightforward investment. This includes cases where what was initially a 'quasi-partnership' has changed its nature. For example, in *Re DR Chemicals Ltd*[168] the company was originally a small member-management company, but the petitioner had done nothing while he was frozen out of management, and the court held that when he finally petitioned he could no longer demand a pro rata valuation of his shares because he was no longer entitled to be treated as more than an investor.

A parallel question is the proper valuation date, which cannot always be the date of the petition or the judgment. For example, it may have to be backdated to take account of the loss of value which has taken place since the conduct complained of began or because the company's capital has in the meantime been reorganised[169] or where the wrongdoers may have deliberately depressed the share prices in expectation of the petition. The nearest thing to a general rule seems to be that, if the company is still a going concern, the shares should be valued as at the date of the judgment or immediately afterwards.

In *O'Neil v Phillips*,[170] the House of Lords emphasised the need for an amicable settlement to be reached when there is a breakdown between the two persons running a company. Legal proceedings should be brought only as a very last resort.[171]

7.15.5 Department of Trade and Industry investigation

This is a final hazard to be faced by the board even where disgruntled shareholders cannot afford to take or continue action in the courts. The DTI has duties and discretions. It must appoint inspectors to investigate:

(1) the company's affairs if the court so directs (s 432(1));
(2) the ownership of particular shares or debentures, when it receives an application from 200 members or members holding 10 per cent of the issued shares, subject to:

   (a) their tendering up to £5,000 to meet the costs of the investigation; and
   (b) the DTI's power to refuse if it considers the inquiry vexatious or to exclude matters from the inquiry that it considers unreasonable to investigate (s 442(3)).[172]

The DTI may appoint inspectors:

(1) to investigate the company's affairs, if 200 members or members holding 10 per cent of the issued capital apply or if the company itself applies (s 431(2));
(2) if it suspects fraud or unlawful conduct of the company's affairs, unfair prejudice to some of the members, other misfeasance or the withholding of information which the members might reasonably expect to receive (s 432(2));
(3) to investigate the ownership or control of the company and to determine who may be the 'true persons' interested in its success or failure (s 442(1)); and
(4) if it appears there may have been contraventions of s 323 (option dealings), s 324 (disclosure of director's holdings in his own company) or s 328 (restrictions on dealings by directors and their families and duties to notify interests) (s 446(1)).

The DTI also has ancillary powers:

(1) to make inquiries about share ownership to anyone reasonably believed to have such information or access to it, *without* appointing any inspectors, a kind of 'in-house' and discreet investigation (s 444);
(2) for the purposes of s 442 or s 444 (above) to impose restrictions on the exercise of shareholders' rights, including dealings, while the investigation continues (s 455);
(3) to require the production of documents, a power which can now be delegated not only to a civil servant but also to any 'competent person' with the result that a limited investigation may now be carried out by a private firm, for example, if the DTI asks accountants to examine the company's records (s 447).

The power to demand the production of documents is, hardly surprisingly, also available to inspectors conducting an investigation, and the Act now makes it clear that any records may be demanded, including those stored in computer or other machine-readable form.[173] Amendments made to s 434 by the 1989 Act also make it clear that inspectors can extend their inquiries to the affairs of other companies, or of individuals, as long as these are relevant to the investigation. They may also require directors and others to answer questions on oath, and at this point the statutory procedures become potentially oppressive since, as we shall see shortly, there is little or no right to refuse to answer or provide information.

The DTI has two further powers which should be borne in mind. First, inspectors are normally expected to report to the DTI, and the report is published; but, under s 432(2A), inspectors may be appointed under that section on the basis that they will not make a public report. This may be a useful provision as the publicity given to a report may damage the company even where no adverse findings are made, but it may also be used where the object of the investigation is to make inquiries with a view to possible prosecutions or regulatory action.[174] Here, the absence of a published report may help to prevent potentially prejudicial pre-trial publicity. Secondly, the DTI has the power – not the *duty* – to stop the investigation in whole or in part if it appears that the inspectors are uncovering criminal offences (s 437(1B)).[175]

One of the reasons for extending the DTI's powers and at the same time making more provision for informal investigations is to meet criticisms often made – that the DTI is too slow and too timid in exercising its powers – and reconcile them with the strictly limited resources available to the DTI and the potential damage to companies under investigation, which is a perfectly legitimate concern of the DTI. If the balance has shifted towards a better-armed investigative regime, it becomes even more important for those who may be investigated to determine what limits there are upon the powers of the DTI and inspectors. An investigation may lead to proceedings by the DTI:

(1) for civil claims in the company's name against directors and others (s 438);
(2) for winding up in the public interest (s 440);[176]
(3) for an unfair prejudice remedy under s 460; or
(4) for criminal convictions under the Companies Act 1985 or the general law.

Limitations do arise from the fact that both the DTI and the inspectors are exercising statutory powers affecting the rights of individuals, in a 'public law' context. Consequently, their actions and decisions must be justified under the Act and under general principles of public law which require them to act for proper reasons,[177] on the basis of relevant considerations and, above all, with procedural fairness. This means, for example, that while neither departmental officials nor inspectors act as judges – the system would not work if they did not take the initiative, or were bound by strict rules of evidence – they must not presume that there has been wrongdoing and must afford some opportunity to those against whom adverse findings may be made to 'meet the case against them'.[178]

Assuming that the conduct of the proceedings is regular in public law terms, there is little further protection for those who may be the subject of an investigation or asked to give evidence or supply information. The inspectors' conclusions as expressed in their report are not admissible against those whom they have criticised insofar as they are matters only of opinion,[179] but uncontradicted findings of fact made in the report may be adopted in court not only by the DTI, but also by some third parties, for example, a member seeking to have the company wound up.[180] Potentially, the most serious problem for directors and others is that the inspectors can compel witnesses to answer questions and produce documents, and refer the matter to the court (with a view to contempt proceedings) if no answers or documents are forthcoming (s 436). There is very little to counterbalance this coercive power. First, once an answer has been given, it is admissible against the speaker in subsequent criminal proceedings whether or not the inspectors cautioned the witness or warned him of any suspicions they might already have entertained.[181] Secondly, there is no general right to refuse to answer. The courts have clearly ruled that the privilege against self-incrimination does not apply to investigations conducted by inspectors appointed under the 1985

Act.[182] The only protection available is that it is, in the end, for *the court* to determine whether the inspectors must be obeyed. It may decide not to treat a refusal to obey the inspectors as a contempt on the basis that the inspector's demands were oppressive and unfair, but the mere fact that an answer to a relevant question or the contents of relevant documents may tend to incriminate the speaker does *not* attract this protection. Conceivably, the court would refuse to allow questions to be put under the threat of contempt proceedings once a criminal charge had already been made against the witness. Certainly, where an investigation is suspended under s 437(1B) (see above), any further criminal investigations will be handled by the police and Crown Prosecution Service or by the Serious Fraud Office (SFO). In the first case, the normal criminal process applies, and suspects must be cautioned and may refuse to answer questions. In the second case, all questions must be answered, but the answers may be used in evidence against the speaker only if: (i) he is charged with lying to the SFO; or (ii) in the course of a prosecution for some other offence, he makes a statement inconsistent with his answer,[183] although statements already made to the inspectors before the investigation was suspended seem to remain admissible in subsequent proceedings. The driving force behind these rules, which treat directors considerably more severely than burglars, is presumably that white-collar suspects do not require as much protection as others, have more time to prepare themselves and take advice – and might be very difficult to prosecute successfully if they were not obliged to give evidence against themselves.

The DTI may also appoint inspectors to investigate possible offences reported to it by the Director of Public Prosecutions on complaint by a liquidator (s 218 of the Insolvency Act 1986).

CHAPTER 7 FOOTNOTES

1 Until the return of a Labour government in 1997, it had been intended that stamp duty on share transfers would be abolished; whether this is still the intention remains to be seen.

2 The move towards 'paperless' shares and share dealings will not cause private company shares and share transfers to change form dramatically, but see note 1 above.

3 *Lindlar's case* [1910] 1 Ch 312.

4 But before this can happen, there must be some concrete proposal for a transfer. Thus, where executors of a deceased member had completed the administration of his estate but the beneficiaries had no wish to acquire the shares, the pre-emption provisions of the Articles did not come into operation: *Safeguard Industrial Investments Ltd v National Westminster Bank Ltd* [1982] 1 WLR 589.

5 *Tett v Phoenix Property Investment Co Ltd* [1986] BCLC 149.

5 Thus, making it clear that the discretion to refuse registration arises only after the pre-emption rights are complied with and preventing a challenge to the exercise of that discretion if the shares have not been offered to the members.

7 The courts will probably imply a procedure, as it did in the *Tett* case (above). However, this involves an avoidable expenditure on litigation and there is no guarantee that the procedure devised by the courts will correspond with the wishes of the company.

8 *Re Smith & Fawcett Ltd* [1942] 1 All ER 542.

9 See note 8.

10 *Re Bede SS Co* [1917] 1 Ch 123.

11 *Moodie v W & J Shepherd (Bookbinders) Ltd* [1949] 2 All ER 1044.

12 *Re Swaledale Cleaners Ltd* [1968] 3 All ER 619.

13 *Re Zinnotty Properties Ltd* [1984] 1 WLR 1249.

14 *Charles Forte Investments Ltd v Amanda* [1963] 2 All ER 940.

15 *Baber v Kenwood Manufacturing* [1978] 1 Lloyd's Rep 175.

16 *Jones v Sherwood Computer Services plc* [1992] 1 WLR 277, CA, disapproving the decision in *Burgess v Purchase and Sons Ltd* [1983] 2 All ER 4, that significant error was sufficient for the court to intervene. Although in *Jones* the parties had expressly agreed that the valuation should be final, this will usually be implicit in an agreement for valuation, including a provision in the company's Articles. Underlying the reluctance to intervene in a valuation, as against an arbitration, is the availability of an action in negligence against the valuer.

17 Ibid, at p 286. The challenge in *Jones* was to the valuer's determination of the number of shares which a purchaser had to provide as part of the purchase price of other shares, but the principles involved are exactly the same.

18 *Re Howie & Crawford's Arbitration* [1990] BCLC 686.

19 In *A Company (No 002708 of 1989) ex parte W* [1990] BCLC 795, a general offer for the shares was held to be an admissible and important consideration even though it occurred shortly after the agreed valuation date because it tended to show what the 'market' regarded as the value of the shares as of that date.

20 Enhanced voting rights will, obviously, explain a valuation in excess of the sum produced simply by reference to asset values and dividends: see *Holt v Holt* [1990] BCC 682.

21 See *Re Bird Precision Bellows Ltd* [1984] BCLC 195, a valuation in pursuance of an unfair prejudice claim under s 459: see **7.15.4**.

22 *Re a Company (No 00330 of 1991)* [1991] BCLC 597.

23 Table A, reg 23 merely prescribes a 'usual' form or a form approved by the board.

24 From the company's point of view, 'debts' may be preferable to 'loans' since the latter word is often construed narrowly and literally to exclude forms of accommodation other than simple repayable advances: *Champagne, Perrier-Jouet SA v H H Finch Ltd* [1982] 1 WLR 1359.

25 It must also be decided whether the power of sale is to override pre-emption rights. If the Articles fail to achieve this, the company may lose the open market value of the shares and be forced to sell at a lower price in accordance with the pre-emption machinery for valuation: see *Champagne Perrier* above.

26 In contrast, a public company may not take security over its own shares unless it is a lending or credit company and the lien or other security is taken in connection with a loan or credit extended to the member in the course of that business (s 150).

27 *Borland's Trustee v Steel Bros & Co Ltd* [1901] 1 Ch 279.

28 *Sidebottom v Kershaw Leese & Co* [1920] 1 Ch 154.

29 *Brown v British Abrasive Wheel Co* [1919] 1 Ch 290.

30 *Dafen Tinplate Co Ltd v Llanelly Steel Co* [1920] 2 Ch 124.

31 *Greenhalgh v Arderne Cinemas Ltd* [1950] 2 All ER 1120.

32 In the case of companies (other than public companies first registered as such) which registered before 22 June 1982, paragraph (2) also applies to pre-emption rights granted by a contract outside the Memorandum or Articles.

33 Except, apparently, for the purposes of s 89(2) and (3), mentioned in paragraph (2), where only the first part of the definition applies.

34 [1994] BCC 857.

35 This authority lasts only as long as the authority conferred upon them to make allotments, but like that authority it may be renewed. The directors may complete a transaction begun before the expiry of this authority if the special resolution or power in the Articles so intends. The resolution must be filed with the Registrar (s 380) and *Gazetted* by him (s 711).

36 The knowing or reckless inclusion in such a statement of material which is misleading, false or deceptive in a material particular is an offence carrying a sentence of up to two years' imprisonment.

37 Admission of Securities to Listing (the Yellow Book) Section 5, Ch 2, § 37. The restriction extends to any 'major' unlisted subsidiary, ie one in which the company has a holding representing 25 per cent or more of the group assets or pre-tax profits. If the subsidiary is itself listed, s 37 applies to it directly.

38 *Belmont Finance Corp v Williams Furniture (No 2)* [1980] 1 All ER 393.

39 *Armour Hicks Northern Ltd v Armour Trust Ltd* [1980] 3 All ER 833.

40 Section 152(2): this includes contingent liabilities. The definition relates to actual value, not book value.

41 *Charterhouse Investment Trust Ltd v Tempest Diesels Ltd* [1986] BCLC 1.

42 Thus, assistance to finance a buyout of resigning directors was under the old law a breach of the Act which might be excused if its purpose was to secure the company's future and stability: *Marine and Industrial Generators Ltd v Mercer* [1982] NLJ 65. Although relief is still available under s 727, such assistance may now be justifiable under s 153 itself (but see the text to notes 44 to 47).

43 See notes 39 and 40 above.

44 [1989] AC 755.

45 It is important to remember that where the company's solvency is in doubt the interests of creditors must be given priority over those of the company or its members: see **5.2.2**.

46 They could have been used in *Brady* if someone had thought it necessary to do so. *Brady* could be regarded as a deliberate attempt to channel directors' conduct towards the private company exemptions, leaving public companies to be dealt with by s 151 unless there were very good reasons for allowing the s 153 exceptions to apply. This explanation would be more convincing, however, if charges alleging a massive share support operation in breach of s 151 had not been dropped at the end of the first Guinness trial on the ground that the issues raised under s 151 were too complex for a criminal court.

47 Under ss 263 to 281 which protect creditors and minorities. This exception allows liquid funds to be used to finance purchases retrospectively, but seeks to prevent the worst abuses by the purchaser.

48 Measured by book value.

49 This is necessary (and not a mere irritant) because private companies are not required to take unrealised losses into account under ss 263–281 governing distribution of profits and assets.

50 Except where the company providing assistance is a wholly owned subsidiary.

51 Unless they acquire them in good faith, for value and without notice of the breach, for example, a bank receiving moneys in reduction of an overdraft.

52 And, if they have parted with the original moneys in return for new property, that property in turn may be the subject of a tracing claim.

53 (1989) 5 BCC 352.

54 It will be seen from **7.7** that all shares are potentially redeemable under ss 162–166, even if not redeemable by their terms of issue under s 159.

55 Preventing capital reductions by the back door.

56 Ie those profits from which distribution may lawfully be made: s 181. As to this see s 263: **4.4.1**.

57 *Report of the Committee on Company Law* (1962) Cmnd 1749, para 167.

58 *Trevor v Whitworth* (1887) 12 App Cas 409.

59 *Re Castiglione's WT* [1958] Ch 549.

60 Of course, the Articles may be altered to add such a power by s 9 (special resolution).

61 'Listing' still relates to the Stock Exchange, but s 163 is extended by the Financial Services Act 1986 to any investment exchange which is recognised under that Act.

62 It may be that the potential vagueness of the authorisation led to the adoption of ordinary resolution procedure (bare majority) rather than the requirement under s 164 above, for a special resolution. But special resolutions may be perfectly general, as where directors are given general authority to make allotments under s 80. In truth, this difference between s 164 and s 166 is mystifying and apparently lacks any justification at all.

63 Or a formula, provided that it leaves no discretion.

64 In this respect s 166 is stricter than the rules for off-market purchases.

65 [1902] 2 Ch 421.

66 A more robust judge might, conceivably, be prepared to find a misrepresentation in the directors' conduct, but silence per se will not do: there is no duty of disclosure.

67 [1942] 1 All ER 378.

68 [1975] All ER 849.

69 A receiver can undoubtedly bring an action: *Belmont Finance Ltd v Williams Furniture Ltd* [1979] 1 All ER 118.

70 The Code, Introduction, para 2.

71 For an early example, see *Dunford & Elliott Ltd v Johnson & Firth Brown Ltd* [1977] 1 Lloyd's Rep 506.

72 *R v Spens* [1991] BCLC 140 (on a charge of conspiracy to induce shareholders to accept a share exchange by dishonest concealment of material facts the court would consider the true meaning of the Code, but the jury could consider whether criminal intent was negated if the accused believed that they were complying with the Code).

73 Because the Panel exercises a 'public law' function, the courts will see that its decisions do not involve such a serious misconstruction of the rules as in effect to be unauthorised by the Code. But the review is likely to be *ex post facto* (*R v Panel on Takeovers and Mergers ex parte Datafin Ltd* [1987] QB 815) and the courts are unlikely to interfere with the purely discretionary elements in the Panel's functions.

74 Defined as in the Companies Act 1985.

75 The director may, therefore, even have to warn his printer not to use or spread the information which he is printing.

76 Ie pursuant to a formal or informal agreement or understanding; this will be presumed, subject to contrary evidence, in certain cases, including that of a company and its directors.

77 Dealings could easily create a false market in the offeror's shares which in the case of a share for share offer would be very serious. There are also Rules restricting or regulating acquisitions once the holding reaches a certain level. In addition, there are the substantial acquisition Rules, also issued on the authority of the Takeover Panel, which regulate the speed at which acquisitions may be made. These Rules do not relate directly to insider dealing.

78 *Report on First Re-investment Trust Ltd. and other Companies* (Department of Trade) (HMSO, 1974).

79 *Gething v Kilner* [1972] 1 All ER 1164. The duties of the board when there is a takeover are considered in Chapter 4.

80 Ie a promise to the vendor to make good the balance between his selling price and the price of any subsequent offer.

81 Which includes failure to make any disclosure, making an inadequate or non-complying disclosure, and even failing to state in the notice that disclosure is made in pursuance of the obligations imposed by the Rules.

82 Prosecutions may be commenced only with the consent of the Department of Trade and Industry or the Director of Public Prosecutions.

83 Including by a contingent right or an obligation which, when fulfilled, would result in an entitlement.

84 One-third suffices.

85 Certain of these exemptions are made by the Companies (Disclosure of Directors' Interests) (Exceptions) Regulations 1985, SI 1985/802 made under s 324(3).

86 Under ss 608, 611 and 612 of ICTA 1988.

87 Forms complying with these requirements can be obtained from legal stationers.

88 Under Sch 13 delivery of shares to a person's order in fulfilment of a purchase contract is actually deemed to be an event as a result of which he ceases to be interested in them. Thus, extraordinarily, he becomes 'interested' when he gets the contract note but when the executed transfer and share certificate arrive, his interest ceases!

89 Excluding weekends and bank holidays.

90 See note 89.

91 This and the following requirements are derived from Sch 13, Part IV as well as s 325 itself.

92 See **7.13**.

93 Including those of shadow directors, and with subsidiary companies.

94 *W Dennis & Sons Ltd v West Norfolk Farmers, etc, Co* [1943] Ch 220.

95 *Butt v Kelson* [1952] 1 All ER 167.

96 *R v Mariguita Mining Co* (1859) 1 E & E 289.

97 These are open to the company's officers at all times (s 222(1)). As to other documents, the courts will generally allow a director to inspect unless he is about to lose office or it is shown that he is likely to misuse confidential information: *Conway v Petronius Clothing Co Ltd* [1978] 1 WLR 72.

98 Entries may be deleted after 20 years from that date.

99 As also provided by reg 5 of Table A.

100 *Langen & Wind Ltd v Bell* [1972] 1 All ER 296.

101 Rules of the Supreme Court, Ord 50, rr 11–14.

102 In the case of listed companies, there are substantial requirements imposed by the Stock Exchange.

103 His later knowledge may arise not only because of share dealings of which he had no immediate knowledge, but by extraneous events such as a capital reduction which takes his holding over three per cent.

104 Including, to preclude easy evasions, control through conditional or unconditional share options (s 203(4)).

105 If the agreement is not a contract, it will still be caught if there is 'mutuality', ie each acts in reliance upon the other(s) acting in a similar way.

106 Indeed, in an effort to block every avenue of evasion, s 205 also provides that if he is a party to more than one agreement, the separate interests acquired under each agreement will be attributed to him.

107 Similarly, a purchaser or vendor using an agent must ensure that the agent keeps him informed.

108 Including foreign companies with no other presence in the UK except the suspected interest: *Re FH Holdings* (1985) *The Times*, 9 April.

109 The definition of interest is slightly wider than for notification purposes.

110 (1985) 1 BCC 99, at p 402.

111 (1987) 3 BCC 528.

112 'Group' being defined by s 289(4)(b) in terms of wholly owned subsidiaries and their parent companies.

113 This is primarily a relief for those who act nominally as directors of 'off the shelf' companies until a buyer is found. 'Dormancy' is defined by s 250, as to which see **4.1.7**.

114 Section 42. Indeed, even notification under s 711 does not seem to give the third party constructive notice of the event in question: *Official Custodian for Charities v Parway Estates Developments Ltd* [1985] Ch 151 (CA).

115 (1843) 2 Hare 461.

116 A technical breach of procedure can usually be corrected by the majority (*Bentley-Stevens v Jones* [1974] 1 WLR 638), so what is at issue will usually be a procedural protection which the majority cannot sidestep. The simplest example is a case where the majority cannot command sufficient

votes to pass a necessary special resolution and seeks to press ahead by ordinary resolution. The 'majority control' aspect of the rule also applies to complaints of damage to *the company*, since in the last resort the majority can determine to overlook the damage or take no action – unless this involves 'fraud' under (4).

117 For example, in *Re a Company (No 005136 of 1986)* [1987] BCLC 82, the judge said that a member has a right to have the board's power to allot shares used only for proper purposes. But although this is a situation in which the courts have allowed actions to proceed, they have also allowed majority control: see, for example, *Hogg v Cramphorn* and *Bamford v Bamford* (**5.4.1**) where the alleged breach of directors' duties was placed in the control of the *majority* at the general meeting.

118 For example, *Devlin v Slough Estates Ltd* [1983] BCLC 497, where it was held that a member had no standing to complain of a failure to prepare proper accounts, a failure which one might have expected to attract the first exception mentioned in the text if not the second.

119 See **8.3.5**.

120 *Smith v Croft (No 2)* [1988] Ch 114.

121 See s 35(3). But see further **8.3.5**.

122 As in *Cook v Deeks* [1916] 1 AC 554, where the directors wrongfully took profitable contracts for themselves instead of the company. It will be seen that the fraud is really on the *company*, whose rights are then vindicated by the minority in the company's name.

123 *Mercier v Hooper's Telegraph* (1874) LR 9 Ch 250.

124 See *Cook v Deeks*, note 122.

125 *Pavlides v Jensen* [1956] Ch 565, where the absence of absolute control by the wrongdoers was also a factor: see note 129.

126 *Daniels v Daniels* [1978] Ch 406.

127 Hence, perhaps, the half-way house solution in the share allotment cases, where the action has been allowed to proceed but subject to a final decision to be taken at a general meeting where the improperly issued shares would not be voted: for example, *Hogg v Cramphorn* [1967] Ch 254.

128 It is also important as a matter of equity if not of logic that the minority is not itself guilty of misconduct, as in *Nurcombe v Nurcombe* [1985] 1 WLR 370, where the member had accepted settlement of his personal claim against the majority and then sought to use the derivative action to improve his position still further.

129 *Prudential Assurance Ltd v Newman Industries Ltd* [1982] Ch 204. It remains unclear at what point – if any – the court will accept that a majority formed of the wrongdoer plus those voting with him through persuasion, influence or interest amounts to sufficient control.

130 Since a rational member may always fear that the costs of the action will exceed the benefits, this decision will often bar a minority action.

131 *Wallersteiner v Moir (No 2)* [1975] QB 373. An indemnity order in a personal action by a shareholder will not be given, but a suitable order for costs may be made if the action does benefit members generally: *Marx v Estates and General Ltd* [1976] 1 WLR 380, at p 392. Even in a derivative action, it has been held that an indemnity should be given only if the action produces some benefit to the members generally, and not merely to those members who are bringing the action: *Watts v Midland Bank plc* [1986] BCLC 15. The procedure is not generally available after appointment of a liquidator, since the majority's sway is ended: *Ferguson v Wallbridge* [1935] 3 DLR 66. The liquidator may then sue or take over an action: *Fargo Ltd v Godfrey* [1986] 1 WLR 1134; if he refuses, the aggrieved shareholder may still be able to sue, subject to providing an indemnity against costs should the action fail.

132 *Re Yenidje Tobacco Co Ltd* [1916] 2 Ch 426; mere exclusion from management after a breakdown is not necessarily within the section – the question is whether it is reasonable for the applicant rather than the others to leave, and whether the terms of departure are reasonable and fair. If the Articles provide for an enforced share transfer with a fair method of valuation, the applicant cannot complain, particularly if he has some other redress such as an action for wrongful dismissal in respect of the actual exclusion: *Re XYZ Ltd* (1986) FT Comm LR, 12 August.

133 *Re Westbourne Galleries Ltd* [1973] AC 360.

134 *Re A & BC Chewing Gum Ltd* [1975] 1 All ER 1017.

135 *Re Paul's Federated Merchants Ltd* (1985) Co Lawyer 40.

136 *Practice Direction* [1990] BCLC 452.

137 [1990] BCLC 342.

138 It is worth noting that however carefully the Articles are drafted, a court which finds them working unfairly in a particular case is entitled to ignore them on the same kind of 'just and equitable' basis as generates the claim to winding up itself.

139 (1988) 4 BCC 80.

140 Section 459 nowhere requires the petitioner to be or represent a minority, and this is one of the situations where statutory relief is available where a common law minority action (above) would be very difficult to bring because the controllers have only de facto control. The resurgence of the *Foss v Harbottle* rule described at **7.15.1** appears, at the time of writing, to be partly responsible for increased activity under s 459.

141 Conduct controlled by a de facto or shadow director ought to be treated as the company's conduct; but *Re Technion Investments Ltd* [1985] BCLC 434, although decided on the technical question whether or not documents were in the control of the company, may indicate a difficulty in actually building up such a case.

142 *Re London School of Electronics Ltd* [1985] BCLC 273.

143 *Vujnovich v Vujnovich* [1990] BCLC 227.

144 *Re R A Noble & Sons (Clothing) Ltd* [1983] BCLC 273.

145 See note 142.

146 *Re Ringtower Holdings plc* (1989) 5 BCC 82. It does not follow, of course, that the conduct of a public company cannot be unfairly prejudicial to the members or some of them, merely that the complaint cannot usually be based on some 'breach of understanding'.

147 *Re DR Chemical Ltd* [1989] BCLC 383.

148 *Re Nuneaton Borough AFC Ltd* [1989] BCLC 454 (provided always that the breaches do in fact prejudice the complainant's position).

149 *Re a Company (No 005287 of 1985)* [1986] BCLC 68.

150 Again, it cannot be overemphasised that the court's task is to look at what has happened as a whole. In the *Ringtower* case (see note 146 above) from which the last example is taken, the majority deleted pre-emption rights and reregistered the company as private so as to facilitate a takeover. But, in the circumstances, there was no unfair prejudice because the intending purchaser at all times intended to offer the minority the same price for their shares as the majority. Had there been some clear 'quasi-partnership' interest in the minority, the majority's action in shutting out the minority from any say in the negotiations might well have been unfairly prejudicial notwithstanding that the purchaser found by the majority was prepared to make such an offer.

151 [1983] BCLC 273, at p 289.

152 [1985] BCLC 80.

153 [1989] BCLC 383.

154 [1991] BCLC 959.

155 [1994] BCLC 354.

156 *Re Castleburn Ltd* [1991] BCLC 89, although matters will be different if the complainant can show bad faith or something seriously wrong with the process for valuing his shares: *Re Boswell & Co (Steels) Ltd* (1989) 5 BCC 145.

157 *Re a Company (No 002612 of 1984)* [1985] BCLC 80. Although unfair prejudice is not based on deliberate oppression or wrongdoing, the complainant's case is all the stronger where this clearly exists. For example, complaints have succeeded where the object of issuing shares was to divert the petitioner's resources away from litigation against the controllers (*Re Cumana Ltd* [1986] BCLC 430) or secretly to reduce the petitioner's holding from 40 per cent to four per cent (*Re a Company (No 005134 of 1986)* [1989] BCLC 383). At this point, of course, there are manifest breaches of fiduciary duty by the controllers.

158 *Re Cumuna Ltd* at note 157 above.

159 *Re Sam Weller Ltd* [1990] Ch 682, where the dividend had not been increased for nearly 40 years: although this affected the interests of all the members, the controllers did not suffer since they were able to rely on remuneration which was *not* similarly frozen!

160 *Re a Company (No 008699 of 1985)* [1986] BCLC 382.

161 For example, to appoint or remove directors or to call proper meetings.

162 For example, to stop a share issue.

163 The company must then file the altered documents with the Registrar in the usual way.

164 *Ex parte Broadhurst* [1990] BCLC 384.

165 [1991] BCC 44.

166 There was also a complete failure to hold AGMs and lay accounts before the members. The court held that these could not be considered as unfairly prejudicial since they affected *all* the members, a finding which was probably wrong at the time and is certainly reversed by the changed wording of s 459 inserted by the 1989 Act (see **7.15.3**).

167 *Re Bird Precision Bellows Ltd* [1986] 2 WLR 158. For the importance of this issue in relation to winding up on the 'just and equitable grounds', see **7.15.2**.

168 [1989] BCLC 383.

169 *Re OC (Transport) Ltd* [1984] BCLC 251.

170 [1999] BCC 600.

171 See also *Re Legal Costs Negotiators Ltd* [1999] BCC 547.

172 The DTI may also conduct a s 444 inquiry (below) instead if it considers that this will meet the needs of the applicants (s 442(3C), inserted by s 62 of the 1989 Act).

173 See s 56 of the Companies Act 1989. Those who select their banks by reference to traditions of secrecy should first read s 69 of the 1989 Act which may well embarrass overseas banks with branches in the UK, since it enables the inspectors or the DTI to obtain bankers' records in most cases where they are likely to need them.

174 For example, disqualification or even winding-up proceedings.

175 This puts an end to the publication of any inspectors' report unless the DTI says otherwise or the inspectors were appointed pursuant to the initiative of the court.

176 For example, because the conduct of the company's business defrauds its customers: *Re Highfield Commodities* [1985] 1 WLR 149.

177 For example, it would probably not be lawful for the DTI to appoint inspectors or the inspectors to question officers *solely* with a view to assisting a minority action.

178 *Re Pergamon Press Ltd* [1971] Ch 388. Having said this, it should be stressed that no one has a right to make representations to the DTI *against the appointment* of inspectors: *Norwest Holst Ltd v Secretary of State for Trade* [1978] Ch 201. Nor is it likely to be easy to show bias against a particular director or officer on the part of the DTI or an inspector: *R v Secretary of State for Trade, ex parte Perestrello* [1981] QB 19. As the last case shows, it is more likely that a formal defect will emerge, such as a demand for documents which is so ill-defined that the recipient cannot tell if he is complying with it or not.

179 *Savings & Investment Bank Ltd v Gasco Investments (Netherlands) BV* [1984] 1 WLR 271. The report would, of course, be admissible as evidence of the fact that the inspectors have formed these opinions (s 441).

180 *Re St Piran Ltd* [1981] 1 WLR 1300. Even when there is a challenge, the inspectors' findings of fact are admissible as evidence in disqualification proceedings (s 441).

181 *R v Seelig* [1991] 4 All ER 429.

182 *Re London United Investments Ltd* [1992] 2 WLR 850, CA. This is consistent with the attitude of the courts to questions put to company officers by insolvency officers under s 236 of the Insolvency Act 1986.

183 Section 2 of the Criminal Justice Act 1987. Nor is there any prospect of challenging the appointment of the inspectors on the basis that if the DTI suspected fraud it should have referred the matter to the police or SFO at once since it is quite clear that a deliberate decision has been made by Parliament to maintain company investigations as a separate but potentially overlapping system of investigation.

Chapter 8

RELATIONS OF DIRECTORS WITH ONE ANOTHER

8.1 DISAGREEMENT ON THE BOARD: MAJORITY DECIDES

We have seen that directors act collectively as a board, although the power to delegate is usually given to them by the Articles (see **3.10.1**). Questions of their relations with one another do not normally arise unless there is disagreement or default or some allegation of personal liability.

What is the position where disagreements occur – as they inevitably will? The Articles usually provide (Table A, reg 88) that questions at board meetings[1] shall be decided by a *majority* of votes, each director having one vote (a director who is also an alternate for another having an additional vote for his absent appointer). Thus, the primary rule is that disagreements are resolved, if necessary, by a simple counting of heads, the chairman having a casting vote in the event of a tie. The size of the shareholding which the director may control or represent is therefore irrelevant so long as the company has not adopted a special Article giving weighted voting rights at board meetings or voting in accordance with the number of shares held. The legal status and responsibility of every director is exactly the same. This is something which has to be borne in mind in private family companies, where the controlling or founding director may be required by the courts, if necessary, to pay due respect to the rights of his colleagues.[2]

8.2 RESPONSIBILITIES OF DISSENTIENTS: *FIRST RE-INVESTMENT TRUST LTD*

Conversely, the other directors must beware of becoming 'yes' men to a dominant chairman or managing director as they, too, run the risk of liability for breach of duty if they fail to play their proper part. The reality of this danger was vividly illustrated in the inspectors' report in the case of *First Re-investment Trust Ltd and other companies*[3] where an entire board of a quoted company was found wanting on this score. The co-directors were all experienced city business men and yet they allowed themselves to get into a situation where they were acting as 'rubber stamps' to the investment decisions of the chairman, who entirely dominated the board.

As a result, the chairman was enabled to buy assets for himself at a price which represented only a fraction of their true value. The chairman knew this; offers had already been made by third parties, which he did not disclose, and shortly afterwards the assets were resold by him at their full value. All the members of the board were found to be in breach of duty, but the report is particularly instructive in indicating the degree of responsibility in each case.

(1) The chairman was acknowledged to be the dominant director; it was he who had the personal interest in the transactions, and he was found to have knowingly broken his duties of good faith and skill and care, and to be guilty of grave mismanagement.

(2) His deputy or 'confidential adjutant' was the only other director who knew the true story, but he claimed to be totally subordinate with a status no higher than that of a clerk.

> 'He stated that he had never learned the duties of a director nor read any book or paper of any kind concerning directors' duties ... he had never formed any independent judgement on the matters under inquiry; and that he did not understand the significance of his actions, in particular that they were capable of constituting breaches of his duty as a director.'[4]

His counsel argued that on the basis of the *Re City Equitable* standard, and having regard to the director's own knowledge and capacity, he was not in breach of duty. The inspectors rejected this; he knew the facts and must have known that breaches of duty were being committed. Moreover, when the chairman failed to make a proper disclosure of his interest at the board meeting, it was the deputy's duty to remedy the omission. This would have been a painful prospect indeed for someone who saw himself merely as a confidential clerk, but the inspectors concluded that nothing less was expected of him. He was, accordingly, found to have been knowingly guilty of the same breaches of duty as the chairman even though the degree of blame was less.

(3) The third director did not know of the chairman's plans and said that he would have been horrified if he had known. Moreover, he had become increasingly unhappy about the autocratic style of management and the 'rubber-stamp' function of the board and he had criticised it. His counsel claimed that on the principles of *Re City Equitable*, he was not negligent and was entitled to rely on the chairman on matters properly delegated to him.[5] But the inspectors pointed out that when being asked to ratify the chairman's investment decisions at the board meetings, he could not escape his duty to exercise his own judgement. Although acting in good faith, he had therefore failed to meet the required standard of skill and care.

The inspectors went on to indicate the positive steps which they thought he should have taken:

(a) criticism he had expressed, but the very fact that he did so should have alerted him to the need for full scrutiny;

(b) formal protests, recorded in the minutes, should have been the next step; followed by

(c) threat of resignation and resignation itself if the situation was not remedied.[6] The director said he did not resign because he felt he could improve matters from within; but this was not good enough for the inspectors. They pointed out that to justify such a view he must have been able to point to genuine improvements in the system, and these had not occurred.

He was therefore in breach of duty.[7]

(4) The fourth director was also ignorant of the scheme and had been equally dissatisfied with the chairman's style of management. He had taken his opposition to the point of resigning from two of the other companies in the group on the ground that 'he was being asked to be a rubber stamp'. Moreover, in the present case he was the only director who sought an explanation of the share price at any board meeting. When asked why he did not resign from the company under investigation, he replied, 'I was foolish enough to think that I could change things. I thought that there were glimmers of light coming.' The inspectors accepted his sincerity but pointed out that he could not escape criticism for his continued participation in this system of management. This should be tempered because of the firm line which he had taken with the other companies and because he had, at least, questioned the chairman in the present case – but he was still in breach of his duty of skill and care.

It will be noted that the conduct of these four directors attracted criticism at four different and descending levels, but in each case it was sufficiently blameworthy to amount to a breach of duty. The lesson seems clear – silence is never enough. A director, however minor or subordinate his role, has a positive duty to apply his own judgement to company matters. If he is not satisfied, he must speak up; then he must record a formal objection in the minutes, and if things still do not change, he must resign unless the company is threatened by insolvency. Otherwise he will bear some of the responsibility for defaults in which he has no part and which he may even have opposed.[8] Since the sort of actions which went unchecked here could easily lead to eventual corporate insolvency, a director would also do well to consider his potential liability for wrongful trading – see s 214 of the Insolvency Act 1986 (**6.2.4**).

It should be added that the rather low subjective standard of care expected of a director in *Re City Equitable* was ignored by Hoffman LJ in *Re D'Jan of London Ltd*[9] where the learned judge said that the standard today is as accurately described in s 214 of the Insolvency Act 1986, namely that a director should show the skill which may be expected of a person in his position.

8.3 REMEDIES

8.3.1 Action in board meeting

Having considered the extent of his responsibilities, our director must now decide what to do if he finds himself in disagreement with the policy of his colleagues.[10]

The first and most obvious step is to raise the matter in a board meeting. If no meeting is in prospect, he should ascertain from the Articles whether he has the right to convene a meeting of the directors. Under reg 88 of Table A, a director may and the secretary on the requisition of a director must, at any time, summon a meeting of the directors. This Article is commonly adopted,[11] but there is, naturally, no certainty that the other members will attend.

If a director raises the matter in dispute at a board meeting and he is outvoted, he must consider whether he will accept the position or whether he will take further action and, if so, what steps are open to him. His decision must largely depend upon the degree of importance which he attaches to the question.

On all but the most important questions – including any matter affecting the company's solvency – a director who has been overruled by his colleagues should accept the decision of the majority. He may regret that he has been unable to make his point and if he judges the matter to be of sufficient importance, he may insist that his dissent is minuted; he may even feel resentful that his advice is not being followed, but nevertheless he should bear in mind that in deferring to the wishes of the majority he may be doing what is best for the company and that the interests of the company should take precedence over his own feelings.

In certain circumstances, however, he is justified in refusing to accept the decision of his colleagues and in taking further action. Indeed, it may not only be his right, but his duty to do so as we have seen in **8.2** above. For example, he may consider that he has not been given a fair hearing before the board, and in that event possibly his best course of action is to circulate to his colleagues a full memorandum setting out his views, so that the matter may be reconsidered.

More serious is the case where a director considers that some action proposed by the majority is illegal, or not in accordance with the standards of conduct which should be observed. Even where he is unable to criticise it on grounds of illegality or as being contrary to business ethics, he may consider that the action proposed will have results which will be so detrimental to the interests of the company that, if persisted in, he cannot take any responsibility for it.

As has been emphasised elsewhere in this book, a director occupies a fiduciary position in relation to the company. If, therefore, he knows that the board are intent upon a course of action which in his view is illegal, or will be disastrous, he is not fully discharging his duties if he merely votes against the proposal at a board meeting. He should, of course, do this and insist on his objections being recorded in the minutes, but having done so he must then consider whether any further action on his part is called for, such as insisting on the company's legal advisers being consulted.

8.3.2   Action in general meeting

If his opposition is unsuccessful, and he feels that the question is so serious as to justify an open conflict with the rest of the board, a director can also ventilate the matters in dispute at a general meeting of the company.

If he controls, or can count on the support of, a substantial proportion of the total voting power, this may prove an effective method of dealing with the matter. It is true that it is not competent for a general meeting to reverse any decision taken by the board, and it may be difficult to find a majority able to bind the board to a course of action which it must follow in relation to matters which under the Articles are vested in the board (see **3.8**), but no board of directors can for long carry out a policy against the expressed wishes of the shareholders.

The form in which the matter could be raised is a resolution that the meeting has no confidence in the policy being carried out by the board, or a resolution for the appointment of a shareholders' committee (possibly with an independent chairman), to investigate the question; or a resolution for the removal of directors and the appointment of others in their place; or, in cases where an investigation is required, a resolution under s 431 for the appointment of an inspector by the DTI. Proper notice of any resolution must be given in accordance with the Act and the Articles, and in the case of a resolution for the removal of directors, this must be 'special notice' as required by s 303 unless the company has adopted a special Article which allows for the removal of a director by some means other than by ordinary resolution under the s 303 procedure, for example, an Article permitting removal by the passing of a special resolution.[12]

The provisions of s 376, regarding the circulation of members' resolutions and statements on requisition, are useful in such circumstances.[13] The general meeting may be the annual general meeting of the company or, if the director cannot wait until the next AGM but can control, or enlist the support of, members holding not less than one-tenth of the paid up shares, he can have an extraordinary general meeting called under the provisions of s 368 (see **9.1.2**).

8.3.3   Resignation

If reference to a general meeting is impracticable, or is unsuccessful, a director can signify his opposition by resigning from the board, and in some cases this is the best course he can adopt. In such circumstances, it may be that, in fairness to the shareholders, he should publish a statement setting out his reasons for the step he is taking.

On the other hand, a director who finds himself in this position should consider carefully before he decides to resign and, in making his decision, he should try to put personal preferences on one side and assess what is in the best interests of the company. He may come to the conclusion that more harm will result from his departure than if he remains on the board and endeavours to put things right. In that case, he may find himself being asked, in due course, to show that he has been able to improve the situation by staying on the board. If he cannot see any signs of such an improvement, he should again consider whether to resign.[14] In regard to resignation when things are going seriously wrong within a company, the case of *Re CS Holidays*[15] is instructive. The case concerned disqualification proceedings against a director. He had formed the view that the company was trading at considerable risk to the creditors and the situation was such that it would have been prudent for him to resign as a director. He did not, however, resign. Chadwick J held that this did not necessarily lead to the conclusion that he was unfit to be concerned in the management of a company. In the circumstances, the director had used such influence as he had to bring trading to an end.

Sometimes a director who is taking a line opposed by the majority will find himself under strong pressure from his fellow directors to resign. This may take the form of a threat to use majority voting power in a general meeting to pass a resolution for his removal from office under the provisions of the Articles or under s 303.

No doubt most directors in this position would, if they considered only their personal preferences, choose to resign rather than be removed, with all the publicity and unpleasantness which the latter may involve. Nevertheless, in this as in other matters, a director should have regard to the interests of the company and this may lead him to the conclusion that he should not give way. After all, if his opponents carry out their proposal to move a resolution for his removal under s 303, he will have the right of having a statement circulated to the members and it may well be his duty, in all the circumstances, to refuse to resign so that his opponents will have to make good their threat before the shareholders in general meeting, when he will be able to put his side of the case.

8.3.4   Inspection by Department of Trade and Industry

Where a director considers that the actions of his colleagues involve serious irregularities, it may be that his best course of action is to invoke the intervention of the DTI who have power under ss 431 and 432 of the Act to appoint inspectors to carry out an investigation of a company's affairs and under s 442 to appoint inspectors to investigate ownership, control or material influence over the company. These powers have been summarised in **7.15.5** above, but it may be useful to re-examine them in relation to the position of a dissatisfied director.

Under s 431, the DTI may order an investigation into a company's affairs on the application of not less than 200 members or members holding not less than one-tenth of the issued shares (in the case of a company not having a share capital, the application must be by not less than one-fifth of the members). Section 431 may also be invoked by the company if the objectors can raise a majority for an ordinary resolution.[16] The application must be supported by such evidence as the DTI may require for the purpose of showing that the applicants have good reason for requiring the investigation and the DTI may, before appointing an inspector, require the applicants to give security, to an amount not exceeding £5,000, for payment of the cost of the investigation. The names of the complainants and the nature of the charges made are not disclosed to the directors of the company, although those who will be censured by the inspectors and possibly disqualified by the courts must, in the course of the investigation, be given a chance to meet the case against them (see **7.15.5**).

Proceedings under s 431, therefore, may be appropriate where a director can obtain sufficient support from other shareholders and the matters complained of are sufficiently grave to warrant the appointment of an inspector.

Irrespective of any application by members, the DTI has also the power to appoint inspectors under s 432. This provides that the DTI *must* order an investigation if the courts, by order, declare that the company's affairs should be investigated by an inspector appointed by the DTI (s 432(1)); and the DTI *may* do so if it appears that the company's business is being conducted or has been conducted in a manner which is fraudulent, unlawful or unfairly prejudicial to some of its members, or its members have not been given all the information with respect to its affairs which they might reasonably expect (s 432(2)(b)).

The provisions enabling the company's affairs to be investigated are, potentially, a powerful deterrent to malpractice. First, there is the threat of publicity. The assumption is that the inspectors' report will be published.[17] Secondly, the report may lead to the DTI taking action by applying for an order under s 460 to protect the members or for disqualification of directors. In an extreme case, the DTI might apply to the court to have the company wound up under s 124A of the Insolvency Act 1986. In any proceedings, whether brought by the DTI or not, the report is admissible as evidence of the inspectors' opinions, and in an application for disqualification based on the report it is evidence of the facts found by the inspectors. There is a third threat. The inspectors have power to compel directors and others to produce documents and answer questions (if necessary, on oath). Refusal may lead to contempt proceedings. It must be said, however, that information so obtained under compulsion cannot be used as evidence in a subsequent prosecution against the director concerned. This was the decision of the European Commission of Human Rights in *Saunders v United Kingdom*,[18] a case which arose out of the conviction of Ernest Saunders following the Guinness investigation (Registrar of the European Court of Human Rights press release 407).[19] The Commission found that it was an infringement of the human right to a fair trial under the European Convention for the Protection of Human Rights that there had been a failure on the part of the prosecuting authorities to prevent the use of a confession obtained under compulsion of law in a criminal prosecution. It might be commented that this is a somewhat disappointing decision in that it ignores the significant difference in intellectual ability between the street criminal being given a particularly hard time in the course of a police investigation, and the successful and experienced businessman being investigated by the DTI. Furthermore, it disregards the origin of the human rights movement in the protection of citizens against over-aggressive States. Whatever epithets might be applied to the DTI, 'over-aggressive' is not one of them.

Having said this, it would appear that such evidence can be used in disqualification proceedings. This was the decision of the Court of Appeal in *R v Secretary of State for Trade and Industry ex parte McCormick*.[20] It was explained that there was a real doubt whether disqualification proceedings were criminal since they could not result in the deprivation of liberty, livelihood or property. If an investigation reveals something seriously amiss, there is now provision for the inspectors' inquiry to be suspended while the matter is investigated by the Serious Fraud Office (SFO). The SFO may itself compel parties to produce documents and answer questions, but there is a limit to the uses to which the SFO is able to put the answers it receives and, unlike the inspectors, it is an investigating authority subject to the requirements of the Police and Criminal Evidence Act 1984. It must caution parties in more or less the same way as the police must caution a suspected burglar. Contrast the position of the director appearing before company inspectors – no caution, no privilege against self-incrimination, and perhaps no warning until very late in the day that he is not a witness but a suspect.

Under s 442, the DTI may appoint an inspector to investigate and report on the membership of a company and otherwise with respect to the company for the purpose of determining the true identity of persons who are or who have been financially interested in the success or failure (real or apparent) of the company, or able to control or materially to influence the policy of the company.

8.3.5 Application to the courts

Sometimes a director can obtain the assistance of the courts against his fellow directors. A director as such has, however, no special standing in court. As we have seen in previous chapters, even a director commanding a majority of the members' votes may not take over the running of the company *via* the general meeting, but only by forcing his opponents off the board and reversing their policies. He cannot therefore get the general meeting to begin or take over litigation in the company's name. If, on the other hand, he does not command a majority, he is in the same position as any ordinary member when it comes to ventilating a dispute in court.

As we saw in Chapter 7, a minority action is restricted by the rule that so long as nothing fraudulent or ultra vires is being done, the courts will not generally interfere in the internal affairs of a company, but will leave it to the members to settle according to the wishes of the majority under the rule in *Foss v Harbottle*.[21] In that case, two members tried to bring an action on behalf of themselves and the other members against the directors to require them to make good losses sustained as a result of the directors selling their own land to the company for more than it was worth. This would, of course, be a breach of duty, but it was held that as there was nothing to prevent the company itself from taking action, the action must fail. In other words, if the board would not sue, it was up to the majority, if they so wished, to remove the directors and appoint others who would take action.

The majority must have their way, at least if the act complained of is one that they could ratify.

To this rule (see also **7.15.1**) there must be exceptions, if there is to be any effective remedy at all for wrongdoing, and the exceptions are as follows.

(1) Where the act amounts to a 'fraud on the minority' (as in *Cook v Deeks*[22] where the offending directors took some profitable contracts for their own benefit) or are in some other way misappropriating company assets.

(2) Where the wrongdoers prevent the company from taking action in such circumstances that the minority are allowed to bring a derivative action against them. In this situation the company is still the true plaintiff, as required by *Foss v Harbottle*, but it is put in motion by the minority. They bring the action in their own name but in reality on the company's behalf. The need for this type of remedy was explained by Lord Denning MR in *Wallersteiner v Moir (No 2)*.[23]

> 'The rule [*Foss v Harbottle*] is easy enough to apply when the company is defrauded by outsiders. The company itself is the only person who can sue. Likewise, when it is defrauded by insiders of a minor kind, once again the company is the only person who can sue. But suppose it is defrauded by insiders who control its affairs – by directors who hold a majority of the shares – who then can sue for damages? Those directors are themselves the wrongdoers. If a board meeting is held, they will not authorise proceedings to be taken by the company against themselves. If a general meeting is called they will vote down any suggestion that the company should sue them themselves. Yet the company is the one person who is damnified. It is the one person who should sue. In one way or another some means must be found for the company to sue. Otherwise the law would fail in its purpose. Injustice would be done without redress.'

In practice, this exception reinforces the first. In most situations, it means simply that where directors are diverting company assets or benefiting improperly at the company's expense they cannot be allowed to vote their own shares at a general meeting so as to ratify their breach of duty or prevent the company's taking action. To invoke the exception the minority must therefore show a fairly serious breach of duty. Thus, no action lies merely because a third party makes a profit at the company's expense because the directors negligently undervalued an asset when selling it,[24] but the minority may be allowed to proceed where there was serious negligence which actually benefited the negligent parties.[25] Lord Denning's reference to 'injustice' must be read in this light. The policy of the rule in *Foss v Harbottle* is to spare the company the expense of appearing in litigation which it has shown itself unwilling to pursue. If it were enough for the complainant to *allege* injustice, the rule would have no effect at all; if the minority were allowed to prove it as a preliminary matter, there would in effect have been a trial which the rule was intended to avoid.[26] It is, therefore, only when the injustice of denying redress is obvious from the admitted facts that it is a ground for allowing the minority to proceed, and there will be few cases of this sort which do not fall into the fraud on the minority or illegality exceptions.

(3) Where the act complained of is illegal or ultra vires. Here, however, the courts have recently drawn a new line. *Threatened* ultra vires acts may be restrained at the suit of a member – he has a personal right to stop these (as is confirmed by s 35(2)), but even here the action must fail if the third party has an enforceable right against the company. Moreover, in *Smith v Croft (No 2)*,[27] it was held that this did not apply to ultra vires acts *already committed*. These are seen as damaging the company. Consequently, it is for the company to complain, and whether it does so is subject to the rule in *Foss v Harbottle*. On this view the majority may prevent the action proceeding unless there is something bringing the case within the fraud on a minority exception. Section 35A(3) now provides that any decision to relieve directors from liability for ultra vires acts must be made by special resolution. Does this bring the situation into (4) below, even when there is no fraud on the minority? The answer is probably not. In terms the section does not apply to a resolution supporting the directors' refusal to *take action* in the company's name against the wrongdoers. Although the consequences of this and of waiving the breach of duty are the same in practical terms, the refusal to take action does not 'relieve' the directors of liability.

(4) Where the act requires something more than the consent of a simple majority of the members, for example, a special resolution (75 per cent), then the *Foss v Harbottle* principle does not apply and any director or member can apply to the courts to prevent it.[28]

(5) Where a director is being wrongfully excluded from the board by his colleagues he may:

(a) apply to the courts for an injunction;[29] or

(b) apply for a compulsory winding up on the 'just and equitable' ground, if the exclusion amounts to a fundamental breach of an agreement between the shareholders;[30] and possibly

(c) apply for relief under s 459.[31] This will be by no means be available as a matter of course, for s 459 relates to the interests of *members*, not directors. If the director of a small company can show that the exclusion left him as a minority shareholder with little chance of realising the full market value of his shares he might succeed, as he would if he were able to point to wrongful conduct apart from the exclusion. The best hope is to show that there was an agreement or understanding between the members that the complainant would have a place on the board. This is unlikely to work in a larger company or a public company, but it is not absolutely impossible.[32]

(6) If his personal rights as a shareholder are being denied, for example, where the other directors are refusing to record his vote at general meetings, a director, or any other shareholder may ask the courts to enforce them[33] or seek an order under s 459 (see **7.15.4**).[34]

8.3.6 Winding up

In an extreme case a director might feel that, having regard to the extent of the disagreement among the members of the board, the only solution is to put the company into liquidation. This may occur in a private company, particularly where it has some of the characteristics of a partnership.

If the necessary three-quarters majority can be obtained for the passing of a special resolution to wind up, the liquidation can be carried out as a voluntary winding up and, provided a declaration of solvency can be made, it can be a members' voluntary winding up so as to be under the control of the shareholders.[35]

If, on the other hand, the three-quarters majority is not available, the director must consider whether an application to the courts for an order for compulsory winding up would be likely to succeed.

As we have seen, one of the grounds upon which the courts may make such an order is that the courts are of the opinion that it is 'just and equitable' that the company shall be wound up (s 122(1)(g) of the Insolvency Act 1986) and it is on this ground that the director will have to rely in his capacity as a member.

He will succeed, however, only if his case is strong. The following grounds have been successful:

(1) the main object of the company has failed;
(2) the business is fraudulent or illegal or non-existent;
(3) there has been oppression, as where the controlling directors have persistently refused to supply accounts or information;[36]
(4) the company is, in substance, a partnership and the 'partners' have become deadlocked or unable to continue the management;[37]
(5) one party is excluded from the directorship or from management and the facts show an obligation to allow him to participate;[38]
(6) some fundamental term of an agreement between the parties is repudiated.[39]

These cases, culminating in *Westbourne Galleries* and *A & BC Chewing Gum* have undoubtedly strengthened the position of a minority director in a partnership situation or where there is some form of contract between the parties. If he finds himself at odds with his colleagues, as not uncommonly happens in private companies, he now has a powerful deterrent against summary dismissal.

A petition for winding up on the 'just and equitable' ground may be refused if: (i) some other 'remedy' is available to the petitioner; and (ii) he is acting unreasonably in seeking winding up rather than pursuing that remedy (s 125(2) of the Insolvency Act

1986). The 'other remedy' might be under s 459 but need not be a statutory remedy. There might be a minority action available at common law, although given the hazards of such litigation it will be rare for the courts to decide that it is 'unreasonable' to pursue the remedy under the Insolvency Act 1986 instead. The other remedy need not, however, involve litigation at all. Thus, where an incorporated partnership broke down, a petition to wind up the company was refused because the petitioner had turned down perfectly fair offers for his shares, and an order was made for the purchase of his shares at a value based on the date of arbitration not on the date when he was excluded from participation in the company's affairs.[40]

Unless the petitioner has an absolute assurance that he will receive the full value of his shares, however, the courts will let him proceed with the winding-up petition. In *Re Abbey Leisure Ltd*, a joint venture company had run its course,[41] and there was no doubt in principle that the petitioner was therefore entitled to have it wound up, even though the Articles provided nothing to this effect. The majority wished to take on new work. The directors offered to buy out the petitioner's 40 per cent stake in accordance with the Articles. The Court of Appeal held that the Articles did not provide an alternative remedy, since if the majority did not like the result of the independent valuation they could, under the Articles, refuse to buy. The *offer itself* provided a remedy, but not one which it was unreasonable to refuse. This was because it gave no guarantee that the petitioner's shares would not be discounted by the valuer as a minority holding. Since exactly the same is often true where the court orders the petitioner's shares to be bought by the majority on a s 459 petition, it seems to follow that the availability of relief under that section will rarely stop a 'just and equitable' winding-up petition. *Practice Direction No 1 of 1990*,[42] draws attention to the undesirability of including a prayer for the winding up of a company as an alternative to an order for relief from unfair prejudice. However, on occasions such an alternative prayer can be useful since in the course of trial fresh evidence may well come to light which points to the desirability of a winding-up order. In *Re Copeland & Craddock Ltd*,[43] the Court of Appeal considered an appeal against the decision of the trial judge to refuse an application to strike out a petition for the winding up of a company on the just and equitable ground or in the alternative for an order under s 459. The petitioner had adduced evidence to suggest that there had been secret transactions in which some of the respondents had sold company property for cash without recording the receipts in the books of the company. The appeal was dismissed. The alleged transactions could be properly investigated in the course of the winding up of the company.

CHAPTER 8 FOOTNOTES

1　The procedure at meetings is discussed in Chapter 9.

2　By an order under s 459; *Re HR Harmer Ltd* [1958] 3 All ER 689.

3　*Dept of Trade 1974* (HMSO) paras 241–324. It will be appreciated that, even at common law, this could have been stopped, and stopped by a minority in all probability. The transactions, if not approved in advance by the general meeting, would also be voidable (s 322). The principles discussed apply, however, to the responsibility of individual directors for breach of duty to the company (to which should be added, on the facts mentioned, liability to indemnify it (s 322(3)).

4　Paragraph 242.

5　But at best this case shows that he would not be liable for acts done at a meeting from which he was absent and where he had no knowledge of those acts. Today, even that might not be sufficient.

6　But if a director believes that his board's conduct or acquiescence may be steering the company into insolvency, resignation is not a sensible course: see **6.2.6** to **6.2.7**.

7　Had he known of positive misappropriation of the company's assets, it is thought likely that he would have had to stay, rather than resign and, if all else failed, alert the members: see **8.3.2** below.

8　As in *Ramskill v Edwards* (1885) 31 Ch D 100 where a director who signed a cheque for an unauthorised loan was held liable, even though he had protested.

9　[1993] BCC 646.

10　See also *Guidelines for Directors* (Institute of Directors).

11　It is arguable that a director has power to summon meetings by virtue of his office unless the Articles actually exclude it.

12　See Chapter 11 below; the resolution under s 303 may be an ordinary resolution, notwithstanding anything to the contrary in the Articles. If, as sometimes happens with older companies, the Articles provide for a special resolution, a 75 per cent majority would be required and it would be easier to follow the special notice procedure, which cannot be excluded by the Articles. The director must also beware Articles giving directors extra votes in general meeting on a resolution for their removal; such Articles are valid: *Bushell v Faith* [1970] AC 1099.

13　Particularly because the special notice procedure ensures that members receive notice of the resolution before the next meeting but does not compel its inclusion on the agenda: *Pedley v Inland Waterways Association Ltd* [1977] 1 All ER 209.

14　And indeed it may be his duty to do so if he is not to be saddled with the responsibility for what his colleagues are doing (see **8.2**); again, however, subject to the proviso that, if the issue relates to the company's solvency, resignation may be counter-productive for the director himself.

15　[1997] BCC 172.

16　In the case of *First Re-investment Trust Limited* (**8.2**) the board passed a resolution requesting the DTI to appoint inspectors and the DTI then exercised its discretionary power under what is now s 432.

17　The inspectors may, however, be appointed under s 432 on the basis that their report will not be published.

18　Application No 19187/910.

19　[1997] BCC 872.

20　[1998] BCC 379.

21　(1843) 2 Hare 461.

22　[1916] 1 AC 554.

23　[1975] 1 All ER 849, at p 857.

24　*Pavlides v Jensen* [1956] Ch 565.

25　*Daniels v Daniels* [1978] Ch 406.

26　*Prudential Assurance Co v Newman Industries Ltd (No 2)* [1982] 2 WLR 31.

27　[1988] Ch 114.

28　*Baillie v Oriental Telephone Co* [1915] 1 Ch 503.

29　*Hayes v Bristol Plant Hire Ltd* [1957] 1 All ER 685.

30　*Re A & BC Chewing Gum Ltd* [1975] 1 All ER 1017: see also the question of removal from office as opposed to exclusion from board meetings in Chapter 11, below.

31　*Re London School of Electronics Ltd* [1986] Ch 211; *Re a Company (No 00477 of 1986)* [1986] BCLC 376.

32 *Re Ringtower Holdings plc* (1988) 5 BCC 82, at pp 93–94. Usually the free transferability of public company shares will mean that the petitioner can simply sell up and go, and it will not be easy to show how his interests as a member have been prejudiced, let alone unfairly.

33 *Pender v Lushington* (1877) 6 Ch D 70.

34 On an application under s 459 the courts have power under s 461 to authorise action in the company's name and, on its behalf, a statutory form of derivative action.

35 Sections 84(1)(b) and 89 of the Insolvency Act 1986.

36 *Loch v John Blackwood Ltd* [1924] AC 783.

37 *Re Yenidje Tobacco Co Ltd* [1916] 2 Ch 426 where the two 50:50 shareholders and directors could not agree about anything. Winding up was ordered even though the company was still profitable.

38 *Re Westbourne Galleries* [1972] 2 All ER 492.

39 *Re A & BC Chewing Gum Ltd* [1975] 1 All ER 1017.

40 *Re a Company (No 002567 of 1982)* [1983] 1 WLR 927.

41 [1990] BCLC 342.

42 [1990] BCC 292.

43 [1997] BCC 294.

Chapter 9

MEETINGS

9.1 SHAREHOLDERS' MEETINGS

9.1.1 Annual general meeting

Directors are actively involved with meetings of two kinds, general meetings of shareholders and board meetings of the directors. Both law and procedure are important and directors must be familiar with the main features.

The holding of an annual general meeting (AGM) of the members is an obligation imposed by the Act as follows.

(1) Section 366 requires the meeting to be held in every calendar year and not more than 15 months after the last one. These are distinct duties, and their object is to ensure that the members have at least one opportunity in every year to hear and to question their directors.

(2) However, s 366A permits a private company to choose, by passing an elective resolution, to dispense with the need to hold an AGM in the year in which the elective resolution is passed, and subsequent years. See **9.7.2(3)** below. If an AGM is to be held, a new company may omit the AGM in its first and second calendar years, provided the first AGM is held within 18 months of incorporation (s 366(3)).

(3) The procedure is governed mainly by regs 36 to 63 of Table A, which are usually adopted. The 1985 Table A does not specify what the business of the AGM is to be. Where Articles do make specific provision as was the case in previous Table A's, business will generally be divided into general or ordinary business:

   (a) consideration of accounts and balance sheets;
   (b) consideration of directors' and auditors' reports;
   (c) declaration of dividends;
   (d) election of directors; and
   (e) appointment and remuneration of auditors; and
   (f) special business, meaning any other business.[1]

If the accounts are not ready for the AGM the meeting should still be held so as to comply with s 366. All the other business can be dealt with save laying of the accounts, and reappointment of auditors and the meeting adjourned to a later date, when the accounts can be presented and the auditors reappointed. Alternatively, the meeting can be closed and an EGM called to receive the accounts.[2]

(4) However, a private company may choose, by passing an elective resolution, to dispense with the need to lay the accounts before the general meeting, and with the need to appoint auditors annually, in respect of the financial year in which the elective resolutions are passed, and subsequent financial years.[3] See **9.7.2(3)** below.

If an AGM is to be held, the duty to call the AGM is that of the directors under their general management functions in reg 70, Table A. Their power to call meetings lies in reg 37. If (rather improbably) the Articles make no provision at all for calling meetings, two or more members holding at least 10 per cent of the issued capital may call a meeting (s 370(3)). If the company fails to hold a meeting, any member may ask the DTI to convene a meeting, which it may do on such terms as it sees fit including, if necessary, a direction that one member present in person or by proxy shall constitute the meeting (s 367).

(5) The penalty for default or failure to comply with the requirements of the DTI is a fine (up to £5,000, or unlimited in the case of conviction on indictment) on the company and every officer in default (s 366(4)).

(6) In addition to the requirements of the Act and the Articles, the AGM is usually the occasion for the chairman's report on the accounts and prospects of the company, and for members' questions.

The chairman's report, although normally circulated with the accounts, is not a statutory or formal document and so can be used for any desired purpose. Thus, he can explain, items in the accounts or, indeed, correct misleading impressions which the statutory information might otherwise create. For example, some companies, without disclosing personal information, state the amount of tax which a typical taxpayer would have to meet, in respect of the directors' remuneration.[4]

(7) Special business of any kind may be taken at the AGM, for example, in regard to alterations of share capital, issuing of new shares, alterations of the Articles, approval of directors' compensation, incentive schemes, borrowing powers. The nature and details of such matters as special business must be specified in the notice calling the meeting (see **9.3**).

9.1.2   Extraordinary general meeting

Any other general meeting is an extraordinary general meeting (EGM) and the following provisions apply.

(1) The directors (by reg 37, Table A) may call such a meeting whenever they think fit.[5]

(2) If there are not, in the UK, sufficient directors to form a quorum, then any director or any member may call an EGM as though they were the board (reg 37).

(3) The directors must call an EGM on the requisition of the holders of not less than one-tenth of the paid up voting capital, regardless of anything in the Articles (s 368).

The requisition[6] must:

    (a)   state the objects of the meeting;

    (b)   be signed by the requisitionists; and

    (c)   be deposited at the registered office.

(4)   If the directors do not call the meeting requested under s 368 within 21 days, then the requisitionists or the holders of more than half of their voting rights may call it themselves within three months and not later than 28 days after the date of the notice calling the meeting (s 368(4)). The directors are regarded as not having duly convened a meeting should they convene it for a date more than 28 days after the date of notice convening the meeting. This is the effect of the new s 368(8) which was inserted by the Companies Act 1989, Sch 19, para 9. Prior to this, s 368 did not specify a time within which the meeting had to take place. Table A, reg 37 provides that the meeting must be convened for a date not later than eight weeks after the receipt of the requisition by the directors. However, Table A could, of course, always be amended, and, in the absence of reg 37, a meeting could be called by the directors to be held on a date several months after the sending out of the notice; see *Re Windward Islands (Enterprises) UK Ltd.*[7] The new s 368(8) prevents this. Thus the maximum time which the directors can exploit between their receiving the requisition and the holding of the meeting is seven weeks. It will accordingly, be necessary for Table A, reg 37 to be amended in due course. Their expenses must be paid by the company which must deduct it from the remuneration of the defaulting directors.[8]

(5)   If the Articles 'do not make other provision', then two or more members holding one-tenth of the issued share capital may call a meeting themselves and presumably bear the cost themselves (s 370(3)). Formerly, most Articles did make 'other provision' (for example, reg 49 of Table A, 1948 version) but the section does now have some substance for companies adopting Table A, 1985 version, which is silent on this matter.

(6)   If it is impracticable to call an EGM in any of these ways, then the court may call a meeting on such terms as it thinks fit – including a direction, if necessary, that one member present in person or by proxy, shall constitute the meeting (s 371). The courts will use this power where minority shareholders (by deliberately absenting themselves) are using the quorum requirements to deny the majority the right to cast their votes. For example, in *Re El Sombrero Ltd*[10] the company had three shareholders. One had 90 per cent of the shares but was not a director. The other two had five per cent each and were the directors. The 90 per cent shareholder requisitioned a meeting at which he wished to remove the directors. Having called the meeting, the directors then failed to attend. Accordingly, there was no quorum and so the business could not be transacted. The court ordered that one member present, whether in person or by proxy, could validly constitute a quorate meeting. This decision was followed in *Re Opera Photographic Ltd.*[11] Here, there were two directors holding 51 per cent and 49 per cent of the shares respectively. A meeting was requisitioned by the holder of 51 per cent of the shares for the purpose of removing the other director. The meeting was duly convened but, since the other director failed to attend, was rendered inquorate. The court was again prepared to allow one director to constitute a meeting. In each of these cases, the court placed emphasis on the entitlement of the majority shareholder to control the affairs of the company.

Although s 371 refers to meetings of the company, it would seem that the power of the court extends to regulate meetings of directors as well. In *Re Sticky Fingers Restaurant Ltd*,[12] the company was owned by two shareholders, one of whom held 66 of the 100 issued shares and the other held 34. The holder of the 66 shares was not involved in the day-to-day management of the business, which was the responsibility of the holder of 34 shares. They were the only directors of the company and a major dispute had arisen between them. The result was that there could be no effective meetings either of the company or the board because the holder of the 34 shares failed to attend. He was, in fact, bringing proceedings for unfair prejudice under s 459. The majority shareholder now made an application under s 371 on the basis that, pending the end of the s 459 proceedings, the company needed an effective board of directors. Davies J ordered that the majority shareholder alone could constitute a general meeting of the company, which order was necessary so as to enable an effective board of directors to be brought into being. The conduct of the minority shareholder in not attending meetings should not be permitted to prevent the running of the company until after the s 459 proceedings had been disposed of. However, it would not, on the other hand, be fair for the majority shareholder to use s 371 so as to remove the minority shareholder as a director or exclude him from taking part in the affairs of the company until the s 459 proceedings were closed. Accordingly, the s 371 order was qualified so as to provide that the meeting would not be used to dismiss the minority shareholder from his directorship or to exclude him from his rights and duties as a director. Moreover, the minority shareholder, who had all along been responsible for the day-to-day conduct of the business, should be allowed to continue to run the business so long as he did so as he had done in the past. This case was distinguished by Harman J in *Re Whitchurch Insurance Consultants Ltd*.[13] Here, again, the company had two shareholder directors, the majority shareholder holding 66 per cent of the shares and the minority shareholder 34 per cent. They were a couple who had lived together as man and wife for a long period of time but sometime before the hearing the relationship had broken down and the parties had ceased to live together. Because the minority shareholder refused to attend any company or board meetings, the business of the company could not be carried on. The majority shareholder was, accordingly, seeking an order under s 371. The minority shareholder was, at the same time, bringing proceedings under s 459. In *Re Sticky Fingers Restaurant Ltd*, Davies J had said 'It is not a proper use of s 371 to use it indirectly to secure the removal of a director while a s 459 petition is pending'. In *Re Whitchurch Insurance Consultants Ltd*, Harman J said that he did not think this was correct.

> 'I cannot think that the mere existence of a s 459 petition at the date of the hearing of the s 371 application is inevitably a bar. It may be a bar. It is obviously a matter which bears upon the discretion of the court, but it is not something which prevents a court exercising its powers . . . I am wholly satisfied that it is impracticable to hold a meeting within the meaning of that word and, in my view, it is plainly right and desirable to get a proper board into this company by allowing the meeting to be held for the purpose of dealing with the present inquorate state, both of board meetings and general meetings.'

(7) Under s 142, the directors of a public company must convene an EGM in the event of a serious loss of capital. This means that the company's net assets have fallen to 50 per cent or less of its called up capital. A meeting must then be called within 28 days of this coming to the knowledge of a director (since failure to do so is a criminal offence in each director who authorises or permits the default 'knowingly and wilfully' it may probably be assumed for practical purposes that actual knowledge is required and not constructive knowledge). The meeting itself must be held within 56 days of the discovery. The business of the meeting is confined by s 142(3) to matters relevant to the capital loss, but some leeway is given by s 142(1) which provides that the meeting is to consider 'whether, and if so what, steps should be taken to deal with the situation'; the relationship between these words and s 142(3) may well give rise to argument.

(8) All business at an EGM is special business, which must be specified in the notice. Moreover, the notice will be confined (in the case of a requisition from members under s 368) to the matters stated in the requisition.[14]

9.1.3 Class meetings

Where a company's capital is divided into different classes of shares, it has been commonly provided by the Articles that the rights attached to each class (for example, the rate of preferential dividend) may be varied by extraordinary resolution at a separate general meeting of members holding shares of that class. However, this provision was removed from Table A (1948 version) for companies registering after 21 December 1980 by s 88 of the Companies Act of that year, and Table A (1985 version) has no special provision. Instead, variation of class rights is governed by the Act itself, to which attention must therefore be paid even in the case of companies whose Articles do contain such a provision. Class rights may be derived from provisions of the Memorandum, from the Articles, or from some other effective source, for instance, the terms of a resolution or issue. The commonest source is the Articles, and the source is, as will be seen, material to the manner in which the rights may be varied.

What actually *constitutes* a 'class right' is another question. The 'norm' is the case where particular shares have special rights or benefits attached to them which are not attached to other shares (for example, a right to dividend or to share in any surplus on winding up). This would probably be so even though the rights are 'personal' to a particular holder in the sense that they come to an end when he transfers the shares, for while he remains owner of those shares they clearly enough constitute a block – or class – to which special rights for the time being remain attached. By way of contrast, purely personal rights not attaching to any particular shares cannot be class rights. Thus, a provision in the Articles that a member should be the company's solicitor will not constitute a class right if it affects no particular shares, and does not affect the member in his capacity as a member.[15] If, on the other hand, rights or benefits do not attach to particular shares, but do affect the member in his capacity as such, his shares may form a second type of 'class', distinct from the 'norm' described above but equally to be treated as giving rise to 'class rights'. Thus, in *Bushell v Faith*,[16] the Articles conferred three votes per share to a director's shares in the event of a resolution to remove him attached to no specified shares, merely the shares which a director held from time to time. This created two classes, shareholders and shareholders who were directors.

Similarly, in *Cumbrian Newspapers Group Ltd v Cumberland & Westmoreland Herald Newspaper and Printing Company*,[17] the Articles were amended to give a new member rights of pre-emption, to appoint a director, and certain rights over unissued shares. This was to put the new member in a position to block a takeover. These rights were held to constitute class rights, attached therefore to the shares held for the time being by the new member and, accordingly, unalterable except in accordance with the procedures described below; they could not therefore be altered merely by passing a special resolution at a general meeting of the company (s 9) any more than would be the case if they were attached to particular shares. The consent of the class members must always be obtained, but how this is to be done depends, among other things, upon how the class rights were conferred.

(1) If the class rights are conferred by the Memorandum, *and* neither the Memorandum nor the Articles contains a power to vary those rights, they may be varied if all the members of the company agree: s 125(5).

(2) If the class rights are conferred in some other way (for example, by the Articles or by resolution) *and* the Articles contain no power to vary them, they may be varied only by:

    (a) the written consent of 75 per cent in nominal value of the class; *or*

    (b) extraordinary resolution (75 per cent majority) passed at a separate class meeting. If there is some other requirement for variation (for example, in the resolution to issue the shares), that requirement must also be complied with: s 125(2).

(3) If the class rights (however conferred) are subject to a power to vary contained in the Memorandum or Articles, then if the proposed variation is connected with *either*:

    (a) an authority to allot shares under s 80, or its variation, revocation or renewal (see **3.3** above); *or*

    (b) a reduction of capital under s 135 (see **1.5.4**) then there must be either:

        (i) written consent of 75 per cent of the class by nominal value; or

        (ii) an extraordinary resolution at a class meeting.

In addition, any further requirement of the Memorandum or Articles governing the power to vary must be complied with: s 125(3).

(4) If the class rights are conferred by the Memorandum, and the Articles contain a power to vary, which was included in the Articles when the company was first formed, the variation must comply with that provision in the Articles: s 125(4)(a).[18]

(5) If the class rights are conferred otherwise than in the Memorandum, and the Articles contain a power to vary (whenever that power was put into the Articles), the variation must comply with that provision in the Articles: s 125(4)(b).
[Note that if the variation is for a purpose falling within paragraph (3) above, *that* paragraph applies, and not paragraph (4) or (5).]

(6) An alteration or insertion of a power in the Articles to vary class rights is itself treated as a variation of those rights: s 125(7). Where class rights are contained in the Memorandum or Articles, the abrogation of those rights is to be treated as a variation: s 125(8).

(7) Section 125 is not quite a complete code for the variation of class rights. If the rights are conferred by the Memorandum, and the Articles do not authorise their alteration but the Memorandum does, they may be varied in accordance with the Memorandum.

(8) Section 125 does not affect the question of what amounts to a 'variation' and two decisions in particular may weaken the statutory protection:

    (a) that the alteration of voting rights of *other* shares under a power in the Articles is not a variation of the *class* rights;[19] and

    (b) that the issue of new shares of the same class is not a variation.[20]

Such action obviously weakens the position of the existing class members. It is possible, but no more, that objection could be taken on the general principle of lack of good faith, without resort to a complaint under the Act.[21]

(9) A variation of class rights may, however, be reviewed by the courts under s 127, which seeks to ensure that variations within the meaning of the Act will not operate unfairly. The holders of 15 per cent or more of the class shares who did not agree to or vote for the variation may within 21 days apply to the courts for cancellation of the variation, which is then suspended until and unless confirmed by the courts. The courts may disallow the variation if satisfied, in all the circumstances, that it would unfairly prejudice class members; otherwise, it must confirm the variation.

In any event, nothing in s 125 above affects the courts' powers:

    (a) under ss 4 to 6 (resolutions to alter the objects);

    (b) under s 54 (objection to a public company reregistering as private);

    (c) under s 425 (company compromising with members and creditors);[22]

    (d) under s 427 (reconstruction or amalgamation); or

    (e) under ss 459 to 461 (protection of minorities).

(10) Sections 369, 370, 376 and 377 (length of notice, voting and members' resolutions) and the ordinary provisions of the Articles govern the procedure for class meetings except to the extent that s 125(6) makes specific provision:

    (a) that the quorum must be two persons holding personally or by proxy at least one-third of the class, except at an adjourned meeting where one member or his proxy suffices;

    (b) that any class member or his proxy may demand a poll.

9.2 COMMUNICATIONS BETWEEN SHAREHOLDERS

Section 376 of the Act gives members representing not less than one-twentieth of the total voting rights, or not less than 100 members holding shares on which there has been paid up an average sum per member of not less than £100, the right to require the company:

(1) to give to the members notice of a resolution[23] which it is proposed to move at the next annual general meeting; this must be lodged with the company six weeks before the meeting;

(2) to circulate to the members entitled to notice of any general meeting a statement of not more than 1,000 words with respect to the business of the meeting; this must be lodged one week before the meeting.

By s 376(1) the cost of doing this must fall upon the requisitionists unless the company otherwise resolves. This is amplified by s 377(1)(b), which excuses the company from its obligation to comply with s 376 unless there is deposited with the company a sum reasonably sufficient to meet the company's expenses in giving effect to it. The court can also, under s 377(3), excuse the company from the obligation to circulate defamatory matter.

9.3 NOTICE OF GENERAL MEETINGS

The question of notice is governed partly by the Act and partly by the Articles.

(1) Section 369 provides that, despite anything in the Articles:

   (a) an AGM requires at least 21 clear days' written notice;
   (b) an EGM requires at least 14 clear days' written notice, unless a special resolution is to be proposed, in which case 21 clear days' notice is required. Under Table A, reg 38 an EGM called for the purpose of appointing a person as a director also requires the giving of 21 clear days' notice. Additionally, 21 clear days' notice is needed for ordinary resolutions following s 379 special notice (see **9.4** below).

(2) An EGM also requires 21 days' notice if an elective resolution is to be proposed.[24]

(3) By reg 38 of Table A, this means clear days' notice, exclusive both of the day of service and of the day of the meeting. Care should be taken if notice is dispatched by post, since a prepaid and properly addressed envelope is, for the purposes of calculating the notice period, deemed by reg 115 of the 1985 Table A to arrive 48 hours after it was posted. Consequently, a notice sent by post on Saturday will be deemed to have arrived on Monday. The first day of the notice period is therefore Tuesday. Interestingly, under the 1948 Table A, reg 131, which still applies to many companies, notices sent by post are deemed to arrive 24 hours after posting. The 1929 Table A, reg 103 provides that notices of meetings sent by post are deemed to be received on the day of posting. And, under the 1908 Table A, reg 110, all notices, whether of meetings or otherwise, are deemed to have been effected at the time at which the letter would be delivered in the ordinary course of post.

(4) Shorter notice may be accepted by:

   (a) all the members entitled to attend and vote in the case of the AGM;
   (b) a majority in number and 95 per cent in value in the case of an EGM.[25]

These provisions are particularly useful for private companies with a small membership, and can be used, if desired, to dispense with the need for a notice period altogether. The members must be made aware, however, that resolutions are being passed, if that is the case, what those resolutions relate to.[26] Additionally, a private company may have passed an elective resolution under which the 95 per cent requirement for an EGM has been reduced. However, even if such an elective resolution has been passed, the required percentage can never be reduced to less than 90 per cent[27] (see **9.7.2**(3) below).

However, if the business of the meeting includes the passing of an elective resolution, the full 21 days' notice should always be given.

(5) Service of notice is to be given to every member under s 370 of the 1948 Act, unless the Articles provide otherwise. Regulation 38 of Table A requires service upon:

(a) every member except those who have not supplied an address within the UK. Service by ordinary prepaid post is sufficient and is deemed to have been effected 48 hours later (reg 115);

(b) every personal representative of a dead member (reg 116);

(c) the trustee in bankruptcy of a bankrupt member (reg 116).

The Articles may exclude certain classes such as preference shareholders, from the right to notice. Accidental omissions are excused by reg 39 of Table A, but this does not include an error of law, such as believing that unpaid vendors were no longer members.[28] However, a procedural irregularity, such as the absence of formal board authority for the meeting, which the majority could cure by going through the proper processes, will not entitle an objector to an injunction.[29]

In addition, the auditors are entitled to receive notice of all general meetings of the company: s 387 and reg 38, Table A.

By Table A, proof that an envelope containing a notice was properly addressed, prepaid and posted is conclusive evidence that the notice was given. A similar provision is contained in s 90(2) in connection with rights issues. Such a rights offer is deemed to be made at the time at which the letter would be delivered in the ordinary course of post. However, it seems that this is superseded by actual knowledge on the part of the directors that the offer has not been received. In *Re Thundercrest Ltd*,[30] the company, having three shareholders, was proposing a rights issue to raise cash for the most noble of causes, the payment of solicitors' fees. The company needed to raise funds to carry on litigation which was likely to result in substantial damages for it. A letter of provisional allotment and form of acceptance was sent by recorded delivery post to the plaintiff. At the time of the allotment of the shares the directors, who were the other two shareholders, had returned by the Post Office this letter of provisional allotment and so they knew that the documentation had not been delivered to the plaintiff. They were also fully aware that the plaintiff wanted to take up his entitlement of shares. At the meeting for the allotment of shares, the other two members took the plaintiff's entitlement equally between them. The plaintiff then brought proceedings under s 359 for rectification of the register. It was held by Judge Paul Baker QC that the actual knowledge that the usual letter of allotment had not been received superseded the deeming provisions of both Table A and s 90. Having said this, it would seem that the decision in *Re Thundercrest Ltd* must be restricted to relatively small companies. As the learned judge explained:

'The purpose of deeming provisions in the case of management of companies is clear. In the case of uncertainty as to whether a document has been delivered, with large numbers of shareholders and so forth, there has to be some rule under which those in charge of the management can carry on the business without having to investigate every case where some shareholder comes along and says he has not got the document. The directors have to proceed and transact the company's business on the basis of the deeming provisions. But, in my judgment, all that falls away when you find it is established without any possibility of challenge that the document has not been delivered.'

(6) Contents of the notice are prescribed as follows.

   (a) Regulation 38 of Table A requires it to specify the place, time, and the general nature of the business.[31] Apart from those matters set out in **9.1.1** which will usually be self-explanatory, there must be sufficient information and, if necessary, explanation for the member to decide whether or not to attend and vote. This may require forethought and care.[32]

   (b) The AGM must be specified as such in the notice calling it.

   (c) The exact wording of special elective and extraordinary resolutions must be set out in the notice which must also specify the type of the resolution (s 378(2)).

   (d) The notice must state with reasonable prominence, the right of every member to appoint a proxy, who need not be a member (s 372).

(7) At common law, the failure to give notice of a meeting to every person entitled to attend and vote invalidated any proceedings at the meeting: see *Young v Ladies' Imperial Club*.[33] To combat the obvious inconvenience of such a rule, Table A reg 39 provides that accidental failure to give notice of a meeting to, or the non-receipt of a notice by, any person entitled to receive such notice shall not invalidate the proceedings at that meeting. The word 'accidental' has, in such circumstances, to be given its specific meaning. For example, in *Re West Canadian Collieries Ltd*,[34] some plates were omitted from an addressograph machine, which resulted in a number of members not receiving notice of a meeting. It was held that this was accidental failure and thus the outcome of the meeting was not affected. On the other hand, in *Musselwhite v Musselwhite & Son Ltd*,[35] a secretary failed to give notice to a member who had sold his shares but whose name had not yet been replaced by that of the purchaser on the register of members. It was held that this was far from an accidental omission. For all that, it was mistaken but it was nevertheless deliberate and so the meeting was invalidated.

9.4   SPECIAL NOTICE

Special notice has nothing to do with notice in the normal sense of notice to the members. It is a technical term used in s 379 for a notice to the company to be given by a party who proposes to move certain types of ordinary resolution at the next general meeting. The procedure is as follows.

(1) Special notice has to be given of intention to propose ordinary resolutions:

   (a) to remove a director (s 303);

(b) unless the Articles provide otherwise, or a special resolution to the contrary has been passed, to appoint a director aged over 70 to a public company or its subsidiary (s 293):

(c) to appoint a new auditor, fill a casual vacancy in the office of auditor, reappoint an appointee of the directors or to remove an auditor (s 388).

(2) The intending proposer of such resolutions must give his special notice to the company not less that 28 days before the meeting. The company must then notify the members either with the notice of meeting or (if that is not practicable) by advertisement or in any other manner permitted by the Articles, not less than 21 days before the meeting. Thus, 21 days' notice is required, even though the resolution to be proposed is an ordinary resolution, normally requiring only 14 days' notice, consent to short notice should not be sought. If the directors call the meeting less than 28 days after the special notice is served on them, the notice is still valid. It may be noted that the result of the 28-day requirement is that shareholders who wish to propose the removal of a director or auditor at the AGM must serve their special notice before they have seen the accounts and the directors' report. But s 379 does *not* entitle the proposer to have notice of his intended resolution to dismiss a director circulated to the other members unless he can raise a requisition under s 376.[36]

(3) The special notice may be left at or posted to the registered office (s 725).

9.5   QUORUM

The quorum (Latin for 'of whom') means the minimum number of members whose presence is necessary in order that business may legally be transacted. The requirements with regard to general meetings are as follows.

(1) Insofar as the Articles do not make any other provision, s 370(4) of the Act provides that the quorum shall be two members present in person.

(2) The usual Articles in fact permit two persons present, being members or proxies or representatives of corporate shareholders: reg 40, Table A.

(3) The quorum should be present at the beginning of the meeting, when it proceeds to business.[37] However, there must be at least two members present throughout the meeting when business is being conducted.[38] The 1948 Table A, reg 53 rather ambiguously provided 'No business shall be transacted at any general meeting unless a quorum of members is present at the time when the meeting proceeds to business'. The 1985 Table A, reg 40 is more straightforward. 'No business shall be transacted at any meeting unless a quorum is present.'

(4) One person cannot constitute a meeting[39] even as proxy for all the members,[40] except:

(a) at a class meeting where he holds all the shares of a class;[41] and

(b) where the court or the DTI order otherwise under ss 367 or 371 of the Act;

(c) where the company is a single member company.

Subject to this requirement, one individual may count as more than one member if he holds shares in two or more capacities, as where he has both a private holding and a trust holding.[42]

(5) A representative of a corporate shareholder counts in the quorum,[43] but not an executor or administrator of a deceased shareholder, unless he has been registered as a member (Table A, reg 3).

(6) If there is no quorum within half an hour of the due time, or the quorum is lost during the meeting, the meeting is (by reg 41 of Table A) adjourned for one week to the same time and in the same place (or as the directors may determine). At the adjourned meeting the same quorum applies.[44] If minority shareholders use the quorum requirements to frustrate the wishes of the majority, by deliberately absenting themselves from meetings, the court will resolve the problem by calling a meeting under s 371.[45]

9.6   CHAIRMAN

The chairman's role is of obvious importance and it may fall to the lot of any director.

(1) Regulation 42 of Table A requires that the chairman of the board[46] shall take the chair at general meetings or, if he is unwilling or not present within 15 minutes, the directors may appoint any one of themselves. Failing that, the members present may elect any one of their number (reg 43).

(2) If there is no provision in the Articles, the members may elect any member as chairman (s 370).

(3) The chairman's duties are:

(a) to preserve order;

(b) to conduct the proceedings in the proper manner;

(c) to allow shareholders to have a reasonable opportunity to speak, but then to propose, if he thinks fit, that the discussion be terminated;[47]

(d) to see that the sense of the meeting is fairly ascertained, if necessary by means of a properly taken show-of-hands or poll;

(e) to decide incidental questions such as the validity of proxies.

(4) By reg 50 of Table A, the chairman has a casting vote in the event of a tie, either on a show of hands or a poll.

(5) Adjournment is not within his sole discretion, but reg 45 of Table A allows him to adjourn the meeting, with its consent (ie by a majority) and he must do so if the meeting so directs. Only the unfinished business may be dealt with at the adjourned meeting and no notice is needed unless it is for 14 days or more, in which case seven clear days' notice specifying the time and place, and the general nature of the business, is required. Apart from reg 45, he may adjourn on his own authority in the case of disorder or order the removal of anyone present who persists in acting in a disorderly manner after being asked to withdraw. If the chairman purports to adjourn improperly, the members may elect another chairman and continue with the business.[48]

An example of an improperly adjourned meeting arose in the case of *Byng v London Life Association Ltd*.[49] Notice was properly given of an extraordinary general meeting of the company to be held at The Barbican in London at 12 noon on a specified day. The location was too small to accommodate all those members who wished to be present at the meeting. Accordingly, the chairman purported to adjourn the meeting to 2.30 pm on the same day at the Cafe Royal, some distance away. The reconvened meeting was duly held and passed the only resolution of which notice had been given. The plaintiff, who was a shareholder in the company, brought proceedings claiming that the chairman had invalidly adjourned the meeting and thus all the business conducted at the reconvened meeting had been invalidly conducted. This was held by the Court of Appeal to have been the case, although the chairman had acted in good faith, his decision to adjourn had not been validly taken.

9.7   RESOLUTIONS

9.7.1   Informal

Before considering the passing of resolutions at general meetings, we may take note of the extent to which they can be passed without formality or the need for a formal meeting at all. The position is as follows.

(1) If all the members are present and assent to a proposal, it does not matter that there has been no formal resolution.[50]
(2) It appears that unanimous assent of the members to any proposal will generally suffice, without any meeting at all. Thus, in *Re Duomatic Ltd*,[51] the agreement of the two sole shareholders could amount to ratification of improperly paid salaries even though there was no shareholders' meeting. This 'principle of unanimity' has been applied even to special and extraordinary resolutions.[52]
(3) Notice of general meetings can be shortened or dispensed with altogether, in the case of:

   (a) the annual general meeting by the consent of all voting members; and
   (b) an extraordinary general meeting by the consent of a majority in number representing 95 per cent of the voting shares (s 369(3), (4)) or, if the company has passed an elective resolution to that effect, some lesser percentage. However, the percentage may not be reduced to less than 90 per cent.[53]

Consent to short notice may be implied if all members attend, even if not all vote.[54] This also means that by agreement the members may waive a defect in the notice of the meeting. However, if the business of the meeting includes the passing of an elective resolution, the full 21 days' notice should always be given.
(4) Regulation 53 of Table A provides that a resolution in writing signed by all the members entitled to vote shall be as valid as if passed at a general meeting. This seems to be envisaged even for special and extraordinary resolutions by s 380 of the Act although not for elective resolutions. The tendency of the courts is to regard a company as bound by any unanimous act of the members no matter when or how it is carried out.[55] But unanimity clears only the immediate procedural hurdle. If there are other requirements, these must be met. For example, an agreement in writing signed by all the members is effective to start a capital reduction under s 135; but the court is unlikely to confirm the reduction unless a special resolution is produced.[56] Certainly, there are procedures under the Act which involve the passing of members' resolutions, where use of a

written resolution pursuant to reg 53 in Table A would render the procedure unlawful. These are procedures involving approval of documents under which the document must be presented to the members at a general meeting. For example, in the case of an off-market purchase of its own shares from a member by a private company, the contract between the company and the member (or if it is not a written contract, a memorandum of its terms) must be approved by a special resolution of the members.[57] The resolution is not effective unless a copy of the contract (or Memorandum) is available for inspection at the meeting at which the resolution is proposed and for 15 days before it. Thus, a reg 53 written resolution would not satisfy the procedural requirements. Additionally, it is likely that the court would strike down a written resolution pursuant to reg 53 which purported to remove a director or auditor. In such cases, special notice (see **9.4** above) is required, the aim of which is to allow the director or auditor time and opportunity to mount a defence. A written resolution would necessarily cut down that time and opportunity, and would not be permitted.

(5)   However, the Companies Act 1989 introduced a new procedure for private companies, whereby written resolutions signed by all the members entitled to vote are given a statutory guarantee of validity, provided that they are dealt with in a certain way.[58] Thus, with two stated exceptions, *all* resolutions, whether special, extraordinary, ordinary or elective, can be passed as resolutions in writing, provided that the new procedure is followed. The two exceptions are resolutions to remove a director under s 303 and to remove an auditor under s 391.[59] This mirrors the likely attitude of the court to use of written resolutions pursuant to reg 53 in Table A to effect these decisions.

As under reg 53 in Table A, the resolution in writing may comprise one instrument signed by all members entitled to vote, or any number of identical instruments, signed by different members but so that all have signed at least one.

Under the new procedure, as it was introduced, a copy of the proposed resolution in writing had to be given to the auditor. Within seven days of receipt, the auditor had either to:

(1)   state that the resolution did not concern him; or
(2)   state that it did concern him but need not be put to a general meeting; or
(3)   state that it did concern him and had to be put to a general meeting.

Thus, it can be seen that the auditor had a right to veto the written resolution procedure. This new procedure, as introduced, left one substantial question unanswered. As has been said, the 1985 Table A, reg 53 envisaged the possibility of a written resolution being signed by all the members of the company. Similarly, reg 73A of the 1948 Table A, substituted by the Companies Act 1981 to take effect from 3 December 1981 envisaged the possibility of a written resolution. (Previous Table As did not contain such a provision.) Supposing that a company had the 1948 or the 1985 Table A provision and such a company wanted to pass a written resolution, could it rely upon its Article and ignore the requirement in s 381 that a copy be sent to the auditor who should have a power of veto? This particular question was never litigated, but it was obviously unsatisfactory that the law should have been uncertain.

For this reason, the Deregulation (Resolutions of Private Companies) Order 1996, SI 1996/1471 was passed and took effect from 19 June 1996. It inserts new provisions into s 381 to clarify the position. By s 381B, if a director or secretary of a company knows that it is proposed to seek to pass a resolution using the written resolution procedure, he must, if the company has auditors, ensure that a copy of the resolution is sent to them or that they are otherwise notified of its contents either at or before the time when the resolution is sent to a member for signature. A person who fails to comply with this provision is liable to a fine. It is, however, a defence for him to prove that the circumstances were such that it was not practicable for him to comply with the requirement to send a copy to the auditor or alternatively that he believed on reasonable grounds that a copy of the resolution had either been sent already to the auditors, or that they had already been informed of its contents. By s 381C, these provisions are stated to have effect notwithstanding any provision in the company's Memorandum or Articles, although they are expressly stated not to prejudice any power conferred by any such provision. Quite what is meant by these words is unclear. However, it is thought sensible that a copy of a written resolution should always be sent to the auditor, if the company has one, since he can in reality now do nothing to prevent its being passed.

9.7.2 Formal

Resolutions passed at general meetings are of four types, special and extraordinary (75 per cent majorities) for certain specified purposes, elective (100 per cent majority) for certain specified purposes, and ordinary (bare majority) for all other purposes. Thus, wherever the consent of the members is required, and nothing more is stipulated by the Act or the Articles, a bare majority of those who attend and vote at the general meeting will suffice.

(1) Extraordinary resolutions are required for:

(a) liquidation on the grounds of insolvency (Insolvency Act 1986, s 84(1)(c));
(b) authorising a liquidator to pay creditors in full or to make compromises (Insolvency Act 1986, s 165);
(c) certain variations of class rights (s 125).

The only practical difference from a special resolution is that it normally requires 14 days', instead of 21 days' notice.[60] The resolution must be set out verbatim in the notice of the meeting and a copy must be filed with the registrar within 15 days.[61] The required majority is three-quarters of those who attend and vote at the general meeting.

(2) Special resolutions are similar in all respects to extraordinary resolutions except that 21 days' notice is specifically required by s 378. They are required for, inter alia:

(a) change of name (s 28);
(b) change of objects (s 4);
(c) change of public/private status (ss 44, 53);
(d) change of Articles (s 9);

(e)   disapplying statutory pre-emption rights (s 95);

(f)   reducing capital (s 135);

(g)   private company assistance for share purchases (s 155) and authority to purchase own shares off market (ss 164, 165) or to redeem shares out of capital (s 173);

(h)   winding up voluntarily (Insolvency Act 1986, s 84(1)(c)) (except where insolvent, when an extraordinary resolution is usually passed);

(i)   authorising a sale of assets by a liquidator in exchange for shares (Insolvency Act 1986, s 110).

All the provisions in respect of extraordinary resolutions (apart from notice) apply, so that the resolution must be set out verbatim in the notice, and a copy must be filed with the registrar within 15 days.[62] Moreover, under s 18 the company must also file a copy of the amended document where the resolution makes an alteration to the Memorandum or Articles. Every special or extraordinary resolution must also be included in or attached to any copy of the Articles which is afterwards issued.[63]

(3)   Elective resolutions were introduced by the Companies Act 1989 as part of a scheme to enable private companies to 'deregulate'.[64] Elective resolutions allow the members of a private company to relax certain requirements of the Companies Acts which would otherwise apply to their company. Members of a public company may not pass elective resolutions. The theme of deregulation has not been well served by the provisions of the 1989 Act. Ironically, deregulation by use of the elective regime is capable of creating more procedural hoops and hurdles than the alternative procedures it is intended to dispense with and simplify.

To pass an elective resolution, 21 days' notice of the meeting is required, and, while there is no express prohibition on calling the meeting on short notice if the requisite proportion of members agree, there is no express authority to do so. It is therefore prudent to always give the full 21 days' notice. The resolution must be set out verbatim in the notice of the meeting.

At the meeting, the resolution must be passed unanimously by the members who are entitled to attend and vote, either in person or by proxy. Thus, if a member is neither at the meeting, nor represented by proxy, the elective resolution cannot be passed. Similarly, if a member, or his proxy, abstains from voting, this is fatal to the elective resolution. A copy of the elective resolution must be filed with the registrar within 15 days. Elective resolutions may currently be passed in five circumstances, although the Secretary of State has power to vary or add to the circumstances without the need for a further Act of Parliament. The five circumstances are as follows.

(1)   An elective resolution may be passed to dispense with the requirement to hold an AGM in the calendar year in which the resolution is passed, and subsequent years.[65]

(2)   An elective resolution may be passed whereby the annual accounts may be sent to members (and the auditors) rather than laid before them at a general meeting.[56] This resolution has effect in respect of the financial year in which it is made, and subsequent financial years. The accounts can be sent at any time not less than 28 days before the end of the period for delivery of the accounts to the Registrar –

which period is 10 months after the end of its accounting reference period for a private company. The accounts must be accompanied by a notice informing each member of his right to require a general meeting to be held in respect of those accounts, at which they should be laid before the members.[67]

(3) By elective resolution, the members may dispense with the need for auditors to stand down every year. The auditors are otherwise required to retire at every general meeting at which accounts are laid. This, of course, does not mean that auditors are irremovable. They can still be sacked using the procedure under s 391.[68]

(4) An elective resolution can be passed whereby the members can authorise themselves to give directors an authority to allot shares which can last for any fixed period exceeding five years, or even for an indefinite period. Without such an elective resolution, the maximum period for which the members can give such an authority to the directors is five years.[69]

The members, having passed such an elective resolution, may then give such an authority to allot shares, containing the requisite reference to a fixed period exceeding five years, or an indefinite period.

(5) An elective resolution can be passed to reduce the percentage of members required to hold an EGM on short notice down to a minimum of 90 per cent.[70]

Elective resolutions cease to have effect if the company ceases to be private, or if revoked by ordinary resolution. Otherwise they continue to take effect year on year.

Elective resolutions are hedged about with procedural difficulty, and should not be passed without professional advice. Particularly, there are rights of objection vested in any member, and in some cases, the auditor, which mean that they should be handled with care!

These rights may be exercised by any member in relation to (1), (2) and (3) above, and by the auditors in relation to (2). The effect of an objection in a particular year is that the elective resolution is suspended in that year. For example, a member who objects in a particular year to an elective resolution to dispense with the AGM, perhaps passed several years before, will, provided that he has lodged his objection with the company not later than three months before the end of the year, require the holding of an annual general meeting in that year.

In the hands of a disgruntled member, these are powerful rights – a procedurally minded member can wreak procedural mayhem if he times his objections carefully, since the procedures which must be observed in respect of an objection are intricate and tedious – enough to exercise the mind of the most conscientious company secretary.

The lesson to be learnt is to consider passing elective resolutions only if there is no likelihood of this procedural weapon being turned on the company. Family companies, companies whose employees are voting shareholders, and companies with outside investors should be particularly careful. If elective resolutions are to be passed, a further tip is that, if any of (1), (2) and (3) are to be passed, pass all three – all or none. The reason for this is that, far from easing the procedural burden on the company, passing only one or two of the three can actually increase the annual procedural requirements for the company.

Finally, while a company does not require authority to pass elective resolutions in its Articles of Association, care should be taken to review a company's Articles if its members are to pass an elective resolution to dispense with the requirement to hold an AGM. Some Articles may require certain matters to be dealt with at the AGM, such as retirement by rotation of the directors. To prevent inconsistencies of this sort from arising, the members will also wish to pass a special resolution to alter the Articles prior to the elective resolution.

Ordinary resolutions are required for all other cases. A bare majority of those who vote is sufficient and the length of notice depends on the type of meeting. There is no statutory definition of what constitutes an ordinary resolution. However, in *Bushell v Faith*,[71] Lord Upjohn explained the position as follows:

> 'An ordinary resolution is not defined nor used in the body of the 1948 Act although the phrase occurs in some of the articles of Table A in Sch 1 to the Act. But its meaning is, in my opinion, clear. An ordinary resolution is in the first place passed by a bare majority on a show of hands by the members entitled to vote who are present personally or by proxy and on such a vote each member has one vote regardless of his shareholding. If a poll is demanded then for an ordinary resolution still only a bare majority of votes is required.'

An ordinary resolution will serve for:

(a) increase of capital (s 121);
(b) removal of a director (s 303),
(c) appointment of a new director;
(d) appointment of auditor;
(e) issue of shares;
(f) increasing directors' borrowing powers;[72]
(g) authority to allot shares (s 80);[73]
(h) authority for market purchases of own shares (s 166);
(i) revocation of elective resolutions. (s 379A(3)).

Amendments and resolutions from the floor are a source of difficulty. Board resolutions are commonly proposed by the chairman himself and Table A does not require a seconder. The position then is as follows.

(1) The chairman should allow a reasonable opportunity to speak to any member who wishes to do so.
(2) Amendments from the floor must be accepted and put to the vote before the resolution itself, provided they are within the scope of the notice calling the meeting. Thus, where notice was properly given of special resolutions to wind up and to appoint a named liquidator, a different liquidator could be proposed at the meeting in place of the second resolution since it was within the scope of the notice and the name of the liquidator need not be stated anyway[74] nor included in a special resolution. The same would have applied to a resolution to appoint directors.

(3) No amendments of substance to special, extraordinary or elective resolutions can be accepted, since these resolutions must be set out verbatim in the notice (s 378).[75] Minor amendments, such as spelling and grammatical corrections are permissible.

(4) Otherwise, however, failure to put to the vote amendments or resolutions which are within the scope of the notice or the ordinary business of the meeting (in the case of the AGM) may invalidate a resolution which has been passed.

(5) Resolutions from the floor must also be put to the vote if they satisfy the same criteria, ie if they have been included in the notice to members under s 376 or if they fall clearly within the business specified in the notice calling the meeting. Moreover, any special requirements of the Act or Articles, such as special notice of a resolution to dismiss a director or auditor must have been given.

(6) In a public company, resolutions to appoint directors must be proposed separately unless a resolution to the contrary is approved nem con (s 292(2)).

As we have seen, the majorities required for resolutions other than elective resolutions are never majorities of the entire voting membership. They are majorities of those who actually vote in person or by proxy, at the meeting in question. Thus, it does not matter how few they are, so long as there is a quorum. However, for elective resolutions, there must be unanimity of all the members entitled to attend and vote – all must attend, all must vote.

9.8 VOTING

Voting rights at general meetings depend upon the provisions of the Articles. The right to vote (where it exists) is something which will be enforced by the courts.[76] The usual provisions are as follows.

(1) In the absence of any special rights or restrictions,[77] reg 54 of Table A provides that:

(a) on a show of hands, members present in person (or via a corporate representative, which is the equivalent of 'in person' for a corporate shareholder) have one vote each – ie proxies do not count – and the size of a member's shareholding is irrelevant;

(b) on a poll, members (in person or by proxy) have one vote per share. If the Articles make no provision, s 370(6) also gives one vote for each share or for each £10 of stock.

(2) Regulation 46 provides that voting in the first instance is by show of hands, the result of which is declared by the chairman. His declaration is conclusive, unless a poll is demanded (either then or earlier) (reg 47). The advantage of this procedure is that it enables non-contentious business to be disposed of quickly, and indeed contentious business also, if the result is in accordance with the wishes of the majority shareholders. In that event, they do not need to ask for a poll and time and trouble is saved. Where there is a seriously disputed issue, however, a show of hands is clearly inadequate and therefore the Articles (and the common law) always provide the right to demand a poll.

(3) Regulation 46 allows a poll to be demanded (on or before the declaration of the result of the show of hands) by:

   (a) the chairman; or
   (b) two members; or
   (c) any member who represents one-tenth of the voting rights; or
   (d) any member who represents one-tenth of the paid up voting capital.[78]

For these purposes, proxies have the same rights as their members.[79] A valid demand for a poll does away with the show of hands which need not then be taken.[80]

(4) The poll is taken as directed by the chairman, except where it is demanded on the election of the chairman or the adjournment of the meeting. In that case, it must be taken at once.[81] In other cases, the chairman can decide the time of the poll, and meanwhile proceed with the other business. He may well decide that the preparation of polling cards and the arrangements for counting require the poll to be taken at a later date. In that event, the poll is complete and the resolution carried or defeated, only when the result is ascertained.[82]

The chairman should fix the hours for polling and may give notice to all the shareholders if there is sufficient time. Members may vote at the poll even though they did not attend the meeting, but proxies may do so only if their proxy forms were lodged in time. Table A, reg 62 requires them to be lodged 48 hours before a meeting and 24 hours before a poll. It also permits lodgment 48 hours before an adjourned meeting; but for this, such proxies would be out of time since the adjourned meeting is merely a continuation of the earlier meeting. Voting should always be in writing and the member's or proxy's signature and the number of shares should appear on each card. Members and proxies may cast their votes in different directions, as they may have to do where they hold shares both personally and on trust for beneficiaries whose interests vary (s 374). There are no provisions in Table A for postal votes so the members or their proxies must attend in the absence of a Special Article allowing postal votes. In such a case, it is thought that a postal vote includes one sent by fax: see *Re a debtor (No 2021 of 1995)*.[83] The chairman and other directors may vote their own shares in their own interests, provided there is no majority oppression of the minority.[84] The chairman has his usual casting vote.[85]

(5) The result is declared by the chairman but he will naturally want scrutineers who are either independent or representative of both sides. The result, whether of a show of hands or of a poll, will always be minuted.[86] The importance of strict compliance with the polling requirements cannot be exaggerated, as if the chairman wrongly excludes a voter, the poll may be invalidated.[87] However, objections to a voter's qualifications cannot be raised after the meeting and the chairman's decision is conclusive in respect of objections which are referred to him in due time.[88] This is provided by reg 58 of Table A but it would not prevent the member himself from applying to the court if his right to vote had been wrongly denied.[89]

9.9 PROXIES

Every director should be familiar with the proxy machinery which is as follows.

(1) The statutory right to appoint a proxy to attend and vote is guaranteed for every voting member by s 372.

(2) Section 372 also provides that:

    (a) the proxy may also speak in the case of a private company;

    (b) a member of a private company can be restricted to one proxy;

    (c) the proxy's voting rights can be restricted to a poll (ie not a show of hands);

    (d) the notice of meeting must state the right to appoint the proxy;

    (e) the lodging of the proxy form cannot be required more than 48 hours before the meeting;

    (f) if proxy forms are sent out at the company's expense they must be sent to all the members, ie the directors cannot simply solicit their known supporters (except where the latter request the form and it is available to all).

(3) In practice, proxy forms are always sent out by listed companies and for this purpose the Stock Exchange requires:

    (a) that the forms should be sent to all those entitled to vote and should provide for two-way voting;

    (b) that the Articles must not preclude two-way proxies;

    (c) that corporate shareholders may execute proxy forms by the signature of an authorised officer;

    (d) that preference shareholders are given adequate voting rights in appropriate circumstances.

(4) In the light of s 372, Table A provides:

    (a) proxies[90] do not vote on a show of hands (reg 54) but only on a poll (reg 59);

    (b) the proxy form shall be in writing signed by the shareholder (reg 60);

    (c) the form must be lodged at the registered office: 48 hours before a meeting or adjourned meeting 24 hours before a poll (reg 62);

    (d) the forms of proxy are specified in regs 60 and 61;[91]

    (e) the proxy form confers authority to demand a poll (reg 46);

    (f) the proxy is not affected by the termination by reason of the member's death, insanity or revocation as long as written notice has not reached the company's office before the meeting, or adjourned meeting (reg 63).

(5) Representatives of corporate shareholders, appointed by resolution of their boards, have the status of members not proxies.[92]

(6) Circulation of proxy forms by the board at the company's expense is not objectionable,[93] provided (as we have seen) the forms are sent out to all members, and are 'two-way' proxies in the case of listed companies. Such circulation can be a two-edged weapon, as the nominated director is then under a duty to demand a poll and to exercise the vote as instructed[94] unless the proxy form gives him discretion.[95]

(7)   Validity of proxies is decided by the chairman whose decision is final (reg 58) in the absence of fraud or bad faith.[96] Stamp duty is not required. It was formerly payable where a proxy form covered more than one meeting, but this has not been required since March 1985. The chairman should not reject a proxy where the defect amounts to no more than a clerical error,[97] and he should bear in mind that a member can still attend in person even when he has given a proxy. In that event, either of them may vote,[98] although tender by the member of his vote is prima facie evidence of revocation on which the chairman would be entitled to act (although not obliged to, in the light of reg 63, above) unless, perhaps, he knew that the member was contractually bound to allow the proxy to vote (but see (4)(f) above).

9.10   DIRECTORS' MEETINGS

9.10.1   Notice

As we have seen **(3.10)**, the directors act collectively as a board and the usual procedure under Table A for calling meetings is as follows.

(1)   Directors may meet and regulate their meetings as they think fit (reg 88).
(2)   Any director may call a meeting at any time and the secretary must do so at his request (reg 88).
(3)   Reasonable notice must be given unless the meetings are held at predetermined intervals. What is reasonable depends on company practice, and may be as short as a few minutes if there is nothing to prevent the director attending. If he wishes to object, he must do so at once.[99] However, a casual encounter cannot be converted into a board meeting against the wishes of a director.[100] Notice need not be given to a director who is abroad (reg 88).
(4)   In the absence of proper notice, the meeting is void, as where a few hours' notice was given, which was far shorter than normal and did not even reach one director until the day after the meeting.[101]

9.10.2   Quorum

(1)   The quorum is fixed by Table A, reg 89 as two directors, unless some other figure is decided by the board. An alternate director counts towards the quorum. For a directors' meeting the quorum can be one, since private companies need have only one director.[102]
(2)   Regulation 90 of Table A, allows the continuing directors to act when they cannot make up a quorum, for the sole purpose of increasing their number or calling a general meeting.
(3)   If, exceptionally, there is no provision in the Articles, the quorum is a majority of the board in the absence of some other practice.[103]
(4)   The quorum for directors' meetings is a more complicated matter than that for general meetings, and the question can easily arise at any time during the meeting and not simply at the outset. When a director has an interest in a contract the Articles (for example, Table A, regs 94 and 95) may exclude him both from voting and from counting in the quorum. In that case, the quorum must be looked

at separately for each item of business in which a director has an interest.[104] The transaction must not be artificially split up so as to defeat the requirements.[105] However, there is nothing to prevent a subsequent meeting with an effective quorum from ratifying an invalid resolution and outsiders will not usually be affected because of the rule in *Royal British Bank v Turquand*.[106]

Care should be taken in a two director company if the Articles permit one director to be a quorum. It may be that, even in such circumstances as this, a decision of a sole director is not validly taken. In *Davidson & Begg Antiques Ltd v Davidson*,[107] the company had Articles which largely followed Table A. By reg 70, the business of the company was to be managed by the directors and a meeting of the directors at which a quorum was present could exercise all the powers of the directors. Under reg 88, there was no need for notice to be given of a directors' meeting to a director who was absent from the UK. Under reg 89, the quorum for a directors' meeting was two, but this was to be modified by reg 7(b) if there were a sole director. By reg 93, a resolution in writing signed by all the directors entitled to receive notice of a board meeting was valid as if passed at a board meeting. A resolution had been so passed by a sole director in circumstances where the other director was abroad. It was held by the Scottish Court of Session (Outer House) that the resolution passed by a sole director in these circumstances had not been validly passed. Regulation commenced with the words 'A resolution in writing signed by all the directors . . .'. This suggested signature by more than one director. A broadly similar situation arose in *Hood Sailmakers Ltd v Axford*.[108] Here, again, a resolution was passed by one director in the UK in circumstances where another director was abroad at the time. Carnwath J found, again, that the resolution was invalidly passed. He did so, however, on the slightly different ground that it would be curious if a director could evade the quorum requirements of the Articles merely by waiting for his fellow director to leave the country. He further found, however, that since the company, including the director who had not taken part in the board meeting, had acted upon the resolution, it was now estopped from denying the validity of the resolution.

9.10.3 Procedure

As we have seen, the directors regulate their own procedure and Table A, reg 91 allows them to elect a chairman for such period as they think fit. If he is absent five minutes after the appointed time, any director may be elected. The following matters may be noted.

(1) An attendance book is often signed but this is not compulsory, unless the Articles require it.[109]
(2) An agenda will normally be circulated a little before the meeting with the minutes of the last meeting and other items, such as accounts, which require prior study.
(3) Voting is normally on the basis of a simple majority on a show of hands with a casting vote for the chairman (reg 88). Thus, size of shareholdings is normally irrelevant, but there is nothing to prevent special voting rights from being given by the Articles.
(4) A meeting may be dispensed with altogether, under reg 93, if the resolutions are signed by *all* the directors.

(5) No director must be excluded, unless the members have so resolved.[110] They can in any case remove a director at any time under s 303.

9.11 MINUTES

After a general meeting or a directors' meeting, it is the duty of the secretary to record the decisions taken in the form of minutes.

In some large companies, it is the practice, following approval of draft board minutes by the chairman, for copies of certain draft minutes to be circulated to other directors who may be particularly concerned with the subject matter. Any amendments made by such directors will then be communicated to the chairman and agreed by him before the minutes are finally recorded in the minute book. The duty to keep proper minutes is imposed by s 382(1) which provides that:

> 'Every company shall cause minutes of all proceedings of general meetings, all proceedings at meetings of its directors and, where there are managers, all proceedings at meetings of its managers to be entered in books kept for that purpose.'

Following the passing of a written resolution of the members, agreed to in accordance with s 381A of the Act, the company is also required to keep a record of the written resolution (and of the signatures) in a book in the same way as minutes of a general meeting.[111] Failure to comply with these obligations involves the company and every officer of the company who is in default to liability to a fine of up to £1,000 and of up to £100 for every day while the default continues.

The statutory obligation is reinforced by reg 100 of Table A, which requires minutes of:

(1) all appointments of officers; and
(2) all proceedings at general and class meetings, including the names of directors in attendance.

9.11.1 Minutes as evidence

In addition to the statutory penalty, however, failure to keep adequate minutes or records of a written resolution may have even more serious consequences if it results in the company's being unable to prove that a particular decision was taken or that the proper requirements were observed in relation to some action.

Although unrecorded business may be proved by other evidence, if available, the best evidence which can be offered is a duly signed minute or record of a written resolution. This is the result of s 382(2) and (4), which provide in relation to minutes that:

> '(2) Any such minute, if purporting to be signed by the chairman of the meeting at which the proceedings were had, or by the chairman of the next succeeding meeting, is evidence of the proceedings . . .
>
> (4) Where minutes have been made in accordance with this section of the proceedings at any general meeting of the company or meeting of directors or managers, then, until the contrary is proved, the meeting is deemed to have been duly held and convened,

and all proceedings had at the meeting to have been duly had; and all appointments of directors, managers or liquidators are deemed valid.'

and s 382A(2) which provides in relation to records of written resolutions:

'(2) Any such record, if purporting to be signed by a director of the company, or the company secretary, is evidence of the proceedings in agreeing to the resolution; and where a record is made in accordance with this section, then until the contrary is proved, the requirements of this Act with respect to those proceedings shall be deemed to be complied with.'

It will be noted that the signed minutes or records are simply 'evidence', not 'conclusive evidence'. This means that while the courts will accept them as prima facie proof of what was done at the meeting in the absence of evidence to the contrary, other evidence, such as the testimony of someone present, can be admitted to show that the minutes or records are incomplete or inaccurate. It was held in *Re Fireproof Doors Ltd*[112] that decisions not recorded in minutes may be proved by other evidence.

Sometimes the Articles go further than s 382 and provide that signed minutes shall be conclusive evidence. For example, reg 47 of Table A, which deals with the demand for a poll following the declaration of the result of a vote by show of hands at a general meeting, contains the following:

'Unless a poll is duly demanded a declaration by the chairman that a resolution has been carried or carried unanimously, or by a particular majority, or lost or not carried by a particular majority and an entry to that effect in the minutes of the meeting shall be conclusive evidence of the fact without proof of the number or proportion of the votes recorded in favour of or against such resolution.'

It was held in *Kerr v John Mottram Ltd*[113] that such an Article is indeed conclusive (as between the members) in the absence of fraud or bad faith. This means that contrary evidence cannot normally be admitted.

9.11.2 Signature of minutes

For minutes to be evidence of the proceedings, they must be signed by the chairman of the meeting of which they are a record[114] or, alternatively, by the chairman of the next succeeding meeting. There is no law that the minutes must be submitted to the meeting for 'confirmation', 'verification' or 'adoption' – all that is required is that they shall be signed by the chairman and he can, if he wishes, do so entirely on his own responsibility and without reference to his colleagues. As a matter of prudence, however, it is invariable practice to submit and obtain approval of them as a correct record. In the case of a company which has no chairman, the minutes may be signed by an officer of the company, but in this instance, the board should not only approve the minutes as a correct record, but might also prudently resolve to specifically authorise the officer concerned to sign the minutes. Obtaining approval of the minutes as a correct record is sometimes described as 'confirming' the minutes, but the word should be avoided as all that is involved is the question whether the proceedings have been correctly recorded, the decisions taken not requiring any 'confirmation'.

It follows that no question regarding the merits of any decision stated in the minutes should be raised when the signature of the minutes is being decided upon, and that only members present at the previous meeting should take part in any discussion as to whether or not the minutes of that meeting are a true record. If the meeting considers that a particular decision, while correctly recorded in the minutes, ought not to have been taken, the proper course is to leave the minutes as a true record of what was done but pass a new resolution rescinding the decision. Where, on the other hand, it is decided that a minute does not accurately record what happened, the necessary correction should be made and initialled by the chairman when he signs the minutes. No alteration should ever be made after the minutes have been signed[115] and mutilation of any minute book will give rise to suspicions of bad faith.[116]

The fact that a meeting approves the minutes of a previous meeting does not of itself make a director who is present at the second meeting, but who was absent from the previous meeting, responsible for the decisions recorded in the minutes. This is a further reason for avoiding the word 'confirmed' which might suggest the contrary.

The usual procedure for submitting board minutes for approval is to circulate a copy to the members of the board in advance of the meeting; thus saving time as well as giving the directors an opportunity to consider them carefully before the meeting.

It is also usual for the minutes of a general meeting of a company to be signed at the next meeting of the board of directors, rather than to leave them unsigned until the next general meeting, possibly a year later. This is quite in order provided they are signed by the chairman who presided at the general meeting. If, however, the chairman of the board meeting is not the same person as the chairman who presided at the general meeting, it would seem that he is not competent to sign the minutes of the general meeting for the 'next succeeding meeting', which for the purpose of s 382(2) is the next general meeting, not the next board meeting. In most cases, the chairman of the board will have presided at the general meeting and will be competent to sign its minutes by that fact alone.

9.11.3   Contents of minutes

Minutes are not intended to be a report of the meeting but are a record of decisions taken, preceded by a very short narrative where necessary, to lead up to the decision.

When there has been a conflict of opinion on any part of the business of the meeting, it is not necessary to record the names of those voting against the decision taken by the majority unless this is specially requested. If, therefore, a director feels strongly that a wrong decision has been taken, he should ask that his objections be recorded in the minutes.[117]

The books containing the minutes of general meetings must be kept at the registered office of the company and must be open for inspection by any member of the company without charge. In addition, any member is entitled to be furnished, within seven days after request, with a copy of such minutes at a prescribed fee (s 383).

Shareholders have no right to inspect or have copies of the minutes of directors' meetings and these should, therefore, be kept in separate books from those containing the minutes of general meetings. The auditors are entitled to have access to the minutes of both general meetings and directors' meetings. A director has a common law right to inspect minutes of board meetings although there is no provision in the Acts.[118]

Section 722 of the 1985 Act provides that any register, index, minute-book or book of account required by the Act to be kept by a company may be kept either by making entries in bound books or by recording the matters in question in any other manner.[119] When entries are made in some manner other than bound books (for example, loose-leaf books), adequate precautions must be taken for guarding against falsification and for facilitating its discovery, otherwise the company and every officer of the company who is in default will be liable to a penalty.

Precautions which are usually regarded as adequate for loose-leaf minute-books are for the chairman, when signing the minutes, to initial each page, and for the book to be provided with a lock, the key being kept by a responsible official. An alternative method is for the typewritten sheets to be initialled or signed and stuck into a bound book.

9.12   IRREGULARITIES AT MEETINGS

We have looked at the effect of failure to comply with some of the requirements for calling and conducting meetings. The general principle under *Foss v Harbottle*[120] is that the courts will not interfere in internal irregularities at the request of the minority. The argument is that it is futile to allow the minority to litigate on such matters when the majority can cure the defect at any time by going through the correct procedure.[121] However, this principle is subject to the exceptions to *Foss v Harbottle* which are discussed in **7.15**. In particular, the rule does not apply, and any member may ask the court for an injunction or a declaration that the proceedings are invalid, where:

(1) his personal rights of membership are being denied, for example, the right to vote,[122] or to object to short notice of the AGM;[123]
(2) what is being done could not be ratified by a bare majority as where rights in the Articles are being infringed, which it would need a special resolution to change;[124]
(3) the matter complained of is illegal or ultra vires or a fraud on the minority[125] or even where a notice is merely misleading because it conceals some benefit which is to be conferred on the directors.[126] Where the objectors consider that the irregularity falls outside *Foss v Harbottle*, they will normally sue on behalf of themselves and the other minority shareholders and, as a preliminary, either side can seek a 'declaration of rights' so as to ascertain whether the minority has the right to sue.[127] Where the objectors are in a majority, the rule presents them with no problem as they can call another general meeting and reverse the disputed resolution, remove the directors and cause the company to sue them for breach of duty.

Even where a dissatisfied member or director is unable or unwilling to apply to the court, he has alternative remedies which may be available including:

(1) a request to the DTI for an investigation (**8.3.4**);
(2) a request for criminal proceedings, as some of the statutory requirements for meetings carry criminal sanctions, for example, s 372 which requires the notice to state the right to appoint a proxy;
(3) a requisition for an EGM under s 368, if he can obtain the support of one-tenth of the paid-up voting capital.

CHAPTER 9 FOOTNOTES

1 The list in the text will be found quite commonly, since it is contained in reg 52 of Table A (1948 version). Special business must be specified in the notice convening the meeting; even if, technically, *all* business has to be treated as such under Table A (1985 version) the requirement to give notice of 'the general nature of the business' reg 38, (1985 version) will not greatly increase the burden upon the secretary in specifying items (a)–(e) above.

2 In which case, the accounts will be 'special business' even under the older versions of Table A.

3 Sections 252 and 386.

4 Listed companies are subject to additional requirements in regard to the AGM under the Yellow Book. Copies of all reports and announcements must be sent to the Stock Exchange (including any additional comments which the chairman wishes to add to his report at the meeting). This is quite apart from the need to obtain approval for circulars and notices other than the most routine.

5 As with all their other powers, the directors must use this power in good faith: *Pergamon Press Ltd v Maxwell* [1970] 2 All ER 809.

6 A requisition need not be in a single document, provided that it is contained in documents 'in like form' and each signed by at least one requisitionist.

7 [1983] BCLC 293.

8 Section 368(6).

9 See also *Re HR Paul and Son Ltd* (1973) 118 SJ 166.

10 [1958] 3 All ER 1.

11 [1989] 1 WLR 638.

12 [1991] BCC 754.

13 [1994] BCC 51.

14 *Ball v Metal Industries* (1957) SC 315.

15 As in *Eley v Government Security Life Assurance* (1875) 1 ExD 20 (the case turning, however, on the contract contained in the Articles, which does not extend to purely 'personal' benefits). This, at least, is the general interpretation of the *Eley* decision. In fact, the most likely ratio of the *Eley* case is that Eley failed because he sued as the solicitor named in the Articles of the company. Accordingly, the statutory contract was, in the words of Lord Cairns, 'res inter alios acta [he was] no party to it' at p 90. In other words, he failed because he had sued in the wrong capacity. In a later case, *Hickman v Kent or Romney Marsh Sheep Breeders Association* [1915] 1 Ch 881, Astbury J analysed the *Eley* decision by saying that 'no right merely purporting to be given by an article to a person, whether a member or not, in a capacity other than that of a member, as, for instance, as solicitor, promoter, director, can be enforced against the company'. This analysis seems to have been adopted by the vast majority of the textbooks. Astbury J however, seems to have ignored earlier cases where the courts have allowed enforcement of Articles giving rights to a member other than in his capacity as a member. For example, in *Quin and Axtens Ltd v Salmon* [1909] AC 442, a power was given to a member in his capacity as managing director of the company to veto the disposal of certain assets of the company. The House of Lords held that he could enforce this Article notwithstanding that he was doing so as a director rather than as a shareholder. In acting as a director, the conduct of the director is overlaid with a fiduciary duty. This would not have been the case had the power been vested in him in his capacity as a shareholder. This distinction between the orthodox approach to the s 14, of CA 1985, contract and what really was the decision in *Eley* was first pointed out by Lord Wedderburn in [1957] Camb LJ 183. See also Gregory (1981) 44 MLR 526.

16 [1970] AC 1099.

17 [1986] 3 WLR 26.

18 Section 125(4) is an enactment of two Scottish decisions *Oban and Aultmore, Glenlivet Distilleries Ltd* 1904 5 F 1141; *Marshall, Fleming & Co Ltd* 1938 SC 873.

19 *Greenhalgh v Arderne Cinemas Ltd* [1950] 2 All ER 1120.

20 *White v Bristol Aeroplane Co Ltd* [1953] 1 All ER 40.

21 *Re Holders Investment Trust Ltd* [1971] 1 WLR 583.

22 Where the courts have power to order class meetings (*Re Savoy Ltd* [1981] Ch 351) and 'class' may mean 'identifiable interest group' rather than merely a formal class with distinct rights; *Re Hellenic and General Trust Ltd* [1976] 1 WLR 123.

23 Since this section may be invoked by dissenting shareholders, it is important to remember that it cannot be evaded by the special notice procedure under s 379. See **9.4** below.
24 Section 379A(2)(a).
25 Sections 369(4) and 378(3).
26 *Re Pearce Duff and Co Ltd* [1960] 3 All ER 222.
27 Sections 369(4) and 378(3).
28 *Musselwhite v C H Musselwhite & Son Ltd* [1962] 1 All ER 201.
29 *Bentley-Stevens v Jones* [1974] 2 All ER 653.
30 [1994] BCC 857.
31 Thus, if the business is 'to elect new directors', additional resolutions to elect new directors can be proposed at the meeting. *Choppington Collieries Ltd v Johnson* [1944] 1 All ER 762.
32 Thus a notice of a resolution for the approval of some improperly paid remuneration was insufficient where it failed to state the amount (£44,876): *Baillie v Oriental Telephone Co Ltd* [1915] 1 Ch 503.
33 [1920] 2 KB 523.
34 [1962] Ch 370.
35 [1962] Ch 964.
36 *Pedley v Inland Waterways Association Ltd* [1977] 1 All ER 709.
37 *Re Hartley Baird Ltd* [1954] 3 All ER 695.
38 *Re London Flats Ltd* [1969] 2 All ER 744: reg 41, Table A.
39 *Re MJ Shanley Ltd* (1980) 124 SJ 239.
40 *Re Sanitary Carbon Co* [1877] WN 223.
41 *East v Bennett Bros Ltd* [1911] 1 Ch 163. By the same reasoning, even one of a number of members might constitute a general meeting if *all* the other shares were temporarily disenfranchised, for example, by death of the only other member.
42 *Neil M'Leod and Sons Ltd, Petitioners* 1967 SC 16.
43 When appointed by resolution of that corporation (s 375). If the corporate shareholder is in liquidation, the liquidator (where there is no liquidation committee or direction from the courts or creditors) may make the appointment himself (*Hillman v Crystal Bowl Amusements* [1973] 1 All ER 379).
44 Regulation 40, Table A. But for companies registered before 22 December 1980, reg 54 of Table A (1948 version) provides that the members present shall be a quorum, 'members' including a sole surviving member: *Jarvis Motors (Harrow) Ltd v Carabott* [1964] 3 All ER 89.
45 *Re HR Paul and Sons Ltd* (1973) 118 SJ 166.
46 He is often referred to as the chairman of the company but under Table A, there is no such office.
47 *Wall v London and Northern Assets Corporation* [1898] 2 Ch 469.
48 *National Dwellings Society v Sykes* [1894] 3 Ch 159 and even where he properly exercises his power to adjourn as a last resort because of disorder, he must not adjourn for longer than is reasonably necessary – probably for no more than about 15 minutes to allow tempers to cool. An adjournment *sine die* is unlikely to be justified (*John v Rees* [1970] Ch 245).
49 [1989] 1 All ER 560.
50 *Re Express Engineering Works* [1920] 1 Ch 466.
51 [1969] 1 All ER 161.
52 *Cane v Jones* [1980] 1 WLR 1451; *Re MJ Shanley Ltd* (1980) 124 SJ 239.
53 Sections 369(4) and 378(3).
54 *Re Bailey Hay & Co Ltd* [1971] 3 All ER 693.
55 *Parker and Cooper Ltd v Reading* [1926] Ch 975, where an unauthorised debenture was ratified by the members separately and on different occasions.
56 *Re Barry Artist Ltd* [1985] 1 WLR 1305.
57 Section 164.
58 Sections 381A–381C and 382A.
59 Schedule 15A, Part I, para 1.
60 Section 369 and reg 38, Table A. Its sole purpose thus appears to be the saving of one week.
61 Sections 378 and 380.
62 The Registrar is to publish in the *Gazette*, among other things, notice of receipt of documents altering the Memorandum of Articles, and resolutions or agreements stating or altering or renaming classes of shares or the rights attached to them.
63 Section 380.

64 Section 379A.

65 Section 366A.

66 Section 252.

67 Section 253(1)(b).

68 Section 386.

69 Section 80A.

70 Sections 369(4) and 378(3).

71 [1970] AC 1099.

72 Expressly provided for by reg 79, Table A (1948). No such provision restricting the powers of the directors appears in the 1985 Table A.

73 Even though this may require amendment to the Articles: if it does then s 380 above must be complied with even though the authority is given by ordinary resolution.

74 *Re Trench Tubeless Tyre Co* [1900] 1 Ch 408.

75 But the members unanimously may agree an amended resolution, waiving what will then be the technical inaccuracy of the notice: *Re Moorgate Mercantile Holdings Ltd* [1980] 1 WLR 227. The chairman should think twice before courting litigation by allowing such amendments, however, especially if the resolution is not self-executing but requires the confirmation of the court. The notice of the meeting must state the resolution verbatim or give an extremely accurate account of it, and it is this requirement which makes the business improperly notified if any amendment of substance is passed. A trivial error in the notice or one which is glaringly obviously an error of the typist or printer, will not be as serious. Thus the court may correct an irrelevant error, for example, when continuing a capital reduction (s 137) where the notice stated unissued shares at 2,073,420 instead of 2,073,417: *Re Willaire Systems plc* (1986) *The Times*, 17 July. But the board should beware, since errors of little more substance than this may be fatal.

76 *Osborne v Amalgamated Society of Railway Servants* [1911] 1 Ch 540.

77 The Articles can prescribe any pattern of voting rights which is desired, ie excluding some shares from voting altogether ('A' shares) and giving multiple rights to others.

78 The Articles *cannot* require more than *five members* or the voting strength mentioned in (c) and (d); s 373.

79 Where the chairman is holding proxies, it may be his duty to demand a poll: *Second Consolidated Trust v Ceylon etc Estates* [1943] 2 All ER 567.

80 *Holmes v Keyes* [1958] 2 All ER 129.

81 A poll cannot be excluded by the Articles *except* on these two matters: s 373.

82 It is not clear if the result must also have been declared, but, for example, new directors may not know whether they are able to act until then.

83 [1996] 2 All ER 345.

84 *Carruth v ICI Ltd* [1937] AC 707.

85 Regulation 50, Table A.

86 Which makes the chairman's declaration conclusive in the case of a show of hands (reg 47).

87 *R v Lambeth* (1838) 8 A & E 356.

88 Whether or not the chairman's attention has been drawn to the objection: *Marx v Estates & General Investments* [1975] STC 671.

89 See note 87.

90 Regulation 68, Table A (1948) expressly provides that a proxy may be a non-member. Table A (1985) omits this, presumably as an unnecessary statement of the obvious.

91 See Appendix C. The two forms are a 'general' proxy where the proxy votes *as he* thinks fit and a special or 'two way' proxy where he is instructed which way to vote.

92 Section 375.

93 *Peel v London and NW Rly Co* [1907] 1 Ch 5.

94 *Second Consolidated Trust Ltd v Ceylon etc Estates Ltd* [1943] 2 All ER 567.

95 See also note 79.

96 *Wall v Exchange Investments Co* [1926] Ch 143.

97 *Oliver v Dalgleish* [1963] 3 All ER 330, where the proxies wrongly referred to 'annual' instead of 'extraordinary' general meeting. There was no possibility of confusion as the date was correctly stated.

98 *Cousins v International Brick Co Ltd* [1931] 2 Ch 90.

99 *Browne v La Trinidad* (1888) 37 ChD 1.

100 *Barron v Potter* [1914] 1 Ch 895.

101 *Re Homer Gold Mines* (1888) 39 Ch D 546.

102 Section 282.

103 *Cork Tramways Co v Willows* (1882) 8 QBD 685.

104 See **5.6.3**.

105 *Re North Eastern Insurance Co* [1919] 1 Ch 198.

106 (1856) 6 E & B 327; or because of s 35 (formerly s 9 of the European Communities Act 1972).

107 [1997] BCC 77.

108 [1997] BCC 263.

109 Regulation 86, Table A (1948) did so require, but reg 100 (1985 version) merely requires attendance to be minuted.

110 *Hayes v Bristol Plant Hire Ltd* [1957] 1 All ER 685.

111 Section 382A.

112 [1916] 2 Ch 142.

113 [1940] Ch 657.

114 Section 145(2).

115 *Re Cawley and Co* (1889) 42 Ch D 209.

116 *Hearts of Oak Assurance Co v James Flower and Sons* [1936] Ch 76.

117 See **8.3.1**.

118 *McCusker v McRae* 1966 SC 253.

119 Computerised minutes are permissible: s 723.

120 (1843) 2 Hare 461.

121 *Bentley-Stevens v Jones* [1974] 2 All ER 653, where the irregularity was a defect in calling an EGM to remove a director. Hence an injunction was refused.

122 *Pender v Lushington* (1877) 6 Ch D 70.

123 Section 369(3).

124 *Edwards v Halliwell* [1950] 2 All ER 1064.

125 *Cook v Deeks* [1916] 1 AC 554, where the directors were passing a resolution to appropriate the company's property for their own benefit.

126 *Normandy v Ind Coope and Co* [1908] 1 Ch 84.

127 *Edwards v Halliwell*, at note 124 above.

Chapter 10

TERMS OF SERVICE FOR DIRECTORS

10.1 REMUNERATION – DETERMINED BY ARTICLES

Directors' remuneration is commonly of two kinds – 'fees' for non-executive services and 'salary' for full- or part-time service as an executive. These are not technical terms but are a convenient means of distinguishing two forms of payment which differ in several aspects.

The first point which a director should impress on his mind is the fact that he has no right to remuneration by virtue of his office.[1] He must therefore be able to show the authority for remuneration before he can safely accept or pay it. Otherwise it is liable to be reclaimed by the company or by a liquidator.[2]

The question depends primarily on the terms of the Articles and the usual position is as follows.

(1) Regulations 82 and 83 of Table A provide that:

   (a) the remuneration shall be determined by the company (ie members) in general meeting;
   (b) it accrues from day to day (so that a broken period can be apportioned);
   (c) expenses can be paid including those of attending board meetings.

(2) If these Articles are adopted the board cannot fix remuneration for themselves.[4] This is clearly unsatisfactory and is widely disregarded in private companies where the directors normally include their remuneration in the accounts[5] which then are submitted to the members at the AGM. It is doubtful whether approval of such accounts is sufficient in itself to comply with reg 82, although members might find it difficult to complain if they approved the accounts after being made aware that they were also approving the remuneration.[6] Approval by *all* the voting shareholders would suffice, without any resolution at the AGM provided that it is genuine remuneration and not a 'disguised gift out of capital',[7] and the accounts must draw attention to the directors' remuneration in order to comply with s 232, Sch 6, Part 1.

(3) Regulation 82 should therefore be supplemented by a special Article, which meets business requirements by authorising the board to fix remuneration. Regulation 84 empowers the board to appoint a director as managing director or to 'any other executive office under the company' upon such terms as they may determine (such directors not being subject to retirement by rotation), and they 'may remunerate any such director for his services as they think fit'. Although this has moved in the right direction, and may justify remuneration, it probably does not go far enough, since such a construction is:

(a) hard to square with reg 82(above); and

(b) equally hard to square with the general tenor of reg 84 itself, which seems to contemplate payment for executive services over and above those of a director *qua* director.

What is often found is a special Article providing for:

(a) a fee for non-executive services; and

(b) a salary and/or commission for any executive services at rates fixed by the board, which is also given full power to settle the general terms of any such employment.

It is not, therefore, common to find a resolution to approve the directors' remuneration at the AGM.

(4) The Article should also specify, as does reg 82, that remuneration accrues from day to day, so that an apportionment can be made, if a director serves for only part of the year.[8]

(5) Whatever the procedure, the courts will construe it strictly and against the directors who are remunerating themselves. Thus, in a case where a resolution to pay remuneration was passed at a general meeting without a quorum, those responsible were made jointly and severally liable to repay.[9]

(6) Where the authority is given to the directors, care must also be taken to comply with the requirements of the Articles as to interests in contracts (see **5.6.3**). In Table A, this means regs 94 to 98 which disqualify a director from voting and from the quorum on matters in which he is interested, although a resolution may be split so that he may vote on other directors' appointments. If he complies with this, he may be appointed to any employment ('executive office' under the company), in conjunction with his office as director, on such terms as the board may decide (reg 84).

(7) The Articles may include provisions for remuneration by way of commission or share of profits and in this case it is again desirable to leave the details to the discretion of the directors. If the Articles attempt to define the terms too closely, difficult questions of definition may arise, which can be resolved only by an alteration of the Articles or an application to the court.[10]

(8) When a director is dismissed from office, he will wish to receive some form of monetary payment. This may take the form of compensation or bona fide contractual damages. By s 312, it is unlawful for a company to make to a director any payment by way of compensation for loss of office, or as consideration for or in connection with his retirement from office, without particulars of the payment, including its amount, being disclosed to the members of the company and approved by them. By s 316(3), such a reference to compensation for loss of office does not include any bona fide payment by way of damages for breach of contract or by way of pension in respect of past services. In this regard, it should be borne in mind that there is a general rule in contract that a person seeking damages must do what he can to mitigate his loss; see, for example, *Yetton v Eastwoods Froy Ltd*.[11] When a director is dismissed, the measure of damages to which he is entitled is based upon what he would have earned during the unexpired period of his service agreement or during the period of notice to which he is entitled. However, against this must be set off a sum to take account of:

(a) what he would have earned in alternative employment;

(b) accelerated payment; and

(c) the rather more lenient tax treatment of a severance payment.

This, however, it must be stressed, is only a general rule. An informative recent decision in the Court of Appeal is that of *Gregory v Wallace*.[12] The plaintiff had been employed by the defendant company as group financial director at a salary of £125,000 pa. His contract of employment anticipated three instances when his appointment might terminate:

(d) his reaching retirement age;

(e) the company terminating the agreement in circumstances specified in the contract;

(f) on the expiry of two years' written notice by the company or one year's notice by the plaintiff.

The agreement further provided that if the company gave notice, the plaintiff could take other employment during the notice period subject to his making himself reasonably available to the company. It also provided that if the company gave notice to terminate, it would be entitled to do so immediately. In such circumstances, the company, at the plaintiff's option, was either to pay the plaintiff his salary by way of monthly instalments over the two-year period or the aggregate of such instalments subject to a discount for early payment. The company went into administrative receivership and subsequently into administration. The administrators at first adopted the plaintiff's contract of employment and then dismissed him, first orally and then confirmed in writing. The plaintiff now claimed two years' salary, subject to a discount for accelerated payment, but without deduction for income that he had received in the course of his new employment. It was held that the plaintiff was entitled to damages resulting from his wrongful dismissal. The measure of damages was to be what he would have earned during the two years' written notice period subject to a discount for accelerated payment, such as was provided in the terms of his agreement. However, no deduction was required to take account of what he had received in the course of alternative employment. This had been permitted by his contract and he could take full advantage of such provision.

10.2 TAXATION

(1) Tax-free payments to directors are prohibited by s 311 which provides that any agreement for payment of a net sum, after deduction of tax shall be treated as though the net sum were gross.[13] Thus, the director must bear tax on the net sum.

(2) The directors' personal liability to tax on remuneration falls under Schedule E and PAYE applies, as it does for employees. The company is therefore liable to account to the Inland Revenue and if it fails to deduct, its remedy is to debit the director and deduct the debt from further remuneration.[14] The PAYE deductions include higher rates of income tax, as well as the basic rate.[15]

(3) Expenses and benefits in kind, are prima facie taxable in the hands of directors and the onus is on them to justify any deductions[16] (see **10.7** below).

(4) Compensation for loss of office is also prima facie taxable except:

    (a)   on loss of office through death or disability;

    (b)   in specified circumstances where the director's employment has included foreign service; and

    (c)   to the extent of the first £30,000; provided it is made 'in connection with' termination of employment.[17]

10.3   SHARE INCENTIVE SCHEMES

Many companies have rewarded the efforts of their directors and employees by giving them options to acquire shares at a favourable price. This has been done either by means of an option in the true sense, or by issuing shares on which a very small part of the capital is paid up or by the provision of loan facilities. Such schemes do not conflict with the prohibition on option dealing in s 323, which does not apply to options to subscribe for shares from the company itself.

The tax treatment of these benefits has changed from time to time and will, no doubt, change again in the future. The basic position is that benefits derived from the schemes are taxed as earned income *unless* they fall within specific exemptions. In 1998, such exemptions included:

(1) Approved Profit-Sharing Schemes – ICTA 1988, ss 186 to 187
Shares in the company are acquired by trustees on behalf of participating employees up to an annual maximum of £3,000 or (if higher) 10 per cent of salary up to a limit of £8,000. They must normally be held by the trustees for at least two years. On subsequent sales, income tax on the original value is chargeable on a sliding scale, falling into nil after five years from the date of acquisition. Such schemes are not open to shareholders having more than 25 per cent of the shares in, or controlling a close company.

(2) Approved Savings-Related Share Option Schemes – ICTA 1988, s 185
Here the employee gets an option to buy shares (at not less than 80 per cent of current market value) out of a SAYE scheme of not more than £250 per month. The scheme operates over three, five or seven years at the end of which (or on earlier retirement age) the option is exercisable. No income tax is then payable but there may be some capital gains tax on disposal. Such schemes are, again, not open to shareholders having more than 25 per cent of the shares in, or controlling, a close company.

(3) Registered Profit-Related Pay Schemes (RPRP) – ICTA 1988, ss 169 to 184
Such pay is free of income tax up to £4,000 or 20 per cent of earnings whichever is the lower, under a profit-linked scheme registered by the Inland Revenue.

Only directors working at least 25 hours per week can participate in schemes 1 and 2 above and all employees must be eligible. In the case of RPRP, the scheme must be open to 80 per cent of employees, the directors' minimum hours are 20 per week and again controlling directors (with 25 per cent holdings) are excluded.[18] In view of the limits on these highly advantageous schemes, directors may be more interested in (4) below. RPRP schemes will be phased out by the end of the year 2000, although new approved share schemes are due to be introduced in that year.

(4) Executive Share Option Schemes – ICTA 1985, s 185

These must be approved by the Inland Revenue and can be limited to specific groups of full-time (ie 25 hours per week) executives and directors, with a maximum per person of £100,000 or four times earnings, if greater. The option price must not be 'manifestly' lower than current market value (after 31 December 1991, this can be reduced to 85 per cent where the company also operates schemes (1) or (2)) and must be exercised between three and ten years after the grant. There is no income tax on exercise but capital gains tax will apply on disposal. A holder of a 10 per cent 'material interest' is excluded from participation.

(5) Employee Share-Ownership Plans (ESOPS) – FA 1987, ss 67 to 74: FA 1992, s 36

These provide corporation tax relief to a company on its contributions to a trust which can distribute shares to employees and provide a market in those shares. All qualifying employees must benefit. This includes worker directors with a minimum of 20 hours per week but in those schemes a five per cent share-holding disqualifies. The trust and the beneficiaries are subject to income tax on any benefits.

Listed companies which introduce share incentive schemes must obtain the approval of the members in general meeting and the schemes must provide (Admission of Securities to Listing, ss 1, 3, 9):

(1) details of qualified participants;
(2) the total amount of securities affected;
(3) the maximum entitlement of any participant;
(4) details of the terms of issue;
(5) disclosure of any interests of the directors in the trustees of the scheme.

Moreover, alteration cannot be made to the advantage of the participants without the shareholders' prior approval.

10.4 LOANS, ETC TO DIRECTORS[19]

A comprehensive code for these transactions is set out in ss 330 to 342. Some apply to all companies, some to 'relevant companies' only; 'relevant companies' means public companies or members of groups containing a public company. The rationale of the rules governing loans to directors is probably accurately expressed in the five following propositions. If they are borne in mind the detailed rules make some sense.

(1) A director really should not take a loan from his company. To do so would give rise to a potential conflict of interest and duty.

(2) Professional advisers might try to explain this to their clients for ever and a day, but many small private company directors regard the company's bank account as merely an extension of their own. If, for example, they are taking their family on holiday, they will write a cheque for, say, £2,000 on the company bank account and it is then for the accountant to sort this out by way of a director's loan account.

(3) Given this is how things are, the real prohibition on taking loans should be on directors of public companies because the likelihood here is that persons other than the controllers of the company will be shareholders.

(4) If the law were to restrict simply loans to directors of public companies, this could be circumvented by the public company wishing to make a loan to a director doing so by way of a subsidiary private company.

Accordingly, in the context of loans (and loans only) the Act refers to relevant companies rather than public companies. A relevant company is any company which is itself public or a member of a group which contains a public company. The main restrictions on the giving of loans lies in respect of relevant rather than non relevant companies.

(5) The Act refers to specific prohibitions in respect of loans. This is a further factor which tends to make rules appear confusing. There are considerable exceptions to the express prohibitions. Accordingly, while it might appear from the prohibitions that certain types of loan cannot be made, it will be discovered that there are exceptions, usually limited as to value, which do permit loans of these types to be made in practice.

10.4.1 The prohibitions

These extend to directors of holding companies, and are as follows.

(1) No company may make a loan, or provide a guarantee or other security[20] for a loan made to the director by a third party: s 330(2).[20]

(2) No relevant company may make a 'quasi-loan' to a director, or to a person connected with him,[21] or give any form of security for loans or quasi-loans made by a third party to a director or a connected person. A quasi-loan is a transaction (it need not be a contract) under which the creditor (the company) pays money on behalf of the 'borrower' (the director or connected person) or reimburses a third party for expenditure incurred on the borrower's behalf, on terms or in circumstances which give rise to an obligation on the borrower's part to repay the creditor.[22] An example would be the provision by a company of a credit card to a director to pay such things as hotel expenses and travel costs, but which credit card the director then uses for this person expenditure; such use is a quasi-loan.

(3) No relevant company may provide credit for a director or connected person (as defined at **5.5**) or provide any form of security where credit has been granted by a third party: s 330(4). For these purposes, a credit transaction is:

    (a) the supply of goods or land under a conditional sale or hire-purchase agreement;[23]

    (b) the lease or hire of land or goods for periodic payments;[24] or

    (c) any other disposal of land or supply of goods or service for deferred payment (s 331(7)).

(4) No company may take over a transaction which, if originally made by the company, would have infringed any of the rules (1) to (3) above: s 330(6). For example, a company which takes an assignment of a loan contract from the lender will infringe this rule if the borrower is a director. Conversely, there will be an infringement if the lender is persuaded to allow the company to take over the director's obligations under the loan agreement. For these purposes, and for the purposes of the many amplifying rules described below (including those governing disclosure), the relevant date is the date when the company arranges to take over the agreement, and not the date when the agreement was made (s 330(6)).

(5) No company may take part in any arrangement under which the company (or another group company) confers a benefit upon a third party who enters into a transaction which, if made by the company, would infringe any of the rules (1) to (4) above: s 330(7). This is a characteristic piece of abstract legislative drafting concealing its real intentions. Two examples may help to illustrate that intention, both being infringements of s 330(7):

(a) a bank agrees to give a director an overdraft (a loan) on favourable terms; in return, the company gives its banking affairs to that bank;

(b) company A and company B are in the same group. Company A agrees to make loans to company B's directors, in return for company B's making loans to those of company A.

10.4.2 The exceptions

Short-term accommodations: s 332
A relevant company may make small quasi-loans provided that:

(1) the debtor must repay within two months of the company's expenditure; *and*
(2) the amount (aggregated with any other quasi-loan[25]) does not exceed £5,000.

Inter-company loans within a group: s 333
Such loans made by one group company to another are permitted, as are quasi-loans and the provision of security. It might seem startling that any such exception should be necessary, but the width of the definition of a 'connected person' and the sub-definition of 'associate' is so great that s 330 might otherwise be read as prohibiting intra-group transactions.

Small loans: s 334
A company may make small loans to a director or to a director of its holding company provided that his total indebtedness in this regard does not exceed £5,000. This, in fact, legitimises the borrowing of £2,000, mentioned above, by a director wishing to take his family on holiday.

Minor and business transactions: s 335
There are two exceptions to s 330(4) (**10.4.1**(3) above) whereby relevant companies can enter into otherwise prohibited transactions with directors:

(1)   a company may enter into a credit transaction or provide security for such a transaction if the total indebtedness does not exceed £10,000;

(2)   a company may enter such transactions or provide security if it does so in the ordinary course of its business and gives the director no more favourable terms than his financial standing would justify if he were an outsider.

Transactions with holding companies: s 336

(1)   A company may make a loan or quasi-loan to its holding company or provide security for such a transaction between the holding company and a third party creditor.

(2)   A company may provide credit for its holding company, or provide security for a credit transaction between the holding company and a third party creditor.

Directors' expenditure: s 337

Where a director incurs expenditure for the company's purposes or to enable him to perform his duties as a director,[26] the expenditure may be funded by the company[27] provided that:

(1)   the general meeting gives its approval after full disclosure of the expenditure, the amount of funds to be provided, and any further liability of the company; or

(2)   the loan or other liability of the director under the transaction is to be discharged within six months of the next AGM if the members have not approved it at that or an earlier meeting.

But the aggregate indebtedness[28] must not exceed £20,000 in the case of a relevant company.

Loans and quasi-loans by money-lending companies: s 338

A money-lending company[29] may make loans or quasi-loans, or provide security in relation to such transactions, up to a total (in aggregate of all transactions with the debtor) of £100,000.[30] However, to qualify, the transaction must be:

(1)   in the ordinary course of the company's business; and

(2)   no more favourable in amount or terms than if the borrower were an outsider of similar financial standing.

The second requirement does not apply to house-purchase or improvement loans if such loans are normally made to employees and the terms are no more favourable than those enjoyed by the employees.

As may be deduced from the outline of these provisions given above, they are of considerable complexity. Professional advice should be sought before a company enters into any of the transactions described. It is particularly important to remember that because lending or some form of financial accommodation is involved, these provisions impose restrictions which might not apply if the board decided to make an outright payment to the person in question.

10.4.3 Breaches of s 330

Civil liability: s 341

The transaction is *voidable* at the company's option, except in the following circumstances:

(1) restitution of the money, or other asset which is the subject of the transaction, is no longer possible;
(2) the company has been indemnified against any loss arising from the transaction by the director or (where relevant) the connected person, or by the directors authorising the transaction;
(3) a third party, acting in good faith and without actual notice of the infringement, has acquired for value rights which would be prejudiced by avoiding the transaction.

In any case, the director, a connected person and the authorising directors will be liable:

(a) jointly and severally to indemnify the company for any loss; and
(b) to account to the company for any gain which he has made, directly or indirectly,[31] by the transaction.

Where the infringement lay in a transaction with a connected person, the 'connected director' may escape liability by showing that he took all reasonable steps to secure compliance with s 330; and the connected person himself, and any director authorising the transaction, may escape liability by showing that he was unaware of the circumstances which constituted the infringement. It does not necessarily follow that the directors involved may not be liable to the company for negligence or other breach of duty; it is possible, however, that s 341 could be construed by the courts as having this effect since the form of liability imposed by it is similar to that imposed by the courts themselves, and it can be argued that in many cases (probably not all) the 'exemptions' should extend to both types of liability if they are to have any real substance.

Criminal liability: s 342

This is confined to infringements involving 'relevant' companies (see **10.4.1** above), their directors and those who procure infringements by such companies. A director is criminally liable for authorising or permitting any transaction or arrangement which he knew or had reasonable cause to believe infringed s 330. The 'procurer' is similarly liable. The company is liable for entering into the transaction, even though s 341 (civil liability) treats it as a 'victim' of the infringement. Punishments are fairly harsh. A magistrates' court may impose a £5,000 fine and/or six months' imprisonment; a Crown Court an unlimited fine and/or two years' imprisonment. The company has a statutory defence, however, if it shows that, at the time the transaction or arrangement was entered into, 'it'[32] did not know the relevant circumstances constituting the infringement.

10.4.4 Disclosure

Directors must disclose transactions falling within s 330 to the board: s 317(6). Disclosure must be made whether or not the transaction or arrangement was prohibited by s 330. It must be made at the first meeting of the directors which considers the transaction or (if later) the first meeting after the directors' interest in it has arisen. Disclosure should be to the board as a whole and not merely to a sub-committee; failure will leave the director holding the benefit as a constructive trustee: see *Guinness plc v Saunders*.[33] Failure to make disclosure is also a criminal offence under s 317(7) and a single director company should ensure that the disclosure is properly minuted.

Section 232 and Sch 6, Part II require transactions and arrangements falling within s 330 to be disclosed in notes to the accounts[34] for the years in which they were entered into or still subsisted. The board has no power to withhold publication on the normal basis that the interest of the director is not 'material'. The note must state details of the transaction, the parties and the amounts outstanding.

There is, however, no need to disclose credit transactions, guarantees of credit transactions or ancillary arrangements with a director or connected person if the total outstanding, allowing for repayments, did not exceed £5,000 at any time during the financial year.

On the other hand, Sch 6, Part III extends the disclosure requirements in the accounts to transactions with non-directorial officers of the company if the sum outstanding at the end of the financial year is £2,500 or more.

If the auditors consider that the accounts do not give proper details of any of these types of transaction, they must include in their report a statement giving the required particulars insofar as they are reasonably able to do so: s 237(4).

10.5   REMUNERATION MAY BE SUED FOR

When properly voted, in accordance with the Articles, directors' remuneration is a debt which can be sued for like any other,[35] regardless of whether the company has made a profit.[36] However, the director's position is, in some respects, different from that of other employees.

(1)   In the absence of a resolution by the appropriate body, they cannot claim a reasonable sum (*quantum meruit*) where the Articles provide for the remuneration to be fixed by the board or by the members. If no sum is fixed, then none is payable.[37] An outsider, on the other hand, is entitled to reasonable remuneration if he works for the company without agreeing his remuneration in advance.

(2)   The Articles, although not themselves a contract between the directors and the company, are evidence of the terms on which a director has accepted office, in the absence of express terms in a service contract. Thus, if they say that a director shall be paid £1,000 pa he may claim it in the company's liquidation.[38] However, by the same token, he takes the risk that the Articles may be altered by the members at any time although in such a case he would have a claim against the company for damages for breach of contract: *Southern Foundries (1926) Ltd v Shirlaw*.[39]

(3) If remuneration is wrongly paid, it may be reclaimed, even though the directors acted in good faith and honestly believed that it was payable.[40]

(4) On liquidation, properly awarded directors' remuneration ranks equally with the other unsecured debts. It is not, therefore, a deferred debt, as are the claims of members for unpaid dividends.[41] Is it on the other hand a preferential debt, on the ground that the director is an employee or (under the pre-1986 insolvency law) a 'clerk or servant'?[42] The courts have rejected this view in the case of a managing director,[43] but accepted it in the case of a secretary,[44] and a director[45] employed as an editor of a paper. The logical distinction would appear to be that between a fee-earning non-executive director who would not qualify, and a salaried executive who would.[46]

(5) A claim for remuneration may, like any other claim, be barred by lapse of time after 6 years, or 12, when the director has a contract under seal.[47] Normally, such a debt will be shown year by year in the balance sheet, and provided that the limitation period has not already expired this may be a sufficient acknowledgment to prevent time from running against the claimant from the date when the remuneration was earned.[48] Where the debt is barred, the liquidator cannot pay it, even if the company is solvent, unless all the members consent.[49]

(6) Waiver of remuneration is binding, if resolved by the board[50] or agreed with the liquidator,[51] but a resolution to take no fees may always be rescinded at a later date.[52]

Particulars of waived remuneration are required to be shown in the accounts (by Sch 6, para 6) of all companies which are parent or subsidiary companies, or whose total directors' emoluments exceed £60,000.

10.6   DISCLOSURE IN ACCOUNTS

Disclosure of directors' earnings is secured by requiring the following particulars in the accounts.

(1) The total amount of directors' emoluments, aggregated into a single figure. This includes fees, commissions, expenses which are charged to tax, pension contributions, and the estimated cash value of benefits in kind. The totals for individual directors are not shown (except where (6) below applies), but the aggregate figure must be divided between directors' fees and other emoluments such as executive salaries (Sch 6, para 1).

(2) The total of directors' or past directors' pensions, excluding those paid under a scheme where the contributions are substantially adequate for maintaining it, but including pensions to widows or dependants and the estimated value of non-cash benefits (Sch 6, para 7).

(3) The total compensation and/or damages paid to directors or past directors for loss of office including sums paid on retirement, and distinguishing between payments by the company, its subsidiaries and other parties and also including the estimated value of non-cash benefits (Sch 6, para 8).

(4) The total consideration payable to third parties for making available the services of a person as a director of the company or a subsidiary (Sch 6, para 9).

(5) Where the aggregates shown under para (1) total £200,000 or more, the following must also be shown:

    (a) so much of the total of these aggregates as is attributable to the highest paid director

    (b) so much of the aggregate of the pension contributions paid as is so attributable (Company Accounts (Disclosure of Directors' Emoluments) Regulations 1997, SI 1997/570).

(6) If the accounts do not comply with these requirements the auditors must state the information (if they can) in their report: s 237(4).

(7) Every director is under a duty to notify the company in writing of his own emoluments, so as to enable the company to show the required information in the accounts.[53] There is, however, no requirement in the section that the notice should be in writing or in any particular form nor that it should repeat information which is clearly apparent in the company's books. It should disclose facts which are otherwise unknown to the company, such as payments from other parties and expenses which have been charged to income tax.

(8) In any prospectus, provisions as to directors' remuneration in the Articles must usually be disclosed[54] and listed companies must give details of waived remuneration and dividends with the directors' report.

(9) Trustee directors, ie those whose appointment is due to a trust shareholding, are under a quite separate duty to disclose and account for their directors' fees to the trust estate.[55] However, this will not apply if the trust gives them specific authority to retain them.[56] Where they have the usual professional charging clause, they may still have to pay over their director's fees, but can render an account for their time spent on board duties. Alternatively, the beneficiaries can, in appropriate circumstances, allow them to retain their fees: *Re Gee, Wood v Staples*.[57]

10.7 EXPENSES

The payment of directors' expenses may give rise to several questions.

(1) Remuneration is regarded as covering travelling expenses and other expenses[58] – unless the Articles specifically permit an additional payment or the members so resolve.

(2) The Articles usually give such authority and reg 83 of Table A provides that:

> 'Directors may be paid all travelling, hotel and other expenses properly incurred by them in connection with their attendance at meetings of the directors or committees of the directors or general meetings or separate meetings of the holders of any class of shares or debentures of the company or otherwise in connection with the discharge of their duties.'

(3) If the Articles are drawn more narrowly than Table A and restrict directors' expenses to those incurred 'in the execution of their offices' then travelling expenses must not be paid.[59]

(4) The taxation treatment of expenses naturally changes from year to year, but the position of directors at the time of writing is as follows.

(a) Directors, whether fee earning or salaried, are holders of an office or employment and with very few exceptions are taxed under Schedule E like any other employee. PAYE will normally apply and will extend to the higher as well as the basic rates of tax.

(b) No matter how low a director's earnings, expenses paid to him (or to higher paid employees: the 'P11D' people after the relevant tax form) are subject to tax under Schedule E by virtue of the elaborate code set out in ICTA 1988 (as amended).[60] Expenses are deductible in the ordinary way, but the onus lies upon the taxpayer to establish this.[61]

(c) Taxable benefits include all benefits provided to the taxpayer or his family or household by reason of his employment, and tax is payable on the 'cash equivalent' of the various types of benefit, such as accommodation, cars or loans.

(d) Since the rather absurd position may be reached in which a taxable 'emolument' in the form of expenses may be reduced to nothing by deductibility (see (b) above), s 166 of ICTA 1988 allows the Inland Revenue to grant the company dispensation if it is satisfied that no additional tax will be payable because of the payments, benefits, etc. This notice will remain in force, freeing the payments from the ICTA code, until revoked.

(e) Any expenses which are chargeable to income tax must be disclosed in the accounts as part of the directors' emoluments under Sch 6, para 1.[62]

10.8 NATIONAL INSURANCE

National Insurance is a political football which is liable to be kicked in a different direction at any time. At the time of writing the director's position under the Social Security Acts of 1975, 1986 and 1988 as consolidated in the Social Security Contributions and Benefits Act 1992 and the Social Security Administration Act 1992 is as follows.

(1) All directors, whether fee earning or salaried are treated as class 1 contributors, if not as employees then as 'office holders' with emoluments chargeable to income tax under Schedule E.[63]

(2) Earnings-related contributions are collected, together with income tax, under the PAYE procedure.[64] The DSS assesses directors' contributions on an annual basis to prevent evasion.[65]

(3) If the director has more than one directorship or source of earnings, he should, in general terms, make contributions on his total earnings. There is however no such aggregation in determining the employer's contribution except in certain defined circumstances.

(4) The Social Security Contributions and Benefits Act 1992, s 44(3) provides for a retirement pension consisting of:

(a) a basic flat rate element; and
(b) an element dependent upon earnings-related contributions.

There is no contracting out of the basic element, but partial contracting out of the second element is permitted, subject to specified conditions, for those subject to schemes approved by the Occupational Pensions Board. Contracting-out affects the amount of contribution payable by the director.[66]

(5) What is said above constitutes only the barest outline of what is now an extremely complex area on which professional advice must be sought (if only because over-payments are sometimes irrecoverable!). It must be borne in mind that the liability to pay employee's contributions is enforced by criminal sanctions in proceedings brought by the DSS, in which the onus is on the defendant to show that the contributions were not in fact due. Where the employer was a company which had failed to pay, contributions could formerly be recovered from any director who knew or should reasonably have known of the failure to pay, and this liability survived the director's retirement: Social Security Act 1975, s 152(4). A director who was thus made liable was not entitled to reclaim from the company the sum which he had been forced to pay from his own pocket.[67] Happily for the director, this rather intimidating provision was repealed by the Insolvency Act 1986.

10.9   SERVICE CONTRACTS

Any executive director has a service contract whether or not it is reduced to writing.[68] There is everything to be said for incorporating the more important provisions in a written agreement, however short or informal, particularly in view of the requirements of employment legislation and s 318 of the Companies Act. A specimen form of agreement is in Sch A. The following points may be noted.

10.9.1   The Employment Rights Act 1996

This Act provides minimum periods of notice as follows.

(1) An employee who has served for one month must give not less than one week (s 86(1)).
(2) An employer must give periods of notice depending on the length of the employee's continuous[69] service:

0 to 2 years	1 week
2 to 12 years	1 week for each year of employment
12 years and above	At least 12 weeks (s 86(1))

(3) These periods are minima, so that they will not apply if a longer period of reasonable notice would be implied by law.
(4) Executive directors with a contract of service, express or implied, are employees for this purpose, but the minimum period of notice will not usually affect them, since reasonable notice in their case will almost certainly be longer.[70]
(5) Either side may still terminate the contract without notice where this is justified, for example, for dishonesty or some other grave breach of the contract.[71]
(6) 'Notice' means an actual period of notice or salary in lieu, and the period of weeks must exclude the day of service and the day on which it is to take effect.
(7) Written particulars of the terms of employment must also be given within two months of the commencement of employment to employees (including employed directors) (ss 1 to 5).
(8) The particulars must include remuneration, pay periods, hours, holidays, sick pay, pensions,[72] redress of grievances and notice on either side.[73]

(9) These requirements do not apply where the director or other employee has a written service contract containing all the relevant matters.

(10) Since the period of notice must be stated, it will usually be longer than the statutory period in the case of directors.

10.9.2   Disclosure

Section 318 provides as follows.

(1) A copy of the director's service agreement, or a memorandum of the terms, if not in writing, is to be kept at an appropriate place. This requirement extends to service agreements with shadow directors and with directors employed by subsidiaries.

(2) Appropriate place means either:

    (a)   registered office; or

    (b)   where the register of members is kept; or

    (c)   principal place of business in England of an English company, and in Scotland of a Scottish company; in the case of (b) or (c) the Registrar of Companies must be notified of the address.

(3) The copies and memoranda must be open to inspection by members (not the public) without charge. There is no right to demand copies.

(4) In default, there are fines on the company and every officer in default.

(5) Two classes of contract are excepted:

    (a)   where the director works wholly or mainly abroad;[74] and

    (b)   where his contract expires within 12 months or can be terminated by the company within 12 months without compensation. This can give rise to difficulty, in particular the question what is the position of a director who has no specific agreement as to the length of notice on termination? In such cases he must be given 'reasonable' notice, and for a senior executive director this might be as much as 12 months. In such cases, therefore, the relevant disclosure should be made unless the director is willing to acknowledge that he is entitled to something less than 12 months' notice.

10.9.3   Notice to terminate

We have seen that this question is relevant to the disclosure requirement under s 318, and that in the absence of specific agreement, notice must be 'reasonable' on both sides.[75] This applies where the director is an employee, but the question of termination of employment in relation to his office as director involves other matters which are discussed in Chapter 11 below. In any event, the meaning of 'reasonable' notice would depend on the circumstances in each case and certainty is clearly preferable. The parties should therefore specify in the service agreement either the fixed term of that agreement, or the period of notice required to terminate, or some combination of the two.

When deciding on the period of service agreements, the board must always bear in mind that they are exercising their discretion in the interests of the company and not of the individual directors. The director's position is clearly strengthened by a long-term agreement, particularly in the event of a change of control, but it is rarely in the interests of the company to enter into a fixed contract for more than five years. The same principles apply to 'golden parachutes', ie contractual guarantees of substantial damages on the termination of service agreements.

Unless the company is a wholly-owned subsidiary,[76] s 319 requires prior approval by the general meeting of any director's employment contract which will or may continue for more than five years[77] if the company has no power, or only a restricted power, to terminate it. Approval cannot validly be given unless a memorandum of the agreement setting out the relevant terms is made available for inspection: (i) for at least 15 days before the meeting, at the registered office; and (ii) at the meeting itself. If valid prior approval is not obtained, the company may terminate the contract at any time by giving reasonable notice, whatever the contract itself may say. The director would have no redress, since the term entitling him to long-term employment is void in those circumstances.

10.9.4   Duties

Duties in the service agreement should be specified as far as possible but, from the company's point of view, it is desirable to give wide discretion to the board, ie 'such duties as the board may from time to time require'.

This is particularly useful in a group where the board may wish to move the director from one subsidiary to another, as circumstances require.[78] The contract should contain the usual power to terminate in the event of breach of duties or failure to carry them out by reason of ill-health or absence, as well as for bankruptcy or conviction of a crime. Sometimes contracts will exclude from the definition of a crime such 'regulatory' offences as convictions for road traffic offences.

10.9.5   Patents and inventions

These should be reserved for the company's benefit where they relate to the company's business, and are taken out or made during the director's period of service. This may well have been implied from the director's fiduciary duties,[79] but s 39 of the Patents Act 1977 provides that inventions made in the course of employment belong to the employer while inventions outside the course of the employment belong to the employee. The effect of s 39 cannot be excluded by contract, and it is therefore very much in the interests of both parties that the employment contract sets out the duties of the employee, since it is only where the employment is such that inventions can reasonably be expected to be made that the employer's rights will arise. It is up to an employee who does obtain title to the invention whether or not to patent it; if he does not, but merely publishes it, the employer may use it just as any member of the public might; there will be much more difficulty if the employee discloses it to the employer in confidence, although here some agreement may solve the problem even if the fiduciary duties of a director do not. Section 40 of the 1977 Act gives an employee the right to compensation if his employer is able to patent the invention belonging to the employer under s 39; the invention must have been of 'outstanding benefit' to the employer, and the employee is entitled to a 'fair share' of that benefit (s 41). No contract is enforceable to the extent that it diminishes the employee's statutory rights (s 42).

It should be noted that these statutory provisions relate only to those who work under a contract of employment; if there is no such contract, written or oral, it may be necessary to fall back on an express agreement as to inventions and patent rights, rather than the possibilities of the director's fiduciary duties.[80]

10.9.6   Restrictive covenants

Naturally, a director acquires knowledge, experience and goodwill, and it would be very damaging to the company if, on leaving, he took these to a competitor. Accordingly, a service agreement may contain a 'restrictive covenant' whereby he undertakes that for a specified period after he leaves the company he will not be engaged in the same kind of business. If such a covenant is to be of any use, however, it must be very carefully drafted, as all covenants of this kind are prima facie in restraint of trade and are accordingly void unless it can be established that having regard to all the circumstances they are reasonable, and the onus of proving that a particular covenant is reasonable is on the party seeking to enforce it.[81] Whether or not a covenant is reasonable depends upon whether it is necessary for the protection of the company's legitimate interests and is not injurious to the public. A covenant which is merely designed to protect the company from legitimate competition by a former director is going beyond the protection of legitimate interests.[82] In deciding whether a particular covenant should or should not be enforced, the courts attach importance to such factors as its geographical extent,[83] its duration in point of time and the activities forbidden. Provided, however, that such an analysis shows that the covenant is reasonable, it can be enforced by injunction.[84] The court will not rewrite a covenant so as to make it reasonable. However, if an offending covenant can be severed from other restrictive clauses, those other clauses may be enforceable. Severance is possible if it is not necessary to add to or modify the wording of the remaining provisions.

A restriction on the director engaging in any other business or occupation while he is serving the company may be inserted in his service agreement, and it may also be provided that he shall account to the company for any remuneration he may receive as director of any other company. In the absence of any clause of this kind, he is entitled to retain such remuneration, just as he is entitled to retain any other profits or earnings so long as they are not 'secret profits' made by virtue of his office and for which he is under fiduciary obligation to account to the company (see **5.6**).

10.9.7   Pensions

The service agreement will usually contain provisions for membership of any pension scheme operated by the company. This is discussed in Chapter 12.

10.9.8   Enforcement

Contracts for personal services are not normally enforced by orders of specific performance. In other words, neither the company nor the director will be compelled to perform the service contract against their wishes. The remedy is, therefore, a claim for damages and if one party refuses to perform his obligations, the loss to the other must be quantified and claimed accordingly.

However, where a company has agreed to give a service contract to a third party, then it may be ordered to enter into the agreement. It was so decided in *C H Giles & Co Ltd v Morris*;[85] the mere fact that the contract itself was not one which would be specifically enforced was not a ground for refusing to decree that the contract should be entered into. The judge added that it should not be assumed that as soon as any elements of personal service or continuous service can be discerned in a contract, the courts will, without more evidence, refuse specific performance.

10.10   SPECIAL DIRECTORS

The office of director is a single entity as far as the law is concerned. A person is either a director in the full sense or no director at all. However, different categories of director are found in practice and it may be useful to take note of them here and to consider what they mean.

(1)   Managing directors are those appointed by the board under reg 84 of Table A or similar provisions. Without such an Article the appointment cannot be made.[86] Table A leaves the duties, powers and remuneration of the managing director entirely to the discretion of the board. The only distinction between him and the other directors, which is recognised by the law, is his implied authority to bind the company by contracts in the ordinary course of business.[87]

(2)   Alternate directors are those appointed by the members of the board to act and speak on their behalf during periods of absence or incapacity. A special Article is needed and Table A, regs 65 to 69 now contain such provisions.[88] An alternate may be another director or an outsider, provided that his appointment is approved by board resolution; subject to this, he is appointed and removed by the director for whom he is to act. As far as notice of meetings, attendance and voting are concerned, he is treated in the same way as a 'normal' director, but (perhaps on the assumption that he will normally be another director) reg 66 provides that, while he may perform 'all the functions of his appointor', he is not entitled to any remuneration for his services as an alternate director. Further, except where the Articles provide to the contrary (which would not be sensible) he is 'deemed for all purposes to be a director' (reg 69). The appointor is not, therefore, responsible for his acts or defaults.

(3)   De facto directors are those who have not been properly appointed but who are 'occupying the position of a director' and are therefore treated as directors by s 741. They therefore bear all the responsibilities of directors without enjoying any of the authority.'[89]

(4)   The notion of shadow directors was introduced in 1980[90] and is defined by s 741 as any person (including another company) 'in accordance with whose directions or instructions the directors of the company are accustomed to act'. The category is relevant for various purposes under the Act (for example, disclosure of share interests and the register of directors, loans and property transactions and disqualification) and under the Insolvency Act 1986 (for example, in relation to wrongful trading). It catches the de facto controller whose formal and informal

connection with the company is not sufficiently concrete to make him a de facto director; there is nothing like an appointment or office, or functions carried out on behalf of the company. Shadow directors bear, therefore, many of the statutory responsibilities of directors because of their power over the company, but they are not treated as directors for all purposes unless they also fall within the definition of de facto directors under (3) above. There are savings for those whose involvement is limited to the giving of professional advice and for parent companies giving instructions to their subsidiaries (for certain purposes).[91]

In *Re Tasbian Ltd (No 3)*[92] Balcombe LJ seemed not to differentiate between de facto directors and shadow directors. In this, he was apparently following the view of Vinelott J in that case at first instance.[93] However, in *Re Hydrodan (Corby) Ltd*,[94] Millett J, making no reference in his judgment to *Re Tasbian* drew a very clear distinction between a de facto director and a shadow director.

> 'Directors may be of three kinds: de jure directors, that is to say those who have been validly appointed to the office; de facto directors, that is to say, directors who assume to act as directors without having been appointed validly or at all; and shadow directors who are persons falling within the definition [a person in accordance with whose directions or instructions the directors of the company are accustomed to act] . . . a de facto director, I repeat, is one who claims to act and purports to act as a director, although not validly appointed as such. A shadow director, by contrast, does not claim or purport to act as a director. On the contrary, he claims not to be a director. He lurks in the shadows, sheltering behind others who, he claims, are the only directors of the company to the exclusion of himself.'

(5) Special, executive, local, regional, assistant and divisional directors are titles which are seen with some frequency, particularly in large companies. The object is usually to give enhanced status to senior executives, without at the same time admitting them to the main board. They are, therefore, the opposite of de facto directors in that they are directors in name but not in fact.

The problem here is that it may not be possible both to have one's cake and to eat it. It is the use of the name alone which is wanted but the responsibilities and powers which go with it cannot be disregarded. Unless the position is absolutely clear from the Articles, an outsider can hardly be expected to know that the 'special director' with whom he is dealing is not really a director at all and the very use of the word must involve a possibility that a de facto directorship will arise under s 741. The prospective holder of such an office should, therefore, be aware that the full rigours of the Acts may well apply to him, particularly as he is bound to be an officer, for the purpose of the criminal penalties on an 'officer in default'.

Where there is a group of companies the solution to the problem is to appoint the executive to the board of the particular subsidiary with which be is most concerned. In that case, there is no doubt about his status as a full director of the subsidiary but not of the parent.[95]

Where, however, a special directorship is desired for senior employees, there must be an enabling provision in the Articles. This is not found in Table A and so a special Article will be needed.

In the light of the problems discussed above, this should give complete discretion to the board with regard to his appointment, removal, duties and title, and should expressly provide, if that is the intention (and for what it is worth), that he is *not* a director for the purposes of the Companies Acts.

10.11 DIRECTORS AS EMPLOYEES

The dual capacity of directors as board members on the one hand, and executives or employees on the other, has already been noted.[96] To the question: is a director an employee? – the answer must unfortunately be – yes – for some purposes and – no – for others.

It may be useful to summarise some of the situations in which a director's status as an employee may be relevant.

(1) The Act effectively recognises that a director may be an employee, for s 153(4)(c) refers to 'persons (other than directors) employed in good faith by the company'. This seems to point to a logical distinction between a salaried executive director who forms part of the 'labour force' under a contract of employment and would qualify as an employee, and a fee-earning non-executive who would not.[97] This distinction is not, however, drawn in every situation and the failure to keep the two capacities separate has led to some confusion.

(2) A managing director has been held not to be a 'clerk or servant' (now an 'employee') so as to have preference on winding up,[98] but there seems no reason why this principle should not be restricted to his fees, leaving him free to claim preference in respect of his salary.

(3) All directors are treated as employees or office holders for the purpose of their liability to Schedule E Income Tax under PAYE and National Insurance Class I contributions under the Social Security Act 1975, as consolidated in the Social Security Contributions and Benefits Act 1992 (see **10.8**).

(4) Under the Employment Rights Act 1996, the right not to be 'unfairly dismissed' applies to those who work under a 'contract of employment' which is defined as a 'contract of service' (see **10.9**).

Here, we seem to have the distinction correctly applied. A non-executive director will not have a contract of employment but a salaried executive director will, and should therefore have the protection of the 'unfair dismissal' provisions.

(5) Similar definitions are used by the 1996 Act for the purposes of redundancy payments and directors with contracts of service, whether express or implied, should fall within their provisions, as employees. However, this may not be the case for smaller companies, see (7).

(6) For some purposes, directors are specifically set apart from *most* other employees, for example:

(a) s 153(4)(c) allows the company to make loans for the purchase of its own shares, to bona fide employees 'other than directors';

(b) all directors are lumped together with 'higher-paid employees' for the purposes of taxable expenses and benefits.[99]

(7) Strong authority for the treatment of an executive director as an employee is to be found in the case of *Lee v Lee's Air Farming Ltd*,[100] where the managing and controlling director of a one-man company was killed in an air crash while carrying out a crop-spraying contract for the company. The Privy Council held that he had entered into a contract of service and was therefore a 'worker' for the purpose of the New Zealand Workers Compensation Act 1922. The contractual obligations were not invalidated 'by the circumstances that the deceased was sole governing director in whom was vested the full government and control of the company'.

The decision in *Lee v Lee's Air Farming Ltd* was distinguished by Mummery J in *Buchan v Secretary of State for Employment*.[101] In this case, Mr Buchan and a colleague were working directors of the company in which they were equal shareholders. The company went into administrative receivership and the administrative receiver dismissed Mr Buchan. The question which the Employment Appeal Tribunal had to decide was whether Mr Buchan had been an employee for the purposes of a redundancy payment. It was found that he was not. While expressly approving the decision in Lee's case, the Tribunal drew a very clear distinction between that situation and the claim in this case for a redundancy payment. In essence, the purpose of a redundancy payment is to protect an employee when the company employing him fails. It is not to provide a cushion for an entrepreneur when he gets it wrong himself. As Mummery J put it:

> 'As beneficial owner of 50 per cent of the shares in the company, he was able to block any decision by the board or of the company in a general meeting with which he did not agree, including a decision as to his own dismissal or terms of service. In other words, Mr Buchan's agreement was necessary before he could be dismissed summarily or on notice. If he did not agree to a decision to dismiss him, then that would not be a "dismissal" within the meaning of the ... Act. It would be a case of what is sometimes called "self-dismissal". The intervention of the administrative receiver did not and could not alter Mr Buchan's legal status vis-a-vis the company.'

A similar approach has been adopted by the Employment Appeal Tribunal in two further cases. In *Evans v Secretary of State for Trade and Industry*,[102] the applicant was once again a 50 per cent shareholder and director of the company. The Employment Appeal Tribunal considered that his payment of income tax and National Insurance contributions as an employee was merely something to be taken into account and not conclusive. He was not an employee for the purposes of a redundancy payment. 'He was very much his own master; he was answerable to no one; he was able to come and go as he pleased'. A similar decision was reached in *Helmsley and Butters v Secretary of State*.[103] Here the applicants were the joint proprietors of a business. The Employment Appeal Tribunal, once again, found that they were not employees for the purposes of a redundancy payment. On the other hand, in *Secretary of State v Bottrill*,[104] the Employment Appeal Tribunal found that the one man running a one man company was an employee for the purposes of a redundancy payment, the learned chairman saying that he felt *Buchan* was wrongly decided. The case went on appeal to the Court of Appeal where the decision was upheld, but the Court decided the case on its facts rather than taking the opportunity to clarify the law in this regard.

CHAPTER 10 FOOTNOTES

1 *Re George Newman & Co* [1895] 1 Ch 674.

2 *Kerr v Marine Products Ltd* (1928) 44 TLR 292, where the board acted ultra vires in sending a director to Australia in a salaried post.

3 Otherwise these cannot be paid and are regarded as being covered by the remuneration; *Young v Naval etc Society* [1905] 1 KB 687.

4 See note 2.

5 As they must do to comply with the Act; see below.

6 *Felix Hadley & Co Ltd v Hadley* (1897) 77 LT 131.

7 *Re Duomatic Ltd* [1969] 1 All ER 161; *Re Halt Garage (1964) Ltd* [1982] 1 All ER 1016.

8 Otherwise a fee of '£X per annum' may imply that a full year must be served; *Salton v New Beeston Cycle Co* [1899] 1 Ch 775.

9 *Re J Franklin & Sons Ltd* [1937] 4 All ER 43.

10 *Johnston v Chestergate Hat Manufacturing Co* [1915] 2 Ch 338 where 'net profits' had to be defined by the courts. It was held that they meant profits *before* tax.

11 [1966] 3 All ER 353.

12 (Unreported) August 1997.

13 Thus '£2,500 per annum net of deductions' was not construed as meaning '£2,500 after income tax is deducted': *Owens v Multilux Ltd* [1974] IRLR 113, NIRC.

14 *Bernard and Shaw Ltd v Shaw and Rubin* [1951] 2 All ER 267.

15 ICTA 1988, s 1(2).

16 Ibid, s 153 et seq.

17 Ibid, ss 148 and 188.

18 Ibid, s 135.

19 Including shadow directors: s 330(5).

20 So a company, to take one example, can neither make a loan to enable a director to buy a house, nor guarantee his mortgage to another lender. The reason for the second prohibition is traditionally this: if he can offer good security, he can borrow from other sources. If he cannot, it is undesirable that the company should give him more credit than a commercial lender would have done.

21 As to 'connected persons', the term is defined by s 346 and is discussed in **5.5** above.

22 Section 331(3). Although such transactions might well be treated as lending in some contexts, in company law terms the tendency has been not to treat them as loans: *Champagne Perrier-Jouet SA v HH Finch Ltd* [1982] 3 All ER 713. The line between them is not obliterated by s 330, but for most practical purposes is immaterial.

23 As defined by s 189(1) of the Consumer Credit Act 1974; but for the purposes of the Companies Act, it makes no difference whether the credit agreement is regulated by that Act or not. A conditional sale is (in simple terms) an instalment sale under which the ownership of goods or land will not pass until payment is complete. Hire-purchase (which relates to goods only) is similar except that the debtor has some form of choice (in theory) whether to complete his payments and acquire ownership of the goods.

24 Many leases of goods are similar, in economic terms, to instalment sales, but the definition is not confined to these.

25 Ie made by the company or its subsidiary, or where the director is a director of the company's holding company, by any other subsidiary: s 332(2).

26 This is hardly generous: Table A, reg 83 entitles the company to discharge such expenditure in any case.

27 Or the company may take steps to enable him to avoid the expenditure.

28 The 'relevant amounts' under s 334. As an approximation, these are the value of the proposed transaction plus the value of or amounts due under other transactions between the company and the director or a person connected with him. These amounts may be (and have been) increased by the Secretary of State: s 345.

29 Ie a company whose ordinary business includes the provision of loan or quasi-loan credit and/or the provision of guarantees for such transactions. This must be a genuine part of the general business: *Steen v Law* [1963] 3 All ER 770.

30 Except in the case of a 'banking company', ie a company authorised under the Banking Act 1987 probably because commercial bankers are not to be disrupted by the £100,000 limits when dealing with companies associated with the bank's directors.

31 This potential liability seems to be very wide indeed, since it covers, on the face of it, all profits made with the loan and all assets acquired under a forbidden transaction. Since the obligations are owed to the company, the company may waive them, with the usual caveat that the general meeting or, perhaps, a minority of the members may be able to stop this. In the midst of the complexities of the Act, it should not be forgotten that 'ordinary' civil redress may be open to the company. It may simply demand repayment as and when it falls due; or, for example, if its guarantee is called up by the creditor, it may demand indemnity from the director under the ordinary law governing suretyship.

32 Given that members of the board are involved, the efficacy of this defence will depend upon the extent to which the courts will impute the offending director's knowledge to the company. If it is to work at all, it must be the case that knowledge of one or two directors not available to the rest of the board is not to be treated as the company's knowledge.

33 [1990] 1 All ER 652.

34 And group accounts; and the disclosure requirement extends to transactions involving shadow directors or connected persons.

35 *Nell v Atlanta Gold etc Mines* (1895) 11 TLR 407.

36 *Re Lundy Granite Co* (1872) 26 LT 673.

37 *Re Richmond Gate Property Co Ltd* [1964] 3 All ER 936.

38 *Re New British Iron Co* [1898] 1 Ch 324.

39 [1940] AC 701.

40 *Brown & Green Ltd v Hays* (1920) 36 TLR 330.

41 Section 74(2)(f) of the Insolvency Act 1986.

42 Schedule 6, para 9 to the Insolvency Act 1986 – preference limited to holiday pay (para 10) and four months' salary up to a figure to be prescribed by the DTI (currently £800 under the Insolvency Proceedings (Monetary Limits) Order 1986, SI 1986/1996.

43 *Re Newspaper Proprietary Syndicate Ltd* [1900] 2 Ch 349.

44 *Cairney v Black* [1906] 2 KB 746.

45 *Re Beeton & Co Ltd* [1913] 2 Ch 279.

46 *Boulting v ACTAT* [1963] 1 All ER 716.

47 Limitation Act 1980, ss 5 and 8.

48 *Jones v Bellgrove Properties* [1949] 2 All ER 198; Limitation Act 1980, s 29. A statement of affairs by a receiver may sometimes constitute an acknowledgement for these purposes, but more usually these speak of past debts rather than continuing obligations: *Re Overmark Smith Warden Ltd* [1982] 1 WLR 1195.

49 *Re Art Reproduction Co Ltd* [1951] 2 All ER 984.

50 *Re Consolidated Nickel Mines* [1914] 1 Ch 883.

51 *West Yorkshire Darracq Agency v Coleridge* [1911] 2 KB 326.

52 See note 50.

53 Section 231(4). The penalty is a £400 fine.

54 Schedule 3, paras 1 and 2.

55 *Re Macadam, Dallow v Codd* [1946] Ch 73.

56 *Re Llewellin's Will Trusts* [1949] 1 All ER 487.

57 [1948] 1 All ER 498.

58 *Young v Naval and Military Co-op Society* [1905] 1 KB 687.

59 *Marmor Ltd v Alexander* (1908) 15 SLT 515.

60 ICTA 1988, ss 153–168.

61 *Taylor v Provan* [1975] AC 194.

62 See **10.6** above.

63 Social Security Act 1975, s 2(1)(a) now Social Security Contributions and Benefits Act 1992, s 2; *McMillan v Guest* [1942] AC 561.

64 The lower and upper earnings limits for contributions were £3,432 and £26,000 per annum respectively for the year 1999/2000. For employees earning less than £66 pw the employee contribution was nil. An employee's contribution on earnings between £66 and £500 was 10 per cent or 8.4 per cent if contracted out. An employer will make the following weekly contributions:

Up to £83 pw   nil

Over £83 pw   12.2%

For employees contracting out of state earnings-related pensions the corresponding figures are reduced between £83 to £500 pw.

65 Social Security (Contributions) (Amendments) Regulations 1983, 1983/1000.

66 See note 64 above.

67 *Re J Burrows (Leeds) Ltd* [1982] 1 WLR 1177. *R v Dickson* [1992] 94 Cr App R 7, CA.

68 But for the purposes of unfair dismissal, even a full-time director was held not to be an employee under an implied contract of service where there was not even an *oral* agreement and his remuneration was recorded in the accounts not as wages or salaries but under a separate heading 'directors' fees': *Parsons v Albert J Parsons & Sons Ltd* [1979] ICR 271. This would not of course affect his liability to Schedule E and Class 1, NIC.

69 Continuous employment for one month is a precondition of entitlement.

70 Probably between 6 and 12 months; *Adams v Union Cinemas Ltd* [1939] 3 All ER 136.

71 It may still be necessary, however, to have regard to the *statutory* provisions governing unfair dismissal which overlap with the common law position and which sometimes produce confusing results. These are set out in Part IX of the 1996 Act.

72 In some cases, this information will be provided by the managers of statutory pension schemes.

73 Changes in these particulars must be notified within one month: s 4.

74 But a memorandum stating his name and the duration of the contract must be kept at the appropriate place.

75 *James v Thomas H Kent Co Ltd* [1950] 2 All ER 1099.

76 If the director is also a director of the holding company, his employment with that company is still within s 319; in any case, employment with a subsidiary does fall within the disclosure requirements of s 318 (**10.9.2**).

77 Except at the option of the company itself. Section 319(2) is designed to prevent evasions so that, for example, if a director after two years of a four-year contract enters into a further four-year contract, approval will be required as if the new agreement were for six years.

78 *Harold Holdsworth and Co (Wakefield) Ltd v Caddies* [1955] 1 All ER 725, where such a power served to defend the board against an action by a disgruntled director who objected to having his powers restricted to one of the subsidiaries.

79 *Fine Industrial Commodities Ltd v Powling* (1954) 71 RPC 253.

80 Ibid.

81 *Nordenfelt v Maxim Nordenfelt Guns & Ammunition Co Ltd* [1894] AC 535.

82 *Morris (Herbert) Ltd v Saxelby* [1916] 1 AC 688.

83 It may be easier to draft a 'solicitation covenant' (against dealing with old customers) than an 'area covenant' (dealing with working in a particular area): *T Lucas Co Ltd v Mitchell* [1974] Ch 129.

84 *Masons v Provident Clothing & Supply Co Ltd* [1913] AC 724.

85 [1972] 1 All ER 960.

86 *Boschoek Proprietary Co Ltd v Fuke* [1906] 1 Ch 148.

87 *Freeman & Lockyer v Buckhurst Park Properties (Mangal) Ltd* [1964] 1 All ER 630. See **3.10.2**.

88 There was no such provision in Table A (1948 version).

89 Thus the dominating group chairman in the *First Reinvestment Trust Limited* investigation was treated by the inspectors as a de facto director of six group companies on whose boards he did not serve. He was, therefore, in breach of his duties to those companies as well as to the others (HMSO, 1974).

90 Even then it was not a complete novelty: Companies Acts since 1917 have recognised the status in all but the words 'shadow director'.

91 Those purposes are (s 741(3)):

s 309 (duty to have regard to interested employees);

s 319 (directors' long-term contracts);

ss 320 to 322 (directors' substantial property transactions);

ss 330 to 346 (loans to directors).

The question whether a bank could be a shadow director was left open in *Re A Company (No 005009 of 1987)* (1988) 4 BCC 424 but would seem to be relevant only in the most exceptional circumstances.

92 [1992] BCC 358.

93 [1991] BCC 435.

94 [1994] BCC 161.

95 See also the comments in *Guidelines for Directors* (Institute of Directors, 6th edn) paras 75–91.

96 **10.1.7** and **10.5(4)**.

97 *Boulting v ACTAT* [1963] 1 All ER 716. For the purposes of defining 'associates', s 435 of the Insolvency Act 1986 states that *any* director is to be treated as employed, but this is, it must be said, a very special provision from which no general conclusion can be drawn.

98 *Re Newspaper Proprietary Syndicate Ltd* [1900] 2 Ch 349.

99 ICTA 1988, ss 153 and 162 respectively.

100 [1960] 3 All ER 420.

101 [1997] BCC 145.

102 (Unreported) 11 July 1997.

103 (Unreported) 20 June 1997.

104 [1998] IRLR 120.

Chapter 11

RESIGNATION, REMOVAL AND RETIREMENT

11.1   VACATION OF OFFICE

Vacation of a director's office may occur for several different reasons.

(1) Resignation (Table A, reg 81(d)).
(2) Removal by the members under s 303 (whether or not involving a breach of any service agreement).
(3) Disqualification by law (for example, s 291(3) or ss 1 to 12 of the Company Directors Disqualification Act 1986).
(4) Automatic vacation under provisions in the Articles (for example, Table A, reg 81).
(5) Retirement (for example, Table A, reg 73 and s 293).

We now consider these events separately.

11.2   RESIGNATION

Regulation 81(d) of Table A, allows a director to resign by notice to the company. With or without such an Article, the position is as follows:

(1) a director may always resign and (unless the Articles forbid or impose specific restrictions) notice to the secretary or to the company completes his resignation;
(2) once given, the resignation cannot be withdrawn, even though there has been no formal acceptance;[1]
(3) the reference to *notice* to the company in reg 81 does not specify the form of notice and a verbal notice submitted and accepted at a general meeting is effective.[2]

11.3   REMOVAL UNDER SECTION 303

Section 303 of the 1985 Act provides that:

> 'A company may by *ordinary*[3] resolution, remove a director before the expiration of his period of office, *notwithstanding* anything in its *Articles* or in any *agreement* between it and him.' (Emphasis added.)

The importance of this section can scarcely be exaggerated – it is the key to shareholder control and the statutory expression of the principle that the majority must ultimately have their way.[4] It means that those who can gather together a bare majority of the votes can remove the *entire board at any time* and replace them with directors of their own choosing.

Several features of this section should be noted.

(1) The power to remove is that of the members in general meeting. The board has no such power unless the Articles specifically provide it (Table A does not).[5]

(2) The procedure to be followed in implementing this section is as follows.

    (a) The proponents of the resolution must give 'special notice' to the company of their intention to propose it at the next general meeting.[6] Since this must be given 28 days before the meeting and they may not know when it will take place, it is sufficient for them to state 'the next general meeting' without specifying the date. If, after receipt of the notice, the directors call a meeting for less than 28 days thereafter, the notice is still valid (s 379).

    (b) The company must give notice of the resolution to the members and if this cannot be included with the notice of the meeting (for example, because it has already been sent out) they must advertise at least 21 days before the meeting.

    (c) If the directors fail to call a meeting, the advocates of the resolution may require them to do so, or (finally) call it themselves by mustering the required one-tenth of the paid-up voting capital.[7]

    (d) A copy of the special notice must be sent by the company to the director, who is entitled to have his written representations circulated or read out at the meeting,[8] and to be heard on the resolution at the meeting (s 304).

    (e) At the meeting the ordinary resolution for the removal of the director (with or without the appointment of a replacement) is decided by a bare majority of the votes cast, either by a show of hands or (if demanded) on a poll.[9]

(3) Although s 303 overrides anything in the Articles, so that an ordinary resolution is always sufficient to remove a director, it does not require that all the shares shall have equal voting rights. Thus, the Articles are free to give special rights to special shares, even if such rights are confined to cases where a s 303 resolution is being proposed. Thus, it was held by the House of Lords in *Bushell v Faith*[10] that an Article which gave a director additional voting rights when his own removal was being proposed was valid and did not infringe s 303 even though it would enable him to defeat any such resolution. If the case had been decided otherwise, the problem would have been to draw the line between acceptable and unacceptable variations in voting rights. There is nothing in statute or common law to prescribe absolute equality, and numerous variations are found in practice, including shares which lack any voting rights at all ('A shares'). Thus, the House of Lords was acknowledging that s 303 could be effectively overridden by appropriately weighted voting rights and there was nothing they could do about it. Such rights are not likely to be found, however, except in close family companies, as the majority of the contributors of share capital will not normally accept a situation where they are put into a permanent minority. The right way to give protection to directors is by means of service contracts of reasonable length.

(4) The special notice procedure, where a director is being removed under s 303, applies also to any resolution to appoint a replacement at the same meeting (s 303(2)). If there is no replacement, the vacancy may later be filled as a casual vacancy (s 303(3)) by the board under reg 79 of Table A. Alternatively, the next

general meeting may make the appointment by ordinary resolution under reg 78, either on a recommendation of the board or on 14 days' notice by a member under reg 76. These requirements for special notice and for notice of resolutions to be proposed from the floor are intended to prevent the springing of sudden and unexpected proposals at meetings and also to ensure that there is time for consideration by all the parties.

(5) Removal under s 303 does not deprive a director of any compensation or damages to which he may be entitled in respect of termination of his office or of any other appointment (s 303(5)). Nor does the section derogate from any other power to remove which may exist separately. There is nothing to prevent the Articles from conferring wider powers, although Table A does not do so.[11]

The question of compensation depends upon the existence of some separate contract which is broken by the removal from office and this is discussed in **11.5** below.

11.4 RESTRICTIONS ON USE OF SECTION 303

Section 303(5) envisages that removal of a director under the provisions of the section may amount to a breach of any separate service contract which he may have. It therefore provides that his right to claim compensation or damages is not affected and such claims are considered in **11.5** below. What it does not say is that he has any right to restrain or object to his removal, as such. Are there any circumstances, therefore, in which removal may be questioned, insofar as it deprives him of any right to hold office as a director, as opposed to his right to serve his contract as an employee?

The answer seems to be as follows.

(1) He cannot prevent the passing of the resolution. This is a legal right of the majority under s 303 and cannot be restrained by injunction or otherwise.[12]

(2) He may be able to claim under s 459 (unfair prejudice). Under the earlier versions of this provision, it was difficult to argue oppression (as then had to be shown) when it related to a person in his capacity as a director rather than in that as a member. However, recent cases do seem to point to the availability of a rather easier remedy under the reconstituted provision. It is necessary for the complainant to be a member of the company or a person to whom shares have been transferred or transmitted (s 459(2)). An equitable interest is not sufficient (see, for example, *Re A Company (No 007828 of 1985)*.[13] There have been several cases reported in which the removal of a director has been found to be unfairly prejudicial, particularly in the cases of a small company. See, for example, *Re London School of Electronics Ltd*,[14] *Re Bird Precision Bellows Ltd*,[15] *Re A Company (No 00477 of 1986)*[16] and *Quinlan v Essex Hinge Co Ltd*.[17] On the other hand, in larger companies, particularly those where there is a provision in the Articles permitting a minority shareholder to extricate himself on just terms without a winding up of the company or where there is free transferability of shares, exclusion from management is much less likely to result

in a successful claim of unfair prejudice. For examples, see *Re Ringtower Holdings plc*[18] and *Re Blue Arrow plc*.[19]

(3) If, however, he can show the sort of quasi-partnership situation, which commonly exists in private companies, he may be able to petition for compulsory winding up under the 'just and equitable' ground in s 122(1)(g) of the Insolvency Act 1986. The courts will make such an order where the facts show an underlying obligation that he should participate in management as long as the business continues.[20] Such a situation might arise where three equal shareholders jointly own and manage the business and where two of them combine together to expel the third, leaving him locked in as a shareholder, but excluded from management remuneration. Such remuneration, rather than dividends, is often the return which owner-managers of this type expect to see on the capital and effort which they have invested. The risk of precipitating a winding up may prove an effective deterrent against such conduct and may limit, in practice, the theoretical freedom of the majority under s 303.

(4) Apart from situations of the *Westbourne Galleries*[21] type, where the company is, in substance, a partnership, there may be an express agreement between the parties for continued participation in management. If this is broken and one party is excluded, there may again be grounds for 'just and equitable' winding up.[22]

11.5   REMOVAL FROM OFFICE AS BREACH OF CONTRACT

We have seen that removal under s 303 does not deprive the dismissed director of any compensation or damages to which he may otherwise be entitled. Under what circumstances then, may he have such a claim?

(1) The distinction must be made between the director's roles, first as a director and second as an employee. This is discussed above in **10.11** and must be clearly borne in mind if the law is to be understood. The right of removal under s 303 relates solely to the director's statutory position as a member of the board. If he is also employed by the company under a contract of service, express or implied, that contract may have been broken by the removal and a claim may arise. It follows that, in the absence of some separate contract or appointment, there can be no such claim, except in the limited circumstances where there is a right to a place on the board under the *Westbourne Galleries* principle, referred to in **11.4** above.

(2) A director who is faced or threatened with removal under s 303 or some familiar provision in the Articles must, therefore, consider the terms of his own service contract and see if they are broken. If he is serving in an executive capacity, he should have either a written agreement or written particulars under the provisions of the Employment Rights Act 1996.

(3) It is possible that his employment will not be affected by his removal from the board, for example, if he has a service contract as accountant or works manager. If this contract can be performed without a seat on the board (and it does not

guarantee him such a seat) then his removal will not affect that contract. No question of damages or compensation will arise as no contract has been broken.

(4)   On the other hand, his position on the board may be a requirement of his service contract, for example, where he is the managing director. In this case, removal from the board will also terminate the service contract and will lead to a claim for damages if it breaks the terms of that contract. Thus, the question in every case is: are the terms of the contract broken?

(5)   The general principle is that a director will be able to make such a claim only if he has a separate contract (ie outside the Articles) which is inconsistent with removal under the Articles or s 303. Thus, an unconditional contract to serve as managing director for a fixed term of four years is inconsistent with a right of removal under the Articles, and such a removal before the end of the period will entitle him to damages for breach of contract.[23] It is an implied term of the service contract that the company will do nothing of its own volition to prevent the director from carrying it out.

(6)   Where no period of office or of notice is specified in the contract, there is nothing inconsistent with the general right of removal and the director cannot complain if he is dismissed, without notice, under a power in the Articles.[24]

(7)   The relevant provision in Table A, which is normally adopted, is reg 84 which provides that the board:

(a)   may appoint a director to the office of managing director or any other executive office;

(b)   may give him a service agreement – such agreement to:

(i)   incorporate such terms and remuneration as they think fit,

(ii)   terminate if he ceases to be a director but without prejudice to any claim for damages for breach of the service agreement.

Such termination resulting from the removal of the director from his membership of the board will be a breach of contract if it is inconsistent with the terms of the service agreement, as it will be if the directors have exercised their powers by giving a fixed-term contract.[25]

(8)   The Articles do not of themselves constitute a contract with the director unless perhaps he is also a shareholder: Chapter 8, see note 11, although they may be evidence of the terms on which he has agreed to serve.

If the director relies entirely on the provisions of the Articles, however, he runs the risk that they may be changed at any time by special resolution (75 per cent majority) even if the change results in his instant removal from office.[26] He can complain only if the alteration is inconsistent with an express term of some separate contract outside the Articles.[27] Alternatively, a provision concerning a director could be included in a shareholders' agreement: as such, it is unalterable except as the agreement might provide or with the consent of all the parties to the agreement (see *Russell v Northern Bank Development Corp Ltd*).[28]

(9)   The conclusion to be drawn from these cases is that it will usually be in the director's interest to secure a long-term service contract outside the Articles with no provision for premature termination. Otherwise he is at the mercy of those who can command a majority of the members' votes at any time, and his position may well be weaker than that of employees who are not on the board.

However, the directors must bear in mind when giving such contracts to their own colleagues that their duty is to the company and not to themselves, and that it will rarely be in the interest of the company to bind itself to service contracts of excessive length.[29] Indeed, such contracts may actually depress the value of the shareholders' interests, since any buyer of the shares would have to calculate the cost of terminating the contracts when making his valuation.

11.6 COMPENSATION FOR LOSS OF OFFICE

11.6.1 The position at law

Where removal from office amounts to a breach of the director's service contract on the principles discussed above, the position is as follows.

(1) As we have seen, the director cannot prevent the passing of the resolution nor can he insist on the performance of the service contract since the courts do not order specific performance of contracts for personal services.

(2) His remedy, therefore, is damages for breach of contract. Damages are intended to compensate for what has been lost, subject to a discount for earlier payment, and the director may therefore have a claim in respect of salary, commission, reduction in pension, loss of life insurance cover, loss of car and other items.[30]

(3) As in all contractual claims for damages, the director is under a duty to mitigate his loss by seeking and taking alternative employment where he might be reasonably expected to do so. His damages will thus usually be reduced by the value of any such employment which was open to him.[31] He is, however, entitled to look for something reasonably commensurate with his status, and a managing director was held justified in refusing a job as assistant managing director at the same salary.[32] His liability for income tax (basic and higher rates) must also be taken into account in calculating the damages.[33] For the distinction between damages and compensation, see **10.6** and **11.6.2**.

(4) An executive director who has no entitlement to damages, because there is nothing in his service contract which is inconsistent with a right of instant dismissal under the Articles may, as a last resort, fall back on the statutory right to minimum periods of notice under the Employment Rights Act 1996.

(5) Such a director may also qualify for a redundancy payment under Part VI of that Act, for a payment related to pay, length of service and age. But see **10.11**. To qualify for a redundancy payment the director must also be regarded in law as an employee. The director must make his own claim against the company within six months of dismissal.[34]

(6) He may also be able to make a claim for 'unfair dismissal' under Part X of the Employment Rights Act 1996. It is for the employer to show the *reason* for the dismissal, but the tribunal is then free to consider, on a neutral and objective basis, whether he acted reasonably (s 98(4)). Redundancy is one of the five grounds on which a dismissal can be fair (the others being capability, conduct, contravention of statute and any other substantial reason) but it is still for the tribunal to decide whether the employer acted reasonably in dismissing on that

ground (s 98(4)). Where he did not, then any redundancy payment will be deducted from the basic award for unfair dismissal (s 122), even apparently if it was ex gratia (*Chelsea Football & Athletic Co Ltd v Heath*[35]).

By s 203(1), any provision in an agreement, whether a contract of employment or otherwise, is void insofar as it purports to exclude or limit any of the provisions of the Employment Rights Act 1996, or to preclude a person from bringing any proceedings under the Act before an employment tribunal. However, this does not apply to any agreement to refrain from instituting or continuing proceedings before an employment tribunal, if the conditions relating to compromise agreements under the Act are satisfied in relation to the agreement. These conditions are as follows:

(a) the agreement must be in writing;
(b) the agreement must relate to the particular complaint;
(c) the employee or worker must have received independent legal advice from a qualified lawyer as to the terms and effect of the proposed agreement and, in particular, its effect on his ability to pursue his rights before an employment tribunal;
(d) there must be in force, when the adviser gives his advice, a policy of insurance covering the risk of a claim by the employee or worker in respect of loss arising in consequence of the advice;
(e) the agreement must identify the adviser; and
(f) the agreement must state that the conditions regulating compromise agreements under the Act have been satisfied.

In this context, the word 'independent' in relation to legal advice received by the employee or worker means that the advice is given by a lawyer who is not acting in the matter for the employer or an associated employer. A qualified lawyer means a solicitor who holds a practising certificate or a barrister.

The maximum awards in September 1998 were:

Unfair Dismissal:	Basic	£6,600
	(For failure to comply with an order to re-engage or re-instate)	
	Compensatory	£12,000
	Additional	£5,720
Total		£24,320

The maximum additional award is increased to £11,440 in cases of race or sex discrimination.

Redundancy: Basic £6,600
These sums are reviewable under the Employment Rights Act 1996

11.6.2 NEGOTIATED SETTLEMENTS

A dismissed director who does qualify for common law damages will normally expect to resolve his claim by negotiation with the company, rather than by litigation. His former colleagues on the board will therefore face the task of considering both the merits of the claim and also their own powers and duties in the matter.

(1) If the Articles include the power (as does Table A, reg 84) to give service contracts to their fellow members, then the power to settle a legal claim for compensation for loss of office must be implied and the board is free to negotiate accordingly. They will, no doubt, take professional advice to satisfy themselves that they are dealing with a '*bona fide* payment by way of damages for breach of contract or by way of pension in respect of past services'.[36]

(2) Where, however, they cannot satisfy themselves that they are dealing with such a legally enforceable claim (for example, because the director has no service agreement which has been broken), so that there is an element of gratuity in the proposed payment, then the position is different. Section 312 provides that it is unlawful to make to a director any payment by way of compensation for loss of office, or as consideration for or in connection with retirement, unless particulars are disclosed[37] to and approved by the members. This means that an ordinary resolution of the members in general meeting must be obtained, unless unanimous approval is obtained in some other way.[38] This section is drawn so widely that it can apply equally to cases where a director is removed altogether from the board, and to those where he remains on the board but loses some other job, such as managing director or secretary.

(3) Where there is such a gratuitous element in the proposed compensation, the board requires not only the consent of the members but a power in the company itself, otherwise the payment may be ultra vires. Such a power is normally conferred by a well-drafted objects clause but, if not, it is conferred by s 719 which authorises the company to provide for employees and former employees on the cessation or transfer of all or part of its undertaking or that of a subsidiary, regardless of the 'best interests' of the company. Unless the Memorandum or Articles authorise the directors, or require a special majority of members to exercise the power, however, there must be approval by ordinary resolution: s 719(3). After the requisite approval in one of these forms, even a liquidator (subject to the control of the courts) may make the payments under s 187 of the Insolvency Act 1986. If winding up has already begun when the question of payment arises, the liquidator may exercise the power if, after the liabilities of the company have been fully satisfied and provision has been made for the costs of winding up, the members approve by ordinary resolution or by any special majority required by the Memorandum or Articles.

However, the position of directors is differentiated from that of other employees by s 322A (introduced by s 109 of the 1989 Act) whereby any transaction with directors in excess of 'their powers under the company's constitution' is voidable by the company and results in any event in an obligation on the director (and any authorising director) to account for any gain and to indemnify the company.

Normally, these payments must be made out of profits available for dividend; in the case of winding up, they may be made out of any assets available to members.

(4) *Section 313*

Where the whole or part of the company's undertaking is being transferred to a third party, particulars of compensation for a director's loss of office must again be disclosed and approved by the members under s 313. If not, the director holds the compensation on trust for the company so that he must pay it over to the company on demand. If the company itself were making the payment, it would fall within s 312, so s 313 must apply to cases where the transferee or some other party is doing so. The object of the section is to ensure that there is no question of secret payments to the directors as an incentive for facilitating the transfer of assets.

(5) *Section 314*

Where there is a conventional takeover by transfer of the company's shares, resulting from:

(a) an offer to the general body of shareholders; or
(b) an offer with a view to the company's becoming a subsidiary; or
(c) an offer for control of not less than one-third of the voting power; or
(d) any other conditional offer;

and a payment is to be made to a director for loss of office or retirement, he must take all reasonable steps to ensure that particulars are sent to the shareholders together with the offer. There are penalties in default.[39]

If this is not done or the payment is not approved by ordinary resolution of the members before the transfer of shares, the director holds the compensation on trust for those who sell their shares as a result of the offer (s 315). He must therefore divide it amongst them.

(6) As we have already seen, these provisions (ss 312 to 315) do not apply where the director has a legal claim to damages and a bona fide payment is made in settlement (s 317). However, s 316 goes on to provide that ss 312 to 315 cannot be evaded by the simple expedient of the bidder's paying more for the director's shares than for those of the other shareholders. The excess is to be treated as compensation for loss of office.

Moreover, payments are, prima facie, to be treated as falling within ss 312 to 315 where they:

(a) form part of the takeover arrangement or are agreed during the three-year period beginning one year before and ending two years after; and
(b) the company or the transferee was privy to the arrangement.

(7) Where gratuitous payments of this type are duly made, the current tax position is as follows:

(a) there is no longer any difference in the tax treatment of gratuitous and non-gratuitous payments;
(b) the first £30,000 is exempt from tax and disregarded;
(c) the excess over £30,000 bears the extra tax which would have been payable if it had been added to the recipient's income for the year in which the employment ends. (ICTA 1988, ss 148, 188, Sch 11.)

As this tax treatment will apply to damages awarded by the courts or to compensation awarded by a tribunal, it is a factor which should be taken into account by the awarding authority, and to that extent *British Transport Commission v Gourlay*[40] should be modified, otherwise the recipient may be taxed twice. (See **11.6.1**.)

Contributions to an approved pension scheme on termination of employment are excluded from charge under s 188 of ICTA 1988, but the unfortunate beneficiary of a specific provision for a payment on termination, in his service agreement or the Articles, will find the whole amount treated as deferred remuneration under Schedule E (*Dale v de Soissons*[41]). Moreover, following a change in Inland Revenue practice in 1991, gratuitous payments on what prove to be permanent retirements may be treated as unauthorised retirement benefit schemes.

11.7   DISQUALIFICATION BY LAW

The courts have statutory power to disqualify in certain circumstances – these are discussed at **2.5.1**.

11.8   VACATION OF OFFICE UNDER THE ARTICLES

The Articles normally contain a list of events which serve equally to remove a disqualified director automatically from office, and to prevent him from being appointed (discussed at **2.5.4**).

Table A, reg 81 lists the following:

(1)   (a)   removal by any provision of the Act,
     (b)   prohibition by law;

(2)   bankruptcy or composition with creditors;
(3)   mental disorder accompanied by:

     (a)   admission to hospital (or treatment under the Mental Health Act 1983), or
     (b)   a court order for detention or the appointment of a receiver;

(4)   resignation by notice to the company;
(5)   absence from board meetings for more than six consecutive months[42] without the permission of the other directors and removal from the board if they resolve to remove him.

The Articles are free to add to and subtract from this list and the following variations may be found:

(1)   provision for a resolution of the board in case (3) above, as otherwise there may be doubt as to whether and when the disqualifying event has occurred;
(2)   exclusion of s 293 (retirement at age 70) in a public company or its subsidiary or compulsory retirement at a specified age, for example, 65;[43]
(3)   removal from office by some procedure additional to that in s 303, for example, extraordinary resolution (75 per cent majority) not requiring special notice;

(4) disqualification on conviction of a crime other than in connection with a motoring offence;

(5) resolution by a specified majority of the board or by other specified parties;[44]

(6) the holding of conflicting directorships, with some procedure for certification by the chairman or resolution by the board as to the existence of the conflict;

(7) on a resolution by the other directors that a particular director, by virtue of mental disability, should cease to be a director (this saves the need for a court order as required by reg 81);

(8) physical disability preventing a director from carrying out his functions.

The effect of such Articles is automatic and cannot be waived by the board[45] or by an ordinary resolution of the members. It can be nullified only by a special resolution (75 per cent) altering the Articles.

11.9 RETIREMENT

11.9.1 By rotation

There is no need to provide for the retirement by rotation of directors. It is, however, common for Articles of Association to prescribe that a proportion of the directors shall retire from office at each annual general meeting, but shall be eligible for re-election, and that those to retire shall be the directors who have been longest in office since their last appointment or election. For example, Table A, regs 73 and 74 provide that, at the first annual general meeting, all the directors shall retire from office and that, at the annual general meeting, in every subsequent year, one-third of them – or if their number is not three or a multiple of three then the number nearest one-third – shall retire.

In *Re David Moseley & Sons Ltd*,[46] the Articles differed from Table A in that, where the number of directors was not three or a multiple thereof, then the number nearest to but not exceeding one-third had to retire. At a particular general meeting, only two directors were subject to retirement by rotation and it was held that on a proper construction of the Articles neither of them need retire. It would have been otherwise had the Articles simply stated that the number nearest one-third should retire as does reg 73. In that case, one of the two directors would have retired.

It is usual for Articles to provide that a managing director shall not be subject to retirement by rotation and shall not be taken into account when computing the number of directors who are to retire. This is because a managing director usually has a contract of service for a fixed term of years. Regulation 84 of Table A, provides that a managing director and any other director holding executive office will be excluded from this requirement. Articles may also name specified individuals as permanent directors, to avoid the need for periodical retirement and in many private companies there is much to be said for dispensing with the rotation provisions altogether.

When choosing the directors to retire by rotation at an annual general meeting, it is often found that a number of them have an equal period of service. Regulation 74 deals with such a situation by providing that as between persons who became directors or were last reappointed directors on the same day, those to retire shall be determined by lot unless they agree among themselves which of them are to retire. In *Eyre v Milton Proprietary Ltd*,[47] the Articles stated that they should be chosen by 'ballot'. The court held that this meant by lot.

Regulation 64 provides that the number of directors will not be subject to any maximum unless otherwise decided by ordinary resolution but will not be less than two. So the board cannot itself increase the number of vacancies if a maximum has been fixed either by the Articles or by an ordinary resolution.

Regulation 75 should also be noted, which provides that if the retiring director offers himself for re-election at the AGM, he is deemed to have been re-elected unless:

(1) another person is elected; or
(2) a resolution not to fill the vacancy is passed; or
(3) a resolution for his re-election is lost.

So if no action is taken, he will be re-elected.

11.9.2   Under age limit (public companies only)

Another contingency which may terminate a director's appointment is the attainment of any age limit imposed by the Articles or, if the company is subject to s 293 of the Act, the statutory age limit of 70 prescribed by that section.

Briefly, the effect of s 293 is that, as a general rule, no one over 70 years of age shall be a director but that there shall be machinery whereby, if with a full knowledge of the facts the shareholders agree, a person aged over 70 can be a director as a special case. Alternatively, the section can be excluded by the Articles altogether.

The first point to note is that the section has no application to a private company unless it is a subsidiary of a public company incorporated in the UK. To put it in another way, the statutory age limit applies only to public companies and their subsidiaries and only to them if they do not exclude it.

In a company which is subject to s 293, no person can be appointed as a director if he has attained 70 years of age unless the company has excluded the operation of the section or his appointment is approved by the shareholders in general meeting by an ordinary resolution of which 'special' notice, stating his age, has been given. 'Special notice' is defined in **9.4**.

Where, in a company to which the section applies, an existing director attains 70 years of age, he must vacate office at the conclusion of the next annual general meeting after he attains that age. This is, however, subject to the same exceptions as apply to the rule against appointing directors over the age limit, that is to say, it does not take place if the company has 'contracted out' of the section and, even if the company has not contracted out, the director may be retained in office by a resolution in general meeting of which special notice, specifying his age, has been given.

If such a resolution is passed, the Act does not impose any express limit on the period for which he shall continue in office, and the resolution may, therefore, either provide that he shall hold office for a specified time or leave this open. In the latter event, unless the company's Articles contain provisions for the rotation of directors, the director can hold office without further reference to the shareholders for the rest of his life or until he is removed. If, however, the usual rules for the retirement of a proportion of the directors each year are contained in the Articles then, when next his turn comes to retire by rotation, he can be reappointed only by the procedure of special notice in which his age is disclosed again.

In this connection, s 293(6) is important.

Under this provision, a person reappointed director on retiring by virtue of s 293(3), or appointed in place of a director so retiring, shall be treated, for the purpose of determining the time at which he or any other director is to retire, as if he had become director on the day on which the retiring director was last appointed before his retirement; but, except as provided by this subsection, the retirement of a director out of turn by virtue of s 293(3) shall be disregarded in determining when any other directors are to retire.

The effect of this is best explained by an example. Let it be assumed that there are eight directors, two of whom have to retire each year under the Articles, those to retire being the directors who have been longest in office since their last election.

'A' is over 70 years of age at the annual general meeting in 1985, but is not one of the two directors who have been longest in office since their last election and is not, therefore, due to retire by rotation until 1988. He must, however, retire in 1986 under the age limit (together with the two others who retire by rotation) and, if he is reappointed under special notice, his reappointment will not alter the rotation of directors so that he must submit himself for re-election again in 1988 despite his reappointment in 1986. In 1988, his reappointment, if made, must be carried out with the same formalities as regards special notice as in 1986. If, on the other hand, he was due for retirement by rotation, as well as under the age limit, in 1986, then he will count as one of the two to retire by rotation and he need not retire again by rotation until the normal period has expired, ie in 1989, as he did not retire 'out of turn' in 1986. The same principle is applied in relation to a director appointed in place of one retiring under the age limit – if the latter retires 'out of turn' the director taking his place steps into his shoes for purposes of rotation, but not otherwise.

Where a director retires because of his attaining the age of 70, no provision for the automatic reappointment of retiring directors in default of another appointment applies. If at the meeting at which he retires the vacancy is not filled, it may be filled later as a casual vacancy.

Reference has been made to the power to 'contract out' of s 293. If it is a new company, it may adopt Articles which contain a clause to the effect that s 293(1) to (6) shall not apply, or that directors shall not be obliged to retire on account of age, or that the retiring age shall be some age other than 70 (for example, 60, or 80); any of these provisions, being inconsistent with s 293, will be sufficient to exclude the statutory age limit. Similarly, an existing company may, by special resolution (75 per cent majority), alter its Articles in order to include one of these provisions so as to exclude the age limit of 70. Thus, Articles which are inconsistent with the statutory age limit prevail over that limit; the only exception is where Articles were in existence on 1 January 1947, and have not been amended in the manner described above. Here, the section prevails except to the extent to which the Articles themselves impose an age limit (s 293(7)). If, therefore, such Articles provide that a director shall hold office for life, the statutory age limit will apply to him, but if they provide that he shall hold office until aged 80, for example, that limit will apply instead of the statutory one.

Section 294 requires a person who has attained the age limit imposed by the Act or the company's Articles, and who is appointed or to his knowledge is proposed to be appointed director of the company, to give notice of his age to the company. Failure to do so, or acting as director under any appointment which is invalid or has terminated on account of age, involves liability to a fine of up to £100 (one-fiftieth of the statutory maximum) per day, for every day while the failure continues or while he continues to act. The obligation to inform the company of his age does not, however, apply in relation to a reappointment on the termination of a previous appointment as director of the company – presumably because his age would be already known.

It is provided in s 293(3) that acts done by a person as a director shall be valid, notwithstanding that it is afterwards discovered that his appointment had terminated by his attaining 70 years of age. This would not, however, apply where his appointment was from the beginning invalid under the section.

11.10   WINDING UP AND RECEIVERSHIP

In a winding up of a company, all the powers of the directors cease on the appointment of a liquidator, except insofar as the company in general meeting or the liquidator sanctions their continuance in a members' voluntary winding up, or in a creditors' voluntary winding up, except insofar as the committee of inspection or, if there is no such committee, the creditors, sanction such continuance (ss 91 and 103 of the Insolvency Act 1986).

In an administrative receivership, the directors' powers cease in relation to the assets covered by the charge, ie all the company's assets in the case of a typical bank floating charge. However, their statutory duties continue as do their powers, insofar as they do not relate to the mortgaged assets,[48] so they can move the registered office and call meetings of members.

In the case of an administration order under ss 8 to 27 of the Insolvency Act 1986, the directors remain in office but are effectively displaced by the administrator, who exercises wide powers of control and management under s 17, with which the directors must not interfere (s 14(4)). Moreover, the administrator may remove any director from office and appoint any person to office under s 14(2).

CHAPTER 11 FOOTNOTES

1 *Glossop v Glossop* [1907] 2 Ch 370.

2 *Latchford Premier Cinema Ltd v Ennin* [1931] 2 Ch 409.

3 This is the only section which prescribes an ordinary resolution, ie a bare majority at a general meeting. However, this is always the type of resolution required unless the Act or the Memorandum or Articles specify a special or extraordinary resolution.

4 In the absence of such a provision in the Act or Articles, there is no inherent power to remove a director before his period of office has expired (*Imperial Hydropathic Hotel Co, Blackpool v Hampson* (1882) 23 ChD 1).

5 Thus, the board must not attempt to exclude a fellow director unless he has been properly removed by the members (*Hayes v Bristol Plant Hire Ltd* [1957] 1 All ER 685). The only exception is where the board may resolve to remove a director on the grounds of six months' unauthorised absence (reg 81(e)).

6 See **9.4**.

7 Sections 368 and 370; see **9.1.2**.

8 Except where the court is satisfied that the privilege is being abused so as to give needless publicity to defamatory matter (s 304(4)).

9 See **9.8**.

10 [1970] 1 All ER 53.

11 Listed Companies must contain an Article of this type (*Admission of Securities to Listing*, Sch VII, Part A) and, in addition, they often give a power of removal by extraordinary resolution (75 per cent majority), which does not require the special notice procedure.

12 *Bentley-Stevens v Jones* [1974] 2 All ER 653.

13 (1986) 2 BCC 98, at p 951.

14 (1985) 1 BCC 99, at p 394.

15 (1985) 1 BCC 99, at p 467.

16 (1986) 2 BCC 99, at p 171.

17 [1997] BCC 53.

18 (1989) 5 BCC 82.

19 (1987) 3 BCC 618.

20 *Ebrahimi v Westbourne Galleries Ltd* [1973] AC 360 and see *Re JE Cade & Son* [1991] BCC 360.

21 [1973] AC 360.

22 *Re A & BC Chewing Gum Ltd* [1975] 1 All ER 1017.

23 *Shindler v Northern Raincoat Co Ltd* [1960] 2 All ER 239, although note the restrictions on the Company's power to give a service contract which may exceed five years under s 319. See **10.9.3**.

24 *Read v Astoria Garage (Streatham) Ltd* [1952] 2 All ER 292.

25 *Nelson v James Nelson and Sons Ltd* [1914] 2 KB 770.

26 *Shuttleworth v Cox Bros and Co (Maidenhead) Ltd* [1927] 2 KB 9.

27 *Southern Foundries (1926) Ltd v Shirlaw* [1940] AC 701 and see *Spencer v Cosmos Air Holidays* (1989) *The Times*, 6 December, CA.

28 [1992] BCC 578.

29 Five years is usually regarded as *long enough*, subject to the procedure specified by s 309. See **10.9.3**.

30 *Bold v Brough, Nicholson and Hall Ltd* [1963] 3 All ER 849.

31 See **10.6**.

32 *Yetton v Eastwoods Froy Ltd* [1966] 3 All ER 353.

33 *British Transport Commission v Gourlay* [1956] AC 185 distinguished in *Pennine Raceway v Kirklees MC (No 2)* [1989] STC 122.

34 For the up-to-date position under this Act, the latest revision of the booklet *The Redundancy Payments Scheme* should be obtained from the Department of Employment.

35 [1981] IRLR 73.

36 Section 316(3).

37 Disclosure must be to all members including non-voting members, *Re Duomatic Ltd* [1969] 1 All ER 161.

38 *Re Gee and Co (Woolwich) Ltd* [1974] 2 WLR 515. Under reg 53 of Table A, a written resolution signed by all the members is as good as if it had been passed at a meeting.

39 On summary conviction a fine not exceeding one-fifth of the statutory maximum currently £5,000, (from October 1992) or such other sum as may be fixed by order (s 74 of the Criminal Justice Act 1982 and s 730 and Sch 24 to the Companies Act 1985).

40 [1956] AC 185, HL.

41 [1950] 2 All ER 460.

42 This will not include involuntary absence through ill-health (*Re London and Northern Bank* [1901] 1 Ch 728).

43 Section 293 does not apply to private companies (except subsidiaries of public companies) and, even where it does apply, it can be excluded by the Articles (see **11.9.2** above). Moreover, the director can be reappointed on special notice.

44 As where a minority investor has the right to appoint and remove a director of his choosing.

45 *Re The Bodega Co Ltd* [1904] 1 Ch 276.

46 [1939] Ch 719.

47 [1936] Ch 244.

48 See *Newhart Development Ltd v Co-operative Commercial Bank Ltd* [1978] 2 All ER 896 where it was held that the directors could exercise their power to take proceedings in the name of the company if it was in the company's interests and did not imperil the charged assets.

Chapter 12

DIRECTORS' PENSIONS

12.1 POWER TO PAY PENSIONS

Executive directors will expect their company to provide them with pensions and the question of pension provision for directors, staff and employees is one which absorbs a growing proportion of the time of the board and of the profits of the company. This difficult and continuously changing subject naturally demands specialist advice, which must be regularly updated. In this chapter, we attempt to draw attention only to some of the more important features of the current scene.

Before considering the alternatives, the director must satisfy himself that the company and board have the power to pay pensions at all. With regard to the *company's* capacity s 35 of the 1985 Act (inserted by s 108(1) of the 1989 Act and summarised in **3.10**) provides that the validity of an act done by a company shall not be called into question on the ground of lack of capacity by reason of anything in the company's Memorandum. So far as the *board* is concerned, under s 35A in favour of a person dealing with a company in good faith, the power of the board to bind the company is deemed to be free of any constitutional limitations. However, these provisions protect third parties, not the directors themselves, in their relations with the members.

The latter can still act to restrain or challenge ultra vires acts of directors as can a receiver, liquidator or administrator in insolvency proceedings.

The usual position is that the Memorandum confers an express power to pay pensions upon the company and the Articles then delegate that power to the board. Both the Memorandum and the Articles should specifically include the directors as potential pensioners, as it has been held that reference to employees alone is not sufficient.[1]

In the light of s 322A of the 1985 Act (as introduced by s 109 of the 1989 Act and expanded by s 322B under the Companies (Single Member Private Limited Companies) Regulations 1992, SI 1992/1699), it is particularly important that the company's constitution clearly gives the directors power to apply company funds to provide for pensions for directors and their families. Section 322A provides that where a company enters into a transaction to which the parties include:

(1)   a director of the company or its holding company; or
(2)   a person connected with such a director or a company with whom such a director is associated;

and the board of directors, in connection with the transaction, exceed any limitation on their powers under the company's constitution, the transaction is voidable at the instance of the company (unless: (i) restitution is no longer possible; or (ii) bona fide third parties would be affected; or (iii) the company is indemnified; or (iv) there is ratification by the members). Whether or not it is avoided, any such party to the transaction as is mentioned in (1) or (2), any director of the company who authorised the transaction is liable:

(1) to account to the company for any gain which he has made directly or indirectly by the transaction; and
(2) to indemnify the company for any loss or damage resulting from the transaction.

If the company's constitution omits the express power to pay pensions to directors or connected parties, then the board's powers may, indeed, be limited and, accordingly, by entering into such transactions, the board would be at risk of exceeding them and of falling within s 322A. The Article (reg 87) normally adopted under the old pre-1985 Table A provides as follows:

> 'The directors on behalf of the company may pay a gratuity or pension or allowance on retirement to any Director who has held any other salaried office or place of profit with the Company or to his widow or dependants and may make contributions to any fund and pay premiums for the purchase or provision of any such gratuity, pension or allowance.'

This is replaced by reg 87 of the 1985 Table A, in the following terms:

> '87. The directors may provide benefits, whether by the payment of gratuities or pensions or by insurance or otherwise, for any director who has held but no longer holds any executive office or employment with the company or with any body corporate which is or has been a subsidiary of the company or a predecessor in business of the company or any such subsidiary, and for any member of his family (including a spouse and a former spouse) or any person who is or was dependent on him, and may (as well before as after he ceases to hold such office or employment) contribute to any fund and pay premiums for the purchase of provision of any such benefit.'

The board must, however, bear in mind that these powers must be exercised only in the interests of the company's business and not otherwise. Thus, a pension awarded to a director's widow five years after his death was not justified as there was no evidence that it was for the benefit of the company.[2] Likewise, where a new service contract was given to an ailing managing director (who would have continued to serve without it) so as to provide his dependants with a pension, it was held that the company could repudiate it after his death (*Re W and M Roith Ltd*[3]). Doubt was subsequently cast on this decision by the Court of Appeal, which upheld a pension scheme where the power was a substantive object in the Memorandum and there was no evidence of bad faith or of a negligent disregard of pending insolvency (*Re Horsley & Weight Ltd*[4]).

When implementing a scheme, the board may either set up their own fund and administration, if the size of the scheme will be sufficient, or contract the scheme out, in whole or in part, to an insurance company. There are many company schemes but the advantages of size, administrative expertise and investment management which the insurance companies can offer are clearly significant.

12.2   STATE PENSION SCHEME

The present state pension scheme was introduced by the Social Security Pensions Act 1975, which has been consolidated into the Pension Schemes Act 1993 and the Social

Security Contributions and Benefits Act 1992 (as amended). It started on 6 April 1978 and combines a basic flat-rate pension with an additional earnings-related pension: SERPS which stands for State Earnings-Related Pension Scheme. A right to a SERPS pension is earned from paying National Insurance contributions, which are discussed at **10.8**. Contracting-out of the earnings-related contributions and benefits are allowed where there is an appropriate personal pension plan or a certified occupational pension scheme (the employee and employer paying rather less in contributions).[5] An employee's contracted-out status can change during his working life. Thus, an individual may have been contracted-in to SERPS for some years and contracted-out for others.

Contracting-out is a highly complex area. Occupational schemes can contract-out on two different bases. The first applies to salary-related schemes known as COSRS (contracted-out salary-related schemes). In these schemes, the alternative to SERPS is a defined benefit. The second applies to money purchase schemes known as COMPS (contracted-out money purchase schemes). In these schemes, the alternative to SERPS is whatever the member's account will buy.

Until 6 April 1997, COSRS used to provide a guaranteed minimum pension (GMP). A GMP was a defined benefit based on the employee's earnings between the upper and lower earning units revalued in line with wage inflation. Employees in a COSR continued to accrue their SERPS benefit which was paid after deducting the GMP received by the employee when they retired. The full value of their SERPS entitlement (including inflation proofing) was therefore guaranteed.

Then on 6 April 1997, the rules changed and COSRS were required to certify that the pension provided under the scheme was 'broadly equivalent to' or better than a pension set out in a reference scheme. The reference scheme test is applied collectively and the scheme will pass the test if 90 per cent or more of the members reach the necessary standard. This means that no individual is guaranteed the standard benefits. The reference scheme test is:

Pension age	65
Accrual rate	1/80th
Salary	90 per cent of earnings between lower earnings limit × 52 and upper earnings limited × 53
Service	years of service to maximum 40 years
Spouse	50 per cent of member's pension

The other change is that since 6 April 1997, employees must accrue benefits under either an occupational scheme or SERPS, so there is no longer a SERPS guarantee. It should also be noted that GMPs that have already accrued will remain in COSRS until the employee dies or they are transferred to a COMP.

Occupational pension schemes which contract-out on a money purchase basis do not have a benefit target. Instead, they are required to invest the members' National Insurance rebates. Before 6 April 1997, these rebates were flat rate although the government also paid incentives to encourage people to contract-out. Since 6 April 1997, age-related rebates have been paid so that older people receive more. The amount of the rebate paid to occupational schemes is less than that paid to personal pension schemes. All personal pension schemes contract-out on a money purchase basis. The money purchase contracted-out benefits accrued in an occupational or personal pension scheme are known as 'protected rights'.

An additional complexity is that, since 6 April 1997, schemes can be COMBS (contracted-out mixed-benefit schemes) providing both a COSR and a COMP alternative within the same scheme. Also, for the first time, schemes which otherwise provide final salary benefits can contract-out on a money purchase basis.

A retired employee may have accrued all or just one of these. They will be paid to him together with his basic State pension and any additional pension (either occupational or personal) he may have acquired from further contributions by himself or his employer. Most schemes pay significantly more than SERPS (which is 20 per cent of band earnings). The Inland Revenue limit for occupational scheme being 66 per cent of (capped) final salary for the tax year 1999/2000 is £90,600.

It should be borne in mind that SERPS, which aimed to bring the State pension up to 25 per cent of an employee's band earnings between the lower earnings limit and the upper earnings limit averaged over 20 years, was not fully effective until 1998 when the first members will have completed 20 years' service. Moreover, the pressures of widely fluctuating levels of inflation and mass unemployment soon combined to bring the scheme into question. The Social Security Act 1986 introduced modifications to SERPS reducing the benefits available, and, therefore, the costs of the scheme. The 25 per cent target remains for those retiring on or before 5 April 1999 and is reduced to 20 per cent for pensioners reaching retirement age after 5 April 2009. For those retiring between these dates the percentage is reduced by 0.5 per cent each year. The cost is further reduced by basing the pension on the average lifetime earnings and not the last (usually the best) 20 years' earnings. The introduction of personal pension schemes and the extension of the contracting-out options,[6] both introduced by the 1986 Act, further reduced the appeal of SERPS.

12.3   PRIVATE SCHEMES FOR DIRECTORS

At present, directors may find their pension arrangements falling under one of several categories.

(1) The board, in exercise of its powers, may simply grant them a pension on retirement. This is a deductible expense for the company, but it has to be borne entirely during the retirement period and has none of the tax advantages of the statutory schemes.

(2) There may be a staff scheme approved by the Inland Revenue under which members may or may not be contracted-out of SERPS. Such schemes come in three forms. They can be insured schemes in which case they are operated by an insurance company. They can be 'self-administered schemes' in which case they are operated by a board of trustees. Finally, they can be 'small self-administered schemes'. These schemes have less than 12 members and (subject to certain safeguards) are operated by the members themselves. They can also be final

salary (when they provide a deferred benefit usually based on a formula like 1/60 × salary × years of service)) or money purchase (in which case contributions are invested and used to buy a pension).

(3)   There may be an individual executive pension plan. These were extended to controlling directors by the Finance Act 1973 and were the true successors to the old 'top hat' schemes which had fallen from favour. They offer the director significant advantages over group schemes and retirement annuity contracts, particularly in flexible retirement dates. Alternatively, by a 'topping-up' scheme, a director may either voluntarily or in combination with the company increase his scheme benefits nearer to the maximum levels.

(4)   There may be private provision by the director himself for a retirement annuity under the Finance Act 1956.[7] They are also known as Section 226 policies but may be funded only by the director himself. It has not been possible to take one out since 1 July 1988 when they were replaced by personal pension schemes.

(5)   There may be a personal pension established by the director himself under ICTA 1988 and this may be funded by the individual and/or by the employer.

(6)   There may be an unapproved arrangement that is funded (a FURBS) or unfunded (an UURBS). These are often used to bring a director's pension up to two-thirds of his full salary rather than his capped salary.[8]

It is not possible to combine certain categories. No one may belong to both an occupational and a personal pension in respect of the same source of earnings, although it is possible to combine either with an unapproved scheme. Items (2) and (3) above are occupational schemes; items (4) and (5) are personal pension schemes. Items (1) and (6) are unapproved schemes.

It is also important to understand that the Inland Revenue limits apply differently to occupational and personal pension schemes. The limits set on personal pension schemes affect the amount of contributions; the limits set on occupational schemes (including money purchase schemes) affect the amount of benefits which can be taken. This benefits limit may include the value of other occupational and personal pension scheme benefits which the director has if his accrual rate in the occupational scheme is more than 1/60th of salary for each year of service.

We can now look at some of the significant features of the above.

12.4   INLAND REVENUE APPROVED SCHEMES

The Finance Act 1970 (now consolidated into the Income and Corporation Taxes Act 1988) introduced a new code of approval and tax treatment of staff pension and death benefit arrangements which superseded the previous system. Controlling directors, with more than five per cent of the shares in companies controlled by the board, were excluded from participation until they were admitted by the Finance Act 1973. They are now in the same position as other employees, except that those with a shareholding of 20 per cent or more must average their pensionable remuneration over any three years within the last 10 and cannot therefore give their salary a boost in the final year, simply to establish a high level for pension purposes.

The benefit levels set out below apply to schemes established after 14 March 1989 and members who joined any scheme after 1 June 1989. Members who joined between 17 March 1987 and the above dates and those who joined before 17 March 1987 have different limits. The Inland Revenue refers to them as having 'continued rights'.

(1) The directors' maximum benefits are essentially:

On death before normal retirement age

(a) Life assurance benefit:
  (i)   4 × capped:[9] final salary (or £5,000 if greater); and
  (ii) a refund of his own contributions.
(b) Widow's pension:[10] two-thirds of the maximum pension which the member could have received at his normal retirement date.
(c) Dependant's pension:[11] two-thirds of the maximum pension which the member could have received at his normal retirement date.

On retirement

(a) Members pension: two-thirds × capped[12] final salary;
(b) Tax-free cash sum: 2¼ × initial rate of pension (excluding pension from additonal voluntary contributions (AVC) or free-standing additional voluntary contributions (FSAVC) (reducing the pension accordingly).[13]

(2) Minimum service for receipt of these maximum benefits is 20 years. Lesser periods reduce the benefits.
(3) Pensions from previous sources may be taken into account when arriving at the permitted limits.
(4) Increases in pensions in course of payment are permitted by a percentage not greater than the percentage rise in the cost-of-living index.
(5) There is no limit on the amount of contributions the employers may make as the limits are imposed only on the emerging benefits. However, there is a limit on the assets of a scheme. These must not exceed 105 per cent of the scheme's liabilities as calculated on the statutory basis. The employer's contributions must respect this limit. See ss 601 and 602 and Sch 22 to ICTA 1988. The director's personal contributions must not exceed 15 per cent of his remuneration. For these purposes, contributions include: compulsory contributions, AVCs and FSAVCs.
(6) For calculating the limits, directors' fees may be included if they fall within the definition of remuneration and 'remuneration' means any emoluments charged to Schedule E tax, but excluding income from shares or an interest in a share. 'Final remuneration' means an average of three successive years ending in the last 10 for directors with shareholdings of more than 20 per cent. The calculation may *not* include any earnings charged to Schedule D.
(7) The scheme must be set up under irrevocable trusts; it may be an all embracing scheme, or may be one limited to specific categories or individuals.
(8) Retiring dates must normally be in the age range of 60 to 75 for men and women.[14]

(9) The company must contribute, and contributions both of company and director are fully deductible from their respective taxable earnings. The pensions, when paid, are taxable as earned income under PAYE. The lump sum benefits on retirement and death are tax-free. The trustees of the scheme are nearly always given discretion as to the application of the death benefit which means inheritance tax is not payable.

(10) The position on leaving employment is that the Pension Schemes Act 1993, as amended, requires that any employee with at least two years' pensionable service must retain the right to any pension earned up to the date of leaving. The benefits may be preserved as they are, or transferred to any suitably approved scheme.

Refunds of contributions for employees who have participated in a scheme for more than two years are not permitted as an alternative. However, members with less than two years' pensionable service are entitled to have their own contributions returned to them. Where the contributions are returned, the administrator of the scheme is charged with tax at 20 per cent of the contributions.

(11) In cases of late retirement, the director must postpone and thus increase his pension as it can be taken only when he actually retires from service. The rule is not so strict for members with continued rights. They may take their benefits at any age after normal retirement age even if they continue working. There can be problems for directors (without continued rights, see **12.4**) who wish to retire early, take their benefits and return to work in a different capacity or on a part-time basis. In most cases, the Inland Revenue will not treat this as retirement and will therefore tax any lump sum benefits taken at the time.

(12) Occupational schemes should provide a member with a chance to make AVCs to improve their benefits. These are counted within the 15 per cent limit referred to at (5) above. Alternatively, members can contribute to an FSAVC set up[15] by an insurer or other provider.

(13) The pension fund itself is exempt from income tax, inheritance tax (IHT) and capital gains tax (CGT).

(14) Inland Revenue approval of schemes is dealt with by the Pension Schemes Office (PSO), Yorke House, PO Box 62, Castle Meadow Road, Nottingham, NG2 1BG.

(15) Contracted-out schemes are also supervised by the Inland Revenue.

(16) Compliance with the Pensions Schemes Act 1993 is supervised by the Occupational Pensions Regulatory Authority (OPRA), Invicta House, Trafalgar Place, Brighton, BN1 4DW.

(17) The option to draw down income rather than buy an annuity is now available to members of COMP schemes.

12.5 SMALL SELF-ADMINISTERED SCHEMES

Small Self-Administered Schemes (SSASs) first emerged in the early 1970s when controlling directors were again allowed to join occupational pension schemes. They were particularly attractive because the pension scheme funds could be used for the business in the form of loan backs and lease backs as well as being used for benefits.

It did not take long for the Inland Revenue to realise that these schemes were being abused. They were not being used for the purpose of funding pensions. The result was a memorandum issued in 1979 (JOM 58) which was followed by the Retirement Benefit Schemes (Restriction on Discretion to Approve) (Small Self-Administered Scheme) Regulations 1991, SI 1991/1614 (the 'SSAS Regulations'). These have been amended by SI 1998/1315 and SI 1998/728.

An SSAS is a scheme which is self-administered (ie not fully insured) which has less than 12 members and where at least one member is 'connected' with another member, a trustee or a scheme employer. Connected is a technical term in the SSAS Regulations and includes family relatives and companies within the members' control.

The SSAS Regulations set out the following requirements.

(1)   All SSASs must have a pensioneer trustee. Pensioneer trustees have to be approved by the PSO. They are individuals with extensive pension experience who have undertaken to the PSO that the scheme will be wound up only in accordance with its requirements. Pensioneer trustees are becoming increasingly responsible for ensuring that their scheme complies with all the SSAS Regulations. A new pensioner trustee must be appointed within 30 days if a pensioneer trustee leaves office.

(2)   SSASs used to have to buy annuities for retired members with five years of their leaving service. This can now wait until the member is age 75. In the meantime, a pension must be taken from the scheme and the actuary must provide a certificate comparing the cost of the annuity and the cost of the pension. Finally, the fund must be sufficiently liquid to be able to buy the annuity by age 75.

(3)   SSASs may borrow, but only up to three times the employer's ordinary annual contributions.

(4)   SSASs benefit from fewer restrictions on investment than larger self-administered schemes. Also they are exempt from the requirement to appoint an investment manager if all the members are also trustees.

(5)   The following investments are prohibited:

(a)   art, jewellery, vintage cars, yachts and other 'pride in possession' chattels;
(b)   residential property;
(c)   unquoted shares which have more than 30 per cent of the voting power or more than 30 per cent of the dividend rights;
(d)   transactions with scheme members or those connected with scheme members;
(e)   trading (this applies to *all* self-administered schemes).

(6)   The following investments are permitted, although they remain subject to the above exclusions. Thus, loans are permitted but not to a member or a person connected to a member:

(a)   loans – including to the employer which are subject to restrictions designed to ensure they are arms-length transactions;
(b)   shares – including shares in the employing company;

(c) commercial property.

(7) As they are occupational schemes, SSAS members are subject to the same benefit limits as are described at **12.4**

(8) The requirements of the Pensions Act 1995 apply to an SSAS, but in a more limited way.

(9) If an SSAS loses its approval, it is subject to an immediate stand alone tax charge of 40 per cent on the value of its assets.

12.6   RETIREMENT ANNUITY CONTRACTS

Facilities for Retirement Annuity Contracts (RACs) were provided originally by the Finance Act 1956 (now Ch III, Part XIV of ICTA 1988, as amended) for controlling directors and self-employed persons who could not participate in approved schemes. No new retirement annuity can be taken out after 1 July 1988. However, for those people who have already taken out a retirement annuity, these facilities are still fully effective. They are a form of money purchase scheme in that contributions are invested then the account used to buy an annuity. The following points may be noted.

(1) There is no limit on the amount of contributions which can be paid to an RAC. There is a limit on the amount which qualifies for tax relief.[16] For the tax years on or after 1987/88, relief is available at the following rates from the director's net relevant earnings.[17] These are uncapped.

Age	percentage of net relevant earnings
Up to 50	17.5 per cent
51–55	20 per cent
56–60	22.5 per cent
61–74	27.5 per cent

However, if the director also has a personal pension scheme, his contributions will be capped by the personal pension scheme limits in any year in which he contributes to both. The RAC limits will apply only in years in which he does not also contribute to his personal pension scheme. Contributions can be paid only by the employee and not the employer and are fully deductible for income tax. When received the pension paid out is taxed as earned income.

(2) The pension itself is not limited, as the limiting factor is the contributions. It may be taken at any age between 60 and 75. However, the Inland Revenue may agree to the benefit being drawn before the age of 60 on the grounds of ill-health.

(3) There can be a cash commutation at pension age of up to three times the annual pension then remaining. The right to the cash sum cannot be assigned or charged, but it is frequently relied on to repay a personal pension mortgage.

(4) The pension cannot be assigned or surrendered and, on death before pension age, the contributor gets only the return of his contributions without interest, or alternatively an annuity for his dependants. However, by virtue of s 622 of ICTA 1988, the pensioner may nominate another person to take the benefit of the contract in the form of a 'substituted contract' for the other's benefit.

(5) The pension can be guaranteed for up to 10 years and part can be given up in return for a widow's or dependants' pension for life.

(6) Up to five per cent of the maximum permitted contributions can be invested in life cover which is freely assignable.

(7) Unused tax relief can be carried forward for six years, but *not* unrelieved premiums in excess of the limits. However, they may be back-dated into the preceding tax year.

(8) It is common to place the RAC in a discretionary trust to avoid inheritance tax. This is sometimes called 'writing the policy under trust'.

12.7   PERSONAL PENSION SCHEMES

On 1 July 1988, personal pensions were launched as a successor to retirement annuities. Personal pensions are savings accounts like RACs. They differ from RACs primarily in the following ways.

(1) Higher percentage contributions are allowed (up to 40 per cent,[18] but they are limited to the appropriate percentage of the earnings cap[19]). Tax relief can be carried forward and carried back in the same way as it could for RACs.[20]

(2) Contributions may be paid by the employer or employee (or self-employed person).

(3) When contributions are paid by an employee they are paid net of basic-rate tax with the tax element recovered from the Inland Revenue by the provider. When they are paid by the self-employed, they are paid gross and the tax claimed back in the annual tax return.

(4) Retirement ages may fall in the range of 50 to 70.

(5) The tax-free cash will be a maximum of 25 per cent of the accumulated fund value.

(6) The personal pension may be used as a vehicle to contract out of SERPS. In these circumstances, it is known as an appropriate personal pension scheme (APPS).

(7) Personal pension schemes do not have to be written under trust as they should be inheritance free. However, directors may prefer to use their own trust. The options available under a personal pension scheme should a member die before retiring are complex and need careful planning.

(8) Since 1 May 1985, it has been possible (if the pension scheme allows) to postpone the purchase of an annuity and draw income from the capital sum instead. There are detailed rules setting out the maximum and minimum amount of income which must be taken.

(9) Some personal pension schemes are self-invested personal pensions (SIPPs). These schemes allow the member to direct how the capital is invested provided the investments are those agreed with the Inland Revenue. The scheme rules will limit investments to those permitted if this type of personal pension scheme is chosen.

(10) Some companies have group personal pension schemes. These are *not* occupational schemes. Each employee has a separate contract with provider (for example, insurance company). The advantages are that the employer may be able to negotiate favourable terms because of the number of members and will usually deduct contributions from payroll.

12.8   UNAPPROVED SCHEMES

Before the cap[21] was introduced, it was not possible to belong to both an approved and an unapproved scheme at the same time. After it was introduced, it became common to provide a pension above the cap by using an unapproved scheme. There are basically two types of unapproved schemes: funded and unfunded.

Funded unapproved retirement benefit schemes (FURBS) operate like funded approved schemes. They are usually set up under trust and are money purchase schemes as it is difficult to fund accurately for a benefit promise when events, like ill-health, cannot be smoothed in a larger group.

Unfunded unapproved retirement benefit schemes (UURBS) are no more than a promise to pay a pension when the director retires. As such, they offer less security than a FURBS because there is no fund available if the employer becomes insolvent. They too can be written under trust.

The tax treatment of the two arrangements is very different.

	FURBS	**UURBS**
Employer's contributions	Corporation tax relief is available provided the employee paid tax on the contribution as a benefit in kind – which he does. National Insurance contributions are payable.	None
Investment return	Income tax payable at basic rate. CGT payable. No IHT payable if it is a sponsored superannuation scheme.	None
Pension	Income tax payable.	Income tax payable
Lump sum	Tax free.	Income tax payable

12.9   INSURANCE COVER

The advantages to directors of joining their staff schemes will often outweigh all other factors except in circumstances where income is likely to fluctuate very widely, when personal pension schemes may offer the most flexible solution. They should also bear in mind the benefits which the staff schemes can give them in respect of group life-cover, regardless of state of health, and permanent sickness cover up to three-quarters of their income. Permanent sickness cover can also provide their contributions to the main scheme until they reach retirement, when they can retire on full pension, even though they may have been incapacitated for many years.

12.10   DISCLOSURE IN ACCOUNTS

Disclosure must be made in accordance with the Company Accounts (Disclosure of Directors Emoluments) Regulations 1997, SI 1997/570 which amended Sch 6 to the Companies Act 1985. These came after the Greenbury Report. They apply to companies with financial years ending after 31 March 1997 and apply to both listed and unlisted companies. They require the accounts to list separately:

(1) the number of directors accruing retirement benefits under:

    (a) money purchase schemes (defined contribution schemes), and

    (b) final salary (or defined benefit) schemes; and

(2) the aggregate value of the company's contributions to any money purchase schemes; and

(3) any increases to directors' pensions in payment greater than allowed for under the rules; and unless *all* members received the same increases; and

(4) details of the highest paid director's retirement benefits if the total of directors' emoluments is over £200,000. In these cases the accounts must show either:

    (a) the accrued value of his retirement benefits if he is in a final salary scheme, or

    (b) the value of the company's contributions if he is in a money purchase scheme.

If the company is listed, it must also comply with Amendment 10 of the Stock Exchange Listing Rules. These apply to companies with financial years ending after 30 June 1997. Details must be given for each director. If the director is in a final salary scheme, the accounts must show the value of his accrued leaving service pension and any increases granted during the year (net of inflation) together with the transfer value of those increases or the means to calculate the transfer value.

CHAPTER 12 FOOTNOTES

1 *Normandy v Ind Coope & Co* [1908] 1 Ch 84.

2 *Re Lee Behrens & Co* [1932] 2 Ch 46 and see also **11.6.2** (3).

3 [1967] 1 All ER 427.

4 [1982] 3 All ER 1045.

5 Pension Schemes Act 1993, ss 41 to 42A. Contracting-out reduces National Insurance contributions on earnings between the lower and upper limits by 1.6 per cent for employees and 3 per cent for employers or if the occupational pensions scheme is a COSR (contracted-out salary-related scheme); and 1.6 per cent for employees and 0.6 per cent for employers if it is a COMP (contracted-out money purchase scheme). Members of appropriate personal pension schemes pay the full National Insurance rate and the provider (for example, insurance company) claims the rebate from the DSS.

6 A personal pension scheme may be used as a vehicle for contracting out of SERPS if it complies with the money purchase test which will result in the reduction of National Insurance contributions (see Chapter 10, note 64). The government is currently paying additional rebates rising from 3.1 per cent at age 15 to 9 per cent for age 53 and over.

7 As consolidated in ICTA 1988 and later amended.

8 Further to the Finance Act 1989, an earnings cap on pensionable earnings has been introduced for both occupational and personal pension schemes. For occupational schemes, it is used to cap the salary which can be used to calculate benefits. For personal pension schemes, it caps the salary which can be used to calculate contributions. The earnings cap applies to all members of a personal pension scheme and to those members of an occupational scheme: (a) who joined the scheme after 1 June 1989 (where such a scheme existed prior to 14 March 1989); and (b) who joined a scheme which came into existence on or after 14 March 1989. The current limit on pensionable earnings is £90,600. Since it was introduced in 1989 the cap has been increased every year in line with RPI except one.

Year	Amount £
1989/90	60,000
1990/91	64,800
1991/92	71,400
1992/93	75,000
1993/94	75,000
1994/95	76,800
1995/96	78,600
1996/97	82,200
1997/98	84,000
1999/2000	90,600

The Inland Revenue has a discretion to modify or waive these provisions where, in their opinion, the facts are such that their application would not be appropriate. Applications to waive these provisions have been made successfully if a director has to change schemes for reasons beyond his control (a company sale or reorganisation) and he is not protected by the transitional Regulations.

9 Ibid.

10 Separate pensions may also be provided for widows and children or other dependants but the total must not exceed the maximum director's pension.

11 Ibid.

12 See note 8.

13 The amount and timing of the payments to AVCs or FSAVCs may be varied to suit the individual. The tax reliefs remain unchanged. No benefits accrued by payment of AVCs may be converted to a lump sum but may be drawn down on income if the scheme rules allow.

14 Since the case of *Barber v Guardian Royal Exchange* [1990] 2 All ER 660, before the European Court of Justice, men and women must have the same normal retirement dates.

15 See note 13.

16 Section 641 of ICTA 1988 enables an individual to elect to carry back a contribution tax made in the current year to the previous tax year, thereby obtaining relief from the previous year of assessment (providing he does not exceed the contribution limits for that previous year). Section 642 provides that any unused relief may be carried forward for to up to six years. Therefore, under s 642, it is possible to pay a greater contribution in any of the following six years than allowed for in a particular tax year, by adding to it relief not already used. It is possible that this right will be lost at the end of the tax year 1999/2000.

17 Such earnings comprise salary or profits after deduction of business expenses, but *not* personal charges such as alimony, charitable covenants and mortgage interest.

18 Tax relief for contributions made are available up to the following limits as a percentage of capped remuneration depending on age. (Tax relief will not be available on the excess contributions mace to one or more personal pension schemes.)

Age	*Contribution limit*
35 or less	17.5 per cent
36–45	20 per cent
46–50	25 per cent
51–55	30 per cent
56–60	35 per cent
60 and over	40 per cent

19 See note 8.
20 See note 16.
21 See note 8.

APPENDICES

JORDANS STANDARD FORM OF MEMORANDUM AND ARTICLES OF ASSOCIATION FOR A PRIVATE LIMITED COMPANY

Resettled by Richard Sykes QC and Andrew Thornton of Erskine Chambers, Lincoln's Inn[1]

The Companies Acts 1985 to 1989
Private Company Limited by Shares
Memorandum of Association of

[With general commercial object clause pursuant to section 3A of the Companies Act 1985]

[company name]   LIMITED

1.   The Company's name is '*[company name]* LIMITED'.

2.   The Company's registered office is to be situated in England and Wales.

3.1   The object of the Company is to carry on business as a general commercial company.

3.2   Without prejudice to the generality of the object and the powers of the Company derived from Section 3A of the Act the Company has power to do all or any of the following things:

3.2.1   To purchase or by any other means acquire and take options over any property whatever, and any rights or privileges of any kind over or in respect of any property.

3.2.2   To apply for, register, purchase, or by other means acquire and protect, prolong and renew, whether in the United Kingdom or elsewhere, any trade marks, patents, copyrights, trade secrets, or other intellectual property rights, licences, secret processes, designs, protections and concessions and to disclaim, alter, modify, use and turn to account and to manufacture under or grant licences or privileges in respect of the same, and to expend money in experimenting upon, testing and improving any patents, inventions or rights which the Company may acquire or propose to acquire.

3.2.3   To acquire or undertake the whole or any part of the business, goodwill, and assets of any person, firm, or company carrying on or proposing to carry on any of the

---

1   Source: P Van Duzer, HGM Leighton and JRM Lowe *Jordans Company Secretarial Precedents* 2nd edn (Jordans, 1997).
   Note: The following devices are employed throughout this predecent
   – *[italic text]* gives instructions on what details are to be inserted.
   – [roman text] gives examples or options of details to be inserted.

businesses which the Company is authorised to carry on and as part of the consideration for such acquisition to undertake all or any of the liabilities of such person, firm or company, or to acquire an interest in, amalgamate with, or enter into partnership or into any arrangement for sharing profits, or for co-operation, or for mutual assistance with any such person, firm or company, or for subsidising or otherwise assisting any such person, firm or company, and to give or accept, by way of consideration for any of the acts or things aforesaid or property acquired, any shares, debentures, debenture stock or securities that may be agreed upon, and to hold and retain, or sell, mortgage and deal with any shares, debentures, debenture stock or securities so received.

3.2.4 To improve, manage, construct, repair, develop, exchange, let on lease or otherwise, mortgage, charge, sell, dispose of, turn to account, grant licences, options, rights and privileges in respect of, or otherwise deal with all or any part of the property and rights of the Company.

3.2.5 To invest and deal with the moneys of the Company not immediately required in such manner as may from time to time be determined and to hold or otherwise deal with any investments made.

3.2.6 To lend and advance money or give credit on any terms and with or without security to any person, firm or company (including without prejudice to the generality of the foregoing any holding company, subsidiary or fellow subsidiary of, or any other company associated in any way with, the Company), to enter into guarantees, contracts of indemnity and suretyships of all kinds, to receive money on deposit or loan upon any terms, and to secure or guarantee in any manner and upon any terms the payment of any sum of money or the performance of any obligation by any person, firm or company (including without prejudice to the generality of the foregoing any such holding company, subsidiary, fellow subsidiary or associated company as aforesaid).

3.2.7 To borrow and raise money in any manner and to secure the repayment of any money borrowed, raised or owing by mortgage, charge, standard security, lien or other security upon the whole or any part of the Company's property or assets (whether present or future), including its uncalled capital, and also by a similar mortgage, charge, standard security, lien or security to secure and guarantee the performance by the Company of any obligation or liability it may undertake or which may become binding on it.

3.2.8 To draw, make, accept, endorse, discount, negotiate, execute and issue cheques, bills of exchange, promissory notes, bills of lading, warrants, debentures, and other negotiable or transferable instruments.

3.2.9 To apply for, promote, and obtain any Act of Parliament, order, or licence of the Department of Trade or other authority for enabling the Company to carry any of its objects into effect, or for effecting any modification of the Company's constitution, or for any other purpose which may seem calculated directly or indirectly to promote the Company's interests, and to oppose any proceedings or applications which may seem calculated directly or indirectly to prejudice the Company's interests.

3.2.10   To enter into any arrangements with any government or authority (supreme, municipal, local, or otherwise) that may seem conducive to the attainment of the Company's objects or any of them, and to obtain from any such government or authority any charters, decrees, rights, privileges or concessions which the Company may think desirable and to carry out, exercise, and comply with any such charters, decrees, rights, privileges, and concessions.

3.2.11   To subscribe for, take, purchase, or otherwise acquire, hold, sell, deal with and dispose of, place and underwrite shares, stocks, debentures, debenture stocks, bonds, obligations or securities issued or guaranteed by any other company constituted or carrying on business in any part of the world, and debentures, debenture stocks, bonds, obligations or securities issued or guaranteed by any government or authority, municipal, local or otherwise, in any part of the world.

3.2.12   To control, manage, finance, subsidise, co-ordinate or otherwise assist any company or companies in which the Company has a direct or indirect financial interest, to provide secretarial, administrative, technical, commercial and other services and facilities of all kinds for any such company or companies and to make payments by way of subvention or otherwise and any other arrangements which may seem desirable with respect to any business or operations of or generally with respect to any such company or companies.

3.2.13   To promote any other company for the purpose of acquiring the whole or any part of the business or property or undertaking or any of the liabilities of the Company, or of undertaking any business or operations which may appear likely to assist or benefit the Company or to enhance the value of any property or business of the Company, and to place or guarantee the placing of, underwrite, subscribe for, or otherwise acquire all or any part of the shares or securities of any such company as aforesaid.

3.2.14   To sell or otherwise dispose of the whole or any part of the business or property of the Company, either together or in portions, for such consideration as the Company may think fit, and in particular for shares, debentures, or securities of any company purchasing the same.

3.2.15   To act as agents or brokers and as trustees for any person, firm or company, and to undertake and perform sub-contracts.

3.2.16   To remunerate any person, firm or company rendering services to the Company either by cash payment or by the allotment of shares or other securities of the Company credited as paid up in full or in part or otherwise as may be thought expedient.

3.2.17   To distribute among the members of the Company in kind any property of the Company of whatever nature.

3.2.18   To pay all or any expenses incurred in connection with the promotion formation and incorporation of the Company, or to contract with any person, firm or company to pay the same, and to pay commissions to brokers and others for underwriting, placing, selling, or guaranteeing the subscription of any shares or other securities of the Company.

3.2.19   To support and subscribe to any charitable or public object and to support and subscribe to any institution, society, or club which may be for the benefit of the Company or its directors or employees, or may be connected with any town or place where the Company carries on business; to give or award pensions, annuities, gratuities, and superannuation or other allowances or benefits or charitable aid and generally to provide advantages, facilities and services for any persons who are or have been directors of, or who are or have been employed by, or who are serving or have served the Company, or any company which is a subsidiary of the Company or the holding company of the Company or a fellow subsidiary of the Company or the predecessors in business of the Company or of any such subsidiary, holding or fellow subsidiary company and to the wives, widows, children and other relatives and dependants of such persons; to make payments towards insurance including insurance for any director, officer or auditor against any liability in respect of any negligence, default, breach of duty or breach of trust (so far as permitted by law); and to set up, establish, support and maintain superannuation and other funds or schemes (whether contributory or non-contributory) for the benefit of any of such persons and of their wives, widows, children and other relatives and dependants; and to set up, establish, support and maintain profit sharing or share purchase schemes for the benefit of any of the employees of the Company or of any such subsidiary, holding or fellow subsidiary company and to lend money to any such employees or to trustees on their behalf to enable any such schemes to be established or maintained.

3.2.20   Subject to and in accordance with the provisions of the Act (if and so far as such provisions shall be applicable) to give, directly or indirectly, financial assistance for the acquisition of shares or other securities of the Company or of any other company or for the reduction or discharge of any liability incurred in respect of such acquisition.

3.2.21   To procure the Company to be registered or recognised in any part of the world.

3.2.22   To do all or any of the things or matters aforesaid in any part of the world and either as principals, agents, contractors or otherwise, and by or through agents, brokers, sub-contractors or otherwise and either alone or in conjunction with others.

3.2.23   To do all such other things as may be deemed incidental or conducive to the attainment of the Company's objects or any of them.

3.2.24   AND so that:

3.2.24.1   None of the provisions set forth in any sub-clause of this clause shall be restrictively construed but the widest interpretation shall be given to each such provision, and none of such provisions shall, except where the context expressly so requires, be in any way limited or restricted by reference to or inference from any other provision set forth in such sub-clause, or by reference to or inference from the terms of any other sub-clause of this clause, or by reference to or inference from the name of the Company.

3.2.24.2   The word 'company' in this clause, except where used in reference to the Company, shall be deemed to include any partnership or other body of persons, whether incorporated or unincorporated and whether domiciled in the United Kingdom or elsewhere.

3.2.24.3   In this clause the expression 'the Act' means the Companies Act 1985, but so that any reference in this clause to any provision of the Act shall be deemed to include a reference to any statutory modification or re-enactment of that provision for the time being in force.

4.   The liability of the members is limited.

5.   The Company's share capital is [£] divided into [*number of shares*] shares of [£] each.

The Companies Acts 1985 to 1989
Private Company Limited by Shares
Memorandum of Association of

[With specific objects clause and 'Cotman v Brougham' multiple objects]
[*company name*] LIMITED

1. The Company's name is '[*company name*] LIMITED'.

2. The Company's registered office is to be situated in England and Wales.

3. The Company's objects are:

3.1.1[   ]

3.1.2 To carry on any other trade or business whatever which can in the opinion of the board of directors be advantageously carried on in connection with or ancillary to any of the businesses of the Company.

3.2 To purchase or by any other means acquire and take options over any property whatever, and any rights or privileges of any kind over or in respect of any property.

[And continue with clauses 3.2.2 to 3.2.23 inclusive of the general commercial object version as clauses 3.3 to 3.24]

3.25 AND so that:

3.25.1 None of the objects set forth in any sub-clause of this clause shall be restrictively construed but the widest interpretation shall be given to each such object, and none of such objects shall, except where the context expressly so requires, be in any way limited or restricted by reference to or inference from any other object or objects set forth in such sub-clause, or by reference to or inference from the terms of any other sub-clause of this clause, or by reference to or inference from the name of the Company.

3.25.2 None of the sub-clauses of this clause and none of the objects therein specified shall he deemed subsidiary or ancillary to any of the objects specified in any other such sub-clause, and the Company shall have as full a power to exercise each and every one of the objects specified in each sub-clause of this clause as though each such sub-clause contained the objects of a separate Company.

3.25.3 The word 'company' in this clause, except where used in reference to the Company, shall be deemed to include any partnership or other body of persons, whether incorporated or unincorporated and whether domiciled in the United Kingdom or elsewhere.

3.25.4 In this clause the expression 'the Act' means the Companies Act 1985, but so that any reference in this clause to any provision of the Act shall be deemed to include a reference to any statutory modification or re-enactment of that provision for the time being in force.

4. The liability of the members is limited.

5. The Company's share capital is [£] divided into [*number of shares*] shares of [£] each.

The Companies Acts 1985 to 1989
Private Company Limited by Shares
Articles of Association of

[*company name*] LIMITED

1. Preliminary

1.1   The regulations contained in Table A in the Schedule to the Companies (Tables A to F) Regulations 1985 (SI 1985 No. 805) as amended by the Companies (Tables A to F) (Amendment) Regulations 1985 (SI 1985 No. 1052) (such Table being hereinafter called 'Table A') shall apply to the Company save in so far as they are excluded or varied hereby and such regulations (save as so excluded or varied) and the Articles hereinafter contained shall be the Articles of Association of the Company.

1.2   In these Articles the expression 'the Act' means the Companies Act 1985, but so that any reference in these Articles to any provision of the Act shall be deemed to include a reference to any statutory modification or re-enactment of that provision for the time being in force.

2. Allotment of shares

2.1   Shares which are comprised in the authorised share capital with which the Company is incorporated shall be under the control of the directors who may (subject to section 80 of the Act and to Article 2.4 below) allot, grant options over or otherwise dispose of the same, to such persons, on such terms and in such manner as they think fit.

2.2   All shares which are not comprised in the authorised share capital with which the Company is incorporated and which the directors propose to issue shall first be offered to the members in proportion as nearly as may be to the number of the existing shares held by them respectively unless the Company in general meeting shall by special resolution otherwise direct. The offer shall be made by notice specifying the number of shares offered, and limiting a period (not being less than 14 days) within which the offer, if not accepted, will be deemed to be declined. After the expiration of that period, those shares so deemed to be declined shall be offered in the proportion aforesaid to the persons who have, within the said period, accepted all the shares offered to them; such further offer shall be made in like terms in the same manner and limited by a like period as the original offer. Any shares not accepted pursuant to such offer or further offer as aforesaid or not capable of being offered as aforesaid except by way of fractions and any shares released from the provisions of this Article by any such special resolution as aforesaid shall be under the control of the directors, who may allot, grant options over or otherwise dispose of the same to such persons, on such terms, and in such manner as they think fit, provided that, in the case of shares not accepted as aforesaid, such shares shall not be disposed of on terms which are more favourable to the subscribers therefor than the terms on which they were offered to the members. The foregoing provisions of this Article 2.2 shall have effect subject to section 80 of the Act.

2.3   In accordance with section 91(1) of the Act sections 89(1) and 90(1) to (6) (inclusive) of the Act shall not apply to the Company.

2.4   The directors are generally and unconditionally authorised for the purposes of section 80 of the Act to exercise any power of the Company to allot and grant rights to subscribe for or convert securities into shares of the Company up to the amount of the authorised share capital with which the Company is incorporated at any time or times during the period of five years from the date of incorporation and the directors may, after that period, allot any shares or grant any such rights under this authority in pursuance of an offer or agreement so to do made by the Company within that period. The authority hereby given may at any time (subject to the said section 80) be renewed, revoked or varied by ordinary resolution.

3. Shares

3.1   The lien conferred by regulation 8 in Table A shall attach also to fully paid-up shares, and the Company shall also have a first and paramount lien on all shares, whether fully paid or not, standing registered in the name of any person indebted or under liability to the Company, whether he shall be the sole registered holder thereof or shall be one of two or more joint holders, for all moneys presently payable by him or his estate to the Company. Regulation 8 in Table A shall be modified accordingly.

3.2   The liability of any member in default in respect of a call shall be increased by the addition at the end of the first sentence of regulation 18 in Table A of the words 'and all expenses that may have been incurred by the Company by reason of such non-payment'.

4. General meetings and resolutions

4.1   Every notice convening a general meeting shall comply with the provisions of section 372(3) of the Act as to giving information to members in regard to their right to appoint proxies; and notices of and other communications relating to any general meeting which any member is entitled to receive shall be sent to the directors and to the auditors for the time being of the Company.

4.2.1   No business shall be transacted at any general meeting unless a quorum is present. Subject to Article 4.2.2 below, two persons entitled to vote upon the business to be transacted, each being a member or a proxy for a member or a duly authorised representative of a corporation, shall be a quorum.

4.2.2   If and for so long as the Company has only one member, that member present in person or by proxy or (if that member is a corporation) by a duly authorised representative shall be a quorum.

4.2.3   If a quorum is not present within half an hour from the time appointed for a general meeting the general meeting shall stand adjourned to the same day in the next week at the same time and place or to such other day and at such other time and place as the directors may determine; and if at the adjourned general meeting a quorum is not present within half an hour from the time appointed therefor such adjourned general meeting shall be dissolved.

4.2.4   Regulations 40 and 41 in Table A shall not apply to the Company.

4.3.1 If and for so long as the Company has only one member and that member takes any decision which is required to he taken in general meeting or by means of a written resolution, that decision shall be as valid and effectual as if agreed by the Company in general meeting, subject as provided in Article 4.3.3 below.

4.3.2 Any decision taken by a sole member pursuant to Article 4.3.1 above shall be recorded in writing and delivered by that member to the Company for entry in the Company's minute book.

4.3.3 Resolutions under section 303 of the Act for the removal of a director before the expiration of his period of office and under section 391 of the Act for the removal of an auditor before the expiration of his period of office shall only be considered by the Company in general meeting.

4.4 A member present at a meeting by proxy shall be entitled to speak at the meeting and shall be entitled to one vote on a show of hands. In any case where the same person is appointed proxy for more than one member he shall on a show of hands have as many votes as the number of members for whom he is proxy. Regulation 54 in Table A shall be modified accordingly.

4.5 Unless resolved by ordinary resolution that regulation 62 in Table A shall apply without modification, the instrument appointing a proxy and any authority under which it its executed or a copy of such authority certified notarially or in some other way approved by the directors may be deposited at the place specified in regulation 62 in Table A up to the commencement of the meeting or (in any case where a poll is taken otherwise than at the meeting) of the taking of the poll or may be handed to the chairman of the meeting prior to the commencement of the business of the meeting.

5. Appointment of directors

5.1.1 Regulation 64 in Table A shall not apply to the Company.

5.1.2 The maximum number and minimum number respectively of the directors may be determined from time to time by ordinary resolution. Subject to and in default of any such determination there shall be no maximum number of directors and the minimum number of directors shall be one. Whenever the minimum number of directors is one, a sole director shall have authority to exercise all the powers and discretions by Table A and by these Articles expressed to be vested in the directors generally, and regulation 89 in Table A shall be modified accordingly.

5.2 The directors shall not be required by rotation and regulations 73 to 80 (inclusive) in Table A shall not apply to the Company.

5.3 No person shall be appointed a director at any general meeting unless either:

(a) he is recommenced by the directors; or
(b) not less than 14 nor more than 35 clear days before the date appointed for the general meeting, notice signed by a member qualified to vote at the general meeting has been given to the Company of the intention to propose that person for appointment, together with notice signed by that person of his willingness to be appointed.

5.4.1   Subject to Article 5.3 above, the Company may be ordinary resolution appoint any person who is willing to act to be a director, either to fill a vacancy or as an additional director.

5.4.2   The directors may appoint a person who is willing to act to be a director, either to fill a vacancy or as an additional director, provided that the appointment does not cause the number of directors to exceed any number determined in accordance with Article 5.1.2 above as the maximum number of directors and for the time being in force.

5.5   In any case where as the result of death or deaths the Company has no members and no directors the personal representatives of the last member to have died shall have the right by notice in writing to appoint a person to be a director of the Company and such appointment shall be as effective as if made by the Company in General Meeting pursuant to Article 5.4.1 above. For the purpose of this article, where two or more members die in circumstances rendering it uncertain which of them survived the other or others, the members shall be deemed to have died in order of seniority, and accordingly the younger shall be deemed to have survived the elder.

6.   Borrowing powers

6.1   The directors may exercise all the powers of the Company to borrow money without limit as to amount and upon such terms and in such manner as they think fit, and subject (in the case of any security convertible into shares) to section 80 of the Act to grant any mortgage, charge or standard security over its undertaking, property and uncalled capital, or any part thereof, and to issue debentures, debenture stock, and other securities whether outright or as security for any debt, liability or obligation of the Company or of any third party.

7.   Alternate directors

7.1   Unless otherwise determined by the Company in general meeting by ordinary resolution an alternate director shall not be entitled as such to receive any remuneration from the Company, save that he may be paid by the Company such part (if any) of the remuneration otherwise payable to his appointor as such appointor may by notice in writing to the Company from time to time direct, and the first sentence of regulation 66 in Table A shall be modified accordingly.

7.2   A director, or any such other person as is mentioned in regulation 65 in Table A, may act as an alternate director to represent more than one director, and an alternate director shall be entitled at any meeting of the directors or of any committee of the directors to one vote for every director whom he represents in addition to his own vote (if any) as a director, but he shall count as only one for the purpose of determining whether a quorum is present.

8.   Gratuities and pensions

8.1.1   The directors may exercise the powers of the Company conferred by its Memorandum of Association in relation to the payment of pensions, gratuities and other benefits and shall be entitled to retain any benefits received by them or by any of them by reason of the exercise of any such powers.

8.1.2 Regulation 87 in Table A shall not apply to the Company.

9. Proceedings of directors

9.1.1 A director may vote, at any meeting of the directors or of any committee of the directors, on any resolution, notwithstanding that it in any way concerns or relates to a matter in which he has, directly or indirectly, any kind of interest whatsoever, and if he shall vote on any such resolution his vote shall be counted; and in relation to any such resolution as aforesaid he shall (whether or not he shall vote on the same) be taken into account in calculating the quorum present at the meeting.

9.1.2 Each director shall comply with his obligations to disclose his interest in contracts under section 317 of the Act.

9.1.3 Regulations 94 to 97 (inclusive) in Table A shall not apply to the Company.

10. The seal

10.1 If the Company has a seal it shall only be used with the authority of the directors or of a committee of directors. The directors may determine who shall sign any instrument to which the seal is affixed and unless otherwise so determined it shall be signed by a director and by the secretary or second director. The obligation under regulation 6 of Table A relating to the sealing of share certificates shall apply only if the Company has a seal. Regulation 101 in Table A shall not apply to the Company.

10.2 The Company may exercise the powers conferred by section 39 of the Act with regard to having an official seal for use abroad, and such powers shall be vested in the directors.

11. Notices

11.1 Without prejudice to regulations 112 to 116 (inclusive) in Table A, the Company may give notice to a member by electronic means provided that:

11.1.1 the member has given his consent in writing to receiving notice communicated by electronic means and in such consent has set out an address to which the notice shall be sent by electronic means; and

11.1.2 the electronic means used by the Company enables the member concerned to read the text of the notice.

11.2 A notice given to a member personally or in a form permitted by Article 11.1 above shall be deemed to be given on the earlier of the day on which it is delivered personally and the day on which it was despatched by electronic means, as the case may be.

11.3 Regulation 115 in Table A shall not apply to a notice delivered personally or in a form permitted by Article 11.1 above.

11.4 In this article 'electronic' means actuated by electric, magnetic, electromagnetic, electro-chemical or electro-mechanical energy and 'by electronic means' means by any manner only capable of being so actuated.

12. Indemnity

12.1   Every director or other officer or auditor of the Company shall be indemnified out of the assets of the Company against all losses or liabilities which he may sustain or incur in or about the execution of the duties of his office or otherwise in relation thereto, including any liability incurred by him in defending any proceedings, whether civil or criminal, or in connection with any application under section 144 or section 727 of the Act in which relief is granted to him by the Court, and no director or other officer shall be liable for any loss, damage or misfortune which may happen to or be incurred by the Company in the execution of the duties of his office or in relation thereto. But this Article shall only have effect in so far as its provisions are not avoided by section 310 of the Act.

12.2   The directors shall have power to purchase and maintain for any director, officer or auditor of the Company insurance against any such liability as is referred to in section 310(1) of the Act.

12.3   Regulation 118 in Table A shall not apply to the Company.

13.   Transfer of shares

13.1   The directors may, in their absolute discretion and without assigning any reason therefor, decline to register the transfer of a share, whether or not it is a fully paid share, and the first sentence of regulation 24 in Table A shall not apply to the Company.

Optional Additional Articles

(A)

[Enhanced voting rights for directors

1.   Every director for the time being of the Company shall have the following rights:
   (a)   if at any general meeting a poll is duly demanded on a resolution to remove him from office, to ten votes for each share of which he is the holder; and
   (b)   if at any general meeting a poll is duly demanded on a resolution having the effect of deleting, amending or nullifying the effect of the provisions of this Article, to ten votes for each share of which he is the holder if voting against such resolution.

2.   Regulation 54 in Table A shall be modified accordingly.]

(B)

[Casting vote

The chairman shall not, in the event of an equality of votes at any general meeting of the company or at any meeting of the directors or of a committee of directors, have a second or casting vote. Regulation 50 in Table A shall not apply to the Company, and regulations 88 and 72 in Table A shall be modified accordingly.]

(C)

[Associate directors

1.   The directors may at any time and from time to time appoint any employee of the Company to the position of associate director.

2.   An associate director shall at the request of the directors advise and assist the directors but shall not attend board meetings except at the invitation of the directors, and when present at board meetings he shall not vote, nor be counted in the quorum, but subject as aforesaid he shall as associate director have such powers, authorities and duties as the directors may in the particular case from time to time determine.

3.   As associate director shall not be deemed a member of the board, nor any committee thereof, nor shall he be a director for any of the purposes of these Articles of Association or for any of the purposes of the Act.

4.   Without prejudice to any rights or claims the associate director may have as employee under any contract with the Company, any appointment as an associate director may be terminated by the directors at any time and shall ipso facto terminate if the associate director shall from any cause cease to be an employee of the Company.

5.   An associate may receive such remuneration (if any) in addition to the remuneration received as an employee of the Company as the directors shall from time to time determine.]

(D)

[**Meetings**

1. In this Article 'electronic' means actuated by electric, magnetic, electro-magnetic, electro-chemical or electro-mechanical energy and 'by electronic means' means by any manner only capable of being so actuated.

2. A person in communication by electronic means with the chairman and with all other parties to a meeting of the directors or of a committee of the directors shall be regarded for all purposes as personally attending such a meeting provided that but only for so long as at such a meeting he has the ability to communicate interactively and simultaneously with all other parties attending the meeting including all persons attending by electronic means.

3. A meeting at which one or more of the directors attends by electronic means is deemed to be held at such place as the directors shall at the said meeting resolve. In the absence of a resolution as aforesaid, the meeting shall be deemed to be held at the place, if any, where a majority of the directors attending the meeting are physically present, or in default of such a majority, the place at which the chairman of the meeting is physically present.]

Explanatory Notes

Introduction

The form of memorandum and articles to which these Notes are attached [Jordans 1997 draft] is intended to provide a basic constitution for a private company limited by shares. Depending on the choice of location of its registered office, such a company may be incorporated in either England and Wales or in Scotland.

Whilst the specimen articles of association are primarily based on the statutory model set out in Table A of the Companies Act 1985, a number of variations have been incorporated. In particular, a number of variations and additional articles relating to other matters [optional articles (A) to (D)] have been provided. These are intended to cater for situations which our clients have found arise regularly in practice.

The attached documents have been drafted by experienced specialist Counsel as integrated documents to be read in conjunction with the relevant provisions of company law. Particular care must be taken when amending any of our standard forms. Redrafting should not be attempted without proper professional advice. COPYRIGHT IS RESERVED IN ALL OF OUR STANDARD FORMS.

Although the attached specimen documents are suitable for most sets of circumstance, we acknowledge that companies are incorporated for a whole host of different reasons. In particular, companies may be incorporated to pursue particular objects or to meet specific circumstances. It is not possible to anticipate all possible sets of circumstance in any standard form document. It is important for those who form companies to obtain appropriate professional advice as to whether our standard form or any of the standard variations and additional provisions are suitable for their particular requirements.

In the first instance, those wishing to incorporate a company should look to their solicitors, accountants, or other appropriately qualified professional advisers for advice in such matters. Jordans are, however, able to provide bespoke drafting services to such advisers to cater for circumstances as defined by those advisers' instructions.

The obligations and responsibilities imposed on persons running limited companies are wide and far-reaching. For those unfamiliar with the responsibilities of running a private limited company, we would recommend 'Running a Limited Company' [Jordans 1996] as a valuable initial guide.

Section 3A of the Companies Act 1985 provides for a company to have a general commercial object. The object and powers set out on pages 359 to 367 are a suggested format for making use of that provision. The articles also make provision for the case where the Company may be, or become, a single member company.

For the purposes of registration, copies of the final draft must be printed for signature by subscribers and for supplying to members in accordance with section 19 of the Companies Act 1985.

Commentary on the form

NOTES TO MEMORANDUM

Clause 2   The country within Great Britain in which the registered office is situated must be stated – either 'England and Wales' or 'Scotland'. Alternatively, a Welsh registered office may be specified and the Welsh words 'cyfyngedig' or 'cyf' substituted for 'limited' or 'Ltd' respectively in the name of the Company. The intended situation of the registered office will be set out on Form 10 filed with the Registrar of Companies as part of the incorporation procedure.

Clause 3   Section 110 of the Companies Act 1989 (which came into force on 4 February 1991) inserted a new section 3A into the Companies Act 1985. Section 3A provides that where a company's memorandum states that: 'the object of the Company is to carry on business as a general commercial company' (as set out in paragraph 3.1 on page 359) – the object of the Company is to carry on any trade or business whatsoever, and the Company has power to do all such things as are incidental or conducive to the carrying on of any trade or business by it. Section 3A draws a clear distinction between objects and powers and the proper construction of this section cannot be to exclude additional powers. Accordingly, if the wording set out in section 3A is used it would be sensible either to add the wording set out in paragraph 3.2 on page 359 followed by the wording of paragraphs 3.2.1 onwards or use other similar means to ensure that the provisions in the Company's memorandum are sufficient for its purposes.

Clause 3.1.1 – Alternative use of specific objects   Alternatively a suitable 'main objects' clause reflecting the principal business to be carried on by the Company may be inserted as clause 3.1.1. This needs to be carefully and comprehensively drafted; an example is set out below, but the version used should be based on the business actually intended to be carried on. This type of main objects clause may still be used and in some circumstances will be more suitable than a general commercial company object under section 3A of the Companies Act 1985.

If an existing business or shares in an existing company are being acquired, reference to such acquisition may be desirable.

Specimen 'Main Objects' Clause

'3.1   The Company's objects are:

3.1.1   To create, establish and maintain an organisation for the export, import, introduction, sale, purchase, distribution, advertising or marketing of products, goods, wares and merchandise of every description; to carry on all or any of the businesses of export marketing specialists, market research advisers and consultants, mail order specialists, manufacturers' agents and representatives, importers and exporters, commission agents, general merchants and traders; and to participate in, undertake, perform and carry out all kinds of commercial, industrial trading and financial operations and enterprises; and to carry out all of the operations performed by commission and general agents, export, import and general merchants, shippers, traders, capitalists and financiers, either on the Company's own account or otherwise; and to carry on all or any of the businesses of haulage and transport contractors, garage proprietors and owners, operators, hirers and letters on hire of, and dealers in motor and other vehicles, conveyances and craft of every description, and all plant, machinery, fittings, furnishings, accessories and stores required in connection therewith or in the maintenance thereof.

3.1.2   To carry on any other trade or business whatever which can in the opinion of the board of directors be advantageously carried on in connection with or ancillary to any of the businesses of the Company.'

The remaining part of clause 3 sets out additional objects which are likely to be applicable and necessary for any trading company. It is necessary for these or equivalent clauses to be set out to enable a company to carry out such objects or exercise such powers. These may be identical in format to paragraphs 3.2.1 to 3.2.23 inclusive on pages 359 to 367 but will need to be renumbered as paragraphs 3.2 to 3.24. The remainder of clause 3 might then be as follows:

'3.24   To do all such other things as may be deemed incidental or conducive to the attainment of the Company's objects or any of them.

3.25   AND so that:

3.25.1   None of the objects set forth in any sub-clause of this clause shall be restrictively construed but the widest interpretation shall be given to each such object, and none of such objects shall, except where the context expressly so requires, be in any way limited or restricted by reference to or inference from any other object or objects set forth in such sub-clause, or by reference to or inference from the terms of any other sub-clause of this clause, or by reference to or inference from the name of the Company.

3.25.2   None of the sub-clauses of this clause and none of the objects therein specified shall be deemed subsidiary or ancillary to any of the objects specified in any other such sub-clause, and the Company shall have as full a power to exercise each and every one of the objects specified in each sub-clause of this clause as though each such sub-clause contained the objects of a separate company.

3.25.3   The word 'company' in this Clause, except where used in reference to the Company, shall be deemed to include any partnership or other body of persons. whether incorporated or unincorporated and whether domiciled in the United Kingdom or elsewhere.

3.25.4   In this Clause the expression 'the Act' means the Companies Act 1985, but so that any reference in this Clause to any provision of the Act shall be deemed to include a reference to any statutory modification or re-enactment of that provision for the time being in force.'

Clause 5   Even if the share capital is to be divided into different classes of shares it is advisable (unless there is a particular requirement to entrench class rights), and usual, to omit any such division or reference to special classes in the memorandum.

Subscription   There must be shown in the memorandum against the name of each subscriber the number of shares he takes and, if the capital is divided into shares of different classes, the class subscribed for should also be stated.

The memorandum of association must be signed by at least one subscriber whose signature must be duly attested by a witness (Companies Act 1985, section 2(6)). Where there are two or more subscribers, it is permissible for one person to act as witness to them all. Underneath the signature of each subscriber and that of the witness there should be printed the full name and address of the signatory.

Notes to Articles

The first 13 articles are standard articles which are followed by special articles which can be selected and added if appropriate.

Article   All the regulations in Table A under the Companies Act 1985 are incorporated in these articles unless specifically stated. Where appropriate, special articles have been substituted or added.

It is convenient to bind a copy of the 1985 Table A with the articles when final prints are made. *Even if Table A changes after incorporation the Company remains subject to the version in force at its incorporation (unless it subsequently adopts new articles referring to a new Table A).*

Table A to the 1985 Act came into force on 1 July 1985 and is set out in the Companies (Tables A to F) Regulations 1985 (SI 1985 No 805). It was subject to minor amendment in the Companies (Tables A to F) (Amendment) Regulations 1985 (SI 1985 No 1052) and this final form applies as of 1 August 1985 and to these articles.

Article 2   Article 2.1 places the shares in the authorised share capital with which the Company is incorporated at the disposal of the directors to allot as they think fit. Shares subsequently created must be offered pro rata to existing members in accordance with Article 2.2. Article 2.3 excludes the statutory pre-emption rights set out in sections 89 and 90 of the Companies Act 1985. Article 2.4 gives authority under section 80 of the Act for the allotment of shares in the initial authorised share capital. This authority is effective for five years and may be renewed. Whenever a resolution is passed creating new shares it will be normal at the same meeting to seek new authority under section 80 by ordinary resolution either in relation to that capital alone or in respect of all capital then remaining unissued. Resolutions to increase share capital and resolutions to give section 80 authority each have to be filed at the Companies Registry. The following is a possible form of resolution to give section 80 authority in respect of all unissued capital at the date of the resolution:

'That the directors be and they are hereby generally and unconditionally authorised pursuant to section 80 of the Companies Act 1985 to exercise any power of the Company to allot and grant rights to subscribe for or to convert securities into shares of the Company up to a maximum nominal amount equal to the nominal amount of the authorised but unissued share capital at the date of the passing of this resolution provided that the authority hereby given:

(a)   shall be subject to the provisions of Article 2 of the articles of association of the Company;

(b)   shall expire five years after the passing of this resolution unless previously renewed, revoked or varied save that the directors may, notwithstanding such expiry, allot any shares or grant any such rights under this authority in pursuance of an offer or agreement so to do made by the Company before the expiry of this authority.'

A different form of wording will be required if the Company has passed an elective resolution pursuant to section 80A and it is desired to give authority for an indefinite period or for a fixed period greater than five years.

Article 3.1   This article extends the Company's lien conferred by regulation 8 in Table A.

Article 3.2   This article increases the liability on defaulted calls imposed by Table A to include costs.

Article 4   Article 4.1 serves as a reminder of the statutory requirements in section 372 of the Companies Act 1985.

Article 4.2 deals with the quorum at general meetings. Article 4.2.2 is declaratory of section 370A of the Companies Act 198S and clarifies the position of an authorised representative when a corporate body is the sole shareholder.

Article 4.2.3 alters regulation 41 in Table A so as to require a quorum to be present at an adjourned meeting and provides for the dissolution of the meeting if a quorum is not then present.

Article 4.3 contains provisions which clarify the circumstances in which and the means by which a sole member can take decisions outside a general meeting.

Article 4.4 entitles a proxy for a member to speak at a general meeting and to vote on a show of hands, contrary to the rule in Table A. Article 4.5 derogates from the inflexible rule in Table A that proxies may not be used unless lodged 48 hours before the meeting or 24 hours before the poll at which they are to be used.

Article 5   Section 13 provides that the persons named in the statement of directors filed on incorporation are to be the first directors. There is no other method of appointment.

Under Articles 5.1.1 and 5.1.2 the number of directors may be fixed by ordinary resolution of the Company. Table A is modified to provide for a sole director if required. It should be noted that a sole director may not act as secretary.

Retirement of directors by rotation is excluded. If it is desired to provide for retirement by rotation the whole of Articles 5.2 and 5.4.2 should be deleted.

Article 5.5 covers the procedure where as a result of death(s) a company has neither directors or shareholders; for example in a single member/director or husband and wife situation as a result of an accident. The last survivor in a simultaneous death is the younger person.

Article 6   Regulation 70 in Table A gives the directors authority to exercise all the powers of the company. This article is added to make it clear that they have unlimited borrowing powers and should be read in conjunction with clause (3.8) (3.2.7) of the memorandum. If it is proposed to issue loan capital giving rights of conversion into share capital the issuing company should ensure that authority to allot rights to convert into shares has been given under section 80 of the Companies Act 1985.

Article 7   This article makes some practical modifications to regulations 65 and 66 of Table A in connection with alternate directors.

Article 8   The powers of the Company as to payment of pensions conferred by the memorandum are wide and extend to directors whether or not they hold or have held any executive office. This article replaces regulation 87 in Table A which limits payment of pensions to directors who have held executive office.

Article 9   Article 9.1.1 varies Table A to enable directors to vote at board meetings without restriction on matters in which they have an interest. Such provision is commonly included in the articles of private companies, but the directors (including a sole director) must still comply with section 317 of the Companies Act 1985 in disclosing interests: Article 9.1.2.

Article 10   Sections 36A and 36B of the Companies Act 1985 (as inserted by section 130 of the Companies Act 1989 and subsequent legislation) provide that a company does not have to have a common seal (although many companies may continue to have one). This article replaces regulation 101 and modifies regulation 6 in Table A so that it will he appropriate whether or not the Company has a common seal.

Article 10.2 enables the Company to have an additional seal for use abroad, in accordance with section 39 of the Companies Act 1985.

Article 11   This new article permits the Company and a member to agree that notices may be given to the member in electronic form (for example by e-mail).

Article 12   The indemnity given by this clause is wider than that provided by regulation 118 in Table A. Article 12.2 empowers directors to purchase and maintain insurance against liability of officers in accordance with the permissive power in section 310(3) of the Companies Act 1985 as altered by section 137 of the Companies Act 1989. Those wishing to take out such insurance should take advice.

Article 13   This gives the Directors absolute discretion to refuse to register a share transfer, without being required to give reasons. Restrictions on share transfers are not contained in the current version of Table A.

In many private companies the members may wish to have the right to transfer their shares to a restricted group, for example, other members or members of their family. It may also be desired to oblige a member to make his shares available for purchase by the other members in certain circumstances, and to regulate the manner in which the price for the shares is determined. Specific transfer articles to deal with such circumstances are available if desired.

Optional articles
The following optional forms may be adopted:

A. Enhanced voting rights for directors

This article reinforces the position of a director who is also a shareholder by giving such director additional votes per share on a resolution to remove him from office or amend or delete this article. Please check that 10 votes for each share is sufficient for this purpose or alter accordingly.

B. Casting vote

This article removes the chairman's casting vote which is normally exercisable under Table A if there is an equality of votes at a general meeting or a meeting of directors. Such a provision can be useful but additional provisions may be appropriate if the articles are designed to create a 'deadlock' situation with intentionally evenly balanced representation of specific shareholding interests.

C. Associate directors
For management purposes it may be appropriate to create a class of associate directors who are given additional status beyond that of an employee but are not members of the board. This can be useful when the appointee is in contact with customers. This additional article makes appropriate provision for a class of associate directors.

D. Electronic attendance

This optional article enables attendance at board meetings to be by telephone or other electronic means, provided that all participants can communicate with all other parties to the meeting and that all proceedings at the meeting are communicated to him.

Appendix B

TABLE A TO THE COMPANIES ACTS 1948–1981

(Incorporating all changes made by the Companies Acts 1967, 1976, 1980 and 1981 and other legislation.)

Regulations for Management of a Company Limited by Shares

Interpretation

1. In these Regulations:
    'the Act' means the Companies Act 1948.
    'the Seal' means the common seal of the company.
    'Secretary' means any person appointed to perform the duties of the secretary of the company.
    'the United Kingdom' means Great Britain and Northern Ireland.

Expressions referring to writing shall, unless the contrary intention appears, be construed as including references to printing, lithography, photography, and other modes of representing or reproducing words in a visible form.

Unless the context otherwise requires, words or expressions contained in these regulations shall bear the same meaning as in the Act or any statutory modification thereof in force at the date at which these regulations become binding on the company.

Share Capital and Variation of Rights

2. Without prejudice to any special rights previously conferred on the holders of any existing shares or class of shares, any share in the company may be issued with such preferred, deferred or other special rights or such restrictions, whether in regard to dividend, voting, return of capital or otherwise as the company may from time to time by ordinary resolution determine.

3. Subject to the provisions of Part III of the Companies Act 1981, any shares may, with the sanction of an ordinary resolution, be issued on the terms that they are, or at the option of the company are liable, to be redeemed on such terms and in such manner as the company before the issue of the shares may by special resolution determine.

4. If at any time the share capital is divided into different classes of shares, the rights attached to any class may, whether or not the company is being wound up, be varied with the consent in writing of the holders of three-fourths of the issued shares of that class, or with the sanction of an extraordinary resolution passed at a separate general meeting of the holders of the shares of that class.

5. The rights conferred upon the holders of the shares of any class issued with preferred or other rights shall not, unless otherwise expressly provided by the terms of issue of the shares of that class, be deemed to be varied by the creation or issue of further shares ranking *pari passu* therewith.

6.   The company may exercise the powers of paying commissions conferred by section 53 of the Act, provided that the rate per cent or the amount of the commission paid or agreed to be paid shall be disclosed in the manner required by the said section and the rate of the commission shall not exceed the rate of ten per cent of the price at which the shares in respect whereof the same is paid are issued or an amount equal to ten per cent of such price (as the case may be). Such commission may be satisfied by the payment of cash or the allotment of fully or partly paid shares or partly in one way and partly in the other. The Company may also on any issue of shares pay such brokerage as may be lawful.

7.   Except as required by law, no person shall be recognised by the company as holding any share upon any trust, and the company shall not be bound by or be compelled in any way to recognise (even when having notice thereof) any equitable, contingent, future or partial interest in any share or any interest in any fractional part of a share or (except only as by these regulations or by law otherwise provided) any other rights in respect of any share except an absolute right to the entirety thereof in the registered holder.

8.   Every person whose name is entered as a member in the Register of Members shall be entitled without payment to receive within two months after allotment or lodgment of transfer (or within such other period as the conditions of issue shall provide) one certificate for all his shares or several certificates each for one or more of his shares upon payment of 12½p for every certificate after the first or such less sum as the Directors shall from time to time determine. Every certificate shall be under the seal and shall specify the shares to which it relates and the amount paid up thereon. Provided that in respect of a share or shares held jointly by several persons the company shall not be bound to issue more than one certificate, and delivery of a certificate for a share to one of several joint holders shall be sufficient delivery to all such holders.

9.   If a share certificate be defaced, lost or destroyed, it may be renewed on payment of a fee of 12½p or such less sum and on such terms (if any) as to evidence and indemnity and the payment of out-of-pocket expenses of the company in investigating evidence as the directors think fit.

10.   [Repealed by the Companies Act 1981]

Lien

11.   The company shall have a first and paramount lien on every share (not being a fully paid share) for all moneys (whether presently payable or not) called or payable at a fixed time in respect of that share, but the directors may at any time declare any share to be wholly or in part exempt from the provisions of this regulation. The company's lien, if any, on a share shall extend to all dividends payable thereon.

12.   The company may sell, in such manner as the directors think fit, any shares on which the company has a lien, but no sale shall be made unless a sum in respect of which the lien exists is presently payable, nor until the expiration of 14 days after a notice in writing, stating and demanding payment of such part of the amount in respect of which the lien exists as is presently payable has been given to the registered holder for the time being of the share, or the person entitled thereto by reason of his death or bankruptcy.

13. To give effect to any such sale the directors may authorise some person to transfer the shares sold to the purchaser thereof. The purchaser shall be registered as the holder of the shares comprised in any such transfer, and he shall not be bound to see to the application of the purchase money, nor shall his title to the shares be affected by any irregularity or invalidity in the proceedings in reference to the sale.

14. The proceeds of the sale shall be received by the company and applied in payment of such part of the amount in respect of which the lien exists as is presently payable, and the residue, if any, shall (subject to a like lien for sums not presently payable as existed upon the shares before the sale) be paid to the person entitled to the shares at the date of the sale.

Calls on Shares

15. The directors may from time to time make calls upon the members in respect of any moneys unpaid on their shares (whether on account of the nominal value of the shares or by way of premium) and not by the conditions of allotment thereof made payable at fixed times, provided that no call shall exceed one-fourth of the nominal value of the share or be payable at less than one month from the date fixed for the payment of the last preceding call, and each member shall (subject to receiving at least 14 days' notice specifying the time or times and place of payment) pay to the company at the time or times and place so specified the amount called on his shares. A call may be revoked or postponed as the directors may determine.

16. A call shall be deemed to have been made at the time when the resolution of the directors authorising the call was passed and may be required to be paid by instalments.

17. The joint holders of a share shall be jointly and severally liable to pay all calls in respect thereof.

18. If a sum called in respect of a share is not paid before or on the day appointed for payment thereof, the person from whom the sum is due shall pay interest on the sum from the day appointed for payment thereof to the time of actual payment at such rate not exceeding five per cent per annum as the directors may determine, but the directors shall be at liberty to waive payment of such interest wholly or in part.

19. Any sum which by the terms of issue of a share becomes payable on allotment or at any fixed date, whether on account of the nominal value of the share or by way of premium, shall for the purposes of these regulations be deemed to be a call duly made and payable on the date on which by the terms of issue the same becomes payable, and in case of non-payment all the relevant provisions of these regulations as to payment of interest and expenses, forfeiture or otherwise shall apply as if such sum had become payable by virtue of a call duly made and notified.

20.   The directors may, on the issue of shares, differentiate between the holders as to the amount of calls to be paid and the times of payment.

21.   The directors may, if they think fit, receive from any member willing to advance the same, all or any part of the moneys uncalled and unpaid upon any shares held by him, and upon all or any of the moneys so advanced may (until the same would, but for such advance, become payable) pay interest at such a rate not exceeding (unless the company in general meeting shall otherwise direct) five per cent per annum, as may be agreed upon between the directors and the member paying such sum in advance.

Transfer of Shares

22.   The instrument of transfer of any share shall be executed by or on behalf of the transferor and transferee, and, the transferor shall be deemed to remain a holder of the share until the name of the transferee is entered in the Register of Members in respect thereof.

23.   Subject to such of the restrictions of these regulations as may be applicable, any member may transfer all or any of his shares by instrument in writing in any usual or common form or any other form which the directors may approve.

24.   The directors may decline to register the transfer of a share (not being a fully paid share) to a person of whom they shall not approve, and they may also decline to register the transfer of a share on which the company has a lien.

25.   The directors may also decline to recognise any instrument of transfer unless:

(a)   a fee of 12½p or such lesser sum as the directors may from time to time require is paid to the company in respect thereof;

(b)   the instrument of transfer is accompanied by the certificate of the shares to which it relates, and such other evidence as the directors may reasonably require to show the right of the transferor to make the transfer; and

(c)   the instrument of transfer is in respect of only one class of share.

26.   If the directors refuse to register a transfer they shall within two months after the date on which the transfer was lodged with the company send to the transferee notice of the refusal.

27.   The registration of transfers may be suspended at such times and for such periods as the directors may from time to time determine, provided always that such registration shall not be suspended for more than 30 days in any year.

28.   The company shall be entitled to charge a fee not exceeding 12½p on the registration of every probate, letters of administration, certificate of death or marriage, power of attorney, notice in lieu of distringas, or other instrument.

Transmission of Shares

29.   In case of the death of a member the survivor or survivors where the deceased was a joint holder, and the legal personal representatives of the deceased where he was a sole holder, shall be the only persons recognised by the company as having any title to his interest in the shares; but nothing herein contained shall release the estate of a deceased joint holder from any liability in respect of any share which had been jointly held by him with other persons.

30.   Any person becoming entitled to a share in consequence of the death or bankruptcy of a member may, upon such evidence being produced as may from time to time properly be required by the directors and subject as hereinafter provided, elect either to be registered himself as holder of the share or to have some person nominated by him registered as the transferee thereof, but the directors shall, in either case, have the same right to decline or suspend registration as they would have had in the case of a transfer of the share by that member before his death or bankruptcy, as the case may be.

31.   If the person so becoming entitled shall elect to be registered himself, he shall deliver or send to the company a notice in writing signed by him stating that he so elects. If he shall elect to have another person registered he shall testify his election by executing to that person a transfer of the share. All the limitations, restrictions and provisions of these regulations relating to the right to transfer and the registration of transfers of shares shall be applicable to any such notice or transfer as aforesaid as if the death or bankruptcy of the member had not occurred and the notice or transfer were a transfer signed by that member.

32.   A person becoming entitled to a share by reason of the death or bankruptcy of the holder shall be entitled to the same dividends and other advantages to which he would be entitled if he were the registered holder of the share, except that he shall not, before being registered as a member in respect of the share, be entitled in respect of it to exercise any right conferred by membership in relation to meetings of the company:

Provided always that the directors may at any time give notice requiring any such person to elect either to be registered himself or to transfer the share, and if the notice is not complied with within 90 days the directors may thereafter withhold payment of all dividends, bonuses or other moneys payable in respect of the share until the requirements of the notice have been complied with.

Forfeiture of Shares

33.   If a member fails to pay any call or instalment of a call on the day appointed for payment thereof, the directors may, at any time thereafter during such time as any part of the call or instalment remains unpaid, serve a notice on him requiring payment of so much of the call or instalment as is unpaid, together with any interest which may have accrued.

34.   The notice shall name a further day (not earlier than the expiration of 14 days from the date of service of the notice) on or before which the payment required by the notice is to be made, and shall state that in the event of non-payment at or before the time appointed the shares in respect of which the call was made will be liable to be forfeited.

35.   If the requirements of any such notice as aforesaid are not complied with, any share in respect of which the notice has been given may at any time thereafter, before the payment required by the notice has been made, be forfeited by a resolution of the directors to that effect.

36. A forfeited share may be sold or otherwise disposed of on such terms and in such manner as the directors think fit, and at any time before a sale or disposition the forfeiture may be cancelled on such terms as the directors think fit.

37. A person whose shares have been forfeited shall cease to be a member in respect of the forfeited shares, but shall, notwithstanding, remain liable to pay to the company all moneys which, at the date of forfeiture, were payable by him to the company in respect of the shares, but his liability shall cease if and when the company shall have received payment in full of all such moneys in respect of the shares.

38. A statutory declaration in writing that the declarant is a director or the secretary of the company, and that a share in the company has been duly forfeited on a date stated in the declaration, shall be conclusive evidence of the facts therein stated as against all persons claiming to be entitled to the share. The company may receive the consideration, if any, given for the share on any sale or disposition thereof and may execute a transfer of the share in favour of the person to whom the share is sold or disposed of and he shall thereupon be registered as the holder of the share, and shall not be bound to see to the application of the purchase money, if any, nor shall his title to the share be affected by any irregularity or invalidity in the proceedings in reference to the forfeiture, sale or disposal of the share.

39. The provisions of these regulations as to forfeiture shall apply in the case of non-payment of any sum which, by the terms of issue of a share, becomes payable at a fixed time, whether on account of the nominal value of the share or by way of premium, as if the same had been payable by virtue of a call duly made and notified.

Conversion of Shares into Stock

40. The company may by ordinary resolution convert any paid-up shares into stock, and reconvert any stock into paid-up shares of any denomination.

41. The holders of stock may transfer the same, or any part thereof, in the same manner, and subject to the same regulations, as and subject to which the shares from which the stock arose might previously to conversion have been transferred, or as near thereto as circumstances admit; and the directors may from time to time fix the minimum amount of stock transferable but so that such minimum shall not exceed the nominal amount of the shares from which the stock arose.

42. The holders of stock shall, according to the amount of stock held by them, have the same rights, privileges and advantages as regards dividends, voting at meetings of the company and other matters as if they held the shares from which the stock arose, but no such privilege or advantage (except participation in the dividends and profits of the company and in the assets on winding up) shall be conferred by an amount of stock which would not, if existing in shares, have conferred that privilege or advantage.

43. Such of the regulations of the company as are applicable to paid-up shares shall apply to stock, and the words 'share' and 'shareholder' therein shall include 'stock' and 'stockholder'.

Alteration of Capital

44. The company may from time to time by ordinary resolution increase the share capital by such sum, to be divided into shares of such amount, as the resolution shall prescribe.

45. The company may by ordinary resolution:

(a) consolidate and divide all or any of its share capital into shares of larger amount than its existing shares;

(b) subdivide its existing shares, or any of them, into shares of smaller amount than is fixed by the memorandum of association subject, nevertheless, to the provisions of section 61(1) (d) of the Act;

(c) cancel any shares which, at the date of the passing of the Resolution, have not been taken or agreed to be taken by any person.

46. The company may by special resolution reduce its share capital, any capital redemption reserve fund or any share premium account in any manner and with, and subject to, any incident authorised, and consent required, by law.

General Meetings

47. The company shall in each year hold a general meeting as its annual general meeting in addition to any other meetings in that year, and shall specify the meeting as such in the notices calling it; and not more than 15 months shall elapse between the date of one annual general meeting of the company and that of the next. Provided that so long as the company holds its first annual general meeting within 18 months of its incorporation, it need not hold it in the year of its incorporation or in the following year. The annual general meeting shall be held at such time and place as the directors shall appoint.

48. All general meetings other than annual general meetings shall be called extraordinary general meetings.

49. The directors may, whenever they think fit, convene an extraordinary general meeting, and extraordinary general meetings shall also be convened on such requisition, or, in default, may be convened by such requisitionists, as provided by section 132 of the Act. If at any time there are not within the United Kingdom sufficient directors capable of acting to form a quorum, any director or any two members of the company may convene an extraordinary general meeting in the same manner as nearly as possible as that in which meetings may be convened by the directors.

Notices of General Meetings

50. An annual general meeting and a meeting called for the passing of a special resolution shall be called by 21 days' notice in writing at the least, and a meeting of the company other than an annual general meeting or a meeting for the passing of a special resolution shall be called by 14 days' notice in writing at the least. The notice shall be exclusive of the day on which it is served or deemed to be served and of the day for which it is given, and shall specify the place, the day and the hour of meeting and, in case of special business, the general nature of that business, and shall be given, in manner hereinafter mentioned or in such other manner, if any, as may be prescribed by the company in general meeting, to such persons as are, under the regulations of the company, entitled to receive such notices from the company:

Provided that a meeting of the company shall, notwithstanding that it is called by shorter notice than that specified in this regulation, be deemed to have been duly called if it is so agreed:

(a) in the case of a meeting called as the annual general meeting, by all the members entitled to attend and vote thereat; and

(b) in the case of any other meeting, by a majority in number of the members having a right to attend and vote at the meeting, being a majority together holding not less than 95 per cent in nominal value of the shares giving that right.

51. The accidental omission to give notice of a meeting to, or the non-receipt of notice of a meeting by, any person entitled to receive notice shall not invalidate the proceedings at that meeting.

Proceedings at General Meetings

52. All business shall be deemed special that is transacted at an extraordinary general meeting, and also all that is transacted at an annual general meeting, with the exception of declaring a dividend, the consideration of the accounts, balance sheets, and the reports of the directors and auditors, the election of directors in the place of those retiring and the appointment of, and the fixing of the remuneration of, the auditors.

53. No business shall be transacted at any general meeting unless a quorum of members is present at the time when the meeting proceeds to business; save as herein otherwise provided, two members present in person or by proxy shall be a quorum.

54. If within half-an-hour from the time appointed for the meeting a quorum is not present, the meeting, if convened upon the requisition of members, shall be dissolved; in any other case it shall stand adjourned to the same day in the next week, at the same time and place or to such other day and at such other time and place as the directors may determine.

55. The chairman, if any, of the board of directors shall preside as chairman at every general meeting of the company, or if there is no such chairman, or if he shall not be present within 15 minutes after the time appointed for the holding of the meeting or is unwilling to act the directors present shall elect one of their number to be chairman of the meeting.

56. If at any meeting no director is willing to act as chairman or if no director is present within 15 minutes after the time appointed for holding the meeting, the members present shall choose one of their number to be chairman of the meeting.

57. The chairman may, with the consent of any meeting at which a quorum is present (and shall if so directed by the meeting), adjourn the meeting from time to time and from place to place, but no business shall be transacted at any adjourned meeting other than the business left unfinished at the meeting from which the adjournment took place. When a meeting is adjourned for 30 days or more, notice of the adjourned meeting shall be given as in the case of an original meeting. Save as aforesaid it shall not be necessary to give any notice of an adjournment or of the business to be transacted at an adjourned meeting.

58. At any general meeting a resolution put to the vote of the meeting shall be decided on a show of hands unless a poll is (before or on the declaration of the result of the show of hands) demanded:

(a) by the chairman; or

(b) by at least two members present in person or by proxy; or

(c) by any member or members present in person or by proxy and representing not less than one-tenth of the total voting rights of all the members having the right to vote at the meeting; or

(d) by a member or members holding shares in the company conferring a right to vote at the meeting being shares on which an aggregate sum has been paid up equal to not less than one-tenth of the total sum paid up on all the shares conferring that right.

Unless a poll be so demanded a declaration by the chairman that a resolution has on a show of hands been carried or carried unanimously, or by a particular majority, or lost and an entry to that effect in the book containing the minutes of the proceedings of the company shall be conclusive evidence of the fact without proof of the number or proportion of the votes recorded in favour of or against such resolution.

The demand for a poll may be withdrawn.

59. Except as provided in regulation 61, if a poll is duly demanded it shall be taken in such manner as the chairman directs, and the result of the poll shall be deemed to be the resolution of the meeting at which the poll was demanded.

60. In the case of an equality of votes, whether on a show of hands or on a poll, the chairman of the meeting at which the show of hands takes place or at which the poll is demanded, shall be entitled to a second or casting vote.

61. A poll demanded on the election of a chairman or on a question of adjournment shall be taken forthwith. A poll demanded on any other question shall be taken at such time as the chairman of the meeting directs, and any business other than that upon which a poll has been demanded may be proceeded with pending the taking of the poll.

Votes of Members

62. Subject to any rights or restrictions for the time being attached to any class or classes of shares, on a show of hands every member present in person shall have one vote, and on a poll every member shall have one vote for each share of which he is the holder.

63. In the case of joint holders the vote of the senior who tenders a vote, whether in person or by proxy, shall be accepted to the exclusion of the votes of the other joint holders; and for this purpose seniority shall be determined by the order in which the names stand in the Register of Members.

64.   A member of unsound mind, or in respect of whom an order has been made by any court having jurisdiction in lunacy, may vote, whether on a show of hands or on a poll, by his committee, receiver, *curator bonis*, or other person in the nature of a committee, receiver or *curator bonis* appointed by that court, and any such committee, receiver, *curator bonis* or other person may, on a poll, vote by proxy.

65.   No member shall be entitled to vote at any general meeting unless all calls or other sums presently payable by him in respect of shares in the company have been paid.

66.   No objection shall be raised to the qualification of any voter except at the meeting or adjourned meeting at which the vote objected to is given or tendered, and every vote not disallowed at such meeting shall be valid for all purposes. Any such objection made in due time shall be referred to the chairman of the meeting, whose decision shall be final and conclusive.

67.   On a poll votes may be given either personally or by proxy.

68.   The instrument appointing a proxy shall be in writing under the hand of the appointor or of his attorney duly authorised in writing, or, if the appointor is a corporation, either under seal, or under the hand of an officer or attorney duly authorised. A proxy need not be a member of the company.

69.   The instrument appointing a proxy and the power of attorney or other authority, if any, under which it is signed or a notarially certified copy of that power or authority shall be deposited at the registered office of the company or at such other place within the United Kingdom as is specified for that purpose in the notice convening the meeting, not less than 48 hours before the time for holding the meeting or adjourned meeting, at which the person named in the instrument proposes to vote, or, in the case of a poll, not less than 24 hours before the time appointed for the taking of the poll, and in default the instrument of proxy shall not be treated as valid.

70.   An instrument appointing a proxy shall be in the following form or a form as near thereto as circumstances admit:

‘   Limited

I/We,   ,

of   , in the County of   , being a member/members of the above named company, hereby appoint

of   , or failing him,   of   , as my/our proxy to vote for me/us on my/our behalf at the (annual or extraordinary, as the case may be) general meeting of the company, to be held on the   day of 19   , and at any adjournment thereof.

Signed this   day of   19   .’

71.   Where it is desired to afford members an opportunity of voting for or against a resolution the instrument appointing a proxy shall be in the following form or a form as near thereto as circumstances admit:

'   Limited

I/We,   ,

of   , in the County

of   , being a member/members of the above named company,

hereby appoint   of   , or failing him,

of   , as my/our proxy to vote for me/us on my/our behalf at the
(annual or extraordinary, as the case may be) general meeting of the company, to be
held on the   day of 19   , and at any adjournment thereof.

Signed this   day of   19 .'

This form to be used *in favour of/against the resolution. Unless otherwise
instructed, the proxy will vote as he thinks fit.
(*Strike out whichever is not desired.)'

72.　The instrument appointing a proxy shall be deemed to confer authority to
demand or join in demanding a poll.

73.　A vote given in accordance with the terms of an instrument of proxy shall be
valid notwithstanding the previous death or insanity of the principal or revocation of
the proxy or of the authority under which the proxy was executed, or the transfer of the
share in respect of which the proxy is given, provided that no intimation in writing of
such death, insanity, revocation or transfer as aforesaid shall have been received by
the company at the office before the commencement of the meeting or adjourned
meeting at which the proxy is used.

73A.　Subject to the provisions of the Companies Acts 1948 to 1981, a resolution in
writing signed by all the members for the time being entitled to receive notice of and to
attend and vote at general meetings (or being corporations by their duly authorised
representatives) shall be as valid and effective as if the same had been passed at a
general meeting of the company duly convened and held.

Corporations Acting by Representatives at Meetings

74.　Any corporation which is a member of the company may by resolution of its
directors or other governing body authorise such person as it thinks fit to act as its
representative at any meeting of the company or of any class of members of the
company, and the person so authorised shall be entitled to exercise the same powers
on behalf of the corporation which he represents as that corporation could exercise if it
were an individual member of the company.

Directors

75.　The number of the directors and the names of the first directors shall be
determined in writing by the subscribers of the memorandum of association or a
majority of them.

76.　The remuneration of the directors shall from time to time be determined by the
company in general meeting. Such remuneration shall be deemed to accrue from day
to day. The directors may also be paid all travelling, hotel and other expenses properly
incurred by them in attending and returning from meetings of the directors or any
committee of the directors or general meetings of the company or in connection with
the business of the company.

77. The shareholding qualification for directors may be fixed by the company in general meeting, and unless and until so fixed no qualification shall be required.

78. A director of the company may be or become a director or other officer of, or otherwise interested in, any company promoted by the company or in which the company may be interested as shareholder or otherwise, and no such director shall be accountable to the company for any remuneration or other benefits received by him as a director or officer of, or from his interest in, such other company unless the company otherwise direct.

Borrowing Powers

79. The directors may exercise all the powers of the company to borrow money, and to mortgage or charge its undertaking, property and uncalled capital, or any part thereof, and subject to section 14 of the Companies Act 1980 to issue debentures, debenture stock, and other securities whether outright or as security for any debt, liability or obligation of the company or of any third party:

Provided that the amount for the time being remaining undischarged of moneys borrowed or secured by the directors as aforesaid (apart from temporary loans obtained from the company's bankers in the ordinary course of business) shall not at any time, without the previous sanction of the company in general meeting, exceed the nominal amount of the share capital of the company for the time being issued, but nevertheless no lender or other person dealing with the company shall be concerned to see or enquire whether this limit is observed. No debt incurred or security given in excess of such limit shall be invalid or ineffectual except in the case of express notice to the lender or the recipient of the security at the time when the debt was incurred or security given that the limit hereby imposed had been or was thereby exceeded.

Powers and Duties of Directors

80. The business of the company shall be managed by the directors, who may pay all expenses incurred in promoting and registering the company, and may exercise all such powers of the company as are not, by the Companies Acts 1948 to 1981 or by these regulations, required to be exercised by the company in general meeting, subject, nevertheless, to any of these regulations, to the provisions of the Companies Acts 1948 to 1981 and to such regulations, being not inconsistent with the aforesaid regulations or provisions, as may be prescribed by the company in general meeting; but no regulation made by the company in general meeting shall invalidate any prior act of the directors which would have been valid if that regulation had not been made.

81. The directors may from time to time and at any time by power of attorney appoint any company, firm or person or body of persons, whether nominated directly or indirectly by the directors, to be the attorney or attorneys of the company for such purposes and with such powers, authorities and discretions (not exceeding those vested in or exercisable by the directors under these regulations) and for such period and subject to such conditions as they may think fit, and any such powers of attorney may contain such provisions for the protection and convenience of persons dealing with any such attorney as the directors may think fit and may also authorise any such attorney to delegate all or any of the powers, authorities and discretions vested in him.

82. The company may exercise the powers conferred by section 35 of the Act with regard to having an official seal for use abroad, and such powers shall be vested in the directors.

83. The company may exercise the powers conferred upon the company by sections 119 to 123 (both inclusive) of the Act with regard to the keeping of a Dominion Register, and the directors may (subject to the provisions of those sections) make and vary such regulations as they may think fit respecting the keeping of any such Register.

84. (1) A director who is in any way, whether directly or indirectly, interested in a contract or proposed contract with the company shall declare the nature of his interest at a meeting of the directors in accordance with section 199 of the Act.

(2) A director shall not vote in respect of any contract or arrangement in which he is interested, and if he shall do so his vote shall not be counted, nor shall he be counted in the quorum present at the meeting, but neither of these prohibitions shall apply to:
   (a) any arrangement for giving any director any security or indemnity in respect of money lent by him to or obligations undertaken by him for the benefit of the company; or
   (b) to any arrangement for the giving by the company of any security to a third party in respect of a debt or obligation of the company for which the director himself has assumed responsibility in whole or in part under a guarantee or indemnity or by the deposit of a security; or
   (c) any contract by a director to subscribe for or underwrite shares or debentures of the company; or
   (d) any contract or arrangement with any other company in which he is interested only as an officer of the company or as holder of shares or other securities;
   and these prohibitions may at any time be suspended or relaxed to any extent, and either generally or in respect of any particular contract, arrangement or transaction, by the company in general meeting.

(3) A director may hold any other office or place of profit under the company (other than the office of auditor) in conjunction with his office of director for such period and on such terms (as to remuneration and otherwise) as the directors may determine, and no director or intending director shall be disqualified by his office from contracting with the company either with regard to his tenure of any such other office or place of profit or as vendor, purchaser or otherwise, nor shall any such contract, or any contract or arrangement entered into by or on behalf of the company in which any director is in any way interested, be liable to be avoided, nor shall any director so contracting or being so interested be liable to account to the company for any profit realised by any such contract or arrangement by

reason of such director holding that office or of the fiduciary relation thereby established.

(4) A director, notwithstanding his interest, may be counted in the quorum present at any meeting whereat he or any other director is appointed to hold any such office or place of profit under the company or whereat the terms of any such appointment are arranged, and he may vote on any such appointment or arrangement other than his own appointment or the arrangement of the terms thereof.

(5) Any director may act by himself or his firm in a professional capacity for the company, and he or his firm shall be entitled to remuneration for professional services as if he were not a director; provided that nothing herein contained shall authorise a director or his firm to act as auditor to the company.

85.   All cheques, promissory notes, drafts, bills of exchange and other negotiable instruments, and all receipts for moneys paid to the company, shall be signed, drawn, accepted, endorsed, or otherwise executed, as the case may be, in such manner as the directors shall from time to time by resolution determine.

86.   The directors shall cause minutes to be made in books provided for the purpose:

(a) of all appointments of officers made by the directors;
(b) of the names of the directors present at each meeting of the directors and of any committee of the directors;
(c) of all resolutions and proceedings at all meetings of the company, and of the directors, and of committees of directors;

and every director present at any meeting of directors or committee of directors shall sign his name in a book to be kept for that purpose.

87.   The directors on behalf of the company may pay a gratuity or pension or allowance on retirement to any director who has held any other salaried office or place of profit with the company or to his widow or dependants and may make contributions to any fund and pay premiums for the purchase or provision of any such gratuity, pension or allowance.

Disqualification of Directors

88.   The office of director shall be vacated if the director:

(a) ceases to be a director by virtue of sections 182 or 185 of the Act; or
(b) becomes bankrupt or makes any arrangement or composition with his creditors generally; or
(c) becomes prohibited from being a director by reason of any order made under section 188 of the Act, or
(d) becomes of unsound mind; or
(e) resigns his office by notice in writing to the company; or
(f) shall for more than six months have been absent without permission of the directors from meetings of the directors held during that period.

Rotation of Directors

89. At the first annual general meeting of the company all the directors shall retire from office, and at the annual general meeting in every subsequent year one-third of the directors for the time being, or, if their number is not three or a multiple of three, then the number nearest one-third, shall retire from office.

90. The directors to retire in every year shall be those who have been longest in office since their last election, but as between persons who became directors on the same day those to retire shall (unless they otherwise agree among themselves) be determined by lot.

91. A retiring director shall be eligible for re-election.

92. The company at the meeting at which a director retires in manner aforesaid may fill the vacated office by electing a person thereto, and in default the retiring director shall if offering himself for re-election be deemed to have been re-elected, unless at such meeting it is expressly resolved not to fill such vacated office or unless a resolution for the re-election of such director shall have been put to the meeting and lost.

93. No person other than a director retiring at the meeting shall unless recommended by the directors be eligible for election to the office of director at any general meeting unless not less than 3 nor more than 21 days before the date appointed for the meeting there shall have been left at the registered office of the company notice in writing, signed by a member duly qualified to attend and vote at the meeting for which such notice is given, of his intention to propose such person for election, and also notice in writing signed by that person of his willingness to be elected.

94. The company may from time to time by ordinary resolution increase or reduce the number of directors, and may also determine in what rotation the increased or reduced number is to go out of office.

95. The directors shall have power at any time, and from time to time, to appoint any person to be a director, either to fill a casual vacancy or as an addition to the existing directors, but so that the total number of directors shall not at any time exceed the number fixed in accordance with these regulations. Any director so appointed shall hold office only until the next following annual general meeting, and shall then be eligible for re-election but shall not be taken into account in determining the directors who are to retire by rotation at such meeting.

96. The company may by ordinary resolution, of which special notice has been given in accordance with s 142 of the Act, remove any director before the expiration of his period of office notwithstanding anything in these regulations or in any agreement between the company and such director. Such removal shall be without prejudice to any claim such director may have for damages for breach of any contract of service between him and the company.

97. The company may by ordinary resolution appoint another person in place of a director removed from office under the immediately preceding regulation, and without prejudice to the powers of the directors under regulation 95 the company in general meeting may appoint any person to be a director either to fill a casual vacancy or as an additional director. A person appointed in place of a director so removed or to fill such a vacancy shall be subject to retirement at the same time as if he had become a director on the day on which the director in whose place he is appointed was last elected a director.

Proceedings of Directors

98.   The directors may meet together for the despatch of business, adjourn, and otherwise regulate their meetings, as they think fit. Questions arising at any meeting shall be decided by a majority of votes. In case of an equality of votes, the chairman shall have a second or casting vote. A director may, and the secretary on the requisition of a director shall, at any time summon a meeting of the directors. It shall not be necessary to give notice of a meeting of directors to any director for the time being absent from the United Kingdom.

99.   The quorum necessary for the transaction of the business of the directors may be fixed by the directors, and unless so fixed shall be two.

100.   The continuing directors may act notwithstanding any vacancy in their body, but, if and so long as their number is reduced below the number fixed by or pursuant to the regulations of the company as the necessary quorum of directors, the continuing directors or director may act for the purpose of increasing the number of directors to that number, or of summoning a general meeting of the company, but for no other purpose.

101.   The directors may elect a chairman of their meetings and determine the period for which he is to hold office; but if no such chairman is elected, or if at any meeting the chairman is not present within five minutes after the time appointed for holding the same, the directors present may choose one of their number to be chairman of the meeting.

102.   The directors may delegate any of their powers to committees consisting of such member or members of their body as they think fit; any committee so formed shall in the exercise of the powers so delegated conform to any regulations that may be imposed on it by the directors.

103.   A committee may elect a chairman of its meetings; if no such chairman is elected, or if at any meeting the chairman is not present within five minutes after the time appointed for holding the same, the members present may choose one of their number to be chairman of the meeting.

104.   A committee may meet and adjourn as it thinks proper. Questions arising at any meeting shall be determined by a majority of votes of the members present, and in the case of an equality of votes the chairman shall have a second or casting vote.

105.   All acts done by any meeting of the directors or of a committee of directors or by any person acting as a director shall, notwithstanding that it be afterwards discovered that there was some defect in the appointment of any such director or person acting as aforesaid, or that they or any of them were disqualified, be as valid as if every such person had been duly appointed and was qualified to be a director.

106. A resolution in writing, signed by all the directors for the time being entitled to receive notice of a meeting of the directors, shall be as valid and effectual as if it had been passed at a meeting of the directors duly convened and held.

Managing Director

107. The directors may from time to time appoint one or more of their body to the office of managing director for such period and on such terms as they think fit, and, subject to the terms of any agreement entered into in any particular case, may revoke such appointment. A director so appointed shall not, whilst holding that office, be subject to retirement by rotation or be taken into account in determining the rotation of retirement of directors, but his appointment shall be automatically determined if he cease from any cause to be a director.

108. A managing director shall receive such remuneration (whether by way of salary, commission or participation in profits, or partly in one way and partly in another) as the directors may determine.

109. The directors may entrust to and confer upon a managing director any of the powers exercisable by them upon such terms and conditions and with such restrictions as they may think fit, and either collaterally with or to the exclusion of their own powers and may from time to time revoke, withdraw, alter or vary all or any of such powers.

Secretary

110. Subject to section 21(5) of the Companies Act 1976 the secretary shall be appointed by the directors for such term, at such remuneration and upon such conditions as they may think fit; and any secretary so appointed may be removed by them.

111. No person shall be appointed or hold office as secretary who is:

(a) the sole director of the company; or
(b) a corporation the sole director of which is the sole director of the company; or
(c) the sole director of a corporation which is the sole director of the company.

112. A provision of the Act or these regulations requiring or authorising a thing to be done by or to a director and the secretary shall not be satisfied by its being done by or to the same person acting both as director and as, or in place of, the secretary.

The Seal

112. The directors shall provide for the safe custody of the seal, which shall only be used by the authority of the directors or of a committee of the directors authorised by the directors in that behalf, and every instrument to which the seal shall be affixed shall be signed by a director and shall be countersigned by the secretary or by a second director or by some other person appointed by the directors for the purpose.

Dividends and Reserve

114.   The company in general meeting may declare dividends, but no dividend shall exceed the amount recommended by the directors.

115.   The directors may from time to time pay to the members such interim dividends as appear to the directors to be justified by the profits of the company.

116.   No dividend or interim dividend shall be paid otherwise than in accordance with the provisions of Part III of the Companies Act 1980 which apply to the company.

117.   The directors may, before recommending any dividend, set aside out of the profits of the company such sums as they think proper as a reserve or reserves which shall, at the discretion of the directors, be applicable for any purpose to which the profits of the company may be properly applied, and pending such application may, at the like discretion, either be employed in the business of the company or be invested in such investments (other than shares of the company) as the directors may from time to time think fit. The directors may also without placing the same to reserve carry forward any profits which they may think prudent not to divide.

118.   Subject to the rights of persons, if any, entitled to shares with special rights as to dividend, all dividends shall be declared and paid according to the amount paid or credited as paid on the shares in respect whereof the dividend is paid, but no amount paid or credited as paid on a share in advance of calls shall be treated for the purposes of this regulation as paid on the share. All dividends shall be apportioned and paid proportionately to the amounts paid or credited as paid on the shares during any portion or portions of the period in respect of which the dividend is paid; but if any share is issued on terms providing that it shall rank for dividend as from a particular date such share shall rank for dividend accordingly.

119.   The directors may deduct from any dividend payable to any member all sums of money (if any) presently payable by him to the company on account of calls or otherwise in relation to the shares of the company.

120.   Any general meeting declaring a dividend or bonus may direct payment of such dividend or bonus wholly or partly by the distribution of specific assets and in particular of paid up shares, debentures or debenture stock of any other company or in any one or more of such ways, and the directors shall give effect to such resolution, and where any difficulty arises in regard to such distribution, the directors may settle the same as they think expedient, and in particular may issue fractional certificates and fix the value for distribution of such specific assets or any part thereof and may determine that cash payments shall be made to any members upon the footing of the value so fixed in order to adjust the rights of all parties, and may vest any such specific assets in trustees as may seem expedient to the directors.

121.   Any dividend, interest or other moneys payable in cash in respect of shares may be paid by cheque or warrant sent through the post directed to the registered address of the holder or, in the case of joint holders, to the registered address of that one of the joint holders who is first named on the Register of Members or to such person and to such address as the holder or joint holders may in writing direct. Every such cheque or warrant shall be made payable to the order of the person to whom it is sent. Any one of two or more joint holders may give effectual receipts for any dividends, bonuses or other moneys payable in respect of the shares held by them as joint holders.

122.   No dividend shall bear interest against the company.

Accounts

123.   The directors shall cause accounting records to be kept in accordance with section 12 of the Companies Act 1976.

124.   The accounting records shall be kept at the registered office of the company or, subject to section 12(6) and (7) of the Companies Act 1976, at such other place or places as the directors think fit, and shall always be open to the inspection of the officers of the company.

125.   The directors shall from time to time determine whether and to what extent and at what times and places and under what conditions or regulations the accounts and books of the company or any of them shall be open to the inspection of members not being directors, and no member (not being a director) shall have any right of inspecting any account or book or document of the company except as conferred by statute or authorised by the directors or by the company in general meeting.

126.   The directors shall from time to time, in accordance with sections 150 and 157 of the Act and sections 1, 6 and 7 of the Companies Act 1976 cause to be prepared and to be laid before the company in general meeting such profit and loss accounts, balance sheets, group accounts (if any) and reports as are referred to in those sections.

127.   A copy of every balance sheet (including every document required by law to be annexed thereto) which is to be laid before the company in general meeting, together with a copy of the auditors' report and directors' report shall not less than 21 days before the date of the meeting be sent to every member of, and every holder of debentures of, the company and to every person registered under regulation 31. Provided that this regulation shall not require a copy of those documents to be sent to any person of whose address the company is not aware or to more than one of the joint holders of any shares or debentures.

Capitalisation of Profits

128.   The company in general meeting may on the recommendation of the directors resolve that it is desirable to capitalise any part of the amount for the time being standing to the credit of any of the company's reserve accounts or to the credit of the profit and loss account or otherwise available for distribution, and accordingly that such sum be set free for distribution amongst the members who would have been entitled thereto if distributed by way of dividend and in the same proportions on condition that the same be not paid in cash but be applied either in or towards paying up any amounts for the time being unpaid on any shares held by such members respectively or paying up in full unissued shares or debentures of the company to be allotted and distributed credited as fully paid up to and amongst such members in the proportion aforesaid, or partly in the one way and partly in the other, and the directors shall give effect to such resolution:

Provided that a share premium account and a capital redemption reserve fund may, for the purposes of this regulation, only be applied in the paying up of unissued shares to be allotted to members of the company as fully paid bonus shares.

128A.   The company in general meeting may on the recommendation of the directors resolve that it is desirable to capitalise any part of the amount for the time being standing to the credit of any of the company's reserve accounts or to the credit of the profit and loss account which is not available for distribution by applying such sum in paying up in full unissued shares to be allotted as fully paid bonus shares to those members of the company who would have been entitled to that sum if it were distributed by way of dividend (and in the same proportions), and the directors shall give effect to such resolution.

129.   Whenever a resolution is passed in pursuance of regulation 128 or 128A above the directors shall make all appropriations and applications of the undivided profits resolved to be capitalised thereby, and all allotments and issues of fully-paid shares or debentures, if any, and generally shall do all acts and things required to give effect thereto, with full power to the directors to make such provision by the issue of fractional certificates or by payment in cash or otherwise as they think fit for the case of shares or debentures becoming distributable in fractions, and also to authorise any person to enter on behalf of all the members entitled thereto into an agreement with the company providing for the allotment to them respectively, credited as fully paid up, of any further shares or debentures to which they may be entitled upon such capitalisation, or (as the case may require) for the payment up by the company on their behalf, by the application thereto of their respective proportions of the profit resolved to be capitalised, of the amounts or any part of the amounts remaining unpaid on their existing shares, and any agreement made under such authority shall be effective and binding on all such members.

Audit

130.   Auditors shall be appointed and their duties regulated in accordance with section 161 of the Act, sections 14 and 23A of the Companies Act 1967, sections 13 to 18 of the Companies Act 1976 and sections 7 and 12 of the Companies Act 1981.

Notices

131.   A notice may be given by the company to any member either personally or by sending it by post to him or to his registered address, or (if he has no registered address within the United Kingdom) to the address, if any, within the United Kingdom supplied by him to the company for the giving of notice to him. Where a notice is sent by post, service of the notice shall be deemed to be effected by properly addressing, prepaying, and posting a letter containing the notice, and to have been effected in the case of a notice of a meeting at the expiration of 24 hours after the letter containing the same is posted, and in any other case at the time at which the letter would be delivered in the ordinary course of post.

132.   A notice may be given by the company to the joint holders of a share by giving the notice to the joint holder first named in the Register of Members in respect of the share.

133. A notice may be given by the company to the persons entitled to a share in consequence of the death or bankruptcy of a member by sending it through the post in a prepaid letter addressed to them by name, or by the title of representatives of the deceased, or trustee of the bankrupt, or by any like description, at the address, if any, within the United Kingdom supplied for the purpose by the persons claiming to be so entitled, or (until such an address has been so supplied) by giving the notice in any manner in which the same might have been given if the death or bankruptcy had not occurred.

134. Notice of every general meeting shall be given in any manner hereinbefore authorised to:

  (a) every member except those members who (having no registered address within the United Kingdom) have not supplied to the company an address within the United Kingdom for the giving of notices to them;

  (b) every person upon whom the ownership of a share devolves by reason of his being a legal personal representative or a trustee in bankruptcy of a member where the member but for his death or bankruptcy would be entitled to receive notice of the meeting; and

  (c) the auditor for the time being of the company.

No other person shall be entitled to receive notices of general meetings.

Winding Up

135. If the company shall be wound up the liquidator may, with the sanction of an extraordinary resolution of the company and any other sanction required by the Act, divide amongst the members in specie or kind the whole or any part of the assets of the company (whether they shall consist of property of the same kind or not) and may, for such purposes, set such value as he deems fair upon any property to be divided as aforesaid and may determine how such division shall be carried out as between the members or different classes of members. The liquidator may, with the like sanction, vest the whole or any part of such assets in trustees upon such trusts for the benefit of the contributories as the liquidator, with the like sanction, shall think fit, but so that no member shall be compelled to accept any shares or other securities whereon there is any liability.

Indemnity

136. Every director, managing director, agent, auditor, secretary and other officer for the time being of the company shall be indemnified out of the assets of the company against any liability incurred by him in defending any proceedings, whether civil or criminal, in which judgment is given in his favour or in which he is acquitted or in connection with any application under section 448 of the Act in which relief is granted to him by the courts.

Appendix C

TABLE A TO THE COMPANIES ACT 1985

(As prescribed in the Companies (Table A to F) Regulations 1985 and amended by the Companies (Tables A to F) (Amendment) Regulations 1985 which came into effect on 1 August 1985.)

Regulations for Management of a Company Limited by Shares

Interpretation

1. In these regulations:

'the Act' means the Companies Act 1985 including any statutory modification or re-enactment thereof for the time being in force.

'the Articles' means the Articles of the company.

'clear days' in relation to the period of a notice means that period excluding the day when the notice is given or deemed to be given and the day for which it is given or on which it is to take effect.

'executed' includes any mode of execution.

'office' means the registered office of the company.

'the holder' in relation to shares means the member whose name is entered in the register of members as the holder of the shares.

'the seal' means the common seal of the company.

'secretary' means the secretary of the company or any other person appointed to perform the duties of the secretary of the company, including a joint, assistant or deputy secretary.

'the United Kingdom' means Great Britain and Northern Ireland.

Unless the context otherwise requires, words or expressions contained in these regulations bear the same meaning as in the Act but excluding any statutory modification thereof not in force when these regulations become binding on the company.

Share Capital

2. Subject to the provisions of the Act and without prejudice to any rights attached to any existing shares, any share may be issued with such rights or restrictions as the company may by ordinary resolution determine.

3. Subject to the provisions of the Act, shares may be issued which are to be redeemed or are to be liable to be redeemed at the option of the company or the holder on such terms and in such manner as may be provided by the Articles.

4. The company may exercise the powers of paying commissions conferred by the Act. Subject to the provisions of the Act, any such commission may be satisfied by the payment of cash or by the allotment of fully or partly paid shares or partly in one way and partly in the other.

5. Except as required by law, no person shall be recognised by the company as holding any share upon any trust and (except as otherwise provided by the articles or by law) the company shall not be bound by or recognise any interest in any share except an absolute right to the entirety thereof in the holder.

Share Certificates

6. Every member, upon becoming the holder of any shares, shall be entitled without payment to one certificate for all the shares of each class held by him (and, upon transferring a part of his holding of shares of any class, to a certificate for the balance of such holding) or several certificates each for one or more of his shares upon payment for every certificate after the first of such reasonable sum as the directors may determine. Every certificate shall be sealed with the seal and shall specify the number, class and distinguishing numbers (if any) of the shares to which it relates and the amount or respective amounts paid up thereon. The company shall not be bound to issue more than one certificate for shares held jointly by several persons and delivery of a certificate to one joint holder shall be a sufficient delivery to all of them.

7. If a share certificate is defaced, worn-out, lost or destroyed, it may be renewed on such terms (if any) as to evidence and indemnity and payment of the expenses reasonably incurred by the company in investigating evidence as the directors may determine but otherwise free of charge, and (in the case of defacement or wearing-out) on delivery up of the old certificate.

Lien

8. The company shall have a first and paramount lien on every share (not being a fully paid share) for all moneys (whether presently payable or not) payable at a fixed time or called in respect of that share. The directors may at any time declare any share to be wholly or in part exempt from the provisions of this regulation. The company's lien on a share shall extend to any amount payable in respect of it.

9. The company may sell in such manner as the directors determine any shares on which the Company has a lien if a sum in respect of which the lien exists is presently payable and is not paid within fourteen clear days after notice has been given to the holder of the share or to the person entitled to it in consequence of the death or bankruptcy of the holder, demanding payment and stating that if the notice is not complied with the shares may be sold.

10. To give effect to a sale the directors may authorise some person to execute an instrument of transfer of the shares sold to, or in accordance with the directions of, the purchaser. The title of the transferee to the shares shall not be affected by any irregularity in or invalidity of the proceedings in reference to the sale.

11. The net proceeds of the sale, after payment of the costs, shall be applied in payment of so much of the sum for which the lien exists as is presently payable, and any residue shall (upon surrender to the company for cancellation of the certificate for the shares sold and subject to a like lien for any moneys not presently payable as existed upon the shares before the sale) be paid to the person entitled to the shares at the date of the sale.

Calls on Shares and Forfeiture

12. Subject to the terms of allotment, the directors may make calls upon the members in respect of any moneys unpaid on their shares (whether in respect of nominal value or premium) and each member shall (subject to receiving at least fourteen clear days' notice specifying when and where payment is to be made) pay to the company as required by the notice the amount called on his shares. A call may be required to be paid by instalments. A call may, before receipt by the company of any sum due thereunder, be revoked in whole or part and payment of a call may be postponed in whole or part. A person upon whom a call is made shall remain liable for calls made upon him notwithstanding the subsequent transfer of the shares in respect whereof the call was made.

13. A call shall be deemed to have been made at the time when the resolution of the directors authorising the call was passed.

14. The joint holders of a share shall be jointly and severally liable to pay all calls in respect thereof.

15. If a call remains unpaid after it has become due and payable the person from whom it is due and payable shall pay interest on the amount unpaid from the day it became due and payable until it is paid at the rate fixed by the terms of allotment of the share or in the notice of the call or, if no rate is fixed, at the appropriate rate (as defined by the Act) but the directors may waive payment of the interest wholly or in part.

16. An amount payable in respect of a share on allotment or at any fixed date, whether in respect of nominal value or premium or as an instalment of a call, shall be deemed to be a call and if it is not paid the provisions of the articles shall apply as if that amount had become due and payable by virtue of a call.

17. Subject to the terms of allotment, the directors may make arrangements on the issue of shares for a difference between the holders in the amounts and times of payment of calls on their shares.

18. If a call remains unpaid after it has become due and payable the directors may give to the person from whom it is due not less than fourteen clear days' notice requiring payment of the amount unpaid together with any interest which may have accrued. The notice shall name the place where payment is to be made and shall state that if the notice is not complied with the shares in respect of which the call was made will be liable to be forfeited.

19. If the notice is not complied with any share in respect of which it was given may, before the payment required by the notice has been made, be forfeited by a resolution of the directors and the forfeiture shall include all dividends or other moneys payable in respect of the forfeited shares and not paid before the forfeiture.

20.   Subject to the provisions of the Act, a forfeited share may be sold, re-allotted or otherwise disposed of on such terms and in such manner as the directors determine either to the person who was before the forfeiture the holder or to any other person and at any time before sale, re-allotment or other disposition, the forfeiture may be cancelled on such terms as the directors think fit. Where for the purposes of its disposal a forfeited share is to be transferred to any person the directors may authorise some person to execute an instrument of transfer of the share to that person.

21.   A person any of whose shares have been forfeited shall cease to be a member in respect of them and shall surrender to the company for cancellation the certificate for the shares forfeited but shall remain liable to the company for all moneys which at the date of forfeiture were presently payable by him to the company in respect of those shares with interest at the rate at which interest was payable on those moneys before the forfeiture or, if no interest was so payable, at the appropriate rate (as defined in the Act) from the date of forfeiture until payment but the directors may waive payment wholly or in part or enforce payment without any allowance for the value of the shares at the time of forfeiture or for any consideration received on their disposal.

22.   A statutory declaration by a director or the secretary that a share has been forfeited on a specified date shall be conclusive evidence of the facts stated in it as against all persons claiming to be entitled to the share and the declaration shall (subject to the execution of an instrument of transfer if necessary) constitute a good title to the share and the person to whom the share is disposed of shall not be bound to see to the application of the consideration, if any, nor shall his title to the share be affected by an irregularity in or invalidity of the proceedings in reference to the forfeiture or disposal of the share.

Transfer of Shares

23.   The instrument of transfer of a share may be in any usual form or in any other form which the directors may approve and shall be executed by or on behalf of the transferor and, unless the share is fully paid, by or on behalf of the transferee.

24.   The directors may refuse to register the transfer of a share which is not fully paid to a person of whom they do not approve and they may refuse to register the transfer of a share on which the company has a lien. They may also refuse to register a transfer unless:

(a)   it is lodged at the office or at such other place as the directors may appoint and is accompanied by the certificate for the shares to which it relates and such other evidence as the directors may reasonably require to show the right of the transferor to make the transfer;

(b)   it is in respect of only one class of shares; and

(c)   it is in favour or not more than four transferees.

25.   If the directors refuse to register a transfer of a share, they shall within two months after the date on which the transfer was lodged with the company send to the transferee notice of the refusal.

26. The registration of transfers of shares or of transfers of any class of shares may be suspended at such times and for such periods (not exceeding thirty days in any year) as the directors may determine.

27. No fee shall be charged for the registration of any instrument of transfer or other document relating to or affecting the title to any share.

28. The company shall be entitled to retain any instrument of transfer which is registered, but any instrument of transfer which the directors refuse to register shall be returned to the person lodging it when notice of the refusal is given.

Transmission of Shares

29. If a member dies the survivor or survivors where he was a joint holder, and his personal representatives where he was a sole holder or the only survivor of joint holders, shall be the only persons recognised by the company as having any title to his interest; but nothing herein contained shall release the estate of a deceased member from any liability in respect of any share which had been jointly held by him.

30. A person becoming entitled to a share in consequence of the death or bankruptcy of a member may, upon such evidence being produced as the directors may properly require, elect either to become the holder of the share or to have some person nominated by him registered as the transferee. If he elects to become the holder he shall give notice to the company to that effect. If he elects to have another person registered he shall execute an instrument of transfer of the share to that person. All the Articles relating to the transfer of shares shall apply to the notice or instrument of transfer as if it were an instrument of transfer executed by the member and the death or bankruptcy of the member had not occurred.

31. A person becoming entitled to a share in consequence of the death or bankruptcy of a member shall have the rights to which he would be entitled if he were the holder of the share, except that he shall not, before being registered as the holder of the share, be entitled in respect of it to attend or vote at any meeting of the company or at any separate meeting of the holders of any class of shares in the company.

Alteration of Share Capital

32. The company may by ordinary resolution:
  (a) increase its share capital by new shares of such amount as the resolution prescribes;
  (b) consolidate and divide all or any of its share capital into shares of larger amount than its existing shares;
  (c) subject to the provisions of the Act, subdivide its shares, or any of them, into shares of smaller amount and the resolution may determine that, as between the shares resulting from the subdivision, any of them may have any preference or advantage as compared with the others; and
  (d) cancel shares which, at the date of the passing of the resolution, have not been taken or agreed to be taken by any person and diminish the amount of its share capital by the amount of the shares so cancelled.

33. Whenever as a result of a consolidation of shares any members would become entitled to fractions of a share, the directors may, on behalf of those members, sell the shares representing the fractions for the best price reasonably obtainable to any person (including, subject to the provisions of the Act, the company) and distribute the net proceeds of sale in due proportion among those members, and the directors may authorise some person to execute an instrument of transfer of the shares to, or in accordance with the directions of, the purchaser. The transferee shall not be bound to see to the application of the purchase money nor shall his title to the shares be affected by any irregularity in or invalidity of the proceedings in reference to the sale.

34. Subject to the provisions of the Act, the company may by special resolution reduce its share capital, any capital redemption reserve and any share premium account in any way.

Purchase of Own Shares

35. Subject to the provisions of the Act, the company may purchase its own shares (including any redeemable shares) and, if it is a private company, make a payment in respect of the redemption or purchase of its own shares otherwise than out of distributable profits of the company or the proceeds of a fresh issue of shares.

General Meetings

36. All general meetings other than annual general meetings shall be called extraordinary general meetings.

37. The directors may call general meetings and, on the requisition of members pursuant to the provisions of the Act, shall forthwith proceed to convene an extraordinary general meeting for a date not later than eight weeks after receipt of the requisition. If there are not within the United Kingdom sufficient directors to call a general meeting, any director or any member of the company may call a general meeting.

Notice of General Meetings

38. An annual general meeting and an extraordinary general meeting called for the passing of a special resolution or a resolution appointing a person as a director shall be called by at least twenty-one clear days' notice. All other extraordinary general meetings shall be called by at least fourteen clear days' notice but a general meeting may be called by shorter notice if it is so agreed:

    (a)   in the case of an annual general meeting, by all the members entitled to attend and vote thereat; and

    (b)   in the case of any other meeting by a majority in number of the members having a right to attend and vote being a majority together holding not less than ninety-five per cent in nominal value of the shares giving that right.

The notice shall specify the time and place of the meeting and the general nature of the business to be transacted and, in the case of an annual general meeting, shall specify the meeting as such.

Subject to the provisions of the articles and to any restrictions imposed on any shares, the notice shall be given to all the members, to all persons entitled to a share in consequence of the death or bankruptcy of a member and to the directors and auditors.

39. The accidental omission to give notice of a meeting to, or the non-receipt of notice of a meeting by, any person entitled to receive notice shall not invalidate the proceedings at that meeting.

Proceedings at General Meetings

40. No business shall be transacted at any meeting unless a quorum is present. Two persons entitled to vote upon the business to be transacted, each being a member or a proxy for a member or a duly authorised representative of a corporation, shall be a quorum.

41. If such a quorum is not present within half an hour from the time appointed for the meeting, or if during a meeting such a quorum ceases to be present, the meeting shall stand adjourned to the same day in the next week at the same time and place or to such time and place as the directors may determine.

42. The chairman, if any, of the board of directors or in his absence some other director nominated by the directors shall preside as chairman of the meeting, but if neither the chairman nor such other director (if any) be present within fifteen minutes after the time appointed for holding the meeting and willing to act, the directors present shall elect one of their number to be chairman and, if there is only one director present and willing to act, he shall be chairman.

43. If no director is willing to act as chairman, or if no director is present within fifteen minutes after the time appointed for holding the meeting, the members present and entitled to vote shall choose one of their number to be chairman.

44. A director shall, notwithstanding that he is not a member, be entitled to attend and speak at any general meeting and at any separate meeting of the holders of any class of shares in the company.

45. The chairman may, with the consent of a meeting at which a quorum is present (and shall if so directed by the meeting), adjourn the meeting from time to time and from place to place, but no business shall be transacted at an adjourned meeting other than business which might properly have been transacted at the meeting had the adjournment not taken place. When a meeting is adjourned for fourteen days or more, at least seven clear days' notice shall be given specifying the time and place of the adjourned meeting and the general nature of the business to be transacted. Otherwise it shall not be necessary to give any such notice.

46. A resolution put to the vote of a meeting shall be decided on a show of hands unless before, or on the declaration of the result of, the show of hands a poll is duly demanded. Subject to the provisions of the Act, a poll may be demanded:

(a) by the chairman; or
(b) by at least two members having the right to vote at the meeting; or

(c) by a member or members representing not less than one-tenth of the total voting rights of all the members having the right to vote at the meeting; or

(d) by a member or members holding shares conferring a right to vote at the meeting being shares on which an aggregate sum has been paid up equal to not less than one-tenth of the total sum paid up or all the shares conferring that right;

and a demand by a person as proxy for a member shall be the same as a demand by the member.

47. Unless a poll is duly demanded a declaration by the chairman that a resolution has been carried or carried unanimously, or by a particular majority, or lost, or not carried by a particular majority and an entry to that effect in the minutes of the meeting shall be conclusive evidence of the fact without proof of the number or proportion of the votes recorded in favour of or against the resolution.

48. The demand for a poll may, before the poll is taken, be withdrawn but only with the consent of the chairman and a demand so withdrawn shall not be taken to have invalidated the result of a show of hands declared before the demand was made.

49. A poll shall be taken as the chairman directs and he may appoint scrutineers (who need not be members) and fix a time and place for declaring the result of the poll. The result of the poll shall be deemed to be the resolution of the meeting at which the poll was demanded.

50. In the case of an equality of votes, whether on a show of hands or on a poll, the chairman shall be entitled to a casting vote in addition to any other vote he may have.

51. A poll demanded on the election of a chairman or on a question of adjournment shall be taken forthwith. A poll demanded on any other question shall be taken either forthwith or at such time and place as the chairman directs not being more than thirty days after the poll is demanded. The demand for a poll shall not prevent the continuance of a meeting for the transaction of any business other than the question on which the poll was demanded. If a poll is demanded before the declaration of the result of a show of hands and the demand is duly withdrawn, the meeting shall continue as if the demand had not been made.

52. No notice need be given of a poll not taken forthwith if the time and place at which it is to be taken are announced at the meeting at which it is demanded. In any other case at least seven clear days' notice shall be given specifying the time and place at which the poll is to be taken.

53. A resolution in writing executed by or on behalf of each member who would have been entitled to vote upon it if it had been proposed at a general meeting at which he was present shall be as effectual as if it had been passed at a general meeting duly convened and held and may consist of several instruments in the like form each executed by or on behalf of one or more members.

Votes of Members

54. Subject to any rights or restrictions attached to any shares, on a show of hands every member who (being an individual) is present in person or (being a corporation) is present by a duly authorised representative, not being himself a member entitled to vote, shall have one vote and on a poll every member shall have one vote for every share of which he is the holder.

55. In the case of joint holders the vote of the senior who tenders a vote, whether in person or by proxy, shall be accepted to the exclusion of the votes of the other joint holders; and seniority shall be determined by the order in which the names of the holders stand in the register of members.

56. A member in respect of whom an order has been made by any court having jurisdiction (whether in the United Kingdom or elsewhere) in matters concerning mental disorder may vote, whether on a show of hands or on a poll, by his receiver, *curator bonis* or other person authorised in that behalf appointed by that court, and any such receiver, *curator bonis* or other person may, on a poll, vote by proxy. Evidence to the satisfaction of the directors of the authority of the person claiming to exercise the right to vote shall be deposited at the office, or at such other place as is specified in accordance with the articles for the deposit of instruments of proxy, not less than 48 hours before the time appointed for holding the meeting or adjourned meeting at which the right to vote is to be exercised and in default the right to vote shall not be exercisable.

57. No member shall vote at any general meeting or at any separate meeting of the holders of any class of shares in the company, either in person or by proxy, in respect of any share held by him unless all moneys presently payable by him in respect of that share have been paid.

58. No objection shall be raised to the qualification of any voter except at the meeting or adjourned meeting at which the vote objected to is tendered, and every vote not disallowed at the meeting shall be valid. Any objection made in due time shall be referred to the chairman whose decision shall be final and conclusive.

59. On a poll votes may be given either personally or by proxy. A member may appoint more than one proxy to attend on the same occasion.

60. An instrument appointing a proxy shall be in writing, executed by or on behalf of the appointor and shall be in the following form (or in a form as near thereto as circumstances allow or in any other form which is usual or which the directors may approve):

'   PLC/Limited

     I/We,

of,

                                                        ,

being a member/members of the above named company,
hereby appoint   of   , or failing him,   of   ,
as my/our proxy to vote in my/our name[s] and on my/our behalf at the annual/extraordinary general meeting of the company, to be held on
      19   , and at any adjournment thereof.

Signed on   19   .'

61.   Where it is desired to afford members an opportunity of instructing the proxy how he shall act the instrument appointing a proxy shall be in the following form (or in a form as near thereto as circumstances allow or in any other form which is usual or which the directors may approve):

'   PLC/Limited
          I/We,
of,

                                                                                                    ,

being a member/members of the above named company, hereby appoint
of   , or failing him,   of   , as my/our proxy to vote in my/
our name[s] and on my/our behalf at the annual/extraordinary general meeting of
the company, to be held on   19   , and at any adjournment
thereof.

This form is to be used in respect of the resolutions mentioned below as follows:
    Resolution No. 1 *for *against.
    Resolution No. 2 *for *against.
*Strike out whichever is not desired.

Unless otherwise instructed, the proxy may vote as he thinks fit or abstain from voting.

Signed this   day of   19   .'

62.   The instrument appointing a proxy and any authority under which it is executed or a copy of such authority certified notarially or in some other way approved by the directors may:

(a)   be deposited at the office or at such other place within the United Kingdom as is specified in the notice convening the meeting or in any instrument of proxy sent out by the company in relation to the meeting not less than 48 hours before the time for holding the meeting or adjourned meeting at which the person named in the instrument proposes to vote; or

(b)   in the case of a poll taken more than 48 hours after it is demanded, be deposited as aforesaid after the poll has been demanded and not less than 24 hours before the time appointed for the taking of the poll; or

(c)   where the poll is not taken forthwith but is taken not more than 48 hours after it was demanded, be delivered at the meeting at which the poll was demanded to the chairman or to the secretary or to any director;

and an instrument of proxy which is not deposited or delivered in a manner so permitted shall be invalid.

63.   A vote given or poll demanded by proxy or by the duly authorised representative of a corporation shall be valid notwithstanding the previous determination of the authority of the person voting or demanding a poll unless notice of the determination was received by the company at the office or at such other place at which the instrument of proxy was duly deposited before the commencement of the meeting or adjourned meeting at which the vote is given or the poll demanded or (in the case of a poll taken otherwise than on the same day as the meeting or adjourned meeting) the time appointed for taking the poll.

Number of Directors

64. Unless otherwise determined by ordinary resolution, the number of directors (other than alternate directors) shall not be subject to any maximum but shall be not less than two.

Alternate Directors

65. Any director (other than an alternate director) may appoint any other director, or any other person approved by resolution of the directors and willing to act, to be an alternate director and may remove from office an alternate director so appointed by him.

66. An alternate director shall be entitled to receive notice of all meetings of directors and of all meetings of committees of directors of which his appointor is a member, to attend and vote at any such meeting at which the director appointing him is not personally present, and generally to perform all the functions of his appointor as a director in his absence but shall not be entitled to receive any remuneration from the company for his services as an alternate director. But it shall not be necessary to give notice of such a meeting to an alternate director who is absent from the United Kingdom.

67. An alternate director shall cease to be an alternate director if his appointor ceases to be a director; but, if a director retires by rotation or otherwise but is reappointed or deemed to have been reappointed at the meeting at which he retires, any appointment of an alternate director made by him which was in force immediately prior to his retirement shall continue after his reappointment.

68. Any appointment or removal of an alternate director shall be by notice to the company signed by the director making or revoking the appointment or in any other manner approved by the directors.

69. Save as otherwise provided in the articles, an alternate director shall be deemed for all purposes to be a director and shall alone be responsible for his own acts and defaults and he shall not be deemed to be the agent of the director appointing him.

Powers of Directors

70. Subject to the provisions of the Act, the Memorandum and the Articles and to any directions given by special resolution, the business of the company shall be managed by the directors who may exercise all the powers of the company. No alteration of the memorandum or articles and no such direction shall invalidate any prior act of the directors which would have been valid if that alteration had not been made or that direction had not been given. The powers given by this regulation shall not be limited by any special power given to the directors by the Articles and a meeting of directors at which a quorum is present may exercise all powers exercisable by the directors.

71. The directors may, by power of attorney or otherwise, appoint any person to be the agent of the company for such purposes and on such conditions as they determine, including authority for the agent to delegate all or any of his powers.

Delegation of Directors' Powers

72.   The directors may delegate any of their powers to any committee consisting of one or more directors. They may also delegate to any managing director or any director holding any other executive office such of their powers as they consider desirable to be exercised by him. Any such delegation may be made subject to any conditions the directors may impose, and either collaterally with or to the exclusion of their own powers and may be revoked or altered. Subject to any such conditions, the proceedings of a committee with two or more members shall be governed by the Articles regulating the proceedings of directors so far as they are capable of applying.

Appointment and Retirement of Directors

73.   At the first annual general meeting all the directors shall retire from office, and at every subsequent annual general meeting one-third of the directors who are subject to retirement by rotation or, if their number is not three or a multiple of three, the number nearest to one-third shall retire from office; but, if there is only one director who is subject to retirement by rotation, he shall retire.

74.   Subject to the provisions of the Act, the directors to retire by rotation shall be those who have been longest in office since their last appointment or reappointment, but as between persons who became or were last reappointed directors on the same day those to retire shall (unless they otherwise agree among themselves) be determined by lot.

75.   If the company, at the meeting at which a director retires by rotation, does not fill the vacancy the retiring director shall, if willing to act, be deemed to have been reappointed unless at the meeting it is resolved not to fill the vacancy or unless a resolution for the reappointment of the director is put to the meeting and lost.

76.   No person other than a director retiring by rotation shall be appointed or reappointed a director at any general meeting unless:

(a)   he is recommended by the directors; or

(b)   not less than fourteen nor more than thirty-five clear days before the date appointed for the meeting, notice executed by a member qualified to vote at the meeting has been given to the company of the intention to propose that person for appointment or reappointment stating the particulars which would, if he were so appointed or reappointed, be required to be included in the company's register of directors together with notice executed by that person of his willingness to be appointed or reappointed.

77.   Not less than seven nor more than twenty-eight clear days before the date appointed for holding a general meeting notice shall be given to all who are entitled to receive notice of the meeting of any person (other than a director retiring by rotation at the meeting) who is recommended by the directors for appointment or reappointment as a director at the meeting or in respect of whom notice has been duly given to the company of the intention to propose him at the meeting for appointment or reappointment as a director. The notice shall give the particulars of that person which would, if he were so appointed or reappointed, be required to be included in the company's register of directors.

78.   Subject as aforesaid, the company may by ordinary resolution appoint a person who is willing to act to be a director either to fill a vacancy or as an additional director and may also determine the rotation in which any additional directors are to retire.

79.   The directors may appoint a person who is willing to act to be a director, either to fill a vacancy or as an additional director, provided that the appointment does not cause the number of directors to exceed any number fixed by or in accordance with the Articles as the maximum number of directors. A director so appointed shall hold office only until the next following annual general meeting and shall not be taken into account in determining the directors who are to retire by rotation at the meeting. If not reappointed at such annual general meeting, he shall vacate office at the conclusion thereof.

80.   Subject as aforesaid, a director who retires at an annual general meeting may, if willing to act, be reappointed. If he is not reappointed, he shall retain office until the meeting appoints someone in his place, or if it does not do so, until the end of the meeting.

Disqualification and Removal of Directors

81.   The office of a director shall be vacated if:

(a)   he ceases to be a director by virtue of any provision of the Act or he becomes prohibited by law from being a director; or

(b)   he becomes bankrupt or makes any arrangement or composition with his creditors generally; or

(c)   he is, or may be, suffering from mental disorder and either:

   (i)   he is admitted to hospital in pursuance of an application for admission for treatment under the Mental Health Act 1983 or, in Scotland, an application for admission under the Mental Health (Scotland) Act 1960, or

   (ii)   an order is made by a court having jurisdiction (whether in the United Kingdom or elsewhere) in matters concerning mental disorder for his detention or for the appointment of a receiver, *curator bonis* or other person to exercise powers with respect to his property or affairs; or

(d)   he resigns his office by notice to the company; or

(e)   he shall for more than six consecutive months have been absent without permission of the directors from meetings of directors held during that period and the directors resolve that his office be vacated.

Remuneration of Directors

82.   The directors shall be entitled to such remuneration as the company may by ordinary resolution determine and, unless the resolution provides otherwise, the remuneration shall be deemed to accrue from day to day.

Directors' Expenses

83.   The directors may be paid all travelling, hotel, and other expenses properly incurred by them in connection with their attendance at meetings of directors or committees of directors or general meetings or separate meetings of the holders of any class of shares or of debentures of the company or otherwise in connection with the discharge of their duties.

Directors' Appointments and Interests

84.   Subject to the provisions of the Act, the directors may appoint one or more of their number to the office of managing director or to any other executive office under the company and may enter into an agreement or arrangement with any director for his employment by the company or for the provision by him of any services outside the scope of the ordinary duties of a director. Any such appointment, agreement or arrangement may be made upon such terms as the directors determine and they may remunerate any such director for his services as they think fit. Any appointment of a director to an executive office shall terminate if he ceases to be a director but without prejudice to any claim to damages for breach of the contract of service between the director and the company. A managing director and a director holding any other executive office shall not be subject to retirement by rotation.

85.   Subject to the provisions of the Act, and provided that he has disclosed to the directors the nature and extent of any material interest of his, a director notwithstanding his office:

    (a)   may be a party to, or otherwise interested in, any transaction or arrangement with the company or in which the company is otherwise interested;

    (b)   may be a director or other officer of, or employed by, or a party to any transaction or arrangement with, or otherwise interested in, any body corporate promoted by the company or in which the company is otherwise interested; and

    (c)   shall not, by reason of his office, be accountable to the company for any benefit which he derives from any such office or employment or from any such transaction or arrangement or from any interest in any such body corporate and no such transaction or arrangement shall be liable to be avoided on the ground of any such interest or benefit.

86.   For the purposes of regulation 85:

    (a)   a general notice given to the directors that a director is to be regarded as having an interest of the nature and extent specified in the notice in any transaction or arrangement in which a specified person or class of persons is interested shall be deemed to be a disclosure that the director has an interest in any such transaction of the nature and extent so specified; and

    (b)   an interest of which a director has no knowledge and of which it is unreasonable to expect him to have knowledge shall not be treated as an interest of his.

Directors' Gratuities and Pensions

87.   The directors may provide benefits, whether by the payment of gratuities or pensions or by insurance or otherwise, for any director who has held but no longer holds any executive office or employment with the company or with any body corporate which is or has been a subsidiary of the company or a predecessor in business of the company or of any such subsidiary, and for any member of his family (including a spouse and a former spouse) or any person who is or was dependent on him, and may (as well before as after he ceases to hold such office or employment) contribute to any fund and pay premiums for the purchase or provision of any such benefit.

Proceedings of Directors

88. Subject to the provisions of the Articles, the directors may regulate their proceedings as they think fit. A director may, and the secretary at the request of a director shall, call a meeting of the directors. It shall not be necessary to give notice of a meeting to a director who is absent from the United Kingdom. Questions arising at a meeting shall be decided by a majority of votes. In the case of an equality of votes, the chairman shall have a second or casting vote. A director who is also an alternate director shall be entitled in the absence of his appointor to a separate vote on behalf of his appointor in addition to his own vote.

89. The quorum for the transaction of the business of the directors may be fixed by the directors and unless so fixed at any other number shall be two. A person who holds office only as an alternate director shall, if his appointor is not present, be counted in the quorum.

90. The continuing directors or a sole continuing director may act notwithstanding any vacancies in their number, but, if the number of directors is less than the number fixed as the quorum, the continuing directors or director may act only for the purpose of filling vacancies or of calling a general meeting.

91. The directors may appoint one of their number to be the chairman of the board of directors and may at any time remove him from that office. Unless he is unwilling to do so, the director so appointed shall preside at every meeting of directors at which he is present. But if there is no director holding that office, or if the director holding it is unwilling to preside or is not present within five minutes after the time appointed for the meeting, the directors present may appoint one of their number to be chairman of the meeting.

92. All acts done by a meeting of directors, or of a committee of directors, or by a person acting as a director shall, notwithstanding that it be afterwards discovered that there was a defect in the appointment of any director or that any of them were disqualified from holding office, or had vacated office, or were not entitled to vote, be as valid as if every such person had been duly appointed and was qualified and had continued to be a director and had been entitled to vote.

93. A resolution in writing signed by all the directors entitled to receive notice of a meeting of directors or of a committee of directors shall be as valid and effectual as if it had been passed at a meeting of directors or (as the case may be) a committee of directors duly convened and held and may consist of several documents in the like form each signed by one or more directors; but a resolution signed by an alternate director need not also be signed by his appointor and, if it is signed by a director who has appointed an alternate director, it need not be signed by the alternate director in that capacity.

94.   Save as otherwise provided by the articles, a director shall not vote at a meeting of directors or of a committee of directors on any resolution concerning a matter in which he has, directly or indirectly, an interest or duty which is material and which conflicts or may conflict with the interests of the company unless his interest or duty arises only because the case falls within one or more of the following paragraphs:

(a)   the resolution relates to the giving to him of a guarantee, security, or indemnity in respect of money lent to, or an obligation incurred by him for the benefit of, the company or any of its subsidiaries;

(b)   the resolution relates to the giving to a third party of a guarantee, security, or indemnity in respect of an obligation of the company or any of its subsidiaries for which the director has assumed responsibility in whole or part and whether alone or jointly with others under a guarantee or indemnity or by the giving of security;

(c)   his interest arises by virtue of his subscribing or agreeing to subscribe for any shares, debentures or other securities of the company or any of its subsidiaries, or by virtue of his being, or intending to become, a participant in the underwriting or sub-underwriting of an offer of any such shares, debentures, or other securities by the company or any of its subsidiaries for subscription, purchase or exchange;

(d)   the resolution relates in any way to a retirement benefits scheme which has been approved, or is conditional upon approval, by the Board of Inland Revenue for taxation purposes.

For the purposes of this regulation, an interest of a person who is, for any purpose of the Act (excluding any statutory modification thereof not in force when this regulation becomes binding on the company), connected with a director shall be treated as an interest of the director and, in relation to an alternate director, an interest of his appointor shall be treated as an interest of the alternate director without prejudice to any interest which the alternate director has otherwise.

95.   A director shall not be counted in the quorum present at a meeting in relation to a resolution on which he is not entitled to vote.

96.   The company may by ordinary resolution suspend or relax to any extent, either generally or in respect of any particular matter, any provision of the articles prohibiting a director from voting at a meeting of directors or of a committee of directors.

97.   Where proposals are under consideration concerning the appointment of two or more directors to offices or employments with the company or any body corporate in which the company is interested the proposals may be divided and considered in relation to each director separately and (provided he is not for another reason precluded from voting) each of the directors concerned shall be entitled to vote and be counted in the quorum in respect of each resolution except that concerning his own appointment.

98.   If a question arises at a meeting of directors or of a committee of directors as to the right of a director to vote, the question may, before the conclusion of the meeting, be referred to the chairman of the meeting and his ruling in relation to any director other than himself shall be final and conclusive.

Secretary

99. Subject to the provisions of the Act, the secretary shall be appointed by the directors for such term, at such remuneration and upon such conditions as they may think fit; and any secretary so appointed may be removed by them.

Minutes

100. The directors shall cause minutes to be made in books kept for the purpose:

(a) of all appointments of officers made by the directors; and

(b) of all proceedings at meetings of the company, of the holders of any class of shares in the company, and of the directors, and of committees of directors, including the names of the directors present at each such meeting.

The Seal

101. The seal shall only be used by the authority of the directors or of a committee of directors authorised by the directors. The directors may determine who shall sign any instrument to which the seal is affixed and unless otherwise so determined it shall be signed by a director and by the secretary or by a second director.

Dividends

102. Subject to the provisions of the Act, the company may by ordinary resolution declare dividends in accordance with the respective rights of the members, but no dividend shall exceed the amount recommended by the directors.

103. Subject to the provisions of the Act, the directors may pay interim dividends if it appears to them that they are justified by the profits of the company available for distribution. If the share capital is divided into different classes, the directors may pay interim dividends on shares which confer deferred or non-preferred rights with regard to dividend as well as on shares which confer preferential rights with regard to dividend, but no interim dividend shall be paid on shares carrying deferred or non-preferred rights if, at the time of payment, any preferential dividend is in arrear. The directors may also pay at intervals settled by them any dividend payable at a fixed rate if it appears to them that the profits available for distribution justify the payment. Provided the directors act in good faith they shall not incur any liability to the holders of shares conferring preferred rights for any loss they may suffer by the lawful payment of an interim dividend on any shares having deferred or non-preferred rights.

104. Except as otherwise provided by the rights attached to shares, all dividends shall be declared and paid according to the amounts paid up on the shares on which the dividend is paid. All dividends shall be apportioned and paid proportionately to the amounts paid up on the shares during any portion or portions of the period in respect of which the dividend is paid; but, if any share is issued on terms providing that it shall rank for dividend as from a particular date, that share shall rank for dividend accordingly.

105. A general meeting declaring a dividend may, upon the recommendation of the directors, direct that it shall be satisfied wholly or partly by the distribution of assets and, where any difficulty arises in regard to the distribution, the directors may settle the same and in particular may issue fractional certificates and fix the value for distribution of any assets and may determine that cash shall be paid to any member upon the footing of the value so fixed in order to adjust the rights of members and may vest any assets in trustees.

106. Any dividend or other moneys payable in respect of a share may be paid by cheque sent by post to the registered address of the person entitled or, if two or more persons are the holders of the share or are jointly entitled to it by reason of the death or bankruptcy of the holder, to the registered address of that one of those persons who is first named in the register of members or to such person and to such address as the person or persons entitled may in writing direct. Every cheque shall be made payable to the order of the person or persons entitled or to such other person as the person or persons entitled may in writing direct and payment of the cheque shall be a good discharge to the company. Any joint holder or other person jointly entitled to a share as aforesaid may give receipts for any dividend or other moneys payable in respect of the share.

107. No dividend or other moneys payable in respect of a share shall bear interest against the company unless otherwise provided by the rights attached to the share.

108. Any dividend which has remained unclaimed for twelve years from the date when it became due for payment shall, if the directors so resolve, be forfeited and cease to remain owing by the company.

Accounts

109. No member shall (as such) have any right of inspecting any accounting records or other book or document of the company except as conferred by statute or authorised by the directors or by ordinary resolution of the company.

Capitalisation of Profits

110. The directors may with the authority of an ordinary resolution of the company:

(a) subject as hereinafter provided, resolve to capitalise any undivided profits of the company not required for paying any preferential dividend (whether or not they are available for distribution) or any sum standing to the credit of the company's share premium account or capital redemption reserve;

(b) appropriate the sum resolved to be capitalised to the members who would have been entitled to it if it were distributed by way of dividend and in the same proportions and apply such sum on their behalf either in or towards paying up the amounts, if any, for the time being unpaid on any shares held by them respectively, or in paying up in full unissued shares or debentures of the company of a nominal amount equal to that sum, and allot the shares or debentures credited as fully paid to those members, or as they may direct, in those proportions, or partly in one way and partly in the other: but the share premium account, the capital redemption reserve, and any profits which are not available for distribution may, for the purposes of this regulation, only be applied in paying up unissued shares to be allotted to members credited as fully paid;

(c) make such provision by the issue of fractional certificates or by payment in cash or otherwise as they determine in the case of shares or debentures becoming distributable under this regulation in fractions; and

(d) authorise any person to enter on behalf of all the members concerned into an agreement with the company providing for the allotment to them respectively, credited as fully paid, of any shares or debentures to which they are entitled upon such capitalisation, any agreement made under such authority being binding on all such members.

Notices

111. Any notice to be given to or by any person pursuant to the articles shall be in writing except that a notice calling a meeting of the directors need not be in writing.

112. The company may give any notice to a member either personally or by sending it by post in a prepaid envelope addressed to the member at his registered address or by leaving it at that address. In the case of joint holders of a share, all notices shall be given to the joint holder whose name stands first in the register of members in respect of the joint holding and notice so given shall be sufficient notice to all the joint holders. A member whose registered address is not within the United Kingdom and who gives to the company an address within the United Kingdom at which notices may be given to him shall be entitled to have notices given to him at that address, but otherwise no such member shall be entitled to receive any notice from the company.

113. A member present, either in person or by proxy, at any meeting of the company or of the holders of any class of shares in the company shall be deemed to have received notice of the meeting and, where requisite, of the purposes for which it was called.

114. Every person who becomes entitled to a share shall be bound by any notice in respect of that share which, before his name is entered in the register of members, has been duly given to a person from whom he derives his title.

115. Proof that an envelope containing a notice was properly addressed, prepaid and posted shall be conclusive evidence that the notice was given. A notice shall be deemed to be given at the expiration of 48 hours after the envelope containing it was posted.

116. A notice may be given by the company to the persons entitled to a share in consequence of the death or bankruptcy of a member by sending or delivering it, in any manner authorised by the Articles for the giving of notice to a member, addressed to them by name, or by the title of representatives of the deceased, or trustee of the bankrupt or by any like description at the address, if any, within the United Kingdom supplied for that purpose by the persons claiming to be so entitled. Until such an address has been supplied, a notice may be given in any manner in which it might have been given if the death or bankruptcy had not occurred.

Winding Up

117. If the company is wound up, the liquidator may, with the sanction of an extraordinary resolution of the company and any other sanction required by the Act, divide among the members in specie the whole or any part of the assets of the company and may, for that purpose, value any assets and determine how the division shall be carried out as between the members or different classes of members. The liquidator may, with the like sanction, vest the whole or any part of the assets in trustees upon such trusts for the benefit of the members as he with the like sanction determines, but no member shall be compelled to accept any assets upon which there is a liability.

Indemnity

118. Subject to the provisions of the Act but without prejudice to any indemnity to which a director may otherwise be entitled, every director or other officer or auditor of the company shall be indemnified out of the assets of the company against any liability incurred by him in defending any proceedings, whether civil or criminal, in which judgment is given in his favour or in which he is acquitted or in connection with any application in which relief is granted to him by the court from liability for negligence, default, breach of duty or breach of trust in relation to the affairs of the company.

THE COMBINED CODE
PRINCIPLES OF GOOD GOVERNANCE AND
CODE OF BEST PRACTICE

Derived by the Committee on Corporate Governance from the Committee's Final Report and from the Cadbury and Greenbury Reports.[1]

Preamble

1. In the Committee's final report we said that, in response to many requests, we intended to produce a set of principles and code which embraced Cadbury, Greenbury and the committee's own work. This Combined Code fulfils that undertaking.

2. The Combined Code is now issued in final form, and includes a number of changes made by The London Stock Exchange, with the Committee's agreement, following the consultation undertaken by the Exchange on the committee's original draft.

3. The Combined Code contains both principles and detailed Code provisions. We understand that it is the intention of The London Stock Exchange to introduce a requirement on listed companies to make a disclosure statement in two parts.

4. In the first part of the statement, the company will be required to report on how it applies the principles in the Combined Code. We make clear in our report that we do not prescribe the form or content of this part of the statement, the intention being that companies should have a free hand to explain their governance policies in the light of the principles, including any special circumstances applying to them which have led to a particular approach. It must be for shareholders and others to evaluate this part of the company's statement.

5. In the second part of the statement the company will be required either to confirm that it complies with the Code provisions or – where it does not – provide an explanation. Again, it must be for shareholders and others to evaluate such explanations.

6. In our report we make clear that companies should be ready to explain their governance policies, including any circumstances justifying departure from best practice; and that those concerned with the evaluation of governance should do so with common sense, and with due regard to companies' individual circumstances.

---

1   The Combined Code has been reproduced by kind permission of Gee Publishing Limited, © The London Stock Exchange Limited.

7. We also make clear in our report that it is still too soon to assess definitively the results of the Cadbury and more especially the Greenbury codes. We see this Combined Code as a consolidation of the work of the three committees, not as a new departure. We have therefore retained the substance of the two earlier codes except in those few cases where we take a different view from our predecessors. We should in particular like to make clear, in relation to the detailed provisions in the Listing Rules on directors' remuneration, that we envisage no change except where we take a different view from the Greenbury committee. With two exceptions, relating to the status of the remuneration committee, and the compensation payable to an executive director on loss of office, these changes are minor.

8. Section 1 of the Combined Code contains the corporate governance principles and code provisions applicable to all listed companies incorporated in the United Kingdom. These would be covered by the statement referred to in paragraphs 3–5 above, which will be required by the Listing Rules. Section 2 contains principles and code provisions applicable to institutional shareholders with regard to their voting, dialogue with companies and evaluation of a company's governance arrangements. These are not matters which are appropriate for the Listing Rules to include within the disclosure requirement. Nevertheless we regard Section 2 of this Combined Code as an integral part of our recommendations; we commend it to the organisations representing institutional shareholders and we hope that at least the major institutions will voluntarily disclose to their clients and the public the extent to which they are able to give effect to these provisions.

9. We have not included in the Combined Code principle D.IV in Chapter 2 of our final report, which reads as follows:

    'External Auditors. The external auditors should independently report to shareholders in accordance with statutory and professional requirements and independently assure the board on the discharge of its responsibilities under D.I and D.II above in accordance with professional guidance.'

    We say in paragraph 6.7 of the report that we recommend neither any additional prescribed requirements nor the removal of any existing requirements for auditors in relation to governance or publicly reported information, some of which derive from the Listing Rules. This recommendation is accepted by The London Stock Exchange. But the existing requirements for auditors will be kept under review, as a matter of course, by the responsible organisations.

Committee on Corporate Governance

June 1998

Principles of Good Governance

Section 1 Companies

A. Directors

The Board

1. Every listed company should be headed by an effective board which should lead and control the company.

Chairman and CEO

2. There are two key tasks at the top of every public company – the running of the board and the executive responsibility of the company's business. There should be a clear division of responsibilities at the head of the company which will ensure a balance of power and authority, such that no one individual has unfettered powers of decision.

Board Balance

3. The board should include a balance of executive and non-executive directors (including independent non-executives) such that no individual or small group of individuals can dominate the board's decision taking.

Supply of information

4. The board should be supplied in a timely manner with information in a form and of a quality appropriate to enable it to discharge its duties.

Appointments to the Board

5. There should be a formal and transparent procedure for the appointment of new directors to the board.

Re-election

6. All directors should be required to submit themselves for re-election at regular intervals and at least every three years.

B. Directors' Remuneration

The Level and Make-up of Remuneration

1. Levels of remuneration should be sufficient to attract and retain the directors needed to run the company successfully, but companies should avoid paying more than is necessary for this purpose. A proportion of executive directors' remuneration should be structured so as to link rewards to corporate and individual performance.

Procedure

2. Companies should establish a formal and transparent procedure for developing policy on executive remuneration and for fixing the remuneration packages of individual directors. No director should be involved in deciding his or her own remuneration.

Disclosure

3. The company's annual report should contain a statement of remuneration policy and details of the remuneration of each director.

C.   Relations with Shareholders

Dialogue with Institutional Shareholders

1. Companies should be ready, where practicable, to enter into a dialogue with institutional shareholders based on the mutual understanding of objectives.

Constructive Use of the AGM

2. Boards should use the AGM to communicate with private investors and encourage their participation.

D.   Accountability and Audit

Financial Reporting

1. The board should present a balanced and understandable assessment of the company's position and prospects.

Internal Control

2. The board should maintain a sound system of internal control to safeguard shareholders' investment and the company's assets.

Audit Committee and Auditors

3. The board should establish formal and transparent arrangements for considering how they should apply the financial reporting and internal control principles and for maintaining an appropriate relationship with the company's auditors.

Section 2 Institutional Shareholders

E.   Institutional Investors

Shareholder Voting

1. Institutional shareholders have a responsibility to make considered use of their votes.

Dialogue with Companies

2. Institutional shareholders should be ready where practicable, to enter into a dialogue with companies based on the mutual understanding of objectives.

Evaluation of Governance Disclosures

3. When evaluating companies' governance arrangements, particularly those relating to board structure and composition, institutional investors should give due weight to all relevant factors drawn to their attention.

Code of Best Practice

Section 1 Companies

A. Directors

A.1 *The Board*

Principle **Every listed company should be headed by an effective board which should lead and control the company.**

Code Provisions

A.1.1 The board should meet regularly.

A.1.2 The board should have a formal schedule of matters specifically reserved to it for decision.

A.1.3 There should be a procedure agreed by the board for directors in the furtherance of their duties to take independent professional advice if necessary, at the company's expense.

A.1.4 All directors should have access to the advice and services of the company secretary, who is responsible to the board for ensuring that board procedures are followed and that applicable rules and regulations are complied with. Any question of the removal of the company secretary should be a matter for the board as a whole.

A.1.5 All directors should bring an independent judgement to bear on issues of strategy, performance, resources, including key appointments, and standards of conduct.

A.1.6 Every director should receive appropriate training on the first occasion that he or she is appointed to the board of a listed company, and subsequently as necessary.

A.2 *Chairman and CEO*

Principle **There are two key tasks at the top of every public company – the running of the board and the executive responsibility for the running of the company's business. There should be a clear division of responsibilities at the head of the company which will ensure a balance of power and authority, such that no one individual has unfettered powers of decision.**

Code Provision

A.2.1   A decision to combine the posts of chairman and chief executive officer in one person should be publicly justified. Whether the posts are held by different people or by the same person, there should be a strong and independent non-executive element on the board, with a recognised senior member other than the chairman to whom concerns can be conveyed. The chairman, chief executive and senior independent director should be identified in the annual report.

A.3   *Board Balance*

Principle   **The board should include a balance of executive and non-executive directors (including independent non-executives) such that no individual or small group of individuals can dominate the board's decision taking.**

Code Provisions

A.3.1   The board should include non-executive directors of sufficient calibre and number for their views to carry significant weight in the board's decisions. Non-executive directors should comprise not less than one third of the board.

A.3.2   The majority of non-executive directors should be independent of management and free from any business or other relationship which could materially interfere with the exercise of their independent judgement. Non-executive directors considered by the board to be independent in this sense should be identified in the annual report.

A.4   *Supply of information*

Principle   **The board should be supplied in a timely manner with information in a form and of a quality appropriate to enable it to discharge its duties.**

Code Provision

A.4.1   Management has an obligation to provide the board with appropriate and timely information, but information volunteered by management is unlikely to be enough in all circumstances and directors should make further enquiries where necessary. The chairman should ensure that all directors are properly briefed on issues arising at board meetings.

A.5   *Appointments to the Board*

Principle   **There should be a formal and transparent procedure for the appointment of new directors to the board.**

Code Provision

A.5.1   Unless the board is small, a nomination committee should be established to make recommendations to the board on all new board appointments. A majority of the members of this committee should be non-executive directors, and the chairman should be either the chairman of the board or a non-executive director. The chairman and members of the nomination committee should be identified in the annual report.

A.6 *Re-election*

Principle **All directors should be required to submit themselves for re-election at regular intervals and at least every three years.**

Code Provisions

A.6.1 Non-executive directors should be appointed for specified terms subject to re-election and to Companies Act provisions relating to the removal of a director, and reappointment should not be automatic.

A.6.2 All directors should be subject to election by shareholders at the first opportunity after their appointment, and to re-election thereafter at intervals of no more than three years. The names of directors submitted for election or re-election should be accompanied by sufficient biographical details to enable shareholders to take an informed decision on their election.

B. Directors' Remuneration

B.1 *The Level and Make-up of Remuneration*

Principle **Levels of remuneration should be sufficient to attract and retain the directors needed to run the company successfully, but companies should avoid paying more than is necessary for this purpose. A proportion of executive directors' remuneration should be structured so as to link rewards to corporate and individual performance.**

Code Provisions

Remuneration policy

B.1.1 The remuneration committee should provide the packages needed to attract, retain and motivate executive directors of the quality required but should avoid paying more than is necessary for this purpose.

B.1.2 Remuneration committees should judge where to position their company relative to other companies. They should be aware what comparable companies are paying and should take account of relative performance. But they should use such comparisons with caution, in view of the risk that they can result in an upward ratchet of remuneration levels with no corresponding improvement in performance.

B.1.3 Remuneration committees should be sensitive to the wider scene, including pay and employment conditions elsewhere in the group, especially when determining annual salary increases.

B.1.4 The performance-related elements of remuneration should form a significant proportion of the total remuneration package of executive directors and should be designed to align their interests with those of shareholders and to give these directors keen incentives to perform at the highest levels.

B.1.5   Executive share options should not be offered at a discount save as permitted by paragraphs 13.30 and 13.31 of the Listing Rules.

B.1.6   In designing schemes of performance related remuneration, remuneration committees should follow the provisions in Schedule A to this code.

Service Contracts and Compensation

B.1.7   There is a strong case for setting notice or contract periods at, or reducing them to, one year or less. Boards should set this as an objective; but they should recognise that it may not be possible to achieve it immediately.

B.1.8   If it is necessary to offer longer notice or contract periods to new directors recruited from outside, such periods should reduce after the initial period.

B.1.9   Remuneration committees should consider what compensation commitments (including pension contributions) their directors' contracts of service, if any, would entail in the event of early termination. They should in particular consider the advantages of providing explicitly in the initial contract for such compensation commitments except in the case of removal for misconduct.

B.1.10   Where the initial contract does not explicitly provide for compensation commitments, remuneration committees should, within legal constraints, tailor their approach in individual early termination cases to the wide variety of circumstances. The broad aim should be to avoid rewarding poor performance while dealing fairly with cases where departure is not due to poor performance and to take a robust line on reducing compensation to reflect departing directors' obligations to mitigate loss.

B.2   *Procedure*

Principle   **Companies should establish a formal and transparent procedure for developing policy on executive remuneration and for fixing the remuneration packages of individual directors. No director should be involved in deciding his or her own remuneration.**

Code Provisions

B.2.1   To avoid potential conflicts of interest, boards of directors should set up remuneration committees of independent non-executive directors to make recommendations to the board, within agreed terms of reference, on the company's framework of executive remuneration and its cost; and to determine on their behalf specific remuneration packages for each of the executive directors, including pension rights and any compensation payments.

B.2.2   Remuneration committees should consist exclusively of non-executive directors who are independent of management and free from any business or other relationship which could materially interfere with the exercise of their independent judgement.

B.2.3   The members of the remuneration committee should be listed each year in the board's remuneration report to shareholders (B.3.1 below).

B.2.4   The board itself or, where required by the Articles of Association, the shareholders should determine the remuneration of the non-executive directors, including members of the remuneration committee, within the limits set in the Articles of Association. Where permitted by the Articles, the board may however delegate this responsibility to a small subcommittee, which might include the chief executive officer.

B.2.5   Remuneration committees should consult the chairman and/or chief executive officer about their proposals relating to the remuneration of other executive directors and have access to professional advice inside and outside the company.

B.2.6   The chairman of the board should ensure that the company maintains contact as required with its principal shareholders about remuneration in the same way as for other matters.

B.3   *Disclosure*

Principle **The company's annual report should contain a statement of remuneration policy and details of the remuneration of each director.**

Code Provisions

B.3.1   The board should report to the shareholders each year on remuneration. The report should form part of, or be annexed to, the company's annual report and accounts. It should be the main vehicle through which the company reports to shareholders on directors' remuneration.

B.3.2   The report should set out the company's policy on executive directors' remuneration. It should draw attention to factors specific to the company.

B.3.3   In preparing the remuneration report, the board should follow the provisions in Schedule B to this code.

B.3.4   Shareholders should be invited specifically to approve all new long term incentive schemes (as defined in the Listing Rules) save in the circumstances permitted by paragraph 13.13A of the Listing Rules.

B.3.5   The board's annual remuneration report to shareholders need not be a standard item of agenda for AGMs. But the board should consider each year whether the circumstances are such that the AGM should be invited to approve the policy set out in the report and should minute their conclusions.

C.   Relations with Shareholders

C.1   *Dialogue with Institutional Shareholders*

Principle **Companies should be ready, where practicable, to enter into a dialogue with institutional shareholders based on the mutual understanding of objectives.**

C.2   *Constructive Use of the AGM*

Principle **Boards should use the AGM to communicate with private investors and encourage their participation.**

Code Provisions

C.2.1   Companies should count all proxy votes and, except where a poll is called, should indicate the level of proxies lodged on each resolution, and the balance for and against the resolution, after it has been dealt with on a show of hands.

C.2.2   Companies should propose a separate resolution at the AGM on each substantially separate issue, and should in particular propose a resolution at the AGM relating to the report and accounts.

C.2.3   The chairman of the board should arrange for the chairmen of the audit, remuneration and nomination committees to be available to answer questions at the AGM.

C.2.4   Companies should arrange for the Notice of the AGM and related papers to be sent to shareholders at least 20 working days before the meeting.

D.   **Accountabilty and Audit**

D.1   *Financial Reporting*

Principle **The board should present a balanced and understandable assessment of the company's position and prospects.**

Code Provisions

D.1.1   The directors should explain their responsibility for preparing the accounts, and there should be a statement by the auditors about the reporting responsibilities.

D.1.2   The board's responsibility to present a balanced and understandable assessment extends to interim and other price-sensitive public reports and reports to regulators as well as to information required to be presented by statutory requirements.

D.1.3   The directors should report that the business is a going concern, with supporting assumptions or qualifications as necessary.

D.2   *Internal Control*

Principle **The board should maintain a sound system of internal control to safeguard shareholders' investment and the company's assets.**

Code Provisions

D.2.1   The directors should, at least annually, conduct a review of the effectiveness of the group's system of internal control and should report to shareholders that they have done so. The review should cover all controls, including financial, operational and compliance controls and risk management.

D.2.2   Companies which do not have an internal audit function should from time to time review the need for one.

D.3   *Audit Committee and Auditors*

Principle   **The board should establish formal and transparent arrangements for considering how they should apply the financial reporting and internal control principles and for maintaining an appropriate relationship with the company's auditors.**

Code Provisions

D.3.1   The board should establish an audit committee of at least three directors, all non-executive, with written terms of reference which deal clearly with its authority and duties. The members of the committee, a majority of whom should be independent non-executive directors, should be named in the report and accounts.

D.3.2   The duties of the audit committee should include keeping under review the scope and results of the audit and its cost effectiveness and the independence and objectivity of the auditors. Where the auditors also supply a substantial volume of non-audit services to the company, the committee should keep the nature and extent of such services under review, seeking to balance the maintenance of objectivity and value for money.

Section 2 Institutional Shareholders

E.   Institutional Investors

E.1   *Shareholder Voting*

Principle   **Institutional shareholders have a responsibility to make considered use of their votes.**

Code Provisions

E.1.1   Institutional shareholders should endeavour to eliminate unnecessary variations in the criteria which each applies to the corporate governance arrangements and performance of the companies in which they invest.

E.1.2   Institutional shareholders should, on request, make available to their clients information on the proportion of resolutions on which votes were cast and non-discretionary proxies lodged.

E.1.3   Institutional shareholders should take steps to ensure that their voting intentions are being translated into practice.

E.2   *Dialogue with Companies*

Principle   **Institutional shareholders should be ready, where practicable, to enter into a dialogue with companies based on the mutual understanding of objectives.**

E.3   *Evaluation of Governance Disclosures*

Principle   **When evaluating companies' governance arrangements, particularly those relating to board structure and composition, institutional investors should give due weight to all relevant factors drawn to their attention.**

Schedule A: Provisions on the Design of Performance Related Remuneration

1. Remuneration committees should consider whether the directors should be eligible for annual bonuses. If so, performance conditions should be relevant, stretching and designed to enhance the business. Upper limits should always be considered. There may be a case for part payment in shares to be held for a significant period.

2. Remuneration committees should consider whether the directors should be eligible for benefits under long-term incentive schemes. Traditional share option schemes should be weighed against other kinds of long-term incentive scheme. In normal circumstances, shares granted or other forms of deferred remuneration should not vest, and options should not be exercisable, in under three years. Directors should be encouraged to hold their shares for a further period after vesting or exercise, subject to the need to finance any costs of acquisition and associated tax liability.

3. Any new long term incentive schemes which are proposed should be approved by shareholders and should preferably replace existing schemes or at least form part of a well considered overall plan, incorporating existing schemes. The total rewards potentially available should not be excessive.

4. Payouts or grants under all incentive schemes, including new grants under existing share option schemes, should be subject to challenging performance criteria reflecting the company's objectives. Consideration should be given to criteria which reflect the company's performance relative to a group of comparator companies in some key variables such as total shareholder return.

5. Grants under executive share option and other long-term incentive schemes should normally be phased rather than awarded in one large block.

6. Remuneration committees should consider the pension consequences and associated costs to the company of basic salary increases and other changes in remuneration, especially for directors close to retirement.

7. In general, neither annual bonuses nor benefits in kind should be pensionable.

Schedule B: Provisions on what should be Included in the Remuneration Report

1. The report should include full details of all elements in the remuneration package of each individual director by name, such as basic salary, benefits in kind, annual bonuses and long term incentive schemes including share options.

2. Information on share options, including SAYE options, should be given for each director in accordance with the recommendations of the Accounting Standards Board's Urgent Issues Task Force Abstract 10 and its successors.

3. If grants under executive share option or other long-term incentive schemes are awarded in one large block rather than phased, the report should explain and justify.

4. Also included in the report should be pension entitlements earned by each individual director during the year, disclosed on one of the alternative bases recommended by the Faculty of Actuaries and the Institute of Actuaries and included in the Stock Exchange Listing Rules. Companies may wish to make clear that the transfer value represents a liability of the company, not a sum paid or due to the individual.

5. If annual bonuses or benefits in kind are pensionable the report should explain and justify.

6. The amounts received by, and commitments made to, each director under 1, 2 and 4 above should be subject to audit.

7. Any service contracts which provide for, or imply, notice periods in excess of one year (or any provisions for predetermined compensation on termination which exceed one year's salary and benefits) should be disclosed and the reasons for the longer notice periods explained.

Appendix E

LAW COMMISSIONERS
DRAFT STATEMENT OF DIRECTORS' DUTIES[1]

The Law Commission report 'Company Directors: Regulating conflicts of interest and formulating a statement of duties' (Law Com No 261, September 1999) recommends:

(1) a 'statutory statement' of a director's main fiduciary duties and his duty of care and skill

(2) drafted in broad and general language as in the Draft Statement

(3) not exhaustive ie specifically subject to other duties which would not be codified

(4) contained in Forms 10(2) (First Directors) and 288(a) (Appointment of director or secretary) so that the director, when signing the Forms would acknowledge that he had read the statement.

Draft Statement

(Appendix A from Report pp 185–186)

General

(1) The law imposes duties on directors. If a person does not comply with his duties as a director he may be liable to civil or criminal proceedings and he may be disqualified from acting as a director.

(2) Set out below there is a summary of the main duties of a director to his company. It is not a complete statement of a director's duties, and the law may change anyway. If a person is not clear about his duties as a director in any situation he should seek advice.

Loyalty

(3) A director must act in good faith in what he considers to be the interests of the company.

Obedience

(4) A director must act in accordance with the company's constitution (such as the articles of association) and must exercise his powers only for the purposes allowed by law.

---

1 As referred to in paras 4.13, 4.25, 4.34, 4.35 and 4.48 of the Report.

  Note: (Cm 4436) Crown Copyright material reproduced by permission of the Controller of Her Majesty's Stationery Office.

No secret profits

(5) A director must not use the company's property, information or opportunities for his own or anyone else's benefit unless he is allowed to by the company's constitution or the use has been disclosed to the company in general meeting and the company has consented to it.

Independence

(6) A director must not agree to restrict his power to exercise an independent judgment. But if he considers in good faith that it is in the interests of the company for a transaction to be entered into and carried into effect, he may restrict his power to exercise an independent judgment by agreeing to act in a particular way to achieve this.

Conflict of interest

(7) If there is a conflict between an interest or duty of a director and an interest of the company in any transaction, he must account to the company for any benefit he receives from the transaction. This applies whether or not the company sets aside the transaction. But he does not have to account for the benefit if he is allowed to have the interest or duty by the company's constitution or the interest or duty has been disclosed to and approved by the company in general meeting.

Care, skill and diligence

(8) A director owes the company a duty to exercise the care, skill and diligence which would be exercised in the same circumstances by a reasonable person having both:
  (a) the knowledge and experience that may reasonably be expected of a person in the same position as the director, and
  (b) the knowledge and experience which the director has.

Interests of employees etc

(9) A director must have regard to the interests of the company's employees in general and its members.

Fairness

(10) A director must act fairly as between different members.

Effect of this statement

(11) The law stating the duties of directors is not affected by this statement or by the fact that, by signing this document, a director acknowledges that he has read the statement.

DRAFT STANDARD FORM SERVICE AGREEMENT FOR AN EXECUTIVE DIRECTOR[1]

THIS AGREEMENT is made the   day of   **BETWEEN**

(1) [   ] Limited (registered number [   ]) having its registered office is at [address] ('the Company').

(2) [*name of employee*] of [address] ['the Director']

IT IS AGREED as follow

1.   DEFINITIONS AND INTERPRETATION

1.1   In this Agreement the following words and expressions shall have the following meanings:

'the Board'	means the board of directors of the Company and includes any committee of the Board duly convened by it.
'the Commencement Date'	means the [ ] day of two thousand and [ ]
'Group Company'	means any company which for the time being is (a) a holding company of the Company, or (b) a subsidiary undertaking of the Company or (c) a subsidiary undertaking of any such holding company (as these expressions are defined in section 736 of the Companies Act 1985).
'Intellectual Property'	means (i) every invention discovery design or improvement, (ii) every work in which copyright may subsist, and (iii) moral rights as defined by section 77 and section 80 of the Copyright Design and Patents Act 1988.

1.2   The heading employed in this Agreement are for the sake of convenience only and shall not affect the interpretation or construction of this Agreement.

1.3   All references in this Agreement to any statutory provision shall be construed so as to include any statutory modification or re-enactment of it or the provision referred to.

---

1   Reproduced with kind permission of Andrew Thornton of Erskine Chambers.

2.   EMPLOYMENT

The Company will employ the Director and the Director will serve the Company on the terms and conditions set out in this Agreement.

3.   DURATION OF EMPLOYMENT

The Director's employment shall be deemed to have commenced on the Commencement Date and (subject as otherwise provided in this Agreement) shall be for an initial period of twelve (12) months and shall continue until terminated by either party giving to the other not less than [*] months' notice in writing save that no such written notice shall take effect until following the expiry of the initial fixed term.

4.   DUTIES OF THE DIRECTOR

4.1   The Director shall perform such duties and exercise such powers in connection with the affairs of the Company generally as may from time to time be assigned to or vested in him by or on behalf of the Board.

4.2   The Director shall be obliged to perform his duties at such location within the United Kingdom as may be reasonably specified to him from time to time by or on behalf of the Board.

4.3   Notwithstanding clause 4.2 above, the Board may from time to time require the Director to carry out his duties at a location outside the United Kingdom save that, without his consent, the Director shall not be required to spend a continuous period of greater than seven (7) days alternatively more than 90 days during any calendar year outside the United Kingdom.

4.4   In the event that the Director is required to work permanently at a place more than [*] miles from his present address the Company will reimburse the Director for any reasonable removal expenses incurred as a result of the Company's requirement up to the maximum permitted tax free under Schedule 11A of the Income and Corporation Taxes Act 1988.

4.5   The Director shall obey all lawful and reasonable directions of the Board and at all times keep the Board promptly and fully informed (in writing is so requested) of his conduct of the business or affairs of the Company and any Group Company and provide such explanations as the Board may require.

4.6   The Director shall work such hours as may from time to time reasonably be required of him for the proper discharge of his duties.

4.7   Save where prevented by reason of disability or ill-health or where otherwise agreed in writing between the Director and the Company, for so long as this Agreement shall remain in force, the Director shall devote the whole of his time attention and abilities to the business and affairs of the Company.

4.8   For so long as this Agreement shall remain in force the Director shall not whether directly or indirectly be engaged on his own account or concerned in any business other than that of the Company or any Group Company or accept any other engagement or public office except with the prior written consent of the Company.

4.9 The provisions of sub-clauses 4.7 and 4.8 above shall not preclude the director from holding a minority interest in the securities of a corporate entity for so long as any such securities are quoted on a recognised investment exchange.

4.10 During the currency of this Agreement the Director will comply with all applicable rules of law any recognised investment exchange regulations and any company policy issued in relation to dealings in shares debentures or other securities of the Company and any Group Company or any unpublished price sensitive information affecting the securities of any other company.

5. REMUNERATION

5.1 The remuneration of the Director shall be a basic salary of £[*insert amount*] per annum (or such higher rate as the Board of the Company or any remuneration sub-committee of the Board shall decide). Such salary shall be deemed to be inclusive of any directors' fees or other remuneration payable to him in any way howsoever in connection with the carrying out of his duties pursuant to this Agreement

5.2 Any increase in the Director's remuneration will become effective upon the receipt of written notice of such increase by the Director from the Company.

5.3 The Director's remuneration shall be payable in arrears in equal monthly instalments on the last day of each calendar month.

6. PROVISION OF A COMPANY CAR

6.1 The Director will be supplied with such car as the Company shall consider fit for the performance of the Directors duties pursuant to this Agreement.

6.2 The Director shall be entitled to use any car supplied to him by the Company for private use.

6.3 The Company shall pay all running costs associated with the Company including but not limited to the provision of a policy of comprehensive insurance, service tax and fuel (including fuel used during private use of the car).

6.4 At all times whilst in possession of a company car, the Director shall ensure that he possesses a current valid driving licence appropriate for the vehicle in question, shall take good care of the car and ensure that the terms of any insurance policy relevant to the vehicle are observed.

6.5 Upon the termination of his employment, the Director shall immediately return the car and all sets of its keys in his possession to the Company's principal place of business or such other place as the Company may reasonably require.

7.   EXPENSES

7.1   Subject to the production of reasonable evidence that the same have been incurred wholly and exclusively in connection with the carrying out of his duties pursuant to this Agreement, the Company shall reimburse the Director all reasonable expenses, including but not limited to travelling, hotel and entertainment expenses.

7.2   The Company shall further reimburse the Director for any annual subscriptions payable by the Director to any professional body in order to enable the Director to maintain his professional qualifications.

8.   HOLIDAYS

In addition to normal bank and public holidays and save as otherwise agreed in writing between the Company and the Director, the Director shall be entitled to [*number*] of days holiday per annum. Such holidays shall be taken at such time as may be agreed between the Director and the Company, the Company's consent to particular dates not to be unreasonably withheld.

9.   MEDICAL EXAMINATIONS

9.1   The Director consents, at the company's request, to attend for medical examination by a registered medical practitioner nominated by the Company, save that the Director shall not be required to attend more than one such examination in any calendar year.

9.2   All expenses of and arising out of such examination shall be borne by the Company.

9.3   The Company shall be entitled to require the medical practitioner to disclose to it any results which the Company reasonably believes may impact on the ability of the Director to carry out all or any of his duties pursuant to his employment. To the extent necessary, the Director shall consent to the results of any such examination being disclosed to the Company.

10.   ILL HEALTH

10.1   For any period of absence through ill health or injury of up to [*number*] days, the Director shall upon his return to work maintain a written record of the reason for his absence.

10.2   In respect of any period of absence through ill health or injury of [*number*] days or over, the Director shall (unless otherwise agreed by the Company) provide the Company with a medical certificate in respect of the whole period of the absence.

10.3   Subject to the compliance with the provisions of sub-clauses 10.1 and 10.2 above and to clause 16 below, the Director shall be entitled to be paid in full for any period of absence due to ill health or injury during the currency of this Agreement. The Company shall be entitled to deduct any statutory sick pay or other state benefits to which the Director is entitled to claim during any such period of absence.

11.   PENSION BENEFITS

11.1   During the currency of this Agreement the Director shall be entitled to become a member of any pension scheme from time to time maintained by the Company for the benefit of employees in the position of the Director and further to be provided with cover under a life assurance policy, the benefits of which payable to the Director upon his death will be equal to not less than three times his annual salary as at the date of the commencement of this Agreement.

11.2   The Director shall be entitled to become a member of any private medical expenses or similar scheme maintained by the Company for persons in the position of the Director.

12.   INTELLECTUAL PROPERTY

12.1   The Director hereby acknowledges that during the course of his employment, he may discover or create Intellectual Property.

12.2   Subject to the provisions of any statute, including but not limited to the Patents Act 1977 and the Copyright, Designs and Patents Act 1988, upon the discovery or creation of any such Intellectual Property, whether alone or in conjunction with others, the Director shall forthwith communicate details in writing of the same to the Company.

12.3   The Director hereby acknowledged that any interest of his in any Intellectual Property created or discovered within the terms of sub-clause 12.2 above shall, unless otherwise agreed in writing by the Company, automatically vest in the Company. The Director agrees to provide the Company with all assistance, including the provisions of any information, including all documents, drawings and technical information in order to enable the Company to obtain protection of its Intellectual Property rights whether by patent, copyright or any other method.

12.4   By this Agreement, the Director irrevocably appoints the Company as his attorney to execute in his name and on his behalf any instrument or any act and generally to use his name for the purpose of giving to the Company the full benefits of this clause 12.

12.5   The terms of this clause 12 shall apply notwithstanding the cessation of the Director's employment in relation to any Intellectual Property discovered or created during the course of his employment and shall be binding upon his heirs and representatives.

13.   CONFIDENTIALITY

13.1   The Director hereby acknowledges that during the course of his employment, the director will have access to and be entrusted with information as to the business, affairs and customers of the Company.

13.2   The Director shall not, whether during the currency of this Agreement or thereafter divulge to any person, whether individual or corporate, in whatever capacity, any information which is confidential to the Company, including but not limited to details relating to the business and financing of the Company, the identity of its customers or the Company's dealings with those customers or any other persons, the workings of any manufacturing process or invention or any other methods formulae technical information and know how used or relating to the business of the Company.

13.3   The Director's obligations under sub-paragraph 13.2 above may be waived whether wholly or partially in writing by the Company and will not in any event apply to information in the public domain.

14.   TERMINATION OF EMPLOYMENT

14.1   The Company shall be entitled to terminate the Director's employment by written notice in the circumstances set out below:-

14.1.1   if the Director shall be guilty of gross misconduct or any repeated breach of any of the terms of this Agreement;

14.1.2   if the Director shall be convicted of a criminal offence (except for a road traffic offence not involving a custodial sentence);

14.1.3   if the Director is adjudged bankrupt or makes any composition or enters into any deed of arrangement with his creditors;

14.1.4   if the Director is disqualified or prohibited by law from being or acting as a director;

14.1.5   if the Director shall become of unsound mind or become a patient under the Mental Health Act 1983;

14.1.6   if the Director resigns as a director of the Company otherwise than at the request of the Company;

14.1.7   if the Director's performance of his duties falls below that which the Company reasonably can expect a person in the Director's position and with the Director's skills and qualifications to exhibit. The Director must be given at least one prior warning in writing of such poor performance and a reasonable opportunity to remedy it.

14.2   In the case of the termination of employment pursuant to this clause 14, the Director shall not be entitled to any further payment from the Company except such sums as shall then have accrued due.

15.   RESIGNATION OF OFFICE OF DIRECTOR

15.1   Upon the cessation of his employment pursuant to the terms of this Agreement, the Director shall resign in writing all offices as director of any Group Company. The Director hereby acknowledges that he will not be entitled to any compensation or other monetary sum in respect of any such resignation.

15.2   If the Director fails within a period of seven days following the termination of his employment to resign in accordance with sub-clause 15.1 above, the Company is hereby irrevocably authorised to appoint some person in his name and on his behalf of sign and execute all documents or things necessary or requisite to give effect to the Director's resignation from all Group Companies.

16. NOTICE IN THE EVENT OF ILL HEALTH

If for any reason, including but not limited to ill health, disability or injury, the Director is unable to carry out his duties pursuant to the Agreement for a period of at least 180 days in any period of 12 consecutive calendar months, the Company may by the giving of three months notice to the Director terminate this Agreement.

17. POST-TERMINATION PROVISIONS

17.1 Following the termination of this Agreement and in the absence of any other Agreement for the employment by the Company of the Director, the Director shall not represent himself as being employed by or connected with the Company or any Group Company.

17.2 For a period of [*enter period*] following the termination of this Agreement, the Director shall not solicit or endeavour to entice away from or discourage from being employed by the Company [*any person* or *specify category of employees*] employed by the Company or any Group Company [of whatever rank], save that the provisions of this sub-clause shall not apply to any person with whom the Director did not have contact in the normal course of his duties as a director or any person who has become an employee of the Company since the date of termination of the Agreement.

17.3 Save with the written consent of the Company, for a period of [*specify period*] following the termination of this Agreement, the Director shall not directly or indirectly and whether on his own account or for any other person, firm or company in connection with any business similar to or in competition with the business of the Company solicit or seek to procure orders from or do business with or endeavour to entice away from the Company any person, firm or company (a) who or which in the [*specify period*] prior to the end of his employment shall have been a customer of or in the habit of dealing with the Company and (b) with whom or which the Executive had personal dealings in the course of his employment in the [*specify period*] prior to the end of his employment.

17.4 Save with the written consent of the Company, the Director shall not for a period of [*specify period*] after the termination of his employment and within [*specify area*] directly or indirectly be engaged concerned or interested (whether as principal, servant, agent, consultant or otherwise) in any trade or business which is in competition with any trade or business being carried on by the Company at the end of the Director's employment [or during a period of [*specify period*] prior to the end of his employment] and with which the Director was concerned in the course of his employment.

17.5 The Director acknowledges:

17.5.1   that each of sub-clauses 17.1 to 17.4 (inclusive) above constitutes an entirely separate and independent restriction on him; and

17.5.2   that the restrictions set out in sub-clauses 17.1 to 17.4 (inclusive) above are reasonable in all the circumstances. If and to the extent that the restrictions embodied in those clauses are adjudged to be void or ineffective for whatever reason but would be adjudged to be valid and effective if part of the wording thereof were deleted or the periods thereof reduced or the area thereof reduced in scope they shall apply with such modifications as may be necessary to make them valid and effective.

18.   RETURN OF COMPANY PROPERTY

Upon the termination of his employment under this Agreement, the Director shall immediately deliver up to the Company or any person nominated by the Company all property of whatever nature belonging to the Company or any Group Company and in the possession of the Director including but not limited to all keys, security passes, credit cards, plans, statistics, documents, records, papers, magnetic disks, tapes or other software storage media.

19.   NOTICES

19.1   Any notice given under this agreement shall be in writing and may be served personally or by registered post.

19.2   The Company's address for service shall be the Company's registered office for the time being and the Director's address for service shall be his last-known address.

19.3   Such notice shall be deemed to have been given:

19.3.1   if it was served in person, at the time of service; and

19.3.2   if it was served by post, on the day on which in the ordinary course of post it would be delivered.

20.   DEEMED TERMINATION OF PRIOR AGREEMENTS

This Agreement is in substitution for all previous contracts of employment express or implied between the Company or any Group Company and the Director which shall be deemed to have been terminated by mutual consent as from the date upon which this Agreement takes effect.

21.   DISCIPLINARY PROCEDURE

The Company does not have any fixed rules for the resolution of grievance or disciplinary problems. In the event of the Director being dissatisfied with any decision taken against him in respect of his employment with the Company, or have any grievance relating to the employment, he should raise the matter in writing addressed to the Chairman of the Board of Directors of the Company.

22.   RECONSTRUTION OR AMALGAMATION

If before the termination of this Agreement the Director's employment shall be determined by reason of the liquidation of the Company for the purposes of reconstruction or amalgamation and the Director shall be offered employment with any concern or undertaking resulting from such reconstruction or amalgamation on terms and conditions no less favourable than the terms of this Agreement then the Director shall have no claim against the Company in respect of the determination of his employment.

23.   EMPLOYMENT PROTECTION (CONSOLIDATION) ACT 1978

Schedule 1 to this Agreement sets out the particulars of employment not contained in the Agreement that must be given to the Executive in accordance with the terms of the Employment Protection (Consolidation) Act 1978.

Schedule 2

Section 1 Employment Protection (Consolidation) Act 1978

The following information is given to supplement the information given in the Agreement in order to comply with the requirements of section 1 of the Employment Protection (Consolidation) Act 1978.

1.   The Director's job title is [specify job title].

2.   The Director's continuous period of employment with the Company commenced on
[*date on which Director's employment with the Company commenced*] and is not continuous with any previous period of employment with any other employer.

3.   [A Contracting-Out Certificate pursuant to the provisions of the Pension Schemes Act 1993 is in force in respect of the Director's employment.]

4.   [There are no collective agreements in force which affect the terms and conditions of the Director's employment.]

IN WITNESS whereof the parties hereto have executed this Agreement as a Deed the day and year first above written.

Signed by [specify name and title] Director and by [specify name] Secretary for and on behalf of the Company and delivered as a Deed in the presence of [specify name]

Signed by the Director and delivered as a Deed in the presence of [specify name]:

INDEX

References are to paragraph numbers and Appendices.